JOHN
STOTT

Timothy Dudley-Smith

JOHN
STOTT

A GLOBAL MINISTRY

The second and concluding volume
of the authorized biography; and a sequel to
John Stott: The Making of a Leader

Inter-Varsity Press

INTER-VARSITY PRESS
38 De Montfort Street, Leicester LE1 7GP, England
Email: ivp@uccf.org.uk
Website: www.ivpbooks.com

First published 2001

British Library Cataloguing in Publication Data
A catalogue record for this book is available from the British Library.

ISBN 0–85111–983–2

Set in Adobe Garamond
Printed and bound in Great Britain by Creative Design and Print (Wales), Ebbw Vale

Inter-Varsity Press is the publishing division of the Universities and Colleges Christian Fellowship (formerly the Inter-Varsity Fellowship), a student movement linking Christian Unions in universities and colleges throughout Great Britain, and a member movement of the International Fellowship of Evangelical Students. For more information about local and national activities write to UCCF, 38 De Montfort Street, Leicester LE1 7GP, email us at email@uccf.org.uk, or visit the UCCF website at www.uccf.org.uk.

CONTENTS

ACKNOWLEDGMENTS

The author has made every reasonable effort to obtain permission to reproduce letters and other material, including photographs, used in this book, and is grateful for the co-operation he has received. Should any copyright holders have been inadvertently missed, they are asked to contact the publishers.

Foreword

'What a series of rediscoveries life is,' wrote C. S. Lewis in his mid-forties to a boyhood friend. 'All the things which one used to regard as simply the nonsense grown-ups talk have one by one come true – draughts, rheumatism, Christianity ...'[1] When the first volume of John Stott's story closed, he was on the threshold of his fortieth year, and the truth of Christianity (or, as he prefers to say, about Jesus Christ)[2] had long been the mainspring of his life and ministry. The start of the 1960s found him well settled as the Rector of All Souls Church, Langham Place, in central London, already something of a world traveller in the course of his ministry, widely known as a missioner to students and as a pioneer in evangelism by the local church. He was a Chaplain to the Queen; looked to as a leader, especially by a whole generation of younger evangelical clergy; and beginning to be the kind of author in demand by publishers as well as readers.

The story recounted in this second volume is of a growing worldwide ministry. It tells of his resignation as Rector after twenty-five years and of his re-licensing as assistant curate. It looks at the question of whether he might have served as a bishop or a college principal (and describes his brief tenure as a Visiting Professor). It shows him as the chief architect of NEAC, the National Evangelical Anglican Congress, at Keele in 1967 and again ten years later at Nottingham, watersheds in twentieth-century UK evangelicalism. He appears working with Billy Graham at Montreux, Berlin and Amsterdam, and especially in pursuit of the Lausanne vision for world evangelization. He is to be found in dialogue, debate and dispute not only with unbelievers but with liberals, charismatics, Anglo-Catholics and Roman Catholics; with Dr Martyn Lloyd-Jones and with Bishop Jack Spong; responding to *Honest to God*, to Bishop David Jenkins, to ARCIC (the Anglican–Roman Catholic International Commission) and its Agreed Statements, and to *The Myth of God Incarnate.* Movements touched on in volume one are here further developed: the great Urbana missionary conventions, EFAC and CEEC (that is, the Evangelical Fellowship in the Anglican Communion, and the Church of England Evangelical Council), ELT and ERCDOM (the Evangelical Literature Trust, and the Evangelical–Roman Catholic Dialogue on Mission). His growth as a biblical preacher is charted, as he adds contemporary application to careful exegesis, and the social implications of the gospel of Christ to the evangelistic imperative of the Great Commission.

From his diaries a number of chapters illustrate his travels, and the growing acceptance accorded him by ecclesiastical authorities initially distrustful of his reasoned and uncompromising evangelical teaching. They round out the accepted picture of him with some unfamiliar incidents: sampling the Duke of Edinburgh's cooking at a barbecue at Sandringham, touring the Australian outback in 'Clancy', the converted ambulance, lost in the Amazon jungle, or diving repeatedly in the cloudy waters of an Arctic estuary to retrieve a body for Christian burial. Later chapters show his ministry in other parts of Latin America, in Eastern Europe and in the seminaries of China; and through his years of travel runs the celebrated 'search for the Snowy Owl'.

Study assistants make their appearance, together with Langham scholars, the London Lectures, the founding of the London Institute. There is the short-lived but not unimportant Christian Foundations series, and the continuing and deeply influential The Bible Speaks Today series, with his own contributions on (among other books) Acts, Romans and the Pastoral Epistles. These are the years of his Lambeth DD and honorary doctorates, and of major books: *I Believe in Preaching, The Cross of Christ, Issues Facing Christians Today* and *The Contemporary Christian.* This final volume of biography concludes with the 1990s, the end of the century; leaving John Stott, bereft now of all his childhood family circle but rich in friends, making careful preparation for the continuation of his work, by this time a ministry primarily for scholars, students, preachers and pastors in the developing world.

It can be seen as a mark of confidence, or perhaps only of temerity, that a writer should urge the re-reading of earlier work. Nevertheless this second volume is best understood in the light of the Foreword to the first, which forms a preamble to the whole. All that is said there about writing the biography of a living subject, and about the distinction between 'telling the story' and exploring the character – what Professor Owen Chadwick likened to the work of an anatomist – applies equally to the pages that follow. 'Alas, Sir,' said the great Dr Johnson feelingly, 'what a mass of confusion we should have if every Bishop ... were to write books.'[3] That earlier Foreword explains how this one comes to be written, and touches also on a number of minor matters such as the handling of quotations and the use of sources; while what is said there should determine the reader's expectations of this present volume also.

There are of course considerable differences between the two books. Many people find childhood and early youth the most readable part of any life-story; and volume one had also the benefit of a strong thread of progression, from home and family circle to schoolboy, student, curate and Rector. All Souls itself was a stable background to the fifteen years of ministry there recounted, and continued to be so for about the first third of this present book. After 1970, although John Stott remained a member of the church and its staff, and All Souls was still very much his church family, accounts of its people and developments once he ceased to be Rector are not generally the concern of this biography.

A further difference is that both writer and reader stand increasingly nearer in time to the narrative as this book progresses. When Isak Dinesen (the Baroness Blixen who wrote the justly celebrated *Out of Africa*) was asked by an interviewer, following the publication of her first short stories, whether it would not have been more natural to write about Africa, she replied that this would have been too soon: 'One must have things at a distance ...'[4] Such distance in this present instance is a luxury available only to future biographers.

There are also fewer accounts of direct evangelistic ministry in this second volume. A generous glimpse of John Stott as university missioner has already been included; and while such elements have never been absent from his ministry there are other things to be recounted.[5] Some may seem a poor exchange: patient years of conferences, committees and consultations; the drafting of reports, covenants and manifestos, unenlivened for the most part (to borrow Alice's famous complaint) by even word-pictures or remembered conversations. But John Stott's story would be seriously incomplete without such references.

A final and obvious difference lies in the assumption that volume one has been read first – or is at least to hand. I tried there to add a word of explanation when a significant new character entered the story, perhaps as the source of some letter, quotation or interview; and I continue to do so, for the most part, in this second volume. But it is not possible, and would soon become wearisome, systematically to reintroduce individuals who have already featured in the earlier book. In the most literal sense the account of those earlier decades, upon which this story builds, must be taken as read.

There is, however, a continuity about both story and treatment which outweighs these differences. It is the same life. There is the same division into self-contained decades, ten years at a time, providing a firm scaffolding of chronology. Alongside his travels and his personal ministry must be seen his continuing work as an author. All his major writings during these forty years are referred to in the appropriate chapters and included in the bibliography.[6] There are, too, other areas of continuity. Though the original request for a 'life and times' is clearly impossible on a world stage, I have nevertheless tried to sketch some background in the UK and in North America, and elsewhere through quotations from the diaries, so as to do something to fulfil this part of my brief. And I have continued the approach adopted by James Boswell of allowing the subject to emerge through the eyes of his contemporaries. Boswell told his readers:

> In the chronological series of Johnson's life, which I trace as distinctly as I can, year by year, I produce, wherever it is in my power, his own minutes, letters or conversation, being convinced that this mode is more lively, and will make my readers better acquainted with him, than even most of those were who actually knew him ...[7]

This tends to make for an excess of references, which are again consigned to the endnotes. Philip Ziegler is reported to have said, when taxed with the quantity of notes in a recent biography, 'I never for one moment imagined that any normal human being would want to consult them – that is why they are not footnotes properly speaking but are confined to a ghetto at the end of the book.' He added, 'Real footnotes I reserve for jokes which I can't fit into the text but am determined to put in somewhere.'[8] Very occasionally my endnotes serve a similar purpose.

The question of hagiography has not been easy. 'A man's biography should be written by a conscientious enemy,' said H. G. Wells.[9] 'Abuse is as great a mistake in controversy as panegyric in biography,' wrote J. H. Newman to his friend Coleridge.[10] I am acutely aware of this and have done my best not to present an unreal picture. If it were only a matter of not suppressing unpalatable information, the task might be painful but would not be difficult: but my problems do not lie there. F. W. Dillistone,

by then an experienced biographer, was driven to admit in the Preface to
his life of Max Warren:

> To write about him has been what a recent biographer of Gladstone
> described as 'an act of homage'. I have often heard warnings about
> the perils of hagiography. I can only say that this man came nearer
> to my own conception of what constitutes a saint than any other I
> have known.[11]

One of my correspondents referred to John Stott's practice of 'disengaging
himself from the high opinion others have of him'; and this has been a
comfort to me as I have tried (especially in the concluding chapter) to
give, with candour as well as accuracy, some glimpses of him as others see
him. A few names are missing, mainly of writers of personal letters. I
regret that there is not room for more correspondence; John Stott's range
of replies to letters on many subjects from across the world contains a
wealth of pastoral and theological insight. But no future biographer
should be able to say that I followed the advice given by D. E. Hoste to
Mrs Howard Taylor when she came to write her two-volume *Life* of
Hudson Taylor: 'If you begin too much letting the public in behind the
scenes you shake confidence.'[12]

As for my sources, far more exists in print than I have been able to
include, and as the endnotes show I have supplemented this with letters,
memoranda and interviews, including many with John Stott himself.
There are, of course, references on the Internet but I have had virtually no
help from them beyond the bibliographical, and very little from the
growing number of doctoral or other academic theses which take him as
their subject. There are at least half a dozen already submitted, and one or
two feature in the bibliography towards the end of this volume. They
tend to deal mainly with aspects of his theology; and when discussing his
life and times cover only familiar ground. During the 1980s and 90s he
was the subject of many published interviews. Some of these, significant
in depth and length, shed light on the contemporary scene as he observes
it. Others, as might be expected, repeat one another both in the questions
asked and in his patient replies to reporters and feature-writers in the
countries he was visiting.

John Stott's personal diaries, which were introduced during the chapter
on overseas missions in volume one, here come into their own. Without
them, and the privileged access I have had to them, I could not have
attempted this book. It may be helpful to offer a word of explanation
about them. He began writing a full diary on his first visits overseas (there
are no diaries when he is not on his travels) so as to be able to send to his
parents a few pages at a time, with a brief accompanying personal letter.

In this way they could follow his activities from place to place, and the diaries could then be sent on to All Souls so that Frances Whitehead and praying friends were up to date with his news. At the end of each tour, they formed a resource from which he could write a brief account for the journal *All Souls*, or later for his 'Cornerstone' series in *Christianity Today*, before they were filed for reference. Having once established the practice, he has continued it ever since. Because of this, the diaries are much more detailed, in terms of background information, geographical, political and social descriptions, and even the local knowledge culled from his preliminary reading, than the word 'diary' suggests. For the most part they were not written up a day at a time, nor even within the daily framework of traditional diarists. He would often record a week or ten days together, settling down in some corner of a crowded departure lounge, or on the flight to his next destination; whether Sydney or Chicago, Hong Kong and Singapore, or Heathrow and home.

Such a detailed record has not been without its problems. These have revolved around the length of the diaries (something like 150–200 looseleaf hand-written pages a year, every year for the four decades covered by this volume),[13] and the fact that even the most significant international conferences are not always calculated, twenty or thirty years later, to grip the attention of the general reader. Conversely, passages higher in entertainment value may not qualify to rank as even a footnote to history. On the first of these difficulties, the sheer size of the record, the only solution is to be increasingly selective. Some of the countries John Stott visited (as with many of the people he met or worked with) find no mention in this book at all. Some references to his travels have to be impressionistic, not to say kaleidoscopic, rather than a chronological catalogue. On the second, I have sought to hold the balance, and to remember that for a biographer (as against a historian) small and sometimes amusing domestic incidents may do more to illuminate an individual than does the spotlight of great events. Increasingly, too, the diaries present a problem over birds. I write as one who has often told John Stott that I lack all ornithological aspiration; but it would be a considerable disproportion if I failed to allow the diaries space to reveal at first hand his passionate, not to say obsessive, enthusiasm for birds of every shape, size and colour, and his all-but-professional expertise. Perhaps one day we shall see a complete edition of the diaries: parts at least of John Wesley's famous journal were published in his lifetime. But then there is no evidence that Wesley was an ardent ornithologist![14]

To the expressions of thanks listed in volume one (no less sincere because I do not repeat them in detail) I must add the names of many referred to in both text and notes, as well as of Nelson Gonzalez, John Yates III and

Corey Widmer, recent study assistants to John Stott, who have given me cheerful, skilled and assiduous assistance. Once again I thank Colin Duriez of IVP; and Frances Whitehead who has typed both volumes and made valuable contributions of her own. When Robert Frost was asked to look over a Princeton thesis on his poetry, he wrote in the margin a line of thanks to the author for 'not insisting on my evaluation of his results … No man is supposed to look at himself in the glass except to shave.'[15] Such a truism only increases my gratitude to John Stott for the help I have had from him. Once again, 'At my insistence, he has read the MS of each chapter and helped me to correct errors of fact. But it has been clear between us from the beginning, and proved in practice in many instances, that the final judgment is always mine.'

I began by asking readers to turn again to the Foreword of volume one. Those who do so will find that it concludes with a recognition of how much I owe in the writing of this work, as in all else, to my wife Arlette. I can only add that the gold shines with a brighter lustre as the years pass.

TDS
Ford, 2000

The 1960s

ONE

An Established Ministry: All Souls and Beyond

1

The 1960s have become notorious as years of discontinuity.[1] Radical and apparently irreversible changes occurred in a climate of political instability and unrest. The decade that began with Yuri Gagarin as the first man in space and ended with Neil Armstrong and Edwin Aldrin on the surface of the moon included the years of John Kennedy, elected in 1960 at the age of forty-three, the first Roman Catholic President, and assassinated three years later; while C. S. Lewis died on the same day, almost unnoticed in the worldwide shock. It was the decade of the Berlin Wall, of Vietnam, of the Prague uprising, of a new wave of sectarian fighting in Northern Ireland. Perhaps even more far-reaching were social changes that appeared of less immediate significance. Ironically, these included the widespread introduction of the contraceptive pill; and, in the same breath, the legalizing of abortion in a way unthinkable a few decades earlier. The publication in 1963 of Rachel Carson's *Silent Spring* now appears as a significant milestone in the early environmental movement; while 1967 saw the first human heart transplant. In Britain the death penalty was abolished. Race relations rose to the forefront of the world's agenda (Martin Luther King's 'I have a dream' of 1963 was followed by his assassination five years later); Nelson Mandela went to prison, first for five years, then for 'life'. All over the West a distinctive youth culture flexed its muscles, encouraged at every turn by the media, and by commerce quick to exploit (and by advertising skilled to create) a new market in fashion and consumer goods. The BBC launched *Top of the Pops* in 1962, the year the Beatles were turned down by Decca. In 1963 they shared in a Royal Variety Performance and in 1965 became MBEs. Meanwhile, the 'Lady Chatterley' verdict of 1960 redefined what was thought acceptable to public morals. The Bishop of Woolwich, John Robinson, was the star witness in support of the book, later describing the 1960s as 'a climacteric in the transition from the paternalistic to the permissive society'.[2] John Stott characterized the decade as revealing 'a hatred of authority figures'.[3] Nevertheless, John Wolfe could write of the 1960s as a time when

> Christianity seemed assured of a prominent place in national and cultural life: in 1953 Elizabeth II was crowned Queen amidst the glories of Anglican ceremonial; the novels and theological writings of C. S. Lewis enjoyed great popularity; while the building of a new Coventry Cathedral, consecrated in 1962, became a potent symbol of reconstruction after the horrors of war.[4]

Across the Atlantic, US church membership had reached unprecedented numbers by the end of the 1950s (the pledge recited by pupils at the start of the school day was enlarged in 1954 to include the phrase 'one nation under God', and the words 'In God we trust' were added to US bills and coins a year later), but there would soon be signs that the tide was on the turn.[5]

By contrast, Paul Welsby saw in the 1960s 'the questioning by many, and the abandonment by some, of traditional values. English society was no longer prepared to accept the Christian framework of a transcendental order or a moral universe of absolute values.'[6] There is plenty of statistical evidence that this flight from morality, expressed in the subversion of accepted norms and the extending of the boundaries of sexual permissiveness, gathered momentum at an increasing rate, with only the utterly unforeseen occurrence of Aids to bring any kind of caution; single-parent families proliferated; the term 'husband' and 'wife' became almost quaint, giving place to 'lover' and 'partner'.[7]

Christendom saw the opening of the second Vatican Council in 1962 and the death of Pope John XXIII in 1963. Three years later Michael Ramsey, the 100th Archbishop of Canterbury, visited Pope Paul VI, the first such meeting for over 400 years.

Adrian Hastings, in a fascinating summary, allows himself to 'simplify things a little wildly to make a point':

> Pope John represented Catholicism without Roman rigidity; the
> young Marx and even Khruschev represented Marxism without
> Stalinism; Kennedy represented American capitalism without
> disregard for the needs of the third world; Teilhard and Zen alike
> represented religion without sin and even without dogma; the pill
> represented sex without unwanted children. Remove Roman
> rigidity, Stalinism, sin and the rest, and what a nice world it would
> be and could not Catholicism, Marxism, American capitalism and
> sex all then go happily together? The early sixties half thought they
> might.[8]

For John Stott, beginning his second decade as Rector of All Souls, these
were to be years of consolidation and development in the life of his
church, but of change in those closest to him: by the later 1960s All Souls
was well on the way to becoming his immediate family. Sister Jordan died
in 1961, the only remaining member of the team who had been there
before him, known him as a curate, and worked with Harold Earnshaw-
Smith. She had taken early retirement, struggling with Parkinson's disease
and diabetes. A few years later Packie, the much-loved house-mother at
the Rectory, retired; as did John Dugan, the church bursar. In the
reshuffle that followed, Frances Whitehead became (as she was to remain)
John Stott's personal secretary.

Joanna, John Stott's elder sister, was married and living with her family
in Derbyshire. Her daughter Caroline, the eldest of his three nieces, was
also his God-daughter. 'Uncle Johnnie' (in the very earliest days she could
only manage 'Wumby-Dumby') had long been a favourite. Even before
she visited The Hookses, he used to talk to her about it, and as a tiny
child he had told her bedtime stories: 'When I was a little boy ...' he
would begin, and tell tales of his naughty childhood. He had given her
Patricia St John's stories and explained to her why he was a Christian, and
he let her see that his nieces were very special to him: 'Wherever he is in
the world, he has always remembered our birthdays.'[9] In 1965 Caroline
came to the Froebel Institute at Roehampton. She would often make the
long bus ride into central London to be at All Souls on a Sunday
morning, and would be asked to lunch in the big dining room at the
Rectory with such curates and residents as happened to be there. Packie,
too, would tell her she was always welcome, 'and to bring a friend'.

John Stott's father, Sir Arnold, had died in 1958. His mother Lily lived
on at Bullens Hill Farm until January 1966, sharing it with her daughter
Joy, who shouldered more and more of the task of caring for her mother
and for the home. Until her stroke Lily was often seen at All Souls, a

warm and popular figure; she acted as hostess for her son at the Annual Garden Party which he gave each summer in the grounds of the London Zoo when George Cansdale was churchwarden, and later at Bedford College, Regent's Park, for the volunteer workers of the church. Somehow, so memory records, it was always fine. Then came her first stroke; and she was soon bedridden. John Stott visited as often as he could:

> She remained her sweet and cheerful self, clothed in pink nightie and bed jacket ... She could speak, but got some words muddled. She started calling me 'George' (for no accountable reason), and when a Gull flew past her window, she exclaimed, 'Look! a bluebottle!' She died peacefully in bed, having been visited by many local inhabitants, with whom she was very popular.[10]

There was too, by this time, a tribe of Godchildren. They ranged in ages from Caroline, his eldest niece, entering her teens as the 1960s began, through the children of friends and curates, to Simon Trapnell, born in November 1960, whose father David was later to be one of John Stott's churchwardens.

Throughout the 1960s All Souls was served by a considerable staff. In the summer of 1959 John Lefroy, the senior curate, had already accepted a living when, only days after the birth of his first child, he fell gravely ill with encephalitis and was rushed to the Middlesex Hospital. Here he remained unconscious for some seven weeks, for the early part of which his life hung in the balance; on recovery he was found to have suffered a permanent hemiplegia on his left side. Following lengthy convalescence and rehabilitation, he returned to All Souls and remained for a further six years until his appointment as Vicar of Christ Church, Highbury, in 1965. Geoffrey Rawlins and Julian Charley continued on the staff until the mid-60s, Julian Charley taking over the role of Clubhouse Warden on the departure of Tom Robinson for his native Canada. Martin Peppiatt left to go to East Africa with CMS at the end of 1963; while Vera Williams, Sister Jordan's successor, remained until November 1965 when she went to join John Lefroy at Highbury.

Constantly in evidence at the Rectory, though in no sense a member of the staff, was the remarkable character 'the Countess'. This was Countess Helle Frijs of Denmark, one of four sisters, cousins to Isak Dinesen, the Baroness Blixen who wrote *Out of Africa*.[11] 'The Countess' had been brought up at Frijsenborg, the family seat, a castle near Aarhus on the east coast of Jutland. She was a strong Anglophile, visiting England regularly; and had made a profession of faith at an All Souls Guest Service in the later 1950s. There was a streak of wildness in her family. In her time she had been a steeplechase jockey: she held a pilot's licence, and had a taste for maintaining mechanical vehicles. It was not long, therefore, before she offered to keep 'the Rector's' small car clean and serviced. Though continuing to patronize the Ritz Hotel and Fortnum and Mason, she lived austerely in a bed-sitting room; and so began to spend more and more time in the Rectory mews, an almost too familiar figure in dungarees, lying on her back tinkering with the brakes or adjusting the steering. She quickly established proprietary rights (and mystified observers by managing to bully the Rector), aggravating, and at times infuriating, the residents of the Rectory by constant demands to enter the small kitchen for a bucket of water. Few visitors to the Rectory about that time will have failed to notice this diminutive, aristocratic, self-appointed, lady mechanic-in-residence.[12]

Towards the end of the 1950s Richard Bowdler left the staff, and the ministry of 'Chaplain to the Stores' passed to Michael Harper. He was a Londoner (the family home had been in Welbeck Street) and he had long been an occasional visitor to All Souls. He was converted to Christ in his first year at Cambridge, and during the vacations had alternated between All Souls and Westminster Chapel. He had met John Stott both in London and through the CICCU, and rubbed shoulders with him at meetings of the Eclectic Society while serving his first curacy at St Barnabas, Clapham Common. It was during Michael Harper's time there that John Lefroy led a mission team from All Souls to St Barnabas; and no doubt this played a part in the invitation to succeed Richard Bowdler in 1958. Michael Harper found John Stott 'a very powerful man but easy to work with – an awesome preacher ...'[13] He was one of six curates under the Rector's eye:

> I felt my relationship with him as a curate to a vicar was ideal ... I felt he didn't interfere, but he did take an interest in my work in the Stores. I remember I would share with him either at staff meetings or privately. I know he was interested: he listened to what I was saying and gave advice and supported me.[14]

It was in September 1962 that Michael Harper had an experience of 'renewal', not at a Pentecostal meeting, but through reading the Scriptures: 'It was earth-shaking ... baptized in the Spirit, everything leapt off the page.'[15]

The phrase 'baptized in the Spirit' represents a key element in what became known as the charismatic movement (or in its earlier days, 'neo-Pentecostalism'). This had crossed the Atlantic some years before, but was only then on the point of becoming a feature of British church life. John Stott had come across it to some degree in the late 1950s through visits to

California. He retains a recollection of an American pastor visiting him at the Rectory:

> He came to see me at 12 Weymouth Street and sat opposite me in an armchair, and in the course of the conversation about this outburst of tongue-speaking said to me, 'Have you ever heard anybody speak in tongues?' Those were his exact words, to which I replied, 'No, I haven't', because I hadn't at that time. So he then said, 'Would you like to?', and to my utter amazement, before I had the opportunity to say 'Yes' or 'No', when I was probably hesitating, he broke into this unintelligible utterance, with his eyes open looking at me.
>
> That experience quite shocked me and made me feel that if this is something you can turn on and off like a tap, it really isn't a gift of the Spirit, in the way that they claim. I think it was after this that Michael Harper had his experience, which came to him through meditating on Paul's prayer at the end of Ephesians 3, and the phrase 'to be filled with all the fullness of God'.[16]

This was a period in which the staff of All Souls, in common with many others, were re-examining the call to holiness and to life in the Spirit. John Lefroy's prolonged illness of a few years before had been the cause of much prayer for his healing, and this, together with George Ingram's persistent concern that the church should know the fullness of the Holy Spirit's power, 'had provoked the staff into a deeper and more systematic study of the doctrine of God's Spirit'. The official history of All Souls church continues:

> They did not reach a unanimous conclusion, indeed there were considerable theological differences, but because they felt a growing sense of the need for both individual and corporate self-examination and repentance leading to spiritual revival, All Souls Day 1963 was made the culmination of a week especially devoted to renewal.[17]

It was in this context that, on a staff away-day, John Stott invited Michael Harper to 'tell the whole story' of what he felt had happened to him. At the end John Lefroy told him, 'Michael, I believe you've been baptized in the Spirit' – an expression which Michael Harper had not met before.[18] Foreseeing the dangers of possible division in the church, John Stott told Michael Harper that while he was perfectly free to speak of his experience in terms of personal testimony, it would be best if he did not preach on the subject. Michael Harper agreed:

At some very early stage, I said to John, 'Look, I will never preach on this; I'm not in the business of splitting All Souls', and I never did. I preached and people used to come up to me afterwards and say 'You're different', this sort of thing … John Stott was very interested, he was very intrigued, very gripped by it, but the turn-off was when I spoke in tongues.[19]

The 'speaking in tongues' began, privately, to divide the staff fellowship – some claiming it as a particular gift of God, some dubious about its theological or biblical basis. It was not surprising that, in Michael Harper's words, 'by this time quite a lot of people were writing to John Stott saying "You've really got to get rid of this Harper man" … but John Stott never ever hinted or intimated to me that I should go.'[20] It was not until two years later, when Michael Harper was on the point of leaving the staff, that John Stott felt ready to declare his mind publicly on these neo-Pentecostal teachings and experiences.

After a period of comparative stability through the early 1960s, the middle years of the decade brought many changes among the eight clergy and two lay pastoral workers on All Souls' full-time staff. Miles Thomson joined as a new deacon in Michaelmas 1963, together with Peter Phenna, who had been Assistant Warden at the Clubhouse for two years before starting ordination training. Like other ordinands of the time, he had come to the ordained ministry after military service and a previous career: in his case, in advertising. Peter Bagnall was another such, converted to Christ through the ministry of All Souls just ten days before sailing as an officer cadet in the Indian Army. He later went on to serve as a missionary in Indian villages and in Karachi; in 1964, on Michael Harper's departure, he became Chaplain to the Stores. The following year saw another older curate, George Swannell, newly returned from East Africa, take over from Geoffrey Rawlins the leadership of the Family Service which had been developed at St Peter's with conspicuous success. At the same time Michael Wilcock joined them, a Londoner who had taught for two years before training at Tyndale Hall, followed by a first curacy at Christ Church, Southport.

With so large a staff, comings and goings were continuous. Peter Bagnall suffered a coronary thrombosis after two years as Stores Chaplain and Denis Shepheard was appointed as temporary replacement; he, too, was older than the usual run of curates, and was looking for his first living. When Peter Bagnall did not return to work, Denis Shepheard's appointment was extended and eventually he followed Peter Phenna as Warden of the Clubhouse in 1969. Up to this point, John Stott's staff of curates had been drawn from among his own circle of friends and contacts, all university graduates, mostly from Oxford or Cambridge.

Denis Shepheard was in a different mould, having served for ten years below decks in the Navy before training for ordination. A special rapport grew up between the Rector and this older curate with his wider experience of life, his humour and his uninhibited testimony. After one Service in All Souls, Denis Shepheard told John Stott he had been so moved and excited that he had almost shouted 'Alleluia'. 'If you had,' replied the Rector (not without a twinkle), 'you would have been sacked.' It was only years later that Denis Shepheard confessed that he had returned later to shout his praises when the church was empty! The new curate received, inevitably, a particular welcome from George Swannell, who had joined the staff only six months before:

> Denis was the only ex-R.N. tattooed curate I've ever met, so we had a lot in common. On one occasion when the atmosphere in the staff meeting was a little oppressive we made semaphore briefly to each other.[21]

Two other members joined the team in different capacities during 1966: Jo Gardner followed Vera Williams as Parish Worker; and Norman Anderson was licensed as Reader. J. N. D. Anderson was a well-known evangelical writer and speaker, Professor of Oriental Laws in the University of London, and a member of the Church Assembly. He would become the first Chairman of the House of Laity when the General Synod was inaugurated in 1970, and was one of the key figures, along with his Rector, at the first National Evangelical Anglican Congress in 1967. It was at this time that his son Hugh, one of the most promising students of his generation, fought for two years his battle against cancer, and died at the age of twenty-one in Mildmay Hospital. John Stott was with his parents round the bed where Hugh lay in a coma, very close to death, and read aloud from Romans 8: 'I am convinced that neither death nor life ... will be able to separate us from the love of God that is in Christ Jesus our Lord.'[22] John Stott and Bishop Trevor Huddleston both spoke at Hugh's Memorial Service in All Souls, with the Prime Minister and four or five members of the Labour Cabinet among a crowded congregation.

In 1969 there were further changes: Denis Shepheard moved to the Clubhouse and Barry Dawson succeeded him as Chaplain to the Stores. Michael Wilcock, by then senior curate, left to become vicar of St Faith's, Maidstone, and Garry Guinness arrived to take over the Family Service. Two other staff appointments at this period were of particular significance: Robert Howarth who joined in 1963, and Ted Schroder four years later.

2

Robert Howarth was born in Kenya, where his parents were coffee farmers. During National Service with the Kenya Regiment he saw action against Mau Mau terrorists. In 1953 he came to London and was converted to Christ during Billy Graham's Harringay Crusade the following year: All Souls became his church. After training with the Navigators in America he returned to Kenya, and in 1957 was 'adopted' as an All Souls missionary.

During John Stott's student mission at the Royal College, Nairobi, in May 1962 Robert Howarth was one of his assistants. On the Sunday they drove to the Amboseli National Park. Miles from any church, they held their 'service' (hymn-singing and all) sitting together in their borrowed Land Rover, 'the rest of the congregation, at a respectable distance, consisting of a buck impala and a couple of warthogs!'[23] Here John Stott asked Bob Howarth to consider returning to London with his wife Sarah and their young family, to take charge of the All Souls International Fellowship. Robert Howarth recalls the background to the invitation:

> The late '50s and early '60s was the period in which many countries of the old British Empire were moving into independence. From the outset it was recognized that if the process were to succeed, large numbers of nationals from these countries would need to be trained for leadership. Facilities for this were very limited for most of them at home, so there began a rapidly growing flood of students coming to Britain.

By the early 1960s there were something like 50,000 overseas students in this country, of whom 35,000 were in London. The British Council had opened an Overseas Centre with impressive facilities almost adjacent to All Souls, in Portland Place; and another was opened soon afterwards in Park Crescent on the edge of All Souls' parish:

> John Stott was quick to see the strategic importance of this great field of opportunity. First of all, there was the church's fundamental duty to welcome these strangers and to show them hospitality. Many of them would have been Christians already, and had come assuming that Britain was a Christian country. How would they return after a few years' exposure to the realities of our national life? Others would have had no experience of the gospel at all ...
> And so, in 1961, ASIF (All Souls International Fellowship) was founded, with a small group of enthusiastic All Souls people to lead it. It was to be an *international* fellowship comprising people of *all*

nations, including our own, 'with men and women of several nationalities represented on its committee. In the promotional leaflet, John wrote: 'Come to All Souls on any Sunday and you will see, in the nave, side aisles and galleries, men and women of every race and colour. It is to us a joy and privilege to welcome them ...'[24]

The International Fellowship had been running for about a year when John Stott invited Robert Howarth to All Souls. With his Navigator training, he proved to be a gifted Bible teacher and gave himself to the befriending, teaching and training of successive groups of potential leaders from countries overseas, mainly in the Third World. He and Sarah transferred to London the unquestioning hospitality which had marked their home in East Africa. 'One could not visit their flat near Regent's Park without tripping over the bodies of guests sleeping on the floor!'[25] The Howarth children, Rowland, Toby and Ben, were favourites with ASIF members; and for many visitors their home became a striking introduction to Christian family life.

From the outset Robert Howarth's brief was to care not simply for students but for all overseas visitors, and to commend Christ to them:

> ... the ASIF team became a recognized sphere of 'commissioned service', and we ran a variety of social activities, outings and groups. Each month we would put on a special event for up to 100, which included a two-course meal and coffee (cooked at home by Sarah, and transported to the hall through the rush hour) ... Most of those who came to these suppers did so at the invitation of an existing regular; but deeper friendships were formed as the team mixed with the guests, and then invited them back to their flats or bed-sitting rooms. It was this kind of hospitality that transformed life for many a lonely visitor who found London to be a strange and hostile place. And of course, that led in turn to a receptiveness to the message of Jesus.

In his letter to the 'Friends of All Souls' in February 1967, John Stott was able to report that at a recent Guest Service, eight of the twelve who came forward were from overseas – from Canada, Malawi, Nigeria, Kenya, Zambia and South Africa. All Souls could truly say with John Wesley, 'I look upon all the world as my parish.'[26] One example of this global citizenship could be seen in the appointment to the staff of the next deacon, Ted Schroder. It was sometimes said that 'you can always hear John Stott at All Souls, even if he is not there', because of the way in which many curates soon began to sound like him in mannerisms and intonation. But Schroder was 'one of the first of whom you could never,

ever have said that … if anyone was going to break the mould of the classical All Souls curate, it would be Ted.'[27]

Ted Schroder, like Bob Howarth, was not originally from Britain. His parents owned and managed a small hotel in Hokatika, on the western shore of New Zealand's South Island, where as he grew up he was often to be found serving behind the bar. While still a schoolboy he was converted through a local parish mission. At the University of Canterbury, New Zealand, while reading politics and economics, he joined the Christian fellowship and soon became its president. He came to England to do a second degree and, having been given an introduction to John Stott, visited him at 12 Weymouth Street. They met again at NEAC '67, which Ted Schroder attended as a theological student: and here he also met Professor Norman Anderson and struck up a friendship with his son, Hugh. Nevertheless, he was astonished to receive not long afterwards a letter from John Stott inviting him to consider joining his staff on ordination. John Stott recalls:

> I liked and admired him from the start because he was a man's man, with a strong mind, absolute honesty and an uproarious sense of humour.
>
> He was determined to relate the gospel to the modern world … but he wasn't much good at biblical exposition. My fault was the opposite. I saw the preacher's task in terms of exposition, while I was inept in application. We often said to one another that we needed to combine our strengths.[28]

It was Ted Schroder's influence that first encouraged John Stott to visit again the theatre and cinema (which, like many of his generation, he had renounced soon after his conversion as compromising and unhelpful) as a way of entering the mind-set of contemporary society. Ted, too, because of his work among students, was continually reminding him of the need to relate the gospel to the youth culture of the 1960s:

> This was the time of the student revolutions, and the Vietnam War. I was ministering at The Polytechnic of Central London (formerly Regent Street Poly and now the University of Westminster) as Chaplain with many Maoists and other left-wing Zealots who had no time for Christianity or any religion … my students knew more about Mao's Little Red Book and the Cultural Revolution in China than about the Bible and what went on inside churches. There was a wave of new music on the scene: the Beatles and other psychedelic groups. Dropping acid (LSD), and smoking hash (marijuana), was all the rage. I was concerned for the preaching at All Souls to

address this culture. On one occasion as John and I recessed out of All Souls after a service at which he had preached I said to him, 'So what?' He had preached a good exposition of the passage but I wanted more application to the modern world.

When the Warsaw Pact troops rolled into Czechoslovakia in 1968 John gave ready assent to using All Souls as a refuge for students and others who had been stranded outside their country on their first visit during the Prague Summer. All Souls began to be known for being hospitable to hippies and Christian students who were very unconventional. The high point of this (or low point depending on your perspective) was when an Australian student helped to take the offering in bare feet![29]

Ted Schroder is also particularly remembered for a small incident far-reaching in its consequences. John Stott himself described it as formative:

It was Monday morning in London, the All Souls church staff team had gathered for our weekly meeting, and I was in the chair. The others were carrying on about something which did not particularly interest me (I now forget what it was), and I am ashamed to say that I had switched off. Suddenly Ted Schroder, who might not unfairly be described at that time as 'a brash young colonial from New Zealand', and who is now a close and valued friend, blurted out: 'John, you're not listening!' I blushed. For he was quite right, and it is intolerably rude not to listen when somebody is speaking. Moreover, the tensions which were surfacing in our staff team relationships at that time were largely due to my failure to listen.[30]

Behind Ted Schroder's immediate challenge in the staff meeting was a deeper sense that John Stott was becoming too immersed in the ever more diverse demands of his own ministry beyond the parish. There was, for example, sometimes a question-and-answer session after the Sunday evening service, which Ted Schroder as Minister to Students was responsible for arranging, and about which he was becoming disturbed:

I felt that John wasn't answering the real questions that were being asked – the question behind the question – the context, motivation, reason for the question that was being asked. My comment in the staff meeting was a transference of that problem when some other member of staff was presenting an issue or concern (perhaps it was myself) and he did not hear, or appear to hear, what we were attempting to say.[31]

It remains John Stott's view that this incident brought into the open the tensions among his staff at a time when they thought he was away from All Souls too much, and was therefore one of the factors which led eventually to the decision to appoint a Vicar, and so to the coming of Michael Baughen.[32] Two perceptive observers, returning to All Souls in 1970 after two years overseas, were struck by the changes in style which could be attributed, at least in part, to Ted Schroder's influence on his Rector:

> Putting it very crudely, previously in sermons (for example) John would use contemporary world events by way of anecdotal illustration; after the period of the late 60s he addressed himself more thoroughly and fully to some of the items on the world agenda, with a full, biblical and theological interface ... we were amazed to find in 1970, not having seen John for two years, that he had grown sideburns and was wearing a flowery tie: we really felt decadence had set in to the heart of British society![33]

It was during this period that John Stott was moving towards the 'double listening' (to the Scriptures and to the contemporary world) which became so central to his thinking.[34]

So throughout the 1960s All Souls continued to expand and widen its ministry. An elaborate pattern of fellowship groups ensured that individuals who might have felt lost in so large a congregation, and those who had little other opportunity to participate, were meeting regularly in different neighbourhoods.

John Stott described the thinking and practice behind the creation of this network of fellowship groups during his pastoral-theology lectures at Durham University in February 1968.[35] They were not simply Bible study groups, and 'Bible reading must not therefore dominate the evening'. They were not simply prayer groups, though they were encouraged to give time to intercession, including missionary prayer. Rather, as the policy statement issued in April 1965 made clear, they were each to express and develop the three aspects of Christian fellowship found in Scripture, 'namely our relationship to God himself, our care for one another, and our service to the world'. But the key to the groups was an element of personal sharing, seeking to create a 'climate of confidence' in which members genuinely cared for one another.

John Stott himself, and the members of the staff, tried to visit a different group every fortnight. To supplement these impressions, a questionnaire was circulated to members of the groups. As a result John Stott was able to assure the Durham theological students that lay leadership was what made the groups work:

We pastors may cherish the illusion that we are needed and missed, but the groups consider that they get on better without us! ... Lay leaders, the questionnaire answers inform us, are 'more human and understanding', particularly because they are themselves living and working in lay situations. Further, as a Korean girl put it candidly, 'if clergy-man leads group I become self-conscious and reserved'.[36]

Such fellowship groups quickly became an obvious second step for new Christians graduating from the 'nursery classes'.

Though often thought of as a 'student church', the old people of the parish had held a special place in John Stott's affections since his days as curate. This gained a new and practical expression when an 'Abbeyfield (All Souls) Society' established a home for a number of elderly ladies in Fitzroy Street, within walking distance of the church.[37] This allowed them to remain among friends and in a familiar neighbourhood: whereas under a local rehousing policy for the elderly, some were being sent as far afield as Essex.

Alongside the growth of areas of specialist ministry the geographical bounds of the parish had been extending further under pastoral reorganization. A map in the church magazine in 1962 showed an area extending westwards almost as far as Selfridges, north to the Euston Road, south to Oxford Street, and eastwards to Tottenham Court Road. From this busy commercial centre, and from the large eclectic element in the congregation, the statistics show confirmations (sometimes by Robert Stopford, the new Bishop of London; more often by the Bishop of Willesden) varying from more than fifty candidates to something under twenty. At a special service each year the newly trained Commissioned Workers received their commissioning; as many as fifty in 1961, but averaging thirty or forty a year. Unlike the figures following Harringay, there is little difference to be seen following Billy Graham's Earls Court Crusade of June 1966. The preaching ministry made its own demands on the staff, increased (but also enhanced) by the formation of the Tape Library. After the Sunday evening services the Rector and the headmaster of the Day School, Mansel Connick, would retire to the School's studio to record tapes of his previous sermons. This was because the pace and projection of a sermon as delivered to a large congregation were found to be less suited to the one-to-one situations in which most of the tapes were used. Mansel Connick recalls:

I saw the real calibre and amazing recall together with the absolute commitment of the man then. Always after a full day's preaching he'd bring out his little black book, go over his notes of a sermon he'd given months before, while I set up the knobs and plugs. He would refer to any Bible references on the back of each page and then begin to record. I can't remember a retake nor a stumble, just pure and utter concentration.[38]

Behind all this activity lay the Hour of Prayer, which alternated weekly with the meetings of the fellowship groups. That was not without its lighter moments. David Trapnell, who became churchwarden in 1967, retained vivid memories of George Ingram, a valiant retired missionary,[39] now very deaf, who was never absent from the prayer meeting. When the time came to kneel, he would place his bowler hat on the seat of the chair in front of him, and as one prayer followed another from different parts of the room an irreverent observer who cared to open his eyes could see George's hearing-aid held aloft like an antenna, rotating as if it were some kind of radar, to catch the prayer being prayed and then respond with a fervent 'Amen'.[40]

In a radio interview on the BBC towards the end of the 1960s, Roy Trevivian asked John Stott for the secret of the 'unusual success' enjoyed by All Souls. John Stott replied:

> I am convinced that Jesus Christ is still attractive to people even in England today where the church puts them off ... If the church came back in loyalty to Jesus Christ and fearlessly preached Jesus as the Lord and Saviour of men, I still believe that England would sit up and take notice.[41]

John Stott was here speaking from experience. He could point to a steady stream of individuals who were ready to 'sit up and take notice' of preaching which was Christ-centred and fearlessly proclaimed. Roger Simpson, while not wholly typical, would be a good example. The son of a pilot with East African Airways, he was at boarding school in England when he first came to follow Christ through a Scripture Union houseparty. His twin brother was experimenting with the drug culture of the day, and Roger arrived at London University, aged eighteen, 'with a headband, beads, very long hair and somewhat confused spiritually and morally'. His houseparty leader had encouraged him to visit All Souls, and he wandered in, 'lost and empty'. He recalls:

> It was through John Stott's preaching that I came to a deep and lasting commitment to Jesus Christ. I will never forget his words (which I have said countless times when leading missions myself): 'As you come forward, you will have to go against the stream; but you may as well learn that now, because it will be like that for the rest of your life.' I battled against the crowd going out and

introduced myself to him, and that is how I began to grow in my faith.[42]

It says something for All Souls that they were able to contain and nurture this student of the swinging 60s. Ted Schroder's presence on the staff was reassuring, since he also had fashionably long hair and sideburns. Presently Roger Simpson found himself a student member of the All Souls PCC – and due to take up the offering during the service, wearing 'a shaggy Afghan coat, jeans with no zip held together with rope, headband, beads and all'. It could never have crossed his mind that in less than ten years' time he would be on the same chancel step, only this time in cassock and surplice, receiving the collection as one of the All Souls clergy.

In 1969 Michael Marshall was appointed vicar of All Saints, Margaret Street, the nearest church to All Souls, and with a reputation for being a bastion of high-church worship and ceremonial. The two men knew each other already (Michael Marshall had been Chaplain to the University of London since 1964) but now acquaintance grew into friendship, each recognizing in the other a love for Christ and a concern to share his gospel of redemption. Soon after Michael Marshall's arrival, John Stott asked him to come to a meal at the Rectory, and they decided to inaugurate a joint meeting between their young ordinands. It would be called 'Saints and Souls', and take the form of an occasional debate on some topic of the day. A few such meetings were held before it ran into the sand. The friendship, however, continued to flourish, so that in the 'Decade of Evangelism' of the 1990s they could be found sharing a platform together.[43] Less easy to achieve was any real relationship with the local Roman Catholic Church of St Charles Borromeo in Ogle Street, just round the corner from All Souls Church Day School. John Stott approached the priests there, and a meeting for theological dialogue was sustained for a year or two. Though little seemed to come from it at the time, it probably played a part as a stepping-stone in John Stott's thinking towards the prolonged and significant Evangelical–Roman Catholic Dialogue on Mission (ERCDOM) of the 1970s and 80s.[44]

3

During the 1960s John Stott continued to receive more invitations as speaker, teacher and preacher than he could hope to fulfil. University missions remained his first priority, but three times during the decade he visited the Keswick Convention to give the Bible readings: in 1962 from 1 Corinthians 1 – 6; in 1965 from Romans 5 – 8; and 1969 from 2 Timothy.

The Keswick Convention owes its name to the small town of Keswick in the Lake District, where it has been held annually since 1875. Its stated purpose is 'the deepening of the spiritual life' (originally 'the promotion of scriptural holiness'). This 'message of Keswick', with its stress on 'the rest of faith' as the God-given means of holiness, 'shaped the prevailing pattern of Evangelical piety for much of the twentieth century'.[45] To be invited as a Keswick speaker therefore implied a particular cachet, a public recognition of evangelical credentials coupled with the gift of addressing an interdenominational audience hungry both for spiritual challenge and for biblical teaching.

At the same time, Keswick was not without its critics. Under J. I. Packer (with the enthusiastic support of Dr Martyn Lloyd-Jones) Anglican evangelicalism in the 1950s was discovering a renewed interest in the Puritans. This in turn led to the establishing of a Puritan Studies Group (later Conference) chaired by Dr Lloyd-Jones and meeting at Westminster Chapel. Alister McGrath, writing as James Packer's biographer, describes how this new grouping

> ... potentially posed a significant challenge to the 'received wisdom' of British evangelicalism on a series of issues, especially the Keswick doctrine of 'sanctification by faith'. While an older generation looked back to Keswick Conventions for their fellowship and teaching, an emerging generation looked instead to the Puritans. The Puritan and Keswick positions were incompatible. Tensions and conflict were thus virtually inevitable within evangelicalism over this significant matter.[46]

The controversy came to public notice through a fifteen-page critique contributed by James Packer to *The Evangelical Quarterly*. Entitled '"Keswick" and the Reformed Doctrine of Sanctification', this took the form of a sustained and critical assault on a recent book which the Chairman of the Convention, Fred Mitchell, had commended as a 'faithful and accurate' account of Keswick teaching. Packer hoped to show in this article that what he understood by the Keswick message was 'attenuated and impoverished; that its teaching rests on a theological axiom which is false to Scripture and dishonouring to God; and that it cannot but prove comfortless and sterile to those who take it as meaning what it says'.[47] The article concluded by summarizing Keswick teaching as Pelagian, shallow, depressing, and delusive: 'After all, Pelagianism is the natural heresy of zealous Christians who are not interested in theology.'[48]

John Stott was among those who were troubled about certain accustomed expressions of the Keswick message at this period. But with many friends on the Council and on the team of speakers, he had no occasion to explore the issues publicly. Harold Earnshaw-Smith had himself been a Keswick speaker; but John Stott was aware that there were Christians who sometimes found what they heard at Keswick confusing, and became distressed as they struggled to reconcile the hope held out to them with their own very imperfect experience of sanctification. James Packer's original misgivings about Keswick teaching 'had primarily to do with its failure to meet his spiritual condition',[49] and this goes far to explain the tone of his article quoted above. In something of the same way, Earnshaw-Smith's daughter Elisabeth had returned from Keswick during one of her father's spells of illness, disappointed and confused over her failure to find the promised 'second blessing' – and it had fallen to John Stott, her father's curate, to sort out her difficulty and put her right.[50] For him to be invited to give the Bible readings highlighted a certain ambivalence, therefore, in his attitude. Bash (E. J. H. Nash) had valued Keswick and encouraged his leaders to attend.

> It was part of my upbringing [John Stott wrote] to revere the Keswick Convention. At the same time, there was widespread uncertainty about the nature of 'the Keswick message'. What were its distinctives? Keswick was reputed to teach three holiness doctrines – first, that the 'Keswick blessing', sometimes called 'the baptism of the Spirit', was the birthright of all Christians as a distinct post-conversion experience; secondly, that Romans 6 teaches a 'death to sin' by which one becomes insensitive and even immune to it, and thirdly, that the way of victory was to 'let go and let God', that is, to surrender passively to the indwelling Spirit without having to make any active contribution to the process of sanctification. I had already come, while at Cambridge, to reject these three teachings, whether or not it was true that Keswick was committed to them.[51]

Accordingly, when John Stott received an invitation from the then Chairman of Keswick, his friend A. T. Houghton, asking him to give the Bible readings at the 1962 Convention, he felt that he could not accept until his uncertainties about the 'message of Keswick' had been aired and answered. He wrote to Canon Houghton asking if he would be expected to subscribe to any particular 'holiness doctrine', and received the reply (after some discussion at the speakers' conference)[52] that the Council were simply inviting him to expound the Scripture as he understood it. Reassured by this, John Stott accepted the invitation, and chose for his four Bible readings the early chapters of 1 Corinthians under the general title 'The Calling of the Church', speaking in turn of its unity, its humility, its ministry and its purity.

In the 1960s the Convention was attracting some 7,000 people annually. For one week in the year it dominated the town. The meetings were held in two vast marquees, the main tent recently extended and the smaller linked to it by the innovation of closed-circuit television. 'A first visitor at the opening Saturday night', wrote John Pollock in his history of Keswick, 'cannot fail to be moved by the mere mass of people united in worship, by the reverent singing of many thousand tongues, by the rank upon rank of faces looking toward the flower-banked platform beneath the great red motto-banner.'[53] The banner proclaimed, as it does still today, a unity which transcends denominational boundaries: ALL ONE IN CHRIST JESUS.

'To say that this was expository preaching at its best', wrote a Church newspaper of J. R. W. Stott's series on 1 Corinthians 1 – 6, 'is hardly to do justice to the immense vigour, fire and love for Christ and His Church. Nor can it quite convey the impression of a man "under" God's Word, using great gifts to unfold the precise meaning and application of almost every phrase.'[54]

'The precise meaning and application of every phrase' was not won without effort. Rowland Appleton was the member of the Keswick Council deputed to welcome John Stott, and was waiting for him on the steps of the hotel to show him to his room:

John went across to the chest-of-drawers under the window, removed the top drawer, turned it over, and re-inserted it upside down. Satisfied that this would make a desk on which he could work, he spent much of his time in Keswick in his room, writing on this improvised desk, and was very little seen in the public rooms of the hotel.[55]

Thanks to the Keswick Tape Library these addresses were heard across the world, sometimes by missionaries in very isolated stations. Charles and Shirley Horne, for example, were working among 'completely Stone Age people, warlike animists' in the Central Highlands of Papua New Guinea with the Unevangelized Fields Mission. They had seen in 1961/62 'a big mass movement, resulting in thousands of people burning their fetishes and weapons, and seeking teaching'. Isolated from fellowship, they received reel-to-reel tapes of the Bible readings on 1 Corinthians: 'John Stott ministered to us through those tapes.'[56]

It was partly this knowledge that many Christian pastors and missionaries would be looking to him for teaching that would shape their own ministries, as well as his own determination to be faithful to the

Scriptures he was expounding, that led to John Stott's attention to careful preparation; and so in turn to his clarity and power as an expositor. In 1965, when he gave the Bible readings on one of the passages much disputed by certain styles of 'holiness teaching' (Romans 5, 6, 7 and 8), he used the journey north to continue his study. Peter Moore was the driver:

> I recall driving up with him to Keswick the year he gave the Bible Readings on Romans 5 – 8. I had no idea how important those readings would be for the history of Keswick or the evangelical understanding of sanctification; but I do recall John being more than usually nervous on the trip up, and working furiously in the back seat of the small car.[57]

4

'Keswick' was an interdenominational week in the evangelical annual calendar. 'Islington', by contrast, was a single day's conference for Anglican clergy. The Islington Clerical Conference, to give it its full name, was the creation of Daniel Wilson the younger, who was Vicar of Islington in the 1830s, following his father, Daniel Wilson the elder, who in 1832 became Bishop of Calcutta, 'leaving behind him a parish proverbial for strength and efficiency'.[58] In 1827 he had invited twelve friends to discuss the subject of prayer, with special reference to the events of the day; and this quickly became an annual event. In the years following, under his son's leadership, the January meeting grew steadily until it was attracting more than 300 clergy. Successive Vicars of Islington maintained the tradition, not always at this level of attendance, and in particular Hugh Gough and Maurice Wood worked hard to revive the Conference in the years following the Second World War.

John Stott had spoken at the 1955 Conference on the subject of parochial evangelism.[59] Maurice Wood then invited him to be the Conference preacher in 1960; and to give a main address the following year on the theme of 'The Word of God in the World Today'. Three years later in 1964, at the invitation of Prebendary R. P. P. Johnston, he gave an address which was to prove far-reaching in its consequences. The theme of the Conference was 'The Holy Spirit in the Life of the Church'; and John Stott's subject was 'The Individual Christian and the Fullness of the Holy Spirit'. The Conference attracted 'the largest attendance in living memory', perhaps a thousand clergy and lay people. The editor of *Crusade* found it 'hard to refute the suggestion that the attendance, up by several hundred on previous years, was greatly influenced by the subject'.[60] Many were looking for guidance in trying to relate this 'New

Pentecostalism' to Scripture. John Stott's reputation as a Bible-expositor, who had first-hand experience of the new movement among his own colleagues at All Souls, ensured a large audience.

The rise of neo-Pentecostalism in America had been brought forcibly to the notice of evangelical Anglicans in Britain by a five-page editorial in the journal *The Churchman* by Philip E. Hughes, a respected scholar. His imagination had been fired by what he had seen and heard, on a visit to the United States in 1962, of Pentecostalism there.[61] From 1962 onwards a stream of occasional articles and pamphlets – many of American origin – kept this issue on the evangelical agenda. A new organization, the Fountain Trust, was established with Michael Harper among the moving spirits. A few years earlier he had been 'singled out ... for particular prayer' among the staff team at All Souls by a little group of lay members (including George and May Ingram, whose great longing was for revival) who wanted him to experience 'a baptism of the Spirit'.[62] George Ingram made no secret of this, and Michael Harper would find 'that familiar elderly voice' on the phone pleading, 'Brother – please don't travel second class to heaven, will you?'[63] By the beginning of 1964 both John Lefroy and Martin Peppiatt (who was leaving to serve with CMS in East Africa) were joining Michael Harper in believing that they too had been baptized with the Holy Spirit.

Roopsingh Carr, then working in London and a member of All Souls, asked John Stott one day whether there was such an experience as 'the baptism of the Holy Spirit', and remembers the reply: 'I do not know, Roopy.'[64] With a number of those close to him already involved in the movement and testifying to blessings received, John Stott set himself during a visit to The Hookses to think through the question in the light of Scripture. Then it was time to share his conclusions. Many hoped for a similar testimony, supported by biblical exegesis:

> But these hopes were finally disappointed at the Islington evangelical clergy conference early in 1964. Before a record attendance attracted by the topic of the Holy Spirit and by news of this new movement, Stott repudiated the concept of a post-conversion Spirit-baptism.[65]

David Watson, at that time a curate in Cambridge, had been assured by Dr Martyn Lloyd-Jones that what he had begun to experience in this new Pentecostalism was indeed the baptism of the Holy Spirit. Looking back some twenty years later, David Watson recalled:

> This was a period of much heart searching, diligent study and many meetings. Because of the growing number of people in the country

claiming to be filled or baptized with the Spirit, John Stott was asked to produce a clear paper setting out the biblical doctrines. This he did with his usual clarity, authority and graciousness, but taking a view diametrically opposed to that of Dr. Martyn Lloyd-Jones.[66]

John Stott's address was neither prepared, nor delivered, as quite the manifesto which these accounts suggest. His aim, as with his Keswick Bible readings, was not to create controversy or to reinforce division, but to teach the truth. Nevertheless it was a timely intervention, since many thoughtful evangelicals – not least those concerned with the student world – had considerable misgivings as to how far this movement, at least in all its manifestations, was solely the work of the Holy Spirit of God. Derek Tidball, in an understated comment, notes that

> Evangelicals have been much affected by the charismatic movement in its various forms but have not always embraced it easily. The involvement of the Roman Catholics, the apparent devaluing of doctrine in favour of experience and the preference for the present word of God, as in prophecy or words of knowledge, as opposed to the written word of God, as in Scripture, have made many evangelicals cautious.[67]

Further, he shows how, at least for a time in the early days, it seemed that 'Pentecost was replacing Calvary' and adds, 'The songs of the movement were particularly noted as having changed the emphasis but it was true of the writing and preaching too.'[68]

It is still sometimes supposed that John Stott's address at the 1964 Islington Conference (particularly when expanded for publication) was a throwing down of the gauntlet, a confrontational challenge. A correspondent writing from California the following year suggested as much. John Stott replied rebutting any suggestion that his view was preconceived:

> When the movement began some years ago in this country I personally searched the Scriptures deliberately in order to discover the truth about the subject. I opened my mind afresh to all that was being said, written and claimed, and spent two years reading, thinking, praying and discussing. It was as a result of this prolonged period of study that I came to my conclusions.[69]

The impression was easily given that certain 'charismatics', by their insistent advocacy of 'baptism in the Spirit' and the gift of tongues, were thereby impugning the standard of discipleship of others. John Martin, sometime editor of *The Church of England Newspaper*, writes of 'a bitter war of words', though he admits that this was generally conducted with courtesy:

> For the most part, charismatics were as polite and gracious as Stott in their language, yet they could not hide the fact that they believed Christians needed this second experience of God's blessing – be it called 'baptism' or 'fullness'. The conservatives could draw only one conclusion from their arguments: that there were first-class Christians who had received this charismatic blessing and second-class Christians who had not. It was hardly a recipe for harmony at parish level.[70]

John Stott's Islington address, both as delivered and in its published form, was firmly directed to the need of the time: 'the recrudescence of "Pentecostalism" in non-Pentecostal churches, which rejoices some and bewilders or even alarms others'.[71] Nevertheless, he made his reasons for speaking (and later writing) clear:

> ... our motive in thus seeking to discern God's purpose is practical and personal, not academic or controversial. We are brethren. We love one another. We are concerned to know God's will in order to embrace it ourselves and commend it to others, not in order to score cheap points off one another in theological debate.[72]

The booklet (it was only forty pages long) laid down as axiomatic that Scripture taught the fullness of the Holy Spirit as a distinctive blessing of the new age, the Christian era; that it was a universal blessing for all Christians, and intended as a continuous blessing. Careful exegesis dealt firmly with what were frequently cited as contrary instances (notably in Acts 8 and 19). His main thesis was that the baptism of the Spirit necessarily accompanies conversion, a once-for-all experience:

> As an initiatory event the baptism is not repeatable and cannot be lost, but the filling can be repeated and in any case needs to be maintained. If it is not maintained, it is lost. If it is lost, it can be recovered. The Holy Spirit is 'grieved' by sin (Eph. 4:30) and ceases to fill the sinner. Repentance is then the only road to recovery. Even in cases where there is no suggestion that the fullness has been forfeited through sin, we still read of people being filled again, as a fresh crisis or challenge demands a fresh empowering by the Spirit.[73]

Finally, he considered the implication of the apostolic command, 'Be filled with the Spirit' (Ephesians 5:18), and added: 'We must assert that neither the baptism nor the fullness of the Spirit need be accompanied by spectacular signs. The initial baptism of the Spirit may be quiet and unsensational while the continuing fullness of the Spirit manifests itself in moral qualities rather than in miraculous phenomena.'[74]

In its original or later form the booklet or book has never been out of print. In 1975 the original booklet was replaced by a rewritten and expanded version, *Baptism and Fullness*. John Stott's purpose in this revision was to clarify and amplify what he had written, and relate it to the growth of the charismatic phenomenon during the intervening decade. But twenty years later, in reply to a question, he added this explanation:

> I practically rewrote the book, principally because I felt I had been less than generous in my evaluation of the movement. So, I wanted to put on record that I had no doubt that God had blessed the charismatic movement to both individuals and local churches. It would be quite impossible and improper to deny that.[75]

But there was also a third and more personal reason. 'During recent years,' he wrote in the Preface to the new edition, 'I have regularly received letters from people who say they have heard that, since writing *The Baptism and Fullness of the Holy Spirit*, I have changed my views. This is not so. The revised edition gives me the chance to correct this false rumour.'[76]

The letters in question continued from many parts of the world for a period of three or four years. John Stott summarized their general content as making five points: 'We hear that you have changed your mind, that you now have been baptized with the Spirit, that you speak in tongues, that you have asked IVP to withdraw the book, and they have refused to do so.'[77] It is not surprising that he was glad of an opportunity to deny all such suggestions and set the record straight. From time to time since then the rumour has resurfaced; but it remains entirely without foundation.[78]

5

The following year, 1965, John Stott was not at the Islington Conference because he was overseas; but he spoke in 1966 and again in 1967, when the theme was 'Pastor and People'. In 1966 the Conference discussed 'Bishops in the Church'. It was indicative of evangelicalism in the 1960s that not only was there no bishop among the speakers, but that none of them was other than plain 'The Reverend' – though in time Peter

Johnston would become Prebendary of St Paul's, John Cockerton Prebendary and Canon of York, and George Marchant Archdeacon of Auckland and Canon of Durham. John Stott's address was on 'The New Testament Concept of *Episkopē*', an exposition of Acts 20:17–38, Paul's farewell to the elders of the Ephesian church. He showed that oversight (*episkopē*) belonged to God and was delegated to presbyter-bishops ('the two terms are in the New Testament convertible and refer to the same office')[79] and that the essence of this oversight was pastoral rather than administrative, was characterized by service rather than authority, and had at its heart the feeding of the flock by the careful teaching of the truth: 'Oh for bishops and presbyters who will take seriously this fundamental character of oversight in the Church today!'[80]

John Stott was then aged forty-four. He had been ordained for twenty years, and Rector of All Souls for fifteen. A few years later, during Edward Heath's premiership, vacant dioceses began to be asked to fill in a *pro forma*, indicating what kind of man they wanted as their next bishop. Bernard Palmer later interviewed Sir Edward Heath in the course of his study of prime ministers as bishop-makers:

> Heath told me that the completed *pro formas* always showed a remarkable similarity. Every diocese wanted a man aged between 44 and 48, married with four children (preferably two at university and two still at school), and with a knowledge both of agriculture and of industry. The only difference that ever arose was that the diocese which had had a High Church bishop usually wanted his replacement to be a little Lower, while a diocese with a Low Church bishop asked for one a little Higher.[81]

It is difficult to believe that John Stott's name was not constantly before the 'bishop-makers' of this period. Indeed, church people made sure that this was so.[82] In November 1963 (Sir) John Hewitt, as Secretary for Appointments to Sir Alec Douglas-Home, had a long talk with the Dean of Windsor, Robert Woods, and made a 'Note for the record' of their conversation:

> In discussing Southwell the Dean asked me whether I had thought about Maurice Wood who, in his view, was very much better and more sensible than John Stott who would be equally acceptable to the evangelicals … I said I thought Maurice Wood might well go to a Diocesan See.[83]

It was clearly not easy filling vacant sees: in the files of this period, certain names regularly reoccur.[84] Less than ten years before, Archbishop

Fisher had been complaining about the difficulty of finding men with the qualities needed for episcopal office: 'we have drained the reservoir dry at the moment'.[85] Certainly John Stott could not produce the wife and four children dioceses seemed to want; but there have been plenty of examples of bachelor bishops, 'married to their dioceses'. Perhaps he had no specialist knowledge of agriculture or industry; but he was a Cambridge double first, a Chaplain to the Queen, a linguist, a naturalist with a love of the countryside, yet committed to urban ministry, enriched by a vastly greater experience of the world beyond these shores than came the way of most bishops-designate. Mervyn Stockwood has described how towards the end of 1959, as Vicar of Great St Mary's, Cambridge, he was asked to become Bishop of Southwark:

> I had an opportunity to talk over the matter with Michael Ramsey, the Archbishop of York, who happened to be in Cambridge. He was reluctant to commit himself, but in his inimitable way he said, 'If you decide to become a bishop I shall be glad to welcome to the bench a man who when all of us, like sheep, are saying 'Yes, yes, yes,' will have the courage to say, 'No, no, no, no, no.'[86]

There is little doubt that John Stott would have found himself in bishops' meetings saying 'No, no, no, no, no.' Michael Saward, as Radio and Television Officer of the Church Information Office, recalls a later talk with Michael Ramsey, then Archbishop of Canterbury:

> Archbishop Michael Ramsey and I were conversing in his car in about 1969. He was grumbling about the fact that 'none of the Evangelical bishops would stand up and be counted.' I suggested that few of them were recognized as being Evangelicals, by my generation. Coming back in the late afternoon the name of John Stott came up. 'I do find that man so intransigent,' he growled. 'Archbishop,' I said, 'you complained about lack of backbone in Evangelicals this morning. You really cannot have it both ways.'[87]

In the inevitable absence of hard evidence, it can only be assumed that what Ramsey felt to be John Stott's 'intransigent' evangelicalism, however graciously expressed, was a major stumbling-block. Owen Chadwick has lifted a corner of the curtain to give a glimpse of Harold Macmillan's mind on the subject of bishops; and though Macmillan had ceased to be Prime Minister in 1963, Ramsey would remain Archbishop of York and then of Canterbury from 1956 until 1974. This was before the days of the Crown Appointments Commission, and therefore at a time when the personal views of either Archbishop must have carried very considerable weight. Michael Ramsey's lack of understanding of (not to say distaste for) Anglican evangelicalism cannot have been without significance whenever John Stott's name came to be mentioned in connection with a vacant See. Macmillan, early in his time as Prime Minister, asked Ramsey down from York so that they could meet:

> And at one point in the conversation they touched on the kind of people who ought to become bishops. Macmillan was very frank about his personal preference. 'He discoursed about his under-standing of the Church and he said that we had to hold the high and the low together but for his part his sympathies were with the high. He added that while the evangelicals had their part in the Church he did not think that on the whole they had the qualities suitable for being bishops.'[88]

The same note constantly reoccurs. When the gentle, disarming Stuart Blanch, a man of 'moderate evangelicalism, was consecrated Bishop of Liverpool in 1966, the same year as this Islington Conference, Bernard Palmer states that 'his churchmanship was never held against him'.[89] The fact that such a denial seems necessary tells its own story; as does the account of Maurice Wood, on his appointment to Norwich in 1971, appearing to some critics 'indelibly tarred with the Evangelical brush'.[90] Perhaps there still remains some atavistic remnant of that 'barrier of psychological association, too rarely recognized' which Owen Chadwick cites as one reason why evangelical Anglicans of an earlier age seemed to bring with them, to high churchmen, 'a touch of the alien intruder'.[91] Perhaps it was simply that a moderate liberal tractarianism had long monopolized ecclesiastical corridors of power. Michael Ramsey recalled that when Maurice Wood's name came before the Queen for the See of Norwich, Her Majesty had not heard the expression 'conservative evangelical' and needed to have it explained to her.[92]

Even as late as 1987, in connection with what was to become the Gareth Bennett tragedy, Robert Runcie (so Bennett wrote in his diary) seemed to be in agreement that 'Evangelicals and Catholics' were not being fairly treated by the Crown Appointments Commission, telling Bennett that this must be laid at the door of the diocesan representatives.[93]

Such references as those quoted above are not nullified by the fact that, with hindsight, it is clear that God had marked out John Stott for a different kind of leadership. Adrian Hastings, a shrewd Roman Catholic observer of the Anglican scene, after recounting something of John Stott's position as 'one of the controlling figures in the councils of international Evangelicalism', goes on to add:

One thing he has not become is a bishop, and doubtless wisely. A modern Anglican bishop has to relate sympathetically to all wings of the Church of England, and in strict Evangelical eyes an Evangelical who accepts a bishopric, like Edward Woods or even Donald Coggan, is almost bound to be judged sooner or later as something of a sell-out. British Evangelical history in fact is replete with lost leaders – men who, as they grew older, have found it impossible or at least undesirable to stick quite closely enough to the movement's doctrines and norms.[94]

Yet for John Stott the ambivalence has remained. Alongside his confidence in God's over-ruling providence he has sometimes felt (but rarely expressed) a sense of very human disappointment that this opportunity was never given to him.[95] Perhaps it was his own understanding of the role of the presbyter-bishop in the New Testament which has sometimes persuaded him, even if only half-seriously, that he would have liked the chance of an English bishopric. In common, perhaps, with many clergy, he sometimes missed a sense of intimate pastoral concern for himself and his ministry from the bishops of his own diocese. He could not but notice how, perhaps over a meal together following a confirmation service,

> ... after what had no doubt been a very busy day, the Bishop would relax and talk about everything under the sun, the Test match and the weather and so on: yet I think it's accurate to say that not once in twenty years did a bishop say to me, 'Well now, tell me, how is the battle going?' or 'Is there anything that you would like to share with me?' or 'Can I help you in any way?' or 'Shall we pray together?' or anything like that.[96]

Seeing himself as an 'evangelical reformer', John Stott had sought in his own ministry to bring 'the local church, exemplified by All Souls, into greater conformity to the Word of God and the vision of the New Testament; and would have liked the chance to try to do the same for a diocese'.[97] Certainly, at least as late as the end of the 1960s, in a memorandum written for himself alone, he confessed to 'the probability of a later invitation to become a bishop'. The question does not feature largely in the published interviews that he has given; but in 1992 Terry Lovell raised this matter with him and reported:

> He would, he admits, in many ways rather like to have been a bishop. Not for the self-gratifying quest for privilege, or the gas-and-gaiters comfort of high office. Rather, for the sheer, naked power.

'Bishops', he said, 'still have a lot of influence, and I would have loved the opportunity to use that influence to serve the people of God and to defend and preach the Gospel.'[98]

We shall probably never know just how near or far John Stott came from being asked to tackle an English bishopric. At different times both the Prime Minister's and the Archbishops' Appointments Secretaries had been to see him – in part, no doubt, because All Souls is a Crown living, but also to talk with him about his own future. John Stott recalls one of them (probably Sir David Stephens or Sir John Hewitt, successive Secretaries for Appointments to the Prime Minister) asking questions about what he might or might not be willing to wear, no doubt with cope and mitre and perhaps chasuble in mind, if he became a bishop. He remembers responding to the effect that the question seemed to him highly improper, and that 'I thought it was very inappropriate to make ecclesiastical millinery the criterion for episcopal suitability'.[99]

Further afield, John Stott had been asked to let his name go forward for bishoprics in Australia, and in the 1950s and again in the 1970s declined specific invitations. He also, at different times, discouraged influential friends who had wished to put forward his name through appropriate channels for a number of English dioceses – Liverpool, Rochester and Winchester, to name but three.

Indeed, in the case of Winchester, matters were taken a little further. When John V. Taylor retired in 1985, Michael Baughen, then Bishop of Chester, felt strongly that if John Stott could be appointed it would very considerably strengthen the cause of evangelical theology within the House of Bishops. Moreover Winchester, being the third senior diocese of the southern province, and with a tradition of episcopal scholarship, would be a not inappropriate appointment. Accordingly, Michael Baughen first consulted the Archbishop, Robert Runcie, who would act as Chairman of the Crown Appointments Commission, the body charged with nominating the new bishop. Dr Runcie indicated that he would be willing to lend his support to John Stott's name, should it come up for discussion, if John Stott himself was ready to let his name go forward and would accept the appointment if it was offered. Michael Baughen then put this idea, with his reasoning behind it, to John Stott at a private meeting at 12 Weymouth Street. John Stott asked for a weekend to ponder the proposal and permission to consult one or two close advisers. Those whom he did consult advised against it; and as John Stott himself wrote later,

I felt I could not now change the whole direction of my ministry without acknowledging that I'd made a mistake. In declining other approaches I believed I'd made the *right* decision, and I had no liberty to change direction now.[100]

This must be seen as final confirmation of Adrian Hastings' judgment, quoted above. Though John Stott might have broken the mould and forged a new type of episcopacy, the care of a diocese would have been a limitation and diminution of the world-wide ministry God has given him. He is often compared with Charles Simeon, not least in Macaulay's tribute to Simeon's powers of example, teaching and oversight: 'If you knew what his authority and influence were, and how they extended … to the most remote corners of England, you would allow that his real sway in the church was far greater than that of any primate.'[101]

It is, on one level at least, a wholly convincing answer to the question why John Stott has not become a bishop.

TWO

Evangelical Leadership: Furthering the Gospel

1

Throughout the 1960s John Stott continued to undertake university missions, both at home and abroad. In 1961/62 he served the first of his three terms as President of IVF (from 1975, UCCF), leading missions at the Royal Agricultural College, Cirencester, in London for the LIFCU, and at Trinity College, Dublin – as well as a six weeks' tour of African universities. In 1963 he was at the University of Manchester in February, and at Aberystwyth (one of the constituent colleges of the University of Wales) in November, with a visit to Asian universities in between.

Aberystwyth 1963 was the only university mission John Stott has led in Wales, and perhaps partly for that reason is still warmly remembered as a remarkable time.[1] It took the form of a series of lecture-type meetings in the Examination Hall of Old College, on 'The Challenge of Christianity'. Attendance was high for the size of the college, with over a hundred students each evening and many personal interviews. Geraint Fielder was a BD student at the time:

The university college was small and so was the CU. The latter existed only intermittently and precariously in a High Church atmosphere extremely hostile to it. There were only a few dozen at the meeting, attended by the authoritarian College chaplain, 'Father Mac', who asked awkward questions ...

During the mission John Stott gave a special lecture to the Presbyterian theological College staff and students. Our New Testament professor in particular was no gospel man, a Bultmannian and dismissive in a jolly kind of way of 'evangelical scholarship'. I recall his expressions of astonishment as during answers to questions John quoted chunks of New Testament verses in Greek off by heart! For the evangelical minority who were much under pressure and who never heard evangelical New Testament scholarship in the College it was a thrilling experience. The church-history professor who welcomed him had a certain amiable dottiness about him and said that though he had never shaken hands with the Queen he was delighted that he had now shaken hands with someone who had shaken hands with the Queen![2]

The following year John Stott was back in Oxford for the OICCU,[3] and in 1965 in Scotland at St Andrew's and at Aberdeen (where he combined the Christian Union mission with the University Sermon) and in Queen's College, Belfast, for a lecture-mission. Three months later, in February 1966, he was at Leeds. Alex Williams, one of the undergraduate members of the CU, acted as aide:

John arrived in February '66 for the mission, and my allotted task was to carry his Wellington boots – at that time Leeds was famous for its sticky mud as well as its green pea-soup fogs, smogs they were called, when smoke was mixed with fog and when, if you stretched your arm out in front of you, you could barely see your hand!

It was a good introduction ... and my perk for carrying the boots was to have him speak at a meeting in my room in my residence – Boddington Hall – to my overseas student friends.[4]

One of these, a nominal Lutheran, came to a personal faith in Christ. Nor was he the only one. A note in John Stott's records written at the time reads: 'Sunday 13 February, 1966 (my 28th spiritual birthday!). In Great Hall after Matthew 11:25–30' – followed by a list of ten names who had responded to the invitation.

In spite of his commitment to the student world and to university missions, John Stott also found time to give the Lent addresses at Charterhouse School in 1964, renewing links which dated back to the 1940s when he was Camp Secretary. The Headmaster's letter of thanks will have been an encouragement:

These talks have gone deep, and I know that both they and your own personal example will be looked to by certain boys as really important things in their lives. I can't promise that we have a C. T. Studd in the school: but I'd like to think so – and that God through you has called forth his service of a lifetime.[5]

But perhaps even more heartening than the Headmaster's letter was another in a schoolboy hand from one of the boarding houses:

Dear Sir,
I am very happy to write to thank you for opening my door.
   That evening, just before lights out, I refused to lend someone my alarm clock, for no reason, except for my own convenience. Then I thought: 'Oh *damn* I've sinned,' and realised that I had sinned again. I sat down on my bed, and added all the sins that I could remember; about ten since I had been down to wash!
   Now I feel some slight, yet deep reassurance, and I am very glad to tell you about it.[6]

A few months after these Lent Addresses John Stott was one of a small group called together (meeting at his Rectory, but not primarily on his initiative) to find ways to develop Christian youth work more widely, following such examples as the old-established Cambridge University Mission in Bermondsey; or the much newer All Souls Clubhouse; or David Sheppard's work at the Mayflower Family Centre in Canning Town. Largely through the vision of Andrew Pierssené of CUM, strongly supported by the longer experience of a few other Christian leaders of open youth-club work (such as Maurice Smith of Streatham or the Venables family of Stafford), an annual conference on 'Youth Clubs as a Sphere of Christian Service'[7] had been running for several years, uniting a faithful but largely unrecognized constituency. In the thinking of those who gathered in Weymouth Street that summer's afternoon, perhaps the time had come to set up a Trust and establish an organization, both to serve those already working in this field, and to try to bring it firmly to the attention of the Christian public. At this first meeting the name 'Frontier Youth Trust' was adopted; and John Stott agreed to be the first Chairman, for one year only, and on the understanding that no publicity be given to his acceptance of the post.[8]
   This embryo committee met again a year later, with John Stott in the chair. It was he who suggested that it might be possible to persuade Scripture Union to second a staff worker to serve the FYT; and he agreed to seek a meeting between himself and the FYT Secretary (at that time his old friend Philip Tompson) and Dr John Laird, General Secretary of

Scripture Union. In the event, FYT was accepted as an associated ministry of the work of Scripture Union: Mr George Venables told the FYT committee that he had written to SU some twenty-two years before, asking them to undertake work of this kind. John Stott's involvement in the work was never widely publicized but (as with the All Souls Clubhouse) it represented something close to his heart. He spoke at its public meetings, and was 'a strong and consistent support and encourager all through the years'.[9] He relinquished his formal connection with the Trust only when its Board of Trustees was reconstituted in 1986.[10]

Alongside the work of All Souls and his punishing schedule of addresses, lectures and missions at home and abroad, the decade saw John Stott closely involved with the organizations and structures of a resurgent evangelicalism. The most notable, the National Evangelical Anglican Congress (NEAC) 1967 at Keele, has a chapter to itself; others included the steady growth of the Eclectic Society and its first residential conference, the early days of Latimer House, the development of the Evangelical Fellowship in the Anglican Communion (EFAC), and the founding of the influential Church of England Evangelical Council (CEEC).

Latimer House was the vision of James Packer, John Wenham and Richard Coates, an idea which took shape during a car journey together late one autumn night in 1958.[11] Tyndale House in Cambridge had been founded a few years before through the initiative of the IVF Biblical Research Committee. Now the need was being felt for an Anglican evangelical research centre to support those who were fighting the intellectual battles and seeking to keep the Church of England true to herself and her formularies. While not himself one of the founders, John Stott fully shared this vision and in October 1959 became Chairman of the embryo Oxford Evangelical Research Trust. He presided over the search for funding, the acquiring and staffing of Latimer House in Oxford, and the formation of the library. Although he resigned the chair in 1973, he continued as a member of the Council for a further eleven years before accepting the office of President.

James Packer was the influential Warden of Latimer House during most of the 1960s, establishing both its role and its reputation, supported by his active and dependable Chairman, whose 'very public endorsement of its goals was of no small significance in its advances'.[12] These advances were considerable: not only were staff members engaged in writing and research, and serving as evangelical representatives on commissions and committees (Dr Packer was an influential member of the Anglican–Methodist Unity Commission, for example), but the House was actively engaged in forwarding the attempts at self-education by almost an entire generation of Anglican evangelicals. John Wenham could write of Latimer House by the end of the 1960s that

… in its decade of existence the tiny staff had done a remarkable work reinforcing the growing band of Evangelicals in many directions. They had set up fifteen study groups which had been working on publications in the fields of Liturgy, Patronage, Missionary Theology, Church and Ministry, Tradition, Law and Morality, Ecclesiastical Polity, Preaching, Church and Community, Pastoral Reorganisation, Church and Sacraments, Ecumenism, Sex and Marriage, Race Relations, Roman Catholicism and Eastern Orthodoxy.[13]

But the real importance of Latimer House lay as much in what it symbolized as in any list of its achievements, impressive though they are. J. I. Packer saw the project as

… able to project an impression or image of the nature of evangelicalism which ran counter to that which prevailed in the church at large. At a time when many senior churchmen dismissed evangelicalism with a finely calibrated condescension, Latimer House demonstrated to the church at large that evangelicalism was still 'a cock with a lot of fight left in it on the theological front'.[14]

Latimer House had as its primary concern the affairs of the Church of England (though it served as a model and inspiration beyond the UK). By contrast, the Evangelical Fellowship in the Anglican Communion (EFAC) was an international vision. The Fellowship was formally constituted in 1961;[15] and while others had a hand in this, the driving force and inspiration came from John Stott. He had seen in his travels that evangelicals in different parts of the Anglican Communion were facing similar problems, sometimes in positions of considerable isolation; and his growing worldwide correspondence underlined the need for some such structured 'network' as the projected Fellowship would provide. He himself (sometimes alone, sometimes with Marcus Loane or Jack Dain) was its Honorary Secretary for the first twenty years of its existence.[16]

It could hardly be expected that the creation of EFAC would be universally welcome. The *Church Times* gave a brief factual report under the heading 'Evangelicals are closing their ranks on a world-wide scale'.[17] In a short historical account written ten years later John Stott sought to reassure those who

… regard as mistaken policy any desire to perpetuate divisions within the Christian Church. Pan-Anglicanism is bad enough; the fostering of a world-wide *Evangelical* Anglicanism appears to them worse still.

In reply to this, I think evangelical Anglicans would want to make a distinction. Anglicanism is largely a historical phenomenon. Its death in any region or nation is not therefore to be regretted, provided that it is followed by a resurrection in a united church which preserves a Biblical Faith. Evangelicalism, on the other hand, is a theological heritage. In so far as it may be shown to embody non-Biblical traditions, it is open to reform. But the Evangelical has no wish to be a 'party' man, owing allegiance to any human group or set of traditions. He desires, if he is true to his own Evangelical principles, to witness to Biblical truth as unchanging divine revelation.

He went on to define the five main aims of the new Fellowship in terms of fostering fellowship, bearing witness to biblical and Reformation principles, formulating policy and exchanging news and information.[18] Once John Stott had been commissioned to create such a Fellowship, he began to correspond with evangelical leaders across the world in order to sound out their ideas and elicit their support. These included Archbishop Hugh Gough in Australia, Max Wiggins in New Zealand, Bishop Alfred Stanway in Tanzania, Desmond Hunt in Canada, Stanley Wakeling in South Africa, Bishop Kenneth Howell in Chile, and Philip Hughes in the USA. Evangelical Anglicanism in America was at a very low ebb. But spurred on by this new vision, Dr Philip Hughes and the Revd Peter Moore founded in 1963 the Fellowship of Witness, as the US branch of EFAC, committed to biblical education and evangelism and to influencing the Episcopal Church for the gospel. A decade later the Fellowship of Witness was to play a key part in the creation of the evangelical Trinity Episcopal School for Ministry, the eleventh accredited seminary in the Episcopal Church.[19] By the end of the 1960s, EFAC had nearly twenty group members, and a number of individuals (as, for example, in the Church in Wales) in parts of the world otherwise unrepresented.

John Stott, as the Fellowship's first Secretary, was also largely responsible for two main central projects, one initiated through the EFAC Literature Committee and the other through the EFAC Bursary Committee.

The EFAC Literature Committee was founded to create and launch a series of small paperbacks known as the Christian Foundations series. Between 1963 and 1968 twenty-two titles appeared at regular intervals, under the imprint of Hodder & Stoughton. In John Stott's recollection, the vision came from Dick Lucas, 'out of the blue', when he was acting as Secretary of the original 'Church of England Group' under the auspices of IVF, which was to lead to the founding of EFAC. 'I think what we need', he is remembered as saying, 'is a contemporary equivalent to the *Tracts for the Times.*'[20] Most of the editorial planning and supervision took place in the Rector's study at 12 Weymouth Street. Philip Hughes was the series editor, joined later by Frank Colquhoun: both contributed titles to the series, Hughes on divine grace and Colquhoun on preaching. John Stott himself wrote the first and last in the series: *Confess Your Sins* (1964) and *Our Guilty Silence* (1967). Other subjects included the church and its ministry; revelation; atonement; the Holy Spirit; the Thirty-nine Articles; Rome and reformation; the open table; and certain practical and ethical contemporary issues such as money and sexual morality.

The project was an ambitious one, a sign of growing evangelical confidence: some 200,000 copies were distributed, including copies to most of the bishops and archbishops of the Anglican Communion.[21] Bishops' post bags are so weighted down with reading matter that the surprise was to find how many found time to read at least some of the series and comment on them. Glyn Simon, Bishop of Llandaff and later Archbishop of Wales, was cited as one on whom these books, coupled with talks with John Stott and Roger Beckwith, 'produced a powerful impression ... and helped remove the various bogeys which had clouded his opinion of evangelicals'.[22] In a longer perspective, this series can be seen as too ambitious for the resources that were then available. Evangelicals were comparatively unused to writing even small books on contemporary issues. The quality and the level of discussion were very uneven from book to book. 'We were not mature enough as a movement to produce influential books,' was John Stott's retrospective assessment.[23]

The EFAC Literature Committee was called into being specifically for this major project. It also lent its name, in the late 1960s, to a small liturgical innovation, the Prayer Book Service of Evening Prayer recast into modern English in what was described as 'a conservative translation', by members of the EFAC Literature Committee.[24] The service was produced very much at John Stott's instigation, with All Souls in mind, but proved deeply divisive to the PCC. With no consensus, it was agreed to wait a year, and then reconsider. John Stott recalls

... kneeling in prayer in my study at 12 Weymouth Street saying, 'Lord, if we can't get modern language at every service, I would accept it once a month in the evening'; and I can well remember the astonishment that when we re-opened the argument we were led to a unanimous decision to have it every Sunday evening.[25]

It is possible to see in the EFAC Literature Committee the seeds which blossomed during the 1970s into the creation of ELT, the Evangelical

Literature Trust; but apart from this, its work was largely achieved with the Christian Foundations series. By contrast, the work of the EFAC Bursary Committee has developed steadily over the intervening decades and is still actively fulfilling its original mandate. This was to give clergy from the younger churches of Africa and Asia the opportunity to come to the UK for theological study and to broaden their experience. The germ of the idea came from Bill Persson, at that time Vicar of Christ Church, Barnet:

> In 1963 we had a Missionary Weekend at which one of the speakers was Amos Betungura. Amos was at the London College of Divinity at the time on a College Bursary of some kind (he later became Bishop of East Ankole, Uganda). It was still the age of sending out as many missionaries as possible – and at one of our meetings, Amos made the suggestion that the church, instead of sending out three missionaries, should send out two, and invite someone over from the Church overseas, as he had been.
>
> We thought the idea over, and during the course of the following year I contacted Greyfriars, Reading, and Edgware Parish Church. Together we agreed we would attempt to fund an overseas bursar at a theological college for two years, meeting his travelling and college costs, and an allowance: the bursar concerned to stay in the vacations in each of our three parishes ... I felt it would be helpful to do the whole thing under wider auspices. So I wrote to John, asking if EFAC might feel able to adopt us.
>
> John invited me over to All Souls to discuss it. He had been evidently floating the idea of a bursary fund – and he asked me if I would take it on, and get a Committee together.

Bill Persson agreed and the committee was convened, with John Stott as Chairman.

> I assumed that they would gently adopt our candidate for the coming year – and work out how to extend things further down the line. Not a bit of it. John said calmly that he proposed we should arrange for five bursaries in the first year, and a similar number the year after.[26]

John Stott's thoughts had been turned to such a bursary fund through conversation with another African, a child of the East African revival, who had been brought to England by well-meaning sponsors, 'but was attending a course which, being more liberal than evangelical, was also more harmful than helpful. Using the language of the East African

revival, he confessed to me that he had "grown cold".'[27] He was the first
of a number whom John Stott discovered to be in a similar predicament.
They had 'found themselves in the wrong company over here' and for
them the fires of revival 'were in danger of being damped down, if not
put out'. The thought came to John Stott that instead of simply rescuing
such overseas visitors from the wrong courses in this country, 'it would be
better to develop an *alternative* scholarship programme of our own so
that they could attend the right courses'.

The scheme as it took shape was a matter of co-operation between
colleges and parishes, colleges reducing their fees and parishes helping to
find the balance: but beyond this, parishes have offered friendship, an
element of pastoral care, and opportunities for ministry: 'the combination
of *study* and *experience*, both contributing to further education, has been
central to the vision'.[28] By 1986, 100 bursars had taken advantage of the
scheme; and, thanks in part to the care taken over the initial selection,
almost all had returned home to place their new experience and
qualifications at the service of their indigenous church. Forty years on, it
is no surprise when a prominent and gifted Third World church leader
turns out to have paid his first visit to England as an EFAC bursar.

It is largely through the network of contacts provided by EFAC that
John Stott has himself been able to contribute towards the training of
Christian leaders in so many parts of the world. Though the occasions
when the Fellowship (or even its international committee) has been able
to meet together have been few and far between, yet the Fellowship has
proved a reality largely through the travels of its Honorary Secretary
during its formative years. Moreover, it was the pattern of the EFAC
bursary scheme (now called Studylink) that was the model for the
Langham Scholars of the next decade.

The same small group who were busy laying the foundations for EFAC
in 1960 and 1961 were conscious that some provision would be needed
for an English group member of the Fellowship. A. T. Houghton, General
Secretary of BCMS, took the chair at their meetings and also kept a diary:

24th March 1960
Got to Church Society at 12.30. Oliver B, Frank, Wilkie, Stibbs,
Hewitt, Mohan and John Stott were there. We formally terminated
the existence of the I.V.F. C. of E. Group and constituted ourselves
as the Church of England Evangelical Council to become first
member of the Evangelical Fellowship in the Anglican
Communion. John Stott had had favourable replies from about a
dozen people overseas. I took the chair and agreed to continue until
the next meeting, without prejudice to the future.[29]

The account of their meeting, headed 'Minutes of the first meeting of the Church of England Evangelical Council', demonstrates that, though work had been going forward towards the formation of such a Council over many months, this was regarded as the actual formation of the new body:

> Upon a resolution proposed by the Rev. L. F. E. Wilkinson and seconded by the Rev. T. G. Mohan, it was agreed that the so-called 'Church of England Group' should cease to exist and that its members become and hereby constitute themselves the members of a new body 'The Church of England Evangelical Council'. The object of this change was to create a public body one of whose main aims was to help to create an International Fellowship.[30]

A. T. Houghton was persuaded to continue as Chairman, and in the following November the Revd R. C. Lucas succeeded Oliver Barclay as Secretary. All was not plain sailing, however. Such bishops as it was hoped would support the new body proved difficult to pin down; requests were made that the word 'The' be dropped from the title so as not to imply an exclusive claim. 'I fear we have no evangelical bishops who have the courage of their convictions,' A. T. Houghton wrote in his diary, and had to report to the committee that 'all three of the bishops to whom we wrote have refused to become Vice-Presidents'.[31] In the end, however, Bishop J. R. S. Taylor consented to remain as President, and the Bishop of Tonbridge agreed to join the Council.[32]

The Council soon proved itself to be one of those institutions which, had it not existed, it would be necessary to invent. In the first year of its life, besides much business to do with the extension of EFAC, the Council considered theological training, Sunday observance (with a memorandum to the Home Secretary's Departmental Committee), 'Tracts for the Times' (which became the Christian Foundations series), Canon Law and Prayer Book revision and, from early in 1963, Anglican–Methodist reunion.

2

In July 1962, mindful of the fact that changes to Canon Law and departures (even experimental) from the *Book of Common Prayer* would need Parliamentary approval sooner or later, the two Archbishops (Michael Ramsey and Donald Coggan) wrote jointly a printed letter to members of both Houses of Parliament. They did not send copies to the press, though it was not long before the press got hold of it. In this letter they asked primarily for 'parliamentary authority for the sanctioning in

the first instance of experimental variations in public worship'. The letter
continued:

> As our Church of England bodies are representative, varying
> opinions will be expressed. There may be differing points of view on
> one or other of the proposals. There will also be constructive
> criticism. Those of us, bishops, other clergy and lay men and
> women, who have introduced them, believe that these proposals
> have the steady support of the great majority in the Church. We are
> convinced that there are adequate safeguards to protect the doctrine
> and historic mission of the Church of England.[33]

Though the letter made semi-jocular allusions to the way Canon Law
prescribed the night-attire of clergy, it made no explicit reference to the
controversial canons which were exercising the minds and consciences of
evangelicals, and seemed to imply only minor and innocuous changes in
public worship. John Stott was one of four leading evangelicals who in
October 1962 followed this letter to MPs with a statement of their own,
setting out their misgivings.[34] In robust language they reminded MPs that
though the Archbishops might believe that the proposals 'have the strong
support of the great majority in the Church' yet, in their own view,

> ... this statement is open to question. The basis for the Arch-
> bishops' assertion is in the fact that the proposals have been
> discussed at length in the two Convocations and in Church As-
> sembly. The Convocations, however, are purely clerical bodies, and
> the unrepresentative nature of the Church Assembly is a byword ...
> It is questionable whether the proposed changes, particularly those
> relating to the Book of Common Prayer, are desired by churchmen
> generally.[35]

Though they could not know it at the time, John Stott and his fellow-
signatories were not alone in their misgivings. James Callaghan, Shadow
Chancellor of the Exchequer and later Prime Minister, wrote as a Free
Churchman to say that he would prefer to cast his vote 'for any measure
that is likely to lead the Church to take action for disestablishment'.[36]
George Thomas, another Free Churchman, then at the Home Office and
later to become Speaker and the first Viscount Tonypandy, took the
opposite view: 'I am far from being anxious to see your church disestab-
lished under present circumstances. I believe this would weaken the
Protestant witness in these Islands.'[37] Perhaps the Attorney General, the
formidable R. E. Manningham-Buller, was nearest to the mark when he
wrote to his own Diocesan, the Bishop of Peterborough, expressing the

view that what was proposed might be the thin end of a wedge towards the reversal of Parliament's decision over the 1928 Deposited Prayer Book. Shrewdly, he added,

> ... while it is not difficult to point to Canons and to parts of the Prayer Book which are obsolete, I do not suppose that the revision of the Canons or the Prayer Book is confined to the excision of what is obsolete.[38]

Once the *Church Times* knew of the Archbishops' letter, and had received a copy of this evangelical response, the editor invited John Stott to make clear to his readers why there was this unease among evangelical Anglicans towards what was represented as a much overdue updating of obsolete provisions. In two articles early the following year, John Stott began by making a number of points about the essential place of Parliament in the decision-making processes of the church ('we do not believe that our ecclesiastical bodies adequately represent the Church of England'). He then challenged the Archbishops' suggestion that the only intention in revision was to bring Canons and Liturgies 'up to date' (whereas some of the proposed provisions involved radical changes: 'Draft Canon B15, for instance ... would put the clock back three hundred if not four hundred years'). He further reminded Members of Parliament that there had been a 40% vote in the House of Laity against the Vestments Canon. And in liturgy, he explained, evangelicals were not against change: 'what we desire is a careful and conservative revision of 1662', retaining a principle of uniformity in worship – 'but why alter the main structure of Cranmer's masterpiece?'[39]

Through all this period of liturgical and legislative change evangelicals needed to be constantly on their guard. Wise, firm and informed theological leadership was called for. A further example of John Stott's willingness to take his share was over the vexed question of 'Reservation'. Early in 1966 the Archbishop of Canterbury, Michael Ramsey, invited him to serve as a member of an informal group under the chairmanship of Robert Stopford, Bishop of London, 'to consider the possibility of agreement upon Rubrics concerning the Communion of the Sick and the Reservation of the Consecrated elements in connection therewith'. The disarming reference to the Communion of the Sick did not conceal the fact that in being asked to consider Reservation – that is, the setting aside of consecrated Bread (and sometimes Wine) at the end of the Communion service, and 'reserving' it in a special place for future use – the group was faced with a contentious issue. Reservation was not sanctioned by the Thirty-nine Articles and was contrary to the historic teaching of the Church of England. Nevertheless, it was common knowledge that in Anglo-Catholic circles Reservation was the regular custom; and that besides the pastoral purposes cited, it was the basis of a cultus, comparable to Roman Catholic practice, whereby the Reserved Sacrament became the focus of adoration and the Roman rite of Benediction. Rubrics in the 1928 proposed Prayer Book would have permitted Reservation under certain circumstances; and it is widely held that these contributed to the book's rejection by Parliament.

John Stott was one of some twenty members of the group, which included such other leading evangelicals as Maurice Wood, Principal of Oak Hill Theological College, and two lawyers, P. H. C. Walker and J. F. Wallace, both members of Church Assembly. Archbishop Ramsey contributed a characteristic 'Note for Discussion' to assist the first meeting, reminding the group that Reservation was not uncommon and that in some parishes 'irregular forms of service are held in connection with Reservation'. Something of the disarray attending the whole subject can be seen in his reference to a ruling by the Dean of Arches to the effect that, while Reservation was illegal, an aumbry (a cupboard in which the Reserved Sacrament might be kept) was 'a reputable form of illegality', whereas a tabernacle (in Roman Catholic practice, an ornamented box for the elements, set into or standing on the High Altar) was not.[40] John Stott could not but note that the thrust of Ramsey's memorandum, which set out alternative possible policies, was towards the continuing and legalizing of Reservation, and did not contemplate the possibility that with the Prayer Book (Alternative and Other Services) Measure under consideration, the bishops should agree to work towards securing conformity with the Thirty-nine Articles.[41]

Following a very unsatisfactory first meeting, the four evangelical members submitted a memorandum stating that they found themselves 'deeply disturbed by the assumption … that rubrics must be provided to permit and regulate the practice of Perpetual Reservation'.[42] Remembering that the terms of reference of the group were primarily directed towards Communion of the Sick, they went so far as to offer, by way of concession to pastoral necessity, that rubrics might be formulated regulating the practice of 'Extended Communion' which would allow the Consecrated Elements to be taken from the church to the bedside under strict conditions. Such a suggestion was not what they themselves would choose, but an attempt to offer a constructive compromise. Having put forward this tentative suggestion, however, they felt it right to make their own convictions crystal clear as representing the authentic position of the Church of England:

We firmly believe that Perpetual Reservation is contrary to Christ's ordinance (as Article 28 says); and that it encourages a view of His localized presence even in the absence of His people which is inimical to the enjoyment of His covenant promise to be present among His people and to dwell in their hearts by faith. For these reasons we feel obliged to oppose it entirely.[43]

Following a second meeting, the group was able to issue a unanimous Report to the Archbishops, recommending that the rubric at the end of the Holy Communion (First Series) should be left unaltered, and suggesting provision by rubric for the Communion of the Sick with no reference to Reservation.[44] In the event the bishops did not accept the policy recommended by the Report. After a further meeting of the group, John Stott was able to lead a small deputation of evangelicals to meet Archbishop Ramsey. In a friendly and constructive time together they were assured that 'there was no surreptitious plot to get Reservation legalised by the back door', and that the rubric in the First Series Holy Communion was by itself, in the view of the lawyers, insufficient to change the law.[45]

Whatever the deficiencies of the Alternative Services and the Revised Canons, it is clear that but for the vigilance and courage of a few evangelical leaders in the 1960s, liturgy and law alike would have strayed further from the ideals of a church true to the New Testament.

3

Proposals for Anglican–Methodist reunion were to be a major preoccupation for both churches during the 1950s and 60s. The story begins in Cambridge, less than a year after John Stott had left Ridley Hall for his curacy. Archbishop Geoffrey Fisher preached on 3 November 1946 his celebrated University Sermon, 'A Step Forward in Church Relations', appealing to the Free Churches 'to take episcopacy into their own system' and so achieve full communion with the Church of England. In spite of the precedent set a year later by the Church of South India, it was taken as axiomatic in most Anglican circles that there was something deficient about a service of Holy Communion conducted by a minister not episcopally ordained.[46] Matters moved slowly. It was not until 1955 that the Church of England and the Methodist Church established official 'Conversations' to explore the way towards intercommunion. Three years later an interim report rejected the idea of mere inter-communion in favour of working towards organic unity. A key element in such a scheme would be a 'Service of Reconciliation' whose studied ambiguity many interpreted as conveying episcopal ordination to Methodist ministers. Indeed Dr James Packer, by then Warden of Latimer House (and an ex-officio member of CEEC), who was himself a member of the 1965 Anglican–Methodist Unity Commission, felt obliged to append a Note making this point to the Report of the Commission:

> Once our two Churches stand pledged to unite in an episcopal Church, there is no good reason why either should decline to accept ministers of the other as they are, without this further ceremony. The Methodist Church could readily do this, but the Church of England has so far hesitated, because existing Methodist ministers have no organic link with the historic episcopal ministry. But, as the 1963 Dissentient View stated, 'historic episcopacy is completely without foundation in the New Testament' (*Report*, p. 59). That an episcopal ministry has value, other things being equal, as a sign of the unity, continuity, and authority of Christ's Church, is un-doubtedly true, but to suspend full fellowship at the Lord's Table on a non-scriptural requirement, this or any other, is sectarian and wrong. I cannot commend or accept a procedure which involves this mistaken principle.[47]

In the summer of 1968 John Stott as Chairman of CEEC was one of the signatories to an 'Open Letter concerning Anglican–Methodist Relations', inviting evangelical clergy to indicate their views on the Scheme, and on the Service of Reconciliation in particular. Archbishop Michael Ramsey was displeased, but in an official referendum of more than 15,000 Anglican clergy the following summer, about a third indicated that they would be unwilling to take part in such a Service of Reconciliation.[48] It was clear, too, that plans were being prepared for both a 'Continuing Methodist Church' and a 'Continuing Church of England' should the Scheme take effect. Instead of creating one church out of two, it would then effectively create three!

The Scheme was eventually submitted to the Methodist Conference and to the Convocations on the same day, 8 July 1969, for a final decision. Special majorities were required. The Methodists approved with a 77% majority; the Anglicans failed to reach the required majority, and though the total vote in favour was 69% the Scheme was rejected. A further 'final vote' was arranged three years later in General Synod, with a similar result.[49]

John Stott wrote about all this at some length to his parishioners in the *All Souls* magazine. He had been involved in discussions opposed to the Scheme not only in CEEC and on the Council of Latimer House, but through his chairmanship of NEAC '67[50] and in his personal capacity as a well-known evangelical leader. He told his readers that a 'yes vote' would have swept under the carpet the theological principle at issue:[51]

This is not a trivial point to be impatiently dismissed. It lies at the root of the Gospel. To require Methodist ministers to submit to a quasi-ordination by episcopal hands is virtually to say that the historic episcopate is necessary for ministry, and therefore for sacraments, and therefore for salvation. But I for one could not possibly subscribe to such a doctrine. It is an ecclesiastical myth totally lacking in biblical warrant.[52]

He attributed the failure of the Scheme to the fact that its terms of reference were too narrowly drawn ('The Church of South India method of uniting churches has not been on the conference table'), and that church leaders were unwilling to take seriously the growing opposition of significant minorities. The evangelicals were not alone. Some Anglo-Catholics had their own reasons for being opposed to the scheme; and evangelicals were accused of an 'unholy alliance' with them. In fact a distinct issue of theological principle lay behind the opposition in each case, even if the theological principles were not the same.[53]

Weighty though these issues were (culminating in a major opportunity lost by an unacceptable Scheme), they represented only one of a number of theological controversies thrown up by the 'discontinuities' of the decade. In the spring of 1963 the Bishop of Woolwich, Dr John Robinson, shook the church, and briefly captured the attention of the nation, with his small paperback, *Honest to God*. It was launched by a specially extracted article taking up the entire front page of *The Observer Weekend Review* of 17 March 1963, a Sunday newspaper with a circulation approaching one million copies. The strident headline, 'Our Image of God Must Go', coupled with the episcopal authorship, ensured huge publicity: 'English religion in the 1960s will always remain more associated with *Honest to God* than with any other book.'[54] Though it appeared to many at the time as a bolt from the blue, the book was in direct succession to, for example, the writings of Alec Vidler (editor of *Soundings*, 1962), Donald Mackinnon, Harry Williams and their friends, who 'did not seriously consider including Dr. John Robinson, then Dean of Clare College. He was thought to be far too conventional.'[55] Others were clear that Robinson must be counted among the members of this 'Cambridge Agnostic Church' which was seen as 'a haven for fundamentalist "free thought"'.[56] Among a number invited to comment in the next week's edition of *The Observer*, C. S. Lewis sought to play down the novelty of the book:

The Bishop of Woolwich will disturb most of us Christian laymen less than he anticipates. We have long abandoned belief in a God who sits on a throne in a localized heaven. We call that belief anthropomorphism, and it was officially condemned before our time. There is something about this in Gibbon ... though sometimes puzzled I am not shocked by his article.[57]

Lewis spoke for the Oxford common-room. Ramsey, as Archbishop of Canterbury, was concerned for the ordinary lay person in the pew. Interviewed on television a week later he was 'positive in praise as well as critical ...' but maintained firmly that it was 'utterly wrong and misleading to denounce the imagery of God held by Christian men, women and children: imagery that they have got from Jesus himself, the image of God the Father in heaven'.[58]

John Stott himself waited until the immediate dust had settled, and then preached a sermon in All Souls on the second Sunday in June.[59] Like Archbishop Ramsey, he sought to commend what could be commended in Robinson's writing, but added:

> Nevertheless, I must immediately go on to say that the essential thesis of this book is incompatible with the teaching of the New Testament ... We are confronted by an inescapable choice: not between two versions of the same religion, but between two different religions: the new radicalism of John Robinson and his fellow travellers and the everlasting gospel of Jesus Christ and His apostles.[60]

When John Robinson resigned his bishopric towards the end of the decade, evangelicals were delighted to find David Sheppard, then Warden of the Mayflower Family Centre in Canning Town, named as the new Bishop of Woolwich. John Stott wrote privately to Mervyn Stockwood, the diocesan bishop, urging that the See be renamed so that Sheppard would not have to live with the theological odium that Robinson's book had brought upon the name of 'Woolwich'. Not surprisingly perhaps, he received a dusty answer!

Throughout the 1960s CEEC continued to hold its regular meetings, moving from the offices of Church Society to the boardroom of the Iraq Petroleum Company in Cavendish Square. Here, month by month, John Stott contributed to or presided over its discussions. Anglican–Methodist reunion was a major preoccupation in which the voice of evangelicals was increasingly heard,[61] but at the same time the Church of England was deep in liturgical innovation. New Services of Holy Communion were written and authorized 'for experimental use'. Series 1 Holy Communion, composed largely of material rejected by Parliament in 1928 (but widely used since) was authorized in 1966. Series 2 followed in 1967, but both services met with much criticism from evangelicals (the proposed Order for Burial with its inclusion of prayers for the dead was defeated); and Colin Buchanan in the Liturgical Commission had severely criticized the element of 'offering' in the new Eucharistic prayers, apart from the offering of praise and thanksgiving, as unreformed and suggestive of Pelagianism. In all this, CEEC and its Chairman sought to be closely informed (Colin Buchanan was himself an influential and active member) and to strengthen the hands of evangelicals in Church Assembly or on the various Commissions which were beginning to see the need for evangelical representatives.

A wide range of issues came before the Council, in addition to the continuing business of EFAC, reunion and liturgical reform. By way of example, they arranged joint meetings with delegations from the Orthodox and Roman Catholic churches. John Stott as Chairman corresponded regularly with the Archbishops on business that had come before the Council, and on occasion led delegations to Lambeth. Questions were raised by the Council on matters of evangelical concern – for example, a Roman Catholic mass in Canterbury Cathedral; to which the Dean replied ingenuously, 'only in the precincts'.[62] Other subjects which concerned CEEC included the ordination of women to the priesthood (1964); capital punishment (1965, to help one of its members, Michael Alison MP, prepare for the debate in Parliament); Anglican–Presbyterian conversations (1965); homosexual law reform and issues on abortion (1966); establishment (1966); consultation on theological colleges (1967); the European Common Market (1967); Christian initiation (1968); race relations (1969) – and this is but to give a flavour of the Council's activities.

Nearer home, the Council was concerned that the traditional structures of evangelical Anglicanism – including such bodies as CPAS (the Church Pastoral-Aid Society) and Church Society – should be equipped to respond to the emerging role of evangelicals in the church of the 1960s. Sweeping proposals for their amalgamation left the Societies concerned largely unconvinced, and CEEC was sometimes regarded as claiming too much for itself. John King, ever an assiduous critic, was not alone in feeling that 'the Church of England Evangelical Council regards itself as having an authority unique among all these organisations, but this view is not widely shared. The CEEC is a self-appointing body and cannot claim to be representative.'[63] Under the urging of Colin Buchanan (among others), CEEC made rigorous attempts in the next decade or so to make itself more representative, more open to election, and more accountable to the Anglican evangelical constituency. As these worthy objectives came to be achieved, however, the real purpose of the Council as a meeting of evangelical leadership began to recede. The diffused authority of a more democratic structure failed to replace the lost authority which formerly derived from the commitment of a nominated membership of key individuals.

Meanwhile John Stott succeeded A. T. Houghton as Chairman, and was acknowledged to be the moving spirit of the Council and the focus of its cohesion through various vicissitudes. But as year followed year the fissiparous nature of the evangelical constituency was ever more clearly demonstrated in this attempt to secure a united and representative voice. In March 1965, for example, the whole continuing existence of the Council was called in question. John Stott himself offered a five-page analysis, 'Has CEEC a Future?'[64] He began by outlining 'our disastrous evangelical disunity', but went on to affirm strongly the role of CEEC as an independent policy-forming advisory body, without executive function:

> It is indispensable to the evangelical cause, and not a waste of time, that we meet to pray, think and talk ourselves clear. At the lowest level, it will help to clarify our differences; the highest prize God may give us is evangelical unity at last.[65]

As will be recounted in the following chapter, the Council played a crucial role in the preparatory work leading up to the 1967 National Evangelical Anglican Congress. From shaky beginnings, both CEEC and EFAC were better established by the close of the decade, with significant tasks still ahead of them, even though unity among evangelical groupings remained elusive.[66]

4

Among the events of the 1960s rooted most firmly in the folk-memory of many evangelicals, both Anglican and Free Church, was an occasion on which John Stott was present not primarily as speaker but as chairman. This was his confrontation with Dr Martyn Lloyd-Jones, the opening speaker at the Second National Assembly of Evangelicals, on 18 October 1966. The Assembly was sponsored and organized by the Evangelical Alliance. Between much of the planning and the event itself there had been a change of General Secretary, Gilbert Kirby moving on to become Principal of the London Bible College, to be succeeded by Morgan Derham. A few years before, the first such National Assembly had set up a Commission to look at the attitudes of evangelicals to 'the ecumenical movement, denominationalism, and a possible future United Church'. It was at the request of this Commission that Dr Lloyd-Jones was invited by the EA Council to give the keynote address on the theme of church unity in the Methodist Central Hall, Westminster. In particular, he was asked to speak in response to the Commission's report, issued the same week, which stated that the time was not ripe for evangelicals to seek to form a united church. He met the EA Council beforehand to share with them what he planned to say, and no objections were raised to the line he intended to take.[67] Reports in the press afterwards that 'he took the EA Council by surprise' can only reflect misinformation or a failure by the Council to recognize the significance of what would be said; or perhaps a difference in presentation which altered the emphasis of the message from analysis to appeal.

The Central Hall, an imposing auditorium, was well filled, with a double row of well-known evangelical leaders representing differing churches and traditions on the platform. Derek Prime, in the middle of his year as President of the Fellowship of Independent Evangelical Churches (FIEC), wrote thirty years later of his clear recollections of being in the vestry before the platform party moved into the hall:

> The atmosphere was warm and friendly. After prayer together, John Stott, the chairman, suggested that we make our way to the platform, and Dr Martyn Lloyd-Jones asked John Stott where he wanted him to sit. 'Sit at my side', John Stott requested, to which the Doctor quickly responded, with a twinkle in his eye, 'Which side? You have *two* sides, John!'[68]

John Stott was given ten minutes for his Chairman's Remarks, and Iain Murray points out that he knew 'the general nature' of what Lloyd-Jones was to say, following a conversation in Oxford earlier that summer at the International Congress of Christian Physicians.[69] It was by agreement, therefore, that John Stott referred to his own conscientious continuing membership of the Church of England on the ground that its formularies were biblical and evangelical, and that evangelicals were therefore the Anglican loyalists, and non-evangelicals the deviationists. And he made four simple points on church unity:

> First, spiritual unity should be expressed visibly. Second, the visibility of this Christian unity must include the mutual recognition of the ministries and sacraments – there must be full communion. Third, this visible unity of the Church must be founded on the Biblical faith. Fourth, this visible unity of the Church must also allow room for divergence of belief and practice in matters of secondary importance.[70]

This was followed by Morgan Derham's appreciation of the main speaker of the evening (remembered by one eyewitness as having 'eulogised the

Doctor with faint praise'[71]), which brought forth the response from Dr Lloyd-Jones when he finally rose to speak, 'It would be churlish of me not to thank Mr Morgan Derham for the remarks he has made, but I wish he had not done so; he has robbed me of my valuable time!'[72] John Stott as chairman introduced Dr Lloyd-Jones as 'in every particular my elder and better; I hold him in great esteem and affection in Christ.'[73]

Lloyd-Jones's address followed; and rapidly began to take the form of an appeal. In its published form, in a book of his collected addresses, it is so entitled: 'Evangelical Unity: An Appeal'.[74] At least twice in the address he speaks of wanting 'to make an appeal to you this evening'; and there can be no doubt that he was explicitly exhorting his hearers, especially 'ministers and clergy, in this congregation at this moment', towards action. Reading his address at this distance it is not entirely clear, for all the passionate rhetoric, what exact step he was urging such men to take; but it is plain that to say – as *The Christian and Christianity Today* reported – that he was urging them 'to leave the major denominations and to form a united church'[75] was quite mistaken. Rather he seems to have pleaded that 'what we need above everything else at the present time, is a number of such churches, all in fellowship together ...'[76]

The effect, however, was sufficiently dramatic, and the urgent note of appeal sufficiently unexpected, for John Stott to feel obliged to offer from the chair an impromptu word of caution against immediate secession. Feelings were running high; one historian speaks of 'the horror of members of the audience who valued their existing denominational allegiances':[77] an eyewitness recalls that 'the atmosphere was electric. None of us had been at an occasion like it ...'[78] The audience included many Anglican clergy for whom John Stott felt a special responsibility:

> From the platform I could see younger men with flushed faces, sitting on the edge of their seat, hanging on every word, and probably ready to go home and write their letter of resignation that very night. I hoped at least to restrain some hotheads from doing this.[79]

Further, the use of the opening address to make an appeal for action seemed to John Stott as chairman an improper anticipation of the business of the Assembly as set out in the agenda of the next two days. It was to foreclose the discussion. When he rose, therefore, to thank the speaker and announce the closing hymn, he felt obliged to add 'with much nervousness and diffidence' that he thought Lloyd-Jones mistaken in his argument from the faithful remnant, as well as in his appeal. As reported in the press, his words were:

I hope no one will make a precipitate decision after this moving
address. We are here to debate this subject and I believe that history
is against Dr. Jones in that others have tried to do this very thing. I
believe that Scripture is against him in that the remnant was within
the Church and not outside it.[80]

As might be expected, this public disagreement produced strong
reactions. J. I. Packer recounts how that night 'my phone rang in Oxford
and a woman's voice greeted me with the words "Jim – is John Stott
mad?" Next day one who had been at the meeting told me that my friend
Martyn Lloyd-Jones had gone off his rocker ...'[81] *The Church of England
Newspaper* described Lloyd-Jones's proposition as 'barmy'! Most people
who spoke to John Stott at the close of the meeting (John Laird, a wise
elder statesman of evangelicalism, General Secretary of the Scripture
Union, not himself an Anglican, among them) expressed their
thankfulness for this timely intervention. Some (for example, Douglas
Johnson of the IVF, who wrote a characteristic six-page memorandum)
complained that John Stott had improperly used his position as
chairman, adding, 'It was said that (though the room may have been hot
and he is naturally rubicund) the chairman was "flushed", "rattled",
"annoyed", "angry" (various terms are used).'[82]

A week or two later John Stott took the initiative and called on Dr
Lloyd-Jones and offered an apology. He went on to describe their meeting
and subsequent relationship in an appreciation written for *The Times* on
Lloyd-Jones's death (though in the event not published by them):

I called on Dr. Lloyd-Jones to apologize – not for what I had said
(which I still believe) but for misusing the chair and almost turning
the meeting (as he put it) into a 'debate'. He told me that he had
scarcely restrained himself from answering me and developing the
debate.

But we continued to have a warm personal relationship. I always
had a strong affection and admiration for him. In an era of theological flux he stood firm for historic, biblical Christianity. And
although he was a polemical speaker, he always distinguished
between principles and personalities, and was at heart a man of love
and peace.[83]

Uncertainty remains, and will probably never be finally resolved, as to
how far the Evangelical Alliance was culpable, as Douglas Johnson
supposed, for a failure adequately to brief the chairman and speaker as to
the nature of the occasion. Indeed, his memorandum goes further, saying
that some of those who had been in touch with him felt that the meeting

had been 'rigged'. Morgan Derham, as the new Secretary of EA, was closely enough in touch with Dr Lloyd-Jones 'to know that something was brewing'; and believed that he 'intended to make the EA Assembly meeting the decisive event in his "crusade" for separationism'. Morgan Derham recalls:

> I rang John and warned him that Lloyd-Jones might well exceed his brief, which was to explain his case, but not to make an 'appeal', and that by doing so I felt he would be violating his rights as a guest at an EA event. If he did so, I felt that John, as chairman, would be well within his rights to challenge MLJ's appeal.[84]

Morgan Derham came to see the whole affair as 'a tragedy for evangelicalism, based on … a monumental error by M.L.J.'.[85] This is also the recent assessment of James Packer's biographer, Alister McGrath. In his view, following the events of October 1966,

> … a broad division opened up within English evangelicalism over the specific issue of whether evangelicals within mainline denominations should stay inside or leave. A bitter dispute arose, where there had hitherto been friendly disagreement. Rightly or wrongly, Lloyd-Jones was criticized for wrecking evangelical unity. It is no exaggeration to say that the 'shadow of 1966' has lingered over English evangelicalism ever since.[86]

This view certainly remains current in some circles. A major historian of evangelicalism writes that 'the effects were catastrophic' with 'a fierce outburst of acrimonious controversy',[87] and the National Assembly had to be cancelled the following year as a direct consequence.[88] For Dr Lloyd-Jones and some of his followers, therefore, it probably could be called a defining moment. James Packer, in his appreciative and enthusiastic review of Iain Murray's second volume of Dr Lloyd-Jones's biography, describes the book 'as a chronicle mostly of compassionate conflict, mostly with other evangelicals', taking its subject, 'Britain's most leaderlike pastoral thinker and greatest preacher, from the middle to the margin of English evangelical life'.[89] Insofar as this is a true assessment, the public disagreement of October 1996 must have played a significant part. Following it, the Puritan Conference (which had enjoyed a very significant measure of Anglican leadership) was re-cast as 'the Westminster Conference', and from the very next year the Westminster Fellowship ceased to offer a welcome to Anglicans.[90] As Dr Packer put it, with saddened realism in an affectionate assessment, '15 years of separatist drum-beating does appear in retrospect as something of a scorched-earth era in English evangelical life'.[91] Yet it remained John Stott's considered view, thirty years later, that the incident had been blown up out of all proportion. He doubted whether, among evangelicals, 'this was a (let alone "the") defining moment in Anglican/Free Church relations'.[92] Certainly the National Evangelical Anglican Congress of 1967 was to prove a bigger cause of division, real or apparent; while the ripples from the Stott/Lloyd-Jones incident of October 1966 quietly faded into the background in most Anglican circles. This is, however, in marked contrast to the feeling of hurt which long prevailed (and lingers still in memory or folk-memory) among those EA supporters whose natural sympathies lay with Westminster Chapel rather than with the Church of England. It is surely significant that the British Evangelical Council (whose constituency, in general, is among evangelical churches which remain outside 'pluralist ecumenical bodies', such as denominations linked to the WCC) should devote the greater part of an issue of their twice-yearly journal to a detailed examination of this incident, thirty years after the event.[93] It suggests that the scars of the occasion and the wider significance it represents in terms of ecclesiology were deeper and longer-lasting in the Independent than in the Anglican evangelical psyche. But even for Anglicans, something of the lesson of that evening remained, and echoes of the need to resist calls for secession could be heard long afterwards.[94]

Eleven years later, for example, John Stott found himself, as President of the Evangelical Alliance, called upon to give an address at their 'President's Night'. Speaking from John 17 (a favourite passage) he took as his subject 'Essentials for tomorrow's Christians' – namely, truth, holiness, unity and mission. Although he made no reference to it, he must surely have had in mind the difficult meeting of October 1966. He told his hearers how

> ... some evangelicals, like myself, believe it is the will of God to remain in a church that is sometimes called a 'mixed denom-ination'. At least until it becomes apostate and ceases to be a church, we believe it is our duty to remain in it and bear witness to the truth as we have been given to understand it. Some of us who do this, however, are thought not to care about the truth. I want to say to you with all the strength of conviction that I possess that we care intensely about the truth, because we believe that God has revealed it fully and finally in Jesus Christ.[95]

While it was possible to remain within the Church of England, he was clear that this was where his duty lay. But asked not long after this in a radio interview on the BBC what he himself would do if 'in a crisis moment' loyalty to the Christian faith clashed with loyalty to the Church, there could be only one answer: 'One would secede from the Church of England.' Having made this plain, he went on immediately to add:

> But I don't see that happening. My understanding of the leaders of the Church of England is that they want to keep evangelicals in the Church, and I would only contemplate seceding if the official doctrine of the Church of England denied the Gospel as I have been given to understand it in any fundamental particular. Then, and not till then, would be the time to secede.[96]

Perhaps as a footnote to the whole incident, now more than a generation ago, can be set the hopes of the present-day Evangelical Ministry Assembly to play some part in repairing bridges between evangelical Anglicans and those in the Free Churches through their annual conference, held originally in St Helen's, Bishopsgate, and more recently in the Central Hall, Westminster, 'the very place where the division of 1966 occurred'.[97]

5

When Cosmo Gordon Lang informed the synod of the Province of Canterbury that he planned to retire as Archbishop in March 1942, he mentioned in passing, among the 'pressure of duties and responsibilities' which weigh upon an archbishop, that of 'unceasing correspondence – a pressure which none can realize but the man who has to bear it'. In his personal account of his feelings at the time he described it as 'ceaseless and wearisome'.[98] More recently Stuart Blanch described how a bishop's post 'comes with sickening regularity through his letterbox'.[99] And to turn over simply the fragments that now remain of John Stott's letter-writing during the 1960s is to demonstrate that this is not a pressure peculiar to the episcopate: he would receive, on average, something like thirty letters a day, six days a week.

Besides such correspondence, every week brought its quota of committees and working parties. Among these, and of strategic import-ance, was the future of the evangelical theological colleges. As the 1960s began, the Church Assembly passed a resolution asking that the Central Advisory Council for the Ministry produce a considered report on the shape of the future pastoral ministry of the Church. They entrusted the work to a sociologist, Leslie Paul, and the result was 'The Paul Report', *The Deployment and Payment of the Clergy*.[100] Crucial to the conclusions of the Report was the number of clergy which the Church might expect to ordain during the next ten years. An actuarial study was commissioned,[101] predicting a remarkably steady increase in ordinations of about twenty-four per year – which, cumulatively, meant an increase from 642 ordinations in 1963 to 809 at the end of the decade. Adrian Hastings later published a table comparing this statistical prediction with the numbers actually ordained:[102]

	1963	1964	1965	1966	1967	1968	1969	1970
Paul Report	642	662	686	713	737	761	785	809
Fact	636	605	592	576	496	478	436	437

So far from being 'conservatively estimated'[103] as the compiler claimed, it soon became obvious as year followed year that the predictions were wildly optimistic. Lower ordinations were the immediate consequence of fewer men in training. Fewer men in training meant empty places in the theological colleges, none of which could continue to operate at a loss for more than a very few years. Faced with this situation the Church of England published in February 1968 a Report, *Theological Colleges for Tomorrow*, written by a small group chaired by Sir Bernard de Bunsen. It recommended for any college a minimum student body of eighty men in training.[104] This was followed a year or two later by 'the Runcie Commission', a triumvirate consisting of Robert Runcie, Kenneth Woollcombe and Derek Wigram. They inevitably became known as 'the Three Wise Men'.[105]

Though the number of evangelical ordinands was declining less quickly than the rest, it was clear that the evangelical colleges would have to consider some far-reaching rationalizations if they were to survive. Seven of the college councils therefore set up a working group of their own ('the Three Wiser Men') to tackle the problem. The members were Hugh Craig, a lay member of the Church Assembly; Douglas Webster, Canon of St Paul's Cathedral; and John Stott as chairman. For six months during 1970 this was a further major preoccupation in his overloaded diary.

What could not be known at the time, save to a very few, was that in other circumstances John Stott might have had a different role to play as the theological colleges sought to come to terms with the new conditions. A year before he had been pressed to leave All Souls and become Principal of Wycliffe Hall, Oxford, which was at that time going through a difficult period. A later Principal, Alister McGrath, has summed up the situation:

> By 1969, the college was in a serious position. Only thirty-one students were enrolled; future recruitment seemed distinctly problematic ... The simple fact was that Wycliffe Hall was widely

seen as being out of sympathy with the forms of conservative evangelicalism which were now gaining the ascendency. Some of its teaching staff were not evangelical; the college as a whole was seen as 'liberal' in its ethos.[106]

Though McGrath does not say so, some at least of the responsibility for the decline in numbers must be laid at the door of the then Principal, David Anderson, who had been appointed only four years before, after a period as Principal of Immanuel College, Ibadan. But in fairness it should be added that the whole tide, in terms of general numbers of candidates, was running strongly against him. Stuart Blanch, Bishop of Liverpool, was Chairman of the Council. He wrote to John Stott, already a personal friend, in the spring of 1969:

> It seems likely now that David Anderson will be resigning as Principal of Wycliffe Hall at the end of the current academic year and quite predictably your name has been mentioned in the Council. I have the delicate task of writing to ask whether, if David should resign and an agreed policy for the future of the Hall should be arrived at, you would be willing at all to consider the possibility of succeeding him. I put it in this highly tentative way for obvious reasons. The numbers at Wycliffe are down to twenty-six, the Theological Colleges' Report recommended that it should merge with Ridley, the buildings are highly unsatisfactory and the financial future is far from secure.[107]

As one would expect, it was a very honest letter. Paradoxically, the very difficulties that it lists may have made the invitation more difficult to decline – at least, without the fullest consideration. There can be few more responsible tasks than the training of the church's future ministers, and the Council of Wycliffe Hall were surely right in their assessment that any college which could name John Stott as Principal would be assured in the short term of as many applications as it could handle, and in the long term of a radical restructuring of such training from biblical first principles.

The invitation came at a difficult moment. John Stott was due to leave at the end of April for three weeks in Australia and New Zealand for two university missions and a programme of conferences; he was therefore struggling to get away to The Hookses to complete his preparation when Stuart Blanch's letter arrived. The following week he sent a four-page reply, going well beyond the question of his own future. He spoke of his astonishment at being approached ('Such a thing had never entered my mind') and of his sense of privilege: 'I certainly feel it right to open my mind to the possibility.' He went on to share his private thoughts:

> What has given me cause for great rejoicing is that your letter
> reveals the Council's willingness to consider the possibility of
> appointing as Principal a man of 'definite' or 'conservative'
> evangelical conviction. If I may say so, I have thought for years that
> this would be right, believing (1) that there would be no other way
> for Wycliffe to be re-established or to fulfil its founders' intentions
> and (2) that the postwar growth of evangelicalism must, for its own
> sake and that of the church, gain a foothold in Oxford and/or
> Cambridge and there demonstrate in intellectual debate and
> exposition its claim to be heard by the whole church.
>
> But in turning to me as a possible candidate I also believe that
> the Council are turning to the wrong person, or at least that I
> should not be the Council's first choice.

The letter continues, 'greatly daring', to commend the name of Dr
James Packer, listing reasons: he was 'the leading theologian' of post-war
evangelicalism; he was a statesman; a gifted teacher; a man of God
concerned for the spiritual as well as for the intellectual development of
students; he was available (Packer had accepted the position of Director
of Studies at the London College of Divinity, but had withdrawn his
acceptance only a month before this); he felt his calling was to 'train
reformed pastors'; he would draw students; he was himself an Oxford and
Wycliffe man.

John Stott concluded:

> I beg you not to be angry with me for writing like this, nor to tell
> me that it is none of my business. Formally, it is not my business, I
> confess. And yet as a clergyman concerned first and foremost for
> God's will and glory, and next for the spread of the gospel and the
> good of the Church, I am constrained to write to you thus. Indeed,
> I would go so far as to say that I would not feel able in conscience to
> consider the Wycliffe Principalship myself unless I knew that Jim
> Packer's candidature had been carefully weighed and for good
> reasons rejected.[108]

John Stott went on to say that, for himself, he still felt it right to
remain at All Souls; but after a further exchange of letters ('Jim Packer's
name will clearly come up for the most serious consideration'), Bishop
Blanch wrote on 9 June to John Stott in New Zealand 'to say that the
Council has unanimously asked me to invite you to become Principal of
Wycliffe Hall from the beginning of the next academic year'.[109]

John Stott then consulted privately a number of friends including Kenneth Grubb (who urged him to accept) and Dick Lucas (who did not). He wrote for his own eyes a detailed summary of pros and cons, questions and counter-questions, from the point of view of the needs of the wider church, of Wycliffe Hall, of All Souls, and of his personal future ('Should I face now the probability of a later invitation to become a bishop ...? NB My fear of becoming a bishop is due largely to present unpreparedness'). It is clear from this that he amply fulfilled his promise to Stuart Blanch to 'give the matter my earnest consideration and prayer'.

But it was not to be. He talked with Bishop Blanch at 12 Weymouth Street face to face on 7 July and finally declined. Stuart Blanch wrote the following day to say, 'You have, I think, made the right decision about Wycliffe, unwelcome though it is to me personally.'[110] The Council of Wycliffe Hall finally appointed as Principal the Revd James Hickinbotham, from St John's College, Durham. When Chaplain of the Hall twenty-seven years before, he had taught Jim Packer as a student. As Alister McGrath's account makes clear, the story had a happy ending:

> Hickinbotham moved quickly to encourage the members of the Hall staff who were not evangelicals to move on to other positions, and appointed committed evangelicals ... in their place. More conservative evangelicals were appointed to the Hall Council. Student numbers began to rise in direct proportion to the confidence in which the Hall was held. By 1977, there were seventy-nine students at the Hall.[111]

By the end of the 1960s John Stott had been twenty-five years in orders, twenty-five years at All Souls, and twenty years as Rector. In that time he had declined many opportunities to move to new work – far more than can be recorded here.[112] Talbot Mohan of CPAS, when dealing with ecclesiastical patronage, had a phrase: 'loosening the roots'. When a man who seemed ready to move declined a number of approaches to do so, Canon Mohan was ready to believe that the time for him to move might not have arrived, but that through apparently abortive offers and explorations, God was at work 'loosening his roots'. Certainly a number of factors contributed to John Stott's sense, towards the close of the decade, that his own future had reached something of a turning-point. It was this that lay behind the major item on the agenda for the All Souls PCC Day Conference in September 1969, 'The Restructuring of the Staff Team'. Just what that meant will become apparent in a future chapter.

THREE

Keele 1967:
Pointing the Way Forward

1

When around the middle of the 1960s a succession of UK opinion polls sought to gauge the religious beliefs of the nation, the results were reassuring. They appeared to give an overwhelmingly affirmative reply to the question, 'Is Britain Christian?' An enquiry commissioned from Gallup for ABC Television, a major independent company, found that almost two-thirds of the population were ready to affirm that Jesus Christ was the Son of God (the past tense being chosen by the questioner).[1] In a similar survey for the Independent Television Authority towards the end of the decade the figure was even higher: 85% among men, 89% among women.[2] But turning from popular attitudes to current intellectual values, in the judgment of a professional historian these

> ... increasingly promoted a discontent with society and its institutions. Advocates spoke of a refusal to accept single solutions, of their rejection of orthodoxies, of 'pluralism' and 'openness'. But in reality the assumptions constituted a new liberal orthodoxy – uncritical in its essential acceptance of the main canons of secular humanism.[3]

This discontent with institutions was soon translated into the hard currency of Anglican ecclesiastical statistics:

> Between 1960 and 1970 there was a 19 per cent decline in regular church attendance and, whereas 636 men were ordained in 1963, this fell to 373 in 1973. Even more significant was the drop in the number of those recommended for training, which in the same ten years fell by 58.9 per cent.[4]

One reason for the contrast between the different conclusions that could be drawn from surveys and statistics was highlighted by Leslie Paul's Report of 1964 in a section 'Statistics of Decline'. 'Realistically', he observed, 'one must speak of a progressive reduction of membership from the impressive multitude of the baptised to the thin minority of Easter or Christmas communicants, the last only 1 in 20 of the home population.'[5]

But against the general decline in church attendance and membership, experienced across the denominations, there was evidence of evangelical resurgence, of which the most striking single example was the National Evangelical Anglican Congress (NEAC) planned for the spring of 1967. Twelve weeks before the start of the Congress, John Stott spoke at the Islington Clerical Conference to explain what lay behind this enterprise, unique in size and scope within living memory. He began with the wider church in a time of change, but soon he went on to show that 'evangelicals in the Church of England are changing too':

> Not in doctrinal conviction (for the truth of the gospel cannot change), but (like any healthy child) in stature and in posture. God is evidently raising up in our generation evangelical churchmen of intellectual and spiritual power. The Church of England has been dominated for a century by the Tractarian and Liberal movements. Now the pendulum is swinging. It is true that a new theological radicalism has arrived on the scene in place of the old liberalism, but at the same time evangelicals are steadily growing in influence.

He regretted that in the church at large evangelicals had a reputation for narrow partisanship (though in the New Testament sense 'evangelical' could never be a party word) and for obstructionism:

> True, we have often been forced into a negative position because proposals have been laid before the Church which in our conviction are contrary to some vital Biblical truth. But we are increasingly anxious to play our part actively and *constructively* in the Church of England ... We do not want to remain for ever on the defensive,

but to take the initiative to speak positively and evangelically to what is going on around us.[6]

2

The origins of NEAC must be sought at least four years before the Congress took place; and, in the opening words of the official Statement, 'it started where it ended, in the North'. Raymond Turvey had moved from London in 1956 to become Vicar of St George's, Leeds. Born organizer that he was, he began to arrange 'small informal meetings of thirty or forty ministers at a time' to allay the feeling of isolation he encountered among clergy, not least a sense of being cut-off from centres of evangelical thought and action in the metropolitan hub of London and the south-east. These sporadic meetings grew into the Northern Evangelical Conference, held first at York in 1963. Canon Colin Craston, Vicar of St Paul's, Bolton, was one of the organizers. He recalls how James Ayre, Vicar of Cheadle, urged the committee to try to mount not only a northern but a national congress:

> At the meeting of the planning group later in 1963 it was decided to follow up the Ayre suggestion which had received strong support. I indicated that John Stott was to be with me for a week-end in November ... and it was agreed that I should raise with him the group's proposals. John was warmly in favour ...[7]

From this personal conversation sprang a more formal meeting between northern representatives including Raymond Turvey, Colin Craston and Cecil Butlin, together with Peter Johnston as Chairman of the Islington Conference, John Goss, Chairman of the Federation of Diocesan Evangelical Unions, and John Stott. With this pedigree, it was inevitable that any national conference or congress should not be in London but in the northern province, somewhere nearer the centre of the country as a whole.[8] In the following spring these ideas came before CEEC. As far as John Stott was concerned there was a sense that the time was ripe:

> I certainly was aware of the Anglo-Catholic Congresses that had taken place in previous decades, and of the influence they had had, and I think CEEC in general were aware that the evangelical movement had grown so considerably in numbers, scholarship, cohesion, and influence that the time had come for us to say something publicly, which would represent both a milestone in our own development and at the same time be an important voice to the church and even to the country ...[9]

CEEC therefore welcomed the proposal and agreed to be among the sponsors of the projected Congress. Though it was to be an Anglican affair, the Minutes carried a note that it was important that the interdenominational Evangelical Alliance should be kept informed as plans developed[10] (this good intention not to part company with evangelicals in other denominations wore thin as the pace quickened). In April it was suggested that the Congress might take place in Oxford, and in June it was firmly agreed that it should be held in 1967, between the projected visit of Billy Graham to London in 1966 and the Lambeth Conference of 1968. It would be best held before Easter, or in September, with a minimum of 400 delegates, either at a holiday camp, or on a university campus. The new buildings of Birmingham University were suggested, as the thoughts of the organizers moved slowly further northwards. Meanwhile, alongside CEEC, the formal sponsorship of other Anglican evangelical bodies was being sought – CPAS, Church Society, the Fellowship of Evangelical Churchmen and the Federation of Diocesan Evangelical Unions.

By August 1964 it was reported that Raymond Turvey had agreed to act as secretary to a NEAC Organizing Committee with John Stott as chairman. During 1965 the committee made good progress. By January the date was fixed for April 1967; by February the new Keele University in Staffordshire had been booked for the period 4–7 April. It was reported that the Congress fee would need to be something over £5 a head for the four days to cover all expenses, and the accommodation was enough for 1,000 people. By May the committee was in full swing: the name 'National Evangelical Anglican Congress' was chosen, to distinguish it from the EA's National Assembly of Evangelicals (an annual event), and the theme title was to be 'Christ Over All'. Again, the CEEC Minutes show that the committee had large ideas. The Congress would be preceded by a preliminary study course in the parishes (eighteen studies from September 1966 to Lent 1967), and followed by further study courses well into 1968;[11] so that when the brochure for the Congress was issued, it made clear that this was 'only one episode in a programme which is planned to last a whole year'. Nor was the projected content less comprehensive in its vision. The chosen speakers would between them cover the contemporary state of Anglicanism, authority, the gospel of grace, salvation, the cross, issues to do with Holy Communion (in the light of the new Alternative Services now being planned), the credibility of the church, local church life, 'Christian worldliness' (which meant involvement in the issues of secular society), and the missionary challenge. Only two of the team of speakers held teaching posts in universities, the most to which the evangelicalism of the day could aspire: all but one were clergy: all were men.

It was originally hoped that both the Archbishops would address the Congress; but it transpired that Donald Coggan, Archbishop of York, would be returning from overseas at the time; and in his place Stuart Blanch, Bishop of Liverpool, was asked to be the preacher at the closing service of Holy Communion. Raymond Turvey, meanwhile, was to invite clerical and lay representation from evangelical churches throughout the country, as well as a wide range of special delegates representing theological colleges, missionary societies and the like. He later looked back on this phase, saying, 'I ended up with over 4,000 clergy on our index, I remember, out of the then 16,000 active clergy; which we thought was an encouraging proportion for those days.'[12]

Early in 1966 (that is, a year before NEAC) a conference, primarily for younger evangelical clergy, was arranged at Swanwick under the title 'Facing the Future'. It was a sign that a certain growing unrest could be detected between the generations, as well as an attempt to meet and counter rumblings about 'secession'. It was hoped that such a conference would allow these concerns to be aired and answered in the company of senior evangelical figures such as Raymond Turvey, Peter Johnston, James Packer and John Stott. To the more aware among the delegates, this arrangement smacked of a rather heavy-handed paternalism. There were mutterings among those who came; and some, like Gavin Reid, decided to stay at home:

> I deliberately stayed away because I felt it was going to be a Conference when the 'oldies' told all the younger folks to step in line. As it happened, I believe, John Stott very quickly realised that the pre-arranged programme was not going to work because very many of those who had gathered for the Conference shared the same feelings that had kept me away.[13]

Michael Walker was one of those who attended, and found it 'an extremely frustrating conference':

> It was clear that every speaker had been told, whatever his subject, to make the point that Evangelicals must not secede from the Church of England. It seemed to me that the leaders who had arranged it were quite out of touch with the younger Evangelicals. I had the opportunity to make a short speech and to voice the frustration of the majority. I ended by saying, 'I am not going to secede from the Church of England; I shall never secede from the Church of England; God has put me in the Church of England, and here I stay.'
>
> I had expected some slight applause but never the enthusiastic

response which those words produced. It was clear to everybody what way the younger Evangelicals wanted to go.[14]

The organizers had arranged that various issues should be addressed in a series of carefully led discussion groups. These included, for example, the problem raised by the rapid growth in numbers of evangelical ordinands, and so of younger evangelical clergy, beyond what the traditional pattern of evangelical parishes could contain. At one point, in the recollection of another of the delegates, John Stott asked for a show of hands from those young incumbents who had been appointed to parishes with no previous evangelical tradition: 'a straw count suggested about 100'.[15] It was originally intended that these various study groups should report back to the final session, but after a hastily convened meeting of the chairmen and secretaries of the groups, it was decided to hold a plenary on the Tuesday afternoon in place of group discussion. Following this, some of the delegates held a late-night meeting of their own, hoping for 'some definite proposals to put forward to CEEC for action'.[16] Recollections are confused; but it is clear that the delegates took control of the agenda, moving on from any idea of secession to voice concern about such issues as liturgical revision or the Anglican–Methodist reunion scheme, and no doubt other current proposals for change. 'It was these which John Stott allowed to take precedence at the final plenary ... it was John Stott's chairmanship that moved us on a generation.'[17] John Stott gave a report to CEEC at its meeting the day following the Conference:

> There was a real spirit of confidence and hope for the future – and a resolve to go ahead at a faster pace. It seemed that the days were past, when we were completely with our backs to the wall: there were now opportunities for a positive and constructive future. The Conference had the desire to see these opportunities taken and used: and that the means for the best use of them should be available.[18]

'Facing the Future' recognized the strategic importance of Latimer House, and asked 'that it should continue its work of identifying the issues which would face the Church of England in the future'.[19] It also asked for the setting up of study groups to address these issues, and a year later thirteen were hard at work.[20] All this helped to prepare the ground, both for the first residential conference of the Eclectic Society in November 1966, and so for NEAC the following spring.

John Stott was now forty-five. He was no longer eligible, on account of age, for membership of the Eclectic Society, but he was present at the conference by invitation as one of the main speakers, and to take the chair. Raymond Turvey continues the story:

In 1966, after a rather disastrous 'Facing the Future' conference at Swanwick, the Eclectics met (John was, of course, no longer in this at that date) and the key personalities, I'm told, sat up till 3am in heated debate and formed a rebel group, revolting over the traditionalism of the patterns of the planned programme [of the projected NEAC]. Philip Crowe was the ring leader with Gavin Reid, Eddie Shirras, George Hoffman and Michael Saward *et al.* They wanted it to be a real conference and suggested it should end by issuing a Statement.[21]

By this time the Congress was less than twelve months away. Nevertheless John Stott listened carefully to what this young group were saying, understood their frustrations, and agreed that their views should be put, with his support, to the NEAC Organizing Committee. This was some twenty strong; though only a much smaller number attended meetings regularly. Gavin Reid recalls:

> I remember I was delegated on behalf of Eclectics to present their views to a meeting of the NEAC Committee: I was already a member because I was working with CPAS on the materials for the Conference. It was a cold day with some early November snow if I remember rightly, and while I was nervously making my case to the Committee, John King of *The Church of England Newspaper* was literally walking up and down the pavement outside praying for a good result!
>
> The Committee was remarkably responsive. I can still remember Peter Johnston saying that he felt relieved to hear the sorts of things I was saying because he had been secretly thinking them himself. In the end I did not feel it was a young-overtaking-the-old movement, but rather a trigger from the younger ones bringing a response that was felt across the board.[22]

One reason why these proposals, based on full participation by delegates rather than simply teaching from the platform, found such ready acceptance is that they self-evidently met the mood of the time. Indeed, there had already been some sense of unease in John Stott's mind[23] as he contemplated a Congress based on the pattern of the last comparable evangelical gathering, 'Evangelicals Affirm', of 1948, when some twenty papers were read to the delegates over two days – and largely sank without trace. John Stott, himself a curate at the time, had been highly critical of the content of that Conference: now it was becoming clear also that its methodology, barely viable even in the 1940s, was quite unsuited to the mood of the 1960s. A majority of the speakers at Evangelicals

Affirm would have described themselves as 'liberal evangelicals' and, in John Stott's cautious phrase, 'the note of distinctly Evangelical affirmation was muted'.[24] A franker statement of his views appears in his correspondence, for as news of the projected NEAC became known he received letters from Canon Bryan Green and Canon Douglas Webster, both leading liberal evangelicals, urging that the evangelical basis of the Congress be broadened to include people like themselves. Douglas Webster wrote a personal and friendly letter 'to one whom I love and respect' to say that he was worried at the way the word 'evangelical' was being monopolized by a single very conservative group, and by what he perceived to be the 'rigidity' of some of the main speakers at the forthcoming Congress.[25] In reply John Stott made it clear that the authority of Scripture remained for him the touchstone of evangelicalism, and it was by the principle of theological submission to this authority that the NEAC Committee had sought to lay their plans. Sending what he called 'a candid reply to a candid letter' he reminded Douglas Webster of this:

> The only precedent we had to guide us was the 'Evangelicals Affirm' Conference in 1948. I expect you will remember it. I recently reread the published report of the addresses, and honestly (with one or two notable exceptions) it is a very pathetic document. There is little 'evangelical affirmation' in it! For example, there was no paper on Biblical authority (only on the use of the Bible in evangelism) and none on Justification (only on assurance) ...
>
> Since 1948 'definite' evangelicals (if I may use this term) have grown considerably in numbers, scholarship, cohesion and confidence. And we have been very anxious to speak to the nation and Church with a clear voice in the midst of the contemporary confusion. Our desire is not just to restate the great evangelical convictions (for we are emphatically not merely going to beat old drums), but to attempt to apply them relevantly to the complicated situations of today. We did not want this message muted by including speakers who, whatever their label, were (in our judgement at least) really more 'liberal' than 'evangelical'.[26]

Neither Bryan Green nor Douglas Webster pursued the matter beyond a letter or two, rather late in the day. Neither was at the Congress, and John Stott remained on friendly terms with both. For his part, the correspondence reinforced his own determination 'to be in a position to affirm something';[27] and therefore to maintain at NEAC the biblical and theological distinctives of an unashamed conservative evangelicalism. Meanwhile a considerable programme of parish study groups was in full swing:

If so large a congress was to do its work responsibly, preparation for churches in general, and delegates in particular, was seen to be a top priority. NEAC was to be a 'grass-roots' affair representing ordinary church people from every part of the country, rather than a working-party of experts and professionals. Preparatory material was carefully planned, first in the form of 'study-course kits' sufficient to serve 12,000 people, produced by Latimer House and the Church Pastoral-Aid Society; and soon more than 700 churches up an down the country had incorporated these 18 group Bible-studies into their winter teaching programme ...

The study kits were followed by the book, *Guidelines*, a collection of major essays by the Congress speakers, the result not only of individual study, but of 'speakers conferences' at which each speaker or writer could share his particular ideas and problems with the team as a whole.[28]

It had originally been intended to publish *Guidelines* at the end of NEAC, as 'the book of the Congress'. But the Committee's eleventh-hour decision to devote the Congress mainly to discussion and debate by the delegates meant that the speakers, instead of delivering to the Congress the papers they had prepared, were now asked to assume that all the delegates had studied these beforehand in *Guidelines*: and so to spend their time re-emphasizing briefly their main themes, and responding to contributions and questions. John Stott wrote to each of them on the following Monday explaining how the Organizing Committee had met for four hours the week before:

Priority was given in our discussion to the growing unrest about the Congress which younger Anglican evangelicals have been expressing both *viva voce* and in the church papers. It seems to centre on two points. First ... the delegates want an opportunity to contribute as well as to listen. Secondly, there is a fear lest all the Congress talk dissipate into thin air without any practical policy being formulated or action recommended. The Congress must speak to the whole Church of England in such a way as to be heard.

The committee felt it right to face honestly this widespread disquiet. We realised that it existed not among destructive critics, but among responsible supporters of the Congress, including one or two speakers. Moreover, as we discussed it, we found that we ourselves were already feeling the same way. So, after prayer for wisdom, and after careful thought, we reached the following unanimous decisions, which I have been asked to communicate to you as one of the speakers.

In brief, the decisions were that the Congress book, *Guidelines*, would be published in advance, as part of the preparation; that the Congress addresses would therefore be elucidation and development of the individual papers, responding also to comments and questions; and that the Congress document, based on a preliminary draft prepared in advance, would be debated and revised in groups and in plenary before (it was hoped) being adopted as the Congress Statement.[29]

In fact speakers eventually had to make their main presentations twice over. There was no single assembly or lecture hall at Keele to seat 1,000 people. Delegates were therefore allocated to one of the two main large halls for these sessions, and the speakers spoke twice on succeeding days, once in each hall.[30] If the delegates were to be able to participate in the way that was now expected, a good deal of homework lay before them. They would be asked to represent the views of the parish study groups from which they came, and to be part of a range of further study groups made up of delegates at the Congress itself:

> As the Congress drew nearer, delegates were gradually briefed and prepared. First they were asked to comment by post on the list of subjects to be discussed. Next, they were asked to state their personal preference among a choice of six study-groups ...
>
> Next (still before the Congress opened) delegates were sent *Guidelines* to read, followed by the original tentative draft of the Congress *Statement*, and a sheaf of further instructions and information. Thus they converged on Keele: some 1,000 delegates, including 110 theological students, together with 30 observers, amongst them Roman Catholic, Greek Orthodox, and Free Church representatives, and members of the Christian Press ranging from the *New Christian* to the *English Churchman*.[31]

Meanwhile, under John Stott's chairmanship, a host of further matters received attention. The 'tentative draft of the Congress Statement' had to be prepared well in advance, and so a drafting committee was set up of Colin Buchanan, Michael Green and Gavin Reid.[32] The status of observers was defined and clarified: besides those referred to above, representing other churches, observers were present from, for example, the Church Information Office, the British Council of Churches, the Mothers' Union, the Cowley Fathers, 'Parish and People', the Franciscans and the Salvation Army.

Practical arrangements had to be considered and confirmed for the serving of meals (the Keele cafeteria would be strained to the limit) and for the welcoming of delegates and their allocation to bedrooms and the meeting-place of their particular study group. The Vice-Chancellor of

Keele was inviting the Archbishop to stay with him: would the committee prefer a sherry party (and if so, large or small?) or a high-table dinner? (In the event, it was dinner.) Worship had to be arranged, and much administrative machinery put in place to prepare and distribute successive drafts of the Statement, from groups to sub-plenaries to plenary sessions. The Press had to be looked after, a handbook prepared, group discussion leaders briefed, and so on.

With less than a week to go, John Stott was given space in the *Church Times* to explain what it was hoped the Congress would achieve. What had begun the year as an event of merely domestic interest to evangelicals had now become (thanks to 1,000 delegate bookings, an impressive array of observers, and the presence of the Archbishop) something command- ing the attention of the church at large. Under the heading 'National Evangelical Congress at Keele – Attempt to Face Today's Crucial Questions', John Stott appealed to readers of the *Church Times* for a better recognition of evangelical distinctives by those who made the big decisions. At NEAC, he told them, 'We want to speak responsibly. But will you listen to what we say?'[33]

It was a courageous plea, showing faith that the Congress would not simply reveal Anglican evangelicals as their stereotypes portrayed them, expose too unkindly their unworldly immaturity, or publicly provoke entrenched division. But many prayers had been offered for the coming week, astonishing feats of administration and logistics had begun to fall into place (thanks, more than anyone, to Raymond Turvey and his team) and the delegates had undertaken serious preparation:

> Present at Keele were the historic elements of the evangelical movement. Let no one think it has ever been a uniform movement! There were the Puritans and Anabaptists who sat uncomfortably in a comprehensive church. There were the pietists who thought the Church of England the best boat to fish from. There were the young charismatics seeking renewal and revival. There were the radicals who wanted to embrace most things modern. In the midst were a group of leaders, young and old, lay and ordained, who held this disparate and sometimes disorderly movement together – in the best tradition of Cranmer, Hooker, Baxter and Simeon.[34]

The tide stood ready to be taken at the flood.

3

Keele University itself was to prove an inspired choice. It was the first of the new universities, founded as the University College of North

Staffordshire in 1949, and receiving university status in 1962. It had hosted other conferences, but none so large as NEAC, with almost as many delegates as the university had students. Keele Hall, for 350 years a family seat, was set in a square mile of farm and woodland, with lakes, lawns and rhododendrons. Modern teaching and residential blocks had been added, and an impressive chapel which would serve as one of the two main halls of the Congress.

John Stott travelled to Keele at the start of the week, nine days after Easter, to find Raymond Turvey and his team already in possession, sorting out rooms, checking lists, going over the needs of the Congress with university staff. Under grey skies, 1,000 participants arrived (519 clergy; 481 laity) including delegates, speakers, observers and Press, to sort themselves out and snatch a cup of tea before the Archbishop's opening address.

After a formal welcome to his diocese by the Bishop of Lichfield, Archbishop Michael Ramsey addressed the Congress on the theme 'Jesus is Lord':

> My subject tonight is the person of Jesus Christ, and I want to do no more than consider with you the meaning of the Easter faith 'Jesus is lord'. Jesus lived nearly 2,000 years ago. Christians claim that he is alive now and that he matters immensely for the human race, but those who are not Christians say that this claim is absurd and may be ignored. I ask tonight: why do we believe the claim to be true, and how does it matter for the world?[35]

It was a straightforward theological paper, going to the heart of the faith in its assertion of the historicity of Christ's resurrection, and the centrality of his cross. It contained almost no explicit reference to the Congress, or to the company among whom it was delivered, apart from a single paragraph appealing for openness across the traditions.[36] Michael Botting confided to his diary, 'a bit dry in the middle but warmed up at the end'.[37] James Packer spoke next, with a call to Christian obedience to revealed truth. He had come to Keele with limited expectation, but found his hopes rising as the Congress tackled its task. Walking from one room to another between meetings, he told John Stott that 'it was very evident that this was an epoch-making conference in which the Holy Spirit was notably at work'.[38]

On the Wednesday morning John Stott expanded on his own contribution to *Guidelines*, 'Jesus Christ, our Teacher and Lord'. He was able to draw on a limited amount of feedback, by letters from delegates and in previous discussion; and, with the draft Statement in mind, to address especially those delegates who would be wrestling with the concept of authority. In *Guidelines*, he had begun with a reminder of theological confusion in the church, 'a basic cleavage in fundamental doctrines': and attributed this to the fact that 'not everybody recognizes the message of Scripture as the message of Christ':

> Let me put it this way. If Jesus Christ were to appear in person on earth today, and if He were to speak to the Church in such a way that His person and His message were clear and incontrovertible, it is charitable to suppose that the great majority of churchmen would heed His message, believe it and obey it ... If we could be certain that what the Scripture says Christ says, that the message of the Bible is the Word of Christ, then surely we would (or at least should) be ready to receive it and conform our lives to it.[39]

From a discussion of the uniqueness and trustworthiness of Scripture, John Stott's contribution to *Guidelines* moved on to a further question. Given that we can trust Christ, can we trust *ourselves* to interpret him aright? His reply drew upon the perspicuity of Scripture and the truth of historical development in theology under the guidance of the Holy Spirit:

> The truth of God is neither what you or I think, nor what the Church teaches, but what the Spirit says to the Church through the Word. And since churches and individuals err when they are 'not governed with the Spirit and the Word of God', the greatest need of the Church in this as in every age is humbly to submit to the authority of the Word and prayerfully to seek the illumination of the Spirit.

The presentation had made much of the word 'submission' in contrast to those prevailing theological attitudes which summoned the Scriptures to the bar of human judgment. Moving towards his conclusion, John Stott was conscious that this might seem to place unacceptable constraints on academic freedom, or to verge simply upon a blind obscurantism. He asked:

> But is not this submission of our minds to the mind of Christ an intellectual imprisonment? No more so than the submission of our wills to the will of Christ is moral bondage. Certainly it is a surrender of liberty, for no Christian can be a 'free thinker'. Yet it is that kind of surrender which is true freedom – freedom from our own miserable subjectivity, and freedom from bondage to the current whims and fancies of the world. Is it stunting to spiritual

growth? No, it is essential to it, for Christian growth is nothing if it is not growth into Christ as Lord and Head.

And if this is true, there are practical consequences. Ministers must preach the Word, Christians must live by it, and it must be the basis of all attempts to reunite churches: 'Only when we thus submit to Jesus Christ as our Teacher and our Lord, is the reunion and the renewal of the Church a realistic possibility.'

Later that afternoon it was time for the delegates to get to work in earnest. The Congress was divided for this purpose into six sections bearing some relation, but not an exact correspondence, to the main presentation from *Guidelines*. They were to study the church and its message; its mission; its structures; its worship; its unity – and the world of which it must be part. Something, perhaps, of almost each of the *Guidelines* presentations spilled over into each different section, and so into different parts of the final Congress Statement. For that Statement to achieve its final form was a logistical *tour-de-force*:

> The discussion groups began their work at 2.15 p.m. on Wednesday, and continued with brief pauses until after 9.15 p.m. The chairmen and secretaries of the groups then met to conflate their reports, and it was 6.00 a.m. the following morning before the last section was complete. Thanks to a team of efficient typists, the revised statement was in the hands of delegates before lunch on Thursday. From then until the last plenary session on Friday, what the *Church Times* described as 'this superhuman programme' rolled on relentlessly as the revisions and redrafting continued ... 'beaten into shape by a thousand people in three gruelling days.'[40]

'Gruelling' was indeed the right word to describe not only the work of the groups, but even more the drafting committee. Philip Crowe, who was at the heart of the process, was said to have had some four hours' sleep during the entire Congress.[41] Raymond Turvey's recollection, nearly thirty years later, was that John Stott survived the first night's drafting, but fell asleep during the second. Quite large numbers were involved, at least in the early stages, since chairmen and secretaries of groups attended the drafting session. Raymond Turvey recalled:

> The nerve centre of the whole Congress was the actual re-drafting of the Statement – which was done *twice*, through the two nights! I think Norman Anderson chaired this group with Stott and Packer. And Philip Crowe had a major part in writing it up. It was presented to the typing pool (Frances Whitehead, Norman Ander-

son's secretary Shelagh Brown, and two others from St George's, Leeds) in the small hours and duplicated, conflated and distributed by lunchtime. I remember that the Roneo rep. from whom we bought a very considerable stock of duplicating paper volunteered to do it for us and brought 6 electric duplicators and locked himself in one of the classrooms and worked all six single-handed![42]

The final editors of this draft Statement due to go before the plenaries of the Congress were John Stott and Michael Green. They had to judge, from the drafts submitted and the resolutions passed by the sub-groups, what was the mind of the Congress; since the structure (and timing) of the Plenaries left little opportunity for further amendment.

Much of the Congress Statement, partly at least at John Stott's insistence in the early days of the planning committee, was a careful theological reformulation of an evangelical understanding of the faith. But throughout the Statement there are distinct contemporary references as the Congress sought to relate their revealed faith to the issues of the day. In the words of one delegate, there was 'a deep sense of something prophetic and forward-looking happening among us. A movement was changing and coming alive in a different way.'[43] The process was laborious and the result inevitably uneven in both coverage and presentation. In his Introduction to the published Statement John Stott commended it as expressing 'the convictions of a large but average evangelical constituency' rather than the work of experts. He explained:

> The Congress Statement represents the common mind of the great majority of the almost 1,000 delegates who were present at Keele. It was composed by them, out of an original and entirely tentative draft, and knocked into shape paragraph by paragraph during many hours of discussion groups and plenary sessions. It is, therefore, a true child of the Congress as a whole.[44]

It was his own conviction that – at least in certain sections – evangelicals had been culpable for generations past in their neglect of scholarship, their lack of social vision, and their insularity within the church. There were shining exceptions, of course; and the church at large must bear some responsibility for the negative image of evangelicals and their withdrawal into 'a church within a church'.[45] Nevertheless in human affairs all new beginnings cannot escape a penitential glance behind; and under John Stott's chairmanship, NEAC '67 was no exception. He wrote in his Introduction to the Statement:

The mood of the Congress was one of penitence for past failures and of serious resolve for the future. This has meant for many of us not a change of fundamental position, but of stance and even of direction. The Statement must not be taken, therefore, as our last and unalterable word. It is more a beginning than an end. As the situation develops, the dialogue increases and the issues clarify, we are sure that we will learn more, and we rather think that we have more to say.[46]

4

The area in which John Stott himself had most to learn, and eventually more to say, was 'The Church and the World'. It was here that the Congress broke new ground for most delegates and signalled a large part of the 'change of direction' attributed to Keele '67. It is noticeable, in the statistical table included in the published Statement, that discussion groups in this section attracted the highest proportion of laity among the six options, ten times those who chose to work on 'The Church's Unity'. Alone among the remaining sections it requires some account here, since it was influential in helping to shape the direction of John Stott's thinking for the remainder of his ministry.

Ten years before NEAC, a perceptive but not altogether friendly critic of evangelicals had neatly impaled them on this very issue.

> Here is IVF [Gabriel Hebert wrote in 1957], with its splendid witness to the authority of the Gospel of God over men's personal lives and the saving of their individual souls. Here it stands in the line of the biblical and Christian tradition. But what has it to say about God's world, and the problems of our social life? For it is not sufficient to say that if only individuals are converted and give their hearts to God all will be well; it is still necessary for them to know how they are to live their lives after they are converted, amid all the problems of business, commerce and social relations.[47]

It was precisely in reply to Hebert's kind of question that Professor Norman Anderson had made his contribution to *Guidelines* on the theme of 'Christian Worldliness – the Need and Limits of Christian Involvement'. The previous week the *Church Times* had featured him in their series 'Portraits of Personalities':

> A tall, willowy and attractive speaker with confident utterance will represent the lay voice at the National Evangelical Anglican Congress at Keele which begins on Tuesday. He is Dr. J. N. D.

Anderson, Professor of Oriental Laws in the University of London and Head of the Department of Law in the School of Oriental and African Studies, Director of the Institute of Advanced Legal Studies and Dean of the Faculty of Laws in the University. His own special subject is, to use his own word, a rather exotic one – Islamic law.

To Professor Anderson belongs the reconciling Evangelical voice which is heard in the Church Assembly; the Evangelicals can congratulate themselves on the presence in their midst of a spokesman who must be among the most academically distinguished in the whole Assembly. Yet he is modest, friendly and informal in manner, with none of that unnerving earnestness sometimes found in Protestantism.[48]

At the outset of his essay, Norman Anderson frankly admitted that Christian involvement in society and its needs was 'a sphere in which the Evangelical has, in recent years, far too often failed', at least by contrast with the Reformation Christians, the Puritans, or the leaders of the Evangelical revival a century before.[49] Speaking to this essay, and developing further some of the concerns, Norman Anderson addressed half the congress each morning. Reflecting on his life, nearly twenty years later, he admitted that he himself had come late to this recognition of the need for Christian involvement in society. He and his friends, he wrote, as students,

> ... had always – in theory at least – recognized 'charity' as a Christian duty; and attempts to help those less privileged than ourselves, in projects like the Cambridge University Mission in Bermondsey, had received a certain amount of support. But for the rest we had largely accepted the inequalities of life as part of the order of things. The urge to evangelize, and to 'witness for Christ', had had signally little counterpart in the sphere of radical social reform.[50]

He goes on to add that it was from his son Hugh, then still at school, but later to be President not only of the Cambridge Union but also of the Cambridge Labour Club, that he and his wife Pat 'had begun to learn a little' of the need for 'Christian worldliness' and a sensitive social conscience.[51] In seeking to analyse the reasons for this failure to engage with the world's agenda, Norman Anderson's essay pointed both to the evangelical's awareness that the world as a system lies under the judgment of God; and also to a not unreasonable fear of 'secular theology'. But it was a failure, nevertheless, and he went on to adduce seven certain principles pointing unmistakably towards a proper Christian involvement with the material order, including 'an attitude to such questions as culture, wealth, politics, morality, law, penology, class relations, race relations, sex, war, education, work and leisure'. And while properly to discuss these (and no doubt other topics) in a single evening was impossible, the basic principle was clear: 'the Christian must recognize man's duty to use all God's gifts ... in a way which corresponds as closely as possible with the Creator's purposes as revealed in the Scriptures'.[52]

By way of example, the paper gave a paragraph or two to a number of contemporary issues as setting the agenda for future study. Besides those already mentioned, it touched on the Christian duty to the democratic state, on welfare provisions and economic issues, on work and industrial relations, the population explosion, divorce and sexual morality, and the sanctity of life. The essay concluded with three reminders of the importance and urgency of secular engagement: the intimate connection between the eternal and the transient; the reformation of society as an expression of God's rule or kingdom; and the hope of Christ's return and 'the restitution of all things' which is in itself 'an incentive to personal holiness and strenuous endeavour'.

By the time this section of the Congress Statement came up for approval at the final plenary session, a considerable agenda had been mapped out. Some of it was rudimentary: a good deal depended on a few activists among the delegates with more prior knowledge of these issues than most. Nevertheless the Statement touches on a number of specific topics, leaving far more to be tackled by a range of post-NEAC study groups. Its importance lies less in what it says on secular issues than in the fact that evangelicals had again begun to address them and to use the Bible to do so. After Keele, they were at least on the agenda. Norman Anderson himself was to say that 'the spark that fired my interest in these issues came from the invitation to address them at Keele', and he followed up his essay by starting work at once on a book which could serve as a better introduction to some of the questions Keele could only note in passing.[53]

Two years after Keele came a further evangelical initiative in this arena in the founding of the Shaftesbury Project, a modest but significant attempt to promote a biblically based evangelical concern for social issues. It was to come to enjoy, in the years that followed, an increasing recognition as a resource centre and think-tank. John Stott and Sir Fred Catherwood were both founding trustees, and John Stott remained so for almost twenty years until in 1988 the Shaftesbury Project merged with another of his ventures, the London Institute for Contemporary Christianity. Roy McCloughry, a later Director of the Project, found him

> ... personally very supportive of the work of the Shaftesbury Project and it gained a great deal from his own pursuit of biblical

approaches to social issues. Over the nineteen years of its life the Shaftesbury Project tackled some of the key issues of the day often in small groups composed of enthusiasts as well as experts who debated and wrote papers on the issues under discussion. There were groups to tackle Race relations, Urban theology, Overseas aid and development, Information technology, Family and sex ethics, Politics and many others. Submissions were drawn up to Government Inquiries and Royal Commissions on issues such as obscenity and pornography. A number of publications came out, notably a handbook on World Development and many monographs on social ethics.[54]

The Project was influential beyond its size. Further and lasting evangelical initiatives owed something of their origin to it, including the magazine *Third Way.* The new social commitment flowing from Keele was also one of the factors contributing, eleven years later, to the first Evangelical Conference on Social Ethics, with John Stott in the chair. It was a sign of how far evangelicals had come along the road that, apart from the Director of the Shaftesbury Project, John Gladwin, the speakers should all be professors or lecturers, drawn from half a dozen British universities or colleges. Among them was the Regius Professor of Moral and Pastoral Theology at Oxford, Oliver O'Donovan, who had sung as a choirboy at All Souls in the early days of John Stott's ministry. The published Report[55] includes an Epilogue from the chairman, 'Tasks which await us'. After reflecting that 'an evangelical conference on social ethics would have been impossible ten years ago', he called the Conference, and through them the evangelical constituency, to three further tasks in this contemporary engagement of biblical evangelicals with secular issues: to go beyond questions to answers; beyond words to actions; and beyond thought and action to passion – prompted by the Christian vision of God himself.[56]

5

By lunchtime on Thursday, the third day of the Congress, all the speakers had finished their presentations twice over, each time to half the delegates, once in the chapel and again in the Walter Moberley Hall. Each delegate had been assigned to one of six sections or study groups, according to choice. Their written drafts had been conflated and edited through much of the night and the Thursday morning session. Now it was time to submit the revised draft statement, section by section, to a sub-plenary, and then (after any necessary amendment) to two further plenaries, at the last of which the whole Statement would be adopted by the Congress. Only an hour could be allowed for the last plenary in a very tight timetable: even so, it started late because the drafters of the section on 'The Church and the World' were still arguing when they should have been drafting, and could not quite meet their final deadline.[57] 'It was really rather confusing,' was Michael Botting's comment, 'as different Halls had decided different things; so one felt one must leave everything to the final drafting committee.'[58]

In spite of the difficulty caused by having to use two halls simultaneously, Philip Crowe remembers moving from one to the other on the last morning, in company with John Stott and Jim Packer, 'and sharing a brief moment of intense relief' that both sessions had gone well, and that the Congress was up to time on a tight final schedule, which meant that the task was nearly complete.[59]

The final morning also included a service of Holy Communion at which Stuart Blanch, Bishop of Liverpool, preached on the Congress theme, 'Christ Over All' from the words of John the Baptist, 'He must increase while I must decrease', applying these to the life of the individual, the church, and the world: 'Most moving,' was Michael Botting's comment.[60]

So with a mixture of euphoria and exhaustion, the delegates prepared to return home. Philip Crowe, editing the Keele Statement for publication the following month, asked some of the observers for their reactions, and included a selection of them. Sir Kenneth Grubb, Chairman of the House of Laity, was short and to the point:

> The Congress has done three remarkable things. It has given Evangelicals a justified sense of their standing; it has emphasized their loyalty to the Church; it has demonstrated that they have much to contribute, not only to individual faith, but also to the great spiritual challenges of contemporary society. Can one expect more?[61]

Canon D. M. Paton, Secretary of the Missionary and Ecumenical Council of the Church Assembly, compared the Congress with Vatican II (but had the grace to add an exclamation mark!). He too had three points: first, the positive and open attitude of the Congress 'confirmed the change of temper among Evangelicals' already noticeable for some time past; secondly, this change was not in doctrine but in 'the way doctrines are held'; and thirdly, a question, are evangelicals prepared to take seriously viewpoints not their own?

He was not the only observer to mention Vatican II. Father Bernard Leeming, the Roman Catholic observer from Heythrop College, wrote of 'the same spirit in which John XXIII summoned Vatican Council II', and noted evidence of great, and unrestricted, charity; and that (as the Statement said) 'Evangelicals and RCs do indeed hold many fundamental doctrines in common'. Others spoke of 'a new willingness to face without fear the winds of change', and of 'a turning point for the whole church'.[62] John Stott himself was later to describe Keele as 'a landmark, a watershed',[63] and as marking 'our Evangelical coming of age, for there we publicly repented of our immature isolationism and resolved to take a more responsible part in the life of both the visible Church and the secular world'.[64] Adrian Hastings' choice of metaphor to describe Keele was as a 'viable road forward', which 'greatly altered the evangelical sense of direction', adding: 'It is hardly surprising if by 1972, 35 per cent of all Anglican ordinands were in the six Evangelical colleges.'[65]

It was not only the church press that recognized that what was happening at Keele was hard news. *The Times* was noticeably reticent, but reports appeared in *The Daily Telegraph* and *The Guardian*, and in more popular papers such as the *Daily Express* and the *Daily Mail*. They picked up and reported a few ecclesiastical issues – senior appointments, baptismal discipline, church reunion – but gave more space to what NEAC (or its speakers) had to say on issues such as abortion, drug addiction or divorce reform. *The Guardian* spoke of 'the impressive and seemingly relentless growth in the last twenty years of the evangelical movement within the Church of England', and quoted in their headline the phrase 'coming out of their ghettoes', which John Stott had used in the press conference.[66] The Roman Catholic *Tablet*, in a full-page article by one of the two RC observers, put forward the view that 'if the competence of the leaders, the thoroughness of the preparation and the enthusiastic commitment of those present are any guide, we may indeed before long be able to speak of new and welcome changes in the atmosphere of English religion'.[67] The radical *New Christian* spoke generously of a *tour de force*: 'John Stott and his organising committee pulled it off and, whatever may be thought of the fruits of their labours, they deserve the warmest of congratulations for a remarkable achievement.' It added that though radicals would find in the theological section of the Keele Statement 'the expected discouragement', and though 'by and large, the radicals are viewed with the gravest suspicion and believed to be selling the pass', nevertheless

> ... a proper examination of the evangelical position may well provide the radical with some pleasant surprises, and it may not be too much to hope that a proper examination of the radical position will give the evangelical some reassurance. In any case, the two groups are the only ones likely to provide the Church of England with any dynamic within the foreseeable future, so the sooner they can learn to share their insights the better for all concerned.[68]

In some of what has been written about Keele there has been an element of overstatement, as though a new evangelical mind was formed almost overnight. But events have causes. D. W. Bebbington, a historian of evangelicalism, points out that 'the trends consolidated at Keele had already been emerging beforehand', for example in the Eclectic Society, in the growing evangelical influence in Church Assembly and in books such as Fred Catherwood's *The Christian in Industrial Society* (1964).[69] The Christian Foundations series (1964–67), to take another example, also had several titles on contemporary issues, though more in the church than in the world. To suggest therefore that before Keele, 'Anglican evangelicals lived in a kind of Christian ghetto',[70] John Stott's phrase that was much overworked at the time, represents only a partial picture of what was happening among evangelicals towards the end of the 1960s.

It was clear to all who came to Keele that John Stott, with some able colleagues, was the inspiration, architect and centre of cohesion for the whole Congress. He was chairman of the organizing committee which had brought it into being, and made it a reality. Though not listed as one of the Congress chairmen (these were given as Canon T. G. Mohan and the Revd R. P. P. Johnston), he and Norman Anderson between them had chaired the unwieldy plenary sessions towards a common mind. Twenty years later David Edwards, with his tongue gently in his cheek, could tell readers of the *Church Times* that John Stott 'has been called the Pope of Evangelicalism';[71] and to those who sought a comparison between Keele and Vatican II such a suggestion was irresistible – the more so because it would be particularly unwelcome to its subject! And in the post-war resurgence of conservative evangelicalism, Alister McGrath is not alone in pointing out that one of the most important factors, if not *the* most important factor, was the personal ministry of John R. W. Stott:

> His impact on a rising generation of evangelical students, through his speaking and writing, though universally acknowledged, cannot easily be measured. If the remarkable growth of English evangelicalism can be attributed to any one person, it is to Stott, who became a role model for a younger generation of evangelical ordinands in England. Stott's parish-based ministry gave evangelical clergy and ordinands throughout England a new awareness of the possibilities open to them.[72]

Because he was regarded as the architect of Keele, John Stott came under fire in a personal way from some of the nonconformists and Independents. Morgan Derham, General Secretary of the Evangelical Alliance, referred in the published Statement, *Keele '67*, to his sense that the Congress 'did not always fully appreciate the feelings of evangelical non-

Anglicans'.[73] But it was his considered judgment, nevertheless, that the Keele Congress and Statement 'represents very great progress in the development of a wholesome, outgoing, uninhibited Evangelicalism'. And though there remained a considerable disagreement between Anglican and non-Anglican evangelicals on ecumenical dialogue, for example, this was not unfamiliar. Evangelicals differed on baptism and on eschatology without breaking fellowship. Could they not also, he asked, agree to disagree on some of the issues raised by Keele?[74]

John Stott felt, with hindsight, that the Congress mishandled this important area 'with only one reference to "our non-Anglican evangelical brethren"'.[75] But at the same time, he felt that more allowance could have been made for the situation with which Keele was confronted: 'We could see an era of change for the Church of England coming, and that unless we were in a position to put our hand on the steering wheel, we should be powerless to see that it remained a church in which we should stay.'[76]

He believed, too, that some of the criticisms were knee-jerk reactions from those who had simply heard NEAC unfavourably reported, or the Statement selectively quoted. Interviewed by the editor of the inter-denominational monthly *Crusade* seven years after Keele, he was un-shaken in his basic support for the Statement. When John Capon commented on the adverse reactions to the Keele Statement on the part of many Free Church evangelicals he 'was met with a courteous but firm rebuff'. John Stott told him,

> I strongly suspect that some of those who criticised us never read the Keele statement ... Like Scripture and every other document it needs to be read as a whole. What they seized on was one or two passages about our desire to enter into dialogue with Christians of ecumenical persuasion. They interpreted this as a definite com-promise of the evangelical position. Our answer was that the first section of the statement was a forthright, outspoken statement of evangelical faith which couldn't be faulted, and that we defined dialogue as a willingness to listen and learn as well as to speak and teach. That represented no compromise of our evangelical position.[77]

A few years later he was again fiercely pressed on this point by Dr Brian Harris, editor of *The Evangelical Magazine of Wales*, in a published interview prefaced by a strong anti-Keele statement representing the position of the journal. Dr Harris asked whether, in John Stott's view, recent years had seen 'a change in evangelicalism ... a division and polarisation in attitudes towards the ecumenical movement'. John Stott replied:

If by the change you mean that at the time of the Keele Conference in 1967 Anglican Evangelicals changed their doctrine of the church, I think that is a misunderstanding. I know a number of non-Anglican evangelicals think so. In my view Anglican theologians such as Dr. Packer have not changed their basic theological positions at all. At Keele there was a clarification of our position, a recognition that we had been too 'pietist' in the sense of withdrawing both from the visible church and the secular world. Now we see that we have to take our position as evangelicals in both of these contexts.[78]

Two years after Keele, John King (who had just handed over the editorship of *The Church of England Newspaper*) wrote a small paperback, *The Evangelicals*. It included a chapter entitled 'Did Keele change anything?', which appeared to give credence, from someone within the Keele circle, to the idea that Anglican evangelicals now preferred to think of themselves primarily as Anglicans who could be described as evangelical. If this were widely true, as John King asserted, it would be a distinct shift of emphasis, and one rightly of concern to Free Church evangelicals. John King wrote, with an imp of mischief at his elbow:

> The outstanding effect of Keele was to deal a death-blow to the idea of an Evangelical unity existing as a kind of alternative to the ecumenical movement. This particular will-o'-the wisp was extinguished once and for all – to the accompaniment of protestations of everlasting friendship to Evangelicals in other Churches than the Church of England. (The protestations were received with coolness by Free Church Evangelicals.)
>
> Keele '67 in fact set Church of England Evangelicals squarely in the historic Church. Loyalty to the historic Church (which, for the present, is the Church of England) came before loyalty to Evangelicals wherever they might be found.[79]

This idea of conflicting loyalties was probably always something of a false antithesis: many Anglican evangelicals found no difficulty in combining a loyalty to those who shared the same gospel across denominational boundaries, with a loyalty to their own church whose formularies they saw as fully biblical. No doubt some could be found, before and after Keele, for whom John King's generalization was true: but, coming from such a source, it seems to have been taken more seriously than it deserved. Paul Welsby quoted this passage in his 1984 *History of the Church of England*[80] without qualification, as did Randle Manwaring in his study a year later,[81] though careful to make it clear that he was quoting an individual's opinion. Kenneth Hylson-Smith, in his definitive study of *Evangelicals in the Church of England*, writes of new post-Keele alignments, giving John King's book as reference.[82] Even more recently, in a serious study published in America in 1994, the same quotation is still at work.[83]

What seems, therefore, at first sight to be a cumulative weight of historical evidence, rests largely on a single common source, offering an individual and indeed journalistic viewpoint. What can be shown beyond doubt is that it did not represent John Stott's personal position. His loyalties to fellow-evangelicals across denominational boundaries remained unchanged. His writing and teaching are as much valued outside Anglicanism as inside it; and in America, much more so. For seven years after Keele he continued as President of Scripture Union; in 1973–74 he was President of the British Evangelical Alliance; on four separate occasions he was President of UCCF – once before Keele, three times afterwards. Twice before Keele he was a Keswick speaker, and again in 1969, 1972, 1975 and 1978 (and also in 2000, though this lies outside the period of this narrative). And on the specific point of where loyalty lies, he made his own life-long position explicit in an address in November 1984, not this time to an interdenominational gathering but to a specifically Anglican one, on the subject of 'I believe in the Church of England':

> First and foremost, by God's sheer mercy, I am a Christian seeking to follow Jesus Christ. Next, I am an evangelical Christian because of my conviction that evangelical principles (especially *sola scriptura* and *sola gratia*) are integral to authentic Christianity, and that to be an evangelical Christian is to be a New Testament Christian, and vice versa. Thirdly, I am an Anglican evangelical Christian, since the Church of England is the particular historical tradition or denomination to which I belong. But I am not an Anglican first, since denominationalism is hard to defend. It seems to me correct to call oneself an Anglican evangelical (in which evangelical is the noun and Anglican the descriptive adjective) rather than an evangelical Anglican (in which Anglican is the noun and evangelical the adjective).[84]

6

What then were the fruits of Keele '67? In what sense can it be called 'the beginning of an Anglican evangelical reformation'?[85] The answer lies not so much in the Statement itself, nor even in the Congress as an event. Foremost, perhaps, was the forging of a new evangelical sense of identity, one which was gaining in confidence, sure of its place within the church, and committed to involve itself further in the life of the church and of society.

Keele also marked a major stage in the process of evangelical self-education. Laity as well as clergy had already begun to take seriously the intellectual challenges, and to realize that though in some areas they had hardly started, yet the longest journey begins with a first step. Keele institutionalized this process, widened it immeasurably, and brought it to the notice of the church at large. It made public commitments from which there could be no going back. It set an ambitious agenda for evangelical parishes, supplemented by a range of 'Congress Conferences' across the country, led by Congress speakers such as Norman Anderson or James Packer, and other leading evangelical figures.

Thirdly, because of the high profile of the event and its open welcome to observers from quite other traditions, the church at large was reminded of the evangelical presence in a new way. For three weeks running, evangelical affairs had been on the front page of the still predominantly catholic *Church Times*.[86] They could no longer be ignored; they must be reckoned with; indeed, they must be genuinely welcomed.

Keele also signified the definitive reversal of the roles of the liberal and the conservative streams of evangelicalism. As with Evangelicals Affirm, the word 'evangelical' had in the past been generally understood in the central councils of the church to mean a Max Warren, a Bryan Green, a Douglas Webster. To the Church of England in general, the structure of evangelicalism was the AEGM, the Anglican Evangelical Group Movement, finding kinship more with the SCM than with the IVF, proud of its liberal distinction. All this of course was changing in the years before Keele: Charles Raven in 1962 had lamented 'the whole liberal Christian movement ... swept away by a flood of neo-orthodoxy ... the sort of thing which the best minds in the previous generation had stood for was abandoned'.[87] Nevertheless it seems at least symbolic, as Alister McGrath has pointed out, that NEAC took place in April, and the final conference of the AEGM in the following July:

> The main business was the Annual General Meeting, which took the decision that the AEGM should 'be dissolved as soon as conveniently practicable' ... Liberal evangelicalism had ceased to be a meaningful organized presence within the church. Conservative evangelicalism had, quite simply, eclipsed it.[88]

Because of Keele and what it represented, evangelicals were better placed than most to weather the secular storms of the 1960s, with their heavy toll upon ecclesiastical institutions. Adrian Hastings writes of how evangelicals 'would for a while combine a clear sense of purpose with pastoral vigour and a willingness to learn that almost no one else could rival'.[89] For John Stott himself, it was important that, alongside so much else that Keele achieved and signified, 'by the end of it, the evangelical constituency made a public penitent renunciation of pietism'.[90] If, as the years passed, the heady promise still proved elusive, that was something to face with realism, and a spur to continue the work. Ten years later Keele '67 would be followed by Nottingham '77, the second NEAC. Writing in one of the preparatory books for that Congress, John Stott reminded the constituency that there were lessons to learn from what happened after Keele. Some of the hopes and expectations for continued study at parish level had proved unsustainable in some local churches:

> Most of us acknowledge that God met with us at the Keele Congress ten years ago. It was in many ways a turning-point for our evangelical constituency in the Church of England. But most of us would also have to agree that the promise of Keele was not fulfilled. The follow-on was disappointing. We failed to maintain and extend the kind of fruitful dialogue which began at the Congress itself. We must not make the same mistake this time.[91]

Perhaps this was not the only mistake at NEAC '67: it would be surprising if it were. But in the various assessments of what had been gained – or lost – and what had finally been achieved, evangelicalism would not want to be measured only by a numerical or organizational yardstick. It was surely the experience of Keele, and what followed from it in the next two years, that enabled David Edwards, a staunch liberal, to write of conservative evangelicals as he did in a review for the *Church Times*:

> They have a burning and shining sense of mission. In an age of religious famine they know God, through Christ … Conservative Evangelicalism is not a fashion depending on great personalities: nor is it a party depending on bureaucracy or on jobs for the boys. It is an emotional reality. It is a reaction against the confusion of our time but more: it is a stirring of the hunger for God.[92]

FOUR

Travels and Writing: God's Word for Today's World

1

The start of the 1960s found John Stott an international figure in the field of student evangelism. Though he conducted numerous university missions in the United Kingdom during those years, he also travelled widely, helped by a loyal and capable staff of curates to hold the fort in London. By the end of the 1960s he was in equal demand as a speaker at clergy conferences; and these two audiences, students and pastors, were to remain his priorities. But it was noticeable that his work with EFAC was part of a more general widening of his interests, with a special eye on the Third World.[1] His own travels, too, made EFAC a reality in many places where there was otherwise little opportunity for Anglican evangelicals to learn from one another. When in July 1968 a pre-Lambeth retreat was held at Oak Hill Theological College for evangelical bishops from across the world, it was clear that, though nominally arranged by CEEC and EFAC, the initiative came from John Stott himself, and very many of the bishops present were personally known to him: 'the response was a clear sign of his growing influence'.[2]

It is not possible in even a long biography to describe in any detail every mission, or every visit: during the decade he was in North America

three times; twice in Asia; three times in Australia and New Zealand; once
(but again at a number of centres) in Africa; in Rome and Berlin, and in
Oslo and Uppsala. Exceptionally, the year 1960 began not with a
'missionary journey' but with a study tour to Israel and Jordan. Dick and
Rosemary Bird, who had both worked in Jordan, were his companions.
By coincidence, he was following hard on the heels of Billy Graham, who
had concluded his series of African crusades with a visit to Jordan and
Israel only a month before. It had been an occasion for much diplomacy.
Time magazine reported that Graham had agreed not to refer to Jesus
when preaching to Jewish audiences. Graham at his press conferences had
disclaimed any intention of proselytizing, while adding, 'I must be grateful to you for proselytizing me. For Jesus Christ was a Jew, all the apostles
were Jews, and the whole early church was Jewish.'[3] Indeed it was for
precisely this reason, to see the land of the Scriptures, that John Stott
chose to go. During the flight home, he wrote down his impressions of
the visit:

> I think that of all the parts of the Holy Land which I have visited
> during the past weeks I have loved, and shall remember, Galilee
> best. Although it is now irrigated and farmed by modern methods,
> it remains beautiful and unspoiled ... the rolling hills and the green
> fertile valleys, and the deep, shimmering blue of the Lake of Galilee
> are the same as when Christ lived and healed and preached there. It
> is not hard to imagine Him in Galilee.[4]

Even as John Stott was preparing to leave for Israel in 1960, Harold
Macmillan was in Cape Town reminding the South African Parliament
that 'the wind of change is blowing through this continent, and whether
we like it or not, this national consciousness is a political fact'. The
Sharpeville massacre the following month demonstrated the truth of his
words. Two years later in the spring of 1962 John Stott embarked on his
second visit to the African continent, not this time to include South
Africa (which had left the Commonwealth the year before), but travelling
only as far south as Salisbury, while conducting university missions in
Sierra Leone, Ghana, Nigeria, Kenya and Uganda, as well as in Rhodesia.
In East Africa he was able to revisit a few people and places he had last
seen in 1959.

The tour was at the invitation of the Pan-African Fellowship of
Evangelical Students, and the opening mission was at the University
College of Sierra Leone in Freetown on the west coast, some 600 miles
north of the equator. The university had grown out of an early CMS
institution for training clergy and catechists, and was now a full-scale
University College of 400 students (90% male) with degrees awarded by

Durham University. At the time of his visit a new campus was being created on the mountainside behind the city. The start was not altogether auspicious:

> I dined with the students. There are three dining halls adjoining one another, linked by a public address system. Today happens to be some special international students' day, dedicated to anti-colonialism, and we were treated throughout the meal to about ten student speeches, one after the other without intermission, shouted down a hand microphone on the violent 'anti-colonialism', 'anti-imperialism' theme. It was impossible to talk to one's neighbours at table. The speeches were rather superficial strings of nationalistic slogans ...[5]

As usual, the days included a number of interviews and receptions: with the local bishop, with members of staff, with the committee of the Students' Union. The main addresses were three evening 'lectures' on 'Fundamental Christian Questions': 'Who was Jesus of Nazareth?', 'Why did He come?', 'What does He demand?' It was encouraging to find that about half the college had turned up for the first meeting, spilling out on to the veranda of the largest lecture hall. After the final lecture a number stayed behind and some came forward 'thoughtfully and with apparent understanding' afterwards. A group of students returned with the missioner to his lodging to continue discussion:

> Shortly before midnight, when the others had gone, there was a knock at the door and in came a Muslim student from Gambia. It is some time since I have talked with such an earnest seeker after the truth. He questioned me closely and intelligently about the Christian faith, about the reason for the cross and the place of Jesus Christ, his big brown eyes searching mine and his whole soul seeming to hunger for God. Was it possible to know God, to 'see' God, he wanted to know. He reminded me of Nicodemus who came to Jesus by night. He went away with a copy of St John's Gospel and a promise to read it. His name is Ishmael. We must pray that as he seeks, he will find.[6]

From Freetown John Stott flew a thousand miles east to Accra to spend a long weekend at the University of Ghana, and then on to Nigeria where he was quickly among friends. Richard Earnshaw-Smith, son of the former Rector of All Souls and recently appointed Bishop's Chaplain, was at Lagos Airport to meet him. He was due to spend the week in Ibadan, staying with Eldryd Parry, senior hospital registrar and an old friend. The mission had to embrace three different institutions: University College ('about eight years old with 1500 students'); University College Hospital ('only five years old ... the biggest and most modern hospital in Africa') with some 400 students; and the new University of Ife, only just constituted. The diary records:

> I'm greatly relieved to find that I seem able to get onto the right wavelength with them. I feared that a combination of my white skin, vocabulary, and European thought forms and thought processes would make effective communication extremely difficult ... probably a majority of the students have been born in a Christian home and received a Christian education in a mission school. They are in fact second or third generation Christians. If asked when they became Christians, they will reply, 'I was born a Christian.' Most have little understanding of the need for a second birth, or of the necessity of a personal commitment to Christ and a firsthand experience of Him.[7]

A much longer flight (via Khartoum and Addis Ababa) took John Stott from West Africa to Nairobi. Here Bob and Sarah Howarth were waiting to take him to the Royal College, a multiracial (and to a limited extent, multifaith) community of about 400 students which had just become one of the constituent colleges of the University of East Africa.

There was no Chaplain: the mission was organized by the Christian Union, under the leadership of a young student, David Gitari,[8] and was the first ever held at the University. More than a third of the College came to the opening lecture, 'Who was Jesus of Nazareth?' David Gitari recalled later:

> Kenya was demanding independence from Britain, and the students of the University Campus were getting more interested in politics than in the Christian gospel. When, however, John Stott gave the first open lecture attended by a large number of students and members of staff he made such a deep impact that every night students of all walks of life attended his lectures. Though there was strong opposition from some quarters especially when the students knew he was the Queen's Chaplain, John Stott was not discouraged ... Some of the Christian leaders in this country who were present as young people during that mission still testify how much they were helped ...'

A week's holiday, not before time, was spent with the Howarths. After an exciting session of photography in the Royal National Park they set off

up the Rift Valley towards Nakuru to stay with George and Maureen
Swannell, and then to visit the Masai-Amboseli National Park on the
border with Tanganyika. Their way took them through Masai villages
with 'low round windowless huts made of sticks and cow dung' to a
Lodge in the heart of the Park with a view of Kilimanjaro. It was on this
brief holiday together, sitting in the Land Rover looking out over the
African bush, that John Stott invited Bob Howarth to consider joining
the staff of All Souls to lead the International Fellowship.[10]

The final engagement of the tour was a week's mission at the
University College of Rhodesia and Nyasaland in Salisbury. On the
Sunday evening beforehand John Stott preached in the Cathedral, a
massive stone building still under construction. The diary records:

> ... into this stronghold of Anglo-Catholicism the Dean welcomed
> 'Father Stott'! I preached on Matthew 11:25–30, and, with the
> Dean's permission, held a continuation service afterwards to which
> almost half the full congregation stayed and in which I explained
> simply the steps to Christ. About a dozen came forward, mostly
> men, some quite elderly, one saying he had wanted to take this step
> for sixty years.[11]

Once again, the heart of the mission was to be three lectures on 'The
Challenge of Christ', held in a spacious modern hall. On the first evening
it was filled with more than half the college, to the evident surprise of the
Student Christian Fellowship who had organized the mission, but seemed
to be spiritually unprepared and disunited among themselves. John Stott
felt much sympathy with a Muslim postgraduate student who came to
him for a personal interview and declared, 'I have a great admiration for
Christianity – but not for Christians.' The diary continues:

> Last night, after the third and last lecture, I had the happiest two
> hours of the week. One of the African students invited seven of his
> African student friends to meet me in a small common room for
> questions and discussion. I just love these Africans. They're so much
> more warm and open and sincere than the rather cold and
> supercilious Europeans. We had a really valuable time, clearing up a
> number of their problems. We talked freely about Jesus Christ as
> the great breaker down of the barriers of race and rank, and I have
> every hope that they will join the Christian fellowship. It would
> certainly be a marvellous thing if the Christians at UCRN were to
> demonstrate within the tensions of the university that a truly
> multiracial fellowship is possible through Christ.[12]

Perhaps it was this kind of personal ministry, as much as the big preaching occasions and the well-attended lectures, which prompted the following assessment half a lifetime later from an African Professor at the University of Nairobi. Referring to what he calls John Stott's 'key role' in the late 1950s and early 1960s in East Africa, he describes how

> ... it was fashionable at that time for college students to dismiss Christianity either on intellectual grounds or as a white man's religion. John Stott's missions to African universities and his writings met the intellectual and spiritual needs of many. They helped to raise an educated class of African Christian leaders and professionals who in turn influenced, and continue to influence, younger people ... Important examples that come to mind immediately include three men who later became prominent church leaders, namely the late Archbishop Janani Luwum, Bishop Misaeri Kauma and Bishop David Gitari. His initiatives and personal friendships have borne much fruit in strengthening the leadership of the church.[13]

2

The following summer, at the invitation of IFES, the International Fellowship of Evangelical Students, John Stott agreed to visit Asia in order to lead student missions in India, Malaya, Singapore and the Philippines. He also planned to try to visit a number of All Souls missionaries and contacts, and so added Iran, Ceylon, Hong Kong and Thailand to his itinerary. Asia, so he told his congregation on the eve of his tour, is home to more than half the world's population, a population growing five times as fast as that of Europe, and including three and a half million students.[14]

His sister Joy brought his mother, by now not in good health, to see him off at London Airport. He flew first to Tehran for an overnight stay, where (as almost universally in his travels) friends from All Souls were waiting to meet him and give him a whistle-stop tour. A change of flight meant that he had to miss both lunch with the British Ambassador, and a visit to the Caspian Sea (a long drive north) at a time when bird migration was at its best: the diary does not indicate which was the greater disappointment. Even in so short a visit he was asked to fit in a talk to an informal gathering which had been arranged in the St Paul's Anglican compound – 'Europeans, Americans, Iranians and Jews, a motley throng'.

So on to India. After a day or two as the guest of Joe and Edith Mullins at their parsonage in Bangalore (Joe was another friend from All

Souls, now a Presbyter in the Church of South India; while Edith was an All Souls missionary), the two men set out by car for the Christian Medical College at Vellore, 120 miles away. The college for medical students, where John Stott stayed, was about four miles from the hospital itself. Since he had been invited by the whole institution, he therefore found himself conducting two concurrent missions, giving the same address twice, once on each site. It quickly became 'one of the most strenuous missions I have ever been on'.

'But', the diary continues, 'we have seen the Holy Spirit at work.' Almost all the students and many of the senior staff attended one of the nightly meetings: some came to all four. In addition John Stott preached twice on Sunday in the local Church of South India (experiencing for the first time the giving of 'the Peace') and was able to get at least a glimpse of local life, including a Hindu festival. 'Birds', he recorded sadly, 'are not numerous ...'

From Vellore he flew next to Ceylon, with a brief call on the Bishop of Madras *en route* ('It was amusing to hear him say he had read two of my books and preached a course of sermons from one of them!'). At Colombo Airport he was met by a large party, including the local Mayor, and found himself garlanded with jasmine amid much clicking of cameras. His host was an Anglican minister, Felix Dias-Abeyesinghe, who had stayed at All Souls a few years earlier. He had laid careful plans for a three-day mission, even arranging for temporary seating to be installed, and his faith was rewarded. Some 2,000 people came, and there was a good response.

Kuala Lumpur, his next stop, was a bustling capital city with high-rise modern buildings and a newly created university some little way out of the city. In a contemporary account Chua Wee Hian gave this description of the visit:

Banners were flying over four strategic points in the campus at Pantai Valley, site of the six-year-old University of Malaya. On walls, steps and trees were attractive notices and handbills advertising a series of lectures on 'The Christian Faith'. On notice boards all over the campus were impressive invitations to attend these lectures. Free transport was promised ...

It was about 4 p.m. and the dark skies could contain themselves no longer. Heavy rain fell. Thunder! Lightning! The first rainstorm for several weeks! One could hear the rapid heart-beats of the members of the Mission committee! The meeting was scheduled for 8 p.m. Would the students go out of their way to hear the Gospel in this heavy deluge? The skies cleared around 6.30 p.m. A quarter of an hour before the main meeting, we were relieved as we saw the crowds pouring in. Over 300 students came – an answer to prayer. Many students remained behind for the Continuation meeting ...[15]

Although at that time it was illegal to seek to evangelize Malays (who were largely Muslim), yet several sat on the stairs of the lecture theatre or listened from doorways. 'Not discouraging,' John Stott wrote home after the first two evenings, 'but only six or eight definitely responding.'[16]

Singapore came next on his itinerary, still one of the Malay States, though due to gain independence during the next two years. Here the university where he was to conduct a week's mission was English-speaking, but 80% Chinese; and the Christian Union, about 100 strong, was celebrating its tenth anniversary. The diary records how

> ... large numbers of Chinese students have absolutely no Christian background whatever. They come from homes where nominal Buddhism or traditional ancestor-worship is practised, and consequently in attending the mission were hearing the Christian Gospel for the first time.
>
> In view of these problems we were all encouraged by the large numbers attending the 'lectures', by the receptive hearing which they gave to the message, and by the small group of fine students who thoughtfully and definitely responded.[17]

On Sunday morning John Stott preached in the Cathedral, after which one of his hosts, Dr Aw Swee Eng, President of the Fellowship of Evangelical Students in Singapore, drove him round the city followed by an enormous lunch in a local restaurant with the mission committee:

> About eighteen of us sat down round two circular tables joined together, under a red illuminated Chinese lantern. Dish after dish was brought and placed consecutively in the centre of the table. The guests all helped themselves in Chinese style, using chopsticks (I with considerable ineptitude!). The custom is not to fill one's plate from the central dish but to keep dipping in for each fresh morsel. I could not begin to describe what we ate. We began with a kind of hors d'oeuvre. I couldn't recognize what the different meats were, but fervently hoped they weren't iguana or crocodile! ... At the end I felt, like Elijah, that I could have gone in the strength of that food 40 days![18]

This was just as well; since, after two hours of interviews, an evening Guest Service at the Cathedral was followed by the Farewell meeting at the university. Early next morning a little bunch of missionaries gathered round the car to pray for John Stott as he left for the airport, 'while monkeys screamed and chattered in the trees nearby'.

By now it was well into September. There remained a final mission at the University of Manila, 1,500 miles across the South China Sea. Once again, besides the evening lectures and many personal interviews, John Stott's days were filled with other speaking engagements: evangelistic meetings both for adults and for young people, a meeting for pastors and seminary students, preaching on Sunday at the Cathedral, a workshop for Christians; concluding with a farewell meeting both for those who during the week had entered into a new experience of Christ, and for the members of the Christian Union who would be responsible to carry on the work.

On the way home John Stott managed a brief visit to Hong Kong, to meet Deaconess Joyce Bennett, one of the All Souls missionaries. After a glimpse of the walled city, she took him to see Bishop Hall, who had refused permission for a proposed IFES mission to Hong Kong students as part of John Stott's tour: 'we had an hour's fairly keen theological debate. We had to agree to disagree, but I hope I was able a little bit to show him that evangelicals are not as black as he has painted us.'[19]

There was yet one more visit, this time to Manorom Hospital in Central Thailand, four hours from Bangkok by train. Here June Morgan and Diana Whitwam, both All Souls missionaries, specialized in reconstructive surgery and rehabilitation for leprosy patients, giving further use to hands and feet ravaged as a result of the disease. John Stott noted in his diary:

> Lepers are not cared for in Buddhism, and the love of God in action which they see in the Christian Hospital at Manorom has led many to Christ. It was a joy to walk through the leprosy wards with June, and see not only the disfigured faces, hands and feet of the sufferers, but their smiling Christian faces too. A strong Thai church is growing up, and the Thai Christians and missionaries seem to be working in the happiest harmony.[20]

While John Stott was in the Far East his mother Lily, aged eighty-three, suffered a stroke. Joy cabled, but he did not receive the message until six days later and was then unable to get in touch with her as storms had caused an entire breakdown of telephone communication between England and Hong Kong. At last news came through that Lily was beginning to improve, but she remained something of an invalid until her death just over two years later, faithfully cared for by her daughter Joy.

3

In 1958 John Stott had paid his first visit to the Australian continent, preaching in Adelaide, conducting university missions in Melbourne and Sydney, and concluding with a brief series of meetings in New Zealand. The 1960s were to see him return to Australia in 1965 and to New Zealand in 1966 and 1969. It was a time of significant change in Australian church life. The new constitution with its General Synod was still very recent, but already there was talk of a new Australian Prayer Book (though in fact publication proved to be more than a decade away). The diocese of Sydney, where Archbishop Hugh Gough was also Primate of Australia, had maintained the original evangelical Anglicanism of the first Christians, but this was by no means true of Australia in general. Stuart Babbage, Dean of Sydney and then of Melbourne, described the position as he saw it in the 1960s:

> In many dioceses there is little respect for, let alone toleration of, evangelical practices. In some cases ordination has been actually refused, in others postponed, in relation to men who have, in conscience, felt unable to wear the eucharistic vestments … At the present time, in most parts of Australia, the tide is running strongly against evangelicals, and the situation is one of agonizing difficulty. There are pressures, both covert and overt, against the profession and practice of evangelicalism.[21]

John Stott's visit in January 1965 was not this time to conduct university missions but to strengthen and encourage the witness of the churches, and to help evangelicals towards a new maturity in their faith. He was to give the Bible readings at three residential Summer Schools of the Australian Church Missionary Society, and at the annual conference of the Australian Inter-Varsity Fellowship. He asked his congregation in London:

> Please pray specially for these young people at the threshold of adult life, that Jesus Christ may capture their wholehearted allegiance and that many may spend their lives in His service.[22]

His route to Australia took him first to America. He flew to Chicago three days after Christmas, to attend the seventh IVCF Missionary Convention at Urbana, Illinois. New Year's Day 1965 found him in Los Angeles, preaching in the Cathedral on the visit of the Magi ('anticipating Epiphany by a few days'), and thankfully returning a box of winter clothes to England: 'overcoat, thick trousers, snow boots, fur cap etc.

which I *certainly* shall not need "down under"'. After a twenty-four-hour stopover in Hawaii he caught the midnight flight to Sydney. Jack Dain, well-known to John Stott as the Missionary Secretary of the UK Evangelical Alliance, and now Federal Secretary of the Australian CMS, was there to meet him.[23]

The CMS Summer Schools were already a regular feature of Australian church life. They had grown in size over the years, and about 1,000 people, many of them students, gathered at Katoomba in the Blue Mountains, 70 miles west of Sydney, for the week ('one evening 1,150 crowded in, with every seat taken and many standing'). Once again, John Stott found that a surprising number of those he met were former friends, or had at least visited All Souls. Bishop Marcus Loane was there, co-secretary with John Stott of EFAC, and Clive Kerle, who was about to become Bishop of Armidale: 'He has been an admirable chairman of the Summer School ... friendly, modest, natural, sensitive, humorous.' A particular joy was to meet, as elsewhere in Australia, several who had committed their lives to Christ as students during the 1958 university missions. There was time, too, for relaxation; mainly some early morning birdwatching, and an occasional afternoon expedition:

> Marcus Loane drove me some thirty miles out of Katoomba to a valley called Scot's River. The scenery was glorious, rolling pastureland studded with different kinds of eucalyptus trees, and the outline of the Blue Mountains in the distance. We came across several flocks of sheep, all recently shorn and looking a bit scraggy. The most exciting birds were Crimson Rosellas – parrots with bright crimson on head, breast and belly, and with bluish-brown wings; Little Lorikeets, dapper little green parrots with scarlet face and crown, flying busily from tree to tree in noisy little flocks; and a pair of Australian Bee-eaters, called the 'Rainbow Bird' because of its gorgeous combination of copper, black, blue and green plumage.[24]

As the week finished, John Stott reflected in his diary on his impressions of Australia, comparing his experiences at Chicago and Urbana with those at Katoomba:

> It has been instructive to come from America to Australia, and to note the differences. The Australians, generally speaking, appear more reserved. One isn't mobbed by autograph-hunters and flashbulb photographers to the same extent! But once their confidence and friendship have been won, they are marvellously warm and loyal. It was quite touching to say goodbye this morning

and to be surrounded by crowds wanting to shake hands and bid one Godspeed.[25]

In between the CMS Summer Schools came the annual IVF Con-ference at Coolangatta on the east coast of Queensland, another holiday resort, followed by a few days' rest at the characterful 'O'Reilly's Guest House' in the Lamington National Park. On the Sunday Ian Hore-Lacy, a staff worker of the Australian IVF, and four students from the IVF Conference who happened to have chosen the same guest house for a holiday, climbed with John Stott to the brow of a nearby hill to hold their own open-air service before breakfast. They found a mountain panorama spread out before them:

> We sang, read and prayed together, and I talked to them for a while on the Biblical warrant for bird-watching! It's interesting how migratory birds which go and return are used to teach us repentance in Jeremiah; how Jesus used sparrows to teach us faith, a quiet trust in Him who feeds and protects the sparrows; and how the author of Psalm 84, who longs to visit the Temple, God's dwelling place, envies the sparrows and swallows which build their nests there![26]

Practising what he was preaching, John Stott added in his diary, 'I seem to have seen about fifty different species over the week-end at O'Reilly's.'

He returned to Sydney for a few days as the guest of the Archbishop and Mrs Gough. The two men took the opportunity to discuss their hopes for the future of EFAC; and John Stott was able to address a private gathering of forty or more evangelical leaders on 'The New Morality', which had yet to gain ground in Australia. Finally, after a relaxing day or two with seals and penguins on Phillip Island ('the whole surroundings reminded me much of Skomer and Skokholm') and even briefer visits to Melbourne, Adelaide and Perth, it was time to go home. A stopover at Karachi meant two or three nights as the guest of Bishop Chandu Ray, the first Bishop of Karachi and a keen evangelist – 'perhaps the only Anglican bishop who preaches regularly in the open-air and does tract and Scripture distribution!'

> Although Christians are a tiny minority in Pakistan, he is obviously well known, respected and even loved. He is in many ways one's ideal for a bishop – deeply spiritual, quite lacking in pomposity, loving and serving his people, and passionately devoted to the cause of making Christ known to all men.[27]

4

In the winter of 1956–57 John Stott had spent six months in the United States and Canada conducting a series of university missions. In the 1960s he was to return three times: in 1961 to give the Payton Lectures at Fuller Theological Seminary at Pasadena, California; and in 1964–65 and 1967–68 to take part in the Urbana Missionary Convention held by the IVCF every three years, over the New Year period, at the University of Illinois, Urbana.

Pasadena lies just to the east of Los Angeles. Here in 1947 Charles E. Fuller, a well-known Christian layman (famous for his coast-to-coast radio programme *The Old Fashioned Revival Hour*), had founded his college with just twenty-seven students. By the 1960s he had built up an impressive campus and a faculty with good academic standing, and the college had grown to some 300 students from a variety of denominations. The Payton Lectures, named after Charles Fuller's wife's parents, were given annually. John Stott, the first English lecturer to be invited, was asked to take a homiletical theme, and had chosen a series of New Testament word studies which he entitled 'The Preacher's Portrait', based on the New Testament pictures of the preacher as steward, herald, witness, servant and father. Among his hearers was the young Michael Cassidy (later to become the founder of Africa Enterprise), whom John Stott had known as an undergraduate in Cambridge, and had encouraged to move on to Fuller for theological training two years before. He remembered 'astonishing clarity of exegesis and exposition':

> I am sure it shaped the thinking about preaching of many of those Fuller Seminary students, as it did for me. Many key concepts came into my life in theology at that time such as the critical importance of understanding the *kerygma* as a fixed deposit proclaimed by a herald (*keryx*) who was not at liberty to change the message and substitute it for his own private opinions on this, that and the next.[28]

John Stott was tired and nursing a heavy cold ('in the last stages of bodily decrepitude'), but he was able to continue with an unremitting programme. On Sunday in Beverly Hills he preached at 9.00am and at 11.00, with a special afternoon service in Los Angeles Cathedral:

> The American churches do not have evening services on Sundays as a rule. This service (at 5pm) was put on specially. I was hoping there might be four or five hundred people at the most, and we were all taken aback to discover the Cathedral packed with over a

thousand. The British and Canadian Consuls read the lessons, and four Canadian Mounties in scarlet uniform (matching my cassock!) were in the procession. Dick Lief took the service, and a Welsh parson the prayers, while the Dean welcomed me. Afterwards he took me outside onto the pavement before the cathedral and I was literally mobbed by hundreds of folk wanting to shake hands: 'I come from Yorkshire', 'I was born in Newcastle', 'my home was in Tunbridge Wells', 'my grandfather lived in Leicester' etc. etc. I told them that so many people had said they were from England, that I wondered there was anybody left in England at all!'[29]

The following week saw a few days of relaxation, picnics and bird-watching, a visit to Disneyland ('I soon became transformed into a schoolboy again') and a much-needed week's holiday in the famous Yosemite National Park. This provided opportunities not only for birdwatching but for sightseeing – including, so the diary records, 'the famous Upper free-fall waterfall, nine times the height of Niagara'; and a family of Black Bears, 'a great black monster of a mother bear with three brown cubs of perhaps a year old'. Two days later, unknown to his companions, was his birthday: 'It was a strange experience to receive no letter, card, present, phone call or personal greeting – as no-one knew my address. But it was appropriate thus to enter the sober forties, perhaps!'[30]

Twice in the decade – and a further four times in the 1970s – John Stott was at the Urbana Missionary Convention of the IVCF. This triennial Convention had originated in Toronto in December 1946, and was always held in the few days immediately after Christmas. It quickly moved to the University of Illinois at Urbana, and was soon attracting well over 1,000 students. By 1964, John Stott's first visit, attendance had grown to more than 6,000.[31] On his way to the Convention, John Stott preached for the Chicago Sunday Evening Club, a regular congregation of something under 1,000, with a radio and TV audience estimated at towards 250,000. It was almost New Year, and he spoke on 'Beginning a New Year with Christ' before 'being bundled into a huge seven-seater Cadillac limousine to be driven 150 miles to Urbana ... we arrived at about half past midnight'.

It was not John Stott's first visit to the University of Illinois, since he had conducted a mission there eight years before. Since then the campus had grown, and the university had just completed a vast circular assembly hall in which the main meetings would be held over the next five days. The Convention would be the largest gathering yet held there, and the administration involved in bringing 6,000 students from all over the United States and Canada, accommodating and feeding them, and providing the most effective Convention programme for them, was daunting to the small IVCF staff. Paul Little, the assistant Convention director, provided for his hard-pressed colleagues a new translation of 1 Corinthians 12:26: 'Your ulcer is my ulcer'.[32]

Enthusiasm was high among the student delegates. Some had been travelling for days to get there, a few even starting on Christmas morning. One father, on hearing that his son planned to attend, gave a grudging comment with the words, 'Go ahead, but if you decide to become a missionary don't bother to return home.'[33] John Stott described in his diary the daily programme:

> My task has been to give a daily forty-minute Bible exposition from 2 Corinthians 3 – 6 ... followed immediately by a panel of speakers from 11–12. This makes possible an early lunch. At 2.15 there's an hour's forum or question-time when the morning speakers are questioned, and then the conference breaks up into groups for 'elective courses' on such subjects as missionary anthropology, radio, education, journalism and literature, linguistics and medicine. After supper is the main evening meeting.[34]

It was not only students who came to hear what was to them a new style and standard of biblical exposition. Arthur Glasser, US Home Director for the Overseas Missionary Fellowship, described how at one of John Stott's Bible readings on 2 Corinthians he found himself sitting next to the minister of a church, who turned to him at the end with these words:

> God helping me, I am never going to enter the pulpit unprepared again and, God helping me, I am going to do biblical exposition. I want to let people hear the Word of God like Stott did this morning. I never realized how fascinating and instructive that kind of preaching is.[35]

The final evening meeting was on 31 December:

> The general public were admitted, as Billy Graham was the main speaker, and I suppose 15,000 or 16,000 people came. When this was over, the hall cleared and most of the students dispersed to do their packing. We reassembled for the concluding Communion Service at 11pm ... a great stillness descended on the congregation, as the administration was silent ... The service finished at midnight, as we rose to sing 'We rest on Thee and in Thy Name we go', and 1965 had dawned.[36]

The Urbana Convention was held every three years, once in each student generation. John Alexander succeeded Charles Troutman as General Director of IVCF in 1964. He wrote later:

> I determined to establish a tradition (following Charles' good example) that for the Urbana triennial conventions the Bible expositor would always be from a non-American nation. For two reasons. First, we felt that the best expositors were from overseas. Second, we wanted to demonstrate that Americans could humbly sit at the feet and learn from non-American Bible teachers.

They therefore wrote to John Stott soon after the end of the Convention, inviting him to return in 1967:

> His response was typically Stottonian. He said he could not accept the invitation and went on to explain that he felt bringing the Bible expositions at Urbana Conventions was such a rare privilege that nobody should enjoy it more than once; that the opportunity should be passed around and shared with other Bible teachers. I admired his generosity and humility. However I wrote back, requesting that he reconsider ...[37]

This time John Stott was persuaded, and after some sabbatical study leave in the summer of 1967, he returned to Urbana in the days after Christmas to give the Bible readings. He chose to expound 2 Timothy, a favourite New Testament letter.[38] Numbers by this time had grown to over 9,000 from some sixty nations. The campus was under snow, with a biting wind and the temperature dropping to 10°F (−12°C). But the Convention managed eight hours of meetings on most of the five days, with over 100 missionary societies represented. Michael Griffiths was there from the Overseas Missionary Fellowship:

> I shall never forget a heart-cry for relevance from a student: 'Dr Stott, you have told us to flee youthful lusts. Will you please tell us, HOW?' ... John was then still expounding objectively, but with less effective application than was later the case.[39]

5

John Stott's visits to Europe during the decade began in August 1960 with a brief but highly significant consultation at Montreux, Switzerland, which paved the way for the Berlin Congress six years later. He also visited Rome when returning from Africa in 1962, the Uppsala Assembly of the World Council of Churches (at which he was an official observer) in 1968, and Oslo, Lund and Helsinki in February 1969 for university missions.

The Montreux Consultation does not figure largely in accounts of the time. Adrian Hastings briefly refers to it when describing John Stott as 'one of the controlling figures in the councils of international Evangelicalism, the man who could be trusted to prepare the key paper on "God's strategy for this age" at the crucial meeting at Montreux'.[40] Billy Graham spent much of 1960 out of the United States because (according to the 1966 authorized biography) 'he did not wish to become involved in a partisan way in the Nixon–Kennedy presidential campaign'.[41] Accordingly, following his Berlin Crusade (immediately before the city was divided by the Berlin Wall), he invited thirty-three Christian leaders from twelve countries to meet him in Montreux, not so much to talk about future crusades as 'to brainstorm about a possible World Congress on Evangelism'.[42] The general title of the Montreux Consultation was 'God's Strategy in Mission and Evangelism', and John Stott was asked to speak on 'The Strategy of Satan', expounding how, in the days of the early church, Satan had sought to obstruct the advance of the gospel through physical persecution (Acts 3 – 4), moral compromise (Acts 5, Ananias and Sapphira) and false teaching (by distracting the apostles from their primary task of teaching the Word of God, Acts 6). John Stott adds: 'Without doubt the seeds of Berlin '66 were sown during those days at Montreux.'[43]

It was six years before the vision came to fruition, but at last in October 1966 the World Congress on Evangelism gathered in the great Kongresshall in Berlin, including 1,200 delegates and observers from 100 nations and seventy-six church bodies. Every major Protestant denomination was represented:[44]

> The delegates' dramatic mile-long march on Reformation Sunday from Wittenbergplatz to Kaiser Wilhelm Memorial Church was the first such public act of witness in Berlin in four centuries, indeed, since a Sunday in December, 1539, when Brandenburg's Prince-Elector publicly embraced the faith of the Protestant Reformation and led a procession from his castle down to the old Cathedral (now St. Margaret's Church in East Berlin) to introduce Luther's Bible and authorize the Reformation teaching. More than 10,000 Berliners joined in the World Congress act of renewal as the clock in the bomb-scarred church tower struck to signal a new hour.[45]

One of the themes that occupied the Congress was the place of social action within the purpose of world evangelization. It was a subject due to resurface at Lausanne later in the decade among a number of issues where battle-lines were drawn in the fight for a genuine 'evangelical ecumenism', in contrast to a withdrawal from the needs of society on the one hand, or on the other the lack of clear doctrinal orthodoxy, which marked the World Council of Churches and their supporters in the search for a redefined evangelism. It was John Stott's task to give three major Bible studies expounding 'The Great Commission' from John 20, Matthew 28 and Luke 24. He could not help feeling that there was 'something vividly symbolic about promoting evangelical unity in mission in the divided city of Berlin', and about the congress title 'One Race, one Gospel, one Task', so contradicted by the reality of the Berlin Wall.[46] In his addresses, John Stott pleaded that along with the church's task of proclamation, there should be a 'compassionate identification':

By his birth, by his life and his death, God's Son identified himself with us. He did not stay apart from us or aloof from us. He made himself one with us. All this was involved in his being sent by the Father into the world.

Now he says to us 'As the Father sent me into the world, so send I you.' I personally believe that our failure to obey the implications of this command is the greatest weakness of evangelical Christians in the field of evangelism today. We do not identify. We believe so strongly (and rightly) in proclamation, that we tend to proclaim our message from a distance ... yet true evangelism, evangelism that is modelled on the ministry of Jesus, is not proclamation without identification any more than it is identification without proc-lamation. Evangelism involves both together. Jesus Christ is the Word of God, the proclamation of God; in order to be proclaimed, however, the Word was made flesh.[47]

In his third exposition, from Luke 24:44–49, John Stott allowed him-self an emphasis (or lack of emphasis) which later caused him some misgivings. In the addresses as printed he speaks of the commission of the church as 'not to reform society, but to preach the gospel',[48] though he soon moves on to the need for Christians, as salt and light, to affect the society in which they live. Again he declared that 'the commission of the church is not to heal the sick, but to preach the gospel';[49] but this is further elucidated in terms of the church today 'having no authority to exercise a regular ministry of miraculous healing'. He concluded his third address by reviewing the three versions of the risen Lord's commission to the church, as recorded by Matthew, Luke and John: 'Our task is to be witnesses to Christ to the ends of the earth; our reward is the presence of Christ to the end of time.'[50]

In the recollection of Jack Dain – a well-qualified but sympathetic judge – the Bible readings 'made the Congress'; so much so that it is from Berlin that he dates the recognition of John Stott as a world figure by international evangelicalism.[51] There were calls that these three addresses should be published for wider circulation rather than simply as part of the official report of the conference. John Stott confessed, thirty years later, to some relief that this did not happen: 'I now consider that I was unbalanced to assert that the risen Lord's commission was entirely evangelistic, not social ... I later argued that at least the Johannine version of the Commission (with its words "as the Father sent me, so I send you") implies in us as in Christ a ministry of compassionate service that is wider than evangelism.'[52]

In the euphoria of a large and successful event, sweeping claims were easily made:

> Carl Henry astonishingly described the Congress as 'an event unique in Christian history. Not even the Protestant Reformation ... offered anything entirely comparable to this.' It was the beginning of the space age and it seemed as if technology, in particular American technology, could achieve anything ... This spirit represents to some extent the switch in power within evangelicalism from Europe to North America.[53]

Nor was this enthusiasm in the wake of Berlin '66 a merely evangelical phenomenon. The *New York Times* referred to it daily: Vatican Radio took sympathetic notice. Billy Graham in his autobiography speaks of 'a new unity among evangelicals' and of the Congress as a 'catalyst for new efforts in evangelism', and saw one of its major contributions as a new emphasis on the theology of evangelism. Numerous other congresses followed to continue its work: in American eyes it marked the emergence of evangelicalism 'as a significant international body'.[54] This was especially so in the context of the World Council of Churches. Dr T. E. Yates, in what has become a standard history, refers to the evangelicals emerging as a force to be reckoned with on the ecclesiastical world stage:

> Certainly, between 1960 and 1980 the WCC was made increasingly aware of a third force with which it had to engage in debate, over and above post-Vatican II Roman Catholicism and the friendly, but often theologically critical, stance of its Orthodox membership.[55]

John Stott would add that after the Berlin Congress Billy Graham himself gained increased credibility and stature as an international Christian statesman; and that it had once more placed the huge task of world evangelism in the forefront of the Christian agenda. Moreover,

> ... it was now evident that the torch of world evangelization, which had been dropped after Edinburgh 1910, and was being fumbled by the World Council of Churches, must be picked up and held high by the worldwide evangelical constituency.[56]

Further, without capitulating to any concept of the social gospel of theological liberalism it had brought home to many evangelicals the idea that the biblical gospel has social consequences. Carl Henry had been urging this on American evangelicals, often to deaf ears, at least since the 1940s,[57] and though the Berlin Congress did not unite its members on this issue, it did give it prominence and credence exactly where it needed to be heard, not least when forcefully articulated by black delegates.[58] Finally, it prepared the way for the Lausanne Congress eight years later, perhaps the most significant international landmark in twentieth-century evangelical concern for bringing the gospel to the world.

There is a certain irony in the fact that John Stott, who regarded the Berlin Congress of 1966 as implying a loss of confidence by evangelicals in the World Council of Churches,[59] should have found himself two years later in Uppsala, Sweden, at the fourth Assembly of the WCC as an official Adviser, invited by the executive committee and authorized to speak (but not to vote). He felt the need to make clear to his All Souls congregation that this was not to be taken as implying any general endorsement of the World Council, which most evangelicals viewed with considerable misgiving:

> Perhaps I may be personal and tell you why after thought, discussion and prayer I felt it my duty to accept, having first made my position clear to the General Secretary of the World Council. I emphasized that evangelicals do not hold that kind of 'ecumenical' position, which seems to regard all divergent theologies as equally legitimate interpretations of Christianity and merely points of view. Rather do we genuinely desire to live under the authority of Scripture. We therefore desire to learn from others if they can improve, deepen, correct or supplement our understanding of Scripture. But Scripture is our fixed point.[60]

Writing after the event in *The Church of England Newspaper*, John Stott defended his decision to attend (though adding, 'I was in a real quandary') and quoted extensively from his letter to Dr Eugene Carsen Blake, the General Secretary, when responding to the invitation. His position was clear:

> I must retain the freedom to disagree with those who disagree with

Scripture, indeed with all those who do not accept Scripture as the supreme and sufficient rule of faith.

Such people I must view not as holding an equally valid or legitimate viewpoint, but as being actually in error. I conceive it to be my Christian duty to such to protest, and to witness to the truth as I see it.[61]

As might be expected, John Stott found himself warmly received and heard with courtesy. Moreover, the participation of evangelicals meant that their contribution was more plainly articulated, and heard with more respect, than at previous gatherings of the WCC. But, in striking contrast to Berlin, the Assembly seemed to be intent on redefining mission largely in terms of material and social needs, and of such issues as race, refugees, world development, oppression, hunger and war.[62] To John Stott, this seemed symptomatic of the failure of the Council to live under the authority of Scripture. Of course, he readily agreed, the social dimension was of critical importance:

An Assembly which ignored these baffling problems could scarcely be called Christian. Much that was said was (to me at least) enlightening, moving and challenging. I do not regret this emphasis at all, *except* that there appeared to be no comparable compassion for the spiritual hunger of the unevangelized millions, no comparable call to go to them with the Bread of Life ... I believe that Jesus Christ is saying to the World Council about their concern for social justice what He said to the Pharisees about their concern for ceremonial observances: 'these you ought to have done, without neglecting the others'.[63]

Moreover, he found (especially among the younger delegates), an intolerance 'of everything which belonged to the past or savoured of the *status quo*'. In their view one was either 'rad' (radical) or 'trad' (traditional) – with no conception of a Christianity anchored unshakeably to the rock of revealed truth, but flexible in everything else:

One felt saddened at Uppsala to be presented with the wrong choice, either of being imprisoned in an ancient system incapable of adaptation, or of being set free from all attachment to the past including Scripture. The former is an unnecessary bondage, the latter an unwarrantable freedom. The truly Christian way is to be conservative in our loyalty to Scripture, but radical in everything else, to struggle to relate God's unchanging word to the ever-changing world of men.[64]

John Stott's work as Adviser lay in Section Two of the Assembly, concerned with world mission. He was in full agreement with evangelical critics (some of whom went so far as to criticize him personally for his very presence there) that there was a sad lack of emphasis on world evangelism. He explained:

> The reason is not far to seek. Section Two is a hodgepodge, a compromise document, a variegated patchwork quilt sewn together out of bits and pieces contributed by delegates and advisers whose convictions were in fundamental disagreement.[65]

And he went on to add that without contributions from Lesslie Newbigin, John V. Taylor, Donald Coggan and others (which, though he did not say so, inevitably included himself) the statement would have been very much worse. Though present only as an Adviser, John Stott felt that in the face of the 'negative stonewalling reaction to our initiative' he must offer an evangelical critique in the plenary session at which the report of Section Two was presented. It was characteristically a combination of courtesy and plain speaking:

> The Assembly has given its earnest attention to the hunger, poverty and injustices of the contemporary world. Rightly so. I have myself been moved by it. But I do not find a comparable concern or compassion for the spiritual hunger of man ... If the report retains this mood (which manifests little or no urgent compassion for the unevangelized) I for one will feel obliged to say that the World Council of Churches does not seem to care much for them. The WCC professes to acknowledge Jesus Christ as Lord. Well, the Lord Jesus Christ sent his church to preach the good news and make disciples; I do not see this Assembly as a whole eager to obey his command. The Lord Jesus Christ wept over the impenitent city which had rejected him; I do not see this Assembly weeping any similar tears.[66]

It was this exposure to the weakness of the WCC, and of much of the ecumenical movement generally in their handling of Scripture and their concept of mission, that led John Stott to study the subject afresh and eventually to make it the theme of his Chavasse Lectures in World Mission given at Oxford in 1975.[67]

Billy Graham tells in his autobiography of an increasing concern for those in material need, seeing it as part of his maturing in discipleship. It was the exposure to 'the stark reality of human suffering' through Third World travel that opened his eyes to this 'larger responsibility';[68] and John

Stott a few years earlier had confessed the same. Interviewed by an American periodical, *World Christian*, in 1989, he spoke of how his understanding of Scripture had changed in the years following the Berlin Congress, where he had believed and taught that the Great Commission was solely a command to preach and teach and make disciples, not a command to heal and to take social responsibility:

> But gradually, and I don't think it was through anybody's particular influence but through my own reflection on the New Testament, I came to see that this view was very narrow and unbiblical. In the early 1960s, I began to travel in the Third World, and I saw poverty in Latin America, Africa, and Asia as I had not seen it before. It became clear to me that it was utterly impossible to take that old view. Since then I have come to a much more holistic position. At the first National Evangelical Anglican Congress in England – in 1967, still seven years before Lausanne – we issued a very clear statement that evangelism and social action belonged together in the church's compassionate and sacrificial mission.[69]

As Francis Bacon remarked long ago in one of his essays, 'Travel, in the younger sort, is a part of education; in the elder, a part of experience.' A second decade of world travel, when moving from his thirties into his forties, and including his first visit to Asia, proved for John Stott to be an enlargement of both education and experience which came in turn to be reflected in his understanding of the Scriptures.[70]

6

During all this period The Hookses, John Stott's Pembrokeshire retreat, provided not only a haven in which to write, but a respite from the pressures of parish life and itinerant ministry. In 1967 he was able to take a few weeks as a kind of unstructured sabbatical and give himself to some long-awaited reading: B. B. Warfield on Scripture; P. T. Forsyth and half a dozen others on preaching; G. K. A. Bell's massive *Life* of Randall Davidson; *Pilgrim's Progress*; *The Lion, the Witch and the Wardrobe*; and even some Gerald Durrell zoological adventures. Usually at The Hookses a major part of each day was given to writing or preparation: but there was also time for some holiday, often enlivened by visits from friends. Tim Hoare was among a small bachelor party invited down in the spring of 1968:

> As soon as I arrived, before I had unpacked, I was led off to the cliffs to admire a Raven's nest on the cliffs, with chicks on show. After

lunch John would have his HHH (horizontal half-hour). Apart from local walks, we had a drive to St Anne's Head to see the Fulmars. Another day we went to St David's where we visited the factory which had made the carpet for All Souls. I noted how slow our drive was through the town as John was always waving or stopping to chat to people ... We took turns to cook but invariably it was stew composed of tins of peas, spam, baked beans, sausages, oxo cubes, potatoes and chicken soup, mixed and cooked in one large pot ... Some fun was had at my expense because of my recent engagement. We sent Felicity [his fiancée] a tape of one of our conversations and John included a message about our excellent bachelor stews and told the story of Montague Goodman who aged 70 was courting a 50 year-old and seemed to need encouragement. She said, 'Monty, I am feeling lonely and my hands are cold.' He replied, 'You have no business to feel lonely as a Christian and you can sit on your hands.'[71]

But even in such congenial company, John Stott would spend some of every morning in his 'Hermitage', pressing on with whatever he was writing at the time. Of the eight books which appeared during the ten years 1960–1969, five were volumes contributed to different series (two of the series, Christian Foundations and The Bible Speaks Today, being largely his creation), two were based on courses of lectures given respectively at Pasadena (*The Preacher's Portrait*) and Durham (*One People*), and the exception was an exposition (originally given at the Keswick Convention) of four key chapters in the epistle to the Romans, *Men Made New*. Also significant in their different ways were two booklets, *The Baptism and Fullness of the Holy Spirit* and *Beginning a New Life with Christ*. And, if this were not enough, there was also a wide range of contributions to symposia, and of articles in periodicals.

The Christian Foundations series had been started as a project of the EFAC Literature Committee in 1964. John Stott contributed the first and last volumes to the series of twenty-two books. The first, *Confess Your Sins*, was sub-titled *The Way of Reconciliation*, a heartfelt plea for confession and repentance as the way to find God's forgiveness through Christ. It included a firm rejection of habitual auricular confession (that is, to a priest): 'God's normal and natural way is not to send us to the confessional but to confront us with himself through his Word.'[72] The concluding book in the series, *Our Guilty Silence*, on the favourite theme of evangelism, was addressed to clergy and laity alike: 'Again and again an opportunity presents itself to speak for our Lord Jesus Christ, but we hold our peace. And what is true of individual believers seems to characterize and paralyse the whole Church.'[73] A substantial extract from the book made a whole-page feature in the *Church Times*[74] under the title 'Failure in Evangelism: the Causes and the Cure'. Roger Roberts, the editor, wrote personally to the author:

> It gave me both pleasure and pride to publish those selections from your really excellent book, the whole of which I have read with appreciation.
>
> What really is worrying me about the Church of England is the continued failure of the top leadership to deal with this threat from those who still call themselves Christians but who, from within the Church, are undermining and trying to destroy the whole essence of the Gospel.[75]

The book was one of a range of writings on the theme of evangelism and proclamation, some in booklet form,[76] from the first half of the decade. *The Preacher's Portrait*[77] was chiefly addressed to clergy, since the lectures had been primarily for seminary students with a lifetime of preaching before them. William Barclay reviewed it enthusiastically in *The Expository Times*, briefly recapitulating much of the argument (with a few *caveats* on the way) and selecting the final chapter on 'The Preacher as Father' as the highlight of the book:

> There is not a preacher in the land who will not be humiliated and challenged and inspired by this chapter, which is worth its weight in gold. Even if a man disagrees with Mr. Stott now and again, there is so much on which no one can possibly disagree with him.[78]

Preaching was a theme to which John Stott would return twenty years later in his much longer study, *I Believe in Preaching*.[79]

The Durham Pastoral Theology lectures were also given to pastors in training in the Divinity Faculty; but this time the aim was to give them 'a theology of the laity'. *One People*, the book containing the published lectures, looks beyond pragmatic arguments ('need, fear and the spirit of the age') to a biblical understanding of (to quote the book's sub-title) *Clergy and Laity in God's Church*. The lecture on 'The Christian Testimony' drew heavily on the experience of All Souls in every-member ministry. Joe Mullins, an expatriate minister in India in the 1960s and '70s, was a good example of those to whom the book offered not only theological insights but a model to adapt to their own situation:

> Taking over a multi-cultural, multi-national congregation of St John's, Bangalore, I needed a strategy to build a congregation, to teach and equip lay leadership, to encourage small group fellowships

and to challenge people in witness and outreach. Solidly based on Biblical principle and using his experience at All Souls as a model, I found *One People* a tremendous help ...[80]

Alongside the Christian Foundations series, Hodder & Stoughton were also publishing a set of small paperback Prayer Book Commentaries, again edited by Frank Colquhoun. John Stott contributed *The Canticles and Selected Psalms.*[81] After a brief historical introduction, this consisted largely of expositions which were to find a whole new lease of life, illustrated in colour, as a kind of 'coffee-table commentary', *Favourite Psalms,*[82] twenty years later. Other series of addresses or Bible readings appeared in print during these years: the three series of Keswick Convention Bible readings in *The Keswick Week,*[83] and the Urbana series in the two Urbana symposia, *Change, Witness, Triumph* and *God's Men: From All Nations to All Nations.*[84]

On an altogether different level was his commentary on the Johannine Epistles,[85] an early volume in the series of Tyndale Commentaries which has stood the test of time. The general editor was R. V. G. Tasker, Professor of New Testament Exegesis in the University of London, who had made it his custom to attend Westminster Chapel from time to time of a Sunday evening. A turning-point in his life came, however, when at the closing meeting of a LIFCU mission he heard Martyn Lloyd-Jones ('the Doctor') preaching on the return of Christ at the end of the age. Leith Samuel, an assistant missioner at the next LIFCU mission, vividly remembered his testimony to this experience:

> The Doctor was, for the last time, giving the main addresses. Once again Professor Tasker was the chairman and I will never forget the electrifying effect of his opening remarks: 'I don't know who else heard Dr Lloyd-Jones speaking in this hall three years ago on the Second Coming of Jesus Christ. But I know one man whose whole life was revolutionised by that address. That man is your chairman tonight!'

Leith Samuel noted two significant consequences that flowed from this spiritual crisis and public witness:

> He forsook liberalism and took a stand in the theological faculty at King's College on the complete trustworthiness of Scripture. This led to considerable isolation from the other members. He once told me he felt as if he had been sent to Coventry! The other consequence was that he approached the Inter-Varsity Press and asked if they would publish his next monograph. He hoped thereby to

burn his theological bridges and be identified with the then rather despised and small group of conservative theological writers in the theological world.[86]

It was a brave and costly decision. Oliver Barclay, who knew him well, has described how he was 'rudely cold-shouldered by his colleagues, and was even told to remember that one of his predecessors (F. D. Maurice) had been deprived of his post when he became out of step with the traditions of the faculty'.[87] For this and other reasons, John Stott felt honoured to contribute to a series under his editorship.

The year 1968 saw the publication of the first in a new series of expositions, of which John Stott himself was the New Testament editor (and also in this instance the author). This was his *The Message of Galatians*[88] in the series The Bible Speaks Today. There is little indication in the original edition that this was the first of a new series, beyond the heading 'The Bible Speaks Today' on jacket and title page. Indeed, the series was notably slow in starting. No further title was added until 1973 when *Guard the Gospel: The Message of 2 Timothy*,[89] again by John Stott, made its appearance; though a memorandum giving his name as General Editor was circulated to a number of possible authors in 1972. The true start of the series therefore belongs properly to the 1970s. But *The Message of Galatians* served as a useful model to later contributors, based as it was on a course of twenty addresses preached at the instigation of Robert Howarth to the evening congregation at All Souls between the autumn of 1965 and the following summer. Michael Wilcock heard many of these, Sunday by Sunday, and was impressed by how 'incontrovertible' was John Stott's exposition: 'You couldn't disagree with what he said without at the same time disagreeing with what the Scripture said, because it was so clearly the same.'[90] The Preface to the book took up the point of how it was based on expositions to a congregation; and was not therefore intended as a detailed commentary, but as having a more direct and contemporary relevance:

> During the months when I was preaching this series, I kept saying this kind of thing to myself: 'Here we are, a comparatively sophisticated congregation in twentieth-century London, giving ourselves week after week to the systematic study of a short letter written in the first century by a then more or less unknown Jewish Christian to obscure little congregations tucked away in the mountains of Galatia.' ... The study has left me more deeply convinced than ever of the divine inspiration, and therefore the permanent authority and relevance, of the Scriptures.[91]   ·

It was the same desire to unfold the teaching of the Bible which lay behind his address on 'The Individual Christian and the Fullness of the Holy Spirit' at the Islington Clerical Conference in January 1964. The subject was the cause of much heart-searching at the time (the early days of the charismatic movement in Britain) and consequently there was an immediate demand for publication. It was revised and expanded and appeared in July as a booklet of forty pages.[92] It was five times reprinted over the next ten years, and in 1975 was further expanded to make a small paperback, *Baptism and Fullness*, which has never been out of print and has been translated into many languages. By some who disagreed with its conclusions it has been seen as a controversial statement, designed to be a check on some of the key elements of the charismatic renewal movement. But as John Stott makes plain in (for example) his 1995 Preface to the Hungarian edition, his concern has been simply to discover and interpret what Scripture says:

> I should like to emphasize that my purpose in this book is not polemical ... I have no desire to hurt or embarrass anybody. My main concern is to try to expound certain important passages of Scripture. And my objective in this is that all of us may grasp more clearly both the greatness of our inheritance in Christ, in order to enter into it more fully, and also the greatness of our responsibility to manifest all the fruit of the Spirit in our lives and to exercise those gifts of the Spirit which in his gracious sovereignty he has bestowed upon us.

From time to time during John Stott's twenty-five years as Rector, All Souls would be asked by the BBC to allow one of their services to be broadcast, either to listeners in the UK or on the World Service. John Stott, while never a 'media personality', was therefore no stranger to the microphone. During 1962 on his visit to Chicago he recorded a series of ten broadcasts on the Apostles' Creed for the Episcopal Radio-TV foundation, and articles based on these appeared later in an American student journal.[93] Two years later his sermon to the Chicago Sunday Evening Club, 'Beginning a New Year with Christ', was broadcast in their 'Hour of Good News' programme: it was the first of a number of similar radio addresses during the 1970s and '80s.[94] This New Year sermon owed something to six broadcast talks delivered in the 'Lift Up Your Hearts' morning slot over the BBC Home Service from New Year's Eve 1962 until 5 January 1963. The title of the series was not 'Beginning a New Year ...', which would have been hard to sustain into the first week of January, but 'Beginning a New Life with Christ'. Although there was little or no invitation to write in, listeners were quick to respond; and it was with this possibility in mind that John Stott had taken the precaution of arranging for the advance publication of the six talks as a booklet.[95] Within days a flood of letters was being sent round by the sack load from Broadcasting House to the Rectory, so that by the end of January Frances Whitehead, with a hastily collected team of helpers, had sent out some 5,000 booklets. John Stott himself sought to reply to more personal letters: and when the immediate pressure eased Frances Whitehead described in *All Souls* something of their varied character:

> We received letters from people not only of every social rank, from the most aristocratic to the road man who wrote, 'You told me Jesus Christ is real today, I thought He had forsaken me, please tell me, will He leave me?', but from high ecclesiastical dignitaries and clergy of all shades and denominations, from all kinds of professional people, and countless everyday folk. The oldest was 99, the youngest 11, and they wrote from all over the British Isles. One had even heard the programme in Holland!

Some of the most moving letters were from Christian people in difficult circumstances who wanted to share their experience of God's faithfulness. Frances Whitehead continued:

> We read of triumph *in sickness* from the man who wrote: 'I am totally blind, bedridden with cancer and old, but happy in the Lord.' Of triumph *in sorrow* from a wife whose 42-year old husband died last year: 'I am a born again Christian and I love the Lord very much. He has been wonderful to me in my sorrow.' Of triumph *in loneliness and old age*: 'I am 81 and housebound but never alone for He has promised never to leave or forsake those who trust Him.' Another wrote: 'I am 90 but am not feeling old and have a very good memory ... but have almost lost my sight ... I gave myself to the Saviour at a CSSM service when I was 12 years old and have been in His glad service ever since.'[96]

'It is easy enough to get published,' C. S. Lewis once told a friend; 'the difficulty is to get people to *read* your stuff.'[97] Compared with most authors, this hardly seems a problem for the author of *Screwtape* and *Narnia*, and it has seldom been a problem for John Stott. Of the books and writings listed in this (and other) chapters, most are still in print, often in revised and updated editions. Some have never been out of print in the ten, twenty, thirty – even forty – years since they were written. Most are published in more than one language besides English, some in a wide range of different translations from every continent.[98] Pastors the world over, preparing to expound to their people a passage from the New Testament, turn before long almost instinctively to their bookshelf: 'I wonder what John Stott has to say on this?' It is then that the long hours of study, preparation and writing bear fruit, so that it is not 'What has John Stott to say?' that matters, but how he can help illuminate the message of the Scriptures for today's world.

The 1970s

FIVE

New Departures: Changes at All Souls

1

To compress into a few paragraphs the events unfolded during a decade is to invite a loss of proportion. Nevertheless the 1970s provides a kind of roll-call of a troubled world. For the IRA, what began with the burning of the British Embassy in Dublin concluded with the assassination of Earl Mountbatten of Burma and his fourteen-year-old grandson. Across the world the war correspondents constantly reported from Vietnam, Lebanon, Cambodia, Angola, Uganda, Iran, Afghanistan, Rhodesia and South Africa. Bangladesh emerged as an independent nation and India as a nuclear power. Solzhenitsyn, Sakharov and Mother Teresa won Nobel prizes; Richard Nixon resigned, the first US President ever to do so; Archbishop Janani Luwum was murdered by Idi Amin's military dictatorship; Mao Tse-tung died in 1976 and Elvis Presley and Charlie Chaplin a year later. Pope John Paul I held office for thirty-three days, and was succeeded by Pope John Paul II, the first non-Italian for 400 years. World oil prices quadrupled and North Sea oilfields began production; Britain embraced a decimal currency and joined the European Common Market; UK inflation reached 25% in 1975, and remained continuously in double figures until 1981. The Duke of Windsor died; the Queen celebrated her Jubilee; and, following a 'winter of discontent', Mrs Thatcher came to power as Britain's first woman Prime Minister. Jumbo jets took to the skies while Concorde landed at Heathrow amid local protests over noise levels; Range Rovers went into production, home video recorders and floppy disks appeared, and a buggy began to explore the surface of the moon. The World Health Organization announced the eradication of smallpox; the first test-tube baby was born.

In Britain the relentless growth in unemployment contributed to the social and moral disintegration which was among the fruits of the previous decade. The Divorce Law Reform Act of 1971 saw the statistics for divorce suffer a sixfold increase between 1963 and 1980. Similarly, by the end of the 1970s 'there were 140 thousand registered abortions a year and more than a million lives had been legally extinguished before birth over the previous decade'.[1] Alarming growth was also evident in the abuse of drugs and alcohol, the spread of pornography (Lord Longford's Commission, of which Professor Norman Anderson and Sir Fred Catherwood were both members, reported in 1972)[2] and the gulf in living standards between the rich and the poor.

In March 1970 the New English Bible sold a million copies – the entire first edition – on the day of publication. In November Her Majesty the Queen inaugurated the first General Synod of the Church of England: Professor Norman Anderson (knighted in 1975) was a founder-member and was immediately elected Chairman of the House of Laity, and so one of the architects of the Crown Appointments Commission of 1976. The long-drawn plans for Anglican–Methodist reunion finally foundered. By an overwhelming vote the Methodists soon afterwards agreed to ordain women, while the Church of England rejected a similar proposal in 1978. One scheme of reunion did come to fruition with the creation of the United Reformed Church in October 1972, but most organized religion was steadily diminishing. In 1976 (according to Adrian Hastings' calculations) one Anglican church was being demolished every nine days.[3] Along with this went a growth in pluralism, reflecting an increasing immigrant population in the UK. William Carey has always been honoured as a pioneer of the British missionary movement, yet 'by the 1970s the Carey Memorial Hall in Leicester was in use as a Sikh temple'.[4]

In America a Gallup Poll had designated 1966 as 'the year of the evangelical';[5] and through the 1970s 'it was becoming increasingly apparent that, while mainline churches were losing members, distinctly evangelical bodies were gaining them'.[6] A 1976 Gallup Poll found that 34% of Americans saw themselves as 'born again' – and eight years later the proportion had risen to 40%. With whatever caution these figures are regarded, they clearly indicate the massive and growing strength of US evangelicalism, largely outside the Episcopal Church.

John Stott himself is seen by Adrian Hastings – a major analyst of post-war trends in the churches of Britain – as a key figure throughout this period:

> Evangelicalism, renewed in the sixties, continued to flourish in the seventies to such an extent that maybe half (and the tougher half) of newly ordained Anglican priests now belonged to it. Behind it the guiding hand of John Stott could still be discerned as it had been for twenty years, nationally as well as internationally – a sort of touchstone of Evangelical respectability. He had become the recognized senior theologian and thinker of world evangelicalism ...[7]

Writing at the start of the 1970s, John Stott began by describing the 1960s, now passing into history, as 'for many people the decade of disillusion', marked by increasing cynicism and even despair: 'True, there has been the phenomenal technical achievement of the Apollo mission to the moon, but there has been no comparable achievement in human relationships on earth.'[8] Nevertheless, in a contribution to a *Festschrift* for Professor Jürgen Winterhager, John Stott was able to identify four marks of evangelical renewal within the Church of England: involvement in theology, in evangelism, in church life and in the secular world. He was able to point to Tyndale House, Cambridge, and Latimer House, Oxford; to NEAC, CEEC and EFAC; to evangelical members in General Synod and on the influential Doctrine Commission and the Anglican–Roman Catholic International Commission. He reported how

> ... it is now becoming respectable once again for evangelicals to enter professions other than the pastoral ministry and the mission field! We have two or three evangelical Anglicans who are Members of Parliament. Others are getting involved not only in medicine and education (always fairly respectable spheres for evangelicals!) but also in the social services, in the mass media of communication (television, radio and journalism), and even in the arts.[9]

It was becoming increasingly clear to John Stott that his own part in this renewed evangelical activity was making demands no longer wholly compatible with the needs of All Souls; and as the 1960s drew to a close, he found himself wondering more and more about his own future. The twentieth anniversary of his institution, followed by his completion of twenty-five years in the ordained ministry, prompted him to ask whether it was time to make a change, and if so, what form such a change should take. On Saturday 20 September 1969 the PCC met in Buckinghamshire for a day conference, with a memorandum from the Rector as their main agenda. In part the ideas it set out had been achieved in consultation with his colleagues. Ted Schroder remembers how

> ... we brainstormed on different ways in which we could bring fresh leadership into the staff. Finally a model from Trinity Church, Wall Street, New York, seemed attractive to us. They had a Rector and a Vicar, with division of responsibility somewhat like a chief executive officer and a chief operating officer in a large business.[10]

In four closely argued foolscap sheets John Stott's memorandum sets out his vision for restructuring the staff, the key proposal being the appointment of a Vicar as chief pastor of the congregation, with both administrative and pastoral leadership. The memorandum spelt out in some detail how this might work in practice, and the PCC and Standing Committee continued to refine the proposals over the next weeks. It became clear that the new Vicar, though legally accountable to the Rector, would be the acknowledged spiritual leader. The Rector's role would be to reside in the parish for part of the year, to share the preaching, and to have some limited pastoral responsibility. For legal reasons, he would retain the freehold of the living.[11]

The urgent question now in John Stott's mind was where to find the right man to be Vicar; and it was while discussing these ideas over breakfast at the coffee shop of the Strand Palace Hotel that Dick Lucas suggested that 'the man you want is Michael Baughen'. Ten years before, Dick Lucas had suggested Michael Baughen to be his own successor as Candidates' Secretary of the Church Pastoral-Aid Society; following that, in 1964, Michael Baughen had moved north to be Vicar of Holy Trinity, Rusholme, in Manchester. To John Stott the suggestion was a surprise: 'I had never thought of flying so high – of somebody who was already a well-known evangelical leader.'[12]

It so happened that John Stott had agreed to preach at Holy Trinity, Rusholme, not long afterwards, and he took the opportunity to raise the possibility, receiving a 'very ambivalent' response. However, when Michael Baughen was in London for the launch of the song book *Youth Praise 2*[13] at the Royal Albert Hall, John Stott renewed his invitation, and this time Michael Baughen was willing to agree. The Bishop of London, Robert Stopford, gave his support. With his churchwardens, John Stott next visited the Crown Appointments Secretary at 10 Downing Street. There Sir John Hewitt told them that since the Crown must retain its sovereign rights, no promise could be made that Michael Baughen would be appointed Rector should the time come for John Stott to resign; although adding some informal encouragement that unless there were cogent reasons, he would not feel obliged to look elsewhere.[14]

So in May 1970 a letter was sent out to everyone on the All Souls congregational register, timed to coincide with Michael Baughen's announcement to his own congregation. After explaining what had led to the restructuring of the church's leadership, John Stott went on to introduce the new Vicar:

> I am very happy to announce that the Rev. Michael Baughen has accepted this new post. Indeed we are extremely fortunate that he is coming to be Vicar, for God has greatly gifted him and blessed his ministry. His wife Myrtle is fully committed as his partner (she is a trained teacher with a special interest in immigrant children), and they have three children – Rachel (11), Philip (7) and Andrew (6).

The letter went on to give some details of Michael Baughen's past and present ministry, and to anticipate some of the questions which would be in the minds of the congregation. In reply to 'What will your position be?' John Stott outlined the plan for him to have more time to read, think, write and travel; but added that he looked forward to being part of the life of the parish and the staff team during some months of each year. On a practical note, the Baughens would live in the Rectory, and John Stott would (eventually) occupy a new flat to be built over the garage. Summarizing the new developments in the Rector's Letter for the parish magazine, John Stott set out the benefits he believed this major change would bring to the church; while, as far as he was concerned, 'it will enable me to respond to the call to a wider ministry, while remaining a member of the team and the congregation'.[15]

There were, of course, considerable financial implications. But about a year before this, the Church Treasurer, Raymond Dawes, investment manager of an assurance company, had arranged to set up the Langham Trust. It was a prescient and timely move. The Trust was separate from the church accounts, and was able to assist with certain general expenses – capital equipment, help with clergy holidays and so on – and also to provide finance for John Stott's wider ministry. Throughout his time as Secretary of EFAC, for example, it was the Langham Trust that absorbed the costs of his Third World travel and much of the cost of administration.[16] With the coming of Michael Baughen as an extra member of staff, and especially with John Stott's resignation as Rector five years later, the work of the Trust became increasingly important. The first accounts in February 1970 showed a total balance of little more than £2,000: by the time Raymond Dawes retired as Chairman over twenty years later the turnover was measured in hundreds of thousands.[17]

As the 1970s progressed a sister fund was set up in the United States as 'the Langham Foundation' and further Trusts followed in Canada (1978) and Australia (1979). By this time three distinct categories of work were being undertaken by the Trusts. First was the General Fund, which helped in the ways described above; and could also stand sponsor for individual projects, as it was to do for the London Lectures in Contemporary Christianity. Then came the 'Stott Fund' which paid for John Stott's office expenses; the salary of Frances Whitehead, his secretary; and his travel to Third World countries. When he was no longer Rector, it was this fund that continued to pay his stipend (though he was entitled as 'curate' to receive from the Rector £5 per annum 'in equal quarterly instalments'). In addition a 'Bursary Fund' was established in a modest way in 1974, to assist Third World scholars to come to the UK for study.

By 1977 this programme was co-ordinated with the EFAC bursary scheme, which by then had already brought some sixty evangelical clergy from Asia and Africa to study in the UK, mostly to gain diplomas and first degrees. Eventually a new joint EFAC/Langham scheme was to finance research scholarships for postgraduate theological study, with a view to enabling Third World students and scholars to become theological educators in their own countries. At the start, three such men were being helped, each with much potential for future leadership. Michael Nazir-Ali was one such, who in 1976 returned to Pakistan after postgraduate studies in Cambridge, and worked there for ten years as 'theological educator, parish priest and bishop'. Advised to leave Pakistan for a period because the safety of his family was threatened, he returned to England and worked as Theological Co-ordinator for the 1988 Lambeth Conference before becoming General Secretary of CMS in 1989, and Bishop of Rochester five years later.[18]

With the appointment of a Vicar to the staff of All Souls, it was clear that the 'Stott Fund' needed some endowment capital to ensure a continuing income. It fell to Jack Dain to approach two or three possible contributors: and in response to his letter substantial gifts were received from Philip Henman, Paul Broomhall and Billy Graham, among other well-wishers.

> My beloved John [Dr Graham wrote], Jack Dain has confidentially shared with me a little bit of your plans. I am absolutely thrilled that the possibility has arisen that you may be able to give more of your time in ministering to the world church.
>
> I am only a steward of the money that the Lord sends me through His people. You have as much right to use it as I do. We will all have to give an account at the Judgment Seat for our stewardship ...[19]

Even as an endowment was being sought, plans were being pursued to create a self-contained apartment out of the old single-room flat above the Rectory garage. This had access only from Bridford Mews, and was in a state of ruinous disrepair. For well over a year John Stott found himself homeless, working (and sometimes sleeping) in the big basement room of the Rectory, or as the elusive guest of David and Elizabeth Trapnell. But early in 1972 his new home was finally ready, with an upstairs living-room and study cantilevered over the Mews to give extra space, and including a kitchenette or galley under the eaves. A twisting staircase leads down to a bedroom and bathroom, with access through to the ground floor of the Rectory and Frances Whitehead's office. The desk in John Stott's living-room looks out through a wide picture window on a typical London city-scape. Up the Mews lies Devonshire Street; to the left and right are the backs of high buildings, a jumble of fire-escapes, drain pipes, TV aerials and chimneys; below are the Mews garages, a single touch of greenery coming from a window-box high up on a distant balcony. One wall of his room is given over entirely to books, with rows of card-index drawers on the floor beneath, classified by biblical references and by subjects – 'Man, Mark, Marriage, Marxism, Materialism, Matthew …' and so on. On the walls, where these are not given to bookshelves, cupboards or windows, are prints of All Souls and of Trinity College, Cambridge; and on the stairs a large contemporary engraving of Charles Simeon with his famous umbrella. He strides out in knee breeches, gaiters and stock, his gown flowing out behind him.[20] A view of The Hookses, painted by Geoffrey Rawlins, a former curate, hangs by the dining table.

John Stott was long ago given the tenancy of this apartment for life. All in all, it offers comfortable if modest quarters. Elizabeth Evans, who had known him since they were children together, used to reflect on the contrast between these two rooms, home of a distinguished 'ambassador for Christ', and the magnificent Embassy that might have been his, had he fulfilled his father's hopes and entered the Diplomatic Service '… and there he is in this tiny little flat with a bedroom that you walk through to get anywhere'.[21] This is literally true: the link between the apartment and the Rectory (including Frances Whitehead's office) is through the only bedroom, which has also to serve as a passageway, and an 'office' for John Stott's study assistant, who has a desk in one corner.

With the arrival of Michael and Myrtle Baughen and their three young children, the Rectory became once more, as it had been in the days of the Earnshaw-Smiths, a family home. Gone were the 'bedsits' for the bachelor curates; 'Packie' and 'the Countess' were only memories. Margaret Shinn concluded almost sixteen years as cook and then cook-housekeeper, during which (so John Stott calculated) she had looked after more than sixty residents.[22] Other changes soon began to be felt. Overnight, it seemed, Christian names became the order of the day. John Stott recalls Michael Baughen in his very early days going down to the Rectory kitchen and saying to the cleaner, 'You're Anne and I'm Michael.'[23] To have a family in the Rectory once more contributed to a growing sense of 'the church family', a favourite phrase of the new Vicar from his Manchester experience: London had to become accustomed to a good many observations beginning 'When I was in Manchester ...' Robert Howarth was on the staff and a shrewd observer:

> From the first day of Michael Baughen's arrival as Vicar in 1970, John Stott stepped back from the day to day responsibility of All Souls. That he was able to watch – more, positively to support – Michael in his leadership, is amazing. For changes began to happen thick and fast; and in them all John was able gently and lovingly to persuade a considerable army of his own devoted admirers to give their loyal support to this newcomer. No doubt it would have been done without allowing himself the luxury of listening to many an unflattering comparison![24]

By no means everybody welcomed every change. George Cansdale soon stepped down as churchwarden when moving to Essex, but he found it a relief to do so since he was out of sympathy with much of the new style and way of doing things.[25] Ted Schroder, who had gone with John Stott to Manchester to persuade Michael Baughen to join them, remembers that 'it was a difficult transition for a while. Michael was sensitive about his independence, and John had to learn not to inquire too frequently about how things were going in case it be interpreted as supervision.'[26] These changes, and the speed at which they came about, were not easy for John Stott. Some of them, the Family Service and the Commissioned Workers Training Scheme, for example, touched what had been 'bedrock All Souls sacred cows',[27] structures which he had himself conceived and initiated, and which had proved their value. It was to the credit of both men that they managed this new and largely unprecedented relationship with harmony and grace. True to his word, John Stott recognized Michael Baughen's sensitivity and remained completely loyal to his leadership, supporting him both in public and in private, even where he might have had misgivings. Sir Norman Anderson remembered how, 'When Michael was away, John would take the service and would say "I would like to say on behalf of the Vicar ..." and so give a word of welcome.'[28]

These were not the only changes on the horizon. Major discussions were also taking place about the future of the All Souls church building. It had been apparent for some time that the cramped quarters of the small meeting-rooms in All Souls Church House, and the lack of a proper hall or adequate catering facilities, were severe handicaps for the kind of ministry that such a church should be exercising in its strategic and unique location. For some time before the appointment of Michael Baughen, in the strictest secrecy, John Stott had been discussing with an inner circle of his church officers the options that might be open to them. David Trapnell remembers 'a group of about six who used to meet and were allowed to talk about pulling down All Souls'.[29] Eric Starling, the architect, was a member of the PCC and one of the group; they rang the changes on a number of possibilities including an ambitious plan to keep the rotunda and the spire, but demolish and rebuild the body of the church with a garage beneath and nine floors of flats above. When the Bishop of London was consulted informally, his wise advice was not to spend the next twenty years fighting officialdom (All Souls was the last Nash church still standing), so the group went on to explore the possibility of finding alternative sites on which to build a 'church centre' within easy reach of the church. This, too, had to be abandoned as impossible: 'Whatever we considered, we were forced back on All Souls.'[30]

It was into this uncertain situation that Michael Baughen found himself plunged when he was installed as Vicar[31] on 19 December 1970. Confidentiality was paramount: it was enough that the people of All Souls seemed to be losing John Stott as their chief pastor, without rumours that they might also lose their church. John Stott, in his final Rector's Letter in the parish magazine, explained that he was to fly to America on Boxing Day and then on to Australia; and it was actually from Perth, speaking to the local Press at the Archbishop's residence during a lecture tour, that this cat was let out of the bag. Lulled into a false sense of security by the remoteness of the setting, John Stott was drawn into answering questions from an innocent-looking young woman journalist about relating ancient buildings to the modern world. He recounted the incident later in a tribute to Michael Baughen:

> I confess to causing him some embarrassment by my unguarded remark at a press conference in Perth, Australia, that we wished someone would bomb the church so that we could rebuild it to meet contemporary needs. So 'Bomb the Church' was the dramatic headline in the national dailies the following morning. The resulting debate was valuable, however, as Michael insisted that the church's calling is to be 'a servant of people not a custodian of antiquities'.[32]

The journalist evidently sold her scoop to Reuter's; *The Daily Telegraph* ran the story under the headline 'Rector says "bomb All Souls" for new church'; and it was clear that John Stott had not hesitated, safely on the other side of the world, to express in colourful language some of his frustrations with whatever impeded the living witness of the church to the gospel:

> Mr Stott said: 'There would be a terrible public outcry if the building went, but the Church cannot be hamstrung for every old building. I would like to sell the English cathedrals to the National Trust, or keep the structures and radically change the insides. The Church should not be the custodian of antiquities ...'[33]

'Peter Simple', who ran for many years a zany column of surrealist humour in *The Daily Telegraph*, provided his own comment on this the following day:

> If bombing the church is seriously in question, I understand that Dr Spacely-Trellis, the go-ahead Bishop of Bevindon, would gladly lend a squadron of his own diocesan air force for the purpose.
>
> This force is being assembled and trained, with funds provided by the World Council of Left-wing Churches, to give air support to the African 'freedom fighters' ... Not long ago, a bomber force led by daredevil Squadron Leader the Rev. Jack ('Jumbo') Nacelle-Harris was sent on a night mission to 'take out' the 12th century Norman church of St Chrysostom-in-the-Ditch. But owing to a navigational error it demolished an almost completed ecumenical family planning clinic and restaurant instead.[34]

Following this storm in a teacup, the church was free to address itself more openly to the problem posed by the lack of an adequate church centre. A document entitled 'Which Way Forward?', presented to the Annual Parochial Church Meeting in April 1971, listed seven possibilities, ranging from total demolition and rebuilding, to a permanent move to St Peter's, Vere Street.[35] Exactly a year later, following the appointment of Robert Potter as architect, the possibilities had been whittled down to one: to raise the floor of the church and create a hall beneath it. In April 1972 Robert Potter watched as a trial excavation uncovered a walled-in 'basement' between the foundations and the floor of the nave, extending over the entire site of the building. Over the next few years, while the church again made their home at St Peter's, Vere Street, some 6,000 tons of earth would be removed and the floor raised to provide space for all the new facilities.

Before this could happen, however, there were to be two further milestones in the life of the church. The first was the celebration of the

150th anniversary of its opening on 25 November 1824. John Stott shared in the 'Special Anniversary Service and Presentation' by the staff, and offered a 'look into the future' based (with apologies) on Martin Luther King's famous speech in Washington eleven years before: 'I have a dream of a church in central London which is a biblical ... a worshipping ... a caring ... a serving ... an expectant church.'[36] Then in the summer of 1975, with the building plans well advanced and Michael Baughen firmly in the saddle, it was time for the next step in John Stott's personal pilgrimage. His own future had been of concern not only to him but to his friends as they watched his time at All Souls stretch from ten to twenty to thirty years, and realized that the day was coming when Michael Baughen could reasonably expect to be Rector, not only in practice but in law and name as well.

Early in 1972 the churchwardens consulted Professor Norman Anderson, himself a former churchwarden, and he in turn wrote at length to Marcus Loane, Archbishop of Sydney:

> The question is what should happen to John in three and a half years' time. He has already, I think, turned down the principalship of two theological colleges, and is scarcely likely to be offered another (though this might, of course, happen). And I very much doubt whether he will be offered a diocesan bishopric in this country. He has a great reputation among Evangelicals, but, rightly or wrongly, is regarded in the Church as a whole as too inflexible for the office of an English Diocesan.[37]

The Archbishop replied saying he had 'never been entirely happy about John's decision to relinquish the main responsibility at All Souls' and that he would be delighted if John Stott would ever consider coming to Sydney, perhaps to Moore College ('unlikely at present'), perhaps to a leading parish church near the city: or possibly, depending on events, as Dean or an Assistant Bishop. Marcus Loane moved quickly, and within a month, on Easter Day 1972, was writing to John Stott with just such an invitation:

> Hitherto I have always felt that it would be a great disservice to you and the Evangelical cause in England even to suggest that you might consider an appointment here in Sydney, ardently as I would welcome it. But I have come to feel that circumstances have now altered so much and that in view of your age (and the effect this might have on any appointment in England), I may write to you with a definite proposal. And as far as Sydney is concerned, the time for that is now.

The letter went on to describe the territory of Parramatta, due to become a new diocese. (At the time of writing the bishop in Parramatta was one of four assistant bishops in the diocese of Sydney.) The present bishop, Gordon Begbie, would retire at the end of 1972, and the Archbishop would therefore need to nominate a new bishop in Parramatta in the course of the next few months: 'I am now writing to ask if you will allow me to nominate you.'[38]

John Stott was in Malaysia when this letter arrived in London. Frances Whitehead opened it as instructed, and sent it on. It reached him in Kuala Lumpur on 22 April and he replied the following day. After an expression of thanks, both for the Archbishop's ministry and friendship, and for his present proposal, his reply continued:

> But I fear my immediate duty is clear, and I have regretfully to say 'no'. As you say, the present All Souls arrangement is for 5 years from Dec. 1970; but this arrangement is a definite commitment to which I feel myself morally bound. Michael Baughen's security of tenure as 'Vicar' depends on my remaining as Rector, and it seemed impossible therefore that he should be invited to become Vicar without being given this assurance by me. It is true that he has several times said to me that, if some invitation were to come to me which I felt I should accept, I should not be bound. But I take a different view ... I wrote to the Crown Patronage Secretary to this effect in 1970 and have declined nomination to posts in UK on this ground. I hope you will understand that I do not consider myself free until December 1975, and therefore am unable to open my mind to the possibility of Parramatta. What lies beyond this period for me, in God's providence, I cannot begin to guess ...

But 1975 was soon upon him. In his newsletter to his friends that February he explained how 'I find myself pulled and pushed in various directions these days, and need divine wisdom to know how to establish priorities'. But it was clear that the time had come to make way for his successor, and to free himself further for the urgent demands being made on him both at home and overseas. In May, therefore, he sent in his resignation to the Prime Minister's Appointments Secretary (by now Colin Peterson, in succession to Sir John Hewitt), who at once consulted the churchwardens about the future. Less than a month later John Stott was able to issue a 'Statement to All Souls Congregation' announcing that his resignation would take effect on September 26, the anniversary of his institution just twenty-five years before, and adding:

> I am very happy indeed to tell you that the Queen has approved the

appointment of Michael Baughen to succeed me as Rector, and that Michael has accepted the appointment.

Now Michael and the PCC have very kindly invited me to remain in the fellowship of All Souls with the title 'Rector Emeritus', and the Bishop of London has said that he will give me his licence to officiate. I am very grateful that in this way I shall be able to continue the present 'mix' of ministry both at All Souls and St Peter's when I am in London, and in the wider world.[39]

In lieu of a personal gift, John Stott asked that any who wished should make a contribution to the 'new' All Souls: and the PCC suggested that these gifts might go towards the new pulpit 'as a continuing mark of the emphasis upon the preaching of the Word at All Souls'.[40] Donors were also invited to send a personal greeting for inclusion in a presentation album to be given to John Stott as he moved from being Rector to Rector Emeritus. In the event, gifts were sufficient to provide not only the pulpit in anodised aluminium, but a matching communion table: photographs of these appear at the front of the album, following the text from John 12:21, 'Sir, we wish to see Jesus.' Then came some 300 individual greetings, some just a name, most with a short message of appreciation and thankfulness. From New Zealand a seven-year-old writes, 'Thank you for baptizing me, Uncle John.' Another mentions the confirmation classes, or *Basic Christianity*, 'which led to my conversion'. One card tells how the writer 'was converted following your Keswick relay talks four years ago'; another writes simply, 'Thank you for showing me the way to Christ.' The messages came from all over the world: from the USA and Canada, the universities of Hong Kong and Singapore, from India and Africa (a missionary writes 'from the swamps of Nigeria'). His sister Joy sent a characteristic card with 'most loving wishes for your next emeritic, exergetic, energetic and happy 25 years'. A succession of churchwardens, organists and curates all have their say. John Lefroy and his wife Sally no doubt spoke for many when they wrote, 'May you long continue to heed the text and disregard the clock!' And a day or two before the date set, Colin Peterson wrote on behalf of the Prime Minister 'to express his gratitude to you for your exceptional service to this Crown living over many years, first as a curate and then as its distinguished Rector'.[41]

It was to be a further two years of prayer, work and giving before the new All Souls could open in all its glory. But by 18 October 1977 the Treasurer could report that enough money was in hand to meet the final bills; and on 2 November 1977, All Souls Day, the doors at last opened again to a congregation, the church above resplendent in new paint and furnishing, the new 'Waldegrave Hall' beneath offering just the accommodation so many had prayed for, for so long.

On the day itself, tiling, painting and cleaning were still proceeding
... As expected, attendance at the Re-opening Service strained the
accommodation to its limits, filling every conceivable space in the
church, with hundreds more participating downstairs by means of
the TV relay. The queue of people waiting to get in stretched up
Langham Place into Mortimer Street. The music from the organ,
orchestra and choir included an anthem specially composed by Noël
Tredinnick ... The first sermon from the new pulpit, on the Pre-
eminence of Christ, was preached by John Stott.[42]

On the old pulpit there had been a brass plaque to catch the preacher's
eye, 'Sir, we would see Jesus'; and this reminder is continued in the new
pulpit from the Revised Standard Version. There is also this inscription:

Many friends of John Stott combined to give this pulpit and
communion table out of deep gratitude for his dedicated ministry as
evangelist, teacher and pastor during 25 years as Rector of All Souls
(1950–1975). He taught us to make God's Word our rule, God's
Spirit our teacher and God's Glory our supreme concern.

2

From 1945 to 1970 the story of All Souls and the story of John Stott
were inseparable. From 1950 when he became Rector, all that happened
in the church was under his inspiration and authority. But from 1970
onwards this was no longer so, although he remained Rector in name and
in law for another five years. Ultimate legal authority may have remained
with him, but it was never called upon. It is significant that what had
always been 'The Rector's Letter' in the opening pages of *All Souls*
became from January 1971 'The Vicar's Letter', with a smiling photograph of Michael Baughen; and that the list of clergy in each issue should
now begin with the Vicar, and John Stott's name come second. He
greatly valued his continuing place within the family, as the church
valued his continued presence, but All Souls now becomes the
background of his life, rather than the main landscape.[43]
Later chapters will look at John Stott's ministry overseas, and at the
study and writing to which he felt increasingly called. But in addition to
these, even in the five years that he continued as Rector, the 1970s were
filled both with continuing commitments, and some new departures.
'Christian Debate' was still meeting regularly, as was the 'Community of
Christian Concern' (which in 1979 dropped the first 'C' from its name),
a group which wrestled largely with problems more related to the world
than to the church: secular culture in the light of Scripture.[44] Typical of a

number of these study circles was the Reading Group, which John Stott described, twenty years later, for an American interviewer. The reading in question did not begin with theology:

> The purpose of starting the reading group was very deliberately to oblige us to listen more attentively and intelligibly to the modern world. I invited about 15 young professional people in our congregation to join the reading group: a couple of doctors, a couple of lawyers, an architect, and a BBC person, etc., all of whom were committed to the gospel, the biblical gospel, and all of whom were modern young men and women eager to relate the gospel to the modern world. We used to meet every other month. And we still meet over 20 years later.[45]

One of the lawyers later described his recollections, which make it clear that the Reading Group did not confine itself to books:

> I remember all those books and films! As well as books, films and plays, we have discussed the values in news broadcasts and in things like *Cosmopolitan* magazine. We have been to the Tate and stood baffled together as one of our number enthused about Mark Rothko's 'Black on Maroon'.[46]

Time had also to be given to the leadership of institutions and organizations. Latimer House, for example, regularly looked to its Chairman in matters of staffing and policy.[47] The Eclectic Society continued to multiply: what had begun as a meeting of friends at the Crown Hotel, Amersham, was now countrywide. By 1977 the national chairman, Christopher Byworth, was quoted as making the sweeping claim that, as regards clergy (it was a clerical society), it had numbered within its membership 'virtually all those who are now influential figures in the evangelical wing of the Church of England'.[48] High morale and a spirit of vigour and enterprise among younger clergy might be expected to contribute towards more young members of live churches being ready to consider God's call to ordination. John Stott noted encouraging signs in his broad survey of worldwide evangelical Anglicanism, written early in the 1970s:

> It is difficult to assess the strength of Evangelical church life in the country as a whole. There are certainly areas where it still seems weak and ineffective. On the other hand, in March 1972, 285 of the 808 ordinands in the English residential theological colleges (35.2 per cent) were in the six evangelical colleges. There is, further, a

welcome new 'radical conservatism' abroad among Anglican Evangelicals ...[49]

The same essay described the growth of EFAC. Within the Eclectic Society, much of the day-to-day leadership had devolved on others as new groups were formed and regional branches established across the country. With EFAC it was different, and John Stott continued as Joint Honorary Secretary of EFAC, with Bishop Jack Dain, throughout both the 1970s and the 1980s.

The task involved almost daily correspondence (the Council itself, being international, could meet only very infrequently). Face-to-face contact with leaders of EFAC branches depended on meetings during John Stott's travels, or on such leaders themselves passing through London, as many did from time to time. Australia was deeply involved, since a local Fellowship had become a founder-member of EFAC in 1961. America, where the Episcopal Church knew little of any evangelical tradition, had at the beginning only a small Fellowship of Witness as the American branch of EFAC – which yet proved 'a cloud no bigger than a man's hand' presaging better things to come. By 1976 John Stott was able to report to the EFAC Council the founding by the 'Fellowship of Witness' of an evangelical seminary within the Episcopal Church with Bishop Alfred Stanway as President.[50] In South Africa the twin Evangelical Fellowships of the Church of England in South Africa and of the Church of the Province were both members of EFAC, suggesting a possible bridge towards some better future understanding. John Stott in his role as Joint Honorary Secretary (but in fact the moving spirit and energizer) sent out a twice-yearly newsletter charting progress. In 1970 he writes of the future of the Burma Anglican Evangelical Fellowship within the new province; in 1972 of the appointment of 'correspondents' in places where no branch is yet possible: for example, in Bolivia, Egypt, Israel, Japan, Singapore, Taiwan, Uganda, India, Pakistan and Ceylon.

As the decade progressed West Africa and Latin America were linked with the Fellowship; and in 1974 the opportunity was taken for a meeting of the Council during the Lausanne Congress on World Evangelization, with twenty members present representing some ten countries. Similarly, many EFAC representatives were able to meet near London, four years later, when visiting England for the 1978 Lambeth Conference. Meanwhile, under John Stott's chairmanship, the EFAC bursary scheme was continuing to bring promising clergy to this country, mainly from Africa but also from Pakistan and South India.

No less demanding throughout the 1970s than the nurturing of EFAC overseas was John Stott's continuing role as Chairman of the English branch of EFAC, the Church of England Evangelical Council. The need for such a Council still seemed undeniable. If Anglican evangelicalism were to be able to speak with a united voice, it could do so only after consulting together. But even with John Stott's personal leadership, it was not easy to make good the claim to represent so fissiparous a grouping, divided by differing shades of evangelical opinion and carrying with them (as with CMS and BCMS, for example) a considerable historical luggage. The Council was forced to spend a disproportionate amount of its resources on seeking improvements to its own structures in an attempt to be 'more representative' or 'more accountable'. Moreover, even with a basis of faith as a condition of membership, the Council inevitably included some of broader views. Oliver Barclay recalls how 'when Alan Stibbs and I were invited to attend a meeting in 1971, he left almost in tears at what he felt was its departure from his hopes for it'.[51] Philip King, who acted as assistant secretary, noted how John Stott's

> ... warm, genial and gracious approach at a personal level was accompanied by an awesome academic and theological rigour in discussion; others were sometimes slow to take him on in debate. It would be unfair to say that he didn't 'suffer fools gladly' but his powerful mind could cause diffidence in others and the result may have had the unintentional effect of complicating what he liked to call dialogue between 'evangelicals and charismatics'.[52]

Throughout these years, meeting monthly with heavy agendas, CEEC was able, in spite of its domestic difficulties and in a way no other single body could achieve, to watch over developments in such disparate matters as women's ministry, liturgical revision, the Nationwide Initiative in Evangelism, the growth of the house-church movement, the Archbishops' Call to the Nation, and a range of moral and theological issues, such as the Nationwide Festival of Light or the credal reductionism of *The Myth of God Incarnate*.[53] Amid the pressures of routine business, four initiatives stand out during the decade; three of them conferences which CEEC helped to arrange or sponsor, and the fourth the Council's response to *The Myth*.

The first of such conferences was in May 1972, jointly sponsored by CEEC and the Evangelical Alliance (of which John Stott would become President the following year). Under the title 'Strategy for Evangelism', it was held at Pontin's holiday camp at Morecambe Bay, Lancashire, and attracted some 850 delegates. Unfortunately it proved to be a bitterly cold late spring, and as the freezing winds blew off the Irish Sea there were said to be cases of hypothermia among missionary delegates from warmer climates. Cliff Richard and Garth Hewitt sang; John Stott gave the Bible readings from the Sermon on the Mount, together with an exposition of

John 17. Five years on from NEAC, it was a valuable reminder to evangelical Anglicans that amid the continuing flurry of self-education and theological muscle-flexing, the sharing of the Good News still lay at the heart of evangelical identity. One of the major emphases of the conference was that, in a changing world, the church must either change or die. Tom Houston spoke of a sub-culture cycle – a 'generation flip' – every four years, and Cliff Richard of a new pop idol every five or six. John Stott's 'summing up' in the official report spoke of six needs confronting both evangelicals and the church as a whole, beginning with the need 'to talk about Jesus', and going on to the need 'to accept (and even welcome) change'.[54]

For some it came as a new and distasteful idea that there should be a relationship between politics and the gospel. David Sheppard, then Bishop of Woolwich and cast as left-wing in his political views, recalls a revealing incident:

> I had been invited to speak on something like 'The Gospel and Social Justice'. During my Paper some walked out. At the end of the three or four days John Stott, who was Chairman, said, 'There was one moment in the Conference when I felt angry. That was when people walked out as David Sheppard was speaking. He gave Biblical reasons for what he was saying. If you disagree with them you should give Biblical reasons to justify your disagreement.'[55]

Two years after Morecambe CEEC helped to sponsor a gathering on a much smaller scale, but of significance in the search for mutual understanding between classic evangelicals and the newer neo-Pentecostal 'charismatics'. In 1973 the Council had discussed 'Charismatic Gifts' (not for the first time), while in the following year the Senior Evangelical Anglican Clergy, many of whom were former members of the Eclectic Society, had heard a major address by Dr J. I. Packer on developments in the seven years since the Keele Congress. His final point was a plea that traditional evangelicals should begin to relate more positively to charismatics within their ranks. 'No-one should hesitate to say', he urged, 'that God is in this thing.'[56]

Michael Harper had made the same appeal in *The Church of England Newspaper*, asking that evangelical leaders should set up a discussion on this subject. He wrote as Director of the Fountain Trust, by now the recognized institutional structure of the charismatic movement in England (and increasingly beyond), concerned about the polarization of the neo-Pentecostal and the classic evangelical position; he had himself made a personal approach to John Stott asking for dialogue towards a better understanding.[57]

In his reply to James Packer's address at SEAC, John Stott made his own position clear:

> Now I could not personally declare 'God is in this thing' *without qualification*, for I would want to qualify this statement in a number of ways. Nevertheless, I confess that I have tended to be too negative towards this movement, and too reluctant to recognise and welcome whatever within it has seemed to be a work of God.
>
> I would also like to make a public apology to Michael Harper that I have allowed our friendship to become tarnished over the years, and that I have been slow to meet him and to talk with him.[58]

He welcomed the proposal for a meeting of minds, warning that he felt it unlikely that any speedy agreement could be reached. His three principles were the objectivity of truth, the centrality of Christ and the diversity of life. So began a series of four whole-day meetings of a group seventeen strong, over a period of some eighteen months, culminating in the issue of a joint statement by CEEC and the Fountain Trust, entitled *Gospel and Spirit*:

> Our task has been to try to articulate widely held and representative attitudes among the so-called 'charismatic' and 'non-charismatic' leaders of Anglican Evangelicalism and to bring both to the bar of Holy Scripture. We have sought to understand each other's views better and to achieve closer harmony and correspondence through examining them all in the light of biblical teaching. We are now issuing this account of our progress, indicating both agreements and disagreements, in the hope that it may help to promote unity where there is discord, and mutual understanding where there has been mistrust.[59]

Probably the process of working together on the Statement was of more significance than the final document. John Stott had a major hand in the drafting of it, and while there was no dissentient 'minority report', few from either side seem to have found it wholly satisfying or convincing. Michael Harper himself saw it as

> ... obviously a compromise document, we didn't reach full agreement; I think there was some very good material in it, and I think it was helpful. I personally may be a bit of a heretic here, but I wonder whether anything very good comes out of written stuff; I think the great thing is meeting people and talking things through ...[60]

Certainly the discussion and the resulting Statement helped to achieve some better mutual understanding and easing of strained relationships. But it did not signal much convergence on disputed points such as spiritual gifts or 'baptism in the Spirit'. Ten years after *Gospel and Spirit*, when John Stott was asked during an interview in Singapore to give his views on the charismatic movement, he denied as firmly as ever any necessity for a baptism of the Spirit as a second and subsequent experience after the new birth: 'that, I believe is mistaken. I think the New Testament cannot be shown to teach a two-stage initiation into Christ.'[61] At the same time he pleaded for balance, and the kind of mutual tolerance and understanding which *Gospel and Spirit* had sought to encourage:

> I think that charismatics and non-charismatics show tendencies of imbalance. You see, we need to come together. Where the charismatics are in command, they should not drive the non-charismatics out of the church and where evangelicals are mostly non-charismatics in the technical sense, they need to make room for the charismatics so that they can feel at home. We should not reject one another, we should accept one another ... people feel strongly about these things but the Holy Spirit is the Spirit of love and Spirit of unity.[62]

This remained an issue on which John Stott himself shared those 'strong feelings' he described. Perhaps some of them go back to the hurtful divisions within his own staff in the early days; some certainly spring from 'the care of all the churches' and a pastoral concern for damaging divisions among evangelicals, unbalanced teaching and mistaken exegesis. But they must also relate to his own experience of ministry, when he had early learned to cast himself upon God and to rely on the Holy Spirit's power:

> One well-known Christian minister (G. R. Harding Wood I think) once asked John Stott at the height of John's ministry in London when All Souls was packed with young professional people and students, 'John, what do you think of as you walk to the pulpit and climb its steps just before you preach, knowing that a thousand people will be hanging on your words?' John replied something like this: 'As I make that journey to the pulpit *I just say over and over again, I believe in the Holy Spirit.*'[63]

If the charismatic movement represented a threat to unity among evangelicals, the publication of *The Myth of God Incarnate* in 1977 was a challenge to fundamental Christian faith common to all orthodox believers.

The Myth of God Incarnate was launched amid great publicity, and 30,000 copies were sold in the first eight months. It consisted of a series of essays in which the New Testament and the development of Christian doctrine were declared to be culturally conditioned. The conception of Jesus as God incarnate, the second person of the Trinity, living a human life, was declared to be a mythological or poetic way of expressing his significance for us. The Chalcedonian Definition of Christology was rejected as incomprehensible to modern man. The whole matter of the incarnation and 'orthodox' Christology was brought into question.[64]

Cynics were saying that its sales were due to the vast number of copies being bought by the oil-rich Arab propagandists as the best statement of the Islamic view of Christ.[65] A visitor to Lambeth Palace about this time, in a delegation which included John Stott among a number of church leaders, wrote later of how

> John Stott told Lord Runcie that a Muslim publishing house in Egypt had quickly translated *The Myth of God Incarnate* into Arabic and that the book was now being widely distributed throughout the Middle East. I was looking straight at the face of the archbishop at that moment, and he was visibly shaken.[66]

John Stott was overseas in Argentina when the book appeared. He found that even there, within a day or two of publication (thanks to media coverage: the doubts of senior ecclesiastics and academics are always newsworthy), 'people were asking me if English churchmen were Christians any longer'.[67] It was not an unreasonable question. Three of the contributors to the book were members of the Doctrine Commission of the Church of England; and 'Don Cupitt, one of the most forceful and publicity minded of the group, published 'only two years later his commitment to objective atheism, *Taking Leave of God*'.[68] Michael Green hastily mounted a rebuttal; and honours were said to be about even. But the controversy was a contributory factor in the verdict that 'the year 1977 may be seen as representing the high water mark of theological liberalism in England ...'[69]

Many have noted John Stott's determination to be fair to those with whom he disagrees, and to build bridges in face-to-face encounter, rather than to conduct a war of words from entrenched positions. Donald English, for example, writes of this from the perspective of the 1990s:

> After the publication of John Robinson's *Honest to God* Stott arranged a meeting between Robinson and a few leading evangelicals to explore areas of agreement and disagreement. He did the

same with contributors to *The Myth of God Incarnate* and, more recently, with David Jenkins, the Bishop of Durham. The aim is not to overpower the other. It is seriously to seek the truth, in obedience to Christ and in accordance with scripture.[70]

Accordingly, when the dust had died down, John Stott set to work through CEEC to arrange a meeting with the contributors to *The Myth*. Writing to Tony Thiselton about the purpose of such a meeting, John Stott had admitted that 'we cannot reasonably expect a half-day conference to change the minds of the four contributors we are to meet':

> Nevertheless, I do believe that God could use our meeting as part of a bigger process to sow doubts and questions in their minds, and so to lead them to re-examine more critically the foundations of their positions. I also believe that a meeting, a face-to-face confrontation, is more likely to challenge them to do this than a book or books whose challenge may be more easily evaded.[71]

In the event, four of the contributors met early in 1979 with John Stott himself and some other members of the Council. Not unexpectedly, perhaps, James Packer reported that 'no real dent seemed to have been made in the "myth" position'.[72] But at least the issue had not gone by default; and there had been a principled attempt at Christian protest by way of dialogue.

Serious, indeed crucial, as were the theological issues raised by *The Myth*, there was a further practical matter of immediate concern, at least as it concerned the Anglican contributors. John Stott raised it towards the end of an article in *All Souls*:

> The third question which this book raises in my mind can be starkly stated: What should the contemporary church do with heretics? Is that a harsh word? I think not. A humble and reverent probing into the mystery of the Incarnation is the essence of true Christological scholarship; attempted reconstructions which effectively destroy that which is supposed to be being reconstructed is Christological heresy. So what should we do with heretics?

A heresy trial would clearly not be desirable: 'heretics are slippery creatures', and trials create martyrs:

> But there are other ways of procedure. The New Testament authors are particularly concerned not so much about false brethren as about false *teachers*, who act like wolves and scatter or destroy

Christ's flock. Although the contributors to *The Myth of God Incarnate* are academics, most are also ordained Anglican clergymen who hold a bishop's licence to preach. Is it too much to hope and pray that some bishop sometime will have the courage to withdraw his licence from a presbyter who denies the Incarnation? This would not be an infringement of civil or academic liberty. A man may believe, say and write what he pleases in the country and the university. But *in the church* it is reasonable and right to expect all accredited teachers to teach the faith which the church in its official formularies confesses, and which (incidentally) they have themselves promised to uphold.[73]

At its Chairman's instigation CEEC pursued this point by further debate resulting in the publication of a small but significant booklet, *Truth, Error and Discipline in the Church*.[74] This argued in some detail for the exercise of ecclesiastical discipline where a licensed teacher of the church, pledged to uphold biblical truth, is found to be promulgating heresy and will neither retract nor resign:

> We recognize that bishops (and their counterparts in other churches) are in a very difficult position; that they are rightly concerned for the peace of the church as well as for its truth; and that in order to avoid a public scandal they prefer where possible to take action privately, and doubtless do so. We recognize also that appearing to make martyrs is not usually the quickest way to discredit fundamental mistakes. Nevertheless, in the last resort, (i) if a central Christian doctrine is at stake, (ii) if the clergyman concerned is not just questioning it but denying it, (iii) if he is not just passing through a temporary period of uncertainty but has reached a settled conviction, and (iv) if he refuses to resign, then we believe the bishop (or other leader) should seriously consider withdrawing his licence or permission to teach in the church.[75]

3

The same year that saw the publication of *The Myth* was the tenth anniversary of the Keele Congress, NEAC '67. Three years earlier CEEC had taken the initiative in setting up a Planning Committee, once again chaired by John Stott, with Norman Anderson and Colin Craston as Vice-Chairmen.[76] The preparatory papers were published by Collins as a series of three paperbacks under their Fountain imprint with the overall title *Obeying Christ in a Changing World*. John Stott was General Editor of the series, as well as editor of volume 1, *The Lord Christ*, whose contributors also included James Packer and George Carey. Other volumes were entitled *The People of God* and *The Changing World*.[77] Of the nineteen contributors, eleven would become over the next few years respectively an Archbishop of Canterbury, four other bishops, an archdeacon, a dean and a provost, a Regius Professor and at least two other holders of professorial chairs. It was a considerable contrast with ten years before.

NEAC '77, like its predecessor at Keele ten years earlier, chose to meet at a university, this time at Nottingham on its impressive campus three miles from the city centre, on 14–18 April. As March began, it was reported to CEEC that 1,900 delegates were firmly booked (in the final count, more than twice as many as attended Keele), while over 12,000 sets of the three preliminary books had been sold, and 8,500 sets of study notes.[78] Delegates were invited to meet in parish study groups and, with the aid of the study notes, to prepare and submit their own views, as written responses to the three books of published papers. From these, a preliminary Draft Statement was hammered out, to be reshaped in its entirety as the Congress developed. Both Archbishops addressed the Congress, but much of the main sessions took the form of interviews, discussions, or practical workshops. Much of the procedure was reminiscent of Keele.

John Stott admitted in a private letter, when it was all over, that he had 'approached the Congress with much apprehension, fearing that the different emphases of our evangelical "coalition" might lead to disarray'. But in the event, though there were difficult moments, and signs of an evangelical constituency a good deal broader than gathered at Keele, disarray was not unduly prominent: 'God kept us together.'[79] The main leader in the *Church Times* on the second day of the Congress offers an insight into how it appeared to contemporary church opinion, as demonstrating the vitality of the evangelical movement. Under the headline 'Evangelicals in the ascendant', the leader continued:

> Probably no other section of the Church of England has the strength to organise such an assembly. The contrast with the inter-war period, when an Anglo-Catholic Congress would be the chief focus of enthusiasm and the High Church school was dominant on the bench of bishops, is almost impossible to exaggerate ... The Evangelical theological colleges are fuller than the others, and the Evangelical lay associations are far more vigorous. In the universities and colleges Christian or Evangelical Unions flourish where the branches of the liberal (or in recent years Leftist) Student Christian Movement have withered away.

The leader-writer went on to speak of that 'heartfelt and confident relationship with the Lord Jesus Christ, person-to-person', which he saw as a continuing characteristic of evangelicalism:

> The religion of the Evangelicals feeds the souls of men and women because all the time it draws very directly on the inexhaustible power of the risen Christ. It is aware of the problems, but it is itself a part of the answer. The end-product is not more worry or doubt or confusion; it is not even discipline or duty. It is joy and peace in believing.[80]

On the Saturday of the Congress John Stott contributed the 'Face to faith' feature in *The Guardian*, spelling out what he felt the church's priorities should be: a serious preaching and teaching ministry, a warm, caring, supportive fellowship; joyful worship expressing the reality of the living God and the victory of Christ: and an imaginative, sensitive and compassionate outreach into the secular community.[81] Not surprisingly, perhaps, it offered in broadest outline some of what the final seventy-page Nottingham Statement[82] would deal with in greater detail. Clifford Longley, Religious Affairs correspondent of *The Times*, was present at Nottingham and published his report on the Monday following, noting how in the years since Keele 'a host of new ideas have been absorbed by the evangelical constituency', and how Nottingham 'brought into the open a fair degree of ferment, and an obvious determination not to go back on the promises made at Keele'.[83] Though he could poke gentle fun at the attempts to grapple with big issues, nevertheless he recognized a genuine attempt to face social problems, to which neither secular politics nor other Christian traditions had found solutions:

> The congress's final statement, conflicting though certain passages are with other passages and having not quite a common thread as it wanders through a world of unemployment, religious pluralism and indifference, racial tension, the rising divorce rate, and so on, nevertheless gives a very different impression from the traditional style of evangelicalism ... The final 'declaration of intent' adopted by the congress, a sort of distillation from the 20,000-word statement, is as much a confession of failure as a programme of action.[84]

Two memories, not necessarily of the most significance, tend to stay in the minds of those who were present, alongside a general impression of sharing in something conceived on a grand scale. The first was an unguarded remark – perhaps hardly more than an aside – by David Watson, who was giving a Bible reading during the main evening worship on the Friday night. It elicited an audible gasp, though the point the speaker was trying to make was (as he always maintained) 'in the context … a perfectly fair statement'.[85] What he is recorded as saying, from his own account written a few years later, was:

> In many ways, the Reformation was one of the greatest tragedies that ever happened to the Church. Martin Luther … never wanted to split the church, simply to reform it. We no doubt glory in the biblical truths that were rediscovered at the Reformation (as I certainly do) but from the Reformation onwards the Body of Christ in the world has been torn from limb to limb into hundreds of separate pieces.[86]

David Watson's biographers, while admitting that in such an assembly this was 'a foolhardy thing to say', record that 'the lions snarled at Daniel hungrily, at the time and for years to come'.[87] 'The lions', here, are presumably those who saw in the growth of the charismatic movement among evangelicals a dependence upon shared experience and a corresponding weakening of doctrinal emphasis and Protestant standards of churchmanship. The evidence suggests that their fears were justified,[88] even if they were wrong to attach much significance to a single error of judgment. Not every slip is a Freudian slip.

The second lasting memory of a NEAC '77 plenary was not unconnected. In his address to the final session, John Stott as chairman chose to remind the delegates that though for many of them the experience of Nottingham '77 had taken them into unfamiliar paths of study, yet they met as Anglican evangelicals, heirs to a definable and honourable tradition. In his introduction to the published version of his address he explained why he felt it right to do this:

> On Friday 15th April, the first NEAC special of the *Church of England Newspaper* carried an editorial in which John King wrote that when I was asked at a press conference, 'What is an evangelical?' I looked slightly dazed. He added that hundreds of delegates would go home happier if they could answer that question without using incomprehensible jargonese. And he concluded with a rather pathetic plea, 'What is an evangelical? Tell us somebody please!' Well, I was very anxious that the delegates should leave the Congress happy, and so as usual I rose to one of John King's baits …

But before describing what constitutes 'an evangelical' and 'what sort of evangelical we Anglicans ought to be now we have had our Nottingham face lift', he took a moment to defend the use of the word:

We do not retain our separate identity because we live in the past and cannot face this exciting new situation in which we are no longer, thank God, a beleaguered minority. On the contrary I suggest we retain the designation because there are certain distinctive convictions that we cherish which we must on no account surrender, and to which we must bear faithful witness so long as there is anybody left who does not share them with us.[89]

In his address, and in the booklet, he then went on to expound two major distinctive convictions: that evangelicals are Bible people (and must go on learning how to learn from Scripture: the word 'hermeneutics' had figured largely in Nottingham discussion): and also gospel people: 'if the first hallmark of the evangelical is biblical supremacy, the second is the centrality of the Gospel'.[90]

NEAC '77 helped to improve the evangelical image in the church at large – and even, to some extent, in society beyond church circles. It continued the massive programme of self-education in the Anglican evangelical constituency begun at Keele: indeed, the writer of the Preface to *The Church of England Year Book* commended the Congress for 'opening to very varied lay audiences a whole range of issues which scholars should not, cannot and (in the main) do not want to keep to themselves'.[91] It helped to show that 'conservative' in theology need not mean 'backward looking in everything else'. Among the many 'observers' was an American from the Trinity Episcopal School for Ministry. He found '2000 Anglicans who rely on Scripture, have found in Christ a gracious Saviour, and who seek to please Christ in all things' almost too good to be believed: 'I don't suppose that before NEAC I had ever seen more than 15 Anglican Evangelicals in one gathering.' His impression was of 'relaxed innovation'.[92]

But it was by no means all gain. It was certainly true that, compared even with Keele, 'less conservative views began to be heard'.[93] James Packer, once again a key contributor, had not wanted such a Congress to be held, feeling it would be a distraction from the continuing study begun at Keele in many local churches. He was not alone in being concerned at some of the methodology, some of the experiential emphasis of charismatic groups, some of the lack of historical perspective in knowing where traditional evangelical roots lay. His biographer, who interviewed him in depth two decades later, is clear that for James Packer Nottingham was 'something of a dud': and helped to convince him that the time had come for him to leave England for Canada.[94] And though Alister McGrath sees the most important long-term achievement of the Congress as the highlighting of the importance of hermeneutics in the search for biblical understanding,[95] this carried dangers with it, none the less real because they were not always clearly perceived by those who had not had to fight the battles of the past:

> Despite the value of hermeneutics rightly applied, the idea spread that the teaching of the Bible was expressed in terms of the culture of its times to such an extent that it could not be related to life today as confidently as it had been. Hermeneutics thus became a tool for mischief as well as for good. As a term of abuse, the phrase 'proof-texting' began to be applied to anyone who used the actual words of the Bible to demonstrate a doctrine. A less clearly definable general sense of Scripture was invoked more often. It became less acceptable to say 'The Bible says'.[96]

In Australia, the Archbishop of Sydney, Sir Marcus Loane, was hearing 'glowing reports' and wrote to his friend John Stott to congratulate him on 'your own tremendous contribution'. He adds, 'I am deeply grateful that God has called out a fresh, young and vigorous band of Evangelicals within the Church.'[97] But his letter went on to speak of some aspects of these reports which disturbed him, and he begged John Stott – 'my dear John' – to use his influence to persuade the younger generation 'to capture the Church of England, not to fracture it'. In reply John Stott admitted that he saw at Nottingham 'disturbing signs of something you don't mention, viz. the beginnings of a new "liberal evangelicalism", perhaps especially at St John's, Nottingham ...'[98] and went on to confess his own disquiet, and the fear that we might soon be facing a new 'battle for the Bible'. After responding briefly to some points in Marcus Loane's letter ('I've attempted to expound this in my little booklet *Balanced Christianity*') John Stott continued:

> On comprehensiveness I entirely agree. While willing to recognize those of other schools of thought as fellow-Christians, this must not lead us into an easygoing doctrinal indifferentism. With you I want to see evangelicals capturing the Church of England for the truth of God. I also agree that in our new concerns for social ethics (owing to some past neglect) we must not lose, or in any way underplay, the central themes of salvation, justification, personal holiness ... I will try to say this more often.[99]

4

During these years John Stott lent his name and his support to the Council of Reference of many good causes (the Nationwide Festival of Light would be a typical example; which, through the work of his friend

Raymond Johnston, developed into CARE, the Christian Action, Research and Education Trust).[100] He also held office as President of a number of evangelical movements and societies: among them the UK Scripture Union and UK Evangelical Alliance, and (twice) UCCF.[101] Work among students continued to hold a high priority, often overseas, and with continued visits to the triennial Urbana Missionary Convention. At home, an article in *All Souls* noted the prediction that within a decade or so, one in every five eighteen-year-olds would be a full-time student, with up to a quarter of them based in London.[102]

The decade had begun with a week's mission in the University of Liverpool. January 1972 again saw him travelling northwards for student evangelism in Nottingham, Leicester and Manchester; and to Newcastle and Durham the following year, with flying visits to Stirling and Belfast and (in 1974) Aberdeen. Only in 1977, after twenty-five years of such missions, did he finally decide the time had come to leave this specialist ministry to younger men. Even so, he continued strongly to support the work of UCCF, whose life to date was so nearly coterminous with his own. Its foundation, as the IVF, is generally traced to 1919,[103] a time when the SCM held an almost undisputed dominance among Christian societies for students. But by the end of the 1950s this was on the wane, and by 1970–80 the IVF/UCCF could point to 'a CU in every major institution of higher education – often the largest of student-run societies', even while the SCM declined to a point where, according to Professor Steve Bruce writing in 1980, 'its continued existence cannot be seen as signifying a continuing interest by students or public in its activities'.[104] John Stott valued the work of UCCF for its stand for biblical authority, its policy of student leadership, its encouragement of thoughtful (rather than emotional) evangelism, and its settled practice of seeking to go on from conversion to discipleship so as to present each convert 'mature in Christ'; a Christian maturity which' included Christlikeness of character and conduct, 'indeed the integration of our whole human personality under the lordship of Christ'.[105]

His last full-scale university mission, therefore, took place where his first had been held exactly twenty-five years before: a full week's mission in Cambridge for the CICCU in its centenary year. Up to 1,000 attended each evening at 8.30pm in the Guildhall, with perhaps 1,200 on the final night. Though others remember 'the meticulous, persuasive and biblical presentation of the addresses',[106] yet John Stott himself later confessed that he 'was fighting some real personal battles during the week of the mission and felt myself to be an object of Satanic attack'.[107] One of the assistant missioners recalls how, after the main address on the first Sunday evening,

... we met for a Missioners' Meeting the following morning. We were somewhat tired and downhearted – not least because John's talk had been pretty solid stuff. There seemed little prospect that people would be drawn to the addresses because they were 'fun'. John listened carefully to the thinly-veiled criticism and then responded; 'A friend of mine once said (I take it he was a friend!), "John, your sermons are like houses without windows and puddings without plums." But you invited me to come!'[108]

When John Stott gave a report of the mission to his praying friends among the All Souls congregation, he wrote:

More impressive than the numbers was the close attention given to nearly an hour's lecture-type address on the basics of the gospel: the evidence for the deity of Jesus, the Christian evaluation of man, the cross, the resurrection, new birth, the church (under the intriguing title 'Christians – cabbages or kings?'), the cost of discipleship etc. More than half then stayed for the optional ten-minute instruction on commitment to Christ.

It was a striking confirmation of the unchanging gospel in a changing age:

Since the first Cambridge mission I led was 25 years ago, before the present student generation were born, I could not help comparing the two. The contrast reflects the accelerating process of secular-isation in post-war Britain. The 1952 mission was held in a church, with all the ecclesiastical paraphernalia of robed clergy, traditional hymns and liturgical prayers; the 1977 mission was held in the city's Guildhall, with no hymns or prayers ... and with the speaker not sporting a clerical collar, let alone clerical robes.[109]

One undergraduate wrote later:

I marvelled most at the discomfort the mission caused, and I think it was intended to do that. A mission stops us in our tracks and challenges us with its stark language. It shouts out an alternative – yes there's more to it than that – and the alternative is Jesus whom a lifetime will never fathom.[110]

But this was not the discomfort born of any kind of manipulative pressure. Though the title of the final address was 'Who's Jesus? – your verdict', yet John Stott made it clear that he believed increasingly in the importance of respecting every person's own integrity: 'This makes thoughtful and definite professions of faith more meaningful.'[111] John Samuel, President of the CICCU, in writing to thank him at the end of the week was concerned to underline this point:

> The professions of faith seem to be deep and strong and durable. I am convinced that is because each person when they turned, did so with the full consent of their mind and personality on the basis of a full disclosure of the facts.

John Samuel went on to tell John Stott of further encouraging signs: forty or fifty coming to the follow-up talks; a good day conference; an immense amount of interest on which to build during the next term or two; quantities of tapes of the 'Who's Jesus?' addresses being ordered – and finally a further dozen or more who professed faith in Christ, unknown to the committee, either during the mission or immediately after it.[112]

5

In the autumn of 1972 John Stott was visiting Trinity Evangelical Divinity School, Illinois, and met there Myra Chave-Jones, a professional psychotherapist from the All Souls congregation, whom he had known in Cambridge in the 1940s when her college, the London School of Economics, had been evacuated there. They talked together about the need for a Christian 'care and counselling service' in London, and were able to consult one or two American specialists in this field.[113] A year later, in October 1973, such an idea came before the All Souls PCC at a Saturday conference, and John Stott was asked to explore it further.[114] By the summer of 1975 he was able to report that such a service was in being, with Myra Chave-Jones as Secretary, and himself as Chairman, of the Council of Management. He described how 'The vision of Care and Counsel has arisen from our awareness of the artificiality and loneliness of much London life, and of the resulting personal and emotional problems of many Londoners,'[115] and went on to speak of three objectives: to co-operate with churches in raising the standards of Christian care; to educate through lectures and seminars; and to work towards the creation of a personal counselling service. The following year Myra Chave-Jones was appointed as the staff-worker of Care and Counsel with the title Consultant and Training Organizer and the brief to expand and develop the work; in 1980 she became Director. By the time she retired in 1983 John Stott had given up the chairmanship of the Council,[116] though the work continued until 1990.

When John Stott resigned the chair of Care and Counsel, it was because he had a new and demanding project in mind, again associated with All Souls but under independent management. This was to be a major annual series of London Lectures, 'to encourage biblical thinking on contemporary issues'. As with Care and Counsel, this had arisen following a visit to the United States, where he had been invited to give the Payton Lectures at Fuller Theological Seminary, California, thirteen years before.[117] Now at last he could pursue a dream, dating back to that time, of an annual series of lectures in central London on a Christian theme. He consulted friends, and found Jim Packer enthusiastic; and the Langham Trust agreed to handle the finances. The creation of a London Lectures Sponsoring Committee with two representatives from the Trust, and others appointed by IFES, UCCF, Scripture Union and All Souls, secured a firm evangelical base.[118] Introducing the Lectures to the All Souls congregation, John Stott wrote of how

> ... the Christianity which most of us prefer is more ancient than modern, more biblical than contemporary ... What Scripture plainly teaches we gladly receive and hold fast, but it is not con-genial to us to develop a Christian mind, informed with Christian presuppositions, and with this mind of Christ to grapple with the great problems of the day, so as to develop a Christian world-view.[119]

The name of the lecturer probably came as something of a surprise to readers of *All Souls*:

> The first series of five lectures is to be given ... by Professor José Míguez Bonino on the topic 'Christians and Marxists – the mutual challenge to revolution'. Marxism is Christianity's most powerful rival today. If Christianity is a worldwide phenomenon (as Hinduism, Buddhism and Islam are not), so is Marxism. Though essentially atheistic, Marxism is tantamount to a religion, claims the allegiance of hundreds of millions, demands total commitment, and sets as its goal the transformation of the world, together with the creation of new men in a new society.
> Yet Dr Míguez refuses to see Christianity and Marxism set over against each other, as neat alternatives ... Christians and Marxists as socially concerned human beings often find themselves involved in a common struggle. Despite all their ideological differences, not all their ideals diverge. Moreover, Christians and Marxists have to learn to listen to each other, as each group challenges the other.[120]

Perhaps not surprisingly, the lectures led to some protest. As late as 1976 a representative of the Christian Affirmation Campaign was writing to the press naming John Stott as 'an evangelical leader whose social thinking has been taken over by Marxist ideology'. Patrick Dearnley, Director of the Shaftesbury Project, was glad to reply:

> Now that the veil has been removed we can see the red face of Comrade Stott shining with the light of truth revealed from his devotional meditation each morning in *Das Capital.* At last the whole ghastly reason for the alterations to All Souls church stands revealed: from its subterranean hall will issue a stream of indoctrinated cadres, their souls nourished by the power that flows from the Tomb in Highgate Cemetery.
>
> When will Commissar Anderson (that renegade bourgeois intellectual) order the hammer and sickle to be unfurled over Church House, Westminster? ...[121]

'Commissar Anderson' represents Professor J. N. D. Anderson, who gave the 1975 London Lectures on 'Issues of Life and Death', dealing with questions of genetic engineering and artificial insemination, abortion, birth control and sterilization, transplant surgery and euthanasia, capital punishment, revolution and war – all within the context of the Christian view of the sanctity of human life.

For the 1976 Lectures the committee chose the journalist Malcolm Muggeridge, whom John Stott had met and befriended through Dr James Houston of Regent College, Vancouver; and who had made a great impression at the Lausanne Congress (perhaps 'more for his amazing command of English than for his message!').[122] He and John Stott had been together on the platform in Trafalgar Square for the Nationwide Festival of Light rally in September 1971. His lectures on 'Christ and the Media' naturally attracted much publicity. His biographer described how

> ... all three lectures were held at All Souls Church, Langham Place, where Stott was rector. That the church was adjacent to the offices of the BBC was an irony that was not lost on Malcolm or his audience. Each night the church was packed to capacity. To give the event added spice and a touch of controversy, the chairmen for the first two evenings were Sir Charles Curran, then Director-General of the BBC, and Sir Brian Young, Director-General of the Independent Broadcasting Authority.[123]

Malcolm Muggeridge made the most of this captive audience. He told them:

> I've always thought myself that there was a very close resemblance

between the BBC and the established Church of England. So that our chairman here this evening would be the primate, and the Chairman of the Governors, Sir Michael Swann, would be the ecclesiastical commissioner, and the various department heads would be bishops, like there might be Alastair television and Edward radio and so on, all entitled to manifest their standing by adding a tiny little microphone to their signatures.[124]

John Stott wrote to Malcolm Muggeridge in his own hand a few days after the first lecture describing it as 'characteristically brilliant' and saying, 'you certainly held us in your hand'. He went on:

Shall I stop there? Or dare I add something on the other side? Because of your hatred of hypocrisy, you don't want to surround yourself with toadies; and Christian friendship means little if it does not involve a high degree of openness. So here goes!

I fear you tended to indulge in the kind of blanket condemnation I'd begged you not to. Of course with your main thrust (that the media feed more on fantasy than on reality) I'm in wholehearted agreement ... But ...

and the letter went on to list four salient points of inner contradiction, distortion, lack of balance or harping too much on the purely negative. 'Dear Malcolm,' John Stott concluded, 'it's unfair to write after only one lecture and it's probably impertinent. But you have two more Mondays in which to redress the balance ...'[125] John Stott also wrote as a matter of courtesy to the Director-General of the BBC, feeling he might have taken personally some of Muggeridge's squibs. Charles Curran replied reassuringly, adding that he hoped John Stott would 'succeed in your efforts to persuade Malcolm to come nearer the heart of the matter in his next two lectures instead of spending all his energy in a kind of pyrotechnic display ...'[126]

Probably the letter arrived too late to change much. Muggeridge's coruscations continued unabated, but with a cumulative effect. If it was impossible not to be critical of his performance, it was equally impossible to be entirely unmoved. John Stott in his chairman's speech at the conclusion of the lectures (hoping he was not 'one of those trendy and long-haired clergymen that Malcolm Muggeridge loses no opportunity to anathematise') called the lecturer 'a true prophet of the twentieth century',[127] marked by courage and perception, adding that prophets were awkward to live with, and prone to exaggerate – both of which were indeed characteristics of the caustic wit and satirical style for which the lecturer was renowned.

In 1997 Professor Donald MacKay took the theme of 'Human Science and Human Dignity'; Raymond Johnston lectured in 1978 on 'Who needs the family?' and in 1979 the Lectures were a symposium on 'Crime and the Responsible Community'. An informal survey after these 1979 lectures revealed that the lectures were attracting a younger element – half of those who attended were under thirty. Over a hundred occupations were represented, from academics and doctors to a night-shelter attendant. It was calculated that forty or fifty magazines (including *New Society* and *Time Out*) had responded to the press release and given free coverage. But that may have had something to do with Chuck Colson being one of the lecturers that year.[128]

6

By 1977, the year of the Nottingham Congress, John Stott was Rector Emeritus. He was therefore free to fly to Venice immediately after the Congress for a first meeting of the Evangelical–Roman Catholic Dialogue on Mission (ERCDOM) whose Report belongs to the following chapter. It was at the end of the 1970s, too, that he became a member of the 'Faith House meetings', a series of theological discussions between Anglo-Catholics, charismatics and evangelicals, named from the offices of the Church Union in Tufton Street, and chaired by Eric Kemp, the Bishop of Chichester, a leading Anglo-Catholic.

It must have been difficult sometimes for John Stott to remember in which particular dialogue he was participating. Yet another, though brief and on a smaller scale, was with what became known as 'the East-end Five', a small group of evangelical Anglican incumbents in inner East London, including Christopher Idle of Limehouse, Charles May of Hackney, Peter Ronayne of Shoreditch, and E. G. (Eddie) Stride of Spitalfields. They were concerned about what they saw as the 'feeble language and needless complications' of the new services emanating from General Synod, as well as their 'departure from biblical norms and Church of England doctrine'.[129] They saw John Stott as a key figure (though he was not of course a member of Synod or of any Liturgical Commission) and he agreed to meet them:

> John understood and respected our concerns, and to some extent shared them. Some he did not agree with; he also expressed a great concern for unity among Anglicans whatever our precise preferences for this or that form of words.

But they were to be disappointed. At the Autumn Conference of the Eclectic Society John Stott spoke on some current trends in the church:

He touched briefly on liturgical matters, and newer services 'which cause offence to those with tender consciences'. Then came the crucial moment; I do not claim to report his exact words, but they were very close to: 'Some others of us may think that their consciences are rather too tender over such matters.' With that, the sort of 'approving conference murmur' went round the room, and we knew that we had lost the battle.[130]

With hindsight it is possible to argue that had stronger, more conservative evangelical leadership resisted some elements of the new services – had CEEC, for example, been able to give a more determined and united lead – things would have been different. But this may be to overlook how much evangelicals owe to those who fought for what they valued, in the various commissions and on the floor of the Synod. Things could easily have been much worse. Perhaps the confidence John Stott reposed in other evangelical leaders in the field sometimes meant that he had to settle for less than what some might have hoped for. Synodical affairs, sadly, are seldom any exception to the rule that politics is the art of the possible.

In the summer of 1978 John Stott attended the Lambeth Conference at the invitation of Archbishop Donald Coggan · as one of twenty consultants, alongside (for example) Professor Henry Chadwick, Canon David Jenkins, later the Bishop of Durham, and Bishop John Robinson, celebrated as the author of *Honest to God*. It appeared even at the time to be a slightly muted affair. The organizers 'were determined that the 1978 Conference should not appear as an English occasion, when those in far-flung subsidiaries came "home" for the decennial visit to head office'.[131] The theme was 'Today's Church in Today's World', with a special focus on 'The Ministry of Bishops', 400 of whom attended, together with a number of members of the Anglican Consultative Council and observers from other churches. They met in Canterbury, at the University of Kent, with the Archbishop presiding. John Stott himself was attached to the group studying mission, who asked him to serve as its secretary: it therefore fell to him to draft the group's submission to the plenary conference, though it does not seem to have been debated. A motion by Bishop Festo Kivengere expressing the conviction that dialogue is no substitute for our continuing responsibility in evangelism was put to the Conference and lost: in John Stott's view, partly because the late hour inhibited debate, and partly because, in the large hall, Festo Kivengere's English pronunciation tended to confuse the issue.

The Conference proved to be notably weak, therefore, on the theme of evangelism. Two pages in the Report on 'Mission and Evangelization' were unexciting, and confusing in their attempt to equate evangelism with meeting the needs of 'poverty, sickness, oppression, persecution, and any form of suffering' as much as those 'ignorant of Christ'. Among the thirty-seven Resolutions the task of evangelism receives almost no significant attention.[132]

Some of the most vivid of John Stott's memories at Lambeth 1978 were his personal encounters. Twenty years later he recalled how

> ... my bedroom at the University of Kent was next to that of the Moderator of the Church of South India, Ananda Rao Samuel. He had recently had a terrible experience. Having disciplined two of his clergy for a financial misdemeanour, they had hired an assassin who, when the Moderator's car had stopped at a crossroads, threw petrol into it and a lighted match. He and his wife were rushed to Vellore Christian Hospital. Mrs Samuel died of her wounds soon afterwards, while he retains dreadful facial scars today. We made friends. Every morning I wakened him with a cup of tea, and we prayed together daily. I'm still in regular touch with him ...[133]

Others had their own recollections. Archbishop Loane told his EFAC readers that among the memories he carried home with him to Australia were 'walking with John Stott through the fields near the University' and, above all, 'the words of the Duchess of Kent to the Archbishop of Papua New Guinea: "Tell them about Jesus: that is what people need to hear."'[134]

John Stott ended 1978 with a private visit to see Dr Martyn Lloyd-Jones; he had tried to do so the previous Christmas but 'the Doctor' had been about to leave London. They met at Dr Lloyd-Jones's home on 19 December: 'he could not have been more affable and welcoming. We sat in his roomy ground-floor study where he does his writing, and Mrs Ll-J brought us coffee and chocolate biscuits.'[135] Both men had written on Ephesians, and John Stott told his host how he had profited from the four volumes of *Ephesian Studies* so far published; and that he had several times quoted him appreciatively in *God's New Society*.[136]

> 'Do you know' [Dr Lloyd-Jones responded], 'I never intended to write up those Ephesian sermons.' Then he explained the 'double commission' he had received in hospital, immediately before having his injection prior to his major operation some years previously. Though he was not the kind of person to hear voices or receive direct messages, yet this had been so direct as to be almost audible, a message as real and clear as his original call to preach. God had said to him two things: (1) 'you are not to go back to Westminster Chapel', and (2) 'you are to put your sermons into writing and to go round encouraging the churches, specially the weaker ones.'[137]

John Stott's main reasons for the visit were personal: to build bridges and to repair a friendship which, though never intimate, was firmly rooted in respect and affection. Their talk went on to speak of 'the Doctor's' outspoken criticism of evangelical Anglicans; and to set right the record, where he had believed (mistakenly) that at NEAC '77 drama had replaced biblical exposition. John Stott reaffirmed his own position:

'Dr Lloyd-Jones, you give the impression that you think we evangelical Anglicans are unprincipled in our commitment to the Church of England. You use expressions like "mixed denomination" and "comprehensive church", as if we gloried in this. Speaking for myself, I'm first and foremost an evangelical.'

'I find that hard to believe.'

'But I am ...'

Later, Dr Lloyd-Jones asked:

'Would you ever leave the Church of England?'

'Yes indeed, I could envisage such a situation, if the church itself compromised officially one of the central doctrines of the faith. I'm not committed to the Church of England irrevocably.'

On a happier note, John Stott observed how, three times in their conversation of not much over an hour, Dr Lloyd-Jones spoke of his desire that the two of them could work together:

'I wish we could be together, you and I. We belong together. Together we could make a terrific impact on the church and the country.'

'But, Dr Lloyd-Jones, we are together – theologically, though not structurally.'

'But we ought to *be* together. If God spares me, and we could be together, I'd say like Simeon "Lord, now lettest thou thy servant depart in peace".'

They never met again; but on Dr Lloyd-Jones's death in 1981 John Stott wrote an appreciation for *The Times*. They did not publish it, but it appeared in a later symposium. He wrote there of his own warm personal relationship, in which 'The Doctor' always distinguished between principles and personalities, and how he was 'at heart a man of love and peace ... a spiritual father to many of us'.[138]

Six

Australia to the Arctic:
A Worldwide Parish

1

The new decade was still young when John Stott was once more on his travels. In January 1970 he was in Ireland for a clergy conference, and then in Liverpool for a university mission; March found him in Sweden and Finland on the same errand. Ever since his four-month visit to American and Canadian universities in the winter of 1956–57 he had sought increasingly to distance the pattern of his missions from ecclesiastical associations. The uncommitted felt more comfortable in a lecture hall rather than a church or chapel; the radical nature of the gospel of grace could be presented, he felt, more freshly and clearly away from church surroundings. He wrote to his congregation, looking back on the missions in the universities of Lund and Helsinki:

I am very thankful that the student mission committees overcame their initial reluctance and agreed to change the pattern in March to a straight series of lectures ... In both Lund and Helsinki I had extremely gifted and fluent interpreters, and I do not think the necessity of interpretation was much of a hindrance to communication. The concentration of the listeners appeared to be good,

although (because of interpretation) each lecture lasted a full hour.
The Christian students also seemed pleased with the numbers
attending ... a maximum of 300 at any time in Lund and 700 in
Helsinki. But there are about 25,000 students in both universities,
and I could not help asking myself about the vast secularized
majority whose only response to the missions was apathetic in-
difference.[1]

Meanwhile he was preparing for a protracted absence from London,
beginning at the end of the year. By that time Michael Baughen as Vicar
would have taken over responsibility for the work at All Souls, and the
Rectory would no longer be John Stott's home. The Baughens moved in
at the end of November, ready for the formal licensing on 19 December.
On Christmas Day John Stott went to join Joy and Auntie Babe at
Bullens; and on the following afternoon Joy drove him to the airport. His
first commitment was the IVCF Conference at Urbana – his third visit –
to give the Bible readings on John 13 – 17, the Upper Room discourse.[2]
He fell into bed about midnight (7.00 in the morning by British time)
and woke to immerse himself in the life of the Convention as one of some
12,000 participants, 10,000 of them students. They came from all across
America, with a few contingents from over the Canadian border.

It was only as the Convention was coming to an end that John Stott
found time to write up his diary:

> The most striking feature of this convention, in contrast to the
> previous two of 1964 and 1967, is the alertness and responsiveness
> of the student body ... At first it seemed a bit inappropriate that,
> for example, a serious Bible exposition should be greeted with
> thunderous applause ... but it was obviously spontaneous student
> exuberance, and a mark of their desire to participate.
>
> Another difference between this convention and the previous two
> has been the increased emphasis on social issues, and their relation
> to world evangelism. Race has been very much to the fore. About
> 1000 Negro students have been here, and several black speakers are
> on the team.

Apart from the four main Bible readings, John Stott made himself
available each afternoon for a 'discussion period', a face-to-face consultation with any students who cared to come; and, as in previous years,
was invited to preside at the final Communion service:

> Although of course it had to be a form of service which was
> interdenominational, I was able to introduce some liturgical bits in

contemporary English, with congregational participation, which they seem to have enjoyed. I also introduced 'the Peace' – a handshake greeting with the words 'Peace be with you', passed down each row from person to person, which went down well. There must have been three or four hundred students 'serving', taking the bread and wine (in tiny individual plastic cups) from row to row, and the administration to 12,000 people took only half an hour.[3]

The service ended just after midnight on New Year's Day with the singing of 'We rest in Thee ... and in Thy Name we go' (which had by now become a tradition) and immediately afterwards the students boarded their long-distance buses, many to begin a two- or three-day journey home. For John Stott himself, the end of the Convention meant an afternoon's birdwatching, followed by a weekend conference for 100 members of the IVCF national staff.

So back to Chicago, to find O'Hare Airport just reopened after a two-foot fall of snow the previous night. David Wells met him and drove him to Trinity Evangelical Divinity School, Deerfield, where he was a member of the church-history department. John Stott dined that evening with the Faculty; and at the Convocation the next day an Honorary DD was conferred on him: 'It was a dignified ceremony and not at all the embarrassment I had feared.'[4] From Deerfield John Stott flew to the West Coast, exchanging the snows of Illinois for the orange trees and palms of California. He used his three hours between planes at Los Angeles to get a tourist's glimpse of Hollywood; and then settled down for the long flight to Sydney. He was booked to speak at three conferences in succession, beginning with the All-Australia CMS Summer School at Katoomba. Held each January, this was a major event in the calendar, not only of CMS but of the Australian church. Attendances ran into four figures, and included missionaries on furlough, new recruits, and numbers of families combining the School with a summer holiday. During the 1960s and '70s it became something of a tradition that John Stott should visit the School immediately after his visit to the triennial Urbana Missionary Convention and repeat the same series of Bible expositions.[5] On this occasion he went from the airport to spend the night as the guest of Archbishop and Mrs Loane at Bishopscourt:

The following morning we drove the 80 or so miles west into the Blue Mountains. The CMS Summer School was due to begin that day, but the Loanes suggested that I should spend the first 24 hours with them in a mountain house nearby which they had rented for the week. As we drove up to the house and stopped, Marcus said to Patricia, 'Darling, I hope you've got the keys.' 'No, darling,' she replied, 'I gave them to you during breakfast!' So there we were, 80 miles from Sydney, with a locked house, and the keys still on the breakfast table at Bishopscourt! Marcus was all for getting into the car and driving straight back to Sydney, leaving Patricia and me to picnic lunch. But I suggested they should take advantage of the presence of an experienced British burglar and allow me to break in! They were not at all keen on the idea, forcible entry being some- what incompatible with archiepiscopal ethical standards ... I spotted a bedroom window with a crack across its top left corner, and with evident reluctance Marcus allowed me to break the corner glass and remove it. The damage done, he then reached through to open the window and insisted himself on clambering through it.[6]

Once again John Stott expounded the Upper Room discourse; and one afternoon spoke on 'The Pastoral Ideal in the New Testament' to 150 clergy. In the discussion that followed, he noted especially

... the tension in the Sydney Diocese between the old and the new, the traditional and the radical, of which one is aware all over the world. The Archbishop himself is on the conservative side, and I've been teasing him about allowing himself to be dragged into the seventies. 'Into the sixties, you mean,' commented his daughter Winsome, who came to breakfast barefoot one morning to His Grace's evident disapproval! I've teased him too about his rather inflexible adherence to the AV of the Bible and the text of the *Book of Common Prayer* (1662), with little or no concession to the demand for modern English – while he has teased me on my side- burns as a throwback to the 19th century![7]

From Katoomba he moved on to Canberra, the Commonwealth capital, to join the IVF/OCF Conference at the Australian National University campus not far from the city centre. The Overseas Christian Fellowship (OCF) is a student group parallel to IVF, but specifically for Asian students, of whom a good number were among the delegates. John Stott found himself requested to speak on God's call to the ordained pastoral ministry. Some sixty students came, and he noted in his diary their disillusion with the institutional church.[8]

Following Canberra, John Stott's itinerary allowed for six days' much- needed holiday in the company of John Reid and Donald Cameron (both later to become Bishops in the Sydney diocese). Their expedition took them deep into deserted valleys, the local habitat of Yellow-tailed Black Cockatoos 'perched in the topmost branches of pine trees and screeching like scalded cats'. Then it was back to work, to join the Christian Medical

Fellowship weekend Conference at Gilbulla. Here about eighty people, mostly doctors and their wives with a sprinkling of medical students, heard John Stott expound Matthew 6 ('The Call to be Different' from the Sermon on the Mount). A formal weekend in Sydney saw John Stott preaching in the Cathedral, and on the Monday ('Australia Day') picnicking and swimming with the Loanes on Warriewood beach amid spectacular surf, before flying on to Adelaide. Here he was to stay with Lance Shilton, Rector of Holy Trinity Church in the heart of the city, with a ministry not unlike that of All Souls in London. It was, as the diary records, a demanding visit:

> Lance Shilton is small of stature, but a living dynamo, and an extremely capable organizer. He had arranged 4 meetings on Tuesday, and made me speak 4 times within seven hours! It made me remember Monty's [Viscount Montgomery of Alamein] saying after a visit to Australia, that he'd given 'more speeches to the square meal' than anywhere else in the world!

The afternoon had been given to watching the Test Match in the Adelaide Oval:

> I confess that my attention was occasionally distracted by the dapper little Australian 'Willie Wagtails' which were disporting themselves on the field, without showing any respect for the test cricket – and by the Silver Gulls, one of which was knocked unconscious by a fast ball and had to be carried off the field (where it was revived by a vet)!⁹

His last Australian visit was to Perth, where a lunch-time gathering of clergy at the Archbishop's House was followed by a large public meeting in the evening, once again on the theme of 'Following Christ in the 70s' (a title proposed by John Stott's hosts in Perth, which he used more than once on this tour).¹⁰

In Hong Kong, the next stop, John Stott had been invited to conduct a week's mission at St Andrew's Church, Kowloon, using the theme of 'revolution': 'The Revolution of Jesus Christ' alone being radical enough to meet the human situation. On the plane, with this in mind, he read Chairman Mao's *Thoughts* from his 'Little Red Book'; and during the mission found himself 'able to draw a number of parallels and contrasts between the Communist and the Christian revolutions, and between the rival ideologies of Marx-Mao and Christ'.¹¹ On the doorstep of communist China such a theme was bound to attract attention; and the posters for the mission included a huge red closed fist with a cross at its heart. There was a large police presence on the opening night, concerned about the nature of this 'revolution'. The church and the adjoining hall (with closed-circuit television link) were filled each evening, while for the Sunday the mission moved to the City Hall concert hall, with almost a capacity crowd of some 1,200. The response was more Chinese than European: 'it has been marvellous to see the serious resolve of a number of student-age Chinese in their commitment to the revolutionary Christ'.

It says something for the changing attitudes of church leaders towards evangelicalism in general, and John Stott in person, that while in 1958 the Bishop of Hong Kong had withheld permission for him to visit the diocese, in 1971 the new bishop met him at the airport, agreed to be Patron of the mission, and personally attended the meetings on four of the seven evenings. Looking back from the perspective of more than twenty-five years, the then vicar summed up his lasting impression of the mission as decisive,

> ... both in the number of people who professed faith and joined the church and on the life of the church itself. Looking back I am sure that the mission marked out St Andrew's as a gospel-proclaiming church. This led to people from all over the colony making it their church and travelling many miles at some inconvenience (crossing on ferries etc.) to attend worship and to get involved in house groups.[12]

On the morning after the final address of the mission John Stott was taken by one of his Chinese hosts, in company with a local ornithologist, to the Mai Po marshes on the south-west tip of the New Territories:

> First we drove to a police post on a hilltop from which we were able
> to see the nearby river which forms the boundary with Red China, the
> wire fence and the paddy fields and mountains of the People's
> Republic beyond. Then we walked out into the marshes, along
> reed-fringed paths, with dykes and water ponds all round. Indian and
> White-breasted Kingfishers flashed by in brilliant blue and red, and
> we saw both Harriers quartering the marshes and White Egrets ...[13]

From Hong Kong he moved on to Singapore: once again there were new birds to see, old friends to meet, All Souls contacts to greet after long absences. He preached twice in the Cathedral, and afterwards in a local Presbyterian church repeated his address on 'Following Christ in the 70s'. There was the usual conference of clergy; and the opportunity to talk with his friend Chandu Ray, formerly Bishop of Karachi, and his new wife Anita.

And so it went on. From this world tour in 1971 John Stott's travels would become more widespread, and continuous. Besides these glimpses of Australia, Hong Kong and Singapore there were brief visits to a host of other cities, and to expectant Christian communities both in Sri Lanka (Colombo, Kurunegala, Kandy) and in South India (Madras, Tiruchchirappalli, Bangalore). Two entries from the diary must serve to suggest something of this round of ministry. On the road from the airport in South India,

> ... we met the special bus chartered by Thavaraj David (yet another EFAC bursar, who spent a month at All Souls), which was crammed with ninety-five of the deaf and dumb children from the school which he and his wife run for them! They garlanded me with 2 gay garlands of roses, drew me into the bus with eager hands and shining faces, and kept crying 'Vanakam' (the Tamil greeting) with as much verve as their little dumb mouths could manage. When they all got out of the bus, they formed a great circle, and one of them, a little girl dressed in a blue skirt and with red decorations in her black hair, performed for me a special welcome dance. The music was tape-recorded. But because she could not hear it, she danced to the rhythm which one of the teachers beat for her. She was a very graceful and accomplished little dancer. When she had finished, there was wild applause from all the other deaf and dumb children, and from the adult spectators.[14]

At the United Theological College in Bangalore a week or so later John Stott conducted the Ash Wednesday 'Quiet Day'. His four addresses were followed by two hours of personal interviews:

> Fifteen students came to talk, and I could see in what personal turmoil many of them are – arriving in many cases from an evangelical background and being plunged (innocent and unprepared) into the radicalism of Bultmann and Tillich. Then at 8.15pm, at my suggestion, we had an open question-time. I'd meant it for students, but most of the faculty came too, and it developed into a straight evangelical–radical confrontation. I think the student spectators quite enjoyed seeing someone daring to stand up to their teachers, but I'm not sure how edifying a spectacle it was. And I wish I could have done better to defend historic Christianity as the Church has for centuries received it ... It grieves one to see so many bowing down and worshipping the latest idol of pop teutonic theology![15]

And so home, after two months away. Sitting in the plane at Prague Airport with snow on the ground, John Stott wrote up his diary, and added his brief reflections on the immense variety of both his ministry and his travels. Next to physical health (a few digestive upsets apart, he was very thankful to have kept well), 'the itinerant Christian minister needs above all to seek and cultivate adaptability' – adaptability to extremes of affluence and poverty, to varieties of social and religious background, to different cultures formed and followed over many centuries. To all these, it remained (he concluded) the task of such a minister to present the biblical gospel of redeeming grace, the totality of its demands, and the uniqueness and finality of Christ.

Sometimes his travels were nearer home. In the spring of 1978, for example, John Stott was in Italy, Greece, Turkey, Lebanon, Syria, Jordan and Egypt. Visiting the Pauline sites in Turkey ('ruins are great places for birds!'), he and his companions came to Tarsus, which they found 'rather dirty and undistinguished'.[16] Here they met a local doctor whose sister was a regular member of All Souls:

> He told us that he had been brought up as a Moslem, but found a New Testament in a shop when 17 years old, and had come to Christ, or 'believed in Jesus Christ' in his own words, as a result. There are 115,000 inhabitants of Tarsus, he told us, but only two Christian families.[17]

They were shown round the local museum by its young curator:

> When we had completed our tour of the small museum, I shared with the curator my surprise that the museum contained no reference to the man who must surely have been one of the most distinguished of all sons of Tarsus, namely Saul of Tarsus. He smiled and nodded. On the spur of the moment, I asked him: 'Supposing I were to donate a professionally crafted exhibit of the life of Saul, without any Christian propaganda, purely factual, would he be willing to accept and display it?' He replied that he would, provided that his superiors in Ankara gave permission.[18]

Back in London, John Stott drafted a careful letter to the appropriate department in Ankara, repeating his offer and expressing surprise that the museum had no Pauline exhibit, since all European and American visitors would immediately link the town of Tarsus with the name of Saul. A member of All Souls translated the letter into Turkish and it was duly sent. Twenty years later no acknowledgment had been received!

In his worldwide ministry John Stott had this singular advantage over many who could pay only occasional visits overseas, that to some of the places he visited – countries, cities, churches, universities and colleges – he would return again and again, not as a stranger but as a friend and pastor. Through his constant travel his name was becoming known even in surprising places. At Kennedy Airport in New York, returning home in 1978, a beautiful blonde was at the check-in desk. She studied his ticket and passport, and then casually enquired, 'Are you any relation to John Stott?'

'Yes, that's my name.'

'But I mean the other John Stott, the Christian apologist who recently died.'

'Well,' John Stott replied, feeling his way, 'I suppose you might describe me as a Christian apologist, but, as you can see, I haven't died yet.'

'There must be some mistake,' she persisted. 'I'm a graduate of Wheaton College, where I heard John Stott speak several times, but I understand he is dead ...'

Only with some difficulty, and to her increasing embarrassment, was John Stott able to set the record straight![19]

So his travels continued and multiplied. In this decade of the 1970s he was, for example, regularly in America; three times in Australia; and in Asia almost every year. His itineraries included visits to Japan, Hong Kong, Manila, Singapore, Thailand, Burma, India, Pakistan and Nepal, sometimes for the third or fourth time. In the Middle East he was in Egypt, Iran and Lebanon. He was in Nairobi in 1973 for a mission in the university: and again for conferences in 1975 and 1976. He visited Tanzania and Uganda and spent a month in the autumn of 1977 in the five English-speaking countries of West Africa. Notably, during the 1970s, he broke new ground in two visits to Latin America, and four to the Arctic.

2

Throughout these years John Stott returned repeatedly to North America. When freed from his responsibilities as Rector he would often make two or even three visits in a single year. This was partly in response to invitations: but there were specific reasons which drew him back. First, according to comments made to him, the Americans particularly valued his style of biblical exposition and preaching, as introducing a new model of such ministry. His triennial visits to the IVCF Urbana Missionary Convention would be a good example. Next, it was clear that he had a particular ministry to an emerging (or re-emerging) evangelical witness in the Episcopal Church, and to a small but growing number of its clergy. To the Fellowship of Witness (the US branch of EFAC) his visits were of strategic importance. Thirdly, he began to find in America a willingness to share the financial responsibilities of the Langham Trust (established there as the Langham Foundation) and then of the Evangelical Literature Trust, in their ministry to leaders and pastors in developing countries.

In the autumn of 1972 he had the opportunity of another more extended stay, in order to spend a term as a guest member of the Faculty at Trinity Evangelical Divinity School in Deerfield, Illinois. It was here that he had received his Honorary DD eighteen months before, which gave him a certain sense of belonging: and he was to return to the college almost annually over the next twenty-five years. His friend David Wells, a member of the Faculty at Trinity, had been urging him to spend time there:

> I had argued with John that he should follow Paul's example in combining travelling with settling down in one place, for a period of time, and teaching. I thought, without presuming to know how God would guide others, that the effects of preaching to people once and then moving on could be ephemeral, whereas staying with those same people over a period of time would give opportunity to reinforce, develop and deepen that teaching.[20]

Interestingly, as John Stott noted in his diary, the start of the new academic year prompted *Time* magazine to carry a substantial news item comparing the falling numbers (and rising budget deficits) of the prestigious and old-established liberal seminaries (it cited Union Seminary, New York, as an example: 'the largest interdenominational divinity school in N. America') with the way in which 'obscure outposts of evangelical conservatism are burgeoning'. Trinity Evangelical Divinity School, Deerfield, and other firmly conservative colleges were mentioned by name. *Time* commented, perhaps with more candour than tact:

> While Union, Yale and Chicago have discarded their language requirements for divinity degrees, these Bible-centered seminaries require their students to master exegesis of Scripture from the original Greek and Hebrew. Traditional piety prevails on their campuses, and cutting chapel is at least as reprehensible as cutting classes. By contrast, an uninitiated underclassman at Union recently drew startled stares in a student meeting when he asked, 'Don't we begin with a prayer?'[21]

John Stott wrote in his September newsletter:

> I am officially labelled 'Visiting Professor of Practical Theology and

Biblical Exposition', which is a rather grandiose way of saying that I am to give one course of lectures and seminars in biblical preaching and two or three other courses in books of the New Testament. These lectures are being concentrated mid-week on Tuesdays, Wednesdays and Thursdays (including a Thursday evening course for visitors from outside the college), so that I shall be free each weekend to fulfil other engagements.

Chief among these other engagements were visits to the ten colleges of a recently formed coalition, the Christian College Consortium, designed to increase the influence of Christian higher education on church and society by enabling its members to speak with a united voice and to co-operate together.[22] In addition, certain weekends were allocated to IVCF student leadership conferences, or to the Fellowship of Witness on behalf of EFAC. John Stott added, 'I am asking to have each Monday off for a birdwatching expedition!'

David Wells was at the airport to welcome John Stott and drove him to the college. He was given an apartment in a small block for married students on the edge of the 25-acre campus, between playing fields and the lake. From his window he could look out on a field and watch the Killdeers, members of the plover family with a noisy and insistent alarm call. By the end of the week he had given the first of his public lecture series on the Sermon on the Mount, the lecture hall packed out and latecomers standing at the back. He also began to invite some of his students, a dozen at a time, to 'coffee and cookies' in his apartment, and they soon reciprocated:

> The Trinity students are being very kind and hospitable, and I find I'm having to turn down numerous invitations to meals. But last Wednesday I went with Dave and Jane Wells to a very pleasant dinner party with three particularly fine married students, which made a group of nine or ten of us. The three students are close friends. Two of them (Paul Cowan and Gene Bourland) are my 'assistants', appointed to keep my class attendance register, get library books for me, grade exam papers on my behalf and help in any other way. Gene is adding to his assignments the task of getting me to and from O'Hare airport every weekend. All three of these students have spent two or three years in Britain …[23]

Half-way through the quarter the college had its annual 'Overseas Missions Institute' with special lectures and forums. John Stott preached through the week in morning chapel to the whole college, faculty as well as students, using as a basis the talks on 'The Great Commission' which he had given at the Berlin World Congress on Evangelism six years before. The following week saw President Nixon elected for a second term. John Stott watched TV until nearly 1.00am: not late enough to hear George McGovern concede defeat but enough to know the outcome. In spite of the huge majority, he noted in his diary, 'a big public scandal is expected when the allegations of Republican corruption are heard in court'.[24]

Life on campus, interspersed with travels on behalf of the Consortium, and long weekends away for IVCF or the Fellowship of Witness, continued at a demanding pace. It was not long before he began to suffer from blinding headaches – so much so that there was even talk of a brain tumour. In the end the cause was traced to the dry heat of the apartment and, with further ventilation (and, perhaps, acclimatization to his new role), the scare was over.[25] However, by Thanksgiving (23 November) he had largely exhausted his advance preparation for lectures, and was needing time to study. Thanksgiving itself was a free weekend with the Trinity campus half-empty:

> All lectures are cancelled, and a majority of students has gone home for the whole weekend to consume turkey and pumpkin pie according to long tradition. Several kind folk have invited me to 'spend Thanksgiving' with them, but I've firmly declined! It seems to be my only wholly free day; so I've barricaded myself into my apartment (like 'sporting my oak' at Trinity Cambridge!), in order to do some rather urgent reading and writing.[26]

A week later, with the end of term in sight, he was writing at his desk after the evening lecture when he heard carol-singers outside his window. Soon they were hammering on his door. When he asked them in, he noticed that several were carrying identical parcels (they looked as if they might be boxes of chocolates) in brightly coloured Christmas wrappings. There were eight parcels, all for him ('I was speechless with astonishment and gratitude'), which turned out to be not 'candy', but the eight volumes of Gerhard Kittel's *Theological Dictionary of the New Testament*, a standard work. It was a parting gift and 'Thank you' from the students of his different courses.[27] John Stott in turn presented the college with a pair of white fantail pigeons, to encourage the members (so he told them) 'in the gentle art of birdwatching'; and to be 'a reminder of the Holy Spirit whose power alone can enable Christian life and ministry'.

Many Visiting Professors with four lecture courses and a pastoral heart towards their students would have found their time fully occupied. But during the few months John Stott was at Trinity he managed ten visits to the campuses of the Christian College Consortium, from Westmont in

California to Gordon in Massachusetts (though most of the ten were a good deal nearer to his base). A typical weekend might involve a lengthy flight, perhaps with a change of planes, then his major lecture 'Your Mind Matters', followed by two or three (sometimes five or six) classes, question-and-answer sessions, or meetings with faculty or students. There would be preaching engagements on the Sunday; sometimes a conference for pastors or students; and one weekend a television address for the Chicago Sunday Evening Club: he spoke on 'The Humility of a Little Child' and had a baby brought to the studio!²⁸ In all his travels, wherever possible, an hour would be snatched in the indefatigable pursuit of birds by binoculars and camera.

The lecture 'Your Mind Matters' was based on the Presidential Address John Stott gave in 1972 for the IVF, published in the UK a month before he left for his term at Trinity.²⁹ It is a powerful thesis against what he described as 'the malady of anti-intellectualism', whether from a distorted emphasis on ritual, on radical social action, or on Pentecostal experience: activities which easily became 'escape routes by which to avoid our God-given responsibility to use our minds Christianly'.³⁰ He wrote in his personal newsletter,

> I hope I see the dangers of the opposite extreme of a dry and barren intellectualism. But I'm increasingly convinced that the contemporary craze for denigrating the mind and enthroning experience is in reality a subtle mode of 'worldliness' (because it is taken over from secular existentialism), and that God intends *truth* (His own revealed truth) to be the criterion of experience and to set our hearts on fire.³¹

In addition to these ten college visits, five weekends were given to student leadership conferences for IVCF, four in the States and the last in Toronto, which proved to be the busiest. He flew in on the Friday evening when, as his diary recounts,

> ... the Canadian IVCF had their annual 'banquet' at a Holiday Inn ... 825 people sat down to dinner! I sat next to Claude Simmons on the one hand (chairman of their Board) and to Samuel Escobar on the other (the South American recently appointed as their General Secretary) with his charming wife Lilly. Samuel told me that the Spanish translation of *Basic Christianity* had received favourable reviews in three Roman Catholic newspapers! The service of dinner was a bit slow, owing to the huge numbers, and I wasn't put on to speak till about 9.45pm!³²

Saturday began with a breakfast meeting for over 100 pastors, followed by a 'teach-in' for most of the rest of the day attended by about a thousand students: 'We romped through the Sermon on the Mount in three sessions.' Sunday saw John Stott preaching in Knox Presbyterian Church, followed by a buffet lunch with eighty IVCF staff, and concluding with an evangelistic service; but over supper with Gordon and Ann Johnson before the evening service (Gordon, an ophthalmologist, was the son of Douglas Johnson, first General Secretary of the IVF), plans began to be laid for a long-awaited trip to the Arctic during the bird breeding season. Monday was honoured as a day off, visiting friends, birdwatching on the shores of Lake Ontario and walking in snow-covered woodlands, before catching the plane back to Chicago and another week's classes and lectures at Trinity.

Talking with David Wells just before the quarter ended, John Stott summed up his feelings about this taste of college life. Much as he had enjoyed it, and in spite of much kindness and signs that his lectures and classes had been appreciated, he was in no doubt that his calling was not to be an academic lecturer but what he called 'a more popular expositor'.[33] He would continue to return regularly to Deerfield, sure of a very warm welcome; but when in due course invitations came to him to join the faculties – either full-time or part-time – at Fuller Theological Seminary or Regent College, Vancouver, or once again at Trinity, his first-hand experience as Visiting Professor led him to decline.

3

That brief Sunday evening discussion in Toronto about a visit to the Arctic was soon to bear fruit. Gordon Johnson busied himself in making preparations, so that John Stott was able to write in his first newsletter of 1973 that following an extensive visit to Asia in May he hoped to cross the Pacific to Canada:

A ministers' conference is planned in Toronto, during the third week of June. Attentive readers will immediately observe that this brings us to the height of the bird breeding season! So several Canadian friends and I are planning to fulfil a (for me, at least) life-long ambition to visit the Arctic tundra during the last week of June and the first of July. It may still prove too expensive, but we live in hopes of seeing and photographing Snow Geese, Snow Buntings, Snowy Owls and other fabulous species in their nesting haunts![34]

John Stott flew from Singapore via Tokyo to Vancouver, to spend a weekend at Regent College before crossing the Rockies and the Great

Lakes to Toronto. There the following morning he was taken by his host, Desmond Hunt, Rector of the Church of the Messiah,

> ... to a marvellous store called 'Thriftys' which sells camping and holiday equipment of every conceivable kind. My main purchase was a pair of cat-tread waterproof leather ankle boots, plus socks, shirt, gloves, mosquito helmet, insect repellent, and dark glasses – not to mention a little 'tele-extender' which effectively doubles the length of any telephoto lens, and an ample supply of film.[35]

Before the expedition could start, John Stott fitted into his programme a three-day clergy conference at the request of the Bishop of Toronto, an informal meeting with some leading members of the Canadian Anglican Evangelical Fellowship (the Canadian group member of EFAC), and a breakfast for ministers. With Gordon Johnson, he then flew north to spend a few days at Churchill on the western shore of the vast Hudson Bay. In spite of poor weather conditions with a thick sea-mist blown off the bay, John Stott recorded in his diary more than fifty bird sightings: 'we left the sub-Arctic well satisfied'.

But the holiday was only beginning: ahead lay the Arctic proper. Their destination was Bathurst Inlet on the northern shore of Canada's North West Territory just inside the Arctic Circle. Here lay Bathurst Inlet Lodge, originally one of the Hudson Bay Company's trading posts and now owned and run by Glenn Warner, a former member of the Royal Canadian Mounted Police, as a lodge for holiday-makers, anglers, birdwatchers and naturalists.[36] John Stott and Gordon Johnson were joined *en route* by Alex Wright, a young British doctor, and by Gordon's wife Ann with their nine-month-old baby David. The last leg of their flight north was from Yellowknife in a twin-propellor DC3, carrying not only the travellers and their luggage, but their food and supplies for the week. John Stott described the flight in his diary:

> It was a clear afternoon, and we found it fascinating to fly over ground which began as thick forest interspersed with innumerable little lakes and gradually gave place to treeless tundra and partially frozen lakes. We landed smoothly on the Lodge's newly built private airstrip. They'd driven a huge bulldozer down 300 miles over the ice from Cambridge Bay, a journey which at 3mph day and night took four days or more![37]

From the airstrip to the Lodge was an hour's journey, first by snowmobile over sand, swamp and thicket to the Burnside River and then by boat. The Lodge itself was part of a small Inuit community, twenty or twenty-five in number including children, the men acting as guides and some of the women staffing the Lodge. The nearest other settlement was 40 miles away, the diary notes, and the nearest shop 75 miles! The entry for 28 June continues:

> We arrived on a beautiful afternoon, with the sun shimmering on the surrounding mountains and the sea. So we had no sooner unpacked and had dinner than the Johnsons, Alex and I set out for a walk along the shore. We were immediately entranced by the Arctic fauna and flora. The sand dunes above the high-water mark were carpeted with Arctic lupins, white and purple saxifrage, moss campion, pale yellow poppies and Indian paintbrushes. It was breathtakingly beautiful. And in among the flowers and dwarf willow undergrowth were flitting tiny Baird's Sandpipers (6" long, not much bigger than a sparrow), Lapland Buntings, Whitecrowned Sparrows and Horned Larks. We found two or three nests without difficulty, and when we'd climbed to the top of the nearest crag we put a couple of Peregrines up from their nest on a precipitous ledge.

The next two days were spent in expeditions, on foot and by boat up the rivers, seeing something of the country and in search of birds. They were able to photograph the Peregrine Falcon, and the (much rarer) Arctic species, the Gyr Falcon, both of which they managed to find nesting.

Sunday was Canada's 'Dominion Day'. John Stott offered to conduct a service, which was arranged for that evening, with the whole Inuit community invited – all Anglicans, though they had not been visited by an Anglican minister since April the year before. It was to be a Communion service, and to include the baptism of the two newest Inuit babies, one of them the child of Joseph and Mary!

> Virtually the whole Bathurst Inlet community gathered, fifteen guests, five staff and about twenty-three Eskimos of all ages. We met in the lounge, having arranged the chairs in a circle, with the children sitting on the floor, and put the Table as central as possible. Another Mary, the sixty-five year old matriarch of the Eskimos, had baked a small round loaf of 'Bannock', a type of Eskimo bread, and the most suitable wine from the bar was a pink sparkling 'Arctic wine', which bubbled and fizzed like Champagne when I poured it from the bottle into the two wine glasses we used as chalices. The font was a small stainless steel dish.
>
> During the afternoon I'd been through the Eskimo hymn-book with John (Mary's husband), and together we'd chosen three well-known hymns which both Eskimos and others would know, and

Trish had carboned copies in English. We began with 'All Things Bright and Beautiful' whose references to 'each little flower that opens, each little bird that sings' seemed particularly appropriate. Next Glenn read the Old Testament lesson from Jeremiah 8 about bird migration. The New Testament lesson was Jesus' teaching about 'the birds of the air' and 'the flowers of the field' from the Sermon on the Mount. John read it first in Eskimo, and Shirley the anaesthetist [a fellow guest at the Lodge] went on to read it in English, after which I spent a few minutes drawing out the lessons which birds can teach us – repentance (migrants go, but always come back) and faith ('if your Heavenly Father feeds them, can you not trust Him to feed you?'). My words of wisdom were somewhat interrupted by baby Connie who started crying, then howling, then screaming! I fear the seed fell by the wayside! When we began the Baptism, Connie's mother was feverishly trying to pacify her infant; out of the corner of my eye I could see her being stripped garment by garment, so that I was eventually handed a half-clad bare-bottomed baby! Each child had both English and Eskimo names, and by dint of some previous practice I think and hope I got them right.[38]

Earlier in the day John Stott had talked with the parents of both babies – in one case, with an older son of the family interpreting – to try to see that they grasped the meaning of Christian baptism; and he made a note to write to the Chaplain at Coppermine, 200 miles west, to ask him to give retrospective consent, and to register the baptisms.

When planning this visit, John Stott had been in touch with Sir Peter Scott, who had made an expedition to the Perry River (200 miles east of Bathurst Inlet) in 1949.[39] He had also approached the Canadian Wildlife Service in Ottawa, which gave John Stott permission for a visit by charter plane to what had now become a bird reserve. This expedition proved the highlight of their visit. The plane, a single-engine Cessna on floats, took them the 250 miles in about two hours, flying low enough for magnificent views of the uninhabited landscape below,

> ... an intricate network of lakes and rivers whose colours ranged from light green through beige and pink to dark brown, due presumably to chemical deposits in the rocks. Nor was it difficult to plot our course on the map. As we approached our destination between the Perry and Simpson rivers, our excitement was quickened by the sight of small compact parties of four to ten white birds on several lakes, which we felt certain were the Geese we'd come to search for.[40]

These were Ross's Geese in particular (the rarest of the North American geese), together with Lesser Snow and Blue Geese. Having landed on a grassy island in Lake Karak, the party were able to photograph them at close quarters, since those with goslings newly hatched remained on their nests even when approached close-to. They spent the afternoon completing the circuit of the southern shores of the island, until, as they approached the very tip, they noticed how

> ... at the summit of the rocks, a cairn had been built. I felt sure it would have contained a message, and sure enough inside the cairn I found an old rusty tin can containing an unspoiled folded piece of paper written by John Ryder in July 1965, announcing his discovery of the lake and naming it 'Karak'. I took the tin and paper to the others, and we wrote a message on the reverse side describing our expedition and then returned it to its tin and cairn. It was rather exciting to think that we were probably only the second group of white people ever to visit the island, and that nobody had set foot on it for the past eight years![41]

A day or two later was American Independence Day, July 4. Since there were Americans in the party, John Stott was again asked to lead a service of worship as he had done on Dominion Day. At the conclusion he found himself appointed 'Honorary Chaplain to the Bathurst Inlet Lodge', and being urged to return the following year as a guest. He noted in his diary: 'It's a tempting offer, and is not impossible if I accept the invitation to speak at the Japanese congress on Evangelism next June. It's also a generous one ...'

In the event, John Stott did accept the Japanese invitation and the following June found him back at Bathurst Inlet Lodge. Because he was two weeks earlier the sea of the inlet was still entirely frozen, though the Burnside River was beginning to melt, helped by a week of unbroken sunshine. Once again, this time as their appointed 'Chaplain', John Stott gave the community a Sunday evening service, a baptism, a wedding and Holy Communion, all within an hour! The marriage was by no means straightforward:

> The bridegroom was Robert, John's twin, who (incidentally) shot seven of the twelve Caribou that afternoon and thus presented his bride with a fine present on her wedding day! The bride was Martha from Cambridge Bay, about 150 miles north, on Victoria Island ...
> Three legal problems arose. First, Martha was seventeen and therefore still a minor. Her adoptive parents were dead and her legal guardian was her elder sister. She agreed to the marriage, I was

THE
1960s

1. *The spire of All Souls: the church in the modern city. Broadcasting House (home of BBC Sound) is to the right of the spire, surmounted by two radio masts*

2. *A defining moment: Martyn Lloyd-Jones and John Stott at the Second National Assembly of Evangelicals, October 1966 (in the background, Gilbert Kirby, centre, and Morgan Derham, right).*
(Photo: Pat Thomas)

3. *December 1964: The triennial student missionary convention of the InterVarsity Christian Fellowship, USA, held at the University of Illinois, Urbana. This was the first of John Stott's six Urbana visits. He spoke from 2 Corinthians 3 – 6*

5. In an Oxford Street department store Michael Harper talks to staff members, November 1961 (Photo: BIPS)

4. (above) Keswick 1965, official group photograph of Council members and speakers. From the left, top row: Rowland Appleton, Kenneth Prior, Eric Alexander, Douglas Thornton, George Duncan, Philip Hacking, Martin Burch, Herbert Cragg and Alec Motyer. Seated: D. Rudbone Pippett (Hon. Secretary), John Stott, Harding Wood, Alan Redpath, A. T. Houghton (Chairman) and John Caiger (Vice-Chairman), Gen. Wilson-Haffenden ('Haffy') (Hon. Treasurer), Hugh Orr-Ewing and Cecil Bewes. In front: John Tanburn and Glyn Owen

6. John Stott in Australia with Marcus Loane, later Archbishop of Sydney and Primate of Australia (centre), and Jack Dain, Assistant Bishop of Sydney

7. Rectory residents 1965, left to right: George Kinoti, Ted Schroder, Serafín López, David Wells, Margaret Shinn the cook, 'Packie' the housemother, John Dugan the Bursar and John Stott

8. *(top) Imaginative reconstruction: All Souls prepares to extend downwards*

9. *(above) With Charles Colson in the Waldegrave Hall under All Souls Church. He delivered two of the 1979 London Lectures on 'Crime and the Responsible Community'*

10. *The IVCF Student Missionary Convention at the University of Illinois, Urbana, 1970*

11. A wartime photograph of Joy, the younger of John Stott's sisters, in ATS uniform

12. Michael and Myrtle Baughen at All Souls (Vicar 1970–75, Rector 1975–82). He became Bishop of Chester in 1982

13. Greeting students at the Urbana Missionary Convention, 1976

THE
1970s

14. *The Lausanne Executive Committee at Springfield, Missouri (September 1978). Left to right: Armin Hoppler, John Stott, Leighton Ford (Chairman), Thomas Zimmerman and Peter Wagner*

15. *John Stott with Nishi tribespeople at the Evangelical Fellowship of India's conference at Gauhati, Assam, January 1975*

16. *Addressing NEAC II, Nottingham 1977*
(Photo: K. W. Coates)

17. *John Stott in the 1970s in his mews flat*

18. *With some of the leaders of NEAC '77 at the University of Nottingham, working towards the draft statement* (Photo: K. W. Coates)

19. The Doctors' service at All Souls, November 1982. Left to right: John Stott; Richard Chartres (Archbishop's Chaplain); the Archbishop of Canterbury, Robert Runcie; Andrew Cornes; June Morgan

20. With Frank Entwistle, Publishing Director of Inter-Varsity Press, at the launch of The Cross of Christ, *October 1986* (Photo: Keith Ellis Collection)

assured, but no written consent had been obtained. Secondly, I held
no licence from the Bishop of the Arctic to officiate at weddings:
would a marriage ceremony performed by me be legally valid?
Thirdly, even if the first two problems could be overcome, the
nearest Anglican marriage registers were hundreds of miles away and
it was certain I couldn't complete or sign one! Yet Robert and
Martha wanted to be officially married, and to have the blessing of a
church service, and it seemed heartless to allow legal problems to
deny them these things owing to the niceties of the law! It was some
comfort to me that Glenn was a former member of the RCMP and
was therefore used to the problems which Eskimos present to
lawyers! In the end I agreed to go ahead with the service, at the same
time warning them that we might later discover (when I reported
the details to the nearest Anglican clergyman) that they were still
not legally married ...[42]

The marriage was duly performed, the bride wearing a coronet of pink
Arctic rhododendrons!

Later in the week the Hon. Chaplain secured permission to visit some
Inuit homes, often with the children (who learned English at school) as
interpreters; the homes themselves were igloos, but green, government-
issue, prefabricated in fibre-glass. He found his hosts very shy, but was
able to say a prayer with them, and rather haltingly to join together in the
Lord's Prayer, he in English and they in their own tongue:

> How much actual communication went on I don't know (we sang
> at Communion from the Eskimo hymnbook 'The Lord's my
> Shepherd' – a concept unintelligible to all but those who've seen
> pictures of sheep and shepherd!), but all are Anglicans and have
> Eskimo Prayer Books if not Bibles, so that they are not without
> some background Christian knowledge. Indeed, it seems distinctly
> odd that they've had only *one* worship-service in twelve months
> (except that the whole community went sixty miles by dog team and
> sled to Bay Chimo to attend an Easter Service); so I've suggested to
> Glenn that *he* should lead a five-minute time of worship *every*
> Sunday morning ... I've left him some suggested Bible passages and
> sample prayers, and have ordered him a book of modern prayers
> plus seven copies of *Good News for Modern Man* (the New
> Testament in 'common language') for those Eskimos who can read
> English.[43]

Once again, much of each day was given to expeditions in search of
birds: the diary mentions Rock and Willow Ptarmigan, Peregrine Falcon

and Arctic Gyr Falcon, a variety of Ducks, Gulls and Waders, as well as three species of Loon: Yellow-billed, Arctic and Red-throated. On higher ground they discovered a carpet of Arctic flowers: 'rhododendron lapponicum, dryas (a white ground rose, the floral emblem of the North West Territories), white Arctic bell heather, Alpine azaleas with tiny pink flowers, and Arctic lupins. Paradise!' It was a brief-lived paradise, only a single week: but when the time came to say goodbye, the Hon. Chaplain left his boots at the Lodge, against a further visit.

Nor was this misplaced confidence: before the end of the decade John Stott paid two further visits, in 1976 and again in 1979. The first of these saw a tragic death among the Inuit community. It was towards the end of his stay. John Stott and a small expedition had made their way to the lake above the Lodge. There some stayed to fish, but he and others set off to walk upstream to a spectacular gorge and waterfall:

> The walk back, still in hot sunshine though now with a cool breeze, was relaxed and invigorating. We reached the lake in good spirits with a tranquil mind. So we were totally unprepared for the tragic news which greeted us: 'Jacob has drowned'.[44]

Jacob Avadluk was a nineteen-year-old Eskimo boy, whose sister and half-sister were both permanent members of the Inuit community at Bathurst Inlet.

> Gradually the pieces of the story were fitted together – Jacob, Sammy, Ikey and Allan, Eskimo boys of nineteen, seventeen, twelve and ten respectively – had all gone swimming off the main landing stage at the Lodge. They'd decided to swim across to the sandbar only about fifty yards ahead, when halfway over Jacob, though physically fit and a strong swimmer, had suddenly disappeared; he surfaced again once and called for help, but then was not seen again … Everybody was dumb with grief.

When the news had reached the Lodge, Glenn Warner had summoned the nearest Royal Canadian Mounted Policeman, who had flown in from Cambridge Bay. They set to work to find the body, first dragging with an improvised grapnel, and then by diving in flippers and a mask. But night was approaching, the weather turned against them, and they had to give up:

> We went to bed shocked and desolate. My own responsibility during the evening had been to visit Lena, Jacob's half-sister, who was disconsolate, sobbing about the nightmares of foreboding

which one of the relatives had had all week, and affirming she could hear Jacob 'howling'.

On Sunday morning the search began again in earnest. Both boats started dragging again.

The policeman and, while he rested, the other men at the Lodge, continued to dive in the icy (but now calm) water:

So now my turn came. Being considerably older and not in good training, I confess that I was fearful. And I'd never worn underwater goggles before, which cover eyes and mouth. But my body soon got used to the cold water after diving in, and I was glad Dr Gibson insisted on staying near in a boat equipped with a lifebelt. When I first dived down, I wondered if I'd ever reach the bottom. The water must have been twelve to fifteen feet deep, and when I did touch bottom, though agreeably surprised that I could see about six feet in each direction, I wasn't prepared for the considerable pressure on my head and ears at that depth. I only seemed to have energy for several strokes, taking me perhaps ten or twelve feet along the bottom before having to push myself hard up to the surface again. I covered the whole distance between the two markers without finding the body, and by then after six or eight dives I was too out of breath to continue. So I came out and resumed my other role of seeking to comfort the sad and distraught.

At last, late in the afternoon, the body was safely recovered. The doctor briefly examined it, and the RCMP stowed it in a canvas body-bag.

The relatives decided that the burial should take place in the graveyard above the Lodge (begun in the 40s when a 'flu epidemic claimed fifteen victims), and several men went to dig the grave. We had planned a Baptism and Communion Service that night, so that it was particularly sad to have to transform this into a funeral. We gathered at about 8.30pm in one of the Eskimo houses, and Henry Kamayok agreed to interpret for me, specially for the two or three older women who speak almost no English. Henry himself spoke about Jacob as a good boy and a good hunter, and I tried to comfort the stricken community with the gospel of God's love, Christ's defeat of death and the hope of new life and resurrection.

Only the men went on to the graveside, about eight pallbearers carrying Jacob's body, still in the bag for a coffin, laid upon a ladder for a stretcher.

I read words from 1 Corinthians 15 after the body was lowered into the grave, and the dozen or so of us who stood round in the twilight of an Arctic evening reflected on life's tragedies in silence before the Eskimo men picked up the spades and shovelled back the earth to fill in the grave.

On Monday morning John Stott conducted a 'Sunday' service for the community, postponed from the previous day. It was held in the igloo-type house of the senior Inuit and again included the blessing of a marriage, a baptism, and Holy Communion with his little flock.

By the time of John Stott's third visit, in July 1979, he was even more determined to find and photograph the Snowy Owl; but in spite of a helicopter flight to the remote Arctic wilderness of the Kent peninsula (to a locality which usually supported a pair or two of Snowy Owls) they were disappointed. However, there was pastoral work to be done:

> During my visits to the Eskimo homes I'd discovered that since my last stay at Bathurst Inlet Lodge three years ago no clergyman had come to see the Inuit community … So here was a marriage to be blessed and two baptisms to be performed, in addition to the Communion Service which the older Eskimos had requested. The Inuit asked for all three services to be held privately, for themselves, without the presence of the white visitors … The Service was held in the Warners' living room, and the whole Inuit community crowded into it, the elders seated, the children on the floor, and the rest standing at the back round the door.[45]

Here John Stott as their Chaplain performed a marriage and two baptisms, followed by a simple service of Holy Communion together.

In the last day or two of his holiday John Stott made further fruitless enquiries and searches for the Snowy Owl. It appeared that there was a shortage of lemmings that year (their staple diet) and so 'no lemmings, no Snowy Owls'. Passing through Yellowknife on his journey home he was able to meet Jack Sperry, the Bishop of the Arctic, over breakfast:

> We talked about Bathurst Inlet Lodge, to which, I'm glad to say, the Warners have invited him to come for a week next summer. He'll then be able not only to minister to the Inuit community at that time, but also to size up the situation in order in future to ensure a more regular ministry for these isolated people. He tentatively invited me one day to teach in their small theological college on the northern shores of Baffin Island in the N.E. Arctic, which I tentatively accepted, provided that my visit could coincide with the bird breeding season![46]

The quest for the Snowy Owl was by no means over.

4

John Stott's 1974 visit to Latin America was at the invitation of the Comunidad Internacional de Estudiantes Evangélicos, the South American branch of IFES. In the strange mix of sometimes primitive Roman Catholicism, the missions (including Anglicans) and the growth of Pentecostalism, he valued the balanced concern that IFES brought to three contemporary needs: a rational and relevant faith; a commitment (in the face of poverty and injustice) to social action; and a longing to reform and renew the churches.[47] So John Stott found himself at Chicago Airport early in January 1974, amid three or four inches of newly fallen snow, leaving behind his overcoat, scarf and gloves – 'and my "Davy Crockett" fur hat' – in the care of his American hosts, as he embarked for Mexico City. His fourth Urbana Conference was safely behind him. He had been pleased to find more student participation on the platform ('though in my view still not enough'). This time his main assignments had been an address on 'The Authority of the Bible'[48] and to preach at the closing Holy Communion service.

His work in Mexico City began with three evening public lectures in a downtown Baptist Church, with his friend Dr René Padilla (IFES Associate General Secretary for Latin America) as translator. John Stott was amused to see in the publicity announcement a reference to the fact that he was from England and therefore had an English concept of time-keeping. At the hour he was due to begin, the church was still packed with wedding guests and the wedding was in full swing! His 7.30 lecture actually started at 8.30: 'nobody thought of explaining, apologizing or even referring to it!'[49]

From Mexico City John Stott and René Padilla moved on to Lima, Peru; once again to speak to Christian leaders and pastors, this time in a short series on expository preaching. They managed a day out together, driving high into the foothills of the Andes, 'with simply magnificent views of a whole family of five Andean Condors ... a huge mountain vulture with a ten-foot wing span ... it was unforgettable'.

Their next location was Santiago, Chile: once again there was a series of public lectures in the evening and often meetings with students during the day. At one of these, which he was to address on 'The Place of the Mind in the Christian Life', he was surprised and delighted to be presented ('*before* I started speaking') with the two-volume standard work on Chilean birds ('in English! ...').

They lunched one day between meetings as guests of the British Ambassador, a Roman Catholic, their talk alternating between discussion on 'what is a Christian', and an attempt to explain the present political situation of the country, ruled by its military junta. John Stott noted in his diary how

> ... soldiers are everywhere. They stand in groups at street corners, most of them apparently conscripts of seventeen or eighteen, with loaded guns or machine-guns. The curfew was extended from 11pm to midnight just before I arrived, but is rigidly enforced. Driving to the airport, we were confronted by an armed guard with his weapon at the ready, standing in the middle of the road! He looked very menacing until he was given a signal to let us pass.
>
> The airline officials told us, when we checked in, that we were not allowed to take *any* hand luggage with us into the aircraft. They then added insult to injury by insisting on weighing briefcases, cameras and all, and telling us we were well overweight and must pay excess. All our protests were of no avail until René Padilla naughtily (and without my knowledge) said that one of the Queen's Chaplains would leave with a poor impression of Chile: – and the demand for excess payment was dropped![50]

As the tour continued, his position as Queen's Chaplain became an embarrassment, so widely was it misunderstood. Because of it, the press in Southern Chile carried news of his visit in front-page headlines; and many of those he met wanted to consult him, in the light of this official position, about the political situation through European eyes.

It was in Southern Chile that he went with Colin Bazley, then the young assistant bishop, and three Baptist pastors to visit Temuco prison:

> They have been paying regular visits there twice a week and distributing New Testaments. As a result of the reading and the preaching appreciable numbers of these men have been converted to Christ. Of the first roundups of political prisoners after the coup on September 11, many suspects have been sent home. Some ninety remain, all members of the MIR ('Movement of the Revolutionary Left') – the extreme Marxist party – and of these about sixty gathered in a circle in the prison yard when we arrived. One of the Baptist pastors climbed onto some wooden steps and led the men in singing hymns and choruses, which they knew by heart. Then one of the prisoners led in prayer. Next I was asked to bring a brief greeting, which René translated. I spoke of the revolution of Jesus, changing persons as well as structures, a revolution of peace (not violence), of love (not hate). Then René preached on the love of God. The men listened attentively. I looked round at their faces.

Perhaps twenty or thirty were students. At least one was a university professor. It was hard to believe they had been (many still were) hard-line communists, and that most had also been interrogated under torture ...'[51]

The final country of this first Latin American visit was Argentina. Here again his theme was often 'Towards Christian Maturity', to congregations of three or four hundred at a time. As well as the familiar public meetings and gatherings for pastors and IFES supporters, he was able to spend six days at the National Student Camp, where he spoke morning and evening but could relax during a long siesta, and for some of the rest of the day. Later, driving to Cordoba Airport, he found himself talking with one of the IFES staff who had pioneered the work in Argentina. He told John Stott how he had known Che Guevara as a boy of twelve but had found no opportunity to speak to him of Christ. John Stott speculated sadly in his diary 'how history might have been different if Che had become for young radicals the world over a Christian rather than a Marxist hero!'[52]

Three years later he returned for a longer stay in Latin America, travelling again with Dr René Padilla, this time visiting seven countries: Mexico, Guatemala and Costa Rica in Central America; and Colombia, Ecuador, Peru and Argentina in the South. In four of these he spoke at pastors' conferences on 'Preaching in the Modern World', again combining this with public meetings and ministry to students. Both among students and pastors, John Stott reported, he found 'a considerable disenchantment'

> ... among students with the institutional churches; and among pastors with the training (or comparative lack of it) many had received. It was correspondingly encouraging to sense a longing to learn, to be instruments of change in the church and the community, and to find biblical solutions to Latin America's colossal problems ... There is no doubt that Latin Americans consider themselves to be an oppressed continent. Some 150 years ago they achieved their independence of Spanish and Portuguese colonial rule, but now they look for other kinds of liberation – from economic dependence on North America, from the oppressive regimes of rightwing dictatorships, and from grinding poverty. It is against this background that the so-called 'theology of liberation' has grown up. I do not think we should quarrel with its defined goal of 'liberation' since the God who made (and makes) human beings in his own image is obviously opposed to everything which dehumanizes them. We may quarrel, however, with the dubious

arguments they use to buttress their position; and also with those theologians who are outspoken advocates of violent revolution ...[53]

His itinerary, demanding as it was, provided the opportunity for a week's birdwatching in the famous Galapagos Islands, associated with Charles Darwin's visit in 1833 and his theory of natural selection. It was here that René Padilla began to evince a real enthusiasm for birdwatching, and to be named as 'my most distinguished ornithological convert'. Sadly, John Stott had to begin his holiday on the Galapagos feeling distinctly unwell from food poisoning (and a trifle depressed from an American mission executive who had asked his age at supper, and hazarded a guess that he must be 'pushing seventy'. In fact he was in his mid-fifties!).[54] They stayed first in the island presbytery of a young and welcoming Roman Catholic priest, fed and cared for by two nuns. With his help, John Stott and René Padilla were able to hire a local boat, the *Cristo Rey*, to take them round some of the islands of the group.[55] After a short voyage they landed on the beach of an idyllic green lagoon and carefully picked their way through a huge colony of sea lions, mostly sleeping:

> As we walked on round the coast I had an orgy of photography –
> bright red crabs on the black basaltic rocks ('Sally Lightfoots' they
> seem to be called), and marine iguanas up to three feet in length,
> black with dark red markings on their back, clambering skilfully up
> the rocks and looking like antediluvian dragons with their sharp
> dorsal comb. And the beautiful endemic Galapagos dove; only five
> inches from beak to tail, with bright blue eye ring and red legs and
> feet, posed nicely for its photograph.[56]

Besides iguanas, they saw the giant tortoises (*galápagos* in Spanish) from which the islands take their name, and innumerable birds Some of these, as Charles Darwin noted, were endemic species, found nowhere else in the world,[57] including the thirteen varieties of Finch which bear his name:

> But we revelled specially in the Waved Albatrosses (whose one and
> only breeding ground in the world is Española island), the Frigate
> birds (the males displaying their fully distended crimson throat
> pouches) and the Redbilled Tropicbirds (trailing behind them their
> pure white and immensely long tail streamers).[58]

It was a welcome break in a long stay.

Looking back, when it was all over, John Stott found himself asking:

So is there any solution to Latin America's problems? I am still convinced that there is more hope in evangelization than in any other single Christian option. We are under the authority of the Lord Jesus who has commissioned us. And nothing is more humanizing than the Gospel. Through it men and women begin to be remade in the image of God. Moreover, the Gospel of God's love supplies the most powerful of all incentives to rescue people from everything that dehumanizes them.[59]

So, in his own mind, he saw the priorities for the South American churches exactly reflecting the characteristics of the newborn church on the day of Pentecost. He had seen for himself how, in Latin America as elsewhere,

> ... the young, with their strong loathing for the inauthentic, quickly detect any dichotomy between the Church and its founder. Jesus has never ceased to attract them. They see him as the radical he was, impatient with the traditions of the elders and the conventions of society, a merciless critic of the religious establishment. They like that. But the Church? Somehow it seems to them to have lost the 'smell' of Christ. So many vote – with their feet. They get out.[60]

But if the church there could regain (as in Acts 2) an authentic contemporary preaching and teaching ministry rooted in Scripture; a warm and caring fellowship; worship that expressed the reality of the living God; and an imaginative, sensitive and compassionate outreach into the community – that would be a different story: as indeed it would be in almost any country one cares to name. These were sobering reflections; but there was time to be playful too. When he was leaving Argentina at the end of his first visit in early 1974, John Stott was asked what he had learned there.

> 'I've learned' (I said) 'three excellent lessons:
>
> (1) to appreciate a long afternoon siesta.
> (2) to renounce that peculiarly English vice called "punctuality".
> (3) to enjoy the liberty of kissing everybody within reach!'
>
> But alas! (I've had to add) I shall have now to unlearn at least the last two lessons, regaining my punctuality and restraining my kisses![61]

SEVEN

World Evangelization: The Lausanne Vision

1

Since the days of the New Testament, Christian leaders have been meeting to confer, often making long journeys to do so. The 1970s saw John Stott travelling to at least seven or eight major conferences, as well as a variety of smaller consultations. In June 1971, for example, he was in Jerusalem for an international evangelical conference on biblical prophecy, and in August at the European Congress on Evangelism in Amsterdam. He was at the Japan Congress on Evangelism in 1974, and in 1975 he attended the World Council of Churches' fifth Assembly in Nairobi: he was there again the following year for the Pan-African Christian Leadership Assembly, PACLA. In 1977 he flew to Venice for the first meeting of ERCDOM, the Evangelical–Roman Catholic Dialogue on Mission, and a year later he attended ALCOE, the Asian Leaders' Conference on Evangelism in Singapore. The inspiration for a number of these gatherings, and more significant than any of them (certainly taking a larger continuing share of John Stott's ministry), was the International Congress on World Evangelization convened in Switzerland at Lausanne in July 1974, which gave its name to the 'Lausanne movement'. It also took him, as part of its follow-up programme, to Mexico City for the first meeting of the Lausanne Continuation Committee in 1975, as well as to Pasadena in the summer of 1977; and to further Lausanne meetings in Bermuda and America the following year.

Each of these has its place in the story of twentieth-century evangelicalism: and because John Stott's involvement was active and significant, this must be seen as a major facet of his many-sided ministry once he began to be free from responsibility for All Souls. Nevertheless, just as the list above is selective rather than exhaustive, this chapter can only touch briefly on a few of the conferences mentioned.

In 1975 John Stott was invited by the Central Committee of the World Council of Churches to attend the Assembly in Nairobi as an 'Adviser', as he had done seven years before at Uppsala. He accepted, though his diary allowed him to be present only for the first week of the seventeen days. The theme chosen was 'Jesus Christ frees and unites'. Preaching in Nairobi Cathedral on the morning before this Fifth Assembly opened, he made the point that there are two freedoms and two unities for which Jesus Christ is concerned:

> On the one hand there is socio-political liberation and the unity of all mankind, for these things are the good will of God the Creator; while on the other there is the redemptive work of Christ who sets his people free from sin and guilt, and unites them in his new community. To muddle these two things (creation and redemption, common grace and saving grace, liberation and salvation, justice and justification) is to plunge oneself into all kinds of confusion.[1]

And 'confusion' remained one of his major impressions of the WCC at work. Though there seemed to be substantially more delegates concerned to uphold historic Christianity (including a number of evangelicals) than had been the case at the previous Assembly, yet what John Stott noted as 'an unprincipled use of Scripture' still prevailed. He felt once again, as he did after Uppsala,

> ... (borrowing somebody's *bon mot* in the House of Commons about an honourable member's use of statistics) that the World Council uses Scripture as a drunk uses a lamp post, namely for support rather than for illumination! Even an otherwise striking presentation of the Parable of the Prodigal Son by the United Bible Societies was marred by their decision to make the real hero of the tale the runaway boy who was bent on liberation![2]

The task of Advisers, each allocated to a work-group of a dozen or so delegates, was to study the Assembly theme (though without making any specific report) and to contribute at the invitation of the chairman. John Stott found himself flung in at the deep end, having arrived late at his work-group after the introductions had taken place:

> As most members were not wearing their name tags I had no idea who they were. The chairman spoke with a slight German accent and was obviously a theologian. I guessed he was one of the Geneva secretariat. Within ten minutes of my arrival I found myself in direct theological debate with him, especially on the relation between evangelism and social action and on the impossibility of talking about 'evangelizing structures'. When it was over, someone came up to me and asked if I knew who the chairman was. No, I replied, I've no idea, – only to be told it was the great Professor Jürgen Moltmann of Tübingen, one of the best-known living German theologians! When I came back to the next session of the group I told him that if I had known who our distinguished chairman was, I would have kept my mouth shut![3]

But when Desmond Tutu, newly elected as Johannesburg's first black Dean ('a colourful personality ... extremely articulate, even loquacious') began to speak, any resolve John Stott might have made to keep silent was quickly set aside. According to the diary, Desmond Tutu said some most outrageous things:

> It was evident he had an antipathy to the apostle Paul. 'Paul was confused', he said; 'he was a prisoner of his own culture and sometimes didn't know what he was talking about. I don't agree with him.' When my blood reached boiling point, I blurted out: 'If I had to choose between the blessed apostle Paul and the Dean of Johannesburg, I would have no difficulty in deciding which to follow!' He didn't seem to mind my outburst, and we became good friends.[4]

Apart from the work-group, John Stott's main task as Adviser was to give a ten-minute response to a plenary address by Mortimer Arias, Bishop of the Evangelical Methodist Church in Bolivia. Time-keeping proved impossible in such an Assembly (in one session devoted to women's issues a High Court judge from Ghana was allocated ten minutes and took forty-five!) and by the time John Stott was due to speak it was 6.00pm and the session was already beginning to overrun. However, the chairman decreed that it should continue into extra time and John Stott was given his ten minutes to a more or less captive (if restless) audience. He used it to list five things which he felt the WCC needed to recover:

> (1) the doctrine of man's lostness (over against the popular universalism of the day), (2) confidence in the truth, relevance and power of the biblical gospel (without which evangelism is impossible), (3) the uniqueness of Jesus Christ (over against all syncretism), (4) the urgency of evangelism (alongside the urgent demands of social justice) and (5) a personal experience of Jesus Christ (without which we cannot introduce others to him).[5]

As may be imagined, it was not a wholly popular analysis. Canon David Paton, the veteran ecumenist[6] and, like John Stott, a Chaplain to the Queen, seemed to appreciate his attempt at a balanced approach in difficult circumstances; by contrast, 'at least one African brother came running up to me afterwards, almost livid with rage that I had dared to criticize the WCC in the way that I had done'.[7] Delegates were seated alphabetically, so that John Stott sat next to the distinguished Swedish theologian from Harvard, Dr Krister Stendahl. When John Stott returned to his seat after speaking from the platform Dr Stendahl leaned over to offer his neighbourly comment: 'I did not agree with one word you said!'[8]

The Pan-African Christian Leadership Assembly (PACLA) the following year was also held in Nairobi, meeting in the new Kenyatta Arena, with forty-five of Africa's forty-nine nations represented. It was largely an initiative of Michael Cassidy, Festo Kivengere and other African leaders. The programme included studies of the relation between gospel and culture, and of the racial tensions of the continent (the large South African delegation consisted of some forty blacks, twenty whites, and the remainder coloured and Indian).[9] John Stott had been asked to speak at a side meeting on 'Theological Tension Points in Ecumenical–Evangelical Relationships',[10] though confessing that he found the title 'misleading because you cannot divide evangelicals and ecumenicals'. He shared his 'evangelical apprehensions' about the WCC attitudes to Scripture and to the gospel; with its confusion between mission and evangelism, between salvation and liberation, and between dialogue and syncretism; and then went on to confess that evangelicals had not been sufficiently concerned about the visible disunity of the church, reminding the Assembly that in John 17 Jesus had prayed for the truth, holiness, unity and mission of the church on earth.

It was here in Nairobi that John Stott gave for the first time a series of Bible studies about the place of mission, developed from a sermon preached in All Souls on World Focus Sunday two years before.[11] He repeated these a week or so later in Urbana, and they were republished, in whole or in part, throughout the 1980s. He took as his theme the missionary nature of God himself and of Jesus Christ, amplifying this at Urbana with two further addresses on the missionary nature of the Holy Spirit and of the Christian church.[12] In the same spirit, Michael Cassidy of Africa Enterprise called for 'a new army of evangelizers, taking the gospel to every corner of Africa in this generation'. Dr Billy Graham, the only American speaker at PACLA, felt it to be 'the most significant African conference in this century'.[13] John Stott himself noted his own reflections on the conference in the form of a question: 'PACLA could yet prove to be the beginning of a much better coordinated and more powerful Christian influence in Africa. And who knows what effect this would have on Africa's political, economic and social problems?'[14]

2

In his speech at PACLA, John Stott reflected on the influence of Vatican II, saying he refused to give up the hope that the Roman Catholic Church might be on the way to reformation: 'There is no knowing what this biblical ferment will do to the ancient monolith of the Roman Catholic Church.'[15] In Nairobi the year before he had made friends with Monsignor Basil Meeking of the Secretariat for Promoting Christian Unity at the Vatican. They had spoken together about the 'convergence' to be noted in the three contemporary statements on evangelism: from the WCC, from international evangelicalism in the Lausanne Covenant, and from the Roman Catholics in Pope Paul VI's apostolic exhortation on evangelism, *Evangelii Nuntiandi*, 'Evangelization in the Modern World'.[16] They were joined by an American scholar, David Hubbard, President of Fuller Theological Seminary; and these three together conceived the idea of ERCDOM, an Evangelical–Roman Catholic Dialogue on Mission. It was at first sight an unlikely partnership. But orthodox Roman Catholics were not likely to be much more impressed by the WCC stance on evangelism than were the evangelicals. Though starting from very different views of authority, might there not be a valuable consensus on what lies at the heart of Christian mission? John Stott was under no illusions about the Church of Rome. He stated firmly in 1977 (when Archbishop Donald Coggan had mooted the idea of intercommunion, to be rebuffed by the Pope), 'I do not think I could bring myself to participate in a Roman Catholic mass, even if it were authorized, until the doctrinal stance of the church has been officially reformed.'[17]

But this did not mean that nothing could be gained by talking to one another. Indeed 'the right way forward seems to be that of personal friendship, joint Bible study, and candid dialogue with Roman

Catholics'.[18] So, in due course, by careful negotiation, just such a dialogue was arranged. The Roman Catholic members were selected by the Vatican, through the Secretariat for Promoting Christian Unity, since they were official delegates of the church. In the absence of an evangelical Vatican, John Stott was made responsible for recruiting an international team of evangelical scholars. The composition of both teams changed a little in the course of the seven years and three major meetings which encompassed the life of ERCDOM (1977–84).[19]

For their first meeting in April 1977 the team gathered in a monastery in Venice, and quickly began to appreciate a measure of common prayer together. Their talks were conceived not as a step towards any kind of negotiation on church unity, but as a search for common ground and better understanding. In the Introduction to the Report the editors spoke of how

> ... it was a demanding experience as well as a rewarding one. It was marked by a will to speak the truth, plainly, without equivocation, and in love. Neither compromise nor the quest for lowest common denominators had a place; a patient search for truth and a respect for each other's integrity did.[20]

In one sense the origin of ERCDOM owed something to ARCIC, the Anglican–Roman Catholic International Commission. Throughout the 1970s this official Commission of the two Communions had been at work, 'in fulfilment of a joint decision by Pope Paul VI and Archbishop Michael Ramsey, expressed in a Common Declaration during their meeting in Rome in March 1966'.[21] Their method was to proceed by way of 'agreed statements', and John Stott had firmly criticized their *Agreed Statement on the Eucharist* in 1972.[22] He sensed, however, that a better understanding would be more likely in a less structured and official gathering: and one in which all the members of each side of the dialogue spoke from their own common basis of faith (in the one case, an evangelical understanding of the authority of Scripture) rather than from the whole breadth of international Anglicanism.

To many, if not most, of those who gathered in Venice, this 'dialogue' was breaking new ground: to some of the Roman Catholic participants it was a wholly novel experience. Some might have had almost no previous acquaintance with mainstream evangelicalism. John Stott was amused to watch their reactions as the dialogue progressed:

> It was fairly evident that they regarded us as a cult, and had thought of us previously as being not very different from Jehovah's Witnesses and Mormons. I remember the delightful Professor from a

seminary in Paris who had written a book on Christology, reading his own paper on the Divine-Human Natures of Jesus in the one Person, and how delighted we were with it. When we said how entirely we agreed with it, his jaw dropped open and he was utterly astonished to discover that we were Chalcedonian Christians.[23]

But there were further discoveries in store. John Stott recalled his surprise in discovering how much common ground there was between the two sides:

> I remember in our section on 'The Church' how much we were able to affirm together: namely, that the church is part of the gospel and the agent of the gospel and the product of the gospel; and even how much we could affirm that baptism must never be isolated from its context of conversion, repentance and faith. They even went so far as to say that they didn't really believe in an *ex opere operato* view of baptism.[24]

The further meetings in Cambridge (March 1982) and in Landévennec, France (April 1984), and the published Report of ERCDOM, belong to the next decade and are recounted in chapter 9.

3

Among this variety of conferences and discussions it is already evident that the Lausanne Congress of 1974 must have pride of place; and that the fruits of Lausanne could already be seen in John Stott's thinking at the WCC Assembly later the same year, at PACLA and in ERCDOM.

The Lausanne Congress began as a child of the Billy Graham Evangelistic Association. The idea for a vast international assembly on the theme of evangelization was entrusted to an international planning committee drawn from sixteen nations, under the Executive Chairmanship of Bishop Jack Dain of Australia (Dr Graham himself being Honorary Chairman).[25] It was held in Lausanne, Switzerland, on the northern shore of Lake Geneva where the Palais de Beaulieu conference centre could provide an auditorium for 4,000, with the necessary facilities for simultaneous translation, and space for innumerable workshops and seminars. *Time* magazine described it as 'possibly the widest ranging meeting of Christians ever held'.[26]

The Congress (officially, the International Congress on World Evangelization, ICWE) opened on 16 July 1974 with some 2,500 members from 150 countries (though missing the USSR and mainland China), some 1,300 other participants such as observers, consultants or guests, and several hundred journalists.[27] As with the planning committee, something like half the speakers and participants were from the Third World. Times had changed since the World Mission Conference in Edinburgh of 1910 which boasted just seventeen non-Westerners among 1,200 delegates.[28]

The aim of the Congress was to develop strategies for the evangelization of the world; or, in the words of the Congress slogan emblazoned above the platform in the six official languages, 'Let the earth hear his voice'. The words would have reminded many participants of Fanny Crosby's rousing hymn 'To God be the glory, great things he hath done',[29] and indeed at the session in the main assembly hall ('a yawning cavern of a place not unlike an aircraft hangar') one observer from the British press was immediately put in mind of Harringay or Wembley with charismatic overtones:

> The main plenary sessions are held from 9am to 10.45am each morning and 7pm to 8.30pm most evenings. The order of service is very reminiscent of a Billy Graham crusade with Tedd Smith and Don Hustad providing the familiar piano and organ accompaniment, and the energetic, ever-smiling Cliff Barrows as master of ceremonies introducing a rather traditional range of musical talent.[30]

John Stott, in a moment of hyperbole, told a student conference some years later that 'the Congress was spoilt for me by one thing only and that was the interminable singing of the word Hallelujah. Do you know that ditty when you sing Hallelujah about twenty times in a crooning voice …?'[31] The mood of the Congress, however, was as far removed from triumphalism as from complacency, set against the sombre background of current world events: the US political crisis, with President Nixon's resignation imminent; the huge rise in world oil prices; the problems of world poverty, with drought in India and famine in Ethiopia; and the growing consciousness that long-neglected issues of world ecology and conservation were coming home to roost.[32]

Dr Graham in his keynote opening address 'reviewed the challenges that evangelism was facing in a world often gripped by crisis', and underlined the single focus of the gathering: 'Here at Lausanne, let's make sure that evangelism is the one task which we are unitedly determined to do.'[33] John Stott had been asked by the planning committee to give an opening address on the nature of biblical evangelism; and especially to provide a biblical definition of the five words, 'mission', 'evangelism', 'dialogue', 'salvation', and 'conversion'.[34] In his first few characteristic sentences he called for 'a note of evangelical repentance' and a willingness to listen to some of the critics of evangelicalism: 'I believe some ecumenical thinking is mistaken. But then, frankly, I believe some of our evangelical formulations are mistaken also ...' And to give point to this, he went on to add this uncomfortable challenge:

> We have some important lessons to learn from our ecumenical critics. Some of their rejection of our position is not a repudiation of biblical truth, but rather of our evangelical caricatures of it.[35]

An eyewitness account sought to describe something of his command over this heterogeneous assembly, his head shown on a vast TV screen above the platform, and his address simultaneously translated into five other languages:

> It was not only what he said, which was the usual helping of patient, lucid exposition, but his manner and presentation. Peering over his fashionable half-moon glasses he consistently managed to make both the profound simple and the simple profound ... His address paved the way right at the start of the congress for the spirit of evangelical repentance and openness to greater social consciousness and cultural integrity to come to the surface – not initially from the lips of a Third World 'rebel' but from someone who spoke from within the Western tradition.[36]

The issue of 'greater social consciousness', and the exact relation between evangelism and social action, was one which might have polarized the Congress into two distinct factions. Some older Western delegates retained a deep suspicion, no doubt influenced in some cases by the activities of the WCC, that where Christian social (let alone political) action prevailed, meaningful evangelism was inevitably threatened. It was not easy for them to listen to radical voices from Third World speakers (who, like René Padilla of Latin America, pulled no punches), highly critical of a Western evangelicalism which seemed to them unaware that it was shaped as much by culture as by biblical understanding. In such a context John Stott's firm and authoritative exposition pleaded for a recognition that to 'go and make disciples' does not stand alone, and that as Christians we are called to serve:

> Is it not in a servant role that we can find the right synthesis of evangelism and social action? For both should be authentic expressions of the service we are sent into the world to give ...
>
> Here then are two instructions, 'love your neighbour' and 'go and make disciples.' What is the relation between the two? Some of us behave as if we thought them identical, so that if we have shared

the Gospel with somebody, we consider we have completed our responsibility to love him. But no. The Great Commission neither explains, nor exhausts, nor supersedes the Great Commandment. What it does is to add to the command of neighbour-love and neighbour-service a new and urgent Christian dimension. If we truly love our neighbour we shall without doubt tell him the Good News of Jesus. But equally if we truly love our neighbour we shall not stop there ... Love does not need to justify itself. It just expresses itself in service wherever it sees need.[37]

To many such an emphasis appeared controversial, a threat to the true calling of the evangelist; while to most Third World participants it seemed self-evident. John Stott himself felt the public debating of differences to be a mark of evangelical coming of age; but also that one of the real achievements of the Congress lay in the fact that

> ... the indispensable necessity of socio-political involvement, along-side evangelism, as part of our Christian doctrine and duty were emphasized more clearly, strongly and positively than at Berlin or indeed (I think) ever before in an international evangelical gathering.[38]

Inevitably a major, if unquantifiable, fruit of such a Congress lies also in the self-education of the participants, and in their openness to a new call from God. The Congress rejected the concept of creating a massive new structure for world evangelicalism (comparable, perhaps, to the WCC), though it did set up a Continuation Committee, of which John Stott was a member, to carry on its unfinished business. But perhaps the most enduring fruit of the Congress is to be found in the Covenant to which it gave its name.

A first attempt to draft what such a covenant might say was made by Jim Douglas on behalf of the planning committee many months in advance: 'it bore no resemblance to the final document'.[39] When the main addresses and papers became available, still some months before the Congress, John Stott was asked to produce from them a draft which might be submitted to the Congress: 'I worked all through the papers in order to try and extract from them what the major thrust of each paper was, and then [at Lausanne] worked on it further in the light of the speeches that were actually given.'[40] A small drafting committee was established, consisting of John Stott, Hudson Armerding (President of Wheaton College) and Samuel Escobar from Peru; with Leighton Ford and Jim Douglas to assist. Day by day during the Congress they continued to refine the draft Covenant, balancing as best they could the conflicting viewpoints and emphases as they emerged. Billy Graham described later in a published interview how

> ... we would meet each night and discuss the happenings of that day. Then we would go over this Covenant phrase by phrase. Then we would give it to Leighton Ford and John Stott to work on during the night and bring a paragraph back the next day. They would read it and we would see how much of it we agreed with and so forth. It was arranged that I had veto power over anything they put in it. So they would come about midnight and read it to me first.[41]

The third complete draft was submitted to the whole assembly, and their comments invited, either as individuals or as groups, and John Stott worked through two whole nights to revise the draft in the light of 3,000 replies,

> ... received (in the official languages), translated into English, sorted and studied. Some proposed amendments cancelled each other out, but the drafting committee incorporated all they could, while at the same time ensuring that the final document was a recognizable revision of the draft submitted to participants.[42]

Given the constraints of such a document and the unwieldy nature of so large a gathering, the Covenant reflects John Stott's particular skill, often noted by those who witnessed it, as chairman and drafter. A similar skill had been exercised by Archbishop William Temple a generation before; his biographer noted how, as a chairman, he was without a rival:

> He was able to rely on an almost infallible memory which was particularly accurate about decisions already reached and resolutions passed that might be relevant to any subject under debate ... Yet the moment always arrived when he would rise and say, 'I wonder whether something like this represents the sense of the meeting?', and his summing-up would be so comprehensive of all the speeches that there was nothing more to be said.

William Temple sometimes called this gift of overcoming difficulties and reconciling divergent views his 'parlour trick'. It could be said of John Stott, as it was of Dr Temple, that such a skill

> ... was never used to better purpose than at oecumenical gatherings, where differences of language, national and ecclesiastical tradition,

and social and philosophic outlook intensified the difficulty of doing justice, in a few unmistakably clear sentences, to the convictions
of all the members.[43]

In remarkably similar phraseology Gordon Landreth, secretary of the
British Evangelical Alliance and one of the delegates, described the final
draft of the Covenant:

> What amazed us at the time was the way this document had
> managed to encompass so many diverse concerns and to tread a
> middle course through so many theological and ecclesiastical mine-
> fields. John's skills were undoubtedly reflected in this. We in the
> British party at Lausanne also felt he was a good counter to Amer-
> ican simplistic and brash formulations of theology and strategy.[44]

Leighton Ford, himself an American and a member of the drafting
committee, is quoted (by William Martin, in his biography of Billy
Graham) as seeing in the final form of the Lausanne Covenant 'one of this
century's exemplary statements on Christian beliefs, concerns and
commitment'.[45] William Martin continues:

> Most of its statements demanded much but occasioned little
> disagreement among people whose very presence signified their
> dedication to evangelism. Several paragraphs, however, represented
> long hours of intense agonizing over precise words and meanings
> and continued to draw attention fifteen years later. One of the most
> controversial addressed the proper balance between evangelism and
> social responsibility. With both the drafting committee and the
> assembly divided on this issue, utmost care was essential if the
> sought-for unity was to last. The result was a set of statements that
> gave unmistakable primacy to evangelism, explicitly defined as 'the
> proclamation of the historical, biblical Christ as Saviour and Lord,
> with a view to persuading people to come to him personally and so
> be reconciled to God,' while making it clear that 'the results of
> evangelism include ... responsible service in the world.'[46]

Even the drafting committee, let alone the Congress, were divided as to
where exactly priorities lay. In the event, however, the Covenant included
the crucial affirmation that 'in the church's mission of sacrificial service,
evangelism is primary'.

> It was a cautious, even hedging sort of statement, and evangelism
> still held its position as the master motive, but the Lausanne

Covenant furnished Evangelical Christianity with a rationale for social action that it had lacked since the days of Charles Finney.[47]

Although successive drafts had been strengthened in this area ('social action' had become 'socio-political involvement' and references to evil, injustice and oppression were forthright), an *ad hoc* group among the participants, calling themselves the 'Theology and Radical Discipleship Group', had felt it necessary to produce an unofficial supplementary statement, less finely balanced and more explicit in its call for social action.[48]

The last full day of the Congress included a prolonged session in which the Lausanne Covenant was presented to the participants:

> Following short reports from the 16 area and functional groups set up at the start of the congress, John Stott, as chairman of its drafting committee, introduced and explained the Lausanne Covenant. It was this performance, perhaps even more than his opening paper, which clearly established him as the key figure in contemporary world evangelicalism. He displayed complete mastery of the complex document in his hand (not surprisingly in view of the fact that he was up until 4.00 a.m. one morning revising it) and expounded it in a way which brought to life the passion beneath the cold print.[49]

The phrase 'the key figure', coming from a British journalist, might be taken as the natural exaggeration of the press, were it not echoed elsewhere. But John Pollock, in his biography of Dr Billy Graham (whose brainchild the Congress was), speaks of John Stott at that time as 'in effect the theological leader of world evangelicalism';[50] Tom Houston described him at Lausanne as 'the giant in the land';[51] while a Third World delegate was sure that 'all of us who attended this conference realised that he carried the entire spiritual burden of the conference on his shoulders'.[52] No doubt these phrases reflect the euphoria of a unique occasion; but they are none the less impressive testimony.

In presenting the draft of the Covenant to the Congress on that final morning, John Stott went out of his way to refer appreciatively to the Theology and Radical Discipleship Group, adding that the drafting committee had had long, friendly and responsible meetings with them and that he personally was willing to sign their call for a more radical discipleship. At the closing Communion service the following morning Bishop Jack Dain and Dr Billy Graham, the two Chairmen, personally signed the Covenant, while 2,000 of the 2,400 participants signed cards to indicate their personal commitment to it. Given the context chosen for the signing, there may be an element of naïvety in John Stott's belief that 'no pressure of any kind was put upon our consciences, and the planning committee were quite ready for the possibility that perhaps only fifty would feel able to sign it'.[53] No doubt the 400 or so who abstained did so for a great variety of reasons. For some, certainly, their misgivings would centre on Paragraph 9, which included what John Stott described as 'the most anxiously debated clause in the Lausanne Covenant'[54] on the adoption of a simple lifestyle:

> One of those who chose not to sign was Ruth Graham, primarily because Stott insisted on inserting the following statement: 'Those of us who live in affluent circumstances accept our duty to develop a simple lifestyle in order to contribute more generously to both relief and evangelism ...' Ruth admires Stott but found his espousal of a simple lifestyle too confining. 'If it said "simpler,"' she told him, 'I would sign it. But what is "simple"? You live in two rooms; I have a bigger home. You have no children; I have five. You say your life is simple and mine isn't.' Stott refused to delete the offending sentence, and Ruth decided, just as she had decided long ago that she did not need to be baptized by immersion, that she could be a quite acceptable Christian without signing something she regarded as a bit self-righteous and precious. Others chose not to sign on various grounds, but signing or not signing was never regarded as a major issue. 'It was a covenant, not a creed,' Leighton Ford ex-plained. 'It was never intended as a testimony of orthodoxy. It was a banner to rally people, not a knife to cut them down.' Interestingly, the names of the signatories were sealed away and never made public.[55]

To John Stott himself the Covenant, not least Paragraph 9, represented 'a very solemn personal commitment' to pray, plan and work together for the evangelization of the whole world.[56]

Big events of this nature generate their own euphoria among participants. Michael Baughen, then Vicar of All Souls, wrote movingly of his impressions of Lausanne. From his hotel room overlooking the Lake, as the Congress moved to a close, he described the warmth of international fellowship among the representatives of 160 countries:

> At meal-tables, in the big meetings, in prayer groups we have met people from all over the world. When we could not speak the same language we communicated by signs and by expression of arms round each other's shoulders to express our oneness in Christ. I have never been to anything so truly international in my life. It has

been a wonderful experience and the stimulus of our brothers from the Third World has humbled us.[57]

John Stott had gone to Lausanne 'without any lively expectation of it being important'; only to find in the event that 'God met with us', and that he had been part of something quite beyond his imagining.[58] In the considered view of a contemporary historian of twentieth-century mission,

> The conference was notable for the maturity of judgement of its participants, not least those from Latin America like René Padilla, Samuel Escobar and Orlando Costas, and from Africa (Bishop Festo Kivengere, the Ugandan Anglican) and Asia (B. V. Subamma, leader of a Christian ashram approach from India and Jonathan Chao, dean of the school of theology at Hong Kong), the breadth of its engagement internationally and missiologically and its success in holding together the evangelistic note, mission as proclamation, with the stress on social justice, concern for the poor and socio-political involvement.[59]

Time magazine was more forthright. In a two-page spread reporting the Congress they made much of the indisputable contrast it presented to the World Council of Churches. Malcolm Muggeridge, in an unguarded moment, told their reporter, 'Anything that does damage to the WCC is a step in the right direction.' Billy Graham was more positive: 'I hope this Congress will get the World Council to re-evaluate its theological position.' Certainly, at least as reported by *Time*, a challenge to the prevailing philosophy of the WCC was overdue:

> Some of the World Council's advocates of ecumenism increasingly have questioned whether Christians even have the right – let alone the duty – to disturb the honest faith of a Buddhist, a Hindu or a Jew. For many in the World Council, the Christian's mission has become more of a campaign to achieve a sort of secular salvation, a human liberation in the political and social sense. To oppose that trend, the Evangelicals at Lausanne laid the groundwork for a post-congress 'fellowship' that could eventually develop into a rival international body.[60]

The Lausanne Covenant, of course, was not without its critics. Looking back a decade later John Stott gave two instances. Some had felt that the statement that Scripture is 'without error in all that it affirms' was an evasion of the issue of inerrancy. He defends the phrase (which was not drafted lightly) as a clarification rather than an evasion: 'not everything contained in Scripture is affirmed by Scripture'. A second criticism was that the Covenant had not distanced evangelical thinking sufficiently clearly from more liberal pronouncements on evangelism. 'Was the Lausanne Covenant clear and definite enough?' John Stott asked himself ten years later. He was able to reply, 'I still think it was':

> Although its thrust is positive and its tone irenic, it dissociates itself from several viewpoints espoused in conciliar [e.g. WCC] circles. It outspokenly rejects 'as derogatory to Christ and the gospel every kind of syncretism and dialogue which implies that Christ speaks equally through all religions and ideologies,' and instead makes an unequivocal affirmation of the uniqueness and universality of Christ (para. 3). It also denies that social action is 'evangelism,' and that political liberation is 'salvation' (para. 5), while at the same time affirming that we should be concerned for 'the liberation of men from every kind of oppression' and that 'evangelism and socio-political involvement are both part of our Christian duty.'[61]

Certainly Lausanne signalled a public shift in mainline evangelical understanding of the relationship between evangelism and social concern. In this it was not original: thinking on this theme had been growing steadily since at least the publication of Carl Henry's *The Uneasy Conscience of Modern Fundamentalism* thirty years before, with its firm declaration that 'There is no room ... for a gospel that is indifferent to the needs of the total man nor of the global man'.[62] But Lausanne was the 'turning point', 'the definitive step', 'a watershed', 'a catalyst' in which such views ceased, in all but the most right-wing circles, to smack of 'social gospel liberalism', and became part of mainstream evangelical understanding of 'mission'.[63] It resonated notably, but by no means exclusively, with a younger generation (for whom John Stott as teacher continued to have a particular appeal, witness the IVCF Urbana Missionary Conventions). Carl Henry's son Paul, more than twenty years after his father's *The Uneasy Conscience of Modern Fundamentalism*, summed up this great divide between the established US evangelicalism of an older generation and the thinking of his contemporaries:

> To say that there is a generation gap between the post-thirty establishment evangelicals and their pre-thirty offspring is not only to state the obvious but to border on understatement ... While the establishment continues to split hairs as to how we are to separate from the world, we wonder how we can become meaningfully involved.[64]

This was the kind of question that not only Carl Henry's son Paul, but also Billy Graham's son Franklin, was wrestling with. Franklin was twenty-two, and attended Lausanne to assist with the complicated arrangements for travel. Until then he had shown little sign of embracing wholeheartedly his parents' faith and Christian commitment:

> At long last the Grahams' patience paid off ... Mingling with Third World Christians and recognizing the physical hardships many of them suffered moved Franklin tremendously. A few weeks later, in a Jerusalem hotel room ... he threw a wadded-up pack of cigarettes in the trash, knelt by his bed, and told God, 'I want you to be lord of my life. I am willing to give up any area that is not pleasing to you.'[65]

Nor was the place of socio-political concern within Christian mission the only area where Lausanne saw a radical, perhaps minority, view begin to be accepted as mainstream biblical evangelicalism for the late twentieth century. Adrian Hastings offers a detached but perceptive insight when he writes of John Stott that

> ... it was due to him that the Lausanne Covenant avoided a commitment to the verbal inspiration of Scripture, made social action a partner of evangelism, and stressed – instead of individual and undenominational evangelism – the collective responsibility of the visible Church. None of this was very acceptable to main-line American Evangelicals ...[66]

'Main-line' here must be a disputable judgment. If to follow Scripture and the teaching of Jesus meant that John Stott was no longer quite the touchstone of evangelical orthodoxy in certain American (and, to a much smaller extent, British Free Church and Independent) circles, that was simply a price to be paid. If such teaching proved divisive (as at least one other aspect of his theological position, his understanding of the possible meanings of eternal punishment, would also prove), then that was a cause of sadness and heart-searching, but not of retreat. Perhaps Lausanne, among much else, signalled a shift in the balance of John Stott's influence as Christian leader away from some sections of evangelicalism in North America, but towards a position of greatly increased respect and stature among leaders and future leaders of Third World Christianity.

Almost as a footnote to Lausanne, there was one further significant gathering in July 1977, this time of evangelical leaders of Europe's confessional churches. John Stott had written at the start of the 1970s to a group of such leaders, concerned that 'with the growing unity of

Europe, there is both a need and a desire to strengthen ties between evangelicals' in churches which owed their origin to the Reformation.[67] It was hoped to issue a regular Bulletin, but in spite of numerous attempts and suggestions (for example, a European edition of *Christianity Today*, or some kind of regular coverage in *The Churchman*), progress seemed to be frustrated. In the wake of Lausanne, however, it was quickly agreed to hold a European Evangelical Theological Conference, with the expectation that this would lead to a European Fellowship of Evangelical Theologians. In the event, the first three words were rearranged, to give the acronym FEET! John Stott was nominated to its Advisory Council, and FEET continues 'to promote evangelical theology in Europe in a spirit of loyalty to the Bible' and to serve the renewal of theological thinking in its member churches.[68]

4

Before the Lausanne Congress ended, participants were asked their views about what should happen next: a large majority voted for a Lausanne Continuation Committee.[69] This was originally conceived as a small group of perhaps twenty-five people; but by the time of its first meeting the following January it had grown considerably, with a particularly large American representation. The events of those few days in Mexico City offered a striking example of the difficulties John Stott found himself facing in these international discussions. He flew in from India, where he had been for the three previous weeks; and described in his diary how Billy Graham opened the proceedings after dinner on the first evening, tracing their progress historically from Montreux in 1960 through the Berlin Congress of 1966 to Lausanne in 1974:

> Then he came to the work of the Continuation Committee and described two concepts of our work which had emerged from the many letters he'd received from participants – 'narrow' and 'broad'. The narrow view was that our paramount task was evangelism, that there was no possibility of evangelicals uniting on any other subject, that to attempt to do everything would be 'a great tragedy', that we must leave other things to other bodies like WEF and instead ourselves be characterized by a 'this one thing I do' commitment. The broader concept was that we should 'get involved in everything God wants done'. Having described the two, Billy made it clear that he favoured the first. If we accepted the second, he added, we'd get 'off the mandate given us at Lausanne', as Lausanne had given us in his judgment 'a rather narrow mandate'. So we must 'not get bogged down in other peripheral matters'. This troubled me very

much, and I stayed up several hours thinking about it and preparing
a rebuttal.[70]

The following morning John Stott was due to give a Bible exposition and
turned once again to Jesus' prayer for his church in John 17, a prayer for
its mission, truth, holiness and unity. He ended by asking whether
Christ's followers had any liberty to cherish a narrower concern than this.
In the open session that followed, the first speaker firmly endorsed the
'narrower' view of the Continuation Committee's role as Billy Graham
had described it the evening before. When he sat down, John Stott caught
the chairman's eye:

> It was an unenviable task to disagree with Billy Graham in public,
> but I felt I had to argue for the wider concept (1) from Scripture
> (Christ calls us to be salt as well as light), (2) from history (the
> church's constant tendency to unbalanced preoccupations), (3)
> from the Lausanne Congress (the Covenant treating a number of
> topics besides evangelism), (4) from the Continuation Committee
> (we were not all evangelists and some of us ought to go home if that
> was to be our exclusive concern), and (5) from the expectation of
> evangelicals throughout the world, many of whom are concerned
> not just for the renewal of the church but for the reform of their
> national life by the Christian penetration of non-Christian society.
> I ended: 'if we go back now, and concentrate exclusively on
> evangelism, it will not be an implementation of the Covenant but
> a betrayal of it'.
> Well, then the fat was in the fire ... !'[71]

Over and above the issue under discussion was the shock felt by some
delegates at this public disagreement with Billy Graham, in the light of
the universal esteem in which Billy was held by the international
evangelical community. Some were in tears about it. Others were soon
openly accusing John Stott of engaging in a power struggle, challenging
Billy Graham for the worldwide evangelical leadership – an allegation so
ludicrously far from the truth as almost to make John Stott himself want
to weep in turn![72] The debate raged for the rest of the morning. Two or
three members were asked to try to draft some broad guidelines, but John
Stott felt their form of words to be unacceptable or inadequate:

> I felt so deeply concerned that we were about to betray Lausanne's
> vision, covenant and spirit that I said I was afraid I would have to
> resign if the Committee decided to go the way they were indicating.
> To my surprise Jack Dain from the chair immediately supported

me, saying that he too would resign, since he couldn't possibly return to Australia with the narrower concept, for Australian participants were *already* implementing the broader vision. We may well have made a mistake in saying this. The Americans interpreted it as a threat, an illicit form of blackmail, even the behaviour of obstinate children who won't cooperate if they don't get their own way. I think there was a cultural difference here, for my statement was not a threat or improper use of pressure, but the only way I seemed to have left to me to indicate the depth of my conviction about the betrayal of the Lausanne vision.[73]

After further drafting, a form of words was agreed which began with the general wider mission of the church, and went on to affirm the primacy of evangelism within it. But John Stott's troubles were not yet over. He soon found himself, with immense reluctance, having to oppose the suggestion that Billy Graham should be, in name at least and by whatever title, the 'Supreme President' of the Lausanne organization. Fearing that the Third World delegates would be too polite and too loyal to Billy Graham himself to voice their real feelings (even though Dr Graham was not present), John Stott once again rose to speak. He began by declaring his personal affection and admiration for Billy Graham and his belief that he would go down in history as one of the greatest Christian leaders of the twentieth century, but went on to urge that he should be one of several equal Co-Presidents, since

> … he himself had consistently said that he did not wish any overall leadership position in the post-Lausanne organization. To be 'Supreme President' would perpetuate the kind of paternalism he wanted to avoid, and would be misunderstood in the Third World.[74]

In fact there proved to be considerable support for this proposal once it had been expressed, and the Committee found itself again divided. It was not until the last day that John Stott was finally able to consult Billy Graham himself:

> I went by appointment to Billy's room at 8.15 and told him face to face what I had said behind his back in committee the previous day, viz. the reasons why I thought the idea of his honorary leadership was not on. Great man that he is, he fully agreed, told me he hadn't slept much that night but had prayed much, that he had given in to the American group's pressure without thought or prayer, and that the Lord had told him during the night that he should be neither

head of the organisation nor even a 'minister-at-large'. Indeed, he added, if he had accepted the leadership the previous evening he would have resigned it that morning!

By this time we were late for the meeting, and coming downstairs the atmosphere was tense.[75]

Billy Graham, however, was equal to the occasion. He read two passages of Scripture (Psalm 133 about dwelling together in unity and James 3 about the peaceable wisdom from above), admitted frankly his mistake in yielding to pressure, and declared his unwillingness to accept a leadership role beyond being Honorary Chairman of the Consultative Council (with which everybody was in agreement). He spoke warmly of John Stott, and his personal friendship and loyalty – and so the wounds began to heal. John Stott was put on the drafting committee to prepare a statement summarizing progress; and this was accepted with a few minor amendments: 'a helpful note of unanimity on which to conclude a rather traumatic conference'.[76]

On the last page of his personal diary for the stay in Mexico City John Stott looked back with the benefit of hindsight on a number of mistakes from which lessons could be learned. He felt, for example, that the Americans tended to hold the floor, while Third World representatives (fewer than there should have been because of visa problems) were more reticent. Time was another factor: three days proved too short adequately to get to know one another and develop mutual respect and understanding. But there was a note of self-criticism also:

> I think I was too quick on the draw. Although I do not regret anything I said, or even the way I said it, for I think I kept my 'cool' and remained courteous, yet I was too quick to cast myself in the role of defending Lausanne and its covenant ... and of acting as protagonist for the Third World. I much regret this now, and wish I could learn to listen longer before speaking!'[77]

The Continuation Committee met again the following year in Atlanta (John Stott remained a member until 1981), and was able to work towards the terms of reference which had been finally agreed at its first meeting:

> ... to further the total biblical mission of the church, recognizing that 'in the church's mission of sacrificial service evangelism is primary' [paragraph 6 of the Covenant], and that our particular concern must be the evangelization of the 2,700 million unreached people of the world.

The pursuit of this defined aim was divided among four working groups. John Stott was appointed Chairman of one, the Lausanne Theology and Education Group, later renamed the Theology Working Group, whose task was 'to promote theological reflection on issues relating to world evangelization and, in particular, to explore the implications of the Lausanne Covenant'. This group organized a series of consultations between 1977 and 1982, some in co-operation with the World Evangelical Fellowship, and these took John Stott as Chairman to Pasadena in 1977 and to Bermuda in 1978.[78]

5

The gathering at Pasadena, South California, at the end of May 1977 was described by the accurate but opaque title 'A Colloquium on the Homogeneous Unit Principle'. The subject, hotly debated in circles that study church-growth theory, was concerned with the propriety of using 'homogeneous units' (that is, groupings of people by social class, ethnic origin, educational background or common culture) as a means to world evangelization. The 'homogeneous unit principle' (HUP) had been developed over many years at the School of World Mission of Fuller Theological Seminary, Pasadena, where the Lausanne delegates now met for two and a half days together. Dr Donald McGavran, Dean Emeritus and Senior Professor of Missions at the seminary, had expounded theories of church growth in a number of seminal books[79] and was a well-known and leading figure in the debate, which gave a structured opportunity for critics of the HUP to voice their misgivings (how, for example, does the principle square with New Testament teaching about unity in Christ transcending all human division?), and for the proponents of the principle to respond. John Stott acted as moderator. He wrote in his diary:

> The twelve of us sat round a square table, three each side, and the twenty-five consultants sat round an outer table. The dynamics were good, and discussion flowed very freely.
>   I was surprised how threatened the School of World Mission team obviously felt and, in consequence, how defensive they were in their presentations and contributions. I did not feel they were really 'open', and it saddened me that when René Padilla [one of the critics of the HUP] got up to speak, they (quite unconsciously, no doubt) put down their pads and pens, folded their arms, sat back and appeared to pull down the shutter of their minds.[80]

By the second day there was little evidence of progress. But John Stott in his role as Moderator had been taking careful notes, and felt he could discern both some areas of convergence and a clearer definition of points of disagreement. He was, inevitably, made chairman of a drafting committee, and in the small hours of the following morning a 3,000-word statement was finished – to be accepted, when the delegates reconvened, with only a few minor verbal emendations. A key section of the statement affirms:

> We have found considerable help in the concept of change. To acknowledge the fact of HUs [Homogeneous Units] is not to acquiesce in the characteristics they possess which are displeasing to Christ. The Christian attitude to HUs is often called the 'realist attitude,' because it realistically accepts that HUs exist and will always exist. We would prefer, however, to call this an attitude of 'dynamic realism' because we wish also to affirm that HUs can change and must always change. For Christ the Lord gives to his people new standards. They also receive a new homogeneity which transcends all others, for now they find their essential unity in Christ, rather than in culture.[81]

Following this Colloquium, it was a logical next step for the Lausanne Theology and Education Group to undertake a study of 'The Gospel and Culture'; and this was the theme of their next meeting, in January 1978, at Willowbank, Bermuda, a Christian guest house spectacularly situated on a cliff top overlooking the ocean. The location lent its name to their 'Willowbank Report'. The group this time was a larger one, with over thirty theologians, anthropologists, linguists, missionaries and pastors from all six continents, including about half from the Third World. Coming from different cultures and different academic disciplines, ordered communication was not easily achieved, and once again John Stott found all his skills called into play:

> Theologians and anthropologists use different methodologies and have different presuppositions; and I as chairman understandably (and rightly) was playfully accused of English imperialism for trying to impose 'Westminster parliamentary procedure' on Africans, Asians and Latin Americans whose cultural ways of discussion and reaching consensus are more leisurely and more emotional. Wordiness and gesticulation come naturally to them; English economy of words, precision and 'sweet reasonableness' do not appeal to them at all! So we had a lively time ...[82]

After a day or two, Bishop Stephen Neill took John Stott aside to say that if he did not stop a South American delegate from dominating the discussion by his verbosity, he, the Bishop, would catch the next plane back to London!

John Stott used his diary to describe the key issue of the Consultation:

> The heart of our concern was the interplay between the three
> cultures which are involved in every attempt to communicate the
> gospel. First, there is the cultural situation within which the biblical
> revelation was given by God. Secondly, there is the cultural
> background of the missionary or evangelist. Thirdly, there is the
> culture of those to whom he goes. How then can a missionary from
> one culture take a message from another to people who live in a
> third?[83]

Seventeen preliminary papers, ranging in theme from 'Hermeneutics and Culture' through 'Mission as Inter-Cultural Encounter' to 'Contextualization of the Gospel in Fiji', prepared the way for the six days of discussion. The starting-point of their thirty-five-page statement is an examination of 'The Biblical Basis of Culture', in which the Report cites first the Genesis account of the dignity and degradation of humankind. But its authors go on to say:

> Many of us evangelical Christians have in the past been too negative
> towards culture. We do not forget the human fallenness and
> lostness which call for salvation in Christ. Yet we wish to begin this
> report with a positive affirmation of human dignity and human
> cultural achievement. Wherever human beings develop their social
> organization, art and science, agriculture and technology, their
> creativity reflects that of their Creator.[84]

The Willowbank Report addresses itself to the place of culture in six areas, namely in the writers and the readers of the Bible (that is, in revelation and interpretation), in evangelism, in conversion, in the church and in ethics. Some of this Willowbank thinking found further expression in the Olivier Beguin Memorial Lecture given by John Stott in Perth, Melbourne and Canberra the following spring. Though the original title was 'The Relevance and Authority of the Bible in the Modern World', the lecture made reference to the work done at Willowbank, and to the need to understand both the culture of the Bible and the culture of the world around us: so much so that, on publication in America, the title chosen was *Culture and the Bible*.[85]

It was the work of these continuing committees and consultations, involving for the chairman much travel, correspondence and preparation, which paved the way for Lausanne II, the second International Congress on World Evangelization of July 1989, whose Manila Manifesto was a call to 'the whole church to take the whole gospel to the whole world'.[86]

Hardly was the Lausanne Congress over than John Stott, along with others, was seeking to arrive at some assessment of it. In the excitement of the Congress extravagant claims were being made. 'It seems to me that the world will never be the same after Lausanne,' wrote a delegate from Latin America; while Billy Graham himself 'ventured a private guess that Lausanne might one day be seen to stand with the three or four decisive moments when church history has changed direction'.[87] In an interview for *His* magazine the following year, John Stott's thoughts were more firmly grounded. He singled out two main lessons: first, that evangelism was no longer a one-way traffic, out from Western Christendom to where 'The heathen in his blindness / Bows down to wood and stone'.[88] Instead, 'the evangelization of the world is being undertaken by the *whole* church in the *whole* world ... this is a new concept of global evangelism'. Secondly, Lausanne had achieved a new understanding of the relationship of evangelism to the culture in which it is undertaken.[89]

More substantial was his assessment in *The International Review of Mission* entitled 'The Significance of Lausanne'.[90] Here he suggested as the first major achievement of the Congress a clarified understanding of the 'mission' of the people of God, and the proper relationship of the nature of evangelism and Christian social action, though careful to emphasize that 'in the church's mission of sacrificial service evangelism is primary'.[91] But he went on to affirm the key message from Lausanne to the rest of the church on the theme of evangelism as 'the need for a recovery of confidence in the truth of God's Word and in the power of God's Spirit'.

Ten years later, describing some of the continuing discussions that had sprung from Lausanne, he was confident in affirming that they had left him even more convinced of the great value of representative international consultations 'despite their cost in money, time and energy'.

It is only when we meet face to face, and struggle to hear and understand each other, that our typecast images of one another (developed in separation) are modified, and we grow in mutual respect and shared conviction.[92]

Ten years on again, in 1995, John Stott offered 'some personal reflections' on the twenty years since the Congress.[93] He spoke of surprise in some quarters that the Lausannne Covenant continued to be influential in evangelical thinking; and after a descriptive historical survey he went on to list five spiritual factors 'without which, whatever the statistics may promise, world evangelization will not be attained'. These were 1. *a greater unity before the task* (as against 'our evangelical tendency to individualism'); 2. *a greater visibility before the world* (personal authenticity in the life of the individual, the local church, and social action); 3. *a greater clarity before the gospel* ('to demonstrate the uniqueness and finality of Jesus Christ'); 4. *a greater consistency before Christ* (the costliness of mission); and 5. *a greater humility before God* (renouncing cultural superiority and confidence in self). And as evidence of continuing life in the Lausanne vision and movement he described how

> ... in the New Year of 1994 the Lausanne Committee, meeting in Stuttgart, announced a new vision and a new beginning, with new structures and new leaders (especially in national, regional and special interest groups), while still serving the same mission as before. The committee discovered that the Lausanne movement 'is more active today than at any time in its history', and mentioned as evidence that in 1993 eleven Lausanne consultations and prayer conferences had taken place in ten countries.

What he would not say of his own part in this, others have said for him. Professor David Wells, in common with many observers of the post-war years, attributes to him 'a large role in the international growth of evangelicalism'. He adds:

> The high-water mark in this resurgence of biblical Christianity was the Lausanne Covenant, the outcome of the International Congress on World Evangelization in 1974 ... The importance of the Lausanne Covenant remains undiminished for its evangelical cohesion, vision, and conviction, and no small part of this remarkable moment belonged to Stott.[94]

Even that is not the whole story. People are, in the end, more influential than structures. Lausanne helped John Stott to reformulate classic evangelicalism and restate it within the contemporary context, in total loyalty to each: a practice conceptualized in his later 'urgent plea for double listening'.[95] Because of this he was able by his personal and pastoral influence to retain within the fellowship at Lausanne the Theology and Radical Discipleship Group which had formed spontaneously among a number of younger and more radical participants during the Congress itself, so that their findings on 'Theology and Implications of Radical Discipleship' formed part of the final 1,400 page Report.[96] In the words of Tom Houston,

> They would have been marginalized but John met with them,

stayed with them, they felt that he was on their side, and he was ready to listen ... I think if you go throughout the world today, you'll find that there is a generation of leadership that was a generation younger than John at that time, who are in important positions today. The pattern probably is like this: they came through the local manifestation of IFES [the International Fellowship of Evangelical Students] and would probably have lost their way in the gap between the student world and the church world ... I think you would get Third World leaders who would say, 'If it hadn't been for John Stott and Lausanne, I wouldn't be an evangelical today.'[97]

EIGHT

Christ and the Scriptures: Letting the Bible Speak

1

John Stott's travels during the 1970s took him increasingly far afield, beyond the churches of North America or Australia, or the established centres of Christian worship and witness in Asia and Africa. Such experiences gave a new focus to his concern for pioneering churches and their witness to Christ in the developing world or where Christianity remained very much a minority faith.

Talking on television in 1978 he expressed his longing that, in a suffering world, Christ should be known:

> Sometimes in recent years I have gone into Buddhist temples, and I have stood in front of the statue of the Buddha with his arms folded and his legs crossed and that seraphic smile upon his face, withdrawn from the suffering of mankind. In my imagination I have turned away from that figure to the tortured figure of Jesus on the cross. And I have seen the pain, and the sweat, and the blood, and the God-forsaken darkness as He bore our sin in His own body, and I have asked myself, 'Which is the more credible of those two?' I could not believe in a God who is withdrawn from the sufferings

of the world, but in Jesus Christ He has entered them and borne our sin and our death.[1]

As his own ministry of writing grew, it was also inevitable that he should reflect on the power and ubiquity of the printed word, and on the contrast between the vast array of titles on offer to the believer, or the Christian worker, in Britain and America, and the pathetically few books available to Third World pastors or students. 'I remember a Christian youth worker in Soweto,' he wrote later, 'whose eyes, when I presented him with a book, filled with tears. He said it was the first Christian book he ever possessed apart from the Bible.'[2] At the same time, his own increasing number of titles in print were beginning to earn significant sums, and he was looking for a way of putting this money to work in the cause of Christian literature.

Such a vision was by no means new. Nicholas Ridley as Bishop of London made it a practice to give away copies of the New Testament to the men of his household.[3] Richard Baxter in the seventeenth century distributed Christian books (including a proportion of each edition of his own works, taken in lieu of payment, expressly to give away). C. H. Spurgeon's wife Susannah ran a 'book-fund' to give books to ministers (starting with her husband's *Letters to My Students*) to help them improve their preaching.[4] The Society for Promoting Christian Knowledge (SPCK), founded in 1698, would be an early institutional example, and Feed the Minds (1964) a more recent one.

So there came into being in 1971 the Evangelical Literature Trust, at first little more than a means of channelling John Stott's own royalties into the distribution of books for the developing world, with the help of a small group of friends[5] already convinced of the power of print and ready to approach other Christian authors to ask them to covenant from their royalties towards the work of ELT. In 1977 they were fortunate to secure Ronald Inchley, just retired from a life's work as Publications Secretary of IVF/UCCF, to succeed Frances Whitehead as their Honorary Administrator. On Ronald Inchley's retirement from the work of the Trust in 1983, John Hayden came from Feed the Minds to take over from him. ELT soon proved to be an idea whose time had come. Third World pastors were a particular concern, and the Trust began by making available the *New Bible Dictionary* and the *New Bible Commentary*, both published by IVP, either as an outright gift, or at prices so heavily subsidized (in part from the funds of the Trust; and in part by negotiation with publishers for special printings at a fraction of the normal retail price) as to be affordable even in Third World churches. Nor was it only pastors who were beneficiaries. ELT began to make grants to theological students, to postgraduate scholars and writers, to college and seminary libraries, and on occasion (as in Eastern Europe) to enable the translation and publication of books of proven usefulness. Twenty-five years after its small beginnings, the Trust was helping annually some 10,000 theological students, 65,000 pastors (15,000 at graduate level), and about 600 colleges, in more than 100 countries in a variety of languages. ELT is thus a practical expression of John Stott's long-held conviction that biblical preaching is the divinely appointed means for securing the health and growth of a church; that theological and ministerial training ought to play a key part in preparing for a preaching ministry; and that continued study (of which books are the life-blood) is crucial in maintaining it: 'the pew is a reflection of the pulpit'.[6]

The 1970s saw a further development in John Stott's provision for his own worldwide ministry of teaching, whether in person or in print, now that he was no longer to be in day-to-day charge of All Souls. This was his employment of the first in a long line of study assistants: a title chosen as at once less pretentious and more accurate than 'research assistant', though research featured among their varied duties. In 1976 Roy McCloughry, newly married, had finished a Master's degree, and was looking for something useful to occupy him before (possibly) starting on a PhD. He secured some part-time teaching in international banking and finance, and also enrolled, with his wife Helen, in what was known as YEAST, a Year of Experience at All Souls with Training. This was the precursor of the All Souls College of Applied Theology (ASCAT) started by Michael Baughen and Andrew Cornes, his curate, whose students came to be affectionately known as AS-Kittens. According to John Stott's recollection, 'I think it was Roy who approached me (perhaps at Andrew's suggestion) to enquire if I could do with a part-time assistant. I jumped at the idea, and the Langham Trust agreed to provide the money.'[7] From the first, John Stott made it clear that he was looking for 'a general assistant', willing to help in any way according to need, and this has remained the study assistants' role. It might involve anything from preparing (and washing-up) for the monthly Prayer Breakfast in the basement of 12 Weymouth Street, to reading whatever John Stott was writing at the time, so as to offer a critique from the perspective of a younger generation:

On the 'study' side, I have asked them to obtain books for me from libraries, track down references, compile an index or bibliography, read MSS and correct proofs. On the more 'general' side, they have helped me to entertain people, done some shopping for me, driven me to engagements, accompanied me on an overseas trip, dis-patched gift books to Third World correspondents, photocopied articles and other documents, and sent faxes and e-mail letters on my behalf.[8]

As far as the assistants were concerned, the opportunity seems to have been universally valued, but often went far beyond the prosaic description above. Roy McCloughry still remembers that

> ... the first thing John Stott asked me to do was to find a Rolls razor for the Archbishop of Burma who had written to him – his had obviously broken. I had to search the highways and byways of London, wondering if I was going to be looking for razors for all the archbishops in the Anglican Communion for the next nine months.[9]

Roy McCloughry helped to establish and shape the new role, which was to embrace a succession of study assistants in John Stott's small team over the next twenty years. To most of them, as to many younger friends, he is known as 'Uncle John', and Roy McCloughry remembers being present at an occasion which helped to establish this tradition. It was at a meeting of student Christian Union leaders in 1976 chaired by John Wyatt, a member of All Souls. John Stott was then in his middle-fifties, and had been concerned for some time (perhaps since the 'swinging sixties' which overdid the breaking down of barriers) that young Christians could easily become over-familiar and lacking in healthy respect towards their seniors, their pastors and teachers. In the course of the meeting, Roy McCloughry recalls, some student whom he had not previously met addressed John Stott just as 'John'. Graciously but firmly, John Stott made it clear that he felt such familiarity was not warranted. John Wyatt, on behalf of a younger generation, explained that no disrespect was implied, and asked what John Stott would prefer:

> John was a bit nonplussed about this. I don't think he'd expected anyone to come back at him. There were a few things suggested which didn't make any headway and then, I can't remember whether it was John Wyatt or myself, one of us suggested 'Uncle John' – I think it was John Wyatt. John Stott visibly warmed to this and he said, 'Oh, yes!' in a very avuncular way. 'Well, if you want to call me Uncle John, I won't protest at that.'[10]

Since then the name has been used by an ever-widening circle, including all the study assistants, as a happy combination of family intimacy and due respect. And to generations of students at the London Institute, 'Auntie Frances' has at times become a parallel address of respect and affection for Frances Whitehead. John Stott is fond of quoting Charles Simeon's reference to himself and his two curates, Henry Martyn and Thomas Thomason, as 'this happy triumvirate', which he transfers (with a fine disregard of gender) to mean Frances Whitehead, the current study assistant and himself.[11]

By the 1970s John Stott was becoming not only an avuncular figure but also something of a legend. He was known for his extreme punctuality, his early rising, his high standards and attention to detail. Successive study assistants tried hard to live up to these ideals. 'He was such a disciplined person', in Roy McCloughry's recollections of the time,

> ... and such a careful person that one of the things that happened was that one was almost over-conscientious about time-keeping or what-have-you. I can remember thinking I was going to be late and taking a very expensive taxi across London to drop me in Devonshire Street outside Bridford Mews. I waited there for thirty seconds then, turning round, walked down the Mews (because he could see everybody who came down the Mews from his window) and rang the bell on precisely the right second ... I thought I was the only one who had ever done this but in fact nearly all the study assistants in the early days told me that they had done that as well in order to be punctual.[12]

Most study assistants, too, shared Roy McCloughry's experience of leaping out of bed at 8.00am to answer the phone, trying to rid their voice of slumber and, in response to John Stott's apologies, to sound as if they had long been at their desk.

A task which often fell to the study assistant was to convene one or more of the various study or discussion groups in which John Stott was involved. Roy McCloughry began by servicing 'Christian Debate', finding and circulating relevant articles, sometimes writing a précis of a book, and on the evening in question helping Frances Whitehead serve coffee or a meal. *The Myth of God Incarnate*[13] proved his undoing:

> My background is in economics ... I started to read this book of academic and liberal theology and was completely nonplussed. I remember sitting at the table in my flat with mounting panic, as I realized that I was not going to be able to do this. I handed in something, which John Stott received very graciously, but somebody told me afterwards he had to read the whole book again and précis it himself. He never told me that, though![14]

Besides 'Christian Debate' they were involved in other study groups;[15] but the Christian study of the contemporary scene was not always without embarrassment. Roy McCloughry suggested that a group should study John Fowles' novel, *The Magus*:

As we were going round the circle saying what we had thought of it, one of the members of the group, a contemporary of mine, said he was very surprised to have been asked to read this book. He found it very unhelpful to him as a Christian and felt that he had nothing to contribute, and was going to leave ... The problem was that there was quite a lot of sexuality in the book. I remember John sitting there, letting him leave and, looking over his glasses at everybody, saying, 'Oh, I think that was most unfortunate. I thought it was erotic, but not pornographic'! For years afterwards people used to say to one another, in a John Stott type of voice, 'It's erotic, but not pornographic', and feel much comforted by the distinction between these two things, which probably John knew but the rest of us didn't.[16]

Roy McCloughry was followed as study assistant by Tom Cooper, a young American preparing for ministry in the Presbyterian Church. He and his wife Karen (the first few study assistants were all married, or soon to be so) arrived when John Stott was at The Hookses. Roy McCloughry met them in London and travelled down to Wales with them by train:

I remember arriving down at The Hookses with them and John giving the task to Tom, as his first study assistant's job, of building a new compost heap. I think this is a real guide to John's sense of humour. Tom put all the energy that the American persona can muster and all the creativity that he could find into building this extraordinarily robust and large compost heap at The Hookses, which can still be viewed as a monument to Tom Cooper's time as study assistant. I think you could compile a list of the first jobs that study assistants were given by John. Mine was the Rolls razor, Tom's was the compost heap ...[17]

A year later Tom Cooper was again at The Hookses, and wrote a private circular letter to friends at home headed 'My first year working with John Stott',[18] in which he singled out what had impressed him most. He described John Stott's handling of Scripture, going back to their first meeting at Regent College, Vancouver, when Tom had been a member of the class:

I had personally never listened to a person speak so clearly, lucidly expounding the text yet unwaveringly speaking to the whole text. He willingly confronted the most difficult passages forthrightly, presenting the full tension of the text open-handedly with great balance and humility ... John seemed not to take sides, but rather to examine every activity and theology through the filter of scripture.

He went on to write of John Stott's birdwatching, his simplicity of lifestyle, his disciplined timetable:

> He awakens early and goes to bed late ... He spends a quiet day each week, when he does not see anyone, or receive phone calls. On these days he reviews his past week, his next week, his next month, the next six months and tries to plan his schedule accordingly. He also thinks, reads and writes on this quiet day. It is not unusual for John to make decisions that are yet one or two years ahead of the current calendar day. I once asked him how he spent his year. He replied that he spends six months a year in London at All Souls, Langham Place, three months a year travelling and speaking, two months a year writing (usually at the Hookses), and one month annually for vacation. I believe that the central reason John is so productive is that he organises his time so well.

Tom Cooper also shared with his correspondents a glimpse of John Stott's worldwide concern for the church ('his office is flooded with hundreds of examples reflecting his personal and caring relationships with people of all kinds'); his meticulous preparation (with a detailed account of the famous 3" × 5" card-indexes of passages, quotes, outlines and illustrations); and his dependence on Frances Whitehead ('her help, I think, has maximised John's ministry'). And he tells how his year as study assistant has replaced 'the "super-star image" we usually have of such men' with that of a 'mere mortal' who has 'consecrated his life to Christ and whom God has elected to use'.

2

> My friends [wrote the apostle Jude], I was fully engaged in writing to you about our salvation – which is yours no less than ours – when it became urgently necessary to write at once and appeal to you to join the struggle in the defence of the faith, the faith which God entrusted to his people once and for all.[19]

Nor is Jude the only apostle who writes in terms of a struggle to defend the faith.[20] Controversy is inescapable in a concern for truth, however much an author might prefer to be 'writing to you about our salvation' rather than about confrontation with other worldviews, disagreements among Christians, and the defence of the faith against its detractors.

However, even those most familiar with the controversies of the apostles seen in their letters and in Acts can be caught unawares by the depicting of Jesus himself as fighting similar battles of the mind and heart. John Stott has described how stimulating and reassuring he found it

> ... when it was shown me, or I saw for the first time, that Jesus was a controversialist, and beyond that, that the principles for which he stood were some of the very principles for which we found ourselves standing as evangelicals. I must confess that this did excite me very much at the time, gave me a new degree of confidence in being a controversialist.[21]

So, following his well-tried principle of teaching before writing, John Stott gave first in the All Souls Bible School, then in Edinburgh and again in New Zealand, a series of lectures which were published in 1970 under the title *Christ the Controversialist*.[22] But in an introductory essay the author showed himself aware that his arguments would not be universally popular. He cites 'Dislike of Dogmatism', 'Hatred of Controversy' and a desire not to expose our divisions to the public gaze or to set church against church as powerful emotional reasons for the aversion some might feel. Some indeed did feel it: Michael Green (an old friend) wrote in his review: 'Just a touch of the hedgehog about the whole book. I confess I prefer Stott the evangelist, Stott the teacher, Stott the pastor, to Stott the controversialist.' But he went on to add, 'So of course does he: but he writes under compulsion ... his concern for truth drove him to become a controversialist, *malgré lui*.'[23] Dr Erik Routley reviewed the book for the influential Free Church *British Weekly* and called it 'beyond doubt the ablest apologia for evangelical Christianity put out in recent years'.[24] But he went on to speak of a 'nagging doubt' and to explain that he felt 'a glacial quality about its very competence and rationality ... I am not really convinced that his Christ loves me ...' An exchange of personal letters followed, notably *un*controversial in tone (Erik Routley was the friendliest of men) in which John Stott thanked him for 'writing fully and thoughtfully, and even to some extent appreciatively', while Erik Routley responded warmly with the confession that 'I think it very likely that if the book was here and there vulnerable to misinterpretation, what I said about it was much more so.'[25]

As its title suggests, the book consists mainly of eight studies in the teaching of Jesus himself, drawn from the four Gospels, where he confronts the traditional religious leaders of his day on specific issues, of a kind which have still an entirely contemporary relevance. These include such themes as the supernatural nature of religion, the seat of authority, the use of Scripture, true morality and the worship of the heart. Michael

Green called it, with some justification, 'perhaps the most scholarly of all his books' up to that time,[26] and he himself thought of it, he told his friends, as 'my "maturest utterance" thus far ... the distillation of my deepening convictions about what authentic Christianity is. My heart and mind have gone into it.'[27] It remains a distinctive landmark, setting out an unmistakable theological and spiritual standpoint which can be recognized in all his later writing.

Two years later there appeared a book about the Bible of a quite different kind: more popular in approach, pastoral rather than controversial, and written (so the Preface made clear) with two distinct kinds of reader in mind. They were the new Christians to whom the Bible was largely a closed book, and also the Christians of some years' standing whose reading of the Bible had become stale and superficial, and had not matured as the readers had ripened personally. The book was written for the Scripture Union, and called *Understanding the Bible*. There is evidence that it still fulfils its author's purpose, helped by numerous translations and reprintings and by a revised edition (based on the New International Version) in 1984.[28]

Towards the end of the decade William Collins published as a Fount Original another paperback directly on a theme of Scripture: *Focus on Christ: An Enquiry into the Theology of Prepositions*.[29] This again was based on teaching originally delivered to a congregation, a course of sermons preached (as Rector Emeritus) at All Souls during July and August 1978. The introduction explains how

> ... this period overlapped the three weeks' residential Lambeth Conference at the University of Kent outside Canterbury. So as a congregation we found ourselves praying, with thousands of others throughout the Anglican Communion, that Christ would be the centre of the bishops' thinking.[30]

This intriguing 'theology of prepositions' turns out to be a study of what the writers of the New Testament mean when they use such phrases as 'through Christ', 'in Christ', 'with Christ', and so on. Perhaps the idea for the series (though not the content) owed something to one of the early Tyndale Lectures, delivered by Dr B. F. C. Atkinson in Cambridge while John Stott was at Ridley Hall, under the same title, *A Theology of Prepositions*.[31] David Edwards reviewed *Focus on Christ* for the *Church Times*: 'These themes are really timeless and spaceless,' he wrote. 'They are found wherever Christianity has in it the original passion of person-to-person love ... St Bernard might have written much of this book in the Middle Ages, or Charles Simeon might have preached it in early nineteenth-century Cambridge.'[32] Indeed, so 'timeless and spaceless' were its themes that an illustrated new edition was published twelve years later,[33] and it has been translated into half a dozen languages.

Among those with particular cause to be thankful for the book was a troubled divinity student at New College, Edinburgh, named Christopher Green. Brought up as an Anglican evangelical, he found himself 'on the brink of severing all my ties with evangelicalism and quite possibly with Christianity'[34] because of an intellectual (and ultimately spiritual) dilemma. He was faced with what seemed an unbridgeable rift between his Biblical Studies course, which 'assumed fairly sceptical conclusions of liberal scholarship, and left the student with little of orthodox Christianity remaining', and the Dogmatics department which seemed determined to disregard this undermining of their roots. Looking back on this period, he wrote:

> I found this split deeply disturbing ... on the one hand the biblical studies were continually threatening to erode my faith in the Bible, and on the other, the systematics studies were rooted in orthodoxy rather than the Bible, and it seemed that nothing would be lost if I surrendered to Barthianism. That way I could be as sceptical as my peers on the Bible, and still as conservative as my teachers on theology. Those I most admired seemed to have taken that same route. But to my mind the biblical studies material would have the final say, for orthodoxy would be based upon a lie, and the only honest way forward would be into an agnosticism.

While struggling with this dilemma, Christopher Green read *Focus on Christ* during the Easter vacation:

> Its subtitle *A Theology of Prepositions*, appealed to an undergraduate systematician. What it modelled was precisely what I lacked: a way of thinking that was simultaneously systematic and biblical, and where the Bible was not merely an authoritative source to be quoted, but the authority by which every other authority is measured ... *Focus on Christ* was thus a very important book for me ... it was a desperately needed evangelical alternative to two roads out of living faith, and I am profoundly grateful I found it that Easter.[35]

Of the three other smaller paperbacks published over John Stott's name during the 1970s, one was an enlarged edition of *The Baptism and Fullness of the Holy Spirit*. The title was shortened to *Baptism and Fullness*, but the length more than trebled. It has remained consistently in print.[36] By contrast, *Obeying Christ in a Changing World: 1. The Lord Christ* was a symposium under his editorship, specifically for NEAC '77 at Nottingham, to which he also contributed the opening chapter. John Stott was General Editor for the series of three books, and (in more detail) editor of the first. They related specifically to the work of the Congress and have not been reprinted.[37]

John Stott's third paperback published in the mid-1970s was *Christian Mission in the Modern World*, a study which has been seen as increasingly significant for an evangelical understanding of some of the central themes of Christian missiology. In the Preface he traces the origin of the book to 'four particular experiences': his attendance as Advisor at the WCC Assembly at Uppsala in 1968; the Baker Memorial Lecture in 1974 in Melbourne which forms a chapter of the book; the Lausanne Congress in the same year where he gave the opening address; and the invitation to deliver the 1975 Chavasse Lectures at Wycliffe Hall, Oxford.[38] The theme of the book (which closely follows the Chavasse lecture series) is the relation between the church and the world, about which most Christians would make some use of the term 'mission':

> But there would be a wide divergence in our understanding of what our 'mission' is, of what part 'evangelism' plays in mission, and of what part 'dialogue' plays in evangelism. I fear further that we would diverge from one another not only in our understanding of the *nature* of mission, evangelism and dialogue, but also in our understanding of the *goal* of all three. Possibly the terms 'conversion' and 'salvation' would figure somewhere in our definition of goals, but again there might be little consensus regarding the meaning of these words. My task, then, is to take this cluster of five words – mission, evangelism, dialogue, salvation and conversion – and to attempt to define them biblically.[39]

John Stott had particularly in mind his own recollections of the poor handling of Scripture at Uppsala, and the way in which 'relations between ecumenical and evangelical Christians (if I may use these terms as a convenient shorthand, for I recognize that they are by no means mutually exclusive) have hardened into something like a confrontation'. However, he was quick to add:

> I have no wish to worsen this situation. Nor, I hope, shall I resort to the dubious device of putting up a few ecumenical skittles in order to knock them down with well-aimed evangelical balls, so that we can all applaud our easy victory! Mind you, I believe that some current ecumenical thinking is mistaken. But then, candidly, I believe some of our traditional evangelical formulations are

mistaken also ... My chief concern, therefore, is to bring both ecumenical and evangelical thinking to the same independent and objective test, namely that of the biblical revelation.[40]

A number of reviewers picked up the author's frank admission that, ten years on from the 1966 World Congress on Evangelism in Berlin, where he spoke on the Great Commission, 'today ... I would express myself differently'.[41] He continued:

I now see more clearly that not only the consequences of the commission but the actual commission itself must be understood to include social as well as evangelistic responsibility, unless we are to be guilty of distorting the words of Jesus.

The crucial form in which the Great Commission has been handed down to us (though it is the most neglected because it is the most costly) is the Johannine. Jesus had anticipated it in his prayer in the upper room when he said to the Father: 'As thou didst send me into the world, so I have sent them into the world' (John 17:18). Now, probably in the same upper room but after his death and resurrection, he turned his prayer-statement into a commission and said: 'As the Father has sent me, even so I send you' (John 20:21). In both these sentences Jesus did more than draw a vague parallel between his mission and ours. Deliberately and precisely he made his mission the *model* of ours ...

The book has had a continuing influence beyond its size, since it expounds in detail some of the thinking that lies behind the conciser statements of the Lausanne Covenant. Defining as it does John Stott's conclusions on the relationship between direct evangelism and Christian social action, it underpins later and longer books – for example, *Issues Facing Christians Today* in the 1980s and the section on Holistic Mission in *The Contemporary Christian* in the early 1990s.[42] It has been used as part of a reading-list for academic studies of missiology, and translated into Chinese, Korean and Malayalam as well as into eight European languages. Remarkably, for a semi-technical study of this kind, the US edition has gone through fifteen reprints.

It was a courageous book, not simply because of its outspoken criticisms of theological weakness in the WCC and the ecumenical establishment, but because it marked a further stage in the author's determination to set forth the truth as he saw it, well knowing that it would diminish in some Free Church and Independent circles his reputation for unswerving evangelical orthodoxy, free from any taint of 'social gospel'. Such evangelicals (who rightly distrusted the 'social gospel' of theological liberalism) did not always accept the crucial distinction between the mistaken identification of the social betterment of society with 'the kingdom of God' (losing thereby much of the New Testament emphasis on the true meaning of salvation) and the legitimate call for a recovery among evangelicals of concern for the social *implications* of the gospel.[43] This kind of misunderstanding of his position was nothing new. Something similar had happened ten years before in his confrontation with Dr Martyn Lloyd-Jones, which had not been forgotten. And because of his resolve to follow Scripture as best he could interpret it, even when this brought him into conflict with a received evangelical understanding of truth or practice, there was a price to be paid in fellowship and reputation which grew heavier rather than lighter as the years passed. On the particular issues raised in *Christian Mission in the Modern World*, he had remained anxious to enter into and understand the views of those represented by

> ... the right wing of the evangelical movement, particularly in the United States, who say no; that the missionary and the evangelist are identical terms and that mission has traditionally been understood in evangelistic terms.

In listening to these 'right-wing evangelicals', he continued,

> I have come to understand better their concern. Their concern is lest those who are called to be cross-cultural missionaries will be deflected from their primary evangelistic task by becoming involved in social, community, medical, agricultural or political activity.

To this he replies:

> I fully understand that many cross-cultural missionaries may be called to specialize exclusively in evangelism. But in the church or in its mission teams, where you may have half a dozen or a dozen people, one or two of whom are specializing in evangelism, there's no reason why others shouldn't specialize in social work, medical work, development work. There is no reason why the local church shouldn't be involved in all these things.[44]

But what were arguably John Stott's most significant books of the 1970s were his three contributions to the series he founded under the title The Bible Speaks Today. This was originally conceived as a ten-year project (in the event, it took over thirty years to complete the New Testament) with three main characteristics, 'accurate exegesis, contemporary application and a readable style'.[45] The first volume – something of a pilot for the series – had been published in 1968 under the title *The Message of Galatians*,[46] and with a second volume from his pen, *Guard the Gospel: The Message of 2 Timothy*,[47] almost complete, it was time to look for other contributors to the series. In a memorandum to accompany his invitation to possible authors, John Stott made clear that he was looking first for accurate biblical exposition, quoting by way of example 'the beloved Simeon', who declared:

> My endeavour is to bring out of Scripture what is there, and not to thrust in what I think might be there. I have a great jealousy on this head; never to speak more or less than I believe the mind of the Spirit in the passage I am expounding.[48]

But exegesis was only the beginning of the author's task:

> The series is deliberately entitled 'The Bible Speaks Today'. It is *today's message* we want our readers to hear and heed ... The application will sometimes be to the burning theological and moral issues of the day, and sometimes to our personal and social respon-sibilities as Christians ... For these reasons I am choosing as contributors an international team of men with 'pastoral' and 'preaching' rather than purely 'academic' gifts (if you will allow the distinction).

Finally, it was made clear that editor and publishers were looking for a readable style, 'a text which flows'.[49]

Perhaps it was not surprising that only one author besides the editor himself was published in the New Testament series during the 1970s: this was Michael Wilcock, formerly curate at All Souls and at that time in his first living at St Faith's Church, Maidstone. His studies on the book of Revelation and on St Luke's Gospel appeared in 1975 and 1979 respect-ively. J. A. Motyer, Principal of Trinity College, Bristol, meanwhile broke new ground with *The Day of the Lion* on the book of Amos, and accepted an invitation to become joint editor of the series with responsibility for the Old Testament. Besides his own book, three others appeared in the later 1970s: Derek Kidner on Ecclesiastes, Ronald Wallace on Daniel, and John Goldingay on selected Psalms.[50]

The task of editor was no sinecure. Not all who were asked to con-tribute accepted the invitation. Not all contributions were suitable when finally submitted. Some manuscripts passed to and fro several times between author and editor before both were sufficiently satisfied. Michael Wilcock had the advantage of having heard John Stott preach the course on Galatians which became the first of the series. When he received a letter asking if he would contribute to the series, and if he had a choice of book, he chose the book of Revelation because he had himself been preaching a series expounding it at his own church. He made, therefore, fewer demands on the editor's time, diplomacy and patience than some later writers.

> I remember his comments on my MSS [Michael Wilcock wrote] as encouraging, perceptive, and thorough; they aimed above all at fidelity to the text, clarity of expression, and application to life (the marks of course of his own writing, and of the BST series). They were almost always *suggestions* – 'don't you think it might be better if … ?' It was, in other words, an easy yoke, and a light one too …'[51]

Meanwhile, John Stott himself continued to contribute to the series. His studies in 2 Timothy had been given first as addresses at Urbana 1967/8, and at Keswick the following year. In the same way his Keswick 1972 Bible readings, 'Christ's Portrait of a Christian: Studies in Matthew 5, 6 and 7', helped to lay the foundation for his third The Bible Speaks Today book, entitled *Christian Counter-Culture: The Message of the Sermon on the Mount.*[52] He had also preached and spoken from these chapters in All Souls, and to various university Christian Unions in the UK and Canada. Such spoken exposition was an invaluable preparation for the books: he recommended it to others whom he invited to write for the series. The American publisher remarked on the trouble he took to shape what began as addresses for the different medium of the printed page:

> It was commonly accepted among all of us at IVP that John Stott was the most meticulous writer we worked with. Almost all speakers accepted their tape transcriptions from the triennial missionary convention (Urbana) as ready for publication. Not John: he knew the differences between print and spoken communication …[53]

By *The Church of England Newspaper* this BST study of the Sermon on the Mount was acclaimed as 'Paperback of the Year'. Richard Holloway, reviewing it for the *Church Times*, was ambivalent. 'I'm in two minds about this book', he began, having read it in the train 'on what the Bishop of Salisbury calls "Ash Thursday"':

> Anyway, there I was at the beginning of Lent on a high-speed retreat conducted by John Stott as I shot from Scotland to London, and he fairly rubbed my nose in my own moral and spiritual feebleness. *Christian Counter-Culture* is an exposition of the Sermon on the

Mount. Unlike a lot of contemporary writers on the Bible, John Stott's intention is to let the Bible speak to us, to confront us with the Sermon on the Mount in a fresh and personal way, without shirking critical issues. In this he has succeeded admirably ... Reading the book was a salutary shock to me, because, like many people who like to be thought of as progressive and up-to-date, I'm a bit soft-centred when it comes to dealing with personal morality, though less so in the area of institutional morality. I need to be re-acquainted with the absolute standard of the holiness of Christ, in private as well as in public behaviour ...[54]

But 'a nagging unease' remained, with the reviewer 'somewhat repelled by the confident and often harsh tone of Dr Stott's frequent admonitions'. Others, however, were attracted: a minister then unknown to John Stott wrote from Belfast in 1983 to tell him how he had been using the book 'here in this city of troubles' as the basis for an adult Bible class:

Within two to three weeks our numbers had doubled until 800 and more people were attending weekly. I have seldom seen such tremendous attention given to public teaching of the Word of God in my lifetime ... You can well imagine when we got to the teaching about turning the other cheek the repercussions for this community were mind-bending! Our lot is to see people slain on our streets virtually every day, and I can only thank God that you took the time to write down what God had laid on your heart so that others of us here in this land, and other lands, could see more clearly the wonderful teaching the Lord Jesus gave on that mountain.[55]

Others too were finding something of the same. Dr Billy Graham's youngest daughter Ruth wrote recalling the Christmas John Stott had spent with her parents when she was a child, 'a kind, warm stranger with a lovely accent'. She went on to recount how she had been using *Christian Counter-Culture* in her own women's Bible study group: 'your wisdom and insights were passed on each week ...'[56]

Only a year after the publication of *Christian Counter-Culture*, John Stott contributed his fourth volume to the series, this time on Ephesians.[57] He explained in the Author's Preface that this too had been hammered out in the lecture hall and pulpit:

During the past five years and more I have been studying the text of Ephesians, absorbing its message, feeling its impact and dreaming its dream. It has been a great practical help in this period to attempt to expound the letter to various groups and to receive their reactions. I began with the responsive and long-suffering con-gregation of All Souls Church, and continued with conferences in India, Nepal, Canada and Mexico, and in July 1975 with the memorable Keswick Centenary convention. No audience is more alert and critical than one composed of students; I have therefore found it specially profitable to share with student groups in India, America, Europe, Australia and Latin America, and to be challenged by the more sustained exposition required in 1976 by the Summer Study Institute at the University of Maryland, USA, and by the Summer School of Regent College, Vancouver.[58]

This BST study on Ephesians, *God's New Society*, was among a number of books by John Stott which an American missionary in Bangladesh had been using to pastor a Russian prisoner converted to Christ in Dhaka Central Jail, a former diplomat falsely implicated in gold smuggling. Writing to tell John Stott of this, the missionary quoted from one of the letters sent to him from the prison:

> I am enjoying very much your Walkman and the cassettes you gave me. John Stott preaching on *Ephesians* is marvellous. I found answers about the Christian attitude (including toward evil) in another of Stott's books that you gave me: *Christian Counter-Culture*. John Stott is nowadays my favourite author with his lucid logic and tremendous persuasion.[59]

By the end of the decade the BST series was firmly established, with nine titles published (most of them already available in up to a dozen languages) and more on the way. A small notice in the front of *God's New Society* must have been a particular pleasure to the author, as an example of how his vision for it was being fulfilled:

> This book was chosen by the Trustees of the Evangelical Literature Trust as their '1980 Bonus Book' for free distribution to some two thousand members of third-world 'Pastors Book Clubs' sponsored by the Trust.

3

Even for a professional author shut away in some academic ivory tower, eight books in ten years would be a mark of considerable industry. Writing, however, as preceding chapters have shown, could be only one aspect of John Stott's ministry. Even so, to the eight books listed above must be added the constant editorial oversight of the BST series, and a number of smaller but still significant publications.

Three booklets require mention. In 1972 John Stott gave his Presidential Address to the IVF annual conference under the title 'Your Mind Matters' and it was published the same year.[60] It was a timely subject. Like many others, John Stott saw the 1970s as 'the decade of the non-rational';[61] but though evangelicalism was popularly supposed to value emotion above intellect, the importance of the mind was by no means a new theme in Christian Union circles. Oliver Barclay has shown how, as far back as the 1930s and '40s, 'DJ' 'drew together a group of like-minded people to plan for serious theological advance at an academic level' under G. T. Manley, who had been Senior Wrangler at Cambridge 'in the year when Bertrand Russell had come sixth!' And in the same book he speaks of how Francis Schaeffer (whose first books were published in 1968) 'helped to remove the lingering fear in CE [conservative evangelical] circles of intellectual and theological involvement'.[62] Timothy Chester, who interviewed John Stott at some length in the 1990s, draws attention to two further influences which helped to strengthen his passionate conviction that 'your mind matters':

> In the early sixties John Stott had been asked by Jim Houston to speak at Regent College in Vancouver, Canada. Stott returned on a number of occasions and was impressed by their attempts to develop a Christian attitude to a range of secular issues and to train lay-people. He also read Harry Blamires' *The Christian Mind* which called for a Christian mind to be developed in response to secularism and this proved influential in his thinking.[63]

It was the substance of this address, 'Your Mind Matters', which John Stott delivered to the ten US Colleges of the Christian College Consortium in the fall of 1972,[64] and it remained a recurring theme of his preaching and writing, especially to students. Twenty years later he was still urging upon his readers the need

> ... to repent of the cult of mindlessness, and of any residual anti-intellectualism or intellectual laziness of which we may be guilty. These things are negative, cramping and destructive. They insult God, impoverish us and weaken our testimony. A responsible use of our minds, on the other hand, glorifies God, enriches us and strengthens our witness in the world.[65]

John Stott returned to the theme of the intellect in another booklet, arising out of his Presidency of the Evangelical Alliance. *Balanced Christianity*[66] is a short study of four 'polarisations' met with in evangelical (indeed, in almost all) Christianity: intellect and emotion, conservative and radical, form and freedom, evangelism and social action. It is a plea for unity, liberty and charity. Three years later another Presidential Address to the Evangelical Alliance was published as a booklet, *Essentials for Tomorrow's Christians*, an exposition of John 17 (a favourite chapter), in terms of the truth, holiness, unity and mission of the Christian church.[67]

Two other significant booklets, not unrelated, were published in the mid-1970s: *Walk in His Shoes*, a powerful plea for Christian compassion, following the example of Jesus, in the face of world need;[68] and an authoritative commentary on the Lausanne Covenant.[69] This thirty-seven page exposition, highly condensed in style and authenticated by a wide range of Bible references, was written during a single week at The Hookses in September 1974 at the request of the Lausanne Committee chairman, Bishop Jack Dain. Because John Stott had himself chaired the drafting committee, the discussions (often lengthy, even heated) behind each of the fifteen sections of the Covenant were still fresh in his mind as he came to draft his commentary two months later. The sections on 'The Nature of Evangelism' and on 'Christian Social Responsibility' again underline the partnership between 'proclamation with a view to persuasion'; and social – even socio-political – involvement in the name of Jesus Christ.

These themes of bringing the Christian mind to bear upon the issues of society found further expression in a long series of articles in *All Souls*, running through most of the 1970s. They represent a brave attempt to say something significant in a page or two for the general Christian reader on major contemporary issues. He included topics current in the church: Anglicans and Methodists, Anglicans and Roman Catholics, disestablishment, the Lambeth Conference; but also such issues as abortion, economic equality among nations, and the simple lifestyle. Some of these were reprinted as, or formed the basis of, an influential monthly series of 'Cornerstone' articles in *Christianity Today* from July 1977 until the summer of 1981. Here he drew on his current experiences in different parts of the world: with Roman Catholics in Venice at work on ERCDOM ('Nothing surprises me more, I think, than our degree of consensus on baptism');[70] with students in Latin America ('"Why can't we form our own university church?" they asked');[71] with the Director of the Tarsus Museum in Turkey ('Would the museum Director accept an exhibition display of Paul if one were presented to him, we asked?').[72] Besides the authenticity of the man on the spot, the articles reveal not only a range of contemporary reading (Hans Küng, James Barr, Steven Spielberg, a Papal encyclical, a UNESCO Declaration, the Brandt Report), but an occasional lightness of touch which engages the attention of the reader, such as the professor who told him, 'I work in an atmosphere so materialistic that the word "spirit" is never mentioned, unless prefaced by the adjective "methylated"!' While perhaps half of the series springs directly from his immediate experience in travels and consultations, problems of peace and war, pro-life issues, economic injustice, work, culture, race and poverty are all addressed.[73]

Even while he was regularly writing these two series, Michael Baughen invited John Stott to preach a number of occasional sermons at All Souls under the title 'Issues Facing Britain Today', and it was from all these sources that his major book *Issues Facing Christians Today* was constructed: a pioneering task in fields largely neglected by evangelical scholars, where it was hard to find serious attempts to relate the teaching of Scripture to contemporary issues, while doing equal justice to both. No wonder that John Stott should confess in the Introduction:

> Several times in the course of writing I have been tempted to give up. I have felt now foolish and now presumptuous to attempt such an undertaking. For I am in no sense a specialist in moral theology or social ethics, and I have no particular expertise or experience in some of the fields into which I trespass. Moreover, each topic is complex, has attracted an extensive literature, only some of which I have been able to read, and is potentially divisive, even in a few cases explosive. Yet I have persevered, mainly because what I am venturing to offer the public is not a polished professional piece but the rough-hewn amateur work of an ordinary Christian who is struggling to think Christianly, that is, to apply the biblical revelation to the pressing issues of the day.[74]

'Struggling to think Christianly' in the quotation above is a clear reference to what John Stott often referred to as 'PIM' – 'pain in the mind'. It is a phrase which Bishop Lesslie Newbigin attributes to G. A. Studdert Kennedy, the 'Woodbine Willie' of the First World War, who 'used to say that any real thinking arose out of a "pain in the mind"'.[75] Bishop Newbigin quotes the phrase in the context of the missionary's task: thinking through the big questions in seeking to communicate the faith. Nor is it only the teacher who feels it: pain can be the experience of all who wrestle with new truth. Vincent J. Donovan, pioneer missionary to the Masai, gives just such an example. He noticed, one morning, among those he had been teaching, an old man named Keriko, in obvious pain:

> I was certain he was ill. But my Masai catechist helper, Paul, chuckled at my concern.

'Are you worried about old man Keriko? Don't worry, he is all right. You see, for a Masai there is not much need to think in life. Almost everything he learns, he learns by memory, by rote. It becomes automatic for him, like tying your shoes or buttoning your shirt is for you. He learns about food and clothes and houses and kraals and cattle and grasses and women by memory – even things about God and religion. When he needs an answer to a question, all he has to do is reach into his memory and come up with the correct answer. He can reach his adulthood without thinking at all. What you are asking Keriko to do is to take the first thought about the Masai brotherhood of the orporor, and the second thought about the human race and the God of all the tribes, and to put the two thoughts together to make a new thought. That is very difficult work. What you are witnessing in Keriko is the pain on the face of a man who is thinking for the first time in his life.'[76]

The act of thinking, 'putting two thoughts together to make a new thought', can indeed demand painful mental effort. But those Christian teachers who wrestle with controversial issues know at least two other aspects of this 'pain in the mind'. The first is well exemplified in his biographer's description of Dr J. I. Packer, and could be echoed in the experience of many others committed to the pursuit of truth:

At times, he found himself at the centre of controversy, sometimes experiencing the pain of arguing with those who were close friends and colleagues. As a public representative of both evangelicalism and 'great-tradition Christianity', Packer has experienced the pain, sadness and bitterness which are so often the lot of those who maintain 'theological watchfulness for the sake of the gospel'.[77]

But in the same ways even more testing is the pain which is felt within, unrelated to friends or critics. 'What, then,' John Stott asked his hearers in 1992, 'is the pain which authors experience? I think it is the challenge to retain one's own integrity.' He went on:

Coming to a problem while writing, one is tempted to conceal it with a carefully chosen formula, instead of wrestling with it. I would go further. If one is called to write in the area of theological controversy, and to seek to defend the faith against its critics, its opponents, a very painful process is involved in which one interiorizes the debate. One has to absorb the arguments on both sides, feeling their strength, and so being pulled most uncomfortably in opposite directions at the same time. But the pain can be creative if what emerges from it is a clarification of the issues and even fresh light or understanding on old dilemmas.[78]

4

Ten years before, at the close of the 1960s, John Stott had been faced with an insistent invitation to move to Oxford as Principal of Wycliffe Hall.[79] He had given this serious prayer and thought before declining on the grounds that his vocation was to be a pastor rather than a Principal; and that he had no clear call to leave All Souls. In the event James Hickinbotham proved the man for the hour, and under his leadership Wycliffe Hall had prospered. Then, at the end of the 1970s, Canon Hickinbotham retired to Devon and the Council again invited John Stott to become Principal. It must have seemed to them that, free now of a parish, this might be a propitious moment to start a new chapter of ministry. But again it was not to be. Four years as Rector Emeritus had given shape to a new calling to teach worldwide, to write, and to work towards his vision of an 'Institute for Contemporary Christianity'. Indeed his final newsletter of 1979 gave a hint of things to come when he wrote of St Peter's, Vere Street, where the fabric was a cause of anxiety:

> It has been closed for over 2 years, owing to a serious attack of dry rot in the roof and other timbers, whose elimination will be fearfully expensive. But the work has been begun, because a local Music College are now renting it, leaving it free for our use in the evenings, at weekends and in vacations ... The prospects of its future are exciting ...[80]

Planning for the London Institute, which was to be the 'future use' alluded to, began seriously in early 1980. Meanwhile Geoffrey Shaw was appointed Principal of Wycliffe Hall.[81] Nor was this all. Hard on the heels of the renewed invitation to Wycliffe Hall came a letter from Illinois inviting, indeed urging, John Stott to become the first full-time President of the World Evangelical Fellowship. It reached him during a visit to the States, and he replied from Fuller Theological Seminary in California making it clear that it was 'out of the question for me to accept. I have too many other commitments which I cannot shed to make it possible for me to contemplate this.' Even if it could be a part-time appointment, there were many reasons that seemed to rule it out of court. But his refusal was not to imply any loss of commitment to the WEF. He told the outgoing President in his reply:

> I hope I do not need to add that I am strongly committed to the

WEF and to all that it stands for. I retain vivid memories of the conference in Holland in 1951 during which the WEF was brought into being. And you know how much I have treasured the times which you and I have spent together, and ... the friendship which has developed between us. I am also very concerned that the right way may be found to bring the WEF and the Lausanne movement into closer partnership.[82]

The 1970s had proved a decade of change in John Stott's professional life and the shape of his ministry. Before they ended, Joy's death was to leave only Joanna and himself from the Harley Street family of his childhood. His father had died in 1958, and Lily in 1966. Then in 1979, while he was in America, his sister Joy was admitted to hospital as an emergency, having taken an overdose.

Joy had faithfully – indeed, heroically – cared for both her parents in their old age, and then for 'Auntie Babe'. In the eighteen months or so after Lily's stroke they enjoyed one another's company in a peaceful and happy relationship. But following her mother's death Joy 'really seemed to lose her way ... she never settled anywhere or to anything'.[83] Though loved and indeed admired by family and friends, she felt herself a failure and struggled with an increasing lack of self-worth. Her mental condition was eventually diagnosed as schizophrenia.

After a rootless period, in trouble with her hearing, she settled on a small house in Chapel-en-le-Frith, not far from her sister. The Derbyshire Dales were a joy to her. Joanna described how

> ... she went out and about a lot in her small car and enjoyed the countryside very much. We tried, my friends and I, to introduce her to the people here, but we were all busy housewives with families and she made no friends; Fanny [Joy's undisciplined beagle] again was no help. Her 'voices' got worse and the medication was very little help: possibly in the end 'they' told her to take all those pills. It was a horrid, cold, snowy winter and although we shopped for her and talked to her it was all too much for her.[84]

As soon as she had taken the drugs Joy phoned her sister and was at once rushed to hospital, critically ill. She lingered long enough for John Stott to see her as soon as he returned to England. She recognized him, but could not sustain a rational conversation and died a day or two later.[85] The inquest was delayed to allow for 'an inquiry', but returned an open verdict. Joanna wrote a full account to her brother (by then again overseas), telling of the Coroner's summing up: 'he was *not* going to give a verdict of suicide, he had seen so many of this type of case – where people with mental troubles took overdoses really to call attention' to themselves and their troubles.[86]

Joy's Roman Catholicism had been short-lived. Her local Anglican vicar in Chapel-en-le-Frith wrote to John Stott after her death, describing how she had talked with him of 'the shattering experience when her faith became meaningless to her',[87] but was himself confident that she died trusting 'in the love of God'. John Stott told his friends of her death in his April newsletter, recalling their shared childhood, her war service, her teaching and lecturing (which included work in Holloway Prison) and the way she had nursed their parents at the end: 'Friends have written charming things about her, that she had "a rare and colourful spirit" and an unusual blend of "fun, mischievousness and eccentricity".' Six months later, writing about the future of The Hookses, he described how Joy had died intestate,

> ... and with my share of the money she left I plan to build a first floor extension behind the house, with two more bedrooms and an extra bathroom. I am going to call the bigger bedroom 'Joy's room' in her memory, and the smaller 'Fanny's room' since that was the name of her much loved, very handsome but totally undisciplined beagle! I am confident that she would approve, indeed does.[88]

The 1980s

NINE

Thinking Christianly: The London Institute

1

The 1980s defy classification. They saw the worst recession since the 1930s, shortly followed by the enterprise culture of the Thatcher and the Reagan years. At one point Great Britain saw the pound fall almost to parity with the dollar. Halfpennies and sixpences and the £1 note vanished in favour of the 20p and the £1 coin. Unemployment in the UK reached three million. They were years marked by unending warfare (the Falklands, the Gulf, Afghanistan, Angola, Lebanon) and by the resurgence of militant Islam; but also by *perestroika*, *glasnost*, the dismantling of the Berlin Wall, and prospects for peace higher than at any time since 1945. New words entered the language or became part of common speech: Yuppie (Young Upwardly-mobile Professional) and Aids (Acquired Immune Deficiency Syndrome), the Space Shuttle, the greenhouse effect, the compact disc, the Chunnel, the Exocet.

Newspapers throughout the decade carried headlines of terrorism and kidnapping (Terry Waite in 1987 was one of many), hijacking, bombing, hostage-taking and assassination: the US President was shot in 1981 and saved only by the small calibre of the weapon; two months later the Pope was severely wounded in St Peter's Square. By May 1982 he was sufficiently recovered to pay the first Papal visit to Great Britain since 1531, entering Canterbury Cathedral to a fanfare of trumpets. War and famine in Ethiopia and Somalia took their terrible toll. The names of places scattered across the globe acquired new and usually sinister significance: Chernobyl, Goose Green, Greenham Common, the Golan Heights, Tiananmen Square, Enniskillen, Lockerbie. Sir Arnold Stott would have been fascinated to read of a patient living for three months with the world's first artificial heart; and perhaps disquieted to learn of the Californian baby who died after twenty-one days with a heart transplanted from a baboon. In 1981 Prince Charles and Lady Diana Spencer shared their wedding with 700 million delighted TV viewers across the world. More substantial cause for celebration came in 1988 when the Soviet Chief of Staff held a press conference in the Pentagon; and delegates from 159 nations stood to applaud President Gorbachev's declaration that 'the use or threat of force can no longer ... be an instrument of foreign policy. This applies above all to nuclear arms.'[1]

In England churchgoing continued to decline, though at a decreasing rate. As the decade began, a census counted 39,000 Christian churches, with 18% of the total adult population claiming church membership. Michael Turnbull, then Chief Secretary of the Church Army, commented on the statistics through Anglican eyes:

> Every week for the past four years 280 people have left the Church of England ... Over the same period other mainstream churches have shown a similar trend while what we, with effortless superiority, sometimes call the fringe churches have shown marked growth in attendance.[2]

Though evangelicalism might claim a high proportion of Anglican ordinations,[3] and largely unite behind Dr Billy Graham for 'Mission England',[4] in other aspects it was becoming a house divided against itself. John Wenham, that shrewd observer and participator in the student scene, returned to Oxford in 1980 after seven years away. He concluded, 'We had lost some ground as well as gaining some. We were a considerable army but we gave the impression that we did not quite know where we were going. We lacked cohesion because we lacked clarity.'[5]

In the US, though there was some evidence of decline in churchgoing, it did not compare with the picture in Britain. Americans who were asked if they had attended a place of worship in the last seven days gave remarkably consistent answers through the 1960s, '70s and '80s, 'in the range of 40–43 per cent'.[6] The 'New Christian Right' came into increasing prominence during the decade (and was said to have contributed to the election of President Reagan, a conservative Republican).

Conservative Protestantism grew, if not absolutely, at least as a proportion of American church life, while liberalism declined in numbers if not markedly in influence.[7]

In 1980 Robert Runcie was translated from the See of St Albans to be Archbishop of Canterbury and spiritual leader of the worldwide Anglican Communion. Among his first tasks was to preside over the introduction of the *Alternative Service Book, 1980*. In 1981 the Synod voted to allow women to join the diaconate; while across the Atlantic at the end of the decade Barbara Harris became coadjutor bishop in the diocese of Massachusetts, the first woman bishop of the Anglican Communion. The twelfth Lambeth Conference called the church to a 'Decade of Evangelism'; and the Papal visit to England brought with it a 'Common Declaration' and a commendation of the work of ARCIC (the Anglican–Roman Catholic International Commission), but no progress whatever – informed circles had expected none – on the question of Anglican Orders.[8] In 1983 the World Council of Churches held its sixth assembly, nearly losing the Church of England from among its members over the WCC's Special Fund to Combat Racism which rendered aid to what some saw as freedom fighting and others as guerrilla warfare.[9] Nearer home, the findings drawn from the 1981 census, coupled with rioting in the streets of a number of British cities (Brixton, Toxteth, Wolverhampton, Birmingham) led to a 'Call for Action by Church and Nation' in the massive Report of the Archbishop of Canterbury's Commission on Urban Priority Areas.[10] *The Times* disliked 'this highly politicized report' and criticized its economics;[11] but it helped to place issues of social justice, including unemployment, racial inequality and urban poverty squarely on the nation's agenda. It was the uncomfortable presence of such injustices which had lent urgency, a year before *Faith in the City*, to John Stott's *Issues Facing Christians Today* with its opening question, 'Involvement: Is it our concern?'[12]

For John Stott himself the 1980s again began with Urbana, the vast US InterVarsity Missionary Convention. It was to be his final visit and he expounded Romans 1 – 5 to an assembly which had grown to number 16,000. By now his life was settling into its new pattern: about three months of the year travelling in the cause of the gospel, with students and pastors still much in mind; another six based in London at his apartment above the Rectory garage, including ten weeks' teaching at the London Institute; and most of the rest at The Hookses[13] preparing addresses and writing. Birdwatching was not neglected; but for the most part was squeezed into the occasional vacation, including expeditions, where possible, in the remoter corners of the globe.[14] Succeeding chapters describe some of the journeys, and some of the books of the 1980s. Taken together, they provide ample justification for the *cri de coeur* with which

Billy Graham began a letter to him early in the decade:

> Thank you for your November letter. Just reading it made me a bit exhausted! How do you do it my friend? If you had a wife, five children, five in-laws – and 15 grandchildren, it would be rather difficult. Please forgive me if I am not able to keep up with you![15]

The year 1981 was supposed to include a six-months' sabbatical in recognition of John Stott's sixtieth birthday, 'Devaluation Day' as he called it.[16] Dick and Rosemary Bird spent it with him at The Hookses, and gave him a present of aubrietias and primroses from the local nursery for his wild Welsh garden. He wrote to Frances, holding the fort in London: 'It was a happy day ... Rosemary had baked a chocolate cake, furnished with six candles, one for each decade.' In the bi-annual newsletter that he sent out to a wide circle of friends he described how

> I sat that afternoon in my favourite nook on the Pembrokeshire cliffs and read the exhortation in Hebrews 12:1 to 'run with perseverance the race marked out for us'. So I prayed for grace to persevere in Christian faith, life and service, and a few months later was encouraged by the promise of Psalm 92:14 that God's people 'will still bear fruit in old age, they will stay fresh and green'. May it be so![17]

High among the 'fruits' of his thinking and planning at this time was the projected London Institute for Contemporary Christianity, of which he became the first Director the following year. It was a major project (a call from God, which he had been seeking to discern during the last few years) and one of three reasons which he gave for declining, when asked in 1981 to allow his name to go forward for election as Archbishop of Sydney, on the retirement of Sir Marcus Loane. Dr Stuart Babbage, a former Dean of Sydney, wrote urging him 'to allow us the privilege of putting your name forward for the gospel's sake'.[18] But to John Stott himself, the proposition was not one he could consider: 'a combination of circumstances puts the matter beyond doubt'. First, Sydney should have an Australian, and good men were available. Second, 'I am too old at 60 to learn the ropes ... I don't think a man can or should be an Archbishop who has not first served his apprenticeship as a Bishop.' But thirdly, 'and decisively', he was committed to make his vision for the London Institute a reality.[19]

In the summer of 1982 Michael Baughen's departure to become Bishop of Chester meant for All Souls a change of Rector, and a seven-month vacancy before Richard Bewes was instituted as his successor the following January. To the eyes of a young graduate working at All Souls while on his way to training for ordination, the change was dramatic:

> As to the changeover between Michael Baughen and Richard Bewes, there was a short period of interregnum during which Andrew Cornes presided (with a rod of kindly iron, quite different from Michael Baughen's more vulnerable and personal style). Then came Richard Bewes, who came across as unbelievably 'laid-back'. At the first full staff meeting with around 20 of us present (following the interregnum in which there had been immense efficiency and productivity) Richard introduced the meeting, following opening prayer, with the question, 'Right, what shall we all do *now*?'[20]

John Stott himself was delighted at the new appointment. Not surprisingly, he was able to report that Richard Bewes had 'kindly invited me to stay on as Rector Emeritus, still living at 13 Bridford Mews',[21] with Frances Whitehead in her office on the ground floor of the Rectory, easily accessible by a communicating door. It was important to him both to make sure that his presence at All Souls was unobtrusive while Richard Bewes settled in, and to see that the proprieties of his position as Rector Emeritus (in the terms of his licence, Honorary Curate) were scrupulously observed.

In his first full year as Director of the London Institute, John Stott found himself in demand (besides his overseas travels) for a number of engagements, remarkable in their variety. He began the year as the guest of the Queen at Sandringham, preaching on the Sunday and staying over the weekend, having had the forethought to hire a dinner-jacket from Moss Bros. He could not resist a letter to Frances Whitehead:

SANDRINGHAM, NORFOLK

Sunday, 9th Jan. 83

My dear Frances,
I did not feel I could spend the week-end here and not avail myself of the Royal Notepaper, provided abundantly in my bedroom!

I had the fantastic privilege last night of being a guest at a Royal Barbeque in a large beach hut which belongs to the Queen, about half an hour's drive away. On arrival I found the Duke of Edinburgh cooking at one end of the porch, and Princess Anne at the other. It was Prince Andrew's last night before rejoining his unit; hence the celebration. Hunks of barbecued beef, half-ducks, sausages and baked potatoes were served. I found myself between the Queen Mother and

> Lady Abel Smith, the lady in waiting. The informality was amazing, and I shall always treasure a memory of the Queen with a Royal Squeegee, mopping up something which had been spilled!

He was up at first light on Monday to visit the RSPB hides at the Snettisham gravel pits ('Pinkfooted, Brent and Barnacle geese; and four Hen Harriers')[22] before returning to London. As on other occasions, the Queen promptly sent a personal gift from her Sandringham estate by way of thanks to the preacher. Toby Howarth, who was to join John Stott as a study assistant, vividly recalls staring out of the window of John Stott's home:

> I noticed a police motorcycle turn into the Mews. Sure enough, it stopped outside the flat and the doorbell rang. Wondering what Uncle John had been up to, I opened the door with some trepidation. The policeman simply opened one of his panniers, lifted out a brace of pheasant, feathers and all, and said, 'For the Revd Dr Stott, with the compliments of Her Majesty the Queen ...'[23]

It is not (or used not to be) the custom for British clergy to call themselves 'Doctor' on the strength of Doctorates awarded overseas. Although in 1971 he had accepted an Honorary DD from Trinity Evangelical Divinity School, Deerfield, Illinois, it was not until Archbishop Robert Runcie conferred on him a Lambeth DD on 18 July 1983 that John Stott accepted the appellation 'The Revd Dr ...'. The Archbishop wrote to him in February: 'I hope you will feel able to accept this as a recognition of the long and positive service you have given in leadership of the Evangelicals in the Church of England', and the official citation spoke of 'your services to the Church as Theologian and Author'.[24] Between the Archbishop's original letter and the conferring of the degree, John Stott received an approach from the Eastern Baptist Theological Seminary in Philadelphia, USA, also offering him an honorary Doctorate of Divinity. He felt he should decline,[25] and framed a careful letter of explanation which stood him in good stead on some similar occasions.[26]

Three months later, John Stott was at Greenbelt, a large-scale Christian festival and rock concert, in company with Cliff Richard. From its early beginnings in a farmer's field ten years before, this had grown to an annual gathering of 28,000 people. Here, over a long weekend in August, he led a series of seminars and Bible expositions, and was one of a panel debating nuclear arms. Interviewed for *Christianity Today*, he told their reporter: 'To see the Communion table in the open air, with 25,000 people gathered around it in a circle – to sense the love, joy, faith, celebration of that crowd – was tremendous. I will never forget it.'[27] To Bob Wismer in Canada, a former study assistant, he described it as 'a fantastic experience', adding:

> Maybe there was a bit too much hand-raising, hip-swaying and jumping for my liking. But it never got out of control. The combination of rock music and serious biblical seminars must be unique. I found the noisy rock beat too dominant, but the seminars were crowded, and I think the Lord helped me to communicate in a situation which could hardly be described as my 'scene'![28]

John Stott was there again in 1984. Since the launch of the London Institute two years earlier he had become known as concerned to relate the teaching of Scripture to contemporary issues; and he hoped that the Greenbelt constituency would be attracted to the courses on offer at the Institute.

John Stott's commitment to theological discussion, and to the social and political consequences of contemporary discipleship, did nothing to blunt his concern for evangelism. Luís Palau preached at All Souls in 1983, and the following year John Stott was at one of the Palau meetings at the Queen's Park Rangers stadium, Shepherd's Bush.[29] He was also the speaker later in the decade at the Prayer Breakfast for the Conference of Commonwealth Speakers and Presiding Officers in 1988 (Michael Alison wrote, 'Your audience was riveted by your ministry') and at the London National Prayer Breakfast the following year attended by the Prime Minister.[30] Michael Alison, MP for Selby, spent nearly five years as Mrs Thatcher's Parliamentary Private Secretary, and because of his long-standing friendship with John Stott (going back to Iwerne Minster in the 1940s) was able to draw him occasionally into such opportunities for witness or testimony. More than once the Prime Minister came with a party of friends to 'Prom Praise', the series of Christian concerts arranged by the All Souls Orchestra and Choir under Noël Tredinnick, first at the Barbican and later at the Royal Albert Hall. It was there in February 1988, with Mrs Thatcher present, that John Stott took the opportunity in a closing address to recount how 'fifty years ago today, on 13 February 1938' a young man knelt at his bedside and 'opened the door of his heart or personality, and invited Christ to come in. I was that young man. I have now had fifty years in which to test the reality of Jesus Christ. Tonight, on my fiftieth spiritual birthday, I want to bear witness to him, and to the length, depth, breadth and height of his love.' Eleven years later Lady Thatcher remembered a visit to Prom Praise as 'a joyous and uplifting evening'.[31] No doubt many others would say the same.

For his sixty-fifth birthday a group of friends nominated John Stott to the Trustees of the Templeton Foundation for their 'Prize for Progress in Religion'. In the event the prize went elsewhere, but John Stott and the Richmond Fellowship for Mental Welfare and Rehabilitation were named as joint winners of the December 1985 Templeton UK Project Awards. *The Church of England Newspaper* carried a whole-page appreciation to mark his birthday, glancing back over some of the landmarks of his ministry, while paying well-deserved tribute on the way to Frances Whitehead for her thirty years of service.[32] Among the birthday cards and letters he received was one from the Vatican, a warm personal tribute by Monsignor Basil Meeking, who had worked closely with him throughout ERCDOM, the Evangelical–Roman Catholic Dialogue on Mission:

> *The Church of England Newspaper* brought word of your 65th birthday. So I wish to add my congratulations and very good wishes. Our Secretariat does greatly appreciate the leadership you have given as a Christian leader and specifically in promoting understanding between Roman Catholics and other Christians. And all of us who took part in ERCDOM have a deep respect for your spiritual gifts.
> Thank you for your friendship and many happy returns![33]

John Stott chose to mark his sixty-fifth birthday (which brought little other evidence of retirement) by calling into being an informal advisory panel appropriately known as AGE; a decision described by one of the founder-members as 'democratizing his life'.[34] In the preliminary letter of invitation to the seven he invited, John Stott indicated that he was not sure whether 'A' in AGE should carry a double meaning:

'AGE' – 'Accountability (or Advisory) Group of Elders'

> I really feel the need of a group who will advise me, and to whom I may to some degree be accountable, and am sorry that I have left it to my declining years before taking action.
> I'm not thinking of a formal committee with motions, votes and minutes, but of an informal group of friends, who will advise me about the apportionment of my time and about which invitations I should accept. I promise both to listen respectfully to your advice and not to go against it whenever it is shared by the great majority of you. At the same time, in contested areas, I imagine you will be willing to let me have a little freedom of decision![35]

The membership changed very little over the next ten years or so. The current study assistant was always included; and John Wyatt, Professor of

Neonatal Paediatrics at University College London, was added to the group.[36] He would sometimes be referred to, with affection as well as amusement, as 'my medical adviser'; and when John Stott was proving intransigent over some more than usually demanding engagement, the other members of AGE would look in the last resort to John Wyatt to restrain him. This they referred to as 'playing the medical card'! David Turner, churchwarden of All Souls and a founder-member of AGE, has described the group at work:

> Richard Bewes 'chairs', though we are and always have been very informal. We meet three or four times a year ... We hear from John what he has been doing and we sift, with him, future invitations ... Our best work has, I think, been to strengthen his hand to refuse certain things and to accept others – in as guilt-free a way as possible. 'Will you *enjoy* it?!', says Richard Bewes with near hedonistic abandon, 'do you *want* to go?' ... We have tried to review travel arrangements, priorities, holidays, rest periods, Institute involvement. We have discussed the need for US trips and all the demands they make. We have talked of energy levels and health issues ... I think JRWS sees himself as truly accountable to us, but we are by no stretch of the imagination legalistic or confrontational! This is ultimately about sensible and concerned friends offering firm advice and support.[37]

To grow older is to suffer the loss of friends. Martyn Lloyd-Jones died, appropriately enough on St David's Day, in 1981, while the following year saw the death of Bash, an even closer 'father figure'. It fell to John Stott to conduct Bash's Memorial Service at All Souls, Langham Place, in June 1982, amid a large gathering of former Iwerne campers and camp leaders. Two years later, in his 1984 personal newsletter, John Stott drew attention to 'Three Notable Deaths': Dr Francis Schaeffer, 'a prophet for the sixties'; Canon David Watson, 'a man of extraordinary faith and courage'; and Bishop Stephen Neill, a scholar-missionary with 'a global ministry of prodigious proportions'.[38] John Stott did not always see eye to eye with them, and could indeed be in marked disagreement; but he paid tribute to them nonetheless as 'Christian men conspicuously gifted and used by God whom the church will sorely miss'.

By contrast, the early 1980s saw the birth of John and of his cousin Hannah, as two more grandchildren to Joanna (John Stott's eldest and only surviving sister) and her husband Derek. With Emily, the eldest, and Joseph born in 1986, 'Uncle John' thus became 'Great Uncle' four times over.[39]

2

Throughout the 1980s, partly through All Souls, and partly on his overseas travels, John Stott found himself constantly engaged in direct evangelism (though the days of regular student missions were now behind him), and in strategic evangelistic planning on a national and international scale. Overseas this often meant work for Lausanne, while at home he was involved in the Nationwide Initiative in Evangelism (NIE),[40] one of the attempts by Archbishop Donald Coggan to establish the priority of evangelism in the life of every local church. John Stott was Vice-Chairman of the group of fifteen theologians from different traditions who drafted the joint Statement, 'The Gospel we Affirm Together'; but since Bishop Lesslie Newbigin, the Chairman, was unable to attend the crucial final meeting, much of the leadership there (including drafting) fell to the Vice-Chairman.[41]

> It will not satisfy those [John Stott wrote a few weeks later], who insist on the inclusion of every jot and tittle of evangelical orthodoxy before we can engage in any common work or witness. Yet the essence of the biblical gospel is recognizably there ... Lacking, from an orthodox Protestant viewpoint, is sufficient precision at three crucial points. Though Jesus is termed God's 'son', his deity is not spelled out. Though the Bible's 'irreplaceable witness' and 'unique authority' are declared, its status as the church's only rule of faith and practice is not. Though the statement includes references to God's grace, the necessity of 'turning in penitence to Christ', and the reception from him of a new life, the freeness of salvation as God's gift through faith is not clearly enough affirmed.[42]

Sadly, though not without positive achievements, NIE quickly lost momentum. The anonymous writer of the *Crockford's* preface had forecast from the start that 'there has not been a great deal of enthusiasm in the Church of England for it';[43] and Paul Welsby's verdict with the benefit of hindsight was that Dr Coggan's desire to see the venture launched before he retired (he had been the driving force from the beginning) meant that its preparation suffered.[44] Paul Welsby also believed, surely optimistically, that parish churches were so immersed in local evangelistic activities that they saw a Nationwide Initiative as an unnecessary distraction.[45]

Thanks in part to the Lausanne movement, and to parachurch activities, much more enthusiastic concern for evangelism was in evidence across the Channel. In 1988, for example, John Stott was to be found speaking at the IFES European Conference on Evangelism in Würzburg, Germany, beneath a vast banner, 'The love of Christ moves us'. He expounded Paul's preaching of the cross of Christ in Corinth, and the objections to his message: intellectual, religious, personal, moral and political. To an audience of 1,000 students from across the continent he went on to describe the first-century Corinthians as 'typical' and to add that the world in which we live today is just as hostile to the gospel:

> We are fooling ourselves if we imagine that we can ever make the authentic gospel popular ... It's too simple in an age of rationalism; too narrow in an age of pluralism; too humiliating in an age of self-confidence; too demanding in an age of permissiveness; and too unpatriotic in an age of blind nationalism ... What are we going to share with our friends? The authentic gospel or a gospel that has been corrupted in order to suit human pride?[46]

He was in Germany again in September, this time to give the keynote address at the European Leadership Conference on World Evangelization at Stuttgart, bringing a challenge to enter other people's worlds: the world of their ideology, and of their alienation and pain.[47]

The issues raised so sharply by NIE and the 'fifteen theologians from different traditions' exemplify what John Stott saw as a continuing task, to wrestle with disagreements among Christians (and Christian churches) over the nature of the gospel; and to try together to submit ecclesiastical tradition and theological enquiry to the bar of Scripture. Throughout the 1980s he was engaged in such an attempt with Roman Catholics, with neo-Pentecostals, with the Anglo-Catholic tradition in the Church of England and with theological liberalism. The Keele '67 Report had called for ecumenical dialogue: 'We are no longer content [as evangelicals] to stand apart from those with whom we disagree ... we wish to talk ...';[48] while ten years later the Nottingham '77 Statement spoke of affirming 'upon scriptural grounds our belief in the visible unity of the church ... marked by a common acceptance of the authority of Scripture and by a rich diversity of expression ...'[49] In a section of the Statement devoted to relations with the Roman Catholic Church, the Congress voted to 'support and encourage opportunities for dialogue between us at all levels'; and, while welcoming the work of the Anglican–Roman Catholic International Commission (ARCIC), called for 'some official denials of past claims and detailed doctrinal clarification'.[50]

Even while NEAC was discussing these issues at Nottingham, John Stott was active as an initiator, and for the next seven years as a leading figure, in ERCDOM, the Evangelical–Roman Catholic Dialogue on Mission. He made it very clear that dialogue, courtesy, a willingness to learn, even a search for unity, implied no doctrinal compromise: 'Reunion with Rome is inconceivable without the reformation of Rome.'[51] ERCDOM met first in Venice in April 1977, and five years later in Trinity College, Cambridge, bringing to John Stott memories of his undergraduate days.

> The evangelical team was inter-denominational as well as inter-national and included such well-known leaders and personal friends as Professor Peter Beyerhaus (Tübingen), Bishop Donald Cameron (Sydney), Dr David Hubbard (Fuller) and Dr David Wells (Gordon-Conwell, and also President of the Langham Foundation). The dialogue was conducted in a remarkable spirit of candour, charity and integrity. Sometimes we were thankful to discover unexpected agreement (e.g. regarding the freeness of God's saving grace), while at other times we experienced sharp, though cour-teous, disagreement (especially over the role of the Virgin Mary in salvation).[52]

The third and final meeting was held in April 1984 on less familiar territory, the Benedictine monastery of Landévenne in Brittany, where John Stott was able to welcome the delegates in French. The membership varied slightly (in the Roman Catholic team, more considerably) from meeting to meeting. John Stott was at all three, and with Mgr Basil Meeking edited the Report.[53] The seven-year project had been for John Stott 'an essay in Christian integrity';[54] and for some of the Roman Catholic delegates a new and totally unexpected appreciation of evangelicals and their theology. Basil Meeking wrote of ERCDOM that John Stott's 'imagination and faith gave it wings', and described him as 'the spiritual father of the group each time it met, giving it a confidence and a sense of direction. He was the theologian who could lead it to the heart of the problem. It was he who kept the discussion on the level of faith so that it never degenerated into polemic.'[55]

Less happy was the need to show constant vigilance over the work of ARCIC and its sequence of official reports. John Stott informed CEEC (the Church of England Evangelical Council) in the summer of 1979 that he was corresponding with his old friend Henry Chadwick, now Regius Professor of Divinity at Cambridge and an Anglican delegate to ARCIC, about the need for the Commission to study justification by faith as a distinct topic.[56] In 1980 CEEC discussed the implications of the proposed papal visit to England in 1982 ('We "should welcome him as John Paul, but not as Peter",' was John Stott's view)[57] and ARCIC continued to feature in CEEC discussions throughout John Stott's time as Chairman. His two most significant contributions to the debate took the form of a detailed Critique of the ARCIC *Final Report* in 1982,[58] and an Open Letter in 1988. The first, drafted on behalf of CEEC, was by no means wholly negative; but it was 'concerned by the absence of an agreed Statement on Salvation in general and Justification in particular'; deeply disturbed by Roman teaching on 'the propitiatory value of the Eucharist'; and insistent on the need 'in both our Churches to correct what the theology of the Bible will not justify', including of course the Marian dogmas and Papal primacy.[59]

In an article in *The Times* John Stott addressed this thorny doctrine, after paying generous tribute to the way 'John Paul II has without doubt captured the hearts of millions ... his smile of pure benevolence ... his concern for the sick and handicapped ... his evident goodness and godliness'. But these are scarcely arguments for primacy. Writing on this fourth and final Report of ARCIC I, John Stott commented on how it related

> ... to the question of the papal primacy, which Archbishop Davidson once called 'that great unremoved mountain of difficulty'. After a fresh and honest re-examination of the Petrine texts, the members of ARCIC reached the surprisingly candid conclusion that the New Testament 'contains no explicit record of a transmission of Peter's leadership'; and therefore offers 'no sufficient basis' for a permanent primacy. But instead of following the logic of their own candour, they went on to defend from analogy, history and pragmatism what Scripture does not require.

Papal primacy, he concluded, would therefore be unacceptable to the great majority of Anglicans, unless balanced by conciliarity and collegiality, and 'unless the Pope were to divest himself of much of his power and glory'. With reluctant realism, he dismissed that possibility as 'extremely remote'.[60]

Six years later John Stott was again called on to assess the work of ARCIC (which now included ARCIC II), this time in the form of an Open Letter commissioned by the Executive Committee of EFAC. Though he was responsible for drafting the letter, a formidable list of signatories was appended from six continents (only Antarctica was missing) and including many church leaders, ordained and lay, as well as professional theologians.[61] Knowing how full are bishops' postbags, and how much paper passes across their desks, the Letter included in an appendix a summary of its main points as it surveyed the five ARCIC Statements to date. Again there were things to welcome as well as much to regret and to reject. One paragraph from the appendix might be taken as a summary of the whole:

Our main criticism of the ARCIC statements is that they betray a
reluctance to allow the Spirit of God through the Word of God to
challenge our inherited beliefs and practices.

'Must we remain for ever prisoners of our past?' the Open Letter asked:
and added characteristically, 'Only Scripture can set us free.'[62] Once
again, as President of EFAC, John Stott found himself writing to *The
Times* to correct the impression that 'the papacy is the most serious stick-
ing point'. On the contrary, substantial agreement would be needed in
many other crucial areas (for example, 'the real presence, eucharistic
sacrifice, ministerial priesthood') before evangelicals could conscientiously
participate in a reunited church.[63] Sadly, what to John Stott seemed a
responsible Christian dialogue in pursuit of truth was taken in other
quarters as a 'betrayal of evangelical Protestantism', and castigated as 'the
compromised stance of men like John Stott ... so-called evangelicals',
with 'no real convictions whatsoever concerning the fundamental soul-
saving doctrines of the faith'.[64] Such hostility from within evangelicalism
to its Anglican leaders is nothing new. Lord Shaftesbury, the great
evangelical social reformer, died in 1885. In the last years of his life he
told his future biographer, Edwin Hodder, 'High Churchmen, Roman
Catholics, even infidels, have been friendly to me; my only enemies have
been the Evangelicals.'[65]

Even while ERCDOM was at work, and John Stott (largely as Chairman of CEEC) wrestling with an evangelical assessment of ARCIC, he
was drawn into yet another series of consultations, this time as a member
of the 'Faith House' group convened by Eric Kemp, Bishop of Chichester,
to try to achieve, if not agreement, at least a better understanding between
Anglo-Catholic, evangelical and charismatic Anglicans.[66]

Both Eric Kemp and John Stott (representing respectively the Church
Union and CEEC) were also participating in a smaller group, meeting
over much the same period. The fruits of their discussion appeared
mainly in a book of essays which took the place of a Report, each chapter
the product of dual authorship between an Anglo-Catholic and an
evangelical Anglican. It was published with an eye to the 1988 Lambeth
Conference;[67] and included a final chapter, 'Mission Agenda for the
People of God', written jointly by John Stott and James Robertson
(Secretary 1973–83 of the United Society for the Propagation of the
Gospel, high-church sister to the Church Missionary Society). The
chapter may have done something to pave the way for the Lambeth 1988
resolution calling for a Decade of Evangelism:

We believe the time is ripe for Anglicans to join other Christians in
that kind of evangelism which combines boldness with humility.

We hope that the 1988 Lambeth Conference will issue a call to mission, and that perhaps it may be initiated by leaders of Third World churches, which are often now more committed to mission than the older churches of the West.[68]

From time to time, as the charismatic movement became more established, John Stott found himself having to restate his own position, and say whether his understanding of Scripture had been in any way modified by the kind of dialogue and discussion that produced the CEEC Report *Gospel and Spirit* in the late 1970s, or by the 'Faith House' discussions (which included Michael Harper) of the 1980s. 'I'm not really "defensive" about charismatic claims', he replied to Bob Wismer (then training for ordination) in 1985,

> for I've been examining them for 30 years! But I believe it's in many ways an unbalanced and unhealthy movement, while recognizing God has used it to bless many churches and individuals. It's because I care about you ... that I don't want to see you deviate from the great biblical Christ-centred highway.[69]

An unexpected opportunity for a further first-hand assessment of new developments in the charismatic movement came in October 1988. John Stott was in Edinburgh for a pastors' conference on preaching when he discovered that John Wimber, whom he had never met, was also in the city. He promptly telephoned and invited him to breakfast. In the two hours they spent together John Wimber did most of the talking, so John Stott was able to take full notes of what he said: 'I was impressed by him as a Christian man, by his relaxed openness and honesty.'

Their main topic was healing. John Stott had read both John Wimber's books, *Power Evangelism* (1985) and *Power Healing* (1986), in which signs and wonders are said to be 'everyday occurrences in New Testament times' and should therefore characterize 'the normal Christian life'.[70] This was not John Stott's understanding either of the New Testament or of contemporary Christian experience:

> My own position is to avoid both extremes, one that miracles 'don't' or 'can't' happen, and the other that they are everyday normality, and to affirm that of course God can and does perform miracles today, but not with the same frequency with which they occurred in the ministry of Jesus and his apostles. So I was curious to know where he stood on this matter.

According to notes made at the time, John Wimber included the following striking statements in his response:

(1) 'All I am asking is that people be open for God to do unique things occasionally, in confirmation of his word.'
(2) 'An ever increasing number of people in our church (the Vineyard Church in Anaheim, California) are *not* healed. I myself am sick in my own body (I am on daily medication). More than about 400 people have come to me saying that the Lord has told them that if they lay hands on me, I will be healed. I have said to them "OK, go ahead", but I have not been healed.'
(3) We both agreed that we have two difficulties, (a) in defining what a miracle is, and (b) in proving a healing in a documentable way. His summary was that about 30% are healed, 30% are blessed but not healed, and 30% receive nothing.
(4) He said that he has never seen major deformities of the body healed, although thousands *say* they have been cured of conditions which cannot be seen.

Before they parted, still with much to say to one another, John Wimber agreed with John Stott's eirenic suggestion that part of the difference in their viewpoints could be accounted for by the tension between the 'already' and the 'not yet', 'Kingdom come and Kingdom coming', 'the new age inaugurated and the new age consummated'.[71]

The same year that John Stott talked over breakfast with John Wimber saw the publication of yet another 'dialogue', this time with David Edwards, Provost of Southwark, on the differences between liberal and evangelical theologies, a book[72] which remains an indispensable guide. But among the best-remembered controversies in which John Stott was involved during the decade was that associated with the name of David Jenkins, Professor of Theology at Leeds University. In the month following the announcement of his appointment as Bishop of Durham, Dr Jenkins appeared on the ITV programme *Credo*, and was asked about his belief in the miraculous elements of the Christian creeds:

The resurrection, said Jenkins, was not a single event, but a series of experiences. Jesus was raised up, that is, 'the very life and purpose and personality which was in him was continuing'. As for the virgin birth, 'I wouldn't put it past God to arrange a virgin birth if he wanted, but I very much doubt if he would because it seems contrary to the way in which he deals with people and brings his wonders out of natural personal relationships.' Next day the *Daily*

Mail headlined the story: 'The fake miracles of Jesus, by a Bishop'. The storm soon came ...[73]

The storm was not diminished by the fact that on 9 July 1984, three days after his consecration in York Minster, the west front was struck by lightning. David Jenkins had delighted the press, as any questioning (not to say doubting) bishop will, and this gave some spectacular headlines.[74] John Stott's response to what in his personal newsletter he later described as the Bishop's 'ill-considered but well-publicized doubts' was both to ask Bishop Jenkins to meet with himself and a few other evangelicals (Michael Baughen, Roger Beckwith, R. T. France)[75] for a discussion of the issues face to face; and also to defend the faith in print. He did this first in *The Times*, setting out the historical nature of Christ's resurrection as a dated event in time; and its significance as 'a divine act of vindication', and the pledge of God's new creation;[76] while in the same year he published under the auspices of the London Institute his 'response to current scepticism in the church', a small book of under 100 pages entitled *The Authentic Jesus*. Five main chapters, on 'The First Witnesses', on his humanity and divinity, his resurrection, his virgin birth and his uniqueness are set in the context of 'The Present Situation'. *The Myth of God Incarnate* (of the late 1970s) was also much in his mind. The book ends with a personal conclusion, wider perhaps in its application than the occasion which gave rise to it:

> Nowadays all kinds of controversy are distasteful, and none more so than religious controversy. Yet to shrink from it is characteristic of the age of uncertainty in which we are living, not of Jesus Christ and his apostles; they contended vigorously for what they believed to be the truth. It is not conducive to the health of the Church to sweep our differences under the carpet or to pretend that all is sweetness and light when it is not. Nor are these subterfuges consistent with Christian integrity. It is more healthy and more honest to bring our disagreements out into the open.[77]

Such were some of the faith issues of the 1980s, touching (as history shows they generally do) both the trustworthiness of revelation, and the uniqueness of Christ, over which John Stott wrestled and agonized in defence of biblical orthodoxy. At the same time, he was deeply immersed in a series of attempts to 'think Christianly' on some of the major concerns not so much of the church as of the contemporary world: war and peace, work and unemployment, race and gender, medical and sexual ethics, and the care of the planet. Further references to them will be found in chapter 11.

3

John Stott relinquished long-standing commitments as the 1980s progressed, to give himself to the establishing of the London Institute for Contemporary Christianity (LICC). He managed, nevertheless, to undertake a fourth Presidential year for UCCF[78] and to serve as President of TEAR Fund (The Evangelical Alliance Relief Fund), a cause close to his heart. Gilbert Kirby and Cliff Richard had agreed to act as Vice-Presidents.[79] TEAR Fund had sprung from very small beginnings during World Refugee Year, 1959/60, the vision of George Hoffman, when a few thousand pounds were given by supporters of the Evangelical Alliance to their Refugee Fund. John Stott had been an early supporter, contributing a chapter to the TEAR Fund study guide for those embarking on work overseas,[80] and preaching on the rich young ruler at the fifteenth anniversary service in All Souls. Especially influential was the booklet he wrote for them to accompany the soundstrip *Walk in His Shoes*,[81] which, so TEAR Fund believes, provided 'for many staff and supporters ... a life-changing moment of understanding'.[82] Indeed, such was his reputation in TEAR Fund circles that when a young staff member heard in the mid-1980s that John Stott was to speak at staff prayers at their Teddington offices, she had to make a quick readjustment to her thinking. Having heard him spoken of as one of the heroes of the faith – almost a Wesley or a Spurgeon – she had supposed him long dead and gone to glory![83]

Until the mid-1980s John Stott continued his close involvement with the Church of England Evangelical Council (CEEC), which he had helped to found twenty-five years before. Such historians as mention CEEC tend to do so in muted terms. They speak of a lack of confidence in its 'evangelical comprehensiveness', of an 'unwillingness to confront differences that everyone knew existed', of having 'limped along underfunded and with only qualified support'. In part, this is undeniable, at least of some aspects of its role, and at certain times in its history. But at its best, especially in the earlier days before 'democratization' and 'accountability' undercut its real strengths, it did indispensable work.[84] In his account of the period, D. W. Bebbington speaks of how 'from 1980 there were broader consultations' leading to the establishing of an Annual Evangelical Assembly (AEA) 'which at last supplanted Islington as the party's main forum'.[85] By 1983 it was possible to claim that

> ... what had begun in 1979 as a Consultation, called as an *ad hoc* response to the sense of a loss of identity within the Church felt by many evangelicals, had finally developed into a new, representative, evangelical gathering. Its sessions were open to the press, its agenda

reflected the nationwide concerns of evangelical Anglicans, its future was based on a constitution adopted by democratic vote, and its role was shaped by its own representative character.[86]

Clifford Longley, Religious Affairs correspondent of *The Times*, described the Assembly as

... the first body to draw together all the strands of this increasingly influential movement in Anglicanism, and the first to be able to claim that its voice is representative. It was founded by the Church of England Evangelical Council, which was itself becoming regarded as the most representative Evangelical grouping in the church ... now to be reconstituted as the Assembly's standing committee.[87]

Two years later, with the Assembly beginning to find its feet, John Stott announced his intention to retire from the chair, and called for a successor to be elected 'who was at the heart of the Church of England and on General Synod'.[88] It was therefore under Mrs Jill Dann's chairmanship that CEEC began to consider a third NEAC, successor to Keele 1967 and Nottingham 1977. Once again, immense care was taken in its preparation; and both attendance and breadth of activity proved impressive.[89] Nevertheless, by contrast with its predecessors it was to leave little lasting impression. The reason was not far to seek, since what began in CEEC's thinking as a 'Congress' was soon transmuted into a 'Festival' (NEWFEST, National Anglican Festival for Worship, Work and Witness),[90] and this was reflected in the choice of some of the main speakers. It was later agreed to continue with the acronym NEAC, but in 1988 the final letter stood not for 'Congress' but for 'Celebration', an indication of the experiential neo-Pentecostal influence which was to change the nature of the event. This became evident in the early days of planning. Gavin Reid, Chairman of the overall Planning Committee, tabled a paper proposing a NEAC III much more in the ethos of the preceding Congresses. But it was not to be: 'It was quite obvious to me that this was not acceptable and the people who had already been put on the group actually to plan the Congress wanted something different.'[91]

Significantly, it was decided to hold NEAC III at a holiday camp rather than on a university campus. Minehead, Skegness, Pwllheli, Ayr, Bognor and Prestatyn were all considered, and eventually it was agreed to book Caister-on-Sea from 28 April to 2 May.[92] A circus 'big top' was hired for the main meetings, and as a setting for united worship. Much of the planning for the worship sessions was entrusted to GROW (Group for the Renewal of Worship) led by Bishop Colin Buchanan; and this served to confirm the impression that 'evangelical' was now synonymous with 'charismatic'. A further departure from precedent was the decision not to frame or publish any final Statement, encapsulating the fruit of study and deliberation. Certainly there had been voices, both at Keele and Nottingham, which felt the production of a Statement to be a kind of tyranny, dominating the event and tying the delegates to a laborious process of drafting. But, so John Stott wrote later,

> I felt that another and more sinister reason lay behind the decision, namely that an assembly of Anglican evangelicals in 1987/8 would not be sufficiently definite or united in conviction to make a Congress Statement possible. To call it a 'Celebration' would clearly indicate that no Statement would be produced, or even expected.[93]

In May 1981 John Stott had been at Australia's second NEAC, held at Monash University, outside Melbourne; and had regretted their decision not to work towards a Statement.[94] In the light of this he made sure that his misgivings were known to the Planning Committee of NEAC '88. He remained firmly of the view that *not* to produce some kind of Statement was both unwise (leading to the event being ignored and forgotten) and selfish (keeping the fruits of the event solely to participants),[95] but these protests went unheard.

John Stott himself was invited by the Planning Committee to give a brief CCTV Bible study (which could be received in chalets) to the different 'cell groups' on three of the four mornings and to work during the weekend with a 'listening group' in trying to discern significant emphases. This would then shape his final address. John Stott tackled this task of collating and synthesizing his listeners' reports with typical thoroughness. Together with Frances Whitehead and Toby Howarth, his study assistant, he was working almost throughout the night prior to his presentation. Chocolate, as always, proved a necessary sustenance and Toby was 'despatched into the misty early morning to find a petrol station where I could replenish the stock of Smarties'.[96] This address became, in effect, the only Report or Statement to emerge from NEAC III. Under the title *What is the Spirit Saying ... ?*[97] it was published as 'A Report from John Stott', and the title page carried the following note:

> John Stott's final address included, at the request of the Executive Team, material supplied by his 'listening group' and by workshop leaders, together with his personal reflections on the Celebration. He has expanded and modified his address in the light of the many responses to it which were submitted by participants. The NEAC 3 Executive Team have authorized its publication, while not

necessarily wishing to endorse every viewpoint expressed in it. They believe it will be a useful basis for further discussion and action.

The final sentences read as a broad hint that though John Stott was still an undoubted leader among Anglican evangelicals, not all of them wished to be his followers.

Though the assembly was popular and well reported, and valuable work was done in a striking range of cell groups and workshops, John Stott was not alone in his disappointment. From the choice of speakers to the style of worship it was clear that this NEAC was under different management, and that evangelicalism was in danger of losing a single core identity. In his 'listening' role, John Stott received a variety of notes from his own team, attending different workshops and events, and sending to him their impressions, some at least of which are still among his papers:

> What is interesting about the hand-written reports, and various unsolicited letters following Caister, is that each one contains a fairly strong (sometimes vituperative) criticism of the 'celebration', or specific parts of it. And not all criticisms were from conservatives ... I think the diversity (and special-interest nature – i.e. abortion, women, charismatic presence) of these negative reactions demonstrated the fissiparous state of the evangelical movement and presaged divisions to come.[98]

Canon Michael Green, then Professor of Evangelism at Regent College, Vancouver, was not the only one among the 'listeners' who sensed coming difficulties. He wrote to John Stott: 'the movement is now so disparate and so multiform that it is hard to see it holding together, especially after the day of your own presidency'. He added, 'There is no individual who looks capable of replacing you.'[99]

For the church at large, much interested in the increasing numbers described as 'evangelical', it was clearly more comfortable to have a widely diverse rather than a closely united movement as bedfellow. Derek Pattinson, Secretary General of the General Synod, wrote some months before NEAC III that 'we wish it well – and don't intend ourselves to miss it'.[100] In the following year he published his impressions in *The Church of England Year Book*, describing Caister in April as 'climatically bracing', the main addresses as 'superb', and John Stott as 'patriarchal'.[101]

The event attracted plenty of media attention at the time, including a front-page headline and the whole of the back page of the *Church Times*.[102] Clifford Longley, Religious Affairs correspondent of *The Times*, devoted a column to the Archbishop's visit and his 'strikingly bold' keynote address, in which Longley claimed to discern a recurrent anxiety that the growth in evangelical size and influence could be harmful to the church as a whole: however, 'his address was warmly received with a standing ovation'.[103] Discerning voices from within evangelicalism found less to celebrate: Melvin Tinker, one of the delegates, described it in *Churchman* as 'A Conference too far?'[104] Peter Williams in *Anvil*, *Churchman*'s younger sibling, reminded his readers that

> Jim Packer has warned that a mood of success 'is regularly the mother of fragmentation, wherever it is found'. The danger signals are there ... The study of recent Evangelicalism reveals how far, at almost every twist and turn of the story of the last thirty years, Stott has engaged with the issues on a very broad front, been prepared to change, to commend change and yet to command the respect and love of all. Anybody well read in Victorian ecclesiastical history knows the difficulties Evangelicalism, strong though it was numerically and close though it had become to the emerging Victorian mores, experienced after the departure of William Wilberforce and Charles Simeon. A similar danger may exist to-day.[105]

The original decision to depart from precedent and frame NEAC III as a celebration ensured that its results would be ephemeral. Perhaps this is most clearly seen in the fact that 1997/8 brought no successor. 'A dynamic, interactive, celebratory event'[106] may be a heady and enjoyable experience, but in the nature of the case can easily become self-centred, transitory and sterile. John Stott summed it up a decade later in terms of an opportunity wasted: 'NEAC III *was* the "Celebration" it was advertised as being ...'[107] NEAC I and II had been so much more ...

A final footnote to this account can be found in a dream which John Stott experienced in the early 1990s. He found himself planning a NEAC IV on the theme of 'Mission through Unity and Truth in Holiness', carefully worked out with four main headings, and detailed sub-headings. 'The whole thing came together in my mind', he explained, 'and I wrote it down on waking up. What an astonishing organ the brain is ...'[108] Some of the questions posed in this dream suggest that his disappointment over NEAC III remains unresolved; and also that NEAC IV would have been – might yet be? – a powerful spiritual challenge:

> Have we shifted our ground on Bible, Cross and Salvation? Are we still content to be a coalition rather than a party, or can we hope to come close together? Is the quest for holiness back on our evangelical agenda? I fear that the quest for spiritual experience and social justice has dislodged the quest for 'scriptural holiness'.[109]

4

Although the post of study assistant ('study asses', as they often called themselves) began with Roy McCloughry, followed by Tom Cooper in the late 1970s, it was the next decade that saw the succession firmly established.[110] After Tom Cooper came Mark Labberton in 1980, and then Steve Ingraham, a former senior student of Moody Bible Institute, who would later work as a prosecuting attorney in Milwaukee. Bob Wismer, an IVCF staff worker in Canada, took over in 1982; followed by Steve Andrews (1984), Toby Howarth (1986) and Todd Shy (1988). Roy McCloughry and Toby were British, Toby being the son of Robert Howarth who was Counsellor to Overseas Visitors at All Souls in the early 1960s, and Bob Wismer was Canadian; the rest were young Americans.

It was Tom Cooper who recommended Mark Labberton, then in his late twenties and reading for an MDiv at Fuller Theological Seminary. He and John Stott had met briefly at Urbana four years before, and again during a Summer School at Regent College, Vancouver. The original plan was for him to work part-time for John Stott, but the intensive preparation for the launch of the London Institute meant that he was soon very fully employed. The role, for him as for all of them, proved an extraordinary combination of the academic and the mundane, each with its own spiritual priority. At one level, the study assistant acted as a kind of domestic chaplain, being someone who could share, support and encourage, a friend and colleague with whom to pray. Every morning at The Hookses, for example, the current study assistant would make his way, rain or shine, to the Hermitage, where he and John Stott would begin the day with prayer together. In London they would meet for breakfast in John Stott's flat every Monday morning, together with Frances Whitehead, and look at the diary for the week and then pray together. Steve Andrews remembers a folder with his name on it which John Stott would produce, with perhaps twenty tasks needing to be done: clothes to the cleaners, a ticket to buy, references to check.[111] Quotations and references proved a continuing preoccupation for all the study assistants: they remember how John Stott

> ... would want to use a quotation he had collected but only if it could be confirmed in context, properly cited, and accurately repro-duced. This sometimes meant searching for the needle (perhaps as little as a phrase of five or six words) with only scant reference detail; for example, it might be in Augustine! When these could be found it was a moment of great glee and joy – and a trophy one was delighted to hand back to the master![112]

Often the current study assistant would accompany John Stott to an engagement, usually driving the car to allow his passenger time to look over his notes by way of final preparation. Mark Labberton remembers such a visit to Oxford:

> I knew that he had been to the place we were going, Wycliffe Hall, and probably knew how to get there. I did not know how to get there so I naturally just asked him to direct me as I was driving. He said with that twinkle of indignation he can use sometimes, 'I couldn't possibly tell you how to get there ... I *disdain* Oxford!'[113]

It often fell to the study assistant to drive John Stott's car about London, delivering a package, fetching a guest from the airport or on some other errand. They did not all find it easy to adjust to British road habits. On one occasion John Stott was threatened with a court summons for non-payment of parking tickets, since it was Bob Wismer's happy custom to ignore such tickets in his home town, and he had simply stuffed them into the glove-pocket of John Stott's Mini-Clubman, out of sight and out of mind![114]

The Hookses was very much part of the study assistant's life, some-times indeed the best part. Steve Andrews, for example, was driven down there by Bob Wismer, his predecessor, two days after his arrival in England. His only previous meeting with John Stott had been a fifteen-minute interview at Regent College some months before, though there had been detailed correspondence; but his enthusiastic welcome, 'a broad smile and warm embrace' soon set any doubts to rest. With John Stott, journeys to The Hookses were usually in the very early morning. Sometimes driver and passenger would share a time of prayer and a reading of Scripture as they drove. Toby Howarth recalls how John Stott found the long drive tedious and the inactivity unwelcome:

> Sometimes he would do some work in the car, or he might sleep, or we might listen to a sermon on tape. Once I played a tape of some old Fred Astaire songs, and we sang along to those! Sometimes the temptation was there to make it a little quicker, and Frances would cast a glance at the speedometer remarking that maybe Uncle John was driving a little too fast. He would respond that if you looked at the needle on the gauge from the passenger seat's angle, it appeared faster than if you looked at it straight from the driver's seat![115]

If, as sometimes happened, the journey to The Hookses meant driving through the middle of the day, the car would be stopped in a layby (on one occasion, to the astonished amusement of Mrs Egtvedt, an early US supporter of the Langham Foundation who was being taken to see The Hookses) so that John Stott could stretch out on the verge by the roadside, instantly fall asleep, and exactly half an hour later wake refreshed![116]

For Toby Howarth (who had known the place for as long as he could remember) life at The Hookses had a quality all its own:

> Although I enjoyed the times in London, especially when Uncle John was there, the times I most looked forward to were at The Hookses ... I would come back from a walk along the cliffs in the morning to arrive at the Hermitage at precisely 7.30. I would tap on the window, and Uncle John would slowly put down his pen and open the door. We would chat briefly together about a bird that he or I had seen, for example. Especially if it was one of those fine and magical Hookses mornings, he would be full of joy about the place. Then we would kneel down and pray about the coming day ... Some of the fondest memories I have of working with Uncle John were at The Hookses when we were laying a concrete doorstep, rebuilding an outhouse or doing something similar.[117]

Sometimes The Hookses' project which fell to the study assistant might be so innovative as to verge on the eccentric. Mark Labberton paid a return visit to The Hookses during Toby Howarth's spell as study assistant, and was drawn in to help with what seemed an unlikely venture for the holders of a degree from Yale and a doctorate from Cambridge:

> Coal dust had been gathering in the coal shed. John thought he remembered a 'recipe' for mixing this coal dust with some amount of cement powder and making coal bricks that would be burnable. This seemed to me and to Toby as taking the 'waste not, want not' theme a little too far, but we were willing to try it. John believed that the appropriate mixture was 10:1 (coal to cement). This was our first attempt and after making hundreds of these little bricks by hand, we went inside for tea, while we watched the rain that had just begun dissolve all of our bricks! Again, not to be deterred, John said that a ratio of 5:1 might have been better, so Toby and I re-mixed the coal dust and did it all again. Toby and I laughed (most of the time!) about this rather extraordinary assignment, and spent a great deal of time discussing what trait(s) it was that caused John to suggest this in the first place, and to pursue it so doggedly. We couldn't decide if it was or was not to be emulated! The bricks were made and burned successfully ... I wasn't entirely sure this was good news for any future study assistants![118]

Some study assistants accompanied John Stott on his tours overseas (in the next decade AGE would insist on this, unless local arrangements made it unnecessary). Mark Labberton went with him to India and Bangladesh early in 1981 'as sherpa and general helper'. Besides the travel, the big meetings, the conferences with local Christian leaders, it was sometimes the tiny incidents that proved memorable. One such was searching with John Stott in a dilapidated quarter of Madras (many of the street signs missing) for the elderly mother of a Tamil he had met in Burma. At last they found her:

> She lived in extremely simple and poor conditions, but was surrounded by what seemed to be her loving family and neighbors. John asked if he could share a brief word from the Bible with them. They enthusiastically accepted and after a very, very small piece of carpet was brought out for John to stand on for this, he proceeded through a translator to share the gospel in the most simple and straightforward way. I was struck then, as at many other points, by the centrality, simplicity, and humility of John's commitment to preach and teach the love of God in Jesus Christ whenever possible.[119]

Toby Howarth, visiting India with him a few years later, was amazed by the contrast between the way in which John Stott was received in India, compared with England. Whatever the reasons, it was palpable:

> We arrived from Sri Lanka to Madras, for example, and were met on the runway by an official delegation complete with garlands and press photographers. Our passports and baggage were taken from us and we were given VIP treatment through the airport without having to clear customs or immigration. Very senior people such as bishops, archbishops and metropolitans were enormously deferential to Uncle John and his very presence enabled some senior church leaders to meet in a way that I was told would not otherwise have been possible. When we arrived at the lovely colonial bungalow of the Bishop of Madhya Kerala, there was an elephant to meet us. The cook had been asked to prepare special 'elephant sweets' for us to feed it ... On one local trip to a village in Kerala that could only be reached by boat, we arrived at the jetty to find it festooned with streamers and banners celebrating his arrival. As the boat moored, firecrackers were set off ...[120]

The elephant had been prepared for John Stott to ride; but he was happy for his study assistant to take his place!

Along with all the respect came an incredible level of demand on his time and energy ... Apart from the talks and Bible expositions that Uncle John gave, there was a constant stream of students wanting to talk personally with him. In the afternoon, when he needed to take a rest, I remember even sleeping by the doorway to make sure people didn't come in and disturb him. In Delhi, later on, he was originally scheduled to preach once or maybe twice in the morning. When we arrived, we found that three churches had advertised that he would preach, even though at least one of these had not even asked him before he arrived. He ended up having to climb down from the pulpit and leave by a side door into a waiting car, to be driven to the next church where the service had already started and was waiting for him to preach, where he would do the same routine.

Sometimes the study assistant, in his role of protector, would become frustrated and even annoyed to see John Stott's goodwill exploited in this way:

Then he would tell me privately, 'I am here as a servant of the church.' Actually, what ended up happening was that if a person got to him, Uncle John would hardly ever turn him away. But it was my task to make sure that there was a limit to the people who got to him. I remember remarking once that I felt like the most unpopular person in the country ...[121]

Chocolate – in minute quantities – was one of few concessions to the weakness of the flesh. But even the largest tube of Smarties did not last long in the crowded social life of hospitable India. Toby Howarth solved this by using a medicine bottle, appropriately labelled. After a meal he would tell John Stott it was time for his 'Vitamin Ch', and shake a few into his hands! They rarely stayed in hotels, but with local people whenever possible, generally sharing a room. They saw few tourist attractions: any spare time was devoted to the local bird-life, oblivious to the stares of passers-by. Steve Andrews was much in favour, having been an ornithologist before he came to England; and so accompanied John Stott on two birdwatching holidays during his years as study assistant, once to the Canadian Arctic, and once to Portugal, to the A Rocha Christian Field Study Centre and Bird Observatory in its early days.[122]

All his study assistants agree that their time with John Stott was a formative period in their lives. It became, however, the received wisdom passed on from each to the next, that 'the first canon of study assistant-ship is not to try to be like John'.[123] Role model he might be, from whom much could be learned in terms of single-mindedness, self-discipline and the mastery of time; but to believe you could simply adopt his principles as your own was to court failure (and probably guilt). Toby Howarth felt this when, at the start, he made it a matter of honour to keep up with John Stott and Frances Whitehead in the pace and pressure under which they lived:

> Both of them were so utterly committed to the work and had such an extraordinary capacity for it, that I felt sometimes left behind. Frances said to me on occasion that working for John was like driving a Mini down a narrow London street with a fire-engine, lights flashing and siren wailing, speeding behind her. I remarked that I felt like I was riding a bicycle in front of them both![124]

Study assistants, anxious to please, soon discovered that they could not sustain rising at 5.00am as John Stott did. Reminiscing at an informal reunion, they were amused to find that at The Hookses more than one of them had set the alarm for 5.00, turned the light on in 'Helen's Hut', where they were quartered, aware that John Stott might notice it – and then dropped quietly off for another couple of hours![125]

One consequence of this pace of life was that it would be made clear to new study assistants, partly by John Stott himself but certainly by their predecessors, that though John Stott would value them for themselves and their friendship (not simply for their work) he would seldom have much time to give to them personally. They were expected (and selected) to be mature enough to manage; though Frances Whitehead is continually remembered as a rock on which all study assistants were glad to lean from time to time.

John Stott himself was anxious that he should not be seen as an inevitable role model to these young men, either in his singleness, or in his call to the ordained ministry: 'he did not want committed Christian young people always to end up getting ordained and taken out of the larger society – especially the professions where they would otherwise be working as salt and light'.[126] Not surprisingly, many of them were already well on the road to ordination either Anglican or Presbyterian, convinced of the call of God; and they could then expect from John Stott full support, encouragement and nurture. He preached for at least one of them at his ordination, and would follow their ministries by prayer, letter and sometimes visit. To Bob Wismer, for example, on his ordination (a couple of years after his time as study assistant), John Stott wrote from The Hookses:

> I think my prayers will focus on your ministerial priorities, which I hope will be three P's – (a) people, whose precious value in God's

sight is stated in Trinitarian terms in Acts 20:28, (b) preaching, as God's Word continues to be the chief means he has ordained for leading his people into maturity, and (c) prayer, without which neither we nor the people we serve will become Christlike.[127]

There was another aspect of the study assistants' lives where they found John Stott's presuppositions might be markedly different from theirs – a culture-gap at once of generation and of geography. From 1986 onwards the current study assistant shared a flat in Queen's Gardens, Bayswater, with Michael Ibsen, who was then a young Canadian musician working for the London Institute for Contemporary Christianity. The flat often provided temporary hospitality to friends who happened to be passing through London and needed a bed for a night or two.

I don't think it ever occurred to Uncle John [Toby Howarth recalled later] that we might have female visitors to stay, just as it never occurred to us that there might be anything wrong with such an arrangement. On this particular occasion, two young American women were sleeping on the floor in the living-room when at 7.30am the telephone rang. The phone was in the living-room so one of the young women picked it up and said, 'Hello.' It was, of course, Uncle John. (Who else would ring at 7.30am?) There was a moment's silence.
   'Is this 46 Queen's Gardens?'
   'Yes,' she replied.
   The caller apologized graciously and hung up. A minute later the phone rang again.
   'Is this Flat 6, 46 Queen's Gardens?'
   'Yes,' she replied.
   By this time, Michael had realized what was happening and had raced from his bedroom to the phone.
   'May I speak to Michael Ibsen please?'
   'No problem,' she replied. 'He's just here.'
   Uncle John did not comment on the incident then, nor ever brought it up later![128]

5

The London Institute for Contemporary Christianity was formally launched in 1982, with a press conference in mid-January and the 'Inaugural School', a ten-week course with twenty-seven students, beginning in April. John Stott was the Director, and the Institute was based at the newly built St Paul's Church complex in Robert Adam

Street. This had replaced the church of St Paul's, Portman Square, where the redoubtable Prebendary Colin C. Kerr had become Vicar a year before Harold Earnshaw-Smith went to All Souls. The Institute was to be 'neither a theological college nor a missionary training college, but a lay institute' with a multicultural student body, and 'a strong input from developing countries'.[129] Behind the public announcement and the launch of the Institute lay seven years of preparation, seeking and sharpening the vision, and finding ways to give effective expression to it. Something of the kind – or perhaps only a conviction that he would discover such a vision – was not far from John Stott's thinking when he retired as Rector, in 1975, to develop a new ministry in his mid-fifties. Interviewed by the editor of *Crusade* a year before his retirement as Rector he spoke of the urgent need for the care of the clergy and the training of the laity:

> Stott would like to see the second of these taken much more seriously, as for instance at the School of Christian Studies recently launched by All Souls and St Helen's Bishopsgate – a six-month evening-class course of weekly two-hour lectures attended by around 200 members of both churches.[130]

And this itself was no new vision. Speaking at the Keswick Convention in 1969, John Stott had shared his now familiar concern for those engaged (or who ought to be engaged) in the intellectual battles of contemporary faith:

> We ought to have a bigger burden for the intelligentsia of the world, in the universities and in the capital cities of the world. Now do not misunderstand me: I am not for one moment denigrating the heroic work of missionaries in villages and simple rural communities. I thank God for them. But have we not sometimes neglected the towns and the universities and colleges, and the intelligentsia?[131]

Such a School of Christian Studies (SOCS), under the joint auspices of All Souls and St Helen's, was therefore a welcome step on the way. But it was not until October 1976 when John Stott met with Professor Andrew Kirk,[132] who was paying a brief visit to England, that they discovered a shared vision for establishing in Britain what they referred to as some sort of 'community of Christian concern'. At this time Andrew Kirk, with a group which included Samuel Escobar and René Padilla, was setting up in Argentina the Kairos Community, partly a research centre on aspects of mission in a Latin American context, and partly a training-centre offering courses and workshops to help Christians relate their faith to their professional life.[133] This tallied closely with the ideas John Stott was turning over in his mind; so that correspondence and memoranda flowed between the two of them, once Andrew Kirk had returned to Buenos Aires, with suggestions of a widening circle of interested people to whom successive drafts adumbrating the project should be sent. Early in 1977 John Stott arranged for a meeting of his 'Christian Debate' group to discuss 'the contemporary need for Christian thinking in public affairs';[134] and in further correspondence with Andrew Kirk he raised the question of how this would relate to existing organizations already in the field, such as the Shaftesbury Project or the Nationwide Festival of Light. Andrew Kirk was prompt to counter John Stott's suggestion that they should hold fire, so as not to divert support from the two bodies. In his view,

> ... neither the Shaftesbury Project nor the NFOL are able to fulfil the kind of function that was beginning to crystalize in your first memorandum, and in mine, concerning the possibilities of a Community or Resource Centre. Nor is it their interest to do so: they are functioning on other levels and with different ends in view. No-one would want to minimize the importance of what is being done and what will be done in the future. But I do not see them as a substitute for the Community, which is based on the premise of a small committed fellowship of people working and acting together, who share the same views concerning the purpose and methodology of the project.[135]

Nevertheless, it was not until 1979 that John Stott felt the time was ripe to convene a meeting with Os Guinness, Andrew Kirk, Oliver Barclay and John Gladwin, the recently appointed Director of the Shaftesbury Project. Os Guinness had been an undergraduate at London University in the early 1960s, and had been urged by John Stott (among others) to do a DPhil at Oxford, with a little help from the Langham Trust. He wrote later of his excitement as the project took shape: 'surely with John's stature, extraordinary administrative gifts, and fund-raising ability, the London Institute would go well. I certainly didn't reckon on what an uphill task it would be ...'[136]

The draft produced by John Stott after brain-storming and consultation among this small circle of like-minded friends was then shared with a wider group, followed by yet further meetings and still more work on the draft. A fourth and final memorandum, incorporating something of each of the preceding three, was produced in August 1980. In eight detailed pages it began by summarizing the need and the vision, before going on to consider staffing, administration and finance. By this time the 'community' had become an 'Institute':

We envisage an Institute for Contemporary Christian Studies dedicated to the integration of Christian faith, life and mission. Our goal would be to help students become more complete Christians in their personal and home life, and more effective Christians in their professional and public life. We hope, of course, that they will also become more faithful and active in local church leadership. Yet our eyes will be mainly on the world rather than the church as the arena in which Christians live and serve. So the Institute will offer courses in the inter-relations between faith, life and mission to thinking Christian lay people who either are graduates (mostly in subjects other than theology) or have equivalent professional qualifications or (for we are anxious to avoid the snare of cultural élitism) are articulate leaders in business, industry and the trades unions.

'Faith', 'Life' and 'Mission' were then set in context, together with the firm statement that 'in all this the Bible would of course be our textbook'.[137]

It was significant that the covering letter which introduced this document was headed 'Re a possible "Regent" in London', since it shows how much the model of Regent College, Vancouver, was in the minds of this working group. Regent College was the brain-child of a group of Canadian Christian Brethren who in 1964/5 were exploring the possibility of a 'graduate School of Theology' in the Vancouver area, 'a Brethren-orientated Seminary for lay people'.[138] As plans progressed, the Canadian committee hoped that F. F. Bruce, himself a member of the Brethren and at that time Rylands Professor of Biblical Criticism and Exegesis in the University of Manchester, might cross the Atlantic to become their founding Principal. He did in fact meet and talk with the committee in the late summer of 1966, but soon made it clear that he was not their man, and recommended another Britisher, J. M. Houston.[139]

James Houston, a Scot and the son of Brethren missionaries, was at that time Bursar and Fellow of Hertford College, Oxford, a distinguished geographer (who would later think of himself as 'a geographer of the soul')[140] and much influenced in his faith through the friendship of C. S. Lewis, with whom he was meeting regularly before Lewis's Cambridge professorship in 1954. He readily acknowledged how 'Lewis influenced me greatly to see the integration of faith and one's own professional standards of intelligence', and how 'the tutorial system also challenged me to nurture students in faith and devotion'.[141] John Stott had sought James Houston's advice in the late 1960s when All Souls was beginning to take more seriously the task of relating the historic Christian faith to the modern world. They met again in Jerusalem at the Conference on Biblical Prophecy in 1971, and in 1974 found themselves visiting Francis

Schaeffer together. Their friendship grew; they shared a few holidays, including a visit to Alaska; John Stott several times lectured at Regent College's Summer School, and at one point James Houston invited him (as he also invited James Packer in the later 1970s)[142] to join the Faculty. When it became clear that this would not happen, he urged John Stott to put his energies into the vision of a 'Regent' in London. James Houston had been talking for some time with a wealthy Dutch Christian couple, Ernst and Erica van Eeghen, who had attended a Regent Summer School in Vancouver: 'They were spiritually renewed in faith and wanted to do something for the Lord. Should it be a mini-Regent in Geneva where they had a house? Or in Amsterdam near their home?'[143] James Houston recommended London, where there was a strong evangelical basis of support, rather than either Switzerland or the Netherlands, and put them in touch with John Stott. Together they urged and encouraged him to pursue his vision for the London Institute, and offered some initial funding.

It was perhaps James Houston, from across the Atlantic, who was best able to understand from his own experience the difficult personal decision which John Stott had to face, as he pondered his own calling to be part of this new venture.

> I have been thinking, and praying deeply about you, John [James Houston wrote at the start of 1980], as you make your decision for the proposed Institute in London. I fully understand that you will blow hot and cold over the scheme, not only because of your own personal involvement but also because leadership in a venture like this does demand nerves of steel. Since you first made the tremendous plunge in going to All Souls, so long ago, life has been reasonably sheltered though the rigours of so much travel have of course cast you so much upon the Lord. But I can deeply understand how weary you must feel at this time in life and wonder whether you do have the stamina and the resources to face such a significant venture of faith. It will be all the tougher because others will expect initiative from you and may not have the same enthusiasm or dreams that you might have about this venture. However, I am willing to stand by you in whatever capacity may be helpful to you to make sure that this venture does get off the ground.[144]

These two strands, the shared vision with Andrew Kirk and others, and the example of Regent College, Vancouver (with the strategic urging of James Houston), were the immediate catalyst for the founding of the London Institute; but, in John Stott's own thinking, some such idea 'had been maturing for over a decade'. When expounding Galatians (expositions which became the basis of the first of The Bible Speaks Today series)[145] at All Souls as far back as the mid-1960s, he had been forcibly impressed by the experience,

> ... namely that a comparatively educated congregation in London in the mid-1960s should think it worth their while to give their minds, Sunday after Sunday, to the task of understanding and applying a letter written in the mid-first century by an ugly Jewish Christian to obscure village Christian communities in the Taurus mountains of Asia Minor, and should find it absolutely relevant to today![146]

During the end of the 1970s, and into the 1980s, John Stott was working on his major study of preaching.[147] From his experience at All Souls and across the world, for publication or in the pulpit, he had come to see contextualization as essential to truly biblical preaching. The aim was relevant application based on accurate exegesis:

> All this thinking, later clarified as 'double listening', was part of the background to the launching of the Institute in 1982. Eight years previously the London Lectures in Contemporary Christianity had begun, so that the expression 'contemporary Christianity' was already being used. But the commitment to serve as Director was a big step. I was already sixty. I realised I could not take on the London Institute for Contemporary Christianity without giving up other commitments.[148]

He therefore relinquished, or prepared to lay down, his work for Lausanne, his long-standing commitment as Honorary General Secretary of EFAC, his joint chairmanship of CEEC/AEA, and his chairmanship of Care and Counsel. He also agreed to reduce his overseas travel, at least in the immediate future, so as to give priority to establishing the Institute on a firm footing, while adding: 'I hope in particular to be able to resume visits to the Third World as soon as possible.'[149] Moreover, he made two conditions on accepting the Council's pressing invitation to be the first Director: that the appointment would be for a limited (five-year) term, and that the Council would also provide an administrative manager. Martyn Eden was therefore appointed as 'Administrative Dean',[150] aided by numerous volunteers and a small staff.

Between the launch in January, and the arrival of the first students in April, John Stott described in an interview something of his own journey to reach that moment:

The London Institute is to some extent for me a culmination of these last fifteen years in which I have begun to struggle with contemporary issues and preach about them, and have seen the need to encourage other people to do the same thing ...

This was primarily a lay Institute, anxious to work with other Christian professional groupings who shared its fundamental basis:

The key words in my thinking are 'integration' and 'penetration'. I think evangelical Christians, if one can generalise, have not been integrated; there is a tendency among us to exclude certain areas of our life from the lordship of Jesus, whether it be our business life and our work or our political persuasion. That sort of integration is crucial to the Institute's vision; the second is the penetration of the secular world by integrated Christians, whose gospel will be a more integrated gospel.[151]

Appropriately enough, Dr James Houston was among the guest lecturers at the Inaugural School (speaking on 'Symbols and Classics of Christian Devotion'), while Andrew Kirk lectured on mission, and John Stott on 'The Use of the Bible Today' together with an exposition of the book of Acts. Twenty-six mature students from fourteen different countries attended the School, 'including all three Third World continents'.[152] There quickly followed a residential Summer School at All Nations Christian College, and in the autumn a 'School of Christian Foundations', whose members numbered (among others) a doctor, a solicitor, a college lecturer, an artist, an engineer, a student worker, a midwife, a pianist, a writer, a singer, a missionary, several business people and a couple of postgraduate students.[153]

As the programme increased, so did the staff. Tony McCutcheon, an Australian, had worked in the Far East as Regional Secretary for Scripture Union. He came to live in London in the 1980s, joined All Souls, and found himself in the same fellowship group as John Stott, whose mission addresses in Melbourne he had listened to enthralled as an embattled Methodist theological student in 1958: 'the most rational exposition of the gospel I'd yet heard'. Tony's wife Margery was already working for the Institute, and Tony was recruited to begin a bookshop, to become a temporary librarian, and to be involved with the work of LICC among senior business executives. Before long he became Bursar. The vision of LICC tallied exactly with the work he had hoped to find in England: 'relating the gospel to every area of life', as he had sometimes told his passengers, while driving taxis in Melbourne after winding up his business there.[154]

Throughout this heady period in which LICC was finding its role and developing courses, its long-term future was still insecure. But of its value to those who were its students there was never any doubt. A not untypical example might be James B. Notkin, a young economics graduate who in 1982 was working as a layman at the University Presbyterian Church in Seattle. John Stott came there to preach at Mark Labberton's ordination, and spoke to the church staff on the theme of 'permeating all sectors' for Christ. He invited James Notkin (who was planning a career in business) to enrol for a course at the LICC: 'when he asked me to come to the Institute I had $27.37 in the bank. Nonetheless I knew I would be there in three weeks.'[155]

Four years later John Stott received a letter from him recalling those early days:

> Since my return home from the inaugural session of the LICC in 1982 I have wanted to write and thank you for the great things I gained in that time. The idea of writing, however, grew increasingly formidable; each passing week, each new adventure in ministry and each opportunity to teach and preach revealed to me benefits of my time in London … So, quite simply thank you. Thank you for dreaming and making the LICC a reality.

Students the world over have always known that the person of the teacher is the most compelling lesson. The early members of Wycliffe Hall, Oxford, used to comment on the first Principal, 'It is not what Chavasse says, but that *he* says it.'[156] Clearly, students at the Institute have found the same. The letter continues:

> The greatest gift you gave us was being with us. You gave an excellent lecture on humility in class, yet your life spoke of it in the dining hall, on the street and in your flat, and it was in those places especially that I heard what the Lord wanted for me to hear from your lectures … perhaps you have spoiled me but it seems now that the professors who have a humility before the Word are the only ones that I learn from, at least the only ones I learn easily from. I have a feeling that long after my notes and tapes from the Institute wear out, the mark God has left on my life by encountering, observing and fellowshipping with you will still be with me.[157]

In one of the early memoranda already quoted John Stott had indicated that 'the purchase of a centre or college is not in mind; we want to stay in the secular city'. At first he had hoped that St Paul's, Robert Adam Street, might prove a permanent base. George Cassidy, the Vicar,[158] was not unwilling; but at about the same time the All Souls PCC began to investigate the future use of St Peter's, Vere Street. After much planning and negotiation (including a Consistory Court hearing) this became the Institute's home,[159] and it was formally opened in St Peter's, complete with offices, library, refectory, kitchen, seminar rooms and lecture hall on 21 October 1983.[160]

At the heart of its annual programme were the ten-week courses on 'The Christian in the Modern World', which continued to attract young graduates from many countries, often including those recruited by John Stott personally in the course of his travels. There was also a course on 'The Church in the World' for pastors and leaders, many of whom, from developing countries, were supported by grants and bursaries. One Tanzanian evangelist was long remembered as having to sell his pig to pay his fare to London for the course.[161] Interspersed with these were single weeks for sixth-formers or students, weekend seminars for professional groups, and workshops on different topics such as 'War and Peace', 'Morals, Law and Social Change', 'Evangelism and Culture', and 'The Sanctity of Human Life'.

At the same time, John Stott committed himself to travelling more widely within the UK, to make the work of the fledgling Institute better known. There is plenty of evidence that even for mature and well-instructed Christians, LICC was offering something new. To those whose evangelical background had tended to caricature secular involvement in negative and pessimistic terms, it was a challenge to try to break through the caricature,

> ... to struggle to understand the issues and forces at work in the world and to develop an authentic and practical Christian response. It was an exhilarating, stretching and life-changing experience. The pessimism was replaced by a new confidence in the relevance and power of Christian truth and by a sense of optimism. In retrospect these experiences changed the direction of my life and Christian service ...[162]

Among a number of Africans who came to the LICC in its early days was Charles Owor, a Ugandan lawyer, already deeply concerned with issues of justice and human rights. At 'The Christian in the Modern World' course, he found his understanding of Christian social responsibility brought into sharp focus, as he re-examined the need 'to relate the Word to the world'. On his return to Uganda he founded a Christian Lawyers' Fellowship, with a primary aim of bringing legal aid to poor victims of exploitation. A later student from Africa, Lawrence Temfwe, Director of the Prison Fellowship of Zambia, who attended the ten-week course at the Institute in the 1990s, returned home 'to share the vision with other Christian leaders in the country', and to find ways to integrate faith and life in contemporary Zambia and Southern Africa. Once again, lasting lessons came not only from the course but from personal friendship and fellowship:

> Perhaps the greatest practical lesson in our ten years' friendship was when I visited his home in London. Uncle John's modest home was a total shock to me ... My prayer since then has been that I grow in godly contentment and learn to invest in things that have eternal purposes.[163]

From Latin America, towards the end of the 1980s, Saúl and Pilar Cruz (whose story belongs to a later chapter) undertook 'The Christian in the Modern World' course at the Institute, and found it 'the most significant moment of definition and decision to launch the ministry of Armonía among the urban poor of Mexico City'.[164]

In contrast, perhaps, to the acclaim received from its students, the Institute struggled behind the scenes to secure its own future. John Stott's agreed five-year term as Director ended with his sixty-fifth birthday in 1986. After fruitless attempts to secure a successor, the Council divided control between Martyn Eden as Dean, and Ernest Lucas as Director of Studies, with John Stott as President. Tony McCutcheon became Development Officer, and volunteers such as Betty Baker, Helen Parry and Margaret Killingray continued to develop key roles, both tutorial and administrative. John Stott told his friends:

> I am very grateful that I shall be able to continue my personal involvement in the London Institute, while at the same time reducing my annual teaching commitment and handing over all executive responsibilities. With the extra time available, I hope to resume more Third World travel (health and strength permitting) and to visit the Hookses more often for study and writing, not least in order to see the New Testament 'Bible Speaks Today' series completed.[165]

A year later he added a postscript:

> People are asking me if 'retirement' from the directorship of the London Institute has altered my lifestyle. Well, let me tell you of two personal resolves, which so far remain uncompromised. First, Frances Whitehead is 'working to rule', arriving a bit later and leaving earlier than she used to each day. And secondly, I am

determined to have a proper day off each week. How's that for a beginning?[166]

Two years later a major reorganization saw the merger of the Institute and the Shaftesbury Project (of which John Stott had been a founding trustee), with staff both in London and Nottingham, under the title of 'Christian Impact'.[167] Meanwhile the London Lectures, since 1986 under the sponsorship of the Institute, continued to attract powerful speakers and interested and often influential audiences. Charles Colson, former Special Counsel to the President of the United States, was one of a team of lecturers in 1979 on 'Crime and the Responsible Community'; though an invitation to former US President Jimmy Carter in the 1980s was unsuccessful. Professor Brian Griffiths, Chairman of the London Institute, gave the 1980 lectures on 'Morality and the Market Place'.[168] Succeeding years saw symposia on the impending millennium, and on a Christian approach to art; while Oliver O'Donovan, Regius Professor of Moral and Pastoral Theology at Oxford, lectured in 1983 on genetic engineering and the whole area of artificial human fertilization.[169] Other series of lectures took as their topics Christian education, the Christian and the State, healthcare, violence, and the revolution in information technology following the development of the microchip. It was a reflection of the difficulties facing the London Institute/Christian Impact that no lectures were given in 1990, breaking the series for the first time since its inception sixteen years before.

In 1995/6 Dr Tony McCutcheon undertook, on behalf of some of John Stott's friends, to collate an application to the Trustees of the Templeton Prize for Progress in Religion. Among those who responded with supporting letters was Andrew Kirk, who had been part of the London Institute vision from the first.

Now, fourteen years later [he wrote], an enormous amount of quite ordinary Christians, earning their living in a wide diversity of secular employments, and from every continent, have benefited from intensive courses of study ... there is no doubt of the revolutionary nature of the experience. The common story is that, often for the first time, the detailed relevance of Christian believing and action has come alive in the context of the real world. Whether it is the world of science, art, journalism, politics, economics, youth, communication, religion, work, the environment, culture, ideologies, and many more, the Christian faith has carefully and thoughtfully been applied. It would be hard to find a centre so dedicated to seeking the right kind of integration between God's revelation and human living ...[170]

TEN

A Global Ministry:
Travels in Six Continents

1

When at the end of the 1980s John Stott came to revise his handbook for Confirmation candidates written some thirty years before,[1] he included a reference to his own experience of the worldwide fellowship of Christian believers:

> Having had the privilege of much travel, I have met fellow Christians on all six continents. I have worshipped with them in some of the great medieval cathedrals of Europe, in makeshift tin huts in Latin American villages, with Eskimos in the Canadian Arctic, and under trees in the tropical heat of Africa and Asia. I have been lovingly welcomed by sisters and brothers in Christ, always with a smile and often also with a hug or a kiss, even when we have never met before and even when our respective languages have been mutually incomprehensible. The fact is that the Christian church is the biggest family on earth, and the only multi-racial, multi-national, multi-cultural community that exists.[2]

Indeed, even as the 1980s began, he was a veteran traveller; and the decade was to see visits, or repeat visits, to something like 100 countries in almost every continent, of which a chapter such as this can give little more than just a flavour. As a tailpiece to his personal newsletter in August 1975 he had included a cartoon representing his various migrations. In April 1979 it reappeared with a caption: 'Several friends have asked me to identify this rare avian species. Having failed to discover it in any of the world's bird books, I hereby name it the "Long-tailed, crowned and spotted Stott-bird"!'

The drawing appeared yet again in his October letter, with a little verse designed both to mark his travels and to mock his ornithological fanaticism:

> The spotters gasp, and murmur: 'What bird
>   Is that, which wanderlust impels?'
> 'The long-tailed, crowned and spotted Stott bird
>   In migratory flight to the Seychelles!'

The same global vision that inspired the incessant travelling was also expressed in other ways. The Evangelical Literature Trust grew steadily in scope and influence, so that from a little office and part-use of a church hall in Ipswich, books by the hundred thousand were sent annually to scholars, pastors and seminary libraries in the Third World. 'Our main concern', John Stott told an interviewer, 'is to raise the standard of discipleship by raising the standard of preaching.'[3] The same aim inspired the choice of Langham Scholars, funded by the Langham Trust to study at a British university.

> It would probably be difficult [wrote one such] for someone in your country to appreciate the problems of a minister of the gospel in India in finding the means or opportunity to grow in Christian knowledge. The few centres of advanced learning are either unsympathetic to evangelical theology or ill-equipped for spiritual growth, or both. Scholarships for advanced study are almost non-existent.[4]

Such scholars were soon proving their worth. Vinay Samuel, the first of them, was shortly to become the moving spirit in establishing the International Fellowship of Mission Theologians, which in turn became the sponsoring body for the Oxford Centre for Mission Studies. John Stott himself had no direct role in the founding or development of either, but was their friend and supporter from the beginning, believing that theologians from the developed West needed to listen respectfully to colleagues from the Third (or Two-thirds) World, 'and will undoubtedly be enriched in the process'.[5]

A third major project which depended on John Stott's overseas travels was EFAC, the Evangelical Fellowship in the Anglican Communion. In some instances it was only his personal visits which kept alive the involvement of isolated evangelical communities, or which added new branches to the Fellowship, often in dioceses or provinces where evangelicalism was little known or undervalued. But the time had come to step down as General Secretary, not least because of the needs of the London Institute; and early in 1981 Canon Alan Neech, just retired as General Secretary of BCMS, took over from him.[6] During these twenty years the Fellowship had grown from small beginnings to embrace members, branches or correspondents in something like fifty countries scattered throughout the Anglican Communion, from the Fellowship of Witness in the American Episcopal Church to EFAC representatives in the Solomon Islands, Sri Lanka or Iran. There were not many Anglican evangelical leaders with whom John Stott had not corresponded. In the files of EFAC 'letters to and from Archbishops abound!'[7]

In 1986 the Council of EFAC invited John Stott to succeed Archbishop Sir Marcus Loane as President: looking back then over twenty-five years, he could record eighteen group members of the Fellowship, a 'group member' signifying a fully constituted national Evangelical Anglican Fellowship in a particular country. In addition, ninety-nine clergy had benefited from EFAC bursaries to gain further theological education or parochial experience in Britain, with the hundredth, a Ugandan, expected in a matter of weeks.[8] Perhaps it could be reckoned that EFAC came of age, at least in the eyes of Anglican circles in England, when in the summer of 1993 it mounted a major international consultation at Canterbury on the theme of 'The Anglican Communion and Scripture', with some twenty-five bishops among the delegates. The *Church Times* gave most of a page to a summary of the Report, calling it 'a ringing statement of mainstream Anglican Evangelical attitudes to the Bible',[9] which indeed it is. John Stott's main task from the platform was a daily Bible exposition. His final study concluded with a personal reference, which was also a reminder of why EFAC was called into being, and some of its continuing purpose. They had been studying 2 Timothy, with Paul's declaration of how he had fought the fight, finished the race, and kept the faith:

> I hope it is not presumptuous, or too personal, for me to apply his words to myself. I am now over seventy years old. I have had my statutory 'three score years and ten'. I am naturally not expecting to live much longer. Any day now my summons may come. So I ask myself: 'Where are the Timothys of the end of the twentieth century, the young men and women who are determined to stand firm against the prevailing winds of fashion and refuse to compromise?' I pray that many may be found among you.[10]

Such a Consultation would have been unthinkable in the days before EFAC: or, indeed, in its early days as a struggling and at times fragile consortium. For more than twenty years it remained the kind of institution aptly described as 'the lengthened shadow of one man'.[11] Canterbury 1993 suggests that in the global village of our shrinking world, the Fellowship will have a continuing, and perhaps increasing, part to play.

2

The Lausanne Movement continued to be a major preoccupation for John Stott during the 1980s. He was one of the convenors of an international consultation on simple lifestyle in March 1980 under the joint sponsorship of the Lausanne Theology and Education Working Group (of which he was Chairman) and the Unit on Ethics and Society of the Theological Commission of the World Evangelical Fellowship, with Ronald Sider as its Convenor. Eighty Christians from twenty-seven countries met for four days at High Leigh, Hertfordshire, to consider the meaning and implication of the deceptively lucid phrase in the Lausanne Covenant, 'to develop a simple lifestyle'. The final report explained how,

> ... above all, we tried to expose ourselves with honesty to the challenges of both the Word of God and the world of need ... We recognized that others have been discussing this topic for several years, and we are ashamed that we have lagged behind them ... we send this statement on its way for the study of individuals, groups and churches, with the earnest hope and prayer that large numbers of Christians will be moved, as we have been, to resolve, commitment and action.[12]

The aim of the drafters of the Report had been to combine thankfulness for the good gifts of a good Creator with the call to simplicity, generosity and contentment, avoiding the extremes of irresponsible indulgence or morbid asceticism.

Three months later John Stott was in Pattaya, Thailand, two hours' drive from the capital, Bangkok, for a further international gathering under the auspices of Lausanne, a major Consultation on World Evangelization (COWE), 'to seek fresh vision and direction for the '80s',[13] six years after the Lausanne Congress. The Consultation was held in the Beach Hotel, the cheapest venue the organizers could find in a Third World country with the facilities needed for a conference on this scale. It was embarrassing to discover later that Pattaya was known as a 'sin city' and the hotel boasted a so-called 'massage parlour'![14]

The COWE Conference was divided at John Stott's instigation into nearly twenty mini-consultations, each focusing on Christian witness to a different people: Hindus, Jews, the urban poor, Marxists and so on. John Stott's task was to co-ordinate their reports, which meant a daily meeting with seventeen chairmen. For him, as for Frances Whitehead and Tom Cooper (his study assistant) who were with him, there was little time to look beyond the immediate needs of the Consultation, apart from brief expeditions in search of birds, and a dip in the South China Sea before breakfast. His major platform task was a plenary address on 'The Place of the Bible in World Evangelization' on the second day of the ten-day conference.[15] He found himself speaking to some 650 participants, drawn from eighty-five countries, and was particularly impressed by the quality of younger Christian leaders from the Third World.[16] He had also hoped that a merger might be proposed between the Lausanne Committee and the World Evangelical Fellowship: but the difficulties loomed too large, and he had to be content with a strong wish expressed by the Consultation for 'growing co-operation with others of like mind'.[17]

During these major conferences John Stott's usual routine had to be thrown to the winds: 'I was up nearly every night till after midnight, and once or twice till two or three in the morning.'[18] Bishop John Reid, his room-mate, the younger by some years and a wiry Australian, found himself caught up in some of this activity:

At the conclusion of the Pattaya meetings the Anglicans met at Christ Church Bangkok for a day conference. I chaired. He was the Secretary. It concluded at 5pm. I was utterly exhausted and he pressed me to accompany him to a public meeting of Christians in Bangkok to hear Leighton Ford speak. He felt we should encourage Ford. I went very reluctantly.

They returned to Christ Church for dinner with the chaplain, and

declined an invitation to drive round Bangkok and see the sights. John
Reid's hopes of an early night were frustrated, however:

> On returning to the room we shared, he then was expansive in
> conversation until 11pm. I excused myself at this stage telling him
> that I had to be up at 5am to catch a plane to Sydney. He said he
> would be up at 5am to write so it was no inconvenience but would I
> mind if he wrote for a little after I went to bed? I was aware that he
> wrote quietly until 2am and then got up at 5am to resume ... I have
> never seen such intellectual stamina![19]

The fruit of John Stott's painstaking drafting will be found in 'The
Thailand Statement', a series of twelve pledges adopted (with perhaps one
dissentient) as COWE ended.[20] Almost every word had been subject to
debate and sometimes fierce scrutiny. A single reference to 'anti-Semitism'
as a hindrance to the gospel provoked in turn Muslim protest, then Israeli
protest at the idea of omitting it. Much excited discussion took place,
with press deadlines looming. Martin Goldsmith, himself a Jewish
Christian, was one of those asked by Jewish representatives to take the
matter up with John Stott and make their position clear to him:

> John brought the workers among Muslims together with us as Jews
> and a new wording was eventually agreed. I still felt that John had
> not understood the strong emotions aroused by this matter and
> with considerable reluctance (I know he hates people doing this) I
> waylaid him after a meeting and reminded him that as Jews we lost
> six million of our people in the gas chambers, a third of our total
> race in four years or so. I remember him bowing his head with a
> new awareness of the horror and pertinence of this fact of the
> holocaust ...[21]

Of the seven major emphases of the Lausanne Covenant of 1974,[22]
none had been the subject of more earnest debate than the issue of
Christian social responsibility. For more than two years the Lausanne
Theology and Education Group, with John Stott in the chair, had been
making careful plans for a further and fuller consultation on the relationship between evangelism and social issues. Their protracted preparations
came to fruition in Grand Rapids, Michigan, in June 1982, when some
fifty participants met together for a week on the spacious campus of the
Reformed Bible College to try to define more clearly this relationship,
particularly in the light of a current polarization of viewpoints between
the World Council of Churches conference in Melbourne in May 1980,
and the LCWE consultation in Pattaya, Thailand, a month later. John

Stott arrived in Grand Rapids with a considerable degree of apprehension. The papers and responses, circulated in advance, had been critical of each other's positions and even in some cases sharply so. He wrote:

> For me it was another and dramatic demonstration of the value of international conferences ... when we meet face to face (or, as our American friends vividly express it, 'eyeball to eyeball'), and listen not only to each other's arguments but to the cherished convictions which lie behind the arguments, then we develop towards one another a new understanding, respect and love. This is not to say that we agree about everything (as our report makes plain), but that our agreements are far greater than our residual differences.[23]

Part of his apprehension was highly personal. Suspicions had been roused, notably in the US (he noted in his diary),

a. that the Lausanne Movement was now going the same way as the WCC;
b. that Lausanne was going soft on the Bible and evangelism, and
c. that JRWS was the villain of the piece, having 'dethroned evangelism' as the traditional and primary task of the church.[24]

This had found expression in Dr Arthur Johnston's book, *The Battle for World Evangelism*; and John Stott had replied in an 'Open Response', published in his 'Cornerstone' series, then running in *Christianity Today*.[25] It was a spirited defence, friendly but firm. In a subsequent conversation with Dr Johnston John Stott suggested that what was needed was 'an international consultation of evangelical leaders to settle this unnecessarily divisive issue'.[26] So the Grand Rapids Consultation had been born. John Stott was again the main drafter of the Report: 'for four nights running I had to burn the midnight oil and secured only three hours' sleep each night'. The final plenary, chaired by Bishop John Reid, asked for some 250 amendments to be incorporated: but in the end both Arthur Johnston and John Stott himself were satisfied with the balance of the statement. 'Cosmos out of chaos', as one delegate wrote on the blackboard in tribute to the drafters.

Fifteen years after Lausanne, a second international Congress was convened at Manila in the Philippines for nine days in July 1989. This was an altogether larger gathering, with some 3,000 participants from 170 countries. The 'Manila Manifesto', which it accepted and commended for further study and response, was primarily a continuing commitment to the Lausanne Covenant, and a renewed call for 'the whole church to take the whole gospel to the whole world'.[27] It therefore came to be known as 'Lausanne II'. Todd Shy, the current study assistant, accompanied John Stott to Manila, sharing in a four-day birdwatching holiday before the Congress began, followed by a local conference arranged by Scripture Union, IVCF, and ISACC (the Institute for Studies in Asian Church and Culture) on 'Developing a Christian Impact on Society'.

Against his will, his considered and reasoned objections ('age ... the pain of discord ... young leaders should be brought forward ... unacceptable on the charismatic issue and to the right-wing American evangelical establishment ...')[28] and his better judgment, John Stott eventually allowed himself to be persuaded yet again to chair the drafting committee. Before travelling to Manila he had read the sixty or seventy plenary papers, and had prepared from them the first draft of the Declaration which the delegates would debate and revise. As the Congress developed, however, this met with a very rough ride. Proposals were put forward that the draft be abandoned entirely, and replaced with 'pithy statements'. It was criticized as too long, too wordy, too vague, too tired: in a word, 'disappointing'. Others wanted to drop the idea of a Manifesto and rename the document a 'Memorandum'; or to send it out, not with the authority of the Congress, but simply over the names of the drafting committee. John Stott found himself personally hurt by these criticisms, dismayed at the prospect of having to begin again,[29] and at one stage, while suffering from a severe headache, unable to go on. But rest brought renewed strength; the corner began to be turned; and eventually the Manifesto was 'received' by an overwhelming majority of the delegates. Only a tiny handful voted against it.

John Stott wrote in his diary:

> I was particularly thankful that afterwards participants of both the 'left' and 'right' expressed their satisfaction and even gratitude. The radicals could see that the Manila Manifesto went considerably further than the Lausanne Covenant in declaring the indispensability of social action, 'good works' making the 'good news' visible. But conservatives were pleased too, especially (I suspect) with the strong theological statements on the human predicament and the uniqueness of Christ. Even Art Johnston, previously critical of my stance, wrote me a delightful note that he had studied it carefully, it might well prove more important than the Lausanne Covenant, and that it was a veritable *chef d'oeuvre!*[30]

In a published interview, John Stott replied to the question, 'What does the Manila Manifesto add to the Covenant or the process of Lausanne?' The gist of his answer was 'to clarify it'; and in particular to try to 'bring evangelism and social action together' rather than considering them as separate topics. It was also able to disarm an impression that had grown up in the intervening years that the Lausanne Covenant was a kind of social gospel: 'In the Manifesto we thought it necessary to repeat that evangelism is primary.'[31] In a private letter written from Manila John Stott described the Congress as something of 'a mixed blessing':

> Wonderful to have 190 nationalities represented in the huge 4000+
> assembly and to sense the universality and diversity of the Body of
> Christ, yet too much American influence and (with a few brilliant
> exceptions) mediocre traditional papers ...[32]

Before flying home John Stott wanted to see at first hand the work of CARE (Christian Action for Reconciliation and Evangelism), run by Melo and Rose Biron in the slums of Manila. The Birons had emigrated to the US some twenty years before, become well-to-do, and found a personal faith in Christ. They determined to return to Manila and work among the poor. So on the day after the Congress they called for Todd Shy and John Stott and drove in the early morning to the North Docks area of Manila Bay:

> Wherever there was a wall, squatters had used it as a way to anchor
> their flimsy plywood and tin-sheet shack, its corrugated roof
> weighed down by an old tyre ... it was horrific to see children and
> even adults scavenging in the refuse like dogs, poking about with
> sticks or with their bare hands to find and salvage what they could.[33]

They came to CARE's headquarters, a modest building with two small offices and a hall just big enough to accommodate fifty or sixty for a Sunday service and to house a preschool playgroup midweek. John Stott met some of the children, 'their black hair shining and their brown eyes twinkling', who sang to him in Tagalog, the basis of Filipino, the national language; after which he taught them the children's chorus 'Two little eyes to look to God ...' Their pastor took him and Todd to see the home of one of his flock, a visit which served to bring into new focus the laborious debates of the preceding days. They found themselves taken

> ... along narrow dark passage ways between more squatters' homes,
> from which eyes peered at us. They looked clean, but were horribly
> overcrowded. I'm glad the Manila Manifesto includes the sentence:
> 'We are outraged by the inhuman conditions in which millions live,
> who bear God's image as we do.'[34]

Including these visits on behalf of Lausanne, John Stott was in Asia on six occasions during the 1980s, now in India and Bangladesh, now in Taiwan, Thailand, Burma or the Philippines. His itinerary would be agreed about two years in advance, but added to as the date drew nearer because of the importunity of his various hosts, until it became a problem to find a rest day amid so many multifarious engagements. One day he would be in a theological or Bible college, meeting students and faculty; the next might find him under a banian tree, expounding the Bible in the open air. There would be endless interviews (including requests for help, bewildering in their variety), consultations with bishops and church leaders, conferences for missionaries, sermons in a range of churches, visits to private homes with simple Christian teaching through an interpreter and much blessing of babies, and once a brief meeting with Mother Teresa. Each day saw pastors' conferences, lectures, addresses, seminars; or less formal meetings with the organizers of a range of local and national evangelistic, social and educational enterprises, many of whom seem to have had links in London with All Souls or the Institute.[35] Wherever he might be, time would usually be found for a birdwatching expedition or two, and (less frequently) for sightseeing: on one occasion, having time in hand at Kuwait International Airport, he visited the airport mosque only to find, once he had emerged and conversation was resumed, that he became 'an object of aggressive Muslim evangelism'.[36] There was an astonishing range and breadth of worship to be experienced, from village churches and open-air gatherings to a style more reminiscent of home: as in Rangoon on Ascension Day, where

> It was a joy to celebrate the exaltation of Jesus at a 7am
> Communion Service in the Cathedral. Although there were only
> seven of us ... and although buses and cars roared by hooting
> outside, and miniature little white-rumped House Swifts whizzed
> by twittering to their nests in the Cathedral porch, we were drawn
> up into 'the heavenlies', as Paul would have said, to bow the knee to
> Jesus and confess with our lips that he is Lord.[37]

3

In May 1981 John Stott returned to Australia. He had many friends there, notably but not exclusively in the Sydney diocese; and his name was widely known from his books and tapes and his seven previous visits. The most recent had been only two years before, in May 1979, when he had delivered a series of addresses in St Andrew's Cathedral, Sydney, during the School of Evangelism of the Billy Graham Crusade.[38]

Evangelical Anglicans in Australia had followed with much interest the

UK Keele Congress of 1967, and its successor at Nottingham ten years later. In 1971 they mounted their own first antipodean NEAC (National Evangelical Anglican Congress), and their second, ten years later, at Monash University, an hour's drive from Melbourne. In May 1981, therefore, John Stott flew out as one of the main speakers (arriving at the auditorium straight from the airport, with perhaps a quarter of an hour to spare: 'I don't know who was the more apprehensive – they or I!'). He spoke to a plenary session of all the 550 participants on the 'Nazareth Manifesto' of Luke 4: 'I tried to bridge the gulf between the two stereotypes of those who entirely politicize and those who entirely spiritualize the gospel.'[39] Confessing in his diary that as 'a hardened conference-goer, I find it hard to enthuse over congresses', he noted that all those whom he talked with seemed to have found it a stimulating experience, though he missed the discipline of working to prepare an agreed Statement; and became steadily more convinced that in England such a platform-dominated congress would not have been tolerated: 'the organizers would have had a grass-roots' riot on their hands'.[40]

Moving to Sydney, he spent the week at Bishopscourt as a guest of the Archbishop and Mrs Loane, fulfilling a busy programme for the Sydney diocese Home Missionary Society – a dozen meetings in eight days. The Archbishop had recently announced his impending retirement, and John Stott found himself being approached, in person or by letter, to ask if he would be willing to be nominated as Marcus Loane's successor: 'It has not been difficult, however, to dissuade them – not least when I mention my firm commitment to the London Institute.'

The third stage of this tour was to Brisbane, on behalf of the Queensland Evangelical Alliance, followed by brief visits to cities strung along Queensland's eastern seaboard to the north of Brisbane, including Gympie, Rockhampton, and Townsville, with the Great Barrier Reef offshore. At intervals between the demands of Christian ministry, Queensland produced remarkable opportunities for ornithology. With a variety of different habitats (coast, foreshore, rain-forest, semi-desert, swamp, woodland, scrub and grassland among them) there were constantly unfamiliar birds to be identified. On one memorable day John Stott and his companions noted more than seventy species, thirty of which were new to him. Sunday was spent in Cairns, further north still, well into the tropical zone:

An interdenominational service had been arranged that evening, and a full church of about 300 gathered. I took the favourite topic 'The Marks of a Renewed Church' (Acts 2:37–47), with a question-time to follow. Because I had said in the talk that the miracles which authenticated the unique ministry of the apostles should not be

expected today, a Chinese Archdeacon ... obviously influenced by
the charismatic movement, rose to his feet and solemnly read the
whole of Mark 16 about the signs which would follow believers,
including healing the sick, drinking poison and taking up snakes
without harm! It seemed to be quite new to him to learn that this
so-called 'Longer Ending' was not part of Mark's autograph but one
of two conclusions added by later copyists.[41]

Finally he returned for a brief stay in Perth with old friends from
Cambridge days, John and Moira Prince. John Stott described John
Prince in his diary as 'hon. co-ordinator for the Western Australian
Evangelical Alliance, a Wykehamist, a former headmaster, a living
dynamo, and my "manager' in Perth'. With them he brought to over 200
the total species of birds seen on this visit, with seventy new sightings;
and fulfilled yet more engagements ('expounding 2 Thessalonians in four
sessions: they were a bit of a flop, I think – though my "manager" denies
it – partly because I was tired ... and partly because the studies
themselves were too "heavy" for a popular audience'). John Stott himself,
used to ministering in countries and cities where he had been before or
might hope to return, questioned the value of these flying visits for single
meetings in more remote areas. John Prince, however, remained convinced that they did much to encourage and inspire clergy and
congregations persevering amid a sense of isolation, as well as 'spreading
the credibility of evangelicalism' and changing the views of some 'deep-
dyed Baptists' in the Australian Evangelical Alliance about the real nature
of evangelical Anglicanism.[42]

John Stott returned to Australia in January 1986 for another visit to
the famous CMS Summer School at Katoomba in the Blue Mountains,
and then moved on to near Melbourne for the Jubilee Conference of
AFES, the Australian Fellowship of Evangelical Students. Here he stayed
with their President, Dr Paul White (the 'Jungle Doctor' of Tanganyika,
now Tanzania), one of the first members of the Sydney student Christian
Union in 1919. At the CMS School John Stott had expounded 1
Timothy in seven sessions; now he was asked to do it again, this time in
six. Towards the last lap of his Australian journey, at a short Summer
School in Adelaide, he had only five sessions to cover the same ground!

A highlight of this visit was an expedition with John and Moira Prince
to the Fitzgerald River National Park, travelling in their converted ambulance, an air-conditioned Dodge 2000 known as 'Clancy'. The name
comes from 'Banjo' Paterson's bush ballad, 'Clancy of the Overflow',
which describes how a letter sent to Clancy the sheep-drover received a
reply from his shearing mate 'written with a thumb-nail dipped in tar',
reporting that

Clancy's gone to Queensland droving,
and we don't know where he are.[43]

The National Park extends over more than half a million acres between Albany and Hopetown, on the south-west tip of Western Australia: mostly dry sand-plain, bush and scrub, divided by small creeks and dried-up rivers, inhospitable to human beings but with its own great variety of birds. Moira and John Prince slept in Clancy, John Stott in a tent nearby. Water was a problem (Clancy carried her own limited supplies) since, according to John Prince, John Stott could not wash up without using three times as much water as they had allowed for. Indeed, after three days, they had to make an emergency return to civilization for fresh supplies. Complete days passed with no other vehicle, no distant aeroplane, no human voices but their own: only innumerable birds.

Towards the end of the week John Stott was sitting with John and Moira Prince on Quoin Head, looking out over the southern ocean towards Antarctica, the nearest land, with huge rollers breaking against the cliffs below and Albatrosses and Shearwaters wheeling above. 'Why doesn't Clancy go droving?' he suggested to his hosts, thinking of the meetings organized for him at the end of the holiday. 'And they won't know where he are!'[44]

4

At midnight on 18 April 1980, the Union Jack was lowered for the last time in Africa. Rhodesia, Britain's last African colony, hoisted instead the red-starred flag of Zimbabwe. Having put from his mind the prospect of a further visit to Africa as the 1980s began, John Stott later found himself persuaded, and went at the invitation of David Gitari, the youngest of the Kenyan bishops, to the Kenyan National Pastors' Conference in September 1980 at Kenyatta University College, ten miles from Nairobi, to minister to 1,000 pastors. They represented over seventy denominations, some of them very quaint indeed, and tragic witness to the fissiparous tendencies of devoted but independently minded Christians. He combined this with some birdwatching at three vast lakes: Turkana, where he was much in awe of ten-foot crocodiles (twenty-footers had been observed); Nakuru ('my fifth visit') and Baringa. He found time to visit Uganda, hospitable as ever but still suffering from the ravages of Amin's reign of terror ten years before. He spoke at Makerere University and at two theological colleges, Namirembe Diocesan College and Bishop Tucker College, travelling (sometimes with an armed guard) in the Archbishop's car, and only in exceptional circumstances at night. He brought with him from Nairobi a suitcase of small gifts for Ugandan

Christians in their shattered economy (eggs cost the equivalent of £1 sterling each, and a bar of soap £7, he noted in his diary). As it turned out, he had chosen well: some clothes, torch batteries, writing materials, twelve bars of soap, aspirins, washing powder, disinfectant, toothbrushes and the like.[45]

On his next visit to Africa, four years later, Uganda was not on John Stott's itinerary, though he flew over it in the course of his travels from the Gambia, Sierra Leone, Togo and Ghana in the West to Kenya on the East Coast, via the Central African Republic, Zaire and Zambia. The purpose of this visit, in February and March 1984, was largely to teach and lecture in a variety of colleges, but meeting in almost every place old friends, EFAC bursars or former members of All Souls, hungry to renew fellowship, exchange news, and entertain him as their guest. He was amused to discover that his passion for ornithology was by now well known, so that on the prepared programme of one visit the first engagement of the day was listed as 'Morning Watch (of birds)'; a new interpretation of Coverdale's translation of Psalm 130:6! On the inevitable visit to Lake Nakuru his host, Ian Marshall, apologized that 'there are only about half-a-million Flamingoes at the moment'.[46]

Most of the month was taken up by college and seminary visits, interspersed by the inevitable frustrations of constant travel: slow and delayed flights, long waits at airports, hours of driving over interminable dusty roads. The colleges ranged from the Sierra Leone Bible College, on the site of an old RAF Station, where the faculty had invited staff and students of both the Pentecostal Evangel Bible College and the Anglican and Methodist Theological Hall to join them ('Believe it or not, the very first time that such a united meeting of the colleges had taken place');[47] to the West Africa School of Advanced Theology ('a slightly pretentious title for the Assemblies of God seminary') in Togo; to the new Nairobi Evangelical Graduate School of Theology, where student residences were being created out of the sheds originally used for intensive chicken farming, forming East Africa's first graduate school of theology. Lectures, seminars, discussions with students (John Stott was always glad when these took place in the absence of faculty members, when participation and question-and-answer flowed more freely), consultations with Christian leaders, and preaching in a variety of churches and cathedrals ensured a busy month of ministry. The list of 'Birds, February/March 1984' appears astonishingly extensive even though it is headed 'selection only' and includes sightings of many species new to him. Pride of place might be assigned to the West African River Eagle, or perhaps (at least for nomenclature) to the Red-bellied Paradise Flycatcher, the Moustached Scrub Warbler or the Blue-cheeked Bee-eater!

His many friends in Africa continued to urge John Stott to make return visits, for a variety of purposes. He was there in the summer of 1988, and again in December. Besides Kenya and war-torn Uganda, there were brief visits to Zimbabwe and Malawi. Denis Osborne, High Commissioner in Malawi, with his wife Christine, were old friends: John Stott had known Denis as President of the DICCU (Durham Inter-Collegiate Christian Union) and had preached at their wedding. On a recent Christmas card they had added an open invitation for John Stott to visit Malawi, hoping that he might be able to help in bringing church leaders together (Christian witness at that time was compromised by inter-church rivalries) and in enabling them 'to discover the power of clear contemporary Bible teaching'.[48] John Stott was therefore able to meet leaders from a number of churches for supper at the High Commissioner's Residence; and next morning gave a three-hour seminar for some 180 clergy. The same evening some thirty distinguished guests were invited to a dinner at the Residence to meet him, together with Richard Francis, Director-General of the British Council, and Nicholas Hinton, Director-General of the Save the Children Fund, who happened to be visiting Malawi at the same time.

One of the main purposes of the summer 1988 visit was to move from East to Southern Africa, and spend time with Michael Cassidy, whom he had known as an undergraduate at Cambridge, and who was the founder and prime mover of Africa Enterprise. Following a brief holiday together in northern Zululand ('little game, but 125 bird species') they paid an even briefer visit to Johannesburg, where John Stott was delighted to have three people come up to him to speak of the blessing they had received at his university mission there nearly thirty years before. With Michael Cassidy he moved on to Cape Town for a series of public meetings, clergy seminars and the like, the former speaking on the current state of South Africa, and John Stott giving addresses on 'Scripture and Culture' and on 'Biblical Preaching in the Modern World'. On the Sunday morning he shared in the Cathedral eucharist ('clouds of billowing incense') while in the evening he preached in the largest 'Church of England in South Africa' (CESA) church, St James's, Kenilworth, to a congregation of some 1,500. His theme was 'salt and light', affirming the place of social concern in Christian discipleship; an appropriate text since many CESA members had been brought up to believe that the church should 'keep out of politics', even in the face of racial injustice and discrimination.

During this visit Michael Cassidy questioned John Stott in a recorded interview on a number of contemporary issues highly relevant to the local situation: 'Was Jesus in any way politically involved?' he was asked; and in reply (after a reminder that Jesus was condemned to death on a political charge) he drew a distinction:

Just simply to say 'The Church has no business in politics' confuses the issue. Politics can have two definitions, one broad and the other narrow. The broad definition of politics is the life of the *polis*, being the Greek word for the secular city. So politics in that broad sense has to do with our life in the community and the art of living together in the community ... and in that sense every Christian must be involved because Jesus sends us into the world, into the human community.

The narrow definition of politics is that it involves parties, policies and programmes with a view to legislative change. And the precise method of securing legislative change in parliament is a highly complex one. And in that sense politics, I think, is for the politicians. But not in the broad sense. It is for all Christian people.[49]

Following a further clergy conference at Pietermaritzburg it was time to head for home. 'What reflections do I feel able to pull together', John Stott asked his 1988 diary, 'after this brief two-week experience of, and exposure to, South Africa's travail?' Three impressions remained with him. First, the seriousness of the situation, with government censorship and the brutal suppression of all dissent (30,000 blacks detained without trial; many, including schoolchildren, facing prison and torture). Secondly, the failure of the church to use the influence it had. With a nominally Christian population of 70% to 80%, disunity inhibited effective action.

But thirdly, he saw grounds for hope that change might yet come. 'As Michael Cassidy says, the certainty that majority rule is coming is "simple mathematics, not politics".' The diary looks forward, prophetically, to the release of Nelson Mandela; and to genuine constitutional negotiations between different ethnic groups meeting as equals, as the only certain way to forestall the 'horrendous bloodbath' of a widespread black uprising.[50]

5

During the 1980s John Stott paid nearly twenty visits to North America, sometimes comparatively brief, more often for three or four weeks, occasionally for even longer. Whatever else he was doing, he was invariably preaching, whether to a thousand in a cathedral, or a dozen in some trapper's cabin in the High Arctic. The diary is full of 'mini-missions', pastors' conferences, lecture series at seminaries and theological schools. One year he might be at the University of Alaska, within 100 miles or so of the Arctic circle; another, at the University of the South in Sewanee, Tennessee (of 'Swany Ribber' fame), where both the university and its seminary are Episcopal foundations. Or he might be found in the far west of Canada, lecturing at Regent College and debating hermeneutical points with Professor Markus Barth of Basel University, himself the grandson of a Professor of New Testament Theology, and son of one of the best-known theologians of the century. An English friend remembers one such visit:

> In Vancouver John seemed altogether different from London. He was much more relaxed in his slacks and tartan jacket. During the Summer School he put on a party for the students and greeted all the girls with a kiss on the cheek. The girls told me that after that they had been careful when washing their faces to leave untouched the spot John had kissed. They called it their 'Stott spot'. It was awful not to have one![51]

Other visits took him to Pasadena, California, 1,000 miles down the coast, participating in a student forum on the Christian and nuclear issues, before preaching to perhaps 'the largest Presbyterian congregation in the US', the same sermon at three consecutive services. Next he might be in Washington for a National Prayer Breakfast, or to teach at the C. S. Lewis Institute;[52] breakfasting with Chuck Colson to discuss future London Lectures, or spending time with former 'study asses' in the area, to meet their families and preach in their churches.

As the work of the Langham Foundation in the US and the Langham Trust in Canada expanded, so John Stott, at their request, agreed to meet annually with their Boards of Trustees, often combining the Chicago meeting with a 'Chicago Sunday Evening Club' broadcast.[53] He noted in his diary that the Chicago meeting was always in January, the coldest time of the year; in 1984 down to 25° below freezing. Moreover, when the US Board arranged to work in four regional 'chapters', where supporters of the work seemed to be concentrated, John Stott agreed an annual visit to each of these as well.

The work of the Evangelical Literature Trust, and the support of the various Third World Langham Scholars, owed much to these visits, and not least to the interest of wealthy Christians in Canada and the US. More than once, John Stott visited Jupiter Island (perhaps 'the greatest concentration of wealth in the USA')[54] as the guest of his friend Mrs Martha Ashe, leading a Bible study group in her home, and speaking at one or two receptions about the work of the Foundation. But his encounters with such a lifestyle always fostered a certain ambivalence. On the one hand, as a guest, he was grateful for hospitality; and especially thankful for generous support of causes close to his heart. But he noted his unease after a meeting of thirty or forty church leaders in a North American city, when they were entertained to a sumptuous outdoor meal in the cool garden of a beautiful home:

I felt uncomfortable [he confided to his diary] when I thought of Calcutta's teeming millions whose only home was the pavement and only possession a blanket, and so felt relieved when [his hosts] told me they had had similar thoughts, leading to a decision to sell their house and build themselves a smaller one. This conscientious desire to simplify one's lifestyle out of solidarity with the world's poor seems to be one of the most significant movements in the contemporary church.[55]

For years past, John Stott had used 'rest days' on his travels, and even brief before-breakfast expeditions, to observe the local bird life. Holiday time, too, was often given to special expeditions: and, with the greater freedom of being Rector Emeritus, these were pursued with ever-increasing determination, often in the company of former study assistants or other like-minded enthusiasts. In 1981, by way of celebrating his sixtieth birthday, he journeyed north with Keith and Gladys Hunt, visiting the Pribilof Islands, 300 miles off the west coast of Alaska, towards the edge of the Arctic circle:

It was inevitable that I should find myself comparing St Paul Island with (say) Skomer Island, and the respective sea cliffs of Pribilof and Pembrokeshire. There was the same colourful carpet of wild flowers, though instead of Thrift, Vetch, Bladder Campion and blue Squills the equivalents were yellow Arctic Poppies in great profusion, purplish-blue Monks' Hood, yellow Fleabane and the dainty little white Bering Sea Chickweed.[56]

He was able to add the Red Phalarope ('though in eclipse'), the Pectoral Sandpiper and the Whistling Swan, among other exotic delights to his list of new sightings. They went on to the Mount McKinley National Park, where John Stott and the Hunts were joined by James and Rita Houston. Keith Hunt had rented a miner's cabin from the Bureau of Land Management for two nights at $2 a night, but the place was so primitive that the Houstons preferred to sleep in their car.[57]

Birds continued to be the main attraction, though bears were also much in evidence. John Stott's diary records eleven grizzlies on a single expedition. Perhaps remembering those schoolboy fishing expeditions with his father, he was persuaded by Keith Hunt, himself an avid fisherman, to take out a one-day licence, since 'we were in prime territory for sockeye salmon'. Keith and Gladys Hunt still recall how his enthusiasm, not much in evidence at the beginning, was soon kindled, taking advantage of the late twilight:

Having landed one good one, John was eager to land some more ...
one more cast and then another and then another. Finally at 11pm
we insisted that we head back, with or without John. We had a mile
to walk through dark woods, making lots of noise as we went to
scare off the bears ... When we reached the location where we were
to cross the river to return to the lodge, there were no boats. We
could see the lodge, but couldn't get there, and in the twilight we
could see the shapes of bears sitting in the rapids catching the
spawning salmon. We called and called for help. Finally one chap
who woke up to use the outhouse-loo heard us and came to pick us
up ... We froze the salmon and John took it home to London and
had two dinner parties with it![58]

Such are the contrasts of the North American continent that it
provided not only 'the quest for the Snowy Owl' (resumed fruitlessly in
1980) but tropical bird adventures, too. In Hawaii, for example, as one of
the few English members of the Hawaiian Audubon Society; camping
with the Howarth brothers on the shores of Whirlpool Lake in the Riding
Mountains National Park; bicycling along the gravel roads of the Delta
Marsh at the University of Manitoba's Field Station; and exploring near
Lake Okeechobee in southern Florida in the company of two local
naturalists who had been asked to act as guides to this distinguished
visiting cleric ('Say, aren't you a Cardinal or something?'). When saying
goodbye, John Stott thanked his guides but told them they had much
enriched his vocabulary (of mild profanity) in a way he would have to
unlearn before returning to London, and especially before he next saw
what one of them referred to quite unselfconsciously as 'the dam' old
Queen'.[59]

6

In January 1980 John Stott paid a further visit to South America, the first
of three during the decade. He was under no illusion, in spite of much
religious revival:

Let me mention [he wrote later] visiting the huge central square of
the capital city of a Latin American republic ... One side of the
square was entirely occupied by the Roman Catholic cathedral. I
tried to get in, but it was closed. On the steps leading up to its main
door, however, were three human beings – a drunk who had
vomited copiously, a blind beggar selling matches, and a prostitute
who was offering herself to passers-by in broad daylight. A drunk, a
beggar and a prostitute, three symbols of human tragedy, and

behind them a locked cathedral, which seemed to be saying 'Keep out! We don't want you'.[60]

It was in Brazil that he began his visit, at São Paulo, 200 miles west of Rio de Janeiro, 'the fastest growing city in the world'.[61] His main purpose there was a pastors' conference on 'The Mission of the Church'; and he took the same theme a week later at a public meeting in Belo Horizonte, a few hundred miles to the north. John Stott had been told in earlier correspondence that this meeting would be public and interdenominational:

> But [he wrote home] I was entirely unprepared for what I found, namely 2,000 people packed into a tin-roofed barn of a hall, with bad public address system, a brass band from an Assemblies of God church whose cacophony was deafening, and most of the audience from a lower middle-class or working-class pentecostal background, who broke into a pandemonium of private prayers when their pastor was supposed to be 'leading in prayer' from the platform![62]

This letter was written from Recife, 1,000 miles or so further north, the most easterly point of the whole continent. The region is sometimes known as 'the other Brazil', being nearer the equator, poorer, less developed, than the Brazil of Rio de Janeiro (forty hours away by non-stop bus) and with fewer Protestants. Here John Stott was to give five studies from the book of Acts to a student congress, a familiar assignment which nevertheless proved less than straightforward:

> Communication by interpretation has been as difficult as ever. It is such a long-winded and laborious process, and the most difficult parts for an interpreter to translate are anecdotes and jokes which often depend for their effect on a turn of phrase, which loses much of its impact in the translation. So the audience sits there impassive, and I miss the ready response to which I'm accustomed when the audience is English. Yet, if one can judge by the kind things people said, especially at the end, more was getting across than I realized, and part of the problem was the extreme heat in an auditorium without fans.[63]

Finally, in this visit, he travelled south to Patagonia, the region of Argentina which stretches southwards between the Atlantic and the Andes to Tierra del Fuego, for a ten-day camping holiday with René Padilla and his family. Their days were full of observation of birds including Rheas, Flamingoes, Turkey Vultures, and Parrots of many species. But they found in addition huge elephant seals, hairy sea lions, and a small armadillo which was temporarily captured for their inspection.

In 1985 he visited Latin America again, flying this time to Ecuador on the north-west coast. Here in Quito, the capital, the IFES Continental Student Leaders' training course, held every two or three years, was meeting for three weeks at a Roman Catholic retreat house, the high perimeter wall patrolled at night by fearsome Alsatian dogs. About eighty students and staff assembled, drawn from some fifteen Latin American republics, the group from Chile travelling by bus for five days in order to attend. John Stott gave two lecture courses on 'The Place and Use of the Bible' and on 'The Authentic Jesus', continually reminding himself of the particular problems faced by some of the delegates. One, for example, was single-handedly pioneering the work of IFES in Uruguay,

> ... one of the hardest of South American countries, having been a secular state for seventy years through the influence of French philosophy. The University of Montevideo has 30,000 students who, on enrolling, sign an undertaking not to speak about religion or politics on campus, and not to engage in political or religious activities on campus either. In addition, they have to promise to report fellow-students who infringe these rules. Several have recently been expelled ... 90% of staff and students are either Marxists or extreme leftwing fellow-travellers.[64]

Four years later John Stott was able to accept an invitation to return to Latin America, in the summer of 1989. He flew to Brazil and stayed briefly in Recife and São Paulo, meeting old friends and speaking at two seminaries; while in Rio de Janeiro he preached in the Presbyterian Cathedral, processing with due dignity among its marble columns: 'Six of us pastors were robed in white Geneva gowns and looked (I thought) more like angels (though wingless) than humans!'[65]

But these were in addition to the two main objects of his visit: to give six addresses to a conference of some 1,500 pastors (with three or four hours of personal interviews each day); and to spend some days travelling on the Amazon through the Islas Anavilhanas National Park. For this, they formed a party of seventeen, including crew, cook, scientists and friends. John Stott's host had been lent the large boat by a prosperous businessman:

> It reminded me of those traditional steamboats on the Mississippi, though without the funnel and the huge paddle wheel. The cabins were small, of course, with bunks, but wood-panelled and supplied with tiny shower, hand basin and loo.[66]

From time to time the scientists put ashore in the boat's aluminium canoes, to erect a mist-net of fine black nylon about 100 yards long in which birds entangled themselves. Every half-hour or so the net would be examined and birds recorded, banded and released. John Stott usually joined the shore party, and in the intervals of examining the catch, would wander off on his own:

> I took my bearings from the sun and followed whatever movements I saw and songs I heard. After an hour or so, I retraced my steps. Or so I thought! For I could not find the mist-net, and some loud shouts failed to elicit a response from the scientists. So, after trying to take my bearings again, I moved steadily in what I believed to be the right direction. But the undergrowth became thicker, my arms got scratched and torn by innumerable spikes and thorns, and I realised I was lost in the Amazon Jungle! However, I also knew that I was on an island, so that I was bound to reach the river or one of its branches at some point.
>
> After struggling slowly and painfully through further jungle, I suddenly heard a cock crow – a sure sign of civilization, and I guessed I was near a clearing I'd seen on the other side of an inlet, on which a house had been built. This was confirmed by the sounds of children's voices ahead of me. So I persevered through the thick, unfriendly undergrowth till I could see the water. But it was down a steep bank and the trees overhung the water so far and so thickly that I could see neither house nor people on the far shore. So I shouted 'Oi!' (Portuguese for 'hi!'), and when a woman's voice replied in Portuguese, I shouted, 'No comprehendo, perdido!' At last I heard the plop of a paddle, and shortly afterwards a very large lady in a very small canoe manoeuvred herself through the screen of trees to the bank on which I was standing. I confess it was with considerable trepidation that I stepped into the canoe. It was already awash under her avoirdupois, and under our combined weight I feared it would sink without trace! But the large lady paddled away with no apparent misgivings, while I kept feverishly baling out the water we were taking in.[67]

In due course he was reunited with the boat and their voyage continued; but it was an experience with which he was to enliven many a dinner-table conversation for some time to come!

7

From time to time during the 1980s John Stott would visit one of the countries nearer home: perhaps on behalf of IFES, or to attend some international congress. In 1983, for example, he was in Sweden for a 'Life and Peace' conference at Uppsala; and in 1988 (just before NEAC III in Norfolk) he attended an international consultation on student evangelism at Würzburg, followed by a gathering of 'University Evangelists and Bible Expositors' at Bischoffsheim, an hour's drive to the north.

Birds continued to feature largely in his travels. In 1982 he joined John and Moira Prince for an ornithological holiday in southern Ireland. ('Why are we stopping?' he would ask when John Prince brought the car to rest at some spectacular viewpoint on the Ring of Kerry. 'I don't see any birds!')[68] He also paid two visits to Portugal to stay at A Rocha, the Christian Field Study Centre, including one in 1985 when the work was only just beginning. Peter Harris, originator of the centre, had been quick to secure John Stott as a founder-member of the Council of Reference, rightly concluding that with his 'almost legendary passion for ornithology' and his published views on Christian concern for the environment, he would prove a staunch supporter of 'such an off-beat project'.[69]

His longer forays into Europe, however, fall into two distinct groups: a couple of birdwatching expeditions, to Lapland in 1981 and Iceland in 1988; and two visits to Eastern Europe in 1980 and 1987 as a teacher of the faith.

For some years past, John Stott's contacts with Eastern Europe had been multiplying. He made friends through conferences at which he met their delegates; through bodies such as FEET (the Fellowship of European Evangelical Theologians); through rare individuals who were able to come to London, perhaps attending All Souls, or even courses at the London Institute. And his name was also becoming known by many who had never met him, through the LICC tapes and through his books, either in imported English editions, or occasionally in the manuscript translations which pastors and scholars in Eastern European countries were beginning to make in the eventual hope of local publication.[70] Nevertheless, it took two years of negotiations before John Stott was able to visit Yugoslavia, Hungary, Czechoslovakia and Poland, in the spring of 1980. His hosts understandably wanted to make the most of him, and had arranged that on arrival in Zagreb (then in Yugoslavia, later the capital of Croatia) he should address the Protestant Theological Faculty that same evening and give four more lectures next day, followed by a public meeting. On his protesting, pleading advancing years, they reduced the programme by omitting just a single lecture![71] He was met at the airport by Alex Williams, who as an undergraduate had carried his Wellington boots during the Leeds University mission of 1966, and was now on the staff of IFES in Eastern Europe.[72] They set off together by car for a pastors' conference at Novi Sad, 50 miles from the capital, Belgrade, where John Stott was also to speak at a public meeting, and where a Yugoslav Evangelical Alliance was to be inaugurated. 'It was worth going to bring them together,' Alex Williams wrote later:

> Yugoslavs were so divided – they spoke in at least one of twelve different languages ... They would not have flocked to hear a Baptist or a Pentecostal speaker – but with an Anglican, a foreigner to all of them with no axe to grind, no enemies, only friends, we could be all brothers together because we are all one in Christ. They took John Stott into their hearts over that weekend and nicknamed him Tata Stotta – Father Stott![73]

John Stott spoke to about 150 pastors from six denominations, with translation into Serbo-Croat. It was, so he was told, the first interdenominational conference they had ever known. His time in Hungary, by contrast, was largely given to holiday (which meant birdwatching) in company with Alex Williams, whom John Stott had previously enlisted as an ornithologist's apprentice.

A few days before, travelling by train from Zagreb to Bled on the Austrian border, Alex Williams had passed Tito's funeral train carrying his body to Belgrade for burial. It was the end of an era. Yugoslavia under Tito had enjoyed a moderate but increasing religious freedom; John Stott noticed Bibles and Christian literature for sale even in secular bookshops. But crossing from Hungary into Czechoslovakia was a different story. All bags were searched, and every book examined to see if it was politically subversive. Even letters to Slovak Christians from friends in England had to be opened and scrutinized. One of the main purposes of this visit was to renew acquaintance with Dr Ludovit Fazekas, a pastor and theologian of the Czech Brethren Church, whom John Stott had met in England at the centenary of the Keswick Convention in 1975, and the following year at a meeting of FEET. Trevor Beeson, writing on behalf of the British Council of Churches in 1974, had described the Evangelical Church of the Czech Brethren as 'easily the most influential of the Protestant churches', though in the early 1970s it had suffered a particularly demoralizing confrontation with the State.[74] By giving formal permission of entry to selected Western visitors, the authorities sought to demonstrate the reality of the religious freedom (a strictly limited freedom, in fact) which they maintained.

John Stott travelled first to Presov, accompanied by Dr Fazekas, where he was to stay with the Brethren pastor and his wife, and preach for him on the Sunday. He did not know quite what to expect by way of congregation:

On Sunday morning, therefore, when I followed the pastor out of his house into the church building (a connecting door links the two), I was astonished to find it packed to the doors, with perhaps 300 seated and another 100 standing two or three deep in all the aisles ... A choir of twenty men sang a Slovak hymn, a dozen little children sat on the bottom step of the platform, and after the service everybody stayed for a further half-hour of questions, so that we were in church for a good two hours.[75]

For the evening service they travelled on to Bardejov, an hour's drive to the north:

What was specially impressive about both services was the heterogeneity of the congregations. The ages ranged from very little children and babes-in-arms through teenagers and young people, adult couples and the middle-aged, to dear wizened old men and ladies, dressed in black, and bearing the stresses and sorrows of long life in their faces. They came from different cultural backgrounds too. There were farmers with tanned skin, and factory workers, alongside students and more educated professional people ... After the service the pastor and I stood at the door. I'd just about learned to say 'Do Videnia' ('goodbye' in Slovak), and some of the men, the bearded and the beardless, felt free to give me the traditional East European greeting, a resounding kiss on both cheeks.[76]

Levice was their next stop, where as an alien John Stott had to go to the police station to register. He was introduced to a retired pastor, seventy-nine years old, busily engaged in translating Christian books (no permit to publish Christian literature was ever issued) who showed him fifteen book-length manuscripts awaiting the day when they could be published. Some Christian books in Slovak, including John Stott's *Basic Christianity*, were printed and published outside the borders (for example, in Austria) and smuggled in. John Stott noted in his diary some chilling examples of how the church was kept under the strictest state control:

All religious activity is confined to church buildings. Churches are officially allowed to continue their traditional practices but only if the state considers them harmless ... Christians are inhibited in a variety of ways. A young man is denied a university place because he is known to be a Christian. Another is denied a passport to permit him to travel. A lecturer has to choose between his faith and his lectureship; choosing the former he is demoted to the status of a research worker.[77]

Pastors as well as people were in fear of the secret police. 'Walls have ears' took on a new meaning, and some conversations had to be conducted with the radio playing to frustrate hidden microphones.

In Bratislava, near the border with Austria and Hungary, John Stott lectured to forty or so local Brethren pastors, lunched with the Praesidium or Church Council, spent an hour and a half with a group of theological students, and spoke at two public evening meetings to about 550 people, some of them standing on every step of the twin staircases of the modern church, which the congregation had built with their own hands. At one point a choir of tiny children sang:

> As the twenty-five or so kids left their seats to mount the front platform, each picked up a single daffodil or tulip from their teacher. This they held up in front of them as they sang, with lips pouted into a large O and eyes fixed on their conductress, a ditty (I gathered) about how the flowers sing God's praises in spring-time. When the song was over, each flower was handed to the oldest girl, and the resulting bunch was then presented to me![78]

Their last visit in Czechoslovakia was to Prague, the capital, though from here they managed a Saturday expedition to a wildlife sanctuary in southern Bohemia. At the small town of Benátky, John Stott preached for the young pastor, Pavel ('Paul') Cerny.

> Here in the vestry [John Stott wrote in his diary] as I was giving a final briefing to my interpreter, a tall and rather burly man, well-dressed and smiling, was ushered in. As we were introduced to each other, he was identified as the Secretary for Church Affairs of the District Council. The pastor had been obliged to report my visit, and he had decided to attend, only his third visit in five years. He was affable, almost obsequious. 'We are honoured to have you visit our community. In the present climate of world affairs it is important for England and Czechoslovakia to come closer together etc. etc.' I thanked him, and the service began. He sat in a pew with the rest of the congregation, although, being a party member and therefore an atheist, it is not surprising that he declined the offer of a hymnbook and took no part in the service. At the beginning of my sermon I acknowledged his presence, referred to the links between our countries since John Hus read John Wycliffe's books, mentioned that the Church Affairs Secretary had said that our relations should be developed, and added that I hoped, when they applied for a passport to visit UK, he would help them to get it! Smiles all round. He seemed to listen carefully as I spoke from the

Sermon on the Mount on the distinction between Christians and non-Christians, as seen in Christ's 'salt' and 'light' metaphors, on the influence which Christians should have on their community, and on the inadequacy of materialism. But when I described the decay of secular society, I thought it more prudent to refer to the condition of England than of the CSSR [Czech and Slovak Socialist Republics]. He was the first out, when the service was over, uttered conventional pleasantries, made no reference to what I'd said, and was gone.[79]

Finally, on this tour, John Stott spent a week in Poland, where the Christian tradition is overwhelmingly Roman Catholic, at a Methodist Ministers' Conference at Ostróda, and at numerous other local engagements. These included a social visit to Metropolitan Basil, head of the autocephalous Polish Orthodox Church: 'I cannot describe him better than as a benevolent Father Christmas'; nor could John Stott recall, according to his diary, a comparable occasion on which theology, whisky, coffee and ecumenical affairs were so harmoniously blended![80]

John Stott returned to Poland and Hungary seven years later, in the early summer of 1987; and this time he was able also to pay a return visit to Romania, 'one of the most ruthless Communist regimes in Eastern Europe', and one in which the Baptists had been singled out for specially strict control: 'probably because they are the only non-Orthodox Church in Romania to have made significant progress in winning the allegiance of ethnic Romanians'.[81] He flew from London to Warsaw, to begin his programme with a weekend student conference, once again in the company of Alex Williams:

> Several hundred students were joined by Christian workers – including some revived Roman Catholics, and maybe some who were not so revived but teaching theology and interested to see what those funny Protestants got up to. John engaged them all in discussion – often resorting to German when they could not cope with English.[82]

This was followed by a gathering for pastors, and then by the International Christian Medical and Dental Association Conference at which he had been asked to speak (to his relief, in English) on 'The physician in the face of death'. He managed a couple of days birdwatching in the Danube Delta and a further conference near Budapest for a group of Hungarian evangelical Lutheran pastors:

> 'Believers' they are called, rather than 'evangelicals', which does not

reflect too well on the bulk of their colleagues in the Lutheran church! About twenty of them came together for a day conference on Thursday, some travelling 200–250 kilometres in order to attend.[83]

He began his stay in Romania with a long weekend of ministry at Oradea, near the Hungarian border, where over the past years the Baptist minority had sent several indirect messages to him by different couriers asking for a visit. John Stott described in his diary something of the background to this invitation:

> In 1958 some 600 Baptist pastors were dismissed, and were either imprisoned or disappeared. The 200 left were mostly elderly, theologically liberal and believed to be informers. Today there are 1000 Baptist churches, but only 160 pastors.

The 1960s and '70s were years of oppression and intimidation. Nevertheless, in 1982 the church called two dynamic lay leaders, both doctors, to serve as their pastors:

> Dr Nic Gheorghita, an endocrinologist, is the older man at fifty-seven, and a delightfully encouraging father figure to the younger men. The other is Dr Paul Negruts, a clinical psychologist, only thirty-four and a born natural leader. But for the last five years the authorities have played a cat-and-mouse game with them over their appointment and over the building of a new church.[84]

Arriving at this church for the morning service, John Stott's expectations were limited. Because of the country's economic straits, that Sunday had been designated by the government as a working day. But in fact 'the place was jam-packed (2,500 in the morning, 3,000 in the evening!)'; and he was told by his hosts that there might well be as many as ten informers among them. Stirred by these experiences, John Stott concluded the diary of his tour:

> I've returned from this two-week visit to Poland, Romania and Hungary with a fresh resolve to try to help our beleaguered brothers and sisters in Eastern Europe; not only in personal friendship, prayer and correspondence; nor only in some careful political agitation on behalf of the oppressed Romanian Baptists; but also and specially in getting more English and German books to them through the Evangelical Literature Trust, in offering some scholarships to London Institute courses, and (???!) in responding to their pressing invitations to return ...[85]

Nor was this an empty resolve. Following his earlier visit John Stott had been deep in correspondence with a Romanian doctor, trying to secure for him from the UK a gastroscope much needed by his hospital, and had written personally to a number of Langham Trust donors asking for contributions towards the cost. He had also written to President Ceaucescu a letter signed by eight leading British Christians, on behalf of the Second Baptist Church in Oradea. When this received no reply he involved the Romanian Ambassador in London and the British Ambassador in Bucharest. And he continued to persevere, following his second visit to Romania, even when the British Embassy was sure he was unlikely to receive any reply.[86] The Embassy's instincts proved to be right. In mid-December 1989 the police attempted to arrest a pastor critical of the President. His congregation formed a human chain round his church and were shot down. Huge demonstrations were then mounted against Ceaucescu; his army rebelled and embraced the cause of the people. After a brief trial he was shot on Christmas Day and a provisional government quickly established. It was the end of yet another era in Romania's turbulent history.

8

On 23 May 1987 John Stott returned to London. He had spent two weeks in Eastern Europe, teaching, travelling, fulfilling a heavy schedule of work (with some serious birdwatching thrown in) in three different countries, constantly meeting a range of friends, new and old, each anxious to make the most of the hours he could spend with them. In spite of Frances Whitehead's efforts to winnow out the non-essentials from his mail, his desk at 12 Weymouth Street would be stacked with post and messages needing his attention: what the diary calls 'the accumulated pile'. Yet the following day, after less than twenty-four hours in England, he was *en route* to Bangkok for four weeks of the same kind of pressurized experience in five Asian countries from Thailand to Indonesia.

To be sure, at this stage of his life (he would be nearly seventy by the end of the decade) his close advisers, notably AGE, Frances Whitehead and the succession of study assistants, were trying hard to limit some of the demands made on him overseas. Toby Howarth travelled with him to Asia the following year, and on his return drafted a memorandum which could be sent to (even if not always observed by) John Stott's overseas hosts. While making the point that the purpose of these visits was to be of service, the memorandum requests a limit of not more than two lectures or addresses a day, provision for a rest (on a bed if possible) after lunch, and a day off each week, 'on which there are neither engagements nor travel but could be (of course!) a little birdwatching, especially if under the guidance of a local expert'. In particular, new meetings or speaking engagements should not be added to an agreed schedule without consulting him. There follow requests about accommodation (a home, however simple, is a perfectly acceptable alternative to a modest hotel, provided he can secure some time to himself); about speaking (two microphones, if possible, one for the translator; a lectern high enough for ageing eyes to read his notes, and leave his hands free); about private interviews; about finance (travel expenses, except in the Third World, met by his hosts *pro rata*; donations to the Langham Trust in lieu of honorarium); and about the numerous presents and mementos which kind sponsors like to make to him:

> Although he greatly appreciates their generous thought, he prefers not to receive personal gifts, partly because of weight problems in travel, but mostly because he is struggling to keep his lifestyle simple, and he lives in two rooms in London, in which he has no space for any more possessions![87]

But why, it is fair to ask, was John Stott at this time of life continuing to arrange and fulfil, year after year, such a demanding programme of four, five – even six or eight – annual visits overseas? No doubt in some way, as perhaps most work of this kind does, it ministered to his own needs, conscious or unconscious. After so many years his own identity was bound up in it, and reaffirmed visit by visit; while even those tours which did not find time for a period of holiday nevertheless included the snatched day or half-day expedition in search of his beloved birds. But there are of course much deeper reasons. First, these visits abroad became increasingly one of the primary ministries (along with writing and, in the early 1980s at least, the London Institute) to which he felt God had called him. Speaking to a group of English clergy, many of them friends of long standing, he told them that 'one of the main burdens God has given me is for the rising Christian leadership of the Third World ... the students and pastors of the Third World are my priority concern'.[88] He described how, in return visits to places like Singapore, he found churches bursting with lively young Christians, so many of whom seemed to acquire only 'a Sunday-School faith' which failed them as they grew older. While health and strength permitted, to play a part in the teaching and nurture of such churches and their leadership was the work to which he had set his hand. Increasing years meant increasing experience, and familiarity, and so only added to his acceptability.

Secondly, he longed to see the gospel known, apprehended with ever-growing understanding, and preached 'in all the world', according to Christ's own commission. Preachers and preaching were God's appointed means. If by teaching and helping local pastors, and putting before students the vision of the pastoral ministry, he could help to raise the standard of preaching and exposition in the places he visited, then that alone made such visits amply worthwhile. Part of what helped to keep him going was the response he met with from those who became, in a real sense, a family to him, united in Christ even in the briefest and most passing encounter. Who would not be heartened, and confirmed in the value of the task, by a note such as this in broken English from a Brazilian student and his fiancée who had attended the meetings in São Paulo:

> We've learned love you of a very special way, like a kind lovely uncle. We could feel the Holly Ghost coming from you to us, and this is the biggest gift that we could receive of you. Thank you, lovely John! we will never forget you![89]

On a larger canvas he felt, for all their inevitable frustrations and the nit-picking nature of the drafting process, that international consultations, especially among evangelicals, had an undeniable claim. He spoke of this in an interview for an American journal: 'Through my long experience, since Lausanne twenty years ago, I'm a great believer in small, private, international, representative consultations in which we're prepared to listen to one another.' After the first few days, entrenched and polarized antipathies begin to yield to personal contact. Then it is possible to listen not just to what is being said, but what lies behind it, the hidden agendas:

> *Why* did they feel this so strongly? What is it that they want to safeguard? The extraordinary thing was that in many cases you find that you want to safeguard it too. And then you reach the point of creative development or creative solutions.[90]

To live in a global village increases the need for Christian to talk with Christian, and to travel to do so: EFAC remains one of the major institutional expressions of John Stott's convictions of this need for 'bridge-building'.[91] But with increasing maturity and recognition (always more noticeable abroad than at home, as successive study assistants were quick to discover) came a unique ministry, almost archiepiscopal in nature, to bishops and church leaders who had come to trust his spiritual wisdom and the perspective of his world vision. In one of his books John Stott refers to conversations in 1987 with Bishop Moses Tay on the charismatic issue and offers a snatch of conversation.[92] But the book does not add that, after John Stott's visit, Bishop Tay wrote to him to thank him 'for spending three whole mornings with our clergy and lay leaders', going on to ask him 'to put your thoughts on paper for our benefit as you reflect on your visit to Singapore and the Diocese'.[93] In reply, after some personal greetings, John Stott wrote:

> Thank you for inviting me to put some of my thoughts on paper, following my enjoyable visit to Singapore. I do not need to write of the new life, the joy and confidence in worship, the loving warmth of fellowship, or the zeal for evangelism, which are all signs of spiritual renewal and which are all very evident in the diocese. But I thought I might express three questions ...[94]

The nature of the questions is not now the point at issue. But these letters indicate a kind of ministry open to very few, which John Stott was enabled to fulfil only by reason of his continued travels. By many senior church leaders in many countries he was received not simply as a distinguished overseas teacher, come to deliver his lectures and move on, but as a confidant, counsellor and friend.

Part of his secret was the humility which he felt, and so expressed, as an English visitor overseas. He would speak of his real love for Africa; but also of his shame over the history of the European slave-trade, and parts of the colonial record and 'the sense of inferiority which Europeans have inculcated in Africans'. And he would go on to speak regretfully of the secularization of Europe, and her lukewarm discipleship. In India he would refer sadly to the 'so-called British Raj mentality', while recognizing much that was valuable in the colonial legacy; and confess himself a lover of the ancient Christian Indian culture, and its spiritual values. 'Jesus Christ', he would sometimes say, 'was not a white man. Certainly Christianity is not a European religion. I come to you as a Christian internationalist, believing ... that it is not neo-colonialism to plead the uniqueness and finality of Jesus Christ.'[95]

It would not be difficult to adduce still further reasons why John Stott steadily continued his arduous programme: and indeed room must be found for yet one more, no less real because it is not easy to define. It has to do with what has just been hinted at, a necessary corrective to an insular and purely Western vision with an appreciation of the immense cultural diversity of the faith, and an opportunity to move beyond that cultural barrier into the existential and eternal reality of 'all one in Christ Jesus'. For him this oneness, both of God's family and of earth's peoples, carried with it a call, however fleetingly, to *be there*. 'Is God on the side of the poor?' he asked the All Souls congregation in the rhetorical question of the preacher; and before going on to consider a biblical answer, offered two complementary approaches:

One could answer this question rationally, with the cool detachment of statistics. There are now over 4,000 million inhabitants of planet Earth, and one-fifth of them (800 million) are destitute. Every day, 10,000 give up the struggle for survival, succumb to starvation, and die. Meanwhile, more than another one-fifth live in affluence, consume four-fifths of the world's income, and contribute to Third World development the derisory annual sum of £20,000 millions, while spending twenty-one times that amount on armaments.

Or one could approach the question emotionally, with the hot-blooded indignation aroused by the sights, sounds and smells of poverty. Arriving in Calcutta in January 1981, I found the city enveloped in a malodorous pall of smoke from a myriad fires fueled with cow dung. An emaciated woman clutching an emaciated baby stretched out an emaciated hand for *baksheesh*. Between a quarter and a half million homeless people sleep on the city's pavements at night, and human beings are reduced to foraging like dogs in its garbage dumps.[96]

His increasing burden for the recapturing of the evangelical social conscience implied for John Stott a need to 'earth' his concern in real situations, if his comfortable (though modest) London quarters, and his modest (though idyllic) Hermitage at The Hookses were not to become escapist, a theorist's ivory tower. When asked to advise a hypothetical 'young North American who wants to spend his or her whole life in the service of the kingdom of God as it relates to the whole world', John Stott began with a cautionary word: 'Remember that everybody cannot do everything. God does call different people to different ministries.'[97] It was advice, obvious though it seems in cold print, that was forged from his own experience. Mark Labberton was with him in India in 1981, and still vividly recalls what was for him a defining moment at the end of their stay in Calcutta (a visit which formed the basis of John Stott's description of the city, quoted above, in his All Souls sermon a month later):

We had been there several days [Mark Labberton writes] and were at the airport getting ready to leave. I asked him if he thought he could actually live in such a city.

His instantaneous response was 'Well, one would count it an honor if one were called, wouldn't one?'

I said, 'Well, one might *want* to count it an honor if one were called, but I'm not sure one *would* – at least if that one were me.'

He said, 'Yes, but doesn't meeting Mother Teresa [we had about forty-five minutes with her in Dacca] make you just want to join her army?'

I believed then and now that John was quite earnest and genuine about this remark. It captures the responsive, humble servant's heart that I believe is real for him.[98]

ELEVEN

Preacher and Writer: Publishing the Faith

1

'I have been preaching for forty-five years,' said Charles Simeon in 1827, 'but for the first seven of those years I did not know the head from the tail of a sermon.'[1] It was his glory, therefore, that having taught himself the art with the aid of John Claude's *Essay on the Composition of a Sermon*, he should have gone on to become 'almost the first man in the history of the English pulpit since the Middle Ages to appreciate that it is perfectly possible to teach men how to preach, and to discover how to do so'.[2]

On the 150th anniversary of Simeon's death, John Stott contributed 'A Personal Appreciation' to an American anthology of Simeon's sermons, acknowledging that 'on many occasions I have had the privilege of preaching from his pulpit in Holy Trinity Church, Cambridge; and, standing where he stood, have prayed for a measure of his outstanding faithfulness'.[3] Simeon's preaching ministry was indeed outstanding, even among the evangelicals of his generation, let alone the broad-church clergy of the day. In *Mansfield Park*, which Jane Austen began in 1811 and published three years later, Mr Crawford can speak of 'a thoroughly good sermon' as 'a capital gratification' and praises 'the eloquence of the pulpit' providing it is exercised 'without offending the taste or wearing out the feelings' of the hearers.[4]

Certainly by the time John Stott knew that he was called to be a preacher, the seriousness with which the Wesleys and their successors in the Evangelical Revival, and many of the Tractarians, regarded the pulpit was long gone;

> ... for this [the 1930s] was pre-eminently the decade in which, in the Anglican pulpit, serious expositions of the revelation of God contained in holy Scripture were going out of fashion, and brief moral pep-talks on current affairs and current problems were coming in.[5]

Bash, of course, pre-eminent as a communicator of the gospel in his own special field, was quick to give the newly converted John Stott opportunities to speak for Christ, and even to preach, while still at school.[6] He soon became a master of the *genre* known as the 'camp talk'; topical rather than expository, though based on, or at least beginning from, a verse or a passage; and always with a view to some practical response in turning to Christ, or in the early steps of discipleship.

Long before he came to All Souls, John Stott had begun to discern that preaching is more than this; and that expository preaching differs from the kind of verse-by-verse exposition of a book of the Bible that had occupied him sometimes three or four evening a week at Ridley Hall, giving Bible readings to CICCU groups in individual colleges. All through his time there, bicycling out on Sunday evenings to Little Shelford or Six Mile Bottom to preach to a village congregation, and then in his busy curacy (made busier by his Rector's illness), he studied what it means to preach, searching for principles, and trying them out in practice. And just as Simeon had sought to share with others what he himself had learned from John Claude, so John Stott in due time began to set down some of what experience had taught him as student, curate and rector. He did this first for the IVF in an article sub-titled 'Some thoughts on expository preaching'. 'What then is this expository preaching?' he asked; and gave the following reply:

> To 'expound' the Word of God is so to treat a verse or a passage from the Bible as to draw out its meaning, its application and its challenge. Exposition is the direct opposite of imposition. The expository preacher comes to the text not with his mind made up, resolved to impose a meaning on it, but with his mind open to receive a message from it in order to convey it to others ... The dearest desire of the expository preacher is so to speak as to let the

Scriptures themselves speak, and so to preach that afterwards the sermon is eclipsed by the growing splendour of the text itself.[7]

In a highly condensed paragraph the article looked at a number of biblical metaphors for preaching: the preacher as sower, builder, herald, workman, steward. When John Stott was asked a few years later to give the 1961 Payton Lectures at Fuller Theological Seminary in California and to choose a homiletic theme, he returned to these metaphors and combined them into a description or portrait of the preacher as the Bible sees him.[8]

All this was prolegomena to John Stott's main work on the subject, *I Believe in Preaching*, 'written with freedom and frankness out of my own experience', but drawing on much else besides.[9] It provides a more reasoned, thorough, systematic and contemporary approach than Martyn Lloyd-Jones's lectures on *Preaching and Preachers* published at the start of the 1970s.[10] The contract for *I Believe in Preaching*, part of a series under the editorship of Michael Green, was signed in April 1977; and it was four years before the manuscript was delivered. It broke for the author a self-imposed ten-year embargo, since in 1970 John Stott had told the Director of Hodder & Stoughton that his confidence in their publishing policy had been badly shaken by their decision to publish John Allegro's *The Sacred Mushroom and the Cross*.[11]

I Believe in Preaching is an exhaustive work in the best sense of the term. Beginning with a historical sketch, and rebutting contemporary objections to preaching as an outdated and discredited relic of a more primitive age, the heart of the book then builds upon biblical and theological foundations a view of preaching as 'bridge-building', crossing the cultural divide (as the title of the US edition, *Between Two Worlds*, suggests) between the revealed Word and the contemporary world. This, the longest chapter in the book, concludes:

> Such preaching will be authoritative in expounding biblical principles, but tentative in applying them to the complex issues of the day. This combination of the authoritative and the tentative, the dogmatic and the agnostic, conviction and open-mindedness, teaching the people and leaving them free to make up their own minds, is exceedingly difficult to maintain. But it seems to me to be the only way ...'[12]

The second half offers more practical help to meet such a challenge with chapters on the call to study, on sermon preparation, and on the preacher himself and his need for sincerity, earnestness, courage and humility. 'This is what preaching is really about', was the heading to an enthusiastic review by Donald Coggan,[13] which the publishers sent, with a copy of the book, to every diocesan bishop in England 'and to key churchmen abroad'.[14] Dr Coggan's review urged Parochial Church Councils to give their clergy a copy of the book. One diocesan bishop offered copies to every deanery chapter, if the clergy would undertake to study it together.[15] The *Church Times* carried full-page extracts on successive weeks together with a long review by Canon Michael Hocking.[16] In general factual and appreciative ('few men better qualified to write about this subject'), this review took issue in particular with the high ideal of study and preparation that was set before the preacher of the Word, and made the point that for most clergy 'the failure to spend many hours every week in study is certainly not laziness. It is a matter of priorities.'[17] It was a criticism which John Stott had foreseen; and one which, in principle at least, he did not accept. He knew from the outset that some readers would find his recommendations idealistic, 'in failing to take sufficient account of the problems under which many clergy labour today'. He admitted that he had mostly in mind churches similar to All Souls 'while trying to remember other situations'. But he went on to add, 'the ideals I have unfolded I believe to be universally true, although of course they need to be adapted to each particular reality'.[18]

In 1981 Dick Lucas and Jonathan Fletcher had run a small conference on expository preaching, inviting mainly younger clergy who were personal friends. Looking back at the end of the 1990s, Dick Lucas could say of it:

> I'm not likely to forget the two days we spent together, nor, I imagine, will any who were there. We recognized that in our official training we had received precious little help in this major responsibility of pastoral ministry; but we were (I think) not quite prepared to discover, as soon we did, how ill-equipped we actually were for the work of expounding the Scriptures accurately.[19]

John Stott's book can therefore be seen as a timely contribution to a revival of serious concern among younger ministers for the task of proclaiming the Word. 'There is nothing we sought to achieve in expository preaching', Dick Lucas is quick to assert, 'that JRWS was not practising in the 1950s!'[20]

Though *I Believe in Preaching* must be counted his definitive work on this theme, John Stott continued to write and speak about it to students and ministers, throughout the 1980s and beyond, often in the context of the power of the Scriptures. This ministry was well summed up by Kenneth Kantzer, editor of *Christianity Today*:

His message is always the same, yet always new and fresh. He simply teaches the Bible! How, you ask, could anyone hold the minds and move the hearts of students from Anchorage to Ouagadougou, and from Belgrade to Boston by simply teaching the Bible? John Stott does it ... When I hear him expound a text, invariably I exclaim to myself, 'That's exactly what it means! Why didn't I see it before?'[21]

This is no accident. His aim as preacher has long been to leave his hearers in no doubt that 'what he said is what the Scriptures say', and so unable to escape the challenge of the Word of God to their own hearts. He told an interviewer in 1995:

> We want to let the congregation into the secret as to how we have reached the conclusions we have reached as to what the Bible is actually saying ... And gradually, as you are doing this in the pulpit, the congregation is schooled not only in what the Bible teaches but in how we come to the conclusion as to what it teaches. So we have to show the congregation what our hermeneutical methods are.[22]

Even so, when seeking to go beyond exposition of the text, the style could still appear to some clergy to be a little removed from life as they experienced it:

> John gave a superb model of expository preaching, that was both a help and a challenge. I discovered, however, that the style needed 'earthing' by greater application in inner city and other contexts.[23]

Many find it easy to be appreciative: sometimes it is a different thing to be attentive. John Stott likes to tell how the Dean of a US cathedral once introduced him, the fulsome language enhanced by a strong southern accent:

> 'When I first read a book by John Stott, I said to myself I would crawl on my knees 500 miles to listen to that man.'
> When he'd finished [John Stott adds], he walked into the sanctuary, sat down and promptly fell fast asleep, and even snored! I could only imagine that his 500-mile crawl had been too much for him![24]

A number of studies have been researched and written on different aspects of John Stott's ministry, including his preaching. In the early 1980s he had as study assistant a young American, Mark Labberton, who for his own interest engaged in a study of his Rector as preacher, while helping with the final stages of *I Believe in Preaching*.[25] He had the opportunity, of course, to hear John Stott regularly in All Souls, but also to accompany him to India and Bangladesh; and to listen to over 100 of his recorded sermons from 1959 onwards. Much of his paper reflects the substance of *I Believe in Preaching*; but he is able, for example, to trace how the pursuit of 'the dominant thought' in a passage of Scripture became steadily clearer through the years, giving as an early example a sermon on the virgin birth with three points, ten sub-points, six additional points, and twenty-five biblical passages cited![26] Mark Labberton traces something of a watershed in the influence of Ted Schroder, and observes at first hand the gains and losses for the preacher who remains unmarried. From his own experience, and from remarks made by others, he lists 'the five traits most frequently repeated, not in any order', as clear, biblically based, balanced, intellectually satisfying, and non-theatrical. Perhaps this last owed something to the framed prayer which hung on John Stott's walls throughout these years:

> When telling Thy salvation free
> Let all-absorbing thoughts of Thee
>   My heart and soul engross:
> And when all hearts are bowed and stirred
> Beneath the influence of Thy word,
>   Hide me behind Thy cross.
>   1 Cor. 1:31[27]

2

For Christian teaching and preaching to be authoritative, it must first be biblical, and then applied. It is no surprise therefore, that the pursuit of relevance should form an increasing part of John Stott's teaching about the Christian and the Scriptures. It could be found, for example, in his Olivier Beguin Memorial Lecture for the Australian Bible Society, delivered in three Australian cities during the spring of 1979.[28] 'The modern world detests authority, but worships relevance,' he began; going on to show that both the authority and relevance of the Bible spring from those of Jesus Christ himself:

> As for his authority, we find it to be liberating rather than oppressive, for his yoke is easy, the hand that fits it is gentle, and under it we find rest. As for his relevance, Jesus Christ is timeless. Though born into a first-century Palestinian culture, he belongs to every culture. He is not dated. He speaks to all people in their vernacular. Christ is our contemporary.[29]

This underlying issue of the nature of the Bible was developed in a more popular way in a series of sermons given to the All Souls congregation as the new decade began, and published two years later as *The Bible: Book for Today*.[30] In his address at St Martin-in-the-Fields on the tenth anniversary of the New International Version of the Bible, John Stott spoke (from 2 Timothy 3 and 4) on 'God's Word for our Time'. He chose to demonstrate from what Paul there urges upon Timothy a 'fundamental correspondence' between 'the historical particularities of the Bible and the immense complexities of the modern world'. He noted how

> ... the Word of God and the mood of the day were, and still are, radically incompatible with one another. And to insist that the Word of God speaks to our time does not mean that the Word of God agrees with our time, because it does not. On the contrary, the Word speaks most authentically to the world when it subjects the world to a rigorous critique ...
>
> We who are members of the Church at the end of the twentieth century, my sisters and brothers, urgently need this summons to continue in the Word of God, not to bow like reeds shaken by the wind of public opinion, not to bow down before the prevailing trends of modern society, its covetousness and its materialism, its relativism and its rejection of the absolutes of truth and righteousness.

From standing firm in the Word of God, he moved to the call to live by it, holding fast 'the God-breathed nature of Scripture' and being ready to make the 'cultural transposition' which would apply biblical principles to the modern world. But this could not be done without scrupulous integrity:

> Cultural transposition is not a respectable way of getting rid of those bits of Scripture that we do not happen to like. On the contrary, cultural transposition is a conscientious way of making our obedience contemporary. And thus it demonstrates that the God-breathed Scripture is profitable in our times.

Finally, the Christian's calling is also to proclaim and share this timeless word of salvation:

> Scripture is nobody's private possession. Scripture is public property. God's Word has been spoken in order that the whole world should hear it, and we must therefore pass it on ... Congregations

live and flourish by the Word of God and languish and die without it. The pulpit is no place for the ventilation of our own private opinions. The pulpit is the place for the opening up of the Word of God.[31]

It was this passionate conviction that lay behind much of his teaching and preaching through these years. The London Lectures in Contemporary Christianity, for example, were evidence of this concern to relate truth to life, the unchanging purposes of God to the often phrenetic and transitory contemporary scene. This was now to come to fruition in a single major work, *Issues Facing Christians Today*.[32] In one sense, it was the inevitable outcome of the determination publicly expressed as far back as NEAC '67 at Keele, where resolution 37 admitted that 'we have not thought sufficiently deeply or radically about the problems of our society', and resolved to do better.[33] In the intervening years this had found expression in various study groups which John Stott (and others) had convened, in his preaching and in his occasional writings, notably his 'Cornerstone' articles for a primarily US reader-ship.[34] More immediate promptings towards a major study can be found in his teaching sessions during the first years of the London Institute, and in a request from Marshalls, the publishers, to Michael Baughen, the Rector, for a projected collection of 'Sermons at All Souls'. Michael Baughen responded by asking John Stott to preach once a quarter on 'Issues facing Britain today', and John Stott agreed to do so:

> Before each sermon, I got Tom Cooper, who was my study assistant at the time, to bring together a little research group of about eight people. I remember particularly that for the one on work and unemployment we got a trade-union leader to come, two un-employed younger people, an employer and an economist, all Bible-believing Christians. I had done some preliminary reading, and I then told them, 'These are my questions, these are my problems; can you throw light on them for me from your point of view and from your expertise? I've studied the biblical aspect; I want you to give me the practical.' Then I sat back and listened for two hours, taking notes, and of course it was very fascinating.[35]

Such were some of the strands which finally came together in the planning and writing of *Issues*. In September 1983 Paul Weston, recently graduated and about to begin ordination training, found himself at The Hookses, and recorded his impressions in a diary written at the time:

> John has been down here for the whole of September working on

his new book on *Issues Facing Christians Today* ... His writing room is very simple in furnishing, with a wide window looking out on a breathtaking view of the West Dale Bay ... by his side is a pair of binoculars in case of ornithological emergency ...

Paul Weston goes on to describe his 'phenomenal' work rate, early rising and long hours at his desk, with the famous 'HHH' ('horizontal half-hour') and work on 'the estate' each afternoon:

The evenings are flexible. When under pressure he works on till 10 pm but, if things are going well, he spends it in the house with us. Last night was one such night. We persuaded him to read a Saki short story to us ... We had *two* readings in the end – the 'Lumber Room' and the 'Stalled Ox' during which JRWS was reduced to tears of laughter by a certain phrase in the latter where the storming ox was described as reducing a prize flower to a 'petal salad'. Off came the half-moon glasses and he rubbed his eyes in laughter ...

A day or two later, instead of his favourite Saki, John Stott read from the draft of the chapter on 'Industrial Relations', just completed:

He read it without trace of self-consciousness. It took over half an hour and he abridged a lot of the final section because he thought he was boring us. The writing was the model of clarity and it read well. It was very long though ... Frances was trying to persuade John to publish in two volumes but he was having nothing to do with it! It's certainly his most ambitious project to date as the whole area is outside his experience and, I suppose, his area of expertise. His desire, and aim, was to bring biblical principles to bear on the issues of today. In this particular chapter he used some verses from the Old Testament on Solomon's harsh treatment of his people so that at the beginning of Rehoboam's reign the people asked for the burdens to be lifted. With this as a basis he tackled the prevailing us/them/non-worker-participation in industry today.[36]

Industrial relations is the subject of only one of the fourteen chapters in the book, which deal in turn with a range of subjects where little was available from a biblical standpoint. John Stott himself had published one or two papers and articles following his preliminary studies in the fields of employment and industry; and had written rather more on the nuclear threat, often in contributions to British or American symposia. Ecology and the environment had become another increasing concern as, for example, in his support for A Rocha; but he had so far written little on global economic inequality (though the Brandt Commission's report appeared in 1980),[37] or on human rights, feminism and gender, or what he called 'the abortion dilemma'. In this chapter of *Issues* he drew attention to the almost unregarded revolution in public attitudes during his lifetime, comparing the cautious provision of the Infant Life (Preservation) Act of 1929 with the two million legal abortions performed in the seventeen years since the passing of the Abortion Act of 1967.[38]

Marriage and divorce presented slightly more familiar ground, if only because he had so often been called on to counsel and pastor those personally involved. A decade before *Issues* he had written on 'Divorce: the Biblical Teaching' for the *Churchman*,[39] as a response to the report of the Archbishops' Commission, *Marriage, Divorce and the Church*.[40] He stressed, as was his invariable practice, that 'the biblical teaching on divorce must never be studied in isolation, but always against the background of the biblical understanding of marriage'.

On homosexual partnerships, however, he was breaking entirely new ground in a chapter which was later to be reprinted in periodicals, symposia and booklet form throughout the next decade; and to undergo successive revisions.[41] In essence, the theme of the chapter, as with John Stott's treatment of divorce, was to begin with God's creation ordinance of marriage; and, working from that (after considering also the other biblical evidences as well as books offering different interpretations) to conclude that 'in sum, the only "one flesh" experience which God intends and Scripture contemplates is the sexual union of a man with his wife, whom he recognizes as "flesh of his flesh"'.[42] But the chapter finds room also for deep pastoral concern, not to say penitence, for the church's past insensitivity to individuals struggling with a homosexual orientation, for its occasional homophobia, and for the lukewarm love within its own fellowship. It was this chapter, more than any other, which was to involve the author in continuous controversy, as a spokesman for biblical orthodoxy; including a public debate with Bishop J. S. Spong in 1993.[43]

The book circulated widely, through successive revisions, in North America, as well as in a variety of translations. Marshalls arranged for Revell to publish the American edition, and John Stott recounts with amusement how

> ... they telephoned me one day, and said, 'We are publishing your book, and we're going to call it *Survival*.'
> I said, 'I beg your pardon?' I went on, 'Have you read the book? It has nothing to do with survival.'
> 'Oh', they said. 'Well, we're sorry, we've already advertised it.'
> So I said, 'Well, I am afraid I withhold permission; you may not

publish it under the name *Survival*: it has got nothing to do with that.'

'We want a short title,' they said. '*Issues Facing Christians Today* is too long; we want one word.'

So I said, 'All right, I'll think.'

Later I rang them back and said, 'What about the word *Involvement*?' So they accepted that, but it was still to be in two hardback volumes and therefore expensive.[44]

Reviewers mostly admired the book, but often with characteristic reservations. George Carey, later to be Archbishop of Canterbury, wondered if John Stott 'had not over-stretched himself', though noting that 'as always Dr Stott is splendidly succinct and courageous' in picking his way through 'a minefield of controversial issues'. Not surprisingly (Dr Carey was then Principal of a theological college training both men and women), he found John Stott's conclusions on women in ministry ('I do not think it biblically appropriate for a woman to become a rector or a bishop') unsatisfactory, and questioned the hermeneutical premise on which the author based them.[45] The *Church Times* was notably appreciative, entrusting the review to Robin Denniston, a distinguished lifelong professional publisher.[46] He and John Stott were well known to each other, and the review included a graceful personal tribute as well as an informed recognition of the magnitude of the task:

> An immense amount of reading has laid the foundations of this valuable and impressive book. To be even partially well informed on such a variety of issues (nuclear war, North-South inequality, unemployment, racism, sex, human rights, feminism and many more), to keep up-to-date, and then not just to repeat received wisdom or common sense on these topics but to give to each informed and critical, tolerant and sensitive judgements, is an achievement of note.[47]

C. S. Lewis wrote once that 'above all other spheres of human life, the Devil claims politics for his own, as almost the citadel of his power'.[48] By the time he came to write *Issues*, John Stott had already affirmed the need for Christian individuals and Christian groups to enter this arena (in Lewis's metaphor, to lay siege to this citadel) by direct political action, and to 'be encouraged from the pulpit to do so'.[49] The book can be regarded as his own contribution in this field (primarily of course a field for lay people in their various vocations and as citizens of a democracy), enabling and encouraging Christians to apply the principles of their faith to the contemporary world.

3

In John Stott's own thinking, his three major books of the 1980s form something of a trilogy. *I Believe in Preaching* was his most substantial contribution to pastoral theology, bigger and weightier, though less original, than *One People* of thirteen years before. *Issues Facing Christians Today* remains his principal study in aspects of moral theology; and in company with them *The Cross of Christ*, which followed hard on the heels of *Issues*, was a major doctrinal exposition in the field of systematic theology. The book is more than this, however, since it is pregnant throughout with a range of thought and feeling affecting the deepest levels of Christian devotion and discipleship. Its author makes no secret of this as far as he himself is concerned:

> I have said and so say that more of my own heart and mind went into that book than into writing any other, so that it is in some sense a personal apologia.[50]

James Gordon, writing five years after its publication, was right to call it 'Stott's magnum opus', in which 'cumulative biblical argument, fruitful trawling amongst historical and contemporary theologians and astute psychological observation, undergird an exposition of the cross which constitutes a personal credo'.[51] That the treatment extends beyond the doctrine of the atonement becomes very plain from the author's Preface. He asks 'what the cross of Christ says to us at the end of the twentieth century':

> I try to show that the cross transforms everything. It gives us a new, worshipping relationship to God, a new and balanced under-standing of ourselves, a new incentive to give ourselves in mission, a new love for our enemies, and a new courage to face the perplexities of suffering ...
>
> In daring to write (and read) a book about the cross, there is of course a great danger of presumption ... it would be most unseemly to feign a cool detachment as we contemplate Christ's cross. For willy-nilly we are involved. Our sins put him there. So, far from offering us flattery, the cross undermines our self-righteousness. We can stand before it only with a bowed head and a broken spirit. And there we remain until the Lord Jesus speaks to our hearts his word of pardon and acceptance, and we, gripped by his love and brimful of thanksgiving, go out into the world to live our lives in his service.[52]

This was not, of course, the first time that he had written about the cross. From his very first book, *Men with a Message*, with its exposition of justification in 'The Message of Paul', through *Your Confirmation*, which included a powerful section on 'Christ's work, or what he did', it was a theme to which he regularly returned. It is never far away in most of his New Testament expositions for The Bible Speaks Today series; and is preached with urgency in the section on 'The Death of Christ' in *Basic Christianity*:

> Sin has separated us from God; but Christ desired to bring us back to God. So He suffered for our sins, an innocent Saviour dying for guilty sinners, and He did it once for all... What He has done can therefore be neither improved, nor repeated. No religious observances or righteous works of ours can earn our forgiveness ... There is healing through His wounds, life through His death, pardon through His pain, salvation through His suffering.[53]

The Preface to *The Cross of Christ* speaks of two surprises. One was the dearth ('until two or three years ago, for nearly half a century') of modern treatments of this topic by evangelical authors for thoughtful readers, as distinct from small paperbacks or weighty works of scholarship. The major surprise, however, was to discover the extreme resistance to any idea of the death of Christ as our substitute (a concept known as 'substitutionary atonement'), even among scholars anxious to be faithful to the biblical record.[54] Indeed, there is something pathetic (in the sense of 'exciting pity or sadness') in the catena of quotations from the Methodist scholar, Vincent Taylor: they reveal him now approaching assent to substitution, dragged unwillingly by the weight of biblical evidence; and now drawing back from the very brink.[55] What 'Vincent Taylor shrank from was not the doctrine itself', John Stott concluded, 'but the crudities of thought and expression of which the advocates of substitution have not infrequently been guilty'. To appreciate John Stott's advocacy of the concept requires a careful study of his book, but the thrust of his thinking can be seen from a key quotation:

> 'Images' of salvation (or of the atonement) is a better term than 'theories'. For theories are usually abstract and speculative concepts, whereas the biblical images of the atoning achievement of Christ are concrete pictures and belong to the data of revelation. They are not alternative explanations of the cross, providing us with a range to choose from, but complementary to one another, each contributing a vital part to the whole. As for the imagery, 'propitiation' introduces us to rituals at a shrine, 'redemption' to transactions in a

market-place, 'justification' to proceedings in a law-court, and 'reconciliation' to experiences in a home or family. My contention is that 'substitution' is not a further 'theory' or 'image' to be set alongside the others, but rather the foundation of them all, without which each lacks cogency. If God in Christ did not die in our place, there could be neither propitiation, nor redemption, nor justification, nor reconciliation. In addition, all the images begin their life in the Old Testament, but are elaborated and enriched in the New, particularly by being directly related to Christ and his cross.[56]

The publication of the book marked part of the Golden Jubilee celebrations of Inter-Varsity Press. John Stott also used it to include a dedication 'to Frances Whitehead in gratitude for 30 years of outstandingly loyal and efficient service 1956–1986'. The evangelical public showed it to be a work for which they had been waiting, since it was reprinting within a week of publication. Some reviewers were enthusiastic: Michael Green in the *Church Times* called it 'a book to buy, digest and teach',[57] and it has certainly become in places (at least in North America) a theological textbook for students in training. Professor James Packer, writing in *Christianity Today*, described the book as 'weightier than Griffith Thomas, though less massive than B. B. Warfield and less metaphysical than Jonathan Edwards', and its author as 'a first-class biblical theologian with an unusually systematic mind, great power of analysis, great clarity of expression, a superb command of his material, and a preacher's passion to proclaim truth that will change lives'.[58] Michael Green suggested that 'it will have to be taken very seriously by scholars'; but as yet there seems little to suggest that a substitutionary view of atonement, however carefully rooted in biblical exposition, will find a hearing in academic strongholds of liberal theology. David Edwards as Provost of Southwark was an exceptional example of one who studied carefully John Stott's arguments in *The Cross of Christ* before rejecting those with which he was not satisfied. His critique, written with friendliness and respect, represents perhaps the best popular opposition to John Stott's exposition. In the book *Essentials* (sub-titled *A Liberal–Evangelical Dialogue*), in which it appears, it is followed by John Stott's ten-page Response (to a chapter of over fifty pages) in which this theological premise of *The Cross of Christ* is defended as fully biblical. 'Perhaps the crucial question between us, then,' John Stott writes to David Edwards at the conclusion of his Response, 'is whether culture is to judge Scripture, or Scripture culture.'[59]

The Cross of Christ circulated in many countries, well beyond the UK and North America,[60] and attracted a weight of correspondence. 'It has stirred, informed and challenged me,' wrote H. F. Stevenson, veteran editor of *The Life of Faith*. 'I am reading it through for the second time ... it has deepened my apprehension of what the cross meant to our Saviour and what it has accomplished for us.'[61] Again, a minister from Australia, writing of John Stott to mutual friends, maintains that

> ... no one in the world has helped me more than he has over the past 37 years ... nothing has thrilled me more than *The Cross of Christ* which I believe should be compulsory reading for all candidates for the ministry. John Stott has, I believe, had more influence on the evangelical Anglican Church in Australia than anyone else ...[62]

From Sri Lanka the National Director of Youth for Christ recounted his copy's adventures. He was half-way through, and 'beginning to feel that it may well be the most thrilling book I have read', when on a bumpy road it fell out of the window of a bus:

> I did not see it fall, but someone else did and we stopped the bus. When I went back to the place the book fell I was told that someone had picked it up and gone in a bus that went in the opposite direction. Fortunately for me, a Police jeep came just at that time. The bus I was in went on its way. I got into the jeep and we gave chase, caught up with the bus and I recovered my book ... I could not replace it with a new copy because it had a detailed outline in front, marginal notes on the sides of the pages and my own index of important points at the back. My only complaint is that the margin is smaller than *I Believe in Preaching*![63]

A missionary doctor wrote ten years after the book's publication to say that he had given a copy of the Urdu translation to a local Roman Catholic schoolteacher in his part of Pakistan:

> He took months slowly and deliberately to absorb the contents of the book and then started a second reading. He said, 'The Holy Spirit really showed the author of that book how to explain things clearly.' Last year [he] was given responsibility for catechising new converts from his own tribal group (low caste Hindu/animists, a number of whom are becoming Christians, mainly Roman Catholic) and prepared a series of lessons for them based on your book.[64]

Nor was the message of the book wholly lost on academia. Professor James Stewart, a former Moderator of the General Assembly in the

Church of Scotland and a notable teacher and preacher, wrote from retirement in Edinburgh: 'This is just a note to say that I have read – and studied quite deeply, going back to it several times – your book on the Atonement ... It made me wish I could have had it at hand for my classes in Theology at the University.' The letter continues:

> More and more I am becoming persuaded that 'substitution', as you expound it here, is indeed the very core of the matter; and I feel that I shall have to rethink this emphasis in the light of what you have written. I hope all Divinity students will ponder, and I am sure that if they do they will benefit by, the sections on 'the Cross and preaching'.[65]

Those who recall the undergraduate John Stott, speaking at camp prayers in the library at Clayesmore School, Iwerne Minster, generally remember how he was entrusted by Bash to tell the story, and unfold the mystery, of the cross of Christ. They still call to mind the dignity, the clarity, the restraint and yet the depth of feeling that held his schoolboy audience. It is therefore no surprise, almost sixty years on, to read his own testimony matured but unaltered through over half a century:

> I could not be a Christian at all if it were not for the cross. What I believe about God himself, about his character and purpose, about time and eternity, about evil, suffering, salvation, reality, faith, love – and everything else besides – is largely determined by the cross.[66]

It remains something of a scandal that as a contribution to theological understanding and debate, in some circles the book might never have been written. So far as the English theological establishment is concerned, with a few honourable exceptions, it must be reckoned a book waiting to be discovered.

4

This major 'trilogy' of books, as John Stott sometimes thought of them, while touching on matters of controversy in each of their fields (preaching, moral issues, the meaning of the cross), were largely pro-active, a carefully ordered presentation on a theme chosen by the writer. But there were also books (and lesser writings) belonging to this decade which were reactive, a response to what was being taught or held as a distortion of the truth.

Earlier chapters have referred to publications resulting from structured consultations with charismatics, Anglo-Catholics, or in ERCDOM; and to *The Authentic Jesus,* which declared itself by the sub-title, *A Response to Current Scepticism in the Church.*[67] A different example of a response to a contemporary debate is found in a short chapter, contributed to a popular symposium, *Hope for the Church of England?,* a book which (according to the editor's Introduction) was designed to address 'the crisis facing England's church'.[68] This 'crisis' was illustrated under various aspects in the Introduction, such as declining membership, current moves towards an unbiblical comprehensiveness, looming issues of church–state relationships, and 'a ferment over ministry'. Following this gloomy analysis, John Stott contributed the opening chapter of the book, nailing his colours to the mast under the title 'I Believe in the Church of England'. He began with a *locus classicus* of his own position as an Anglican evangelical Christian, taking the phrase in ascending order: a Christian, 'first and foremost, by God's sheer mercy'; then an evangelical; then an Anglican.[69] From there he went on to affirm a robust loyalty to the church of his baptism, upbringing and ordination, upholding it as a historical, confessional, liturgical and national church, while admitting that in practice such a description was 'more of an ideal than a reality'. He went on:

> In the last few years there has been what some have called an 'Anglican evangelical identity crisis'. I never liked the expression myself; I think it was alarmist and inaccurate ... It is mainly due to the period of rapid change through which we have been passing, and to the difficulty we all have in adapting to change. It is not easy to maintain our own identity when other identities are changing all around us.[70]

What then, John Stott asked, should evangelical churchmen do in the face of unwelcome changes in the church? Secede, perhaps, or compromise? Or, 'the most painful of the three options', seek for ways of 'comprehensiveness without compromise ... a limited and principled kind of comprehensiveness which lays down clear lines of demarcation'? To achieve this last, he urged the maintaining of evangelical witness in theological dialogue, in teaching the truth and resisting error, and in the unremitting pursuit of holiness of life, 'an indispensable characteristic of all authentic evangelicalism'.

Brief and popular though this was, both as an occasional address and as a chapter in an ephemeral symposium, nevertheless it well represents John Stott's own conclusions in his personal struggles with the less acceptable faces of his church.

> So I do believe in the Church of England [he concluded], in the rightness of belonging to it and of maintaining a faithful evangelical

witness within it and to it. For I believe in the power of God's word and Spirit to reform and renew the church. I also believe in the patience of God. Max Warren wrote in his *I Believe in the Great Commission* that 'the history of the Church is the story of the patience of God'. He was right. I do not think we have any liberty to be less patient than God has been.[71]

A few months after the publication of *Hope for the Church of England?* David Edwards invited John Stott to lunch.[72] They discussed and agreed a proposal from David Edwards that he should write a book provisionally entitled *Evangelical Thought: The Written Contribution of John Stott*, and that John Stott should himself contribute a brief 'response' to David Edwards' assessment. By this means, as a church historian, David Edwards wanted to pose a question and invite John's reply: how 'conservative' do evangelicals have to be, if they are to be faithful to the truth, including the gospel?[73] As these things will, the idea changed as it developed. The title became *What is Essential for Evangelicals?* and then *Essentials*, with the sub-title *A Liberal–Evangelical Dialogue*: a tricky phrase, not referring (as first sight suggests) to liberal evangelicals, but to dialogue between liberals and evangelicals, as represented by David Edwards and John Stott. The word 'dialogue' also indicated that John Stott's response would not be by a single postscript or epilogue, but chapter by chapter. David Edwards prepared a synopsis immediately after their lunch together, and by that summer had completed his part of the book.[74] John Stott took the manuscript to The Hookses in August to prepare his response; and wrote to Bob Wismer, his former study assistant, now ordained and serving a curacy in Montreal, to report progress:

> I don't think you'll know about *What is Essential for Evangelicals?* It's a book which David Edwards (Provost of Southwark, scholar, church historian, liberal) has written about what he calls my 'published works'. It's a pretty devastating critique (once he's through with the flattery!), with chapters on the Bible, the Cross, Miracles, Ethics, Eschatology and the Gospel for Today. I've taken 35,000 words to respond chapter by chapter, seeking to defend our precious evangelical faith against this liberal attack! Tim Dudley-Smith, Dick France and Roger Beckwith have read my Response and made some helpful suggestions. Publication by Hodders early next year.[75]

The relaxed tone of this letter ('liberal attack' must be interpreted by the exclamation mark) belies the fact that, as Steve Andrews, his former study assistant, recalled, 'John was very exercised about the book now that he had seen David Edwards' MS.' It was small comfort that Steve Andrews could reflect, wise before as well as after the event, that he had discouraged John Stott from agreeing to the idea in the first place.[76]

The book was launched, amid considerable interest, at a press conference in April 1988. Unusually, perhaps, the Editorial Director of Hodder & Stoughton opened the meeting, after a brief welcome, with the prayer that stands as a frontispiece to the book, a prayer used by John Stott before preaching:

> Heavenly Father, we bow in your presence.
> May your Word be our rule,
> your Spirit our teacher,
> and your greater glory our supreme concern,
> through Jesus Christ our Lord.

David Edwards spoke first, beginning with a personal word about his fellow-contributor:

> The chapter in the book that I found easiest to write was the first which was a tribute to John's ministry. In so far as I am anything at all, I'm a church historian, and I do sincerely think that he is the most influential clergyman in the Church of England in the twentieth century, apart perhaps from Archbishop William Temple. And I do believe that he has earned that influence by being the leading spokesman of the conservative evangelical or simply evangelical movement, which is the most vigorous spiritual movement in this country ...[77]

He went on to offer five 'urgent questions' to evangelicals; questions to which, in turn, John Stott was able to respond. Because the whole exercise was one of amity as well as seriousness, David Edwards had sent him in advance of the press conference a nine-page handwritten copy of what he planned to say. Though the book itself covers wider ground – the miraculous, moral questions, universalism and so on – at the heart of the dialogue (because at the heart of the difference between a liberal and an evangelical theology) lay the question of Scripture and its authority. In his response to the chapter in *Essentials* on 'The Authority of the Scriptures', John Stott had pressed David Edwards on this issue. He did so by first identifying 'the fundamental difference between us' as the evangelicals' resolve to believe and obey whatever Scripture may be shown to teach.[78] He then put the direct question:

Such an open, unconditional commitment to Scripture would not be acceptable to liberals, would it, David? True, you write that 'these books read us', but are you willing for them to teach us too? Sometimes you seem anxious to demonstrate that your position is more biblical than mine. I wonder why? I mean, if you could prove this to me, I would want to change my mind and position at once. But if I could show you that my position is more biblical than yours, would you be willing to change? I guess your reply would be conditional … As Luther said to Erasmus, 'The difference between you and me, Erasmus, is that you sit above Scripture and judge it, while I sit under Scripture and let it judge me!'[79]

Both in the book, and in his response at the press conference, John Stott made it plain that this evangelical commitment to Scripture sprang from a commitment to Christ. He told the journalists present that 'as far as we can tell', it was a characteristic of Jesus that he did himself submit to the authority of Old Testament Scripture in his acceptance of its moral standards, in his understanding of his messianic mission, and in his public debates with Pharisees and Sadducees:

It was submission to Scripture which shines through them all. It is then – to us – inconceivable, that the disciple should be greater than his teacher. Our evangelical view of Scripture is a direct consequence of our desire to be loyal to Jesus Christ, and the tenacity with which we hold on to our doctrine of Scripture, is due to the tenacity with which we desire to be loyal to Jesus.

Turning perhaps from his audience to David Edwards himself, with his unwavering conviction lightened by the well-known twinkle in his eye, he added:

So you will never persuade me to be a liberal, David, unless and until you can persuade me that Jesus was a liberal. Then I will gladly join you in your liberalism. But liberals need to understand that it is our desired loyalty to Christ that lies at the foundation of our attitude to Scripture.[80]

Reviewers were, in general, kind to the book; and united in praise for the spirit of charity and friendship which it evinces. The journal *Theology*[81] hoped it might prove a prelude to 'mutual recognition of each other's total theological position'. Richard Holloway in the *Church Times* said 'David Edwards wants to make us think: John Stott wants to make us holy. We need to hear both challenges but John Stott's challenge is the primary one … my verdict would be a draw.'[82] *Themelios* devoted a three-page Editorial to it, with four conclusions: the seriousness of the theological debate, the need to hear and understand those with whom we disagree; the place of humility in intellectual encounters; and 'the loving, respectful tone of the book'.[83]

Dr Oliver Barclay, John Stott's lifelong friend, reviewing the book for the Victoria Society (the Philosophical Society of Great Britain), was able from his knowledge of student evangelism to make a singularly cogent point, about commending the gospel to the unchurched. On this issue, he wrote,

> Stott avoids putting in the knife as I think he might have done. Edwards starts with an acknowledgement of the success of the evangelicals and pleads that if only they would become less distinctively evangelical and a bit more liberal, they might reach the outsiders better. He thinks substitutionary atonement unintelligible to the modern man. Stott could have replied that it is precisely that kind of Gospel preaching that has been so successful ... Why has the school of thought that Edwards represents been such a relative evangelistic failure? One does not question Edwards' sincerity in believing that a more liberal stance would be more successful, but the facts of this century's history are not on his side.[84]

For North American reviewers, among the most significant parts of the book were those pages in which, tentatively and carefully, and with a proper sense of awe, John Stott responded to a direct challenge from David Edwards to explain his thinking on the fate of the lost. *Christianity Today* noted how

> Evangelicals will find in John Stott an articulate spokesperson of evangelical conviction, giving thoughtful responses to the most frequently heard objections. Stott is venturesome in places – note his positions on eschatology and his views on those who never hear the gospel – but at those points he admits that he is moving into positions that are not shared by all evangelicals.[85]

This issue of eternal punishment – an issue acutely painful, in the nature of the case, to all who approach it as more than an intellectual exercise – became especially so by the way in which this section of his response was made the basis of attacks upon his evangelical orthodoxy (and even his loyalty to Scripture), sometimes by those who gave little impression of having read his words with any care. The whole passage in *Essentials* (not a long one) is careful to set in context two thorny problems. To the blunt enquiry 'Who will go to hell?' John Stott discusses briefly a range of answers before stating his conviction that 'the most Christian stance is to remain agnostic on this question':

> When somebody asked Jesus, 'Lord, are only a few people going to be saved?', he refused to answer and instead urged them 'to enter through the narrow door' (Luke 13:23–24). The fact is that God, alongside the most solemn warnings about our responsibility to respond to the gospel, has not revealed how he will deal with those who have never heard it.[86]

But John Stott makes it clear that (for all its attraction to the tender-hearted) universalism is not a biblical position: 'I am not and cannot be a universalist.'[87]

Still more controversial to many is John Stott's careful discussion of whether hell, in Scripture, points in the direction of eternal conscious torment or of annihilation. He does not conceal how much he would prefer to believe the latter, but that is not the point:

> As a committed Evangelical, my question must be – and is – not what does my heart tell me, but what does God's word say? And in order to answer this question, we need to survey the biblical material afresh and to open our minds (not just our hearts) to the possibility that Scripture points in the direction of annihilation, and that 'eternal conscious torment' is a tradition which has to yield to the supreme authority of Scripture. There are four arguments ...[88]

A key word in the passage quoted above is *possibility*. John Stott added:

> I do not dogmatise about the position to which I have come. I hold it tentatively. But I do plead for frank dialogue among Evangelicals on the basis of Scripture. I also believe that the ultimate annihilation of the wicked should at least be accepted as a legitimate, biblically founded alternative to their eternal conscious torment.[89]

Christianity Today, quoted above, called this 'moving into positions that are not shared by all evangelicals', and was accurate in doing so. Within worldwide evangelical bodies, close-knit in faith, fellowship and mission, there have always been divergent views, not only on church order (episcopacy, for example) but on the sacrament of baptism (of infants? only by immersion?), on election and freewill (the old Arminian–Calvinistic controversy); and the outworking in practice of a whole range of subsidiary issues (male headship, for example, or divorce and

37. *On the occasion of his seventieth birthday, John Stott with Archbishop George Carey and his wife Eileen, Lambeth Palace, April 1991* (Photo: Richard Bewes)

38. *With students at the Theological Seminary of the Coptic Evangelical Church, Cairo, 1996*

THE
1990s

39. (above) John Stott with some of George and Maureen Swannell's grandchildren at The Hookses

40. Honorary DD, Brunel University; with Dr Derek Tidball, Principal of the London Bible College, and Frances Whitehead 14 October 1998

remarriage). Perhaps because this is a subject of such sensitivity, John Stott's words in this chapter provoked continuing and sometimes bitter controversy (not to say calumny). It would be difficult to trace the full repercussions of this tentative statement through the wide range of publications which (together with statements along the same lines from other sources) it seemed to provoke. To take one example from North America:

> If there is anything sadder than seeing Philip Hughes fall into the terrible error of denying God's eternal punishment of the impenitent wicked, it is seeing the one sometimes called the 'pope of the evangelicals,' John Stott, do the same.[90]

The author writes a few pages further on of John Stott 'seemingly without hesitation' wresting Scripture from its plain meaning; and on 'John Stott's denial of hell'. Much of this kind of thing might have passed without comment, had not John Stott's old friend, Professor J. I. Packer, mentioned him by name both in America and in Australia, suggesting that those prepared to consider the possibility of conditional immortality (as opposed to unending conscious torment) were wilfully (or at least emotionally) rejecting 'the obvious meaning of Scripture'.[91] Though the first published version is of the lecture in Australia, the more significant gathering (in which some of the same key points were made) was in Deerfield, Illinois, in May 1989. This was a four-day meeting of some 350 evangelical pastors, teachers and church officials, under the auspices of the National Association of Evangelicals, to frame a series of theological affirmations. Dr Packer spoke on salvation, referring to John Stott by name; and in a manner which, though motivated by a passion for truth, sounded to some 'not friendly'. The assembly debated the question of whether annihilationism was compatible with evangelical belief: a very significant minority held that it was not.[92]

In this exposed position, open to attack by those who on this issue sought to impugn his right to be called an evangelical, John Stott was of course in good company. This had been Dr Basil Atkinson's view, in the days when John Stott had been an undergraduate, and that in turn had led John Wenham to the same conclusion. Edward Fudge is an example of a leading figure taking the same view among North American evangelicals;[93] and the name of Philip Hughes has already been cited. Beyond evangelicalism, it is a view widely held. C. S. Lewis gave it as his opinion that the teaching of Jesus does not commit us 'to all the later pictures of the "tortures" of Hell'.[94] In the Church of England, the Doctrine Commission of the General Synod, reporting in 1995, took much the same position as Lewis, expressed rather more dogmatically.[95]

It was claimed by some who were dismayed to read John Stott's words (or, sometimes, simply to hear misleading reports of them),[96] that this Response in *Essentials* indicated a recent change of mind, perhaps due to too much exposure to liberal friends like David Edwards. In a personal statement which John Stott prepared in reply to a number of correspondents who asked him about this, he declared: 'my position has been the same for about fifty years'.[97] The statement referred, with obvious pain, to one (unnamed) speaker or writer who might be taken to represent a number ready to exclude John Stott from their understanding of evangelicalism:

> One scholar has referred to me as 'that erstwhile evangelical'. But the hallmark of authentic evangelicalism is not that we repeat traditional beliefs, however ancient, but rather that we are always willing to submit them to fresh biblical scrutiny. This is not adjusting to liberalism, but being open to Scripture.

He concluded:

> There is no 'knockdown' argument on either side which effectively settles this issue; both sides are faced with difficult texts. I am disturbed by the excessive dogmatism of those who claim that only one view is biblical. I plead for greater humility of judgment. We evangelical people need to give one another liberty in areas in which Scripture is not absolutely plain. F. F. Bruce wrote to me in 1989 that 'annihilation is certainly an acceptable interpretation of the relevant New Testament passages'. He added, 'For myself, I remain agnostic.' My position is similar.

It had been a comfort to him to have this support from F. F. Bruce, a Brethren scholar who had devoted a distinguished academic career to biblical studies.[98] Professor Bruce had written a few years earlier that the New Testament answer to the question about the destiny of those who live and die without God 'is much less explicit than is frequently supposed', and that in this situation what was called for among those who accept the Bible as their rule of faith was not polemic but 'the fellowship of patient Bible study'.[99] Now he wrote to his friend John Stott:

> Annihilation is certainly an acceptable interpretation of the relevant New Testament passages ... For myself, I remain agnostic. Eternal conscious torment is incompatible with the revealed character of God. I'd *like* to be a universalist, and Paul sometimes encourages me in this (cf. Rom. 11:32; 1 Cor. 15:22), but only (I fear) when he is read out of context. Our Lord's teaching seems plain enough:

there are some who persist irretrievably in impenitence, and refuse to the end the only salvation that is available for them.[100]

F. F. Bruce added that he would like to be more dogmatic: it was not fear of controversy or criticism that deterred him. 'If I were sure in my own mind, I *would* commit myself.' John Stott might well have said the same.

5

Contrary to predictions that television would spell the end of reading, and that word must shortly yield to image, the number of new book titles published in the UK came near to doubling in the twenty years between 1970 and 1990. Books classified as 'religious' held their own as a stable proportion of the whole, accounting for just over 3.5%.[101] But these were new books: and while John Stott contributed his own new titles to this list, his backlist of older titles remaining in print was steadily growing decade by decade. Of books written before the 1980s, at least a dozen continued to sell steadily, while others, unobtainable for a period, returned to the shelves in new editions during these years. *Favourite Psalms* was the first example of a number which were to reappear in handsomely illustrated editions through the work of Tim Dowley and Peter Wyart and their enterprise Three's Company.[102] Most if not all of these were co-editions with translations and overseas editions in several countries.

His three early contributions to The Bible Speaks Today New Testament series (which he continued to edit through the 1980s and '90s) remained in print, though sometimes in revised editions, and sometimes changing their titles slightly as the series grew. Though no new titles in the series appeared from his own pen in the 1980s, he was busily engaged in preparing to contribute three major studies early in the next decade, on Acts, 1 and 2 Thessalonians, and Romans. Easter Day 1989 found him at The Hookses, writing to Bob Wismer in Canada, telling him (among other things) to maintain his birdwatching: 'I was glad to read of the Snow Buntings and American Goldfinches at your feeder: keep it up!' He adds: 'This week I'm revising and polishing the BST exposition of *Acts*. It has been a real but satisfying challenge, and I pray it will help people.'

When Charles Simeon published in 1819 the full seventeen volumes of his sermon outlines ('skeletons' as he called them) they earned for him some £5,000,

... a prodigious sum in the book world of those days. In fact it was twice the amount that Boswell received in his lifetime for his famous biography. But Simeon did not enrich himself on these profits. In a letter to his publisher he mentions how his royalties had become 'the actual property of three societies. If God be honoured and my fellow-creatures benefited, it is all I want.' This was his special contribution to raising the standard of biblical preaching in the Church of England. 'If it leads the ignorant to preach the truth, and the indolent to exert themselves, and the weak to attain a facility for writing their own, and the busy and laborious to do more and with better effect than they otherwise could have done, I shall be richly repaid for my labour.'[103]

Many, perhaps most, Christian authors with unexpectedly large royalties have followed suit. In our own day, Owen Barfield helped C. S. Lewis set up his 'Agape Fund' in the 1940s (*The Screwtape Letters*, probably his most reprinted book, was published in 1942) as a charitable trust 'into which he could direct most of his royalties'.[104] J. B. Phillips in turn benefited from C. S. Lewis's advice and experience and set up his own 'small private non-profit-making company' in 1961.[105] Billy Graham's books and writings, though fewer in number than either C. S. Lewis's or John Stott's, continue to sell in large editions: *Peace with God*, his most famous title, dates right back to 1953. One of his biographers, after commenting that he could 'easily amass considerable wealth' from this source, sets out what actually happens:

> Since 1960 all his royalties have gone into a general trust administered by the First Union National Bank in Charlotte, which disburses it to facets of his ministry or to other charities ... he has the right to make an exception and hold out a portion of the money each year but said in 1989, 'I've only done it once and that was this last year because Ruth and I felt we just had to have some extra money coming in. We had to help some of our children and grandchildren a little bit ...' Then, quite accurately, he added, 'Of course, I could have kept it all.'[106]

John Stott could say the same: but at a meeting in 1992 to discuss the future of his writings it was made clear that he has irrevocably assigned some 95–98% of his royalty income to charitable trusts: the great majority to ELT, some to the Langham Trust,[107] and some distributed according to needs, mostly to Third World causes.[108] Occasionally, as with *The Cross of Christ* or *The Birds our Teachers*, his books carry a note saying that all royalties go to ELT, 'which distributes books to pastors, theological teachers and students, and seminary libraries, in the developing world'. It took some years for John Stott to overcome his distaste for such an announcement ('it did seem rather boastful'), but he was persuaded that it might encourage other Christian writers to use at least some of their royalties in the same way.[109] Exact figures are not easy to come by, but it is clear that the sums involved, over the full period of his writing, totalled well over £500,000 by 1996 and so substantially more by the end of the decade.

English copyright continues for seventy years after the author's death, so John Stott's literary executors will eventually oversee his continuing ministry of the printed word, a ministry whose influence will continue for as long as there are readers wishing to learn what the Scriptures have to say to them.

The 1990s

TWELVE

Seventy Plus: Pressing On

1

Those who were young in England between the wars may remember their school atlases and how fully a quarter of the world was coloured pink to denote the British Empire. Indeed in 1936 the last words of the dying King George V were reported as 'How is the Empire?'[1] Nor was Britain alone. empires were the order of the day, engines of progress and civilization. Modern colonial empires had arisen with astonishing speed: the twentieth century chronicles their even swifter decline.

Yet forces are always at work with consequences more far-reaching than even global political change. When Queen Victoria died at Osborne in January 1901 she was eighty-one years old at a time when the average life expectancy across the world was calculated to be only forty-five years. By the end of the 1990s, it was said to be seventy-five years.[2] As the arrival of the 1990s ushered in the closing years of the troubled century, shaken by the inhumanity of successive wars, its single most significant characteristic must surely be the growth of population. By 1927 world population had risen to two billion; by 1974 it had doubled to four. A fifth billion was added in the 1980s and a sixth in the late 1990s.[3] Mission statistics show that the proportion of Christians in this rapidly expanding population remained remarkably constant at about one third. The numbers of those who have not heard the gospel all but doubled during the century from some 800 million to 1,500 million.[4]

With this alarming growth in world population came a belated concern for the environment: the 'silent spring', acid rain, the greenhouse effect, the destruction of the tropical rain-forest, assumed a new and disturbing significance for any parent concerned for a future generation. Alongside the horrors of the hydrogen bomb there began to breed apocalyptic nightmares of a wasted earth:

> In the end the globe may become uninhabitable: too many people; too much poisonous CO_2 produced by them; too many chemicals altogether in the soil and the air and the waters, even the oceans ...
> At the same time, we are eradicating a growing number of species. Will humans be one of those on the death list before long?[5]

In the midst of unprecedented material and scientific progress, famine, disease and cruelty – sometimes inextricably linked to disastrous civil wars – continued to haunt the civilized world.[6] Europe still survived the various knife-edges of Cold War politics, though by no means unscarred: in the late 1980s ethnic terrorism in the Balkans, and in the 1990s the disintegration of Yugoslavia, were grim reminders of past events as well as present tragedies. South Africa offered the world a fragile sign of hope when at last a multiracial parliament confirmed, more peacefully than could have been predicted, the final end of apartheid; but in other parts of the continent, as elsewhere, genocide, Aids and famine continued largely unchecked, even while the world was becoming a single community of information instantaneously shared.

In 1994 the ratification of the Maastricht Treaty sealed the UK's commitment to what would henceforth be renamed the European Union. In England and Wales the institution of marriage was at a low ebb. Well over a third (37%) of all babies were born outside marriage and the divorce rate had quadrupled over the last three decades.[7] In 1996 the Prince and Princess of Wales ended their marriage by divorce: a sad prelude to her death a year later amid national (and international) mourning, a mass movement verging at times upon hysteria. In the same year the cloning of Dolly the sheep dramatized the ever-extending possibilities (to some, chiefly sinister possibilities) of genetic manipulation. New legislation provided for the widespread opening of shops on Sundays and (in the Church of England) the ordination of women priests. As the century ended, devolved assemblies for Scotland and Wales placed a small question-mark against the future of the United Kingdom.

When John Stott became Rector of All Souls in 1950, a quarter of all

British adults identified themselves as Christian. Forty years later, as the 1990s began, this figure had been halved. Nor was much comfort to be had from the growth of New Age religion and a renewed interest in the occult or paranormal. In the opinion of one professional sociologist, writing in the mid-1990s:

> The Christian churches have lost their ability to shape popular thinking. In so far as many people in Britain continue to think that there is more to the world than meets the eye, their images of the supernatural are no longer structured by Christian precepts. They are amorphous and idiosyncratic and have few, if any, behavioural consequences.[8]

A survey conducted as the new millennium began revealed that nine out of ten people in Britain found their country more materialistic compared with the 1950s; while official figures showed that the average person was ten times more likely to be depressed, and forty times more prone to violence and more likely to suffer from alcoholism and drug problems.[9] At the same time a public opinion poll showed the church to be 'one of the least-respected institutions in Britain'; and that while respect for public figures generally had fallen, 'only the police are held in lower regard than the members of the Church'.[10]

In America Richard Nixon died in 1994 but the Presidency continued to be beset by scandal and litigation. A youth sub-culture of drug abuse and social deprivation marred the American dream, and sent chilling signals to the rest of the Western world:

> Every eight seconds of the school day, an American student drops out of school. Every 67 seconds, a teenager has a baby. Every seven minutes a child is arrested for a drugs-related offence. Every year the American school system graduates 700,000 young people who cannot read their diplomas.[11]

A country richer than Britain, America (aided by the tax regime) was also more generous, with something approaching three-quarters of charitable giving going to religious institutions. In the immediate post-war years of financial stringency in Europe, 'American religious organizations, taken together, actually enjoyed a higher annual income than the whole of the British government'.[12] Though the figures show evangelicals as less prosperous than other groups in the US, yet their generous support of the Langham Foundation, the London Institute and the Evangelical Literature Trust was highly significant in the development of what was becoming increasingly the main thrust of John Stott's ministry.

2

For John Stott himself, the decade marked his progression from later middle years to at least the threshold of old age. In his personal newsletter of November 1991 he quoted Barbara Cartland (then aged ninety) as saying, 'The scintillating seventies are the gateway to the exciting eighties'; and though there was some talk of 'GMR', 'a Greater Measure of Retirement', this was hardly discernible until the decade was well advanced, and even then but faintly. His year continued to be divided between overseas visits, interspersed with lecturing for the London Institute and a general (often demanding) oversight of its affairs; together with an unceasing worldwide correspondence, much of it still concerned with the care of EFAC (the Evangelical Fellowship in the Anglican Communion), ELT (the Evangelical Literature Trust), and the Langham Scholars programme. With this went spells at The Hookses, long days working on the current book or lecture series, broken only by an afternoon given first to HHH ('horizontal half-hour', of which the middle H was beginning occasionally to be abandoned) and an hour or two of gardening or work on the property.

In recognition of the need to concentrate his energies, John Stott resigned the Presidency of EFAC at a supper and reception in Oxford in September 1990. 'Where is the next John Stott?' asked Bishop Michael Nazir-Ali, General Secretary of CMS: 'The answer is that there will not be another John Stott. But because of his ministry there are and there will be many John Stotts throughout the world.'[13] Regional Secretaries, present for the annual meeting of the Executive, made affecting speeches and brought gifts from their region. Some could look back to EFAC's small beginnings, and recall John Stott as the first General Secretary and the architect of the Fellowship from 1961 for the next twenty years. His concern and interest in its affairs continued unabated, and he was present in Canterbury during June 1993 at the first EFAC International Consultation, on the theme of 'The Anglican Communion and Scripture'. Some of the speakers were his own former EFAC bursars or Langham Scholars: or men (such as Peter Moore) whom he had befriended since their student days. His own task as Founder-Secretary and Past President was to give five major Bible expositions on aspects of God's revelation in the Scriptures.

Other celebrations helped to mark the period of his seventieth birthday. Two *Festschriften* had been in preparation, recognizing his long association with the world of evangelical scholarship on both sides of the Atlantic, and his concern for Third World and missiological issues.[14] *The Gospel in the Modern World: A Tribute to John Stott* was presented to him at a luncheon party sponsored by the publishers and held at St Peter's,

Vere Street, home of the London Institute, attended by family and friends from America as well as Britain. His sister Joanna, with her three daughters and their families, made him a birthday present of a TV, 'determined to drag me back into the modern world, from which I slipped about ten years ago when my first set went *kaput* and I decided not to have it replaced!'[15] The second symposium, *AD 2000 and Beyond*, carried a Foreword from his old friend Billy Graham, describing him as having 'unquestionably been one of the most influential individuals of the 20th Century in bringing about a renewal of biblical faith throughout the world. As a pastor, scholar, evangelist, theologian, and writer he has been used of God to touch countless lives for Christ.'[16] Four particular areas were singled out: as evangelist, as theologian, as church leader and as 'a modern day prophet'. Billy Graham, himself one of the most-travelled of all Christian leaders, added: 'Few have understood the situation of the world church more clearly, and few are as able to address the church's problems and failures – and opportunities – on as broad a scale.'[17]

On 19 April 1991 George Leonard Carey was enthroned in his Cathedral as the 103rd Archbishop of Canterbury with the All Souls orchestra participating. Already, as Archbishop-designate, he had attended the WCC Assembly at Canberra, and chaired his first Primates' Meeting in Ireland:

> The new boy, unknown to them at the start and with the briefest of time in episcopal orders [he had been Bishop of Bath and Wells for barely three years] won their affection and respect, and Eileen similarly with their wives ...[18]

Five days later Dr Carey hosted a reception at Lambeth Palace to mark John Stott's birthday, largely for early members of the revived Eclectic Society. Canon Michael Saward, who had devised the occasion, presented John Stott with a copy of Archdeacon Pratt's notes of the meetings of the original Eclectic Society some 200 years before:[19] Charles Simeon had been a member or visitor from the beginning until 1811, and an occasional leader of their discussions.[20]

Two more particular sources of pleasure helped to mark his seventieth birthday. The first was a handsome album from Todd Shy, the current (and longest-serving) study assistant and his seven predecessors, with tributes to what they had learned from him and the value they placed upon his friendship. The second was his appointment by Her Majesty the Queen as an 'Extra Chaplain', an honour only exceptionally bestowed on a few of her chaplains once they reached the retiring age of seventy.[21] This meant that throughout the 1990s his engagements still included an occasional visit to preach at the Chapel Royal. 'Dale Day' in

Pembrokeshire was an annual event, as was his regular series of lectures on the authority and interpretation of Scripture at the London Institute in the ten-week course, 'The Christian in the Modern World'. He was still at All Souls whenever he was in London, preaching regularly; and he began once again to accept more invitations from colleges and universities, though not for missions. About every second or third year he visited the CICCU and the OICCU (declining, however, an invitation from the Oxford Union to participate in a debate on the motion that 'This house believes science has exposed religion as a confidence trick').[22]

He preached at the opening of the restored and rebuilt St Andrew the Great in Cambridge in 1994, the new home of 'the Round', which, under his old friend Mark Ruston, had ministered so significantly to generations of both town and gown.[23] Nor was it only Oxbridge that could draw him. He lectured at the University of East Anglia (the Vice-Chancellor had to ask students crowding the gangways and sitting on the steps and in the aisles to move to the foyer in the interests of safety), and preached to students in Durham, Newcastle and Aberystwyth. He spoke, too, at Diocesan Evangelical Fellowships, at meetings on behalf of TEAR Fund or the Evangelical Alliance, and at Conferences such as SEAC (Senior Evangelical Anglican Clergy), the Anglican Evangelical Assembly, or Word Alive; but he gave priority in his UK travels to seminars and lectures related to the work of the London Institute. On its behalf he would set off for Durham, Leeds or Bradford; for the south coast or the home counties; for Edinburgh, Newport or Belfast, delivering to provincial, Scottish, Welsh or Irish audiences the lectures first given at the Institute's London courses, so extending its influence and seeking to broaden its base of membership and support.

3

Disparate though some of these activities may appear, the 1990s saw the sharpening of a single long-held and integrated purpose. One day in Philadelphia in 1993 John Stott was speaking on behalf of Scripture Union: David Jones, an old friend and later President of the Langham Foundation, was with him on the platform as President of SU. He took the opportunity to ask John Stott,

> 'In the remaining years that God gives you, what do you feel he most wants you to accomplish?' Without skipping a beat, John replied, 'Assisting the Church in the developing world through books and scholarships for pastors and seminary students.'[24]

There were a number of ways in which he continually pursued this vision, most obviously through the Langham Scholarships, through ELT, and through his own writing. Alongside these can be set his concern for the London Institute, much of whose work increasingly related to the developing world, either in the training of young overseas graduates who would return better equipped to their own countries: or in imparting a biblical and global concern to the future Christian leaders of the West. And not least there was the directly personal contribution made by his own pastoral and teaching visits overseas. In his mind these were all parts of the single objective summed up in his reply to David Jones.

The Evangelical Literature Trust, which began 'mainly as a way to re-cycle my book royalties', was described in his personal newsletter of 1993 as 'one of my major preoccupations since it was founded twenty-one years ago'. All that time John Stott had been Chairman of the small group of trustees,[25] and would soon be the last of the founder-members still serving the Trust. In 1993 he handed over the chairmanship to Nigel Sylvester, followed in 1999 by David Cansdale.[26]

Some indication of growth could be found in the statistics quoted: books in a variety of languages distributed to the retail value of £1 million annually; two carefully chosen books sent each year to about 12,000 graduate pastors, and two simpler books to about 50,000 non-graduates; 10,000 seminary students enabled every year to buy six or seven basic reference books, to form the nucleus of their personal library, at heavily subsidized prices; with grants to scholars teaching in colleges or universities, to seminary libraries, and to Christian publishers in Eastern Europe.

> In western houses [John Stott wrote] books line our walls, are piled on our tables and even spill over onto our floors. Not so in the Third World, however, or in Eastern Europe. In those major regions of the world, reliable and helpful Christian literature is often in disastrously short supply.

Nowhere was this need more pressing than among teachers of the faith:

> ELT focuses on books for pastors and theological students. The logic behind this can be simply stated. The healthy growth of the local church depends, more than anything else, on the quality of preaching it receives. If individuals live and flourish by the Word of God (as Jesus said they do, quoting Deuteronomy), so do churches. But if churches depend on preaching, preaching depends on study, and study depends on books. Books have a key role in the life and development of the church.[27]

Through his overseas travels John Stott could speak from first-hand experience of what books could mean to Third World Christians. He told a Christian Booksellers' convention, 'It is this hunger for books which the Evangelical Literature Trust is seeking to satisfy, particularly in pastors, seminary students and scholars.'[28]

John Stott had relinquished the day-to-day leadership of the London Institute for Contemporary Christianity in 1986, becoming President. He continued to work for its welfare, recruiting students for its courses on his overseas visits, and lecturing both at St Peter's and across the country at seminars and meetings connected with its work. In 1988, partly driven by finance, it had merged with the Shaftesbury Project under the new name of Christian Impact.[29] But by 1990 the whole project was in serious difficulties. Tony McCutcheon, caught up in staff conflicts, had resigned as bursar ('John Stott came to my office saying, "We need a Christian mind about resignation"').[30] and there was a sense that the ship would founder. John Stott had tried hard to distance himself from the running of LICC 'so that it would grow up without him', but it seemed unlikely even to survive. He is remembered as talking sadly in the kitchen of the Rectory after one of the prayer breakfasts to the effect that if he were only ten years younger 'I would take the bit between my teeth' and set to work again to rebuild it. The desire to save the work he had founded, and the resolve to stand back from executive action long ago placed in other hands, were in what seemed irreconcilable conflict. He had disengaged himself partly in order to be free to wrestle with his study of Romans in The Bible Speaks Today series, and this too was weighing on him. Eventually he agreed to help the Council in making a personal 'crisis appeal' to supporters of the Institute, and this quickly brought in some £130,000 in gifts or pledges. John Stott himself studied and analysed the hundreds of donors' response forms, and reported to the Council that he could identify six areas 'made prominent by repetition' demanding urgent attention before the Institute could be relaunched with Elaine Storkey as the Director. These had to do with the need for strong and integrated direction under tight budgetary control; the need to operate on several levels, academic and popular, and to be less tied to a London base; and the need to broaden both co-operation with other like-minded groups (EA, CARE, UCCF, theological colleges and so on) and the support base among churches, groups and individual members.[31]

Throughout the 1990s the LICC lecture series, 'The Christian in the Modern World', continued annually as one of its flagship study courses. For ten weeks each autumn it drew to London a wide variety of participants, including a number from developing countries and from Central Europe on scholarships which often met the full costs of the tuition and board. John Stott himself contributed a regular series of eight or ten lectures on the authority and interpretation of the Bible, and the quoted aim of the course was to create for those few weeks in central London 'a microcosm of Christ's worldwide family, a concentrated period of stimulating and joyful learning, a preparation for creative Christian service, and an opportunity to make friendships for a lifetime – and beyond'.[32]

In November 1998 Elaine Storkey retired after seven years as Director: she travelled widely in the interests of the Institute, and was often at her best when giving a BBC 'Thought for the Day' and when meeting people on the frontier between faith and unbelief. A few months later, John Stott as President was able to report the appointment of Mark Greene, Vice-Principal of the London Bible College, as her successor. He wrote to the Institute's supporters describing the new Director's theological credentials and adding:

> But Mark is far from being an ivory tower academic. He worked with an advertising agency for ten years in London and New York. In addition, he is a journalist, consultant, pioneer and poet. He is also a family man … All this makes me excited about the future. I have just returned from visiting five great Asian cities (Bangkok, Taipei, Hong Kong, Shanghai and Nanjing) and am amazed how widely known the Institute is.[33]

Institutions do not last for ever. No-one can assess how far the present viability of LICC is due to John Stott's presence, his name, and his worldwide contacts and travels. But he remained committed to it, his enthusiasm continually renewed by the response of the students who come to its courses, and who can be found in increasing numbers holding positions of Christian leadership in developing countries.

The same concern for the Christian education of Third World leaders had led, thirty years earlier, to the EFAC bursary scheme. In January 1974 a further development saw the funding of 'PhD bursars', quickly renamed 'Research bursars'. By 1976/7 the Langham Trust, with help from its sister organization in America, the Langham Foundation, had agreed to take over responsibility for their funding; and they became known in consequence as 'Langham Scholars'. The World Council of Churches had trodden this road earlier in the century with (in its own terms) notable success through their Theological Education Fund. This was inaugurated following the Tambaram Assembly in 1938 with a gift from John D. Rockefeller Jr of $2m matched by a further $2m from nine North American mission boards. It was said to have brought about 'a radical change in the quality and strength of the theological education in the younger churches'.[34] In 1963/4 a comparable Christian Literature Fund was set up, with a capital of $3m.[35] This whole initiative, under the name 'Programme for Theological Education', proved of enormous influence. In John Stott's view, indeed, 'one could argue that their policy of sending potential Third World leaders and scholars to liberal seminaries in the West, where they were indoctrinated, has been a major cause of the WCC's theological decline'.

He himself had become increasingly convinced that the seminary is the key institution in the church, 'since all the church's future clergy pass through the seminaries, and it is there that they are either made or marred, either equipped for ministry or ruined through loss of faith and vision'.[36]

In the spring of 1997 John Stott spoke in Toronto at the Ontario Theological Seminary, taking as his subject 'The Importance of a Strategic Theological Education for the Christian World Mission'. From this unwieldy title he developed the sevenfold logic, refined now over many years, which lay behind the Langham Trust and the ELT:

> First, God's concern is focused on the maturing of the church, not merely the conversion of individuals.
>
> Second, it is the faithful teaching of the Word of God that produces mature churches.
>
> Third, God's Word reaches churches mainly through pastors.
>
> Fourth, pastors cannot teach and preach the Word of God adequately without books ... many godly pastors in poor countries do not have access to or money to buy books of any kind.
>
> Fifth, seminaries and Bible colleges are the settings for future pastors to acquire the habit of lifelong learning. Therefore, they need to have good, basic libraries.
>
> Sixth, seminaries need top leaders ... outstanding as scholars and as men and women of God.
>
> Seventh, in order to teach in a seminary and thus influence the future leaders of the church, one needs an earned doctorate from a major university or theological seminary that will be recognized anywhere in the world. Thus, it is strategically essential that the evangelical church encourage its best and brightest to earn doctorates and to take their places as members of the faculty of the theological schools around the world.[37]

In the same address in 1997, John Stott was able to report:

> Of the fifty Langham scholars who have completed doctorates, four are now principals of theological seminaries, twelve are academic deans, and the majority of the others are seminary or university

lecturers. Those not engaged in teaching within an educational institution are likely to be found in church or mission leadership throughout the world. Twenty-four younger scholars are currently engaged in theological research.

Every year John Stott continued personally to encourage likely applicants from developing countries to apply to the Trust, which had, from the outset, always sought to establish and maintain a strong personal and pastoral link with those whom it supported. Each year he spoke at a brief orientation course (arranged jointly by the Langham Trust, the Oxford Centre for Mission Studies and the Whitefield Institute) for those beginning their doctoral studies. His title was usually 'Maturity and Research', and his theme was how to grow in academic excellence and in personal godliness at one and the same time:

> For there is a real danger that a scholar may return home after three or four years an academic success but a spiritual failure, a 'doctor' (qualified to teach) but no longer a 'disciple'; possessing a new degree and a new title, but possessed by no new vision, power or holiness ...
>
> Helmut Thielicke, in his small but suggestive book entitled *A Little Exercise for Young Theologians*, urges us to think about God in the second person ('you'), and not slip into the third person ('he'): 'This transition ... from a personal relationship with God to a merely technical reference ... is the first step towards the worst and most widespread ministers' disease.' My own hope is that Langham scholars, while being competent teachers of theology, will truly know and worship the God they talk about.[38]

Independent but associated Langham Trusts or Foundations were by this time at work in Australia and Canada as well as in Britain, while the Langham Foundation in the United States, begun in a small way in the 1970s, was experiencing dramatic growth. In the early 1990s its annual income stood at $250,000, and this had doubled by 1995, and quadrupled to $1m by the end of the decade. The Foundation began to be responsible for the support of Langham Scholars studying in the US as well as the UK, and to oversee the literature work begun by ELT in Latin America. In 1997 David B. Jones left the Scripture Union staff to become the Foundation's first full-time Executive Officer, with John Stott continuing to attend the twice-yearly meetings of the Board. While his presence has always been requested and appreciated, the US members observed how 'he will rarely offer advice unless directly asked for it, and even then he will start his response by saying, "I am not sure that it is appropriate for an innocent Englishman to respond to this American issue!'"[39]

Because John Stott usually has existing invitations from various churches in the US, it is relatively easy for the Director to arrange fund-raising events around them: 'John is not shy in offering a cogent presentation about the efficacy of our work to potential donors, but often leaves the financial aspects of the presentation to me!'[40]

Before his appointment as Director, David Jones had served on the Langham Foundation, and in 1996 had led the Board through a strategic planning process:

> One clear point raised was the need for a new name. In the States, Langham does not mean anything, and the word Foundation implied that we were in the grant-making business, supporting other ministries! Once we discussed this issue, it became clear that John Stott was our greatest attribute and 'attention-getter', so we felt that his name needed to be in our name. David Spence helped put the final touches on the new name, 'John Stott Ministries for Biblical Preaching and Scholarship'. These discussions moved very quickly, as John was not present to express his embarrassment! But then the question arose, how do we tell John about this decision made by the crazy American Board?[41]

Wisely, they asked Mark Labberton, a Board member and a former study assistant, to break this news, believing that John Stott would respect his judgment. Dr Labberton (who had himself proposed the motion) wrote a long letter some ten days later summarizing the various decisions of the recent Board meeting and explaining in detail the thinking which lay behind the proposed change of name (initially 'The John Stott Society for Evangelical Preaching and Scholarship'). He added:

> Other names were considered. Making no name change was also discussed. But when this possible new name was found, the Board unanimously believed, with all due respect, that its benefits to the ministry both now and in the future outweighed anticipated objections. This new name honors our founder, it acknowledges our partnership, it clarifies our identity, it affirms our purpose. Imagining your blushed face in hearing of this change, John, we hasten to offer ourselves to you as the scapegoats: Blame us!![42]

John Stott replied immediately ('I'm off to China today!') reluctantly acknowledging the cogency of the arguments, and giving permission for the use of his name, while suggesting that 'Society' was not the right word. In the end the Board settled on 'John Stott Ministries'. It remains a source of embarrassment to him: 'John refuses to use it. He speaks diffidently about "the foundation with which I am associated", or sometimes he will bravely say "JSM", but no more fully!'[43]

In the closing years of the decade the Board of John Stott Ministries committed themselves to a New Millennium Fund, aiming to raise $4.5 million by John Stott's eightieth birthday, not as a capital endowment, but to spend on scholarships and books during the first decade of the new millennium. In addition, they began to branch out into a Langham Writers Program, Preaching Seminars, and a ministry of 'Senior Langham Associates' to continue something of John Stott's personal contacts with Christian leaders in different regions of the world. But the vision remains the same: 'that every church in developing countries be served by conscientious pastors who sincerely believe, diligently study, faithfully expound, and relevantly apply the Word of God'.[44]

4

When, early in the 1990s, John Stott reached and passed his seventieth birthday, it brought no noticeable decline in the number of his overseas visits. Perhaps the time available for birdwatching expeditions and holidays in remote locations increased a little: but the demands for his presence and ministry continued relentlessly. During these ten years he visited some forty countries, many more than once, and the USA and Canada (because of his links with JSM and the Canadian Langham Trust) almost twenty times. Within each of these countries he would usually travel to a number of different centres. He would preach and teach in modest halls and vast auditoria, undistinguished churches, great cathedrals, and sometimes in the open air. He would be found especially in seminaries and universities, delivering lectures during the day, with a public meeting in the evening. There would be retreats and study conferences for pastors and missionaries, endless interviews, and a unique ministry of counsel and friendship to the senior leaders of indigenous churches, and of movements such as IFES and SU, who were frequently his hosts and sponsors.

His modest luggage would usually be weighed down with books to give to pastors and students, sometimes as many as a hundred copies divided between his suitcase and briefcase, and his study assistant's backpack. According to what he knew of their needs he would try to take to Third World countries small supplies of unobtainable essentials as a gesture of thanks for hospitality – pens and pencils, soap, toothpaste, simple toiletries, clothing and medicines. For himself, he would use the flight to catch up with his reading or his sleep, helped by sleeping pill, earplugs and eyeshade ('by now a well-tried trio').[45] There was not often much time for sightseeing: given the choice, he would generally opt for his elusive birds: for a nature reserve, a swamp, a forest, a patch of tundra, desert, bush or prairie. Nevertheless, during these years he saw the Taj Mahal, Red Square and the Kremlin, the Great Wall of China, the Murchison Falls and the passion play at Oberammergau. He reflected on this latter experience, and found himself 'impressed ... a traditional expression of medieval Catholic piety ... it all became very real, even if afterwards at the stage door it was somewhat shattered by watching the young Christ emerge in blue jeans, sign autographs, and ride off on his bicycle!'[46]

He travelled not only by scheduled airlines but by tiny Cessnas, rubber boats and dugout canoes, by 'Clancy' the converted ambulance, by limousines, trucks and local taxis, by all-terrain vehicles and snowmobiles, and sometimes by bicycle. On one occasion at the age of seventy-four he set off alone on a dirt track into a Cuban forest on a hired bike (a million bicycles had been imported from China as cars and petrol became restricted) in search of birds and, having miscalculated the distance, returned saddle-sore and aching as the light faded, bumping and pedalling for 25 kilometres.[47] One month might see him in the Marxist culture of Cuba or Eastern Europe: the next in rural Africa or the Far East. He might find himself expounding the Scriptures for the Mar Thoma church of South West India at their famous Maramon Convention, held on a sandbank in the river Pambra, said to be 'the largest annual Christian gathering in the world'.[48] By way of contrast, he would reflect on what he saw of the problems of Christian life and witness under Islamic culture, perhaps when paying a return visit to Egypt in 1996 ('If a Muslim convert's family report him or her, the convert is jailed. So baptisms take place in strict secrecy, and no statistics are published ...').[49] But there was also something to challenge the Western church:

> For both Marxism and Islam offer a comprehensive worldview. Each claims to be able to explain everything, and each demands from its adherents a radical allegiance. As I watched Marxists at work and Muslims at prayer, I could not help asking myself whether our Christian commitment is comparable in its coherence or depth.
>
> Further, as European culture drifts ever further from its original Christian moorings, I pondered the daring affirmation of the apostle Peter that Jesus is 'Lord of all' (Acts 10:36) and asked myself how much it would take for bold uncompromising Christians to bring Europe to his feet again.[50]

In Africa he might find himself invited (as he was in 1998 by David Gitari, Archbishop of Kenya) to conduct a residential retreat for the Archbishop, his diocesan bishops, and 150 senior clergy.[51] Every tour brought new experiences: in Canada the singing at Sunday worship might be led by Navaho Indians; in Kiev he was one of several successive preachers, taking turns during the same long service (made still longer by the need for translation); in Papua New Guinea he helped to give substance to the Lambeth Conference 'Decade of Evangelism'. Audiences, congregations and occasions were bewildering in their variety. In 1997, for example, in Croatia, speaking in a pink-washed former synagogue, he gave the graduation address for the Evangelical Theology School in Osijek to mark their silver jubilee year. In 1999 he delivered the 'Bishop Festo Kivengere Memorial Lecture' in Kampala on 'Christian Witness in the Public Arena', an appropriate theme by which to commemorate one of the twentieth-century heroes of the African church. In South and Central America or parts of Asia he might be distracted by some noisy elements of charismatic worship, trying to remind himself of cultural differences, yet wondering whether 'the Holy Spirit's presence is measured in decibels', and on one occasion concluding that 'to me the whole thing was contrived. It savoured more of a charismatic sub-culture than of authentic freedom in the Spirit.'[52] A rather more dampening experience was lecturing on mission to 2,600 students in a vast natural open-air amphitheatre in South Korea, where one night 'I found myself addressing an undulating sea of umbrellas'; while on the next night (when, being fine, umbrellas had been left at home) an unexpected storm arose: 'I naturally stopped, expecting everybody to take cover ... nobody stirred' and the meeting continued, 'although by the end of the evening many must have been drenched to the skin'.[53]

In some parts of the world, his private motto became 'Expect the unexpected'. Assured that a visit to a college was simply as a guest to meet the faculty, a door would open into an auditorium. A large and expectant gathering would then be told by the Principal that 'John Stott would now address them'. Standards of interpretation varied unpredictably from the fluent, theologically aware and highly professional, to the slow and stumbling. Hospitality, too, presented astonishing contrasts. In remoter Third World areas, or (especially) on birdwatching safaris, he would find himself cooking, or being entertained to, the simplest of meals; and staying in the most basic (not to say primitive) accommodation. Elsewhere up to thirty-five dishes might be on the table. He would be the guest of honour at twelve-course exotic feasts in fashionable Eastern restaurants, while staying (not at his own request) in the presidential suite of an international-class hotel. Once at least he lunched on beans and bacon cooked over a primus on an ice-floe (amid many warnings not to go too near the edge!) during a seal hunt in the Canadian Arctic. It says much for his internal constitution that mostly he kept well, and nearly all the time was able to fulfil a relentless schedule of engagements whether theological or ornithological. Indeed, as the years passed, more and more entries in the diaries record an ever-mounting tally of exotic birds, often lovingly, lengthily and enthusiastically described. One such entry in 1998 triumphantly announces '155 bird species altogether in our three days'![54]

The 1990s brought to a conclusion the long 'search for the Snowy Owl' which had been a feature of his several visits to the Arctic. In the summer of 1991, when camping near Cambridge Bay, Victoria Island, they searched day after day until they were rewarded with 'a momentary glimpse of the wings of a large white bird ...' It reappeared: 'I could see the whole bird now, flying east, with the lazy flip-flop flight of an owl hunting low over the ground, but again it soon disappeared behind a ridge. We were elated. A Snowy Owl at last!'[55] A few pages later he described how the Eskimos call the Snowy Owl both 'Ookpik' (in Inuktituk) and, less romantically, 'the Arctic chicken', since that is what it tasted like! Spurred on by these tantalizing and mouth-watering glimpses, the search for a fuller sighting continued; until five years later this uncompromising tenacity was rewarded, again at Cambridge Bay. Within a few minutes of his arrival by air from Yellowknife he and four friends were taking advantage of the midnight sun to drive out into the wild in a ramshackle truck:

> We'd only gone three or four miles before we'd seen our first pair of Snowies and were walking across the tundra to its eggs. There they were – eight off-white shiny oblong or pear-shaped objects. No! Wait a moment, there were *seven*, and the eighth was a newly hatched little chick! The 'nest' was only a scraping of bare earth, and the site typical of what I've read – on a slight eminence, at the foot of a small rock for protection, and commanding a 360° view of any approaching enemy predators.[56]

With mounting excitement they managed to erect a hide, and here over the next few days John Stott crouched, sometimes for six hours at a stretch, his camera at the ready:

> As I looked at the bird through my 500mm mirror lens, her head and body filled the picture. She stared, even glared, at me with her penetrating yellow eyes. Indeed, it was as if we stared unblinking at each other (tho' I realise she couldn't see me), eyeball to eyeball. I could even watch mosquitoes landing on her feathered face. They even walked on the surface of her eyes until she blinked and shook

her head vigorously to dislodge them. The midnight sun was bright enough for me to take a number of close-up photos.[57]

Not everyone will enter as fully as he did into what John Stott calls 'the excitement of sitting in a hide, or blind, for hour after hour only a few yards from the bird of my dreams!' But for him 'It was the culmination of a twenty-five year search for a truly sensational bird. I felt I could now say my *Nunc Dimittis*: "Lord, now lettest thou thy servant depart in peace … for my eyes have seen …" (Luke 2:29, 30).'[58]

An equally characteristic final glimpse of John Stott in the high Arctic is his description of how he and Steve Andrews, former study assistant and at that time Dean of the Cathedral in Prince Albert, Saskatchewan, prepared for a Sunday service. This was to be held at Sachs Harbour, the only settlement on Banks Island, the most westerly island in the Arctic archipeligo. There had been no regular service in the little wooden Anglican church since a brief period four years before.

> On Saturday morning we cleaned the church, undoing the shutters to let in some light, dusting all surfaces, sweeping the floor littered with dead blue-bottles, and polishing the brass cross, candlesticks and communion rail with Brasso until they shone almost as if new …
>
> Having been assured that the inhabitants of Sachs lie abed on Sunday mornings, we had decided to have our projected Communion Service at 2pm, and posted a notice to this effect on the Co-op notice-board, trusting to the bush telephone to communicate the news throughout the village.

At 1.50 on Sunday a young boy arrived to ring the bell ('vigorously but erratically') but by 2pm only the mayor and his wife had joined them. Then in dribs and drabs a few more turned up:

> In the end we numbered a dozen people, which looked fairly full, since there are only fourteen chairs! Steve presided, and did well to relate the service to the local community's concerns.

John Stott gave a ten-minute address on the way in which birds teach us repentance ('Just as they go away on migration but always return, so if we are conscious of straying from God we must return to him.'). At the end he added, 'to be continued next Sunday'.[59]

At the opposite pole from Banks Island and Cambridge Bay lie the 6 million square miles of Antarctica. Twenty-five years earlier he had identified this as the only continent he had not yet visited ('love to study the penguins … not enough people there, let alone evangelicals, to justify a visit').[60] When in December 1990 he finally achieved this ambition with a visit to the Falkland Islands, his diary includes fifty-five pages of personal notes before the narrative begins. There are sections on varieties of Penguins, Albatrosses, Whales and Seals; notes on the Islands' history, people, language and culture; abstracts of books, including the life of Allen Gardiner, and stanzas from Coleridge's 'The Rime of the Ancient Mariner'. The visit itself was at the request (probably not unprompted) of the Chaplain, Rector and 'Dean', his old friend Canon J. G. M. W. Murphy, also a Chaplain (formerly Domestic Chaplain at Sandringham) to the Queen. John Stott was there over Christmas and New Year, staying in the Deanery, sometimes leading tiny informal services at remoter outposts for a congregation of two or three; helping with a burial and a baptism; or visiting some of the elderly and housebound to sit chatting round a peat fire. On one occasion, 'when the time came for me to leave, I asked if they would allow me to read and pray with them, and (when permission had been granted) if I might borrow their Bible'.

His hostess vanished into her bedroom and seemed to be away a long time:

> Eventually she emerged with a little old black volume. 'I think this is one,' she said, handing it to me. It turned out to be a dilapidated 19th century Congregational Hymnbook! Unperturbed, I looked for 'The Lord's my Shepherd' or 'The King of Love my Shepherd is'. They weren't in the index. Instead I found the most archaic metrical version of Psalm 23 imaginable, which I had difficulty in understanding myself, let alone making it intelligible to my host and hostess![61]

On Christmas Eve he joined the carol-singers on the green next to the Cathedral, gathered round the Whalebone Arch; and preached at the midnight service of Holy Communion as part of a teaching ministry which included a 'mini-mission', held in the Stanley primary school, on three basic questions of identity: 'Who am I? Who is Jesus? Who is a Christian?' This was supported by the three churches of the town and attended by fifty or sixty islanders. Free days before and after Christmas were given mostly to birdwatching (John Stott) or fishing (Gerry and Joy Murphy); and to visits to the off-shore islands where they were made welcome on sheep farms and by the Rector's friends. Never far away was the sense of struggle faced by the islanders. Relics could still be seen of the 1982 conflict with Argentina. One Sunday John Stott was taken for a walk up to 'Wireless Ridge', just outside Stanley:

> At the top all sorts of military 'detritus' was to be found – gun

emplacements, old rusty ammunition boxes, an anti-tank gun, and even some bits of uniform. At several places too are simple crosses, with an engraved stone to commemorate the loss of British soldiers in a particular battle. So Islanders do not forget.[62]

But hardly less evident was the continuing economic struggle, amid the rugged, almost treeless natural environment, exposed to the rigours of the South Atlantic only a few hundred miles from Cape Horn.

From Port Stanley John Stott embarked on the *Society Explorer* for an Antarctic voyage, a seventieth-birthday present from a group of generous friends. A programme of lectures, bird photography, and shore exped-itions filled all the waking hours:

> Each day we landed by zodiac (an inflatable rubber dinghy invented by Jacques Cousteau) on several different beaches, and revelled in many varieties of penguins and seals against a magnificent backdrop of snow-covered mountains and glaciers ... Sometimes we experienced authentic Antarctic weather – wind, snow, cold and fog. But at other times, especially when we began our return journey northwards, the fog lifted and the sun came out, exposing the grandeur of sea and mountain, icebergs and icecliffs. The dreaded Drake Passage (between the Antarctic and Cape Horn) lived up to its reputation of being the roughest sea in the world. Yet Wandering Albatrosses accompanied us, at home in the fiercest weather. This creature, being with its twelve-foot wingspan the largest of all flying birds, circumnavigates the whole southern hemisphere four or five times a year, and deserves to be called 'the king of the oceans'.
>
> On the two Sundays the Captain gave me permission to lead a brief service of worship, both of which were attended by about fifty passengers and crew. I also had some opportunities for personal ministry, and met with one of the expedition's leaders daily at 5.30 a.m. for an hour's heart-to-heart discussion.[63]

Nor was this the only cruise undertaken in these years. The following summer he served as 'Chaplain' aboard the square-rigged *Sea Cloud*, the largest four-masted private tall ship afloat, 'for a fantastic voyage to the great Pauline sites round the Aegean sea'. The organizer, David Spence, was President of the Langham Foundation Board; and John Stott was able to find many opportunities among his sixty (mainly) wealthy fellow-passengers to enlist prayer partners and supporters. He repeated this in January 1995 in the Caribbean, enjoying a natural and amused rapport with what was mainly a North American ship's complement. David Jones recalls how

... one of the passengers was a 'good old Southern boy' (complete with wild Hawaiian shirt) who would greet everyone with, 'Hey, how y'all doin'?' Once, in front of a number of other passengers, he turned and greeted John with this same greeting. John replied, in a slow, southern twang, 'Purrty good, buddy!' Needless to say, the whole group erupted into laughter! We continue to greet each other with 'Hey, buddy' or 'How y'all doin'?'[64]

5

In October 1995 John Stott was excited to receive an official invitation from the China Christian Council to visit four of the country's leading seminaries. His name was known through his visits to Hong Kong, Taiwan and other parts of East Asia; and already some of his books, perhaps as many as thirty, were circulating in translation there. He wrote to ELT supporters:

> China is so huge – in both territory and population – that it is probably inaccurate to generalize about anything Chinese. Yet, at least in contrast to the decade of terror (1966–76), euphemistically known as 'the Cultural Revolution', when the Red Guards went on the rampage, churches were desecrated and Christian leaders imprisoned and tortured, there is today in China an amazing degree of religious freedom. The churches are open again (both registered buildings and unregistered 'meeting places'), large numbers of bibles are being printed, and all thirteen seminaries are fully functional. The churches' greatest and most urgent need is for more and better-trained pastors and teachers. So the top priorities of the China Christian Council are (1) to upgrade their seminaries, (2) to train lay preachers, and (3) to publish suitable books.[65]

He was also able to report that permission had been given for him to correspond with each of the thirteen seminaries and offer them help from ELT to improve the English section of their library; and that a number of church leaders wanted to negotiate for the publishing in Chinese of some of the BST titles, with print-runs of perhaps 100,000 each.

Though capitalist expansion was fast changing the traditional and economic face of China (and bringing with it a long list of social evils, from crime and corruption to environmental pollution), yet tight control rather than independent freedom, not least in matters of religion, had proved the successor to past repression:

The political structure held firm as the Chinese watched the Soviet Union collapse. The lesson of Gorbachev's fall taught Chinese leaders only that political freedoms brought chaos and disintegration. As long as they possibly could, accordingly, they would hold off from allowing such freedoms to their own people, and cling as tightly as possible to their own reins of power.[66]

The China Christian Council, recognized by the government and treading warily, was an expression of this continuing control. Nevertheless the Council had been able to invite Dr Billy Graham and his wife Ruth (herself brought up in China as the daughter of missionary parents) to pay fruitful visits during the 1980s and the early 1990s.[67] John Stott's primary invitation was to visit the four main seminaries: in Hangzhou, capital city of Zhejiang, China's smallest province; in Shanghai and Beijing (government-controlled municipalities with a combined population of some 24m) and in Nanjing, a city the size of Manchester and containing nearly as many people as Chicago. There was no shortage of believers, churches or 'meeting-places', but a great dearth of trained pastors. In Zhejiang province alone there were said to be 1,250,000 Protestant Christians and 2,400 churches. Yet the seminary had only sixty full-time students 'in austere conditions (ten students to a bedroom in bunk beds, I was told)'.[68] John Stott addressed them through an interpreter in each of the seminaries, beginning with a disarming personal introduction along these lines:

> I have come to China with feelings of great respect and humility. I think of your ancient dynasties and cultures ... long before Europe even existed. I think of your 10 million square kilometres of territory, in contrast to little England, which is a tiny, somewhat insignificant, offshore island of Europe! I think of your 1,200 million citizens, approximately one fifth of the world's population.
>
> These statistics are extremely impressive ... but I think I do not need to feel intimidated by your history, your geography, your population or your culture. For I come to you quite simply as your fellow-Christian, as your brother in Jesus Christ, indeed (at the age of 75) your older brother, for I know how much in Chinese culture old age is honoured![69]

There would then often be an exposition of Acts 2:42–47 on 'The Marks of a Renewed Church', followed by a lively period of questions. In Shanghai he was the guest of the East China Theological Seminary, where 100 students were taking a four-year course, with hundreds more engaged in 'distance learning'. At Nanjing (where the college had been local HQ to the Red Guards, who had burned almost every book in the library) the lecture on Acts was particularly well received among an élite student body drawn from all China, many of whom understood a little English:

> In the two previous lectures the students looked taciturn and stern, hardly ever smiled and never laughed, but instead maintained that inscrutable expression for which the Chinese are famous. But here in Nanjing seminary there was a lot of listener response, and I even contrived to squeeze a laugh or two out of them.

While in Nanjing John Stott and his companions were taken to see the Amity Printing Press, producing four million Chinese Bibles a year with the most advanced equipment.[70] Here too they met by appointment 'the most powerful executive authority in the Chinese church', Dr Han Wen Zao, Acting General Secretary of the China Christian Council, and found him 'open and flexible' in discussions about the possibility of translation and publication of theological textbooks, and of the BST series. In the next room, they were introduced to Bishop K. H. Ting, aged eighty-one, 'the grand old man of the Chinese Protestant Church', to whom they delivered special greetings from the Archbishop of Canterbury. John Stott was astonished to be told by Bishop Ting that he had read and enjoyed the recent interview by Roy McCloughry in *Christianity Today*.[71] At dinner that evening, sitting next to Bishop Ting, John Stott learned that while the official description of Christianity in China was still 'the opiate of the people', this Marxist definition was no longer (since 1979) regarded as adequate because of the emergence of more educated 'cultured Christians' in touch with the international Christian community.

Beijing proved at first something of a disappointment: no-one seemed to have realized that there would be no students since the seminary was shut on Saturdays. But at least this made possible a visit to the Great Wall and the so-called Forbidden City. Here as elsewhere there were significant meetings with religious leaders, a substantial programme of preaching in local churches, with public meetings (in Beijing some 2,000 assembled, some braving the cold in an open-air courtyard), the obligatory banquet or two, and in any free moment an equally arduous and determined pursuit of the local birds: perhaps the Orange-breasted Trogon or the Greater Racquet-tailed Drongo. At the end of most student sessions not only were there questions and discussion, photographs and autographs, but groups and individuals would cluster round with questions of their own:

> 'I'm a new believer,' said one, and 'I've been a believer for a month, but have not yet been baptized,' said another. Then after these

introductions a flood of questions was let loose. 'How soon should a new believer be baptized?' 'What happens if I sin again?' 'How can I learn to pray?' 'Should I give up smoking and drinking?' 'Can I pray lying on my back?' 'What should I do to succeed in the Christian life?' It was really fascinating to witness their spiritual hunger and the enthusiasm of their new-found faith.[72]

Before leaving Beijing, the small party drove round Tiananmen Square 'and paid our silent tribute to the brave students who had paid with their lives seven years before'.

Three years later, in 1999, John Stott paid a further visit to Nanjing and Shanghai, as well as to Bangkok, Taipei[73] and Hong Kong, which was by then under Chinese rule. This time the major focus was on seminars and courses for pastors and church leaders: 'A New Vision for the New Millennium'. Some ten miles outside Shanghai a Bible college had recently been opened for lay leaders and elders.

They had taken their final exam of the first term earlier that morning [wrote John Yates, who was accompanying John Stott as study assistant], so they were all sitting quietly in the chapel waiting for our arrival at 10.30. John spoke to them on 'New Timothys for the new millennium'. Most of the students were in their 20s and were very attentive to what he had to say as he stood in front of them in the unheated chapel sporting a heavy overcoat and bright red nose. Lunch in the dining hall with the students after the lecture was fun. They were especially impressed by our facility with chopsticks![74]

Characteristically, John Stott concluded the brief account of the 1996 visit which he gave in his personal newsletter with the words, 'I very much hope ... that soon we will be able to welcome a Chinese lecturer as a Langham Scholar.' Indeed, by the 1990s it was noticeable that as John Stott criss-crossed the globe from one continent to another, he was continually meeting former Langham Scholars or students, or members of one or more of the LICC courses, now in positions of Third World Christian leadership. In 1994, at Trinity Theological College in Singapore, both the Principal (John Chew) and the Dean (Simon Chan) were former Langham Scholars. In India David Samuel, Director of TAFTEE, The Association for Theological Education by Extension, was another. In Cuba the IFES worker who acted as translator had done the course on 'The Christian in the Modern World' (CMW) at the Institute, as also had a number of pastors and lay leaders whom he had last seen as students in London and now met again in Africa or Eastern Europe.

Visiting East Asia in 1999 he was able to meet again four Langham Scholars exercising influential ministries.

Among the most striking examples of those who benefited from the CMW course in its early days were Sergio and Hortensia Sánchez and Saúl and Pilar Cruz from Mexico. John Stott was able to visit Mexico City in the spring of 1992 to meet them again and see at first hand the work they were doing. He wrote in his diary:

> The former have launched 'AMEXTRA' ('the Mexican Association for Rural and Urban Transformation'), with centres in several parts of the country, while the latter have set up 'Armonía' (Spanish for 'harmony', and equivalent of the Hebrew *shalom*, the biblical vision of social peace and wellbeing), which works only in Jalalpa, one of Mexico City's worst slums. Both have arisen from an understanding of Christian 'mission' as combining evangelism and social action, especially among the poor. Both also perceive that a sense of personal powerlessness, arising from a lack of self-worth, lies at the root of many social problems, and both are therefore developing a 'participatory' principle by which the poor are encouraged to express what *they* see to be their greatest needs and to share in alleviating them.[75]

AMEXTRA had begun in 1983 in three local communities; by the time of John Stott's visit they were at work in eighty, seeking by careful listening to identify, and then respond to, each community's most pressing social problem in the name of Jesus Christ. Their efforts were towards needy Indian villages and urban Mexican neighbourhoods.

Armonía was the vision of Saúl Cruz, a clinical psychiatrist, and his wife Pilar, a teacher; a dream which finally took shape during their studies at the London Institute. The centre of this unique ministry was Jalalpa,

> ... a huge slum of approaching three million inhabitants. Their dwellings are perched on two sides of a deep ravine along which flows a river of untreated sewage, known locally as 'The Ditch'. Many have for their home no more than a shack of cardboard, and especially of waterproof milk cartons. There is no hospital to serve this vast population. There are only two schools, though perhaps 60% are children and young people. And there are no active or effective churches ...[76]

In this daunting environment Armonía shared directly in almost all the local concerns, from putting pressure on government to act over dangerous subsidence (a member of the Armonía team 'happened' to be an expert in soil science and geology) to a self-help housing programme aided by TEAR Fund; and even a kind of marriage bureau to make it possible for couples, unable to afford it otherwise, to be married and so acquire the joint legal ownership of their new homes.[77]

Here in Jalalpa John Stott left behind the imprint of his hand in wet plaster, alongside many smaller imprints, when he was enlisted as an honorary member of an Armonía youth group. He wrote in his diary:

> Another fascinating development is the group of children (from about four to seventeen) who have been enrolled as 'Muskateers' (the name having been taken from a Disney cartoon). In order to qualify, the children have to give evidence of their willingness to serve in various ways, and to promise to love God and their neighbour, to respect their own body, their family, their community and the authorities. Their motto is Psalm 133:1, 'See how good it is to live together in harmony (*armonía*)'. In the enrolment ceremony each is invested with a white apron, the badge of servitude, and then makes an imprint of the palm of his/her hands on the wet plaster of a wall.
>
> I found myself being press-ganged into honorary membership of the Muskateers, and promising with the children to 'share my toys, candy, crayons, friends, notebooks, pencils and Bible' with others!! Further promises included the pledge not to 'hit or punch' in order to settle differences, not to 'bother or tease' others, to tell the truth, to obtain good grades at school, to be clean, friendly, agreeable and co-operative! The thirty or so children who have already been enrolled are clearly very proud of it, and it seems to me a marvellous way to inculcate self-esteem, standards and a spirit of service in them.[78]

Looking back, it is clear that Saúl was being prepared long beforehand for those decisive months at the LICC. In junior high school he was given a copy of the Spanish edition of *Basic Christianity*, read it right through three times, and committed his life to Christ. Two years later at the age of fourteen he travelled over 300 miles, against his father's wishes, to meet John Stott in person:

> But, although he introduced himself, he could speak no English, so that communication was minimal. Saúl sat on the back bench during the first lecture. But, being tired and hungry, he slept throughout and afterwards hitch-hiked his return home!

Their next meeting took place in 1971, when he was seventeen and John

Stott came to give a series of addresses to the students of Compañerismo, the Mexican member movement of IFES. Saúl came up from Oaxaca by bus, and during the meetings was given a copy of the booklet TEAR Fund had commissioned, entitled *Walk in His Shoes*. He was struck by the compassion of Jesus.[79]

Before long, 'reaching out to sinners like himself, and serving the poor' became the overriding vision of Saúl's life. Again in 1976 he talked with John Stott in Mexico at the Wycliffe Bible Translators' annual conference; and in 1978, when he and Pilar were married, they both met John Stott at further conferences in connection with the work of IFES. Eight years later, while working for World Vision, Saúl read the two volumes of *Involvement* (the US edition of *Issues Facing Christians Today*); and in 1987 he and Pilar arranged to come to London to attend the CMW course at the London Institute. 'We can truly say', he testified later, 'that that was the most significant moment of definition and decision to launch the ministry of Armonía among the poor of Mexico City.'[80]

Nor has the vision diminished with the years. Armonía has plans and dreams for a school, a clinic, even a fire service. 'I was profoundly impressed by both *Armonía* and *Amextra*', John Stott wrote to his friends, 'and am anxious to do what I can to encourage and support them. Both are inspired by the compassion of Christ and seek to live out his love for the poor.'[81]

6

Many overseas visits were not so far afield. Theological conferences or consultations, for example, were often held in Europe. John Stott was in Germany in 1991 for a student conference and in 1995 to give an address at the Frankfurt Book Fair. In the summer of the following year he was there again for the conference of FEET (Fellowship of European Evangelical Theologians) and at Marburg in 1997 for the IFES Jubilee European Conference on student evangelism. Sometimes in pursuit of birds, more often in the cause of the gospel, he also visited Austria, Belgium, Czechoslovakia, France, Holland, Norway, Poland, Romania, Spain and Switzerland, as well as Russia, Siberia and the Ukraine.

More and more it was the countries of Eastern Europe and the former Communist Bloc that were on his heart. In 1997 he managed to visit the three Baltic countries of Estonia, Latvia and Lithuania, in which he had felt a personal interest since the early years of his ministry when

> ... a group of Baltic émigrés held an annual service in the newly renovated and re-opened All Souls church, in order to remember their friends and relatives enslaved and oppressed by the Soviet

Union and to pray for the liberation of their countries. Probably their faith and hope burned dimly in those days of arrogant and tyrannical Russian imperialism.[82]

In spite of *perestroika*, all was not well. The collapse of communism had left a void. What goal, what worldview, had replaced it?

Nothing has emerged yet. And Christianity does not appear to be a realistic candidate, since it is represented largely by ancient traditional churches (Orthodox, Catholic, Lutheran) which themselves lack visionary dynamism … The spiritual vacuum is there; who or what will fill it?[83]

It was therefore with a special sense of urgency and relevance that he paid these visits; in 1997 largely on behalf of Scripture Union, speaking on 'The Church and the Scriptures' and tackling questions of authority, interpretation, preaching and church life. Numbers were often small, sometimes as low as twenty-five. In Moscow his only opportunity of ministry, in what was little more than a stopover *en route* to Siberia, was an informal gathering of perhaps thirty university and professional people in the small Scripture Union regional office. Later in the year he returned to East and Central Europe, visiting Prague in what was then still the Czech Republic, Odessa in the Ukraine, Osijek in Croatia and Budapest in Hungary. Pavel Cerny had arranged the programme, which was largely given to visiting post-communist seminaries, then struggling with the urgent need of a trained ministry for the emerging churches. In Hungary John Stott was the main speaker at a two-day conference for students and pastors in the panelled hall of the Reformed Seminary, beneath the gaze of 'gold-framed, full-length portraits of earlier Reformed worthies'. 'It seemed to go well,' John Stott wrote in his diary, 'except that one of my interpreters contrived to make the translation of each sentence about four times as long as my English sentence!'[84]

This problem of translation was ever present. A few years earlier in Korea he had reflected on his experience:

Speaking by interpretation continues to seem to me a bigger communication problem than most people realise or concede, even though I have been given experienced and talented translators, and have spent up to an hour with them beforehand, going through each message. Korean seems to European ears a very difficult language. Although I have managed at the beginning of each address to please the audience with the greeting '*Anyang haseyo!*', I do not of course understand what people are saying, and many times I have felt frustrated and even disconcerted when they have carried on an animated conversation in Korean for five, ten or fifteen minutes, ignoring my presence and not thinking to tell me what they were discussing![85]

Nor was translation the only difficulty. Adequate briefing could also be a problem. The Chairman of the Korean Lausanne Committee, for example, invited John Stott to give a lecture on 'The theological, biblical and missiological implications of the Lausanne Movement' – a tall order by any standards!

This I had prepared in London [John Stott wrote in his diary], assuming that a hundred or so academics, missiologists and clergy would attend it. Imagine my horror when I arrived at the church (late because of a standstill traffic congestion) to find the church packed with some 3,000 people, all singing in a happy-clappy mood! I broke into a cold sweat. The 'lecture' I had prepared would be entirely inappropriate for such an audience. I turned to my interpreter for advice. 'Do as the Lord leads you,' he responded unhelpfully. But indeed I had no alternative but to cry in desperation to the Lord for guidance, and in the end decided to keep much of my outline, while abandoning my script in favour of a much more popular presentation *ad lib*. It is still not what I would have said if I'd been properly briefed, but at least it was more suitable than the prepared lecture would have been![86]

Before leaving South Korea, John Stott was able to visit a border post of the Demilitarized Zone, accompanied by local Christian leaders, on the fortieth anniversary of the ceasefire which ended the Korean War and sealed the fateful division of the country. Though the area was out of bounds to civilians, the small party made their way to the high wire fence which marked the beginning of the Zone:

Chaplain Kim and I both prayed, this time holding on to the fence with both hands, and crying to God that as he had broken down the dividing wall of hostility between Jews and Gentiles, so he would break down the barrier separating North and South Korea.[87]

In 1999 John Stott was again in South Korea, this time to attend the IFES World Assembly, and give his Vice-Presidential address on the theme of 'Evangelical Essentials'. Nearly 4,000 students, staff workers and board members were gathered from 135 countries. By now he was known by name, by face and reputation, and by his writings, to the worldwide

IFES membership.[88] He found himself lionized, not altogether un-pleasurably:

> On Thursday, the Assembly's penultimate day, there was a lot of
> book-signing, plus photographing. Everybody seems to have a
> camera, and there were endless permutations and combinations of
> groups, couples and individuals wanting to be pictured with 'Uncle
> John' or (less acceptably) with 'Papa Stott'![89]

Before the key IFES personnel dispersed to their home countries, John Stott had arranged to spend Saturday morning with some of them to explore the question of the continuation (perhaps in association with IFES) of the worldwide ministries he had made his own, when his travelling and speaking days were over. Not surprisingly, the desire for some degree of partnership between 'Langham' ministries and IFES was very positive. A further and more structured consultation was arranged for later in the year, the results of which belong to the next chapter.

THIRTEEN

Still in Print: Serving the Contemporary Christian

1

In October 1995 John Stott was the preacher at the Frankfurt Book Fair and chose as his theme 'Words Matter', taking his text from 2 Corinthians 4:13. 'We are meeting this weekend in Luther's country,' he reminded his congregation.

> Luther had great confidence in words. He was convinced that it was neither political intrigue, nor military might, which established the Reformation in Germany. It was *the Word*. 'I simply taught, preached, and wrote God's Word', he wrote. 'Otherwise, I did nothing ...' And in Luther's great hymn (Ein' feste Burg), which we shall sing at the end of this service, he contrasts the power of Christ and the power of the devil, adding: 'Ein Wörtlein kann ihn fällen' ('one little word will fell him').[1]

It was in this conviction that John Stott used the comparative freedom from institutional oversight, a freedom which the 1990s increasingly brought to him, in order to write. The tally for the decade would be impressive for a full-time author; but, as the previous chapters have shown, John Stott was never that. Yet these ten years saw the writing or publication of eight new books (four of them major New Testament expositions), continuous editing (for The Bible Speaks Today series and of the Lausanne documents)[2] and the revision and reissue of six or eight of his earlier works. Such output would have been impossible but for his 'happy triumvirate' of Frances Whitehead and the current study assistant.

By 1990 Todd Shy, the longest-serving among such assistants, had already been with him for two years. It fell to Todd to visit libraries (for older books, it was generally the British Library), check references, read typescripts and proofs for BST *Acts* and *Thessalonians*; but especially to help with the first revision of *Issues Facing Christians Today* in which (for example) contemporary references and statistical information needed to be brought up to date over the wide range of 'issues' explored in the book. It was painstaking and meticulous work, reading and rereading manuscript, typescript and proofs. As Todd Shy gained experience, John Stott would consult him on points of detail or interpretation, asking, 'Is this clear? Have I got the balance right?' It was not always easy for a young man only recently graduated:

> I always felt sort of incapable, but he would say, 'Tell me what you think honestly; mark anything you wish.' But I never really knew how much he really wanted you to say what you thought, or how much he just wanted a little bit of approbation, or whatever. I never could gauge the dynamic ... to be as helpful as you could, but still being honest, was always tricky.[3]

Todd Shy returned to America in the summer of 1992 and for a year John Stott managed without a study assistant. Then Nelson Gonzalez joined him in 1993, and for the next three years combined his work for John Stott with his own studies. How much John Stott valued the help of his younger assistants can be traced, at least in part, from the Prefaces of these years. Hardly a book appeared without some acknowledgment to one or more. *Issues Facing Christians Today* is a good example. The first edition (1984) thanked, among others, Steve Andrews and the '"apostolic succession' of my Study Assistants – Roy McCloughry, Tom Cooper, Mark Labberton, Steve Ingraham and Bob Wismer – who have compiled bibliographies, assembled groups for the discussion of sermon topics, gathered information and checked references'. The revised second edition (1990) added Toby Howarth and Todd Shy to this list; and the further revision of 1999 gave a deeper insight into his dependence on their labours:

> I reserve my special gratitude for John Yates, my current study

assistant. Not only has he given himself the chore of reading the book's second edition several times over, made his own insightful suggestions, and updated the statistics, but he has also followed up our consultants' proposals, done some redrafting himself and advised me which books and articles I needed to read and ponder myself.[4]

John Yates, formally John W. Yates III, succeeded Nelson Gonzalez in 1996, the son of a family John Stott had known for many years, and whose father was Rector of Falls Church, Virginia. His successor, Corey Widmer, arrived at a time when John Stott was coming to depend increasingly on his study assistant for help in travelling, especially now that (because of impaired vision in one eye) he was no longer allowed to drive.

Issues was the most recent, and perhaps the most significant, but by no means the only one of John Stott's books to be revised and reissued in the 1990s. *Your Confirmation* was another, originally written thirty years before and hardly out of print since then. Besides a revised and illustrated edition for confirmation candidates, a more general worldwide co-edition appeared under the title *Christian Basics*.[5] The revision proved surprisingly demanding; so much so that, in John Stott's words,

> I found that the world, the church and I have all changed so much that it was impossible. Instead, I have virtually had to write a new book although keeping the old outline. Because the average age of confirmation candidates in Britain is steadily rising, and more than one-third of them are now adults, I have tried to write for them.[6]

Other new editions were more straightforward, for example the revised American edition of *Understanding the Bible*, written originally for Scripture Union in 1972;[7] or his small IVP paperback of 1982, *The Bible: Book for Today*, which was reissued in America in the 1990s as *You Can Trust the Bible*.[8]

It was mainly John Stott's association with Tim Dowley and Peter Wyart, begun in 1988 with *Favourite Psalms*,[9] which introduced some of his earlier writing to a new generation. *Favourite Psalms*, a reissue of parts of *The Canticles and Selected Psalms* from the 1966 'Prayer Book Commentaries' (long out of print), was followed in the same large-size colour-illustrated format by *What Christ Thinks of the Church* (1990), an exposition of the Letters to the Seven Churches from Revelation, chapters 1 – 3.[10] First published in 1958 as part of a series, 'Preaching for Today', it had been twice reprinted in the 1950s and '60s but then unavailable for some twenty years. The new, almost 'coffee-table' format, with colour photographs of the ancient sites and a text now based on the New International Version, brought these letters to life for Christians of the 1990s. Quick to exploit demand, Tim Dowley and his small design team Three's Company (by now a partnership rather than a trio) followed this with *Life in Christ* (1991), a welcome reissue of a Fount Original, also long out of print.[11]

Last in this series of reissues was the first book John Stott ever wrote, *Men with a Message*. In this case he entrusted the task of revision to Stephen Motyer, lecturer at the London Bible College. Dr Motyer replaced the first chapter on 'The Message of Jesus' with chapters on Mark and Matthew, and added some other new material.

> The aim [he wrote, in his Preface to the book] has been to make its content accessible to further generations, by lightening the language, relating it to recent biblical scholarship, and incorporating the text into the 'user-friendly' publication format associated with the products of Three's Company. John Stott allowed me great freedom in the revision, but I felt very much at home with his emphases and analyses.[12]

Translations of John Stott's books continued to appear in a variety of scripts and languages. Occasionally small books were published of which no UK edition is available, though some were translations of addresses given in English, and perhaps first published in a report or journal.[13] In something of the same way Africa Enterprise published as a paperback the substance of six lectures given in 1988, entitled *The Lordship of Christ in South Africa*.[14] Two books offering a different kind of reprint of earlier works were also published in this decade. *Authentic Christianity* is an anthology from well over a hundred of his writings, books, articles, published addresses and contributions to symposia;[15] while in 1999, to coincide with volume one of this biography, the same publishers conceived the idea of a double volume containing reprints of two of John Stott's major works, *The Cross of Christ* and *The Contemporary Christian*.[16] Bound together in this way they made a book of 650 pages. There was some discussion between author and publishers as to the title. The publishers planned to call it *The Essential John Stott* (Macmillan had published *The Essential C. S. Lewis* ten years before),[17] a play on the word 'essential' as indicating both 'the essence of' and 'indispensable for the understanding of' their author's mind. John Stott protested. He wrote to IVP: 'The "happy triumvirate" here has reacted very negatively to the proposed title – *The Essential John Stott*. Would you consider as an alternative *The Cross and the Christian*?' But to no avail: the book appeared under the publishers' title, described as 'a double volume for a new millennium', making available for the first time *The Contemporary Christian* between hard covers as well as in paperback.

2

Since its first publication in 1984 *Issues Facing Christians Today* has been the starting-point for many groups or individuals wanting to discern a Christian mind on such diverse but pressing contemporary questions as nuclear pacifism, race relations, feminism, abortion or homosexual partnerships. On a variety of preachers' bookshelves it remained a standard work of reference. But the changing nature of such issues, and the working out of a biblical ethic in contemporary practice, present a moving target. In 1990, and again in 1999, much revising and updating were needed. John Stott reminded his friends in 1990 that

> ... six years have passed since the first edition appeared. Not only have détente and disarmament begun, but AIDS has reached epidemic proportions, the green movement has gathered momentum, and techniques of human fertilization have received wide public coverage. I have tried to offer a Christian comment on these and other issues of today.[18]

Nine years later, he had to report that 'the shape of every debate has changed', and embarked on a second revision.[19] The book (in America, two books) no longer represented the ground-breaking and pioneering study which had characterized the first two editions. It was partly a measure of its own success, and of the new engagement by evangelicals in ethical and social issues for which John Stott had so consistently called, that perceived weaknesses were (to at least one critic) almost more significant than strengths. A full-page review article in the journal *Third Way* questioned in a friendly fashion whether what the book offered could really be called 'evangelical ethics' at all, suggesting that the author's thinking owed too much to William Temple's exposition of 'the congruity between Christian and non-Christian moral reason'; and noting that 'while his contemporary range of reference is wide (from Marshall McLuhan to Demos), there is little sense of the crises of modernity: post-modernity gets a two-page appendix'.[20] Nevertheless, to many intelligent Christians and pastors wrestling with the bewildering world around them, the book offered biblical insights applied to modern problems in a way which, over the sixteen years of its life, no other similar work had yet attempted with the same breadth of interest and overriding faithfulness to Scripture.

The first edition of *Issues* had included a major section on 'Sexual

Issues', and within this a chapter on 'Homosexual Partnerships?' In writing on this theme, John Stott was well aware that he was entering a highly charged contemporary debate; and that, as with the Lausanne movement in the 1970s, or nuclear issues and peacemaking in the early 1980s, he would have to return to it continually, unable to prevent his name being drawn more and more into the discussion. The chapter sets out to address the question, 'Are homosexual partnerships a Christian option?' From the start it makes careful distinctions between homosexual orientation and physical practices – 'being' and 'doing' – and also between casual acts of promiscuity and mutually committed relationships.

The main biblical passages are examined, a page or two to each, succinct but by no means superficial (though of course whole shelves of books have been written on each). In the process the weaknesses or omissions in the treatment of this biblical material by some well-known – and some lesser-known – writers on the subject are exposed. A longer section on 'Sex and Marriage in the Bible' lays the positive groundwork for any discussion of human sexuality within the purpose of God, demonstrating that, in sum, 'the only "one flesh" experience which God intends and Scripture contemplates is the sexual union of a man with his wife, whom he recognizes as "flesh of his flesh"'.[21] Four 'contemporary arguments' are then considered, to do with Scripture and culture, creation and nature, the quality of relationships, and what the gospel means by 'acceptance'. A longer concluding section applies Paul's triad of faith, hope and love to this consideration of homosexually orientated people, with a call to abstain from homosexual practice and partnerships as a deviation from God's norm.

To this, the second edition (1990) added a new section on the Aids epidemic, primarily addressing the question of how far this represented 'the judgment of God on practising homosexual men'. After a grim survey of facts and figures, John Stott concluded:

> I think we have to answer 'yes and no'. 'No' because Jesus warned us not to interpret calamities as God's specific judgments upon evil people (Luke 13:1–5). 'No' also because AIDS victims include many women, especially faithful married women who have been infected by their unfaithful husbands, with a substantial minority of innocent haemophiliacs and children. But 'yes' in the sense that Paul meant when he wrote: 'Do not deceive yourselves; no-one makes a fool of God. A person will reap exactly what he sows' (Galatians 6:7 GNB). The fact that we reap what we sow, or that evil actions bring evil consequences, seems to have been written by God into the ordering of his moral world ... Moreover, this cause-and-effect mechanism is viewed in Scripture as one of the ways in which

God's 'wrath', that is, his just judgment on evil, is revealed (Romans 1:18–32) ... AIDS may rightly be seen, then, as 'part of God's judgment on society'.[22]

In the summer of 1993 John Stott agreed to take part in a major debate or dialogue on Christian sexual ethics with Dr John Shelby Spong, Bishop of Newark, New Jersey, since 1976. The dialogue was sponsored jointly by Regent College, Vancouver, the Vancouver School of Theology, the Anglican Diocese of New Westminster (which includes Vancouver), Christ Church Cathedral and the Langham Trust. Neither the subject nor his fellow-participant was of John Stott's choosing. When a public debate or dialogue had been proposed for his visit to Vancouver, he had in mind the theme of 'Issues of Life and Death', about which he had been speaking recently, and on this provisional basis agreed to take part.

> Some time later, however [he recalled in his diary of the visit], I received a call from Michael Ingham, the Dean, suggesting a change of topic. He had discovered that Bishop Spong would be in Vancouver at the time, and would I be willing to have with him not so much a point-scoring 'debate' as a 'discussion' on 'Christian Sexual Ethics Today'? I asked for twenty-four hours in which to reflect, called Harry Robinson for advice, and decided to go ahead, although proposing 'dialogue' as a better and more precise word than either 'debate' or 'discussion'. He and I were to be given twenty-five minutes each to make our own independent statement (having tossed a coin in the Vestry to determine who would go first), followed by five minutes each in which to critique one another's position. Then there would be about twenty minutes for questions from the floor, concluding with five minutes each in which to sum up. It certainly seemed a fair and potentially productive structure.[23]

John Spong was well known for the passionate liberalism of his convictions. He describes in his autobiography how in the 1960s, following his courageous stand on civil rights as Rector of Tarboro, North Carolina,

> ... the Ku Klux Klan decided that the time had come to hold a countywide rally in a field just outside of Tarboro, where they could burn a cross with impunity. I was denounced at this rally as public enemy number one of the KKK in Edgecombe County. It was among my highest compliments. A program of character assassination was also begun by this hate-filled organization. The

common wisdom of the mentality present in the Klan assumed that there were only two possible reasons that a white man would assist what was at that time called 'the Negro cause'. Either he had some 'nigger blood' in him or else he had a Negro mistress.[24]

Because the Rector's pale skin made the first improbable, the KKK worked assiduously to suggest the second as a means to destroy his reputation and influence. By the 1990s, however, Bishop Spong was better known for his stand on homosexual issues. The *British Columbia Report* made detailed reference to this in their account of the debate:

> Ordaining homosexuals brought the bishop of the diocese of Newark, New Jersey, to national prominence in the United States. In December 1989 he caused a furore when he became the first bishop to ordain a gay priest. In 1990, in a national assembly, the bishops of the Episcopal Church condemned Bishop Spong for violating a church policy prohibiting the ordination of non-celibate gays.
>
> Bishop Spong has ordained three gay priests to date and has sixteen gay, lesbian or bisexual priests in his diocese. The sixty-two-year-old cleric also favours abortion, the ordination of women and the blessing of homosexual relationships.[25]

In a recent book, Bishop Spong had described his upbringing in a devoutly Christian home, and himself as one who, raised as a biblical fundamentalist, had had 'a lifetime love affair' with the Bible: 'there was for me no authority beyond the affirmation "the Bible says"'.[26] But he went on to write of how he became 'disillusioned with the literal Bible'; and how this 'rethinking of the meaning of Scripture' led him to some speculations and conclusions startlingly at variance with an orthodox, let alone an evangelical, view. It was going to be difficult to debate from any agreed biblical premise with one who saw passages in the Gospels as portraying Jesus of Nazareth 'as narrow-minded, vindictive, and even hypocritical', and 'guilty of what we today would surely call anti-semitism'; or believed that, looking at the evidence of Acts and the New Testament letters, 'nothing else accounts for this data as well as the possibility that Paul was a gay male'.[27] Even more explicit were the conclusions reached in his earlier book, *Living in Sin?*, in which he asserted that 'the Bible presents us with ambiguous, contradictory, and sometimes absolutely unacceptable standards for making sexual judgments today'; and urged his readers to abandon their prejudice and 'the prejudice of Holy Scripture'.[28]

On the evening of 7 July 1993 some 1,300 to 1,600 people (published estimates differ) crowded into Christ Church Cathedral, 'with another

300 turned away at the door'.[29] John Stott found himself seated at a table in the nave, facing the usual battery of microphones and lighting for TV and video-recording. On his right was the moderator of the debate, Dr Maxine Hancock, an English scholar and Canadian TV personality; and beyond her, Dr Spong.[30] John Stott had feared that the local homosexual lobby might turn up in force and disrupt the meeting; but in fact he was given an attentive hearing.

Following a disarming introduction listing five disabilities ('A Brit ... male ... single ... seventy-two years old ... a church member'), John Stott began his twenty minutes by celebrating human sexuality and love-making, drawing on the Song of Songs and New Testament teaching. Next he moved on from 'Celebration' to 'Limitation': 'The same God who created sex, also established the context of sex, namely marriage.'[31] And marriage, defined in Genesis 2:24, in words later endorsed by Jesus himself, is monogamous and heterosexual, the loving union of one man and one woman. Thirdly, under the heading 'Liberation', John Stott spoke of the gospel as good news of a new beginning. For a humanity fallen short of God's standard for human sexuality, 'rest, freedom and joy are to be found, not in discarding the yoke of Christ, but in submitting to it'. And the gospel speaks, he concluded, not only of good news for individuals but of a new community; and at the last, a new world.

He did not seek to defend the church's record. Having spoken of 'a new community characterized by love', he quickly added:

Do I hear someone beginning to snigger, because you say the church as you know it is far from being a community of love? You have found it unsympathetic, judgmental, dismissive, homophobic. I know. It's true. Some churches *are* like that. And we need deeply to repent that any church of Jesus Christ could be like that. But there are other churches, you know, that are authentic communities of love – welcoming, caring, compassionate and supportive.

Again, as the Church of England bishops say, homosexual people are in every way as valuable to and valued by God as heterosexual people, and should find the church to be a community of love. Now that doesn't mean that the church should give its approval to the homosexual lifestyle. If we genuinely love people we will want to help them to attain God's standards and to obey God's will and we shall not want to encourage them to break these standards or defy his will. So the church is the community of righteousness as well as love, called both to a prophetic witness to monogamous, hetero-sexual marriage and also to a ministry of pastoral compassion towards those who cannot attain these standards.

Then it was Dr Spong's turn. He, too, eased himself into his stride with a playful introduction: 'John, I'm sorry you come with so many liabilities. I do want you to know that I am married to a Brit. and it is wonderful. Here she sits ...' Soon, however, he took up the theme of the oppression of women and how 'the Bible was quoted time and again to prove that that's the way God intended it to be'. He declared:

But I also come before this audience as a committed Christian. I come as one who cherishes the Bible. I come as one who has made the study of the Bible the primary work of my entire life. Every book I have written, including even my book on sexual ethics, is in the final analysis nothing but a book about the Bible. I speak also as one who loves the Bible so much I am not willing to stand by idly while the Bible is used as a weapon to defend the sexist definitions and stereotypes of yesterday, and to justify a blatant homophobia toward gay and lesbian people.

Before long this had to be qualified: 'A Bible that reflects tribal, racial, nationalistic, and sexual prejudices needs to be confronted.' This confrontation did not hesitate to say of part of Paul's first letter to Timothy: 'This is not the word of the Lord. These are the words of a first century man locked inside the cultural definitions of his day, and trying to support his prejudices by an appeal to God.' Many sections of Scripture, New Testament as well as Old, received similar treatment, from Genesis, Exodus and Leviticus to the Pauline letters. And so to the issue of homosexuality:

Let me be quite specific. I regard homosexuality as a given, not a chosen; as a minority but perfectly normal position on the human sexual scale, not as an abnormality; and as an enriching part of the human experience ...

John Stott, as he sat listening, noted the bishop's skill in advocacy and his powers of passionate communication (Dr Spong was a former radio sports announcer). He also found it difficult to pin down the main areas of disagreement in this diffuse and fast-talking presentation, strong in fervour and conviction, lacking in linear logic. He chose three points to be the subject of his five-minute response; that though the world's view on ethical issues may have changed, Christians are not bound to agree with it; that in Bishop Spong's treatment of Scripture 'he is guilty of a great deal of selectivity'; and finally that 'if we genuinely desire to be submissive to our Lord Jesus Christ, we cannot treat his teaching in the cavalier way in which I fear that Bishop Spong is doing'.

By way of his response, Dr Spong returned to his attack on parts of the biblical record; and again made reference to an issue on which he has long been a campaigner:

He [John Stott] talked about monogamous marriage. I favour monogamous marriage with every part of my being. I understand and I appreciate the phrase, 'what God has joined together, let no one put asunder'. I intend to be monogamously married to the most wonderful woman in the world, and I covet that relationship of faithful monogamy for all of God's people, including God's gay and lesbian children.

Questions followed, to which both participants responded: and to conclude the evening each was given a further five minutes for 'closing comments'. John Stott used his to share his anxiety about what the audience had heard during the evening of the treatment of Scripture:

But if you are scrupulous in your use of proper principles of the biblical interpretation, far from manipulating and controlling Scripture, you'll find that Christ as Lord controls you, your thinking and your living, through the Scriptures. That is, I think, the area that we need to develop.

Then, to his surprise, he found that Bishop Spong used his final five minutes to read from a prepared statement, introducing new points of argument, and ending with an impassioned appeal, so placing John Stott (according to his diary) 'at a considerable disadvantage' as the evening came to an end. So strongly did he feel this that when the editor of *Crux* proposed to carry a transcript of the debate, John Stott wrote and asked to be allowed, in writing, a brief further response. This was agreed, and prefaced by the following editorial statement:

The editor noted during the dialogue that Bishop Spong read from a prepared statement during his closing remarks, a statement which did introduce new points of argument. According to standard debating procedures, this would be ruled out of order. Thus, in fairness to Dr Stott, the following appendix is attached.

The appendix itself, only some 500 words or so, speaks of three major presuppositions in the field of Christian sexual ethics. The first is about creation, God's intentions for human life: 'When Paul described certain kinds of sexual behaviour as either "natural" (*phusikos*) or "unnatural" (*para phusin*), he was not referring to individual orientation but to God's created order.' The second was about self-control, in reply to the Bishop's suggestion that with earlier puberty, it is unrealistic to expect chastity before marriage. 'It is part of the glory of our humanness', John Stott replied, that we are capable of moral choice and control; while as Christians we experience God's grace, with self-control as a fruit of the Spirit. Finally, he spoke of God's love, seeking not necessarily the immediate gratification of his children, but their highest good.

Bishop Spong, as might be expected, took considerable exception to John Stott's printed postscript to the debate; and in due course said as much in a detailed and bitter account of his own treatment at the hands of evangelicals, published in his diocesan newspaper.[32] As soon as a copy reached him, John Stott replied in an eirenic personal letter, setting out the grounds on which he felt Bishop Spong had overstepped the accepted rules of debate. A considerable correspondence followed, apparently to little effect beyond what John Stott expressed in his final letter of the series: 'I think the nature and extent of our disagreements has been clarified.'[33]

Listeners who were present in Christ Church Cathedral on that July evening will hardly have been in doubt about the nature and extent of the disagreement between the participants. But because of the lack of any shared basis of presuppositions it could not be called a very satisfactory or productive debate. Bishop Spong's views were already well known. John Stott had at least been able to offer an exposition of traditional Christian sexual ethics firmly rooted in Scripture. 'In all evangelism,' he wrote once, 'I find it a constant encouragement to say to myself, "The other person's conscience is on my side".'[34] Perhaps the same thought could be applied to some of the congregation in Christ Church Cathedral that July evening, striving to gain a clearer view of God's purposes through the clouded waters of the debate.

Though John Stott remained unsatisfied with his own courageous part in the encounter, this was by no means a general assessment. Harry Robinson wrote to him a week later to say,

> It seems to have been a tremendous encouragement to the brethren:
> I think a lot of lay people very much needed the dialogue in order
> to understand clearly what the issues are and how they are
> understood ... I was quite overwhelmed at the thought of the
> personal cost to you engaging in such a dialogue. To have the
> intellectual ability, the physical strength and the emotional stability
> required by such an encounter was a wonderful example of the grace
> of God in your life.[35]

Michael Ingham, Dean of the Cathedral, reflected on the evening in the

Canadian *Anglican Journal*. He took the ingenuous position that 'from my point of view, both speakers were correct, given that the Bible is in different use by these two men'.[36] John Stott put his finger on the point when, writing to the Dean after his return home, he urged that the next such debate should be on the authority and interpretation of Scripture.[37] Without a greater measure of agreement here, debates on Christian ethical issues were unlikely to see productive engagement.

The Regent College journal *Crux*, which carried the transcript of the debate, included in the next issue three reflections on it; one by Dr Maxine Hancock as moderator, and two by members of the Faculty. Dr Hancock noted how, in contrast to John Stott's 'reasoned and somewhat dispassionate presentation', Dr Spong was able to engage (some would say manipulate) the audience at the level of their emotions, in a way that was 'fundamentally rhetorical':

> ... that is, he used specific techniques for controlling the responses of his audience, for eliciting at least partial agreement with him, and for suppressing intellectual opposition to his arguments. Whether he used these devices intuitively, with a master's sense of how to manage an audience, or calculatingly is not ours to judge and is beside the point of this analysis. The net effect, either way, was the same. Stott's delivery was directed primarily to the minds of his listeners, Spong's to their emotions.[38]

Her conclusion sums up at once some of the strengths and weaknesses of the debate:

> In the face of the emotional appeal of Spong's skilled rhetoric, Stott's blunt and even waspish honesty was certainly less immediately attractive. Nonetheless, his analytic clarity of thought provided, finally, what was the breakthrough point of the entire debate, the point at which the discussion could indeed move beyond polarization into thoughtful and Spirit-led discussion.

This 'breakthrough point' was the plea for a way forward based on agreed hermeneutical principles, the same point that John Stott had made in his letter to the Dean.

No doubt it was with this unsatisfactory debate still in his mind that John Stott turned, a few years later, to the revision of his chapter in *Issues* on the theme of homosexual partnerships. 'Same-sex partnerships?' was the new title of chapter 16, a subject which continued to be a storm-centre of controversy in many churches of the Anglican Communion. It was already foreseen that such partnerships would be a major topic of the

1998 Lambeth Conference. Besides the change of title, John Stott added new material to the chapter. Current statistics were cited to show the small size of the homosexual minority: 'less than 2% of the male population, and less than 1% of the female, are exclusively homosexual in inclination and practice'.[39] There were also responses to more recent publications, such as 'Michael Vasey's sincere but misguided attempt … to combine evangelical faith with homosexual advocacy';[40] and also to the 1991 statement by the Church of England House of Bishops, *Issues in Human Sexuality.*

Because the Lambeth Conference was to meet in the summer of 1998, and *New Issues* would not be published until the following year, it was arranged to publish chapter 16 separately in advance. It made a small book of fifty-five pages, and carried a striking commendation from the Archbishop of Canterbury.[41] At Richard Bewes's request, John Stott preached in All Souls on this theme, drawing on material from the revised chapter 16. He began, not with the biblical passages generally cited (and therefore much disputed) which he expounded and defended in the book, but with God's purpose for human sexuality revealed in the creation ordinance of marriage. Nearly 1,000 cassettes of the recorded sermon were sent by Richard Bewes and All Souls to the bishops and archbishops of the Anglican Communion across the world.

As was predicted, the debate on this issue at the Lambeth Conference was an uncomfortable one:

> The venomous hostility to some of the Lambeth resolutions by some bishops and journalists was, and continues to be, disturbing. The particular issue giving rise to the most heated responses was that of human sexuality and the debate about the practice of homosexuality. In the event, the Anglican bishops worldwide voted very heavily for a pastorally charitable but ethically clear conservative view, to maintain the catholic and evangelical tradition that sex is for men and women who are in the relationship of marriage. People who are caught up in the problem of having same sex desire were affirmed as people in the church, but not given permission to break the Christian ethic.[42]

Though the Conference has no legislative authority, this remained the decisive view of Anglicanism, prayerfully arrived at, in the light of much open discussion, and informed by reliance upon Scripture.

Perhaps there will always be those who disagree and take matters into their own hands.[43] Bishop Spong used his final presidential address to his diocesan convention to describe Lambeth '98 as 'the most disillusioning experience of his whole ministry' and to declare the office of Archbishop of Canterbury tragically weakened by its present occupant. The *Church Times* set his speech in context by reporting how,

> … during his episcopate, Newark had been 'open to the gifts of self-accepting, out-of-the-closet gay and lesbian clergy'. Gay or lesbian clergy were now in charge of 20 congregations. Other openly gay clergy were serving as assistants and as the heads of special diocesan ministries. Two of the core staff were homosexual, the Bishop said.[44]

A note in the editorial of the same issue described how before the Lambeth Conference Bishop Spong had published on the Internet a series of personal theses, 'appearing to deny most of the historic tenets of Christianity'. Perhaps it had therefore been unrealistic to suppose that in the course of a single evening John Stott could engage him in productive dialogue; nevertheless, orthodox morality had been publicly defended.

Between the first and second revisions of *Issues* came the publication of what was described as 'a companion volume', entitled *The Contemporary Christian*.[45] 'Double listening is painful,' John Stott had written in *Issues*,[46] referring to the need to listen carefully to what feminists were saying on women's issues, and equally to listen to what Scripture has to say. Now in this new book he applied the principle more generally, with major sections on the gospel, the disciple, the Bible, the church and the world. On the proven principle of writing what he had first preached, or made the subject of lectures followed by questions and discussion, some of this was the fruit of earlier preparation for addresses and lecture-series in different parts of the world.[47] Dr James Packer reviewed the book for *Christianity Today*, describing it as 'a pastoral essay, a sermon on paper aimed at changing people'; and, more succinctly, as 'vintage Stott':

> In it, as usual, we find him digesting and deploying a wide range of material with a symmetry matching that of Mozart, a didactic force like that of J. C. Ryle, and a down-to-earth common sense that reminds one of G. K. Chesterton. So the book is an expository treat.[48]

Not all critics were so appreciative. The *Church Times* reviewer, Peter Forster, felt that in this book 'Stott remains open to a charge of neo-fundamentalism' and that 'it contains far too many half-grasped nettles', giving as an example the relationship between the author's discussion of the quest for community and love, 'and the actual experience many have of Evangelical Christianity as moralistic and judgmental'.[49]

Perhaps this was to mistake what James Packer readily discerned: the pastoral nature of the book. A vicar describing himself as an Anglo-

Catholic wrote to thank John Stott for it ('so excellently unfolding the paradox and tensions of being a Christian today') and added a graceful compliment: 'I think it was Newman in *The Idea of a University* who said that the qualities of teacher and scholar are seldom found in the same person. The Lord has very much used you to combine the two.'[50]

3

A continuing preoccupation throughout the 1990s, in John Stott's programme of writing, was his desire to see the New Testament volumes of The Bible Speaks Today (BST) series completed. As editor, he was in correspondence with one contributor or more almost month by month throughout these years: with Donald English, President of the Methodist Conference 1990–91 (the Gospel of Mark, 1992); with Bruce Milne in Canada (the Gospel of John, 1993); with Dick Lucas and Christopher Green (2 Peter and Jude, 1995). *The Message of Matthew* presented particular difficulties. John Stott had tried Michael Green without success; and then had high hopes that Mutava Musyimi, Minister of Nairobi Baptist Church, would prove the right choice; but additional responsibilities as General Secretary of the National Christian Council of Kenya made it impossible for him to continue and in 1994 he agreed to be released. A fresh start had to be made with a new author and, to the pleasure of both editor and publishers, Roy Clements, Minister of Eden Baptist Church, Cambridge, already well known as an able pastor, scholar and writer, agreed to take it on with the help of Peter Comont, one of his assistants. But this too proved fruitless when in the summer of 1999, with the work half done, Roy Clements withdrew from his church and other Christian activities following a crisis in his personal life. *The Message of Matthew*, the one missing volume in the BST New Testament series as the century ended, was finally contributed by Michael Green, John Stott's original choice of author.

Editing the series was no sinecure, even with able and willing authors. John Stott's attention to detail, in preserving the uniform nature and purpose of the series, was proverbial. There would be praise: 'I believe this is going to be a very fine book.' Then a concern that the text, in this place or that, might be more 'reader-friendly': 'I advise you to add more full stops, breaking long sentences into two, and more commas ...' Next perhaps would come advice on the number of biblical references: 'the test might be whether you realistically hope your readers will turn to them'. The letter might include a discussion of the balance between too colloquial and too literary a style, illustrated by examples from the draft manuscript; and, to conclude, perhaps thirty or forty detailed questions and comments on individual paragraphs, sentences or expressions.[51]

As the decade began, John Stott found himself committed to contribute no fewer than four titles to the series, covering six New Testament books, Acts and Romans among them. Back in the summer of 1983, when he was working on *Issues*, Dick Lucas visited him at The Hookses, and was even then 'urging John to forget about *Issues* and give us a good commentary on Acts'.[52] When, seven years later, *The Message of Acts* appeared, John Stott explained his aim in writing it:

> I have tried to do what commentaries tend not to do, which is face questions of contemporary application. I am not thinking only of charismatic phenomena (the baptism of the Spirit, glossolalia, and the occurrence of signs and wonders), but also whether, for example, the economic sharing of the Jerusalem church, the unusual accompaniments of Saul's conversion and the apostle Paul's missionary methods are meant to be replicated in our experience today.[53]

Though the learning is worn lightly, a characteristic of the book is the breadth of reading behind it. One reviewer, after some high praise, added, 'This is not to say that I think the book is perfect ... I am sure many readers will find Stott's careful refutation of liberal scholars unnecessary and tedious.' But this was quickly answered by a correspondent in the next issue:

> I wish to assure your reviewer that neither this reader nor his wife find such passages in the commentary in the least tedious. My wife teaches RE to 'A' level. In that capacity she has to cope with liberal criticism and constantly laments the lack of evangelical books which deal with it ... Nor is her case unique. We are personally acquainted (as must be many of your readers) with cases of promising young people who went to college to study theology, biblical studies or to train as teachers, only to find their faith undermined, if not totally destroyed, by liberal arguments ... So please do not dismiss Stott's efforts as tedious and unnecessary, but rather thank God that at least one evangelical theologian has tried to grapple with the problem.[54]

Only a year after *The Message of Acts* came *The Message of Thessalonians*: 'these letters reveal the authentic Paul ... we can hear his heart-beat and see his tears'.[55] As the Preface explains, they offer revealing insights into the life of a local church: 'its continuous evangelism, pastoral care, ethical standards, reciprocal fellowship, public worship, obedience to apostolic teaching, and future hope'.[56] For this reason the sub-title chosen was

Preparing for the Coming King, and the US title, *The Gospel and the End of Time*.

Over twenty years before, John Stott had launched the BST series with his exposition of 2 Timothy, *Guard the Gospel*. In 1996 he contributed his final volume, this time on 1 Timothy and Titus, with the US title *Guard the Truth*. The story of his recurring engagement with the Pastoral Epistles all through his ministry is set out in the Author's Preface, which goes on to show how 'contemporary culture is being overtaken and submerged by the spirit of post-modernism' and its offspring, pluralism; and how by contrast Paul's concern is with the eternal and unchanging truth, that it may be faithfully guarded and handed on. It was, for an author now in his mid-seventies, a theme close to his heart but not without its difficulties.

> I've been battling on with 1 Timothy [he wrote from The Hookses], and am now a third of the way through, having completed three chapters out of nine. You can imagine the hard time I had with 1 Timothy 2:11–15, feeling Dick Lucas looking over my left shoulder, Jim Packer over my right, and (if only I had three shoulders!) the liberal feminists on and over the whole of my back. If only one could see things simplistically as an either-or, or as an unqualified 'yes' or 'no' to women presbyters! But I've tried to retain my integrity and ask what Paul really was affirming and prohibiting! The result is (of course) much too long, and too involved.[57]

Readers of his final published version will see that he finds space to preface his exposition with a discussion of hermeneutical principles, and the place of cultural transposition in determining what these verses mean in the life of the church today. Yet in spite of the author's struggles, and much 'pain in the mind', he is not able to offer 'a slick solution to all our questions about sexual roles'. Perhaps the book would be of less value had he claimed to do so. In the celebrated words of John Robinson, pastor to the Pilgrim Fathers, in 1620: 'The Lord has more truth yet to break forth out of his holy word.'[58]

Two years earlier, however, between the volumes on *1 Timothy* and *Thessalonians*, John Stott contributed to the BST series its longest volume, and arguably its most important: *The Message of Romans: God's Good News for the World*. It had originally been planned, with more optimism than realism, for 1986.[59] He confessed to 'what could be termed a "love-hate" relationship' with Romans:

> It began soon after my conversion, with chapter 6 and my longing

to experience that 'death to sin' which it seemed to promise. I toyed for many years with the fantasy that Christians are supposed to be as insensitive to sin as a corpse is to external stimuli. My final deliverance from this chimera was sealed when I was invited to give the Keswick Convention 'Bible readings' on Romans 5 – 8 in 1965, which were subsequently published under the title *Men Made New.*[60]

'Bash' was of course John Stott's mentor and pastor at the time of his conversion and (with increasing detachment but unswerving friendship) until Bash's last years. Bash himself was fascinated with Romans 6, and often quoted it in prayer and conversation. He explained 'dead to sin' (verse 7) by the analogy of a dead dog in the gutter. A touch of the foot would show if it was only sleeping: it would instantly respond where a dead dog would not. Similarly, to be dead to sin meant to be unresponsive to it. John Stott would look back on this over the intervening years. He recalled:

> Bash was not satisfied with his own teaching. He liked the illustration (it was easy for boys to understand); but he knew that it wasn't true to experience, whether his own or anybody else's. The plain hard fact is that Christians are not insensitive to the approach of sin. On the contrary, temptation is real and can be strong. We are not invulnerable to it. The problem of how to exegete Romans 6 remained.

In his 1965 Keswick Bible readings John Stott had grasped the nettle represented by Bash's interpretation, which was generally held in many evangelical circles, showing it to be contrary to experience.[61] From this, he went on to give a rather different meaning to the phrase, based in part on the way Paul applies it both to Christ himself (verse 10) and to believers (verses 2, 11) in the same paragraph. In this interpretation, Paul is writing in terms of sin's penalty, as being the essential relationship between sin and death. 'We have both', John Stott argues (that is, both Jesus and ourselves), 'died to sin in the sense that in Christ we have borne its penalty. Consequently our old life has finished; a new life has begun.'[62]

In writing about Romans 6, John Stott was able to draw heavily on *Men Made New*, but when he came to chapter 7, he was to treat it rather differently from his exposition of thirty years before. The crux comes in verses 15–17, and concerns the identity of the 'I' who confesses his enslavement and cries out for deliverance: 'What a wretched man I am! Who will rescue me from this body of death?' (verse 24). In 1966 John Stott had taken the Reformers' view that Paul was describing his experience

... as a Christian man, who knows the will of God, loves it, wants it, yearns to do it, but who finds that still *by himself* he cannot do it. His whole being (his mind and his will) is set upon the will of God and the law of God. He longs to do good. He hates to do evil – hates it with a holy hatred. And if he does sin, it is against his mind, his will, his consent; it is against the whole tenor of his life. Herein lies the conflict of the Christian.[63]

He goes on to outline anew the alternative position, that Paul's cry is that of an unregenerate man: 'the human being in Adam, not in Christ';[64] before confounding the reader (already wrestling with two different interpretations) with the uncompromising statement: 'There is an inherent contradiction here, which makes both extreme positions unacceptable.'

John Stott's 'change of mind'[65] over this passage is seen most clearly in the tentative suggestion that this 'I' is an Old Testament believer (Romans 7, as Bishop Handley Moule pointed out, makes no reference to the Holy Spirit), perhaps 'typical of many Jewish Christians of Paul's day, regenerated but not liberated, under the law and not yet in or under the Spirit'.[66] Finally, in this section, John Stott applies these verses to some who 'today might be termed "Old Testament Christians" ... they are like Lazarus when he first emerged from the tomb, alive but still bound hand and foot'.

Paul's letter to the Romans covers much ground beyond these intractable chapters. Wrath and grace, Jews and Gentiles, church and state, the 'already and the not yet', are all considered in this highly compressed apostolic 'spiritual trumpet' (as Chrysostom described the letter sixteen centuries ago). Though John Stott's study of the book went back to the days of his conversion, his work on *The Message of Romans* required much fresh reading and could not be hurried. It was his major writing commitment of 1992, he told his former curate, Denis Shepheard. 'You are kind to enquire about Romans', he wrote to a former study assistant, in a letter from The Hookses that December:

I expect you know about the bomb which Professor E. P. Sanders has tossed into Pauline studies. So I've been struggling with his thesis about Palestinian Judaism. But I've now begun to write. A huge task still lies before me. I'm specially praying for the ability to bring Romans within reach of the busy pastor and the educated lay person, – i.e. *one* volume (unlike Cranfield, Dunn, Moo, Hodge, Murray, Haldane etc., – not to mention Lloyd-Jones' *nine* volumes!) and *readable / simple*, though without sacrificing integrity.[67]

Through most of 1993 *Romans* remained high on his agenda. He told his friends that, following his return from South Korea, 'I spent all the time I could on Romans. Since it is a storm centre of contemporary controversy, in which old traditions are facing new challenges, I have found my studies at times a painful struggle.'[68] But not quite all the time: for alongside that should be placed an earlier letter from The Hookses in the days of pondering, praying and studying, before starting on his manuscript. 'Here I am,' he wrote, 'wallowing, immersed, submerged (though not yet drowned!) in Paul's great, glorious, though sometimes arcane, text. What a joyful privilege!'[69]

4

Two further books, both published in the final year of the decade, were each in the nature of a swan-song for the passing millennium and perhaps proleptically for the author also. It was time to look to a future whose leadership would be in other hands. It was in this spirit that, over a period of a few months during 1998, he wrote his *Evangelical Truth: A Personal Plea for Unity*. He confessed:

As I approach the end of my life on earth, and as this year I complete sixty years of privileged Christian discipleship, I would like to leave behind me, as a kind of spiritual legacy, this little statement of evangelical faith, this personal appeal to the rising generation.[70]

When he was called on at NEAC '77 to answer the question 'What is an evangelical?' John Stott chose to do so, in the very limited time and space available, in terms of Bible and gospel:

For the Bible witnesses to Christ, as Christ witnessed to the Bible. And the Gospel is the good news about Christ and it is Christ who sends us into the world to preach it. So in the end what matters most of all to an evangelical is not a label, nor an epithet. It is not a party ticket; it is not even in the end the Bible and the Gospel. It is the honour and glory of Jesus Christ which are bound up in the Bible and the Gospel.[71]

Twenty years on, he chose a trinitarian approach to evangelical truth, based on the revelation of God, the cross of Christ and the ministry of the Holy Spirit. To those who might ask, 'What is specially evangelical in that?', the book offers three disclaimers: that the evangelical faith is not an innovation, or a deviation from Christian orthodoxy, or a synonym for fundamentalism.[72] The trinitarian chapters follow, beginning with an account of God's self-revelation as the unshakeable ground of Christian truth and how 'the four major pillars of Enlightenment confidence are all crumbling', its bubble pricked by postmodernity, which is itself 'the sworn enemy of claims to absolute truth'. But amid this clash of titans, Christians still argue that truth is truth, and that 'Scripture is the sceptre by which King Jesus reigns'.[73] The book concludes (apart from a brief Postscript) with what the sub-title promised, a plea for evangelical integrity, stability, truth, unity and endurance.[74] Though the author might disclaim the comparison, it is difficult at moments not to be reminded of Paul's farewell to the Ephesian elders in Acts 20.

Those aware of John Stott's difficulties with neo-Pentecostal evangelicalism will find that his 'plea for unity' embraces and affirms the evangelicalism found within much of the charismatic movement without abandoning his reservations; reservations expressed, for example, back in the 1960s in *Baptism and Fullness* with its theological critique of charismatic teaching and exposition.[75] He wrote in 1999:

> On the one hand, there is the recognition that pentecostalism is today the fastest-growing Christian movement in the world, providing abundant evidence of God's blessing upon it. On the other hand, there is genuine anxiety that it is often growth without depth, so that there is much superficiality everywhere. My personal conviction is that what unites evangelicals in our doctrine and experience of the Holy Spirit is considerably greater than what divides us, and my concern in this chapter is to concentrate on the former while not concealing the latter.[76]

Yet such divisions continued to trouble him, exacerbated from time to time by new (and occasionally sensational) manifestations. Writing to Billy Graham in 1995 ('What a joy to see Cliff, and Franklin too, recently in All Souls!'), John Stott confided:

> Though there is much to thank God for in the current scene, there is also much which seriously troubles Richard [Bewes] and me, and others of our perspective – not least the rapid spread of anti-intellectual 'charismania', focussed at the moment on the Toronto phenomena.[77]

To those who sought his counsel, he would do his best to give substance to these misgivings. He wrote to a correspondent in New Zealand not personally known to him:

Although I never feel it appropriate to criticize other people's claimed experiences of God, and I am prepared to be something of a Gamaliel in regard to Toronto, I nevertheless have some grave hesitations.

First, it is an avowedly anti-intellectual movement. One of the first promoters said: 'Don't analyse; don't ask questions; simply receive.' I think that advice is both foolish and dangerous.

Secondly, I am dismayed that, so far as I know, charismatic leaders have not disassociated themselves from the animal noises which some Toronto people have been making, roaring like lions, barking like dogs etc. The whole Bible tells us not to behave like animals.

Thirdly, there is no biblical basis for uncontrollable laughter. In addition, the main characteristic of true revival has been weeping rather than laughing.

Fourthly, there are a few examples in Scripture of people falling down, but they have invariably fallen on their faces after a vision of the majesty and holiness of God. This is quite different from the Toronto phenomenon ...

To a friend in Africa, contemplating a visit to Toronto to meet 'the blessing' at first hand, he elaborated on some of these points. He regretted 'the wrong-headed lust for the spectacular and the physical', and added:

The idea of travelling to Toronto in order to 'get the blessing' is very strange. It's a return to the Old Testament (God's localized presence in Jerusalem) or a Roman Catholic practice (pilgrimages to holy places). But we believe that the Holy Spirit has universalized the presence of Jesus, and that God has pledged himself to his people, wherever they are, not to places or buildings. We live in the era foretold by Jesus when worshippers will worship neither on Mt Gerizim nor on Mt Sion but 'in Spirit and in truth' (John 4:23ff.).[18]

And though the charismatic emphasis of the work based on Holy Trinity, Brompton, and the spectacularly popular Alpha course, fell far short of the extremes of Kansas or Toronto, John Stott was able to express to some of the leaders his misgivings about aspects of their teaching, notably his feeling that the teaching on the experience of the Holy Spirit which Alpha promoted appeared to him contrived, leading people to the expectation of the miraculous; whereas (in healing, for example) God's activity today is primarily as God of nature and history rather than of miracle. Nor was it only with leaders in the charismatic churches that he engaged in dialogue, personal or public. He talked with pioneers in the

Restoration movement (and debated some of their principles with his friend Gerald Coates, in a session at the London Institute in the summer of 1988). He spoke too, on different occasions, with some of the committee of the Anglican group Reform, making the point that most of their platform beliefs are common to nearly all evangelicals, the inadmissibility of the ordination of women being the exception.

> I do not myself believe that the present situation is new [he wrote]: I do not agree with the dogmatic statements which have been made about the ordination of women, namely that it is 'plainly contrary to Scripture'. It is nothing of the kind. The issues are much more subtle and complex, and involve the whole area of cultural transposition. I find myself personally in reaction against excessive evangelical dogmatism, and therefore against what I hear *Reform* people saying.[79]

He regretted that the founders had not talked in detail with CEEC before launching a new movement likely to weaken the evangelical cause by further division, and added, 'the resort to violence (and quota-capping comes under this heading) is always a confession of failure'. Nevertheless, in spite of these uncompromising comments, he had a personal sympathy for Reform on most of the doctrinal issues which concerned them; and indeed attended their first Swanwick Conference as a mark of solidarity.

How far this 'plea for unity' will be heeded, coming from an elder statesman less well known to many British evangelicals than to their parents, only the future can show. But there is no question, looking backwards, as to what such a tradition of leadership has helped to achieve for evangelicals within the Church of England:

> The fact that they have remained *in the Church*, over more than two centuries, is something like a miracle. In almost every other national Protestant Church in Europe, Evangelicals have either been driven from the Church or seceded from it themselves. The 'Pietists' of Württemberg in southwestern Germany are one of the very few other evangelical constituencies to have remained within the established Church of the region. And even there, and certainly in most of Germany, the distinction between 'evangelisch' (recognized *bona-fide* Protestant 'state-church' Christians) and 'evangelikal' (conservative evangelicals scarcely recognized officially within the regular church structures) is a hard-and-fast one. This was, since Charles Simeon, and is, through the leadership of John Stott, not the case in England. The Evangelicals are at home in the Church of England. They are not always comfortable, and they have not

always been 'team players', but they 'have a place at the table'. Their voice is heard, and few in the Church are now able to stop their ears.[80]

John Stott's second 'swan-song' for the old millennium was of a different nature. Through much of the 1990s his thoughts had been returning to the idea of a book about birds: or, more accurately, about birds and the gospel. The designers, Three's Company, had shown what they could do with colour illustration, and he had by this time a very considerable collection of bird photographs, the fruit of arduous treks through bush and jungle, and long motionless hours in tropical or Arctic hides. A tentative working-title, *Reflections*, suggested a book looking back on some of his many overseas visits; a combination of Christian ministry with bird photography. But it proved an elusive concept, hard to pin down, and the more difficult since he had already made available the personal diaries for this biography. Then came a totally unexpected phone call from a North American publisher who had been told of his knowledge of birds: would Mr Stott be willing to write the text for a children's pop-up book of animated cut-outs of selected birds? Had 'Mr Stott' been as familiar with the works of P. G. Wodehouse as with the stories of H. H. Munro ('Saki'), he would have been irresistibly reminded of Jeeves's suggestion that Mr Corcoran's chorus-girl fiancée Muriel should ingratiate herself with his rich uncle, a fanatical ornithologist, by writing 'a small volume, to be entitled – let us say – *The Children's Book of American Birds*'.[81]

It is in the nature of pop-up books that the text does not attempt any exhaustive treatment of the subject. Nevertheless, John Stott was amused and intrigued by the proposal and gave it consideration. And it was from this, and his attempts to give shape to *Reflections*, that there came at last a culmination in book form of his life-long enthusiasm, *The Birds our Teachers*, with the descriptive sub-title *Essays in Orni-theology* and more than 150 photographs in colour by the author.[82]

The text itself is built around eleven lessons to be learnt from birds: in faith, from God's feeding of the ravens, for example; or in joy, from the lark's song. Most of these had been the subject of brief and much-repeated addresses, often during open-air Sunday devotions with a few hardy friends in the remoter places of almost every continent. The book contains a photographic record of the celebrated 'search for the Snowy Owl', a bird for which John Stott confessed 'a life-long romantic fascination, which I cannot rationalize',[83] together with a wealth of biblical references, beginning with the words of Jesus in the Sermon on the Mount: 'Look at the birds in the sky …' (Matthew 6:26).

Against what some felt to be the balance of probabilities, the book proved an immediate success. The standard of photography, as of reproduction, was highly professional. Those who bought the book on the strength of the author's name were given glimpses of 'John Stott as you never saw him before', peering through his telescopic lens, riding the tundra on an all-terrain buggy with Steve Andrews, or fraternizing with King Penguins in South Georgia. What, in bare description, sounded like vanity publishing, or a twentieth-century Mrs Gatty's *Parables from Nature* (pure Victoriana by the author of *Aunt Judy's Tales*) proved in the end a wholly appropriate, not to say triumphant, conclusion to the devoted study of a lifetime.[84] John Stott the birdwatcher is always on the lookout for likely converts to ornithology (as successive study assistants have been quick to discover). *The Birds our Teachers* is a persuasive manifesto, so designed (in the form of a worldwide co-edition, thus achieving dramatic economies of scale in colour printing) to follow the author's other writings into a variety of translations and overseas editions. Indeed, co-publication had been secured in some ten countries before the book was off the press.[85]

The Birds our Teachers can be seen as one expression of a continuing concern for God's creation. In 1997 John Stott was the guest preacher at the Sunday morning service, arranged by A Rocha, during the annual British Birdwatching Fair at Rutland Water, on the theme 'Let the birds be your teachers'. A few years before he had preached at the tenth anniversary celebration of the A Rocha Trust. He invited the A Rocha supporters gathered in St Paul's Church, Robert Adam Street, in London,

> ... to reflect with me on a phrase that occurs about a hundred times in the Psalter. Although I understand that the Hebrew words are somewhat different, nevertheless the idea is repeated again and again in the expression 'the works of the Lord', the mighty works of Yahweh. What is vital to notice, because it is often missed, is that sometimes 'the works of the Lord' are his mighty works of *creation*, bringing the universe into being and sustaining it by his Word of power.[86]

In the same year he contributed a Foreword to Peter Harris's personal story of the beginnings of A Rocha, *Under the Bright Wings*, answering the question, 'can ecological involvement properly be included under the heading of "mission"?'

> Yes, it can and should. For mission embraces everything Christ sends his people into the world to do, service as well as evangelism. And we cannot truly love and serve our neighbours if at the same time we are destroying their environment ... true incarnational

mission involves entering into other people's worlds, including the world of their social and environmental reality.

The gospel itself includes God's creation as well as his work of redemption …[87]

5

On 27 April 1996 John Stott turned seventy-five. In contrast to the London celebration that marked his seventieth birthday, the day was spent quite alone at The Hookses, working on his compilation of documents from the Lausanne movement.[88]

> It's spring migration time down here [he wrote to a friend]. Two days ago I heard the raucous call of a Sandwich Tern, looked up, and saw four in West Dale Bay flying North to their North Wales ternery. Yesterday I heard the 'seven-whistle' call of the Whimbrel, and there were nine flying north to breed in the Scottish Highlands – marvellous![89]

Nor were these sightings the only treat allowed him to mark his three-quarters century. He added: 'I drove to Haverfordwest to do my weekly shop at Tesco's (*Tesco, ergo sum!*) and bought myself a box of choc ices to celebrate: pig!'[90]

For John Stott himself, such a milestone brought with it a deliberate determination to secure the future of the ministry he had made his own. He had always sought to nurture prospective talent and to give younger men their opportunity. When his former colleague Michael Baughen, then Bishop of Chester, invited him to speak at the Evangelical Anglican Leaders Conference in 1995 he replied in terms which could apply to many similar invitations at this period:

> I really am 'in the wings' now, and rightly so. I'm conscious of diminishing intellectual vigour, and I'm no longer abreast of current issues and their literature. I think my days of controversy are over. And, more important still, I question the wisdom of wheeling on a geriatric who belongs to the Keele-Nottingham era. The rising generation must pick up the baton and run with it. To recruit the old guard is to signal that you lack confidence in their successors. It gives the wrong image and message.[91]

A few years later, in reply to a request from the Billy Graham Evangelistic Association inviting him to be one of the main speakers at 'Amsterdam 2000', he went further:

You have obviously secured a strong team of speakers. At the same time, I feel a certain degree of dismay that nearly all of them are American or European, or Third World people who have adopted European or American culture.

Secondly, although I do not know every name on the list, it seems to me that there are too many geriatrics like me! I would want to urge you to secure some more under 50s, and at least to make sure that each of the three blocks of the Third World (Africa, Asia and Latin America) has a major speaker who is a younger evangelical leader in his or her continent.[92]

This need to recognize and use the talents of younger Third World Christian leadership was a recurring theme. Speaking in the US in 1995 he was reported by a local newspaper:

'I see the future of the church in the Third World,' Stott said in an interview. 'Christianity in the West is tired. It is like uncorked champagne: it has lost the fizz.'

Non-white, non-Western Christians outnumber those in the West, and their numbers are skyrocketing, he said.

'There is a vitality and freshness about the Third World (churches) that is delightful to behold,' he said. 'We are going to have to get used to the idea that they are going to be sending missionaries to America ...'

'I am personally full of hope. I count among my friends younger Third World Christian leaders. Many here would be astounded to discover what high-quality people they are personally, spiritually, morally and intellectually,' he said. 'They have no idea of the calibre of leadership arising.'[93]

In 1993 John Stott received an honorary Doctorate of Divinity from Wycliffe College, Toronto. Though he had declined the honour from a number of American colleges or universities in the twenty years since Trinity Evangelical Divinity School, Deerfield, had awarded him an honorary DD, he felt able to accept since Canada was another country. Four years later, on home ground, he accepted his first Doctorate from a British college or university, a DD from Brunel at the instigation of one of its affiliated colleges, the London Bible College, who had first invited him to lecture in the days of his curacy, just fifty years before.[94] 'Tonight a wrong has been righted, an omission remedied,' were the opening words of the Principal, Derek Tidball; who went on to ask why no British university had recognized John Stott's contribution before:

Perhaps the problem with the universities, as Alister McGrath has pointed out, is that they do not recognise what Antonio Gramsci, the Marxist, called an 'organic intellectual' – a thinker who arises from within a community and gains authority for who he is rather than because of any academic appointment held. To evangelicals that is crucial. Theology needs to be done within the church as much as within universities, and John Stott has been for us such an 'organic intellectual'.[95]

In the same year he received the Golden Word award from the International Bible Society 'for his outstanding contribution as a Christian teacher and author': the Archbishop of Canterbury wrote of how it would be difficult to overestimate his contribution to the life of the Church of England, the Anglican Communion and evangelism worldwide.[96] Increasingly he became the subject of interviews, tributes and appreciations in the Christian press. Rowan Williams, soon to be Bishop of Monmouth, reviewing the *Festschrift, AD 2000 and Beyond*, spoke of his work 'in transforming the evangelical landscape'.[97] Across the Atlantic David Wells in *Christianity Today* marked John Stott's seventy-fifth milestone with a moving tribute: 'As an evangelical leader he views the world as a pastor. He has been pre-eminently a steward of God's truth and a herald of the biblical message.'[98]

In 1985 John Stott had been named a joint winner (with the Richmond Fellowship) of the Templeton UK Project Award. Ten years on, a group of friends prepared a submission to the International Board of Trustees, this time for the even more prestigious Templeton Prize. It was submitted in the name of Professor R. J. Berry,[99] supported by thirty testimonials, four brochures, seven books and a bibliography of his writings! Together they were said to represent 'the most thorough and extensive application' the Trust had ever received.[100] Among those who submitted testimonials were bishops (Anglican and Roman Catholic) and archbishops (including the Archbishop of Canterbury), academics, scientists, industrialists, professors and politicians from Asia and Australasia, Africa and Latin America, as well as the United States and Europe. Though on this occasion (the submission was held over for a year because of a confusion over dates) the prize went elsewhere, the cumulative effect of the testimonials and other documents submitted remains overwhelming. How could one lifetime have embraced this breadth of achievement?

Inevitably increasing years brought a certain physical frailty even to so sound a constitution; though, apart from a very brief spell off work following an operation to repair a hernia, he could claim in his early seventies, 'I don't think I've had a day in bed for forty years.'[101] A medical check-up in 1991 in Chicago pronounced his general health 'superb'.[102] Then in May 1998, while birdwatching with friends in Lebanon, he experienced difficulty with his vision. One eyepiece of his binoculars appeared faulty, but on handing them to his companion, it was clear that the trouble was not with the binoculars but with his eye. This was followed by acute abdominal pain which deferred his flight home by twenty-four hours. He arrived at Heathrow in a wheelchair, and was seen by his friend and medical adviser, Professor John Wyatt. Tests showed that he had suffered two embolisms, one of which had permanently impaired the vision of his left eye, and were the probable cause also of some atrial fibrillation – an irregular heartbeat – and of the abdominal pain. After a few days in St Luke's Hospital (where 'I remembered Bash's fascination with the interpretation of Romans 6, and wrote a couple of pages about it'),[103] he was able to return home. He was quite determined to continue with his future overseas engagements, so new guidelines for his hosts were prepared, with John Wyatt's medical report attached. This gave a brief account of the cause of the trouble, insisted that his schedule should include time for rest and recuperation and required that he should, where possible, remain within reach of medical care. It added:

> Following treatment with digoxin the heart rhythm has reverted to normal although, sadly, the visual loss has not improved significantly. Despite this visual impairment John is able to read, write and preach without difficulty, provided that he has a good light. He occasionally trips over obstacles and needs to take care when ascending and descending stairs.[104]

Almost at once it was clear that he should not drive again, though he retained his car so that he could be driven, usually by Frances Whitehead or by his study assistant, to his various engagements and (especially) to and from The Hookses. Shaking hands became difficult to judge, and he began to find himself bumping into people when walking in London, with the occasional tumble. He suffered a chest infection towards the end of his stay in China in February 1999;[105] and later in the year became unwell when visiting Salisbury for the Diocesan Evangelical Fellowship. On his return to London he was at once admitted to hospital and found to be suffering from pneumonia. For a day or two there was serious concern; but after what Richard Bewes (who visited him in St Mary's Hospital) described as 'a sensational recovery',[106] he was quickly back at work, demonstrating the robustness of his constitution.

Meanwhile his sister Joanna had been taken ill while visiting The Hookses during the summer, and died in hospital at Haverfordwest aged eighty-seven. He wrote:

She had been a wonderful wife to [Sir] Derek Hilton (formerly President of the Law Society), mother to Caroline, Sarah and Jenny my three nieces, and grandmother of four. She was the last surviving member of my immediate family circle, and her death has naturally been a further reminder of my own mortality.[107]

The future of what he thought of collectively as 'Langham ministries' (mainly ELT, the Langham Scholars programme, and the support given to these by the overseas 'Langham' branches) had been occupying John Stott's attention for some time past. It looked as if the work of JSM (John Stott Ministries) in the US was now on a firm and independent footing, poised for further growth with David Jones as its full-time executive. Might this be the way forward in the UK and elsewhere? Some provision for the future had already begun, in the appointment of literary executors who, on John Stott's death, would become responsible for the administration of his many copyrights (though almost all the income was already 'irrevocably assigned'). Similarly The Hookses had been passed to the Langham Trustees in perpetuity, though with John Stott, by happy agreement, retaining the use of 'the Hermitage' for as long as he needed it.

By Easter 1999 a more cohesive vision for the future was taking shape, and John Stott was able to issue a lengthy memorandum 'about the future of five third world ministries' for which he felt responsible.

We believe [he wrote]
(1) that God wants his redeemed people to grow into maturity in Christ;
(2) that it is principally the Word of God ('the sword of the Spirit') which matures the people of God; and
(3) that he intends his Word to come to them specially through preaching.

It was to this end that ELT and the Langham Scholars programme had been built up. Now it was proposed to add to them a team of teachers, pastors and consultants ('Senior Langham Associates'), another of authors ('Langham Writers'), and an ongoing multilevel programme of training for preachers. By way of background, John Stott added two further points to his memorandum.

First, there is the recognition that I am approaching the end of my active ministry, indeed of my life on earth. Secondly, there is the desire (shared by the four Langham boards and by me) that the five programmes described below will not only outlive me, but will expand, so long as they are perceived to be necessary and are still wanted by Third World Christian leaders ...

Our motive is emphatically neither to perpetuate my memory, nor to institutionalize what began in the form of personal ministries. In any case, we acknowledge the sovereignty of God, who may wish to develop other plans and raise up other people. We also recognize our need to be open to the possibility of co-operating with other groups which share our vision.[108]

The first of these 'other groups' in John Stott's thinking was IFES, the International Fellowship of Evangelical Students, to which John Stott had for years felt strongly committed, and which already had in place a world-wide network of trained and committed staff. Accordingly John Stott took the opportunity of the IFES World Assembly in South Korea during the following July to meet with Lindsay Brown, IFES General Secretary, seven of their regional secretaries, and a number of their executive committee. A possible framework of co-operation was developed, designed to include a central Langham Trust co-ordinator, engaged in a travelling and preaching ministry of his own and in the general oversight of the whole work. It would be his task to develop close co-operation with and between the autonomous regional boards, and the directors of ELT and the scholarship, training and writing programmes. In addition, it was hoped to appoint regional co-ordinators, probably part-time (for two or three months a year), possibly members of the IFES regional teams.

All this seemed promising, and these tentative proposals were then brought to a residential conference in November, when a group of thirty-six, representing each aspect of the current or proposed 'five ministries', met at the Wycliffe Centre at Horsleys Green. To an American participant it appeared as

> ... an eclectic crowd, ranging from the very young, to the very old, from the lean aristocratic Englishman, to the stout tanned Brazilian, from the London barrister to the West African biologist. We represented four different organizations, many different countries, and one common purpose ... On everyone's mind was the thought that we were seeking to replace an irreplaceable man, and as a result many of the participants were sceptical of what could be accomplished in such a meeting ...

There was an understandable concern that a personal vision and ministry might, with the best intentions, become merely a bureaucratic institution. No-one wanted this to happen, least of all those present (and there were many) whose lives John Stott had touched for Christ at some decisive moment:

> Ziel Machado, IFES Regional Secretary for Latin America, stood up and recounted that as a university student in Brazil he wrestled constantly with doubt and discouragement over his Christian beliefs. Somehow he received a Portuguese copy of *Your Mind Matters*, and reading it finally clarified and confirmed his struggling faith. Las Newman, IFES Regional Secretary for the Caribbean, talked about an occasion when John Stott visited the Caribbean and in one visit stirred up the Christian leaders of Jamaica to a firmer dedication to Scripture. Indeed, as Michael Baughen put it, he had served as the 'cement' for all these ministries, holding them under a common purpose by his personal care.[109]

John Stott prepared (as he had so often done for innumerable meetings over the years) a memorandum summarizing the consensus that emerged as the day progressed. No votes were taken, but there was a clear mandate for the appointment of an International Director to succeed John Stott himself as the focus of the work. He or she would be accountable to an International Council (yet to be formed); but in the meantime a Steering Committee would find and nominate the International Director, begin to wrestle with the legal and financial implications of the new structure, and devise lines of accountability and communication between the various components. The proposal for Regional Co-ordinators would be on their agenda in consultation with IFES; one or two pilot 'Preaching Seminars' would give experience in this new field; other exciting possibilities, including 'Senior Associates' and 'Langham Writers' (Third World and Eastern European scholars supported and assisted in the writing of strategic works while on sabbatical) were in various stages of development, thanks to the initiatives already agreed by JSM. All this would have the attention of the new Steering Committee on what would clearly be an Olympic-sized agenda![110]

6

Charles Simeon was present at the famous meeting of the Eclectic Society in March 1799 when John Venn asked about what methods they could use 'effectually to promote the knowledge of the gospel' across the world. As the discussion proceeded, Simeon himself, 'with characteristic distinctness of purpose and promptitude of zeal', proposed three questions: 'What can we do? When shall we do it? How shall we do it?' Exactly two centuries later the Horsleys Green consultation addressed the same question for a new millennium, called together by one who exhibited much the same 'characteristic distinctness of purpose and promptitude of zeal'. And in their discussions the consultation must surely have had in mind that 'chief principle' which John Venn laid down (for what was to become the Church Missionary Society), namely:

> Whatever success is expected, must be expected entirely through the influence of the Spirit of God. His agency must enlarge the hearts of Christians. His providential guidance must lead the way and open the door.[111]

FOURTEEN

Leader, Pastor, Friend, Disciple: Life in Christ

1

In the same year that his first book was published, John Stott contributed an introduction to a biography of John Sung, missionary and evangelist in China.[1] It was published at the time of Dr Billy Graham's ground-breaking Harringay crusade. In his six-page Foreword John Stott recounted how, when D. L. Moody died, Dr R. A. Torrey wrote a searching booklet entitled *Why God Used D. L. Moody*, giving seven reasons.[2] Like Torrey's seven reasons, John Stott singled out four features which he identified in both John Sung and Billy Graham. He noted the same commitment, surrender, or dedication; the same reliance on the power of prayer, of the Word of God, of the cross of Christ and of the Holy Spirit; the same genuineness and reality; and the same determination to work with and through the churches. These were all lessons which John Stott had set himself to learn in the differing aspects of a lifetime's ministry.

Not long before, in 1952, as President of the Berean Band (a small society to encourage the memorizing of Scripture) he had written for them a pamphlet, *Ezra the Scribe*,[3] portraying Ezra as 'a man to imitate ... the last of the great spiritual men who appear in the history of the Old Testament'.

It was Ezra's greatness, he maintained, to seek the law, to obey it and to teach it. Twenty-five years later Derek Kidner summed up 'the secret of Ezra's lasting influence' in words which, looking for an Old Testament parallel, might describe John Stott himself as one of Ezra's imitators:

> He is a model reformer in that what he taught he had first lived, and what he lived he had first made sure of in the Scriptures. With study, conduct and teaching put deliberately in this right order, each of these was able to function properly at its best: study was saved from unreality, conduct from uncertainty, and teaching from insincerity and shallowness.[4]

Again, writing of the apostle John, John Stott used words which could equally be applied to himself in the character of Christian teacher and expositor, and to his worldwide ministry and readership:

> John is above all else a pastor, entrusted with the care of a group of local churches, and anxious to help their members to learn how to think and live Christianly. At the foundation of their Christian thinking must be a right grasp of the unique divine-human person of Jesus, and at the foundation of their Christian living a transparent integrity of righteousness and love.[5]

But the most natural New Testament comparison must be with the Paul of Acts, of the missionary journeys and the apostolic letters, whose blazing commitment and sometimes tortuous thought-patterns John Stott has expounded personally to students in every continent, as well as by his writings. At first the resemblance is not to Paul but to his younger protégés:

> It was as a comparatively young man that I began a serious study of the Pastoral Letters, so that I found no problem in sitting beside Timothy and Titus, listening through their ears to the elderly apostle's admonitions.

It is a posture of submission to apostolic teaching which no Christian outgrows. Yet in another sense, John Stott continues,

> ... the situation has changed. I am almost certainly older than the apostle was, and it is natural for me to sit beside Paul. Not of course that I am an apostle. But I think I feel something of his concern for the future of the gospel and for the younger generation whose responsibility it is to guard it and pass it on.[6]

For himself he would never presume further than this 'sitting beside'. But it is not difficult to draw out striking similarities, perhaps because Paul is a prototype of all post-ascension Christian ministry. There is the life-changing encounter with Jesus in conversion and new birth; the theological wrestling with a worldview built round the person and work of Christ; the urgency of preaching, the constant travelling, the single eye for the sake of the Name. John Stott had long ago chosen Charles Wesley's 'Jesus! the name high over all' for his funeral, with its fervent outpouring of the preacher's soul:[7]

> Jesus! the name to sinners dear,
>   The name to sinners given;
> It scatters all their guilty fear,
>   It turns their hell to heaven ...
>
> O that the world might taste and see
>   The riches of His grace;
> The arms of love that compass me
>   Would all mankind embrace ...
>
> Happy, if with my latest breath
>   I might but gasp His name;
> Preach Him to all, and cry in death:
>   Behold, behold the Lamb![8]

It is a choice that Paul would surely have recognized and approved!

The comparison holds true also for the darker side of Paul's life and ministry: the shared sense of utter unworthiness ('less than the least of all saints') and of the continuing burden of human sinfulness even while struggling with 'the already and the not yet'. There is the same rigid self-discipline ('I am my body's sternest master', J. B. Phillips); and the constant care, if not for all the churches, at least for so many of God's people in a world at once wider and yet vastly more accessible than Paul's.

All such similarities, of course, are flawed and partial. They are hardly comparing like with like. The gap, even allowing for our shared humanity and discipleship, between the apostle and all other Christian ministers is unbridgeable. Yet imagination may still draw parallels. If John Stott could write of 'the Jesus in whose shoes we are to walk',[9] he could follow in Paul's footsteps and even suppose the apostle to be a fellow-ornithologist:

As I once traced his route from Lystra to Derbe, I could not help wondering if his spirit had also been cheered by the spectacular, snow-capped mountain peaks around him, by the White Storks nesting on the village rooftops and by the pretty song of the Calandra Larks.[10]

A still more striking comparison is to be found nearer home, and reference has been made to it more than once in these pages: the idea of John Stott as a latter-day Charles Simeon. Simeon is frequently quoted in John Stott's own writings; for example, Simeon's great aim 'to bring out of Scripture what is there, and not to thrust in what I think might be there',[11] or Simeon's letter to John Venn on his ordination, with its exalted view of Christian ministry:

> My dearest Friend, I most sincerely congratulate you not on a permission to receive £40 or £50 a year, nor on the title of Reverend, but on your accession to the most valuable, most honourable, most important, and most glorious office in the world – to that of an ambassador of the Lord Jesus Christ.[12]

John Stott himself confessed to a friend:

> Charles Simeon of Cambridge remains something of a guru to me, since he warned, 'Beware of the systematizers of religion!' Instead, he affirmed his submission to everything Scripture teaches, including the antinomies which cannot be neatly systematized or reconciled to one another ... As Simeon constantly said, the truth lies neither at one extreme, nor at the opposite extreme, nor in a 'confused admixture of both extremes', but at both extremes, even if we cannot reconcile them.[13]

In the opinion of one of his closest colleagues, John Stott's Introduction to the anthology of Simeon's sermons, *Evangelical Preaching*,[14] 'was the closest to autobiography that he had ever written'. The parallels between the two men are certainly striking. Both were privileged sons of comparatively affluent parents, educated at public schools, undergraduates at Cambridge. They shared a transforming experience of conversion to Christ, early and severe trials and testing, and virtually a lifetime's ministry in a single church. Each cultivated habits well beyond the norm for early rising, disciplined prayer and the study of Scripture. Each became a mentor to students, and a leader to younger clergy as well as among his contemporaries. They shared a call to the single life, and to the rediscovery (and subsequent teaching) of the art of expository preaching. Like John Stott, Simeon had a world vision (as one of the founders of the Church Missionary Society) and a grasp of strategic organization, as in the patronage trust which he founded and which still bears his name. Each was a believer in the power of the printed word, and published many volumes of Bible exposition.

In *Evangelical Preaching* John Stott writes of Simeon's 'unalloyed personal authenticity' and of his faith as 'the religion of a sinner at the foot of the cross'. And there is surely not simply objective approval, but personal identification, in the story of Simeon he chooses to recount:

> At one of his weekly tea-parties somebody asked Simeon: 'What, Sir, do you consider the principal mark of regeneration?' It was a probing question. With the current popularity of the 'born-again movement,' one wonders how the average evangelical believer would reply today. This was Simeon's answer: 'the very first and indispensable sign is self-loathing and abhorrence ... This sitting in the dust is most pleasing to God ... give me to be with a broken-hearted Christian, and I prefer his society to that of all the rest ... Were I now addressing to you my dying words, I should say nothing else but what I have just said. Try to live in this spirit of self-abhorrence, and let it habitually mark your life and conduct.'[15]

Sir Marcus Loane is one of those fascinated by the comparison between the two men:[16]

> I find myself thinking more and more of the parallels with Charles Simeon [he wrote]. Not in personality, but in single-minded dedication, centred on the Word of God, based on a particular church and pulpit, but influential beyond all local borders. Thirty years ago, I wrote a little book with a dedication to John. I have always thought it one of my better books! But now I wonder if there ought not to be a fresh dedication ... and wish it could be on a plaque to be placed in All Souls. Something like this:
>
>
>
> In honour of
> John Robert Walmsley Stott
> who like Charles Simeon
> for 54 years in the heart of Cambridge
> has now for 54 years in the heart of London
> exercised a ministry
> which has touched the ends of the earth for God
>
>
>
> John would not like it! Perhaps the people of All Souls would ...[17]

All this, however, is to look mainly to the past; and John Stott's own pattern for Christian discipleship cannot be found in the past alone.

Speaking to Canadian students, when accepting an honorary DD from Wycliffe College, Toronto, he raised this question:

> How can Christianity be contemporary, you may be asking. Is it not an ancient faith? Did not its Founder live and die some two millennia ago? Isn't Christianity an antique piece? a period relic; a fossil ...?
>
> My concern tonight is to argue that there is such a thing as contemporary Christianity, and to urge those of you who are graduating today and going out into the world to serve, to determine that you will become authentically contemporary Christians.[18]

It is a determination very much his own. Beyond the parallels with Ezra, John and Paul, or with Charles Simeon of Cambridge, 'the contemporary Christian' forms perhaps the closest and most convincing model of John Stott's personal discipleship.[19]

2

The first volume of this biography carried the sub-title *The Making of a Leader*, a claim which succeeding chapters have sought to justify. Professor Howard Gardner, in his psychological and sociological study of what he calls 'an anatomy of leadership', defines the term as meaning 'persons who, by word and/or personal example, markedly influence the behaviours, thoughts and/or feelings of a significant number of their fellow human beings'.[20] He makes the fascinating points, buttressed by sociological observation, that future leaders have often lost fathers at an early age; or have experienced contrasting relationships with their two parents. Both these factors, in some sense, were part of John Stott's early life. From his study of case histories, Howard Gardner builds up the imaginary picture of an 'Exemplary Leader', whom for the purpose of his illustration he thinks of as female, and christens 'E.L.'. He describes E.L. as a skilled speaker with a keen interest in people, shown at an early stage: 'Individuals who observe E.L. comment on her general energy and resourcefulness, rather than on her specific talents: there is consensus that she will accomplish something, but it is not yet apparent in which spheres that accomplishment will occur.' This accurately describes the young John Stott, at least up to 1950.

Of the early markers of leadership that Gardner notes, 'the most telling indication is a willingness to confront individuals in authority'. Perhaps this can be seen not only in John Stott's obdurate resistance to his family over war service, but in his rejection of the liberal theology he was taught at Cambridge. E.L. as Gardner describes her also stands out because of a concern for moral issues; she 'expands her experiences and viewpoints by travelling outside her homeland' (embryo tyrants, it seems, are more likely to stay at home). Future leaders who are creative have been found to take 'a decade to master the domain in which each ultimately effects a breakthrough': John Stott was five years at Cambridge and five years assistant curate. Moreover, 'the aspiring leader like E.L. – or an individual, like Martin Luther King, Jr., or Eleanor Roosevelt, who is propelled by circumstances – must be attuned to an audience that is posing basic questions and searching for guidance, particularly regarding issues of identity'. Here, perhaps, is the leader of the younger clergy of the Eclectic Society, uneasy with the clerical identity of an earlier generation.

Professor Gardner's study of his hypothetical E.L. goes on to speak of her charisma, of physical gifts, and of the establishing of an organizational base (EFAC, perhaps?). 'Opportunity for reflection' is another feature (the days out of London, solitude at The Hookses?), what has been called 'the uncluttered mind'. So is an optimistic temperament:

> It is important to note that E.L., by and large, is not thrown by apparent failures. Tough and robust, she expects that there will be downs as well as ups. Sometimes, indeed, she is energized by setbacks and returns to the fray with new vigour ... Perhaps only the ordinary leader-manager can reasonably expect to appear successful to her immediate successors, but this success comes at the cost of little significant change. In contrast, the exemplary leader may well appear to have been ineffective immediately after the end of her term; but there remains the chance that she will ultimately prove to have set into operation a series of events that have long-term consequences.

Perhaps this is prophetic, at a time when it can seem (not least to John Stott himself) that, in the UK, his star is on the wane and some of his achievements are unremarked by a younger generation. In Howard Gardner's studies, significant change is like a hand on the helm of a great ship, taking time to become apparent, but no less effective in the long run.

Howard Gardner is only one of many who have sought to describe and analyse the elusive quality of leadership. Aspects of John Stott's powers of leadership were summed up in different ways by those who supported a submission on his behalf for the Templeton Prize, referred to in the previous chapter: 'His work has caused people to change their minds'; 'he has persistently challenged the drift of modern theology into secular paradigms'; 'a new phenomenon' in the church; 'the representative evangelical of his age'; 'his leadership was all about the discovery of other leaders'. It is not surprising that when Dr Billy Graham contributed the Foreword to an international collection of essays marking John Stott's seventieth birthday, 'leadership' was one of four areas singled out as characteristic of his ministry, this time on the world scene:

> Few have understood the situation of the world Church more clearly, and few are as able to address the Church's problems and failures – and opportunities – on as broad a scale. Even those who have disagreed with him could not deny that he speaks with deep conviction, love, and a charitable spirit.[21]

Dr Vinay Samuel, one of the editors of this *Festschrift*, amplified this judgment from his own experience: 'I do not know any context in Asia, Africa and Latin America where key evangelical leaders do not regard Dr Stott as a pastor, friend and theological mentor.'[22]

John Stott chose to conclude his study of *Issues Facing Christians Today* with 'A Call for Christian Leadership', which, appearing during the peak years of his ministry, inevitably reflects his own experience.[23] He identifies five qualities in the shaping of Christian leadership: vision, industry, perseverance, service, discipline. They have all been illustrated in his own life, as preceding chapters have shown: *vision* for All Souls, for Third World leaders, for a more truly biblical evangelicalism, for the power of the printed word.

> It is clear that John is a visionary [writes a member of the JSM Board]. People of the organization are numerous; visionaries are few and far between. By this I simply mean that he sees solutions and conceives of strategies where others only see dilemmas and problems. He sees where we need to go. Much of the resurgence of post-war evangelicalism has his stamp upon it one way or another for this reason from the Church of England, to the Lausanne Committee for World Evangelization, to the Langham Scholars.[24]

His *industry*, too, is indomitable: if sheer labour can accomplish the task, it will certainly be completed. Through tiredness, distraction and preoccupation he managed to retain what Walter de la Mare held in others to be the mark of genius, 'a sovereign energy of mind'.[25] Similarly, *perseverance* – what Bash used to describe to him as 'stickability' – can be seen in the decades devoted to EFAC, to the follow-up of NEAC, to Lausanne, to the London Institute. None of these, in the years he gave to them, was without problems and setbacks, sometimes apparently terminal. None was abandoned. His tenacity was noticed by all who worked with him. Sometimes, indeed, it became an unwillingness to let go which led him (and them) into a morass of difficulties which might have been avoided had his determination not verged so closely upon the obstinate. Imminent absence overseas could mean that others were left trying to handle problems which had become intractable.

Moreover, tenacity and perseverance have been essential ingredients in John Stott's faithfulness to his roots and his convictions. During a public interview, Richard Bewes said to him:

You've helped a lot of us about the Bible. I'd like to ask: have you ever yourself felt tempted to give up and cave in to the liberal side of life? To David Edwards or John Habgood? Have you ever felt tempted not to be an evangelical, not to take the Bible seriously in that sense?

John Stott's reply lifts the curtain to give a glimpse of how vulnerable he had sometimes felt as a defender of orthodoxy:

Well, the first temptation (to which I'm more exposed than that, I think) is to run away; not to give in, but to – what is the word? – to leave. I sometimes say my favourite text is from Psalm 55: 'Oh for the wings of a dove, that I may flee away and be at rest.' So I've found this constant controversy, this constant battling for the truth, very wearing ...[26]

His tenacity has already been illustrated in his loyalty to the church of his baptism and ordination. When in 1993 an American interviewer asked about the attitude of the Anglican Church to homosexual practice with specific reference to the views of Bishop Spong, he replied:

I think we have got to distinguish between the church's official teaching on the one hand and the teaching of an eccentric minority on the other. What Bishop Spong teaches embarrasses me as an Episcopalian, but I am able to say, Well, that is one individual's view. He may have a following, but it is not the official view of the church. If it ever became the official view of the Anglican church, I would find it very difficult to stay in. But I'm confident it won't.[27]

Seven years later he further qualified his position by saying that even if the official view changed, he would be minded, not without pain, 'to stay on and continue the battle for some time':

Once it became clear that the battle was lost and that the church had become apostate by abandoning some essential of doctrine or ethics, it would no longer be the church, and to leave would not be schism.[28]

The practice of *service* to others, learned first by example from his parents, was a family tradition before it was a Christian calling. All his life he has sought to follow the example of a Master who came not to be served but to serve. From time to time his guests (sometimes, indeed, his hosts) tell of finding John Stott cleaning their shoes for them, as a more acceptable service than offering to wash their feet![29] Perhaps he carried with him, persuasive even when unremembered, the words carved above the doorway from the dining hall at his theological college: 'I am among you as he that serveth.'

Finally, to those who know him in countries worldwide, his *discipline* is legendary. 'I am not as disciplined as you think I am,' he would say sometimes in an address to younger clergy.[30] But the testimony of the study assistants is different: 'his daily routine of rising at five and retiring at ten or eleven was vainly imitated by many of us (though the discipline of the Horizontal Half-Hour was usually adopted with great ease!)'.

Writing and travelling are both contributory aspects of his leadership. Neither was deliberately chosen but originated in the invitation of others. It was only as his ministry progressed that he was able to describe himself (looking back over fifty years) as becoming 'less of an activist ... more of a thinker'.[31] Books had always been important to him; but as he began to be increasingly engaged in the intellectual struggle and to discover in his travels what it meant to lack books, he became their constant advocate. 'We should be unashamed', he told a Christian Booksellers Convention, 'in declaring that Christian reading is a neglected "means of grace".'[32]

A moment earlier in this same address he quoted J. H. Newman's comparison of the writing of a book to 'a gestation and child-birth'. On another occasion Newman spoke of himself in words which could apply equally to John Stott in spite of his many travels: 'I *do* think that my influence among persons who have *not* seen me has been infinitely greater than among those who have.'[33] In the nature of the case, this must be true of many writers, and certainly of John Stott, whose books have circulated widely in translation as well as in English. 'Jesus is my hero,' an African pastor (whom he had never met) wrote to him once, 'but the day I saw your picture in a magazine I cut it out and put it in my album ...' and, earlier in the same letter, 'when I am asked about who discipled me I point to your writings'.[34] And what is true of geography, that writings reach those their authors have never met, is also true of chronology, that writings can have a continuing ministry when the author's pen is stilled. The sales of C. S. Lewis's works, so Walter Hooper wrote in 1975, 'have more than trebled since his death in 1963'.[35]

A final word about John Stott's ministry of writing sums up the nature of the books which will form his continuing legacy, in a way which readers of them will be quick to recognize:

His work has been driven by evangelistic, pastoral, and ethical concerns. His books, then, have not pressed back the frontiers for theologians. They have, instead, sought to make the Scriptures accessible ... Thus he combines the urgency of the evangelist, the conviction of the dogmatic theologian who is also a pastor, the generosity of a wide-ranging churchman who has discovered unexpected affinities with those he once took to be implacable opponents, some of the caution of an upper-middle-class English diplomat, much of the charm of an instinctive persuader, the considerable self-awareness of a person who is both brave and humble enough to acknowledge having much to repent of and much to learn, and the unselfconscious love that results from an unusually close relationship with the Lord. This is a most effective combination which has ensured that his books, articles, and contributions to conferences have been as popular with committed and serious evangelical church members as they have been largely ignored by most academic theologians.[36]

In successive interviews with journalists over more than twenty-five years, John Stott has emphasized what he has gained, rather than what he has been able to contribute, through world travel. 'An educative experience', he called it in the 1970s: 'all of us need to be delivered from the prison of our own culture'.[37] In the 1980s he developed this further:

Travel has been one of the formative influences in my life. I began to look at my own cultural upbringing, both in terms of social class and in terms of evangelical sub-culture, through the eyes of people in other cultures ...[38]

Ten years later, he was citing 'our cultural defences' as a barrier to the understanding of Scripture: 'I believe that every Christian ought to be an internationalist. Paul is our model here, in that he was familiar with three cultures: Jewish, Roman, and Greek.'[39] Third World Christian leadership continued to impress him, just as exposure to Third World deprivation pricked his social conscience. But he was not starry-eyed over this:

We have to say that the idea of the First, Second and Third Worlds is out of date and that even if you're thinking of the developing world as the Third World, there is a lot of affluence in parts of the developing world, whether it's the Middle East with their petro-dollars, or whether it's Singapore and Japan and Korea and Hong Kong and Taiwan and so on ... What I think we mean is that there is a great deal in the Bible about God's concern for the poor. Poverty ... in the sense of lacking the basic wherewithal for survival, that kind of poverty – isn't really on the evangelical conscience yet.[40]

But behind this concern lay more than simply humanitarian compassion. Corey Widmer went with him to Africa as study assistant in February 2000, and asked him 'what had originally sparked his interest in the developing world. He responded, "The Bible". Its emphasis to love the poor he took as an unavoidable call.'[41] On the same visit, Corey Widmer described what was a common experience among those who accompanied John Stott overseas, that they saw him with new eyes:

I have been in awe of Uncle John and his ministry with these people. I have never seen him as I have seen him here – so vibrant, alive, strong, compassionate, and brimming with kindness and wisdom. His teaching is powerful as usual, but the joy and sincerity of Christ that he carries away from the pulpit is what attracts the crowds to him ... I find myself becoming quickly annoyed and frustrated with the endless barrage of people but he is ever willing to see another face that is glowing to meet him. The Africans approach him with visible and unconcealed excitement; the Americans and westerners approach with a cool self-confidence but with the same childish eagerness beneath ...[42]

In his study of Lord Runcie, Humphrey Carpenter recounts a conversation with Richard Chartres, then soon to be appointed Bishop of London:

Towards the end of lunch, he remarked to me that Runcie belonged to 'the last generation of ten-talented men who thought they could change the world by being ordained into the Church of England. During his lifetime,' Chartres continued, 'that belief has become totally implausible.'[43]

Perhaps, with the rarest exceptions, it always was. John Stott must rank among the ten-talented leaders of his generation, but at the time of his ordination there is no suggestion that world-changing ambitions were remotely in his mind. Fifty years on, the idea does not seem quite so implausible. Who knows what redrawing of the map of faith this twenty-first century will see, or to what hidden sources future historians will look as, under God, the agents of far-reaching change?

3

It would have come as a surprise to some readers to find John Stott, in an interview in his mid-seventies, denying that he had ever had 'a love for souls'. It must have seemed to confirm the suspicion that his emphasis on the social implications of the gospel had blunted the edge of his concern for evangelism – something for which there is no evidence and which he has always expressly denied. He went on to explain what he meant:

> I have never had a love or passion for souls; I can't envisage a soul as being an adequate object of my love, affection or passion. What God has done is create human beings, and human beings are more than a soul: they are body-souls and they are body-souls-in-a-community. Therefore, if I truly love my neighbour, the second great commandment obliges me to serve my neighbour in his or her physical, social and spiritual dimensions.[44]

To those who worked and travelled with him, there was no doubting his love and concern, if not for 'souls', yet for individuals, colleagues and neighbours, for the wider community, and for the church of Christ:

> He cared a lot about people, the church and the world. I noticed this in his attitude to Frances and me, as well as others; in the way that he talked about events that were going on in the world. His love for the church was evident when we travelled in India and saw how fragmented and corrupt the church could be there, and when he talked about evangelical disunity and backbiting in Britain. It was really the love of a shepherd over sheep; it pained him.[45]

This concern for the whole person had been reflected in his evangelistic preaching and counselling from the earliest years of university missions. Those who worked with him noted how carefully he put before his hearers the total transformation a new life in Christ would mean – in a word, 'the cost of discipleship'. Chua Wee Hian gives a picture not often remembered of the pain of finding no response to the offer of Christ:

> On one occasion, when he invited those who had prayed a prayer inviting Jesus into their lives to come and speak to him so that he could give them a booklet and introduce them to a counsellor, there was no movement or response from the crowd. I was standing next

to him and, with a heavy heart, he lamented over the unbelief of his hearers. He longed passionately for folk to repent of their sin and to receive the free offer of salvation in Christ.[46]

An assistant missioner at one of the CICCU missions remembered a talk with a student who told him that what he really respected about 'Mr Stott' was that he did not press for a decision. 'If you're not ready, I beg you not to make it.'[47] Yet a conversion to Christ (though he later preferred to emphasize 'regeneration')[48] always warmed his heart. He was never as attracted as some of his contemporaries to the writings of C. S. Lewis, feeling that, though credally orthodox, he did not address the question of authority: they met only briefly and hardly knew each other.

> But what made me feel more at one with him than anything else [John Stott wrote later] was his description of his conversion, beginning with rich metaphors of grace like the angler, the hounds after the fox, the cat and mouse, and finally 'checkmate', together with the eloquent description, 'the Prodigal Son at least walked home on his own feet. But who can duly adore that Love which will open the high gates to a prodigal who is brought in kicking, struggling, resentful, and darting his eyes in every direction for a chance of escape?'
>
> Such an appreciation of Sovereign grace makes one ready to excuse innumerable theological peccadillos![49]

As pastor, counsellor and friend (the three often indistinguishable), he took pains to buttress his amazing memory for names and circumstances by careful notes of the people he had met, conversations, plans, family relationships. If some experienced a certain resentment (perhaps most keenly in his early days as Rector) that he was so inaccessible to social callers, there must be set against this his availability as pastor:

> I needed a lot of guidance as a young Christian. John Stott never refused a request to let me come to see him and talk ... I think there is a particular pastoral gift which John Stott has, which says, when one comes to him for advice, that at that moment when the penitent one or the bewildered one is consulting him, this seeker is the most important person in the world, really the only person in the world ...[50]

He felt, of course, a particular responsibility to those who were members of All Souls. Many shared an experience such as this:

John had me to tea, and I remember leaving 12 Weymouth Street with my heart burning because a man whom I admired and revered so much in the pulpit, should have found the time to talk personally to a measly undergraduate ... I can never get over his blend of love for the Lord Jesus, ruthless – and frightening – self-discipline, and marvellous warmth and humanity.[51]

Nor did one need to be a promising student or key Christian worker to experience his pastoral instincts. As Rector Emeritus he could often be found at Christmas time visiting 'shut-in' members of All Souls, usually the elderly and alone, to take them Holy Communion, much as he had done as Harold Earnshaw-Smith's curate forty years before. Old or young, it made no difference. His host on one of the Australian tours tells of how once, after a busy schedule of meetings, he took John Stott

> ... through the bush to the home of Yurik Orlowski, a boy of fifteen who had come to the Lord a few months before, but who couldn't attend the meeting on the previous evening because the poor chap had scarlet fever. John read a verse of Scripture and prayed with Yurik ...
>
> About eight years later I met John again and one of the first things he asked was, 'How is that boy, Yurik? I have prayed for him regularly ...'[52]

One reason why 'a love for people' is a better description than 'a passion for souls' is that it not only embraces the whole person, but speaks of John Stott's concern (like the apostle's) for Christian maturity, 'to present each one of you as a mature member of Christ's body'.[53] Friendship here becomes almost an aspect of pastoring, with growth in holiness an inescapable part of Christian maturity. A letter telling of John Stott's friendship and his visits to their home included this observation: 'As a wife I'm aware that every time [my husband] was with John he returned more committed to becoming a humble, godly man. It was a gift to our family every time they went birdwatching!'[54]

It did not seem to matter whether an individual was already known as a friend, or an unnamed member of a crowd: an American pastor wrote recalling his student days and John Stott's visits to his seminary campus:

> On the occasions you would be speaking, I would try to get to chapel early, and observe the man ... Two things from your actions stood out to me; first, a few minutes before chapel when your face suddenly lit up, your cheeks a cheery glow as you rushed down from the platform to embrace an African brother equally as joyous at

seeing you. On his cheeks were tribal markings, in contrast to your own, a picture of the transcending and unifying love of Christ! The second is your behaviour after chapel. When flight schedules permitted, you would stand patiently on the platform while many students lined up to speak with you. Each was given a smile, a warm handshake and undivided attention. You never seemed to look past anyone to the line behind them. I watched but I guess never had the wisdom to know what questions to ask! Yet I still learned by observation.[55]

Several instances have already been given to show how this concern and respect for people as individuals determined John Stott's attitude to controversy. Wherever possible, in the case of public controversy in the church, he sought to meet face to face, to discuss rationally, to represent the best and not the worst of a position he felt bound to confront. In 1996, and again in 1997, he set out something of his practice in reply to letters he had received: the first, to an American correspondent, made a single but crucial point about Christian controversy:

My main response lies in the area of polarisation. It may be that I am now suffering from a hardening of the arteries, and from the kind of theological and moral compromise which are associated with senility! But in theological debate I think it is important not to push people to the opposite extreme to the one we occupy ourselves, unless the facts warrant it. It is also important for us to confess our own tendencies to imbalance ...[56]

The second sets out his own established practice, with four principles he had developed as a personal guide. In this instance it was in an aspect of charismatic teaching, an area about which he was often consulted:

Over the years, because I have become embroiled in several debates, I have developed some principles to which I try to adhere.
    First, I do not initiate a conversation or correspondence on a controversial matter, but only respond to somebody else's specific questions.
    Secondly, I do not speak about such matters publicly, from platform or pulpit, but only in private and in confidence.
    Thirdly, I do not say behind anybody's back anything I have not said to his or her face.
    Fourthly, I do not speak negatively about anybody without first affirming what I can positively.[57]

Sometimes, of course, his quarrel was of an entirely different nature, as for example with President Ceausescu of Romania about toleration for evangelical Christians; or a long-running (and, it has to be said, one-sided) correspondence with Frederick Chiluba, President of Zambia, on behalf of prisoners under sentence of death, some of whom had written to him after finding his name in a Christian journal in the prison library. It often seemed, to the despair of his over-pressed colleagues, that few appeals remained unanswered during these crowded years if it should appear even remotely within his power to help.

The same love and respect for people have allowed John Stott to outgrow a certain wariness in his relations with women which marked his early days; not with those admitted to the circle of his friendship or pastoral care, but sometimes felt by others who would have liked to be closer to him. The easing of constraint signified a new emotional free-dom, gained both from personal maturity and from the uninhibited expressions of pleasure and affection met with in Latin America or Africa. What had always been his view in theory ('emotion, genuine feelings legitimately aroused – these must be expressed, not suffocated')[58] he became more able to practise. By 1989 he was writing to a former study assistant 'to send you a greeting and a hug (I'm now a life-member of the Institute of Hug Therapy!)'.[59] Yet he did not allow emotional liberation nor mere politeness to overcome his instincts as a pastor:

> After a midweek evening meeting, I was standing close to John when a rather gushing lady came up to talk with him. John listened, and then said something like 'I am surprised that you talk to me about this, for I thought you were going to apologize for the way you behaved last week.' She blushed a very deep scarlet, and I wondered if I would have had the courage to exercise that kind of pastoral care, for John's manner was courtesy itself ...[60]

It is, as one of his study assistants described it, the courage that prevents a pastor declining into a man-pleaser. Nor was he without social armoury if he felt he was being foolishly lionized, or his natural reserve was not respected on first acquaintance:

> John was staying at our house in Ann Arbor during a weekend conference ... Afterwards we gave a supper for some of the univer-sity students at our home. A friend of mine also came who was new to the Bible and things Christian. At one point she sat on the sofa near John, and finding him attractive, said to him in a cozy fashion, 'Tell me about yourself.' John smiled sweetly and said, 'Oh, I'm just a fellow-sinner like everyone else.' She was completely disarmed ...[61]

Over the years he has come to epitomize in many valued friendships what he has written on the relationship of men and women: 'If women need men, men also need women ... Without woman, not necessarily as wife but certainly as companion and helper, man is but a pathetic apology for a human being.'[62]

Children, too, are drawn to him (as earlier chapters have shown) by his genuine interest in them, taking seriously their concerns and sharing their sense of fun. Visiting Kampala, he walked with Corey Widmer, his study assistant, up the hill to the cathedral to show him the graves of earlier Ugandan martyrs:

> It is remarkable to watch the way Uncle John loves people. He will stop completely, approach a person, and with great affection set them at the centre of his attention. He knows so much about their past history and culture, sometimes more than the Ugandans themselves. This afternoon he started singing to a young altar boy in the cathedral, 'Tukutendereza Yesu' (We are washed by the blood of the Lamb). The boy couldn't believe Uncle John knew the song and started singing with him.[63]

An American mother once wrote to him, enclosing a page extracted from her daughter's schoolwork: 'I thought you would enjoy seeing it – even with her honest appraisal!'

Mr Stott, by Missy Larson

It was a Saturday and my aunt was having a party. My Mom told me to say hello to everyone at the party. 'Yuck!' I was meeting everybody and saying 'hello', when I came up to one man he said, 'hello' and kissed my hand.

He was an old man with gray hair, and had a warm smile. He was tall and wearing a brown business suit.

Mr Stott was nice and kind that's why I remember him. It always seems that travling sales men ignore you but not Mr Stott. Mr Stott made me feel grown up and important.[64]

At the same time he was always a realist, well aware, when it came to tiny children, that there is a big difference between an 'uncle' and a father. Sitting in the car next to a small girl steadily smearing herself with chocolate cake, he assured her parents, 'My call to bachelorhood is confirmed!' Yet beneath the jesting references to his single state there lay the consciousness that it represented a costly element in his own discipleship. Rosemary Bird remembers staying at The Hookses with her eighteen-month-old grandson Andy, and John Stott taking the child by the hand. He told her, 'I suddenly realized what I was missing by not having a family.'[65] Marriage might have driven a coach-and-horses through the bachelor lifestyle which alone made possible his vast output; but the emotional side of his nature recognized in marriage a fulfilment beyond what even Christian friends can offer. Meanwhile, he made sure that what was for him a particular calling was not an example to be blindly followed. 'Thank you for discouraging my youthful thoughts about staying single …' a former study assistant wrote to him from the heart of a growing family. An Indian, once a student in London, tells the same story of how, in his mid-twenties,

> I used to fancy myself as a bachelor worker for the Lord. However, to my annoyance John Stott told me that I would be a much better Christian after marriage. I did think then, 'How dare he suggest this, being a bachelor himself.' In fact, he was right.[66]

But, for himself, John Stott had no doubts once he had fully discerned this aspect of his call. He put a brave face on it. 'How do you manage to write amid the pressures?' Keith Weston asked him once, to receive the answer: 'Retain the bliss of singleness.'[67]

4

'Good characters in fiction are the very devil', C. S. Lewis wrote. 'Not only because most authors have too little material to make them of, but because we as readers have a strong sub-conscious wish to find them incredible.' And in reply to Joan, a small girl from Florida who had written to him as the creator of Narnia, he offered some advice to a future writer:

> Don't use adjectives which merely tell us how you want us to *feel* about things you are describing. I mean, instead of telling us a thing was 'terrible', describe it so that we'll be terrified. Don't say it was 'delightful'; make *us* say 'delightful' when we've read the description. You see, all those words (horrifying, wonderful, hideous, exquisite) are only like saying to your readers, 'Please will you do my job for me.'[68]

There are two problems here which apply not only to fiction but to such a biography as this. First, taken together, so many of John Stott's friends and colleagues from across the world describe him in words which, standing alone, might do little to suggest a credible and real humanity. And secondly, to avoid mere adjectives, a life-story must try, at every stage (as preceding chapters have tried), to portray something which epithets can only name. Intellectual qualities come high in all such descriptions. John Stott might think of himself as 'in no sense a New Testament scholar',[69] but the technical accuracy of the statement belies the disciplines of study. Again, 'structured, accessible, articulate' is one description of the many memoranda (in this case to do with LICC) which probed to the heart of an organizational problem. But (by another hand) these are also characterized as 'visionary, far-sighted and strategic', with a penetrating eye for detail. 'John could easily have been a Chief Executive Officer or Managing Director in business, but ... was always first and foremost a man of God, pastor and theologian.'[70] His incisive mind (which he had to train, generally with success, to patience when dealing with those whose pace was slower) could come as a surprise to those with a stereotyped image of the clergy, or who had their own way of doing things. A study assistant describes an encounter with the media:

> Once, a man made an appointment to interview him for a radio show. He arrived while Uncle John was out, a couple of hours before he was expected back to his flat, and spent the time laboriously setting up his equipment. I asked how long he expected Uncle John to speak.
>
> 'Oh, I will only need six minutes, but I expect to interview him for half an hour or longer and then edit it down to what I want.'
>
> When Uncle John arrived, he would have none of the half-hour chat.
>
> 'Exactly what do you want me to say,' he asked, 'and for how long?'
>
> He then thought in silence for about thirty seconds, asked if the man was ready, and proceeded to deliver a beautifully crafted piece for precisely six minutes on exactly the topic required without any hesitation or repetition.
>
> The man told me afterwards, as he laboriously packed up all his equipment, that he had never heard anything like it.[71]

In similar vein, Michael Cassidy recalls a question-and-answer session with students in Africa, which could be paralleled in most other continents. He was impressed by the extraordinary eloquent, precise and articulate way John Stott would, off the cuff and extempore, answer questions from the floor:

> The answers were never superficial or trite, or theologically imprecise, but always manifested an extraordinary lucidity and grasp

of the issues, no matter what they were. And everything came at him from gender and women's issues and the homosexual issue, through to racial matters, capital punishment, conscientious objection and everything else which was pervasive in the dying throes of the apartheid era, when everything for all of us in South Africa was trauma.[72]

'Precision' is a common description of his use of words, taught first by his study of French and German. One of his curates congratulated him in All Souls vestry after a memorable sermon: 'That was vintage stuff, but what was a miasma?'

'A foggy cloud,' John Stott told him.

Thereafter he might find the same curate, 'after one of John Stott's more testing sermons', saying off-handedly in the vestry, 'A bit miasmic this evening!'[73]

He has never been afraid of reusing the same material, particularly a series which would eventually become the basis of a book. But familiarity with his material – even with an actual script – was all the more reason for prayerful preparation before each occasion:

> As we travelled throughout Latin America, he would sometimes preach the same sermon or sermons in different places. And yet, no matter how many times he had already given a Bible reading, he would still spend hours (at least two or three) in preparation for the next delivery of the very same message.[74]

When expositions on the same New Testament passages were given in different continents, they would be carefully contextualized. Again, Michael Cassidy noted in Africa how 'John had inevitably done a tremendous amount of preparation and it was wonderful how he was able to exegete the biblical text in a way which was relevant to the South African situation at the time. In every centre ministers poured out to meet with him, sit at his feet, ply him with questions ...'[75]

Perhaps because of these qualities of mind, John Stott can appear on occasion to place too much confidence in pure reason, and to believe that it holds the same self-evident pre-eminence for others as it does for him. Those whose cast of mind is more lateral than linear, and whose hearts respond more to imagery than to logic, can find themselves left behind by the relentless pursuit of the argument. Sometimes, too, he wrestles with issues to the point where they can be summarized almost too neatly, too symmetrically, to carry conviction; as when Michael Green spoke of how, in one of John Stott's expositions, 'St Paul might be pleasantly surprised to see how neatly he had subdivided his material when writing this Epistle.'[76]

Exceptional qualities of intellect are balanced by human attributes more widely shared: a mischievous sense of humour (Eddie Shirras, just ordained, attending a committee in a collar and tie: 'Mr Chairman, as a new deacon …' JRWS: 'You don't look like one!'),[77] a sunny and generous disposition, a prayerful spirit, a peacemaker (witness his 'swan-song' call for evangelical unity'),[78] kind, contented and unassuming, authentic, genuine, consistent. Consistency and integrity, indeed, come in for special mention from those closest to him: 'He is passionate to live what he teaches others. And he is passionate about integrity, about being pure in heart and speech, about being truthful before God and others, and about living by his deepest convictions.' Or, more simply, 'He is the same man in the pulpit as he is in the garden at Hookses.'

John Stott's personal lifestyle has always been unpretentious. In the early days of his ministry he had very little money and, when his books began to earn some, he gave nearly all of it away. But following the Lausanne Covenant he has deliberately cultivated simplicity, in solidarity with the poor, from a concern for the environment, and in the spirit of the slogan 'Live simply that others may simply live'. There are few clothes in his wardrobe; he hates shopping apart from his weekly ten minutes in Tesco, and sometimes his inexperience and unworldliness (or is it his sense of mischief?) shows:

> He went one day to look for a new sports jacket and found himself rather attracted by a Cashmere one which, as he said, 'felt nice and soft'. He, of course, had no idea what these things cost and enquired of a sales assistant. 'Four seventy-five, sir,' he was told. 'That sounds extremely good value,' replied John, blissfully unaware that what was required was £475, not £4.75!'[79]

On his own, his diet can verge on the alarmingly frugal for days at a time: a bowl of muesli, a sandwich, a piece of chocolate (but not in Lent), perhaps ice-cream if there should be any in the freezer compartment. As a guest, he refuses second helpings on principle (wily hosts know this, and make sure he has a proper first helping!). He watches his weight, and if the scales suggest it, he misses a meal. Since the 1960s when, urged on by Ted Schroder, he abandoned his earlier teetotal principles, his kitchen cupboard has generally contained a modest bottle of sherry (and, at The Hookses, wine for dinner-parties) which he can offer guests. Characteristically, he can still recall the occasion which precipitated the change:

> While Rector I was invited to dinner with a Nigerian couple. I'd expected to be one of a party and found to my surprise I was the only guest. During the meal they produced a bottle of wine which

had obviously been bought in my honour, and I felt it would be such a breach of charity that I broke the practice of twenty-five years.[80]

Many books are sent to him by their authors or publishers; others are borrowed from libraries; few are bought, and those that are will often be given away, perhaps to the library of the London Institute where many of his books have gone. As an undergraduate he found half an hour a day to read *The Times* ('worshipping his idol', his friends called it); but for years now he has taken only a weekly paper, originally *The Times*, later *The Guardian*, asserting that the news of the day is presented in better perspective – and takes less time to read. He is of necessity a diligent and disciplined reader, mostly in connection with whatever he is writing at the moment, or in preparation for his next lecture or overseas visit. Sometimes he will read a few pages of his current Trollope or Dickens ('I try to keep a book for pleasure going'); or, at The Hookses, Saki of an evening. He will listen to tapes in the car (Sherlock Holmes has been known); and usually manages to watch some of what seems significant in the cinema or the London theatre, often by taking visitors or friends.[81] He is an unlikely fan of James Bond (the playful Registrar of the London Institute enrolled him with the membership number 007), which appeals to the small boy who can often be found not far beneath the surface:

> Whenever we finish a meal [one of his American hosts recounts], I will turn to him and ask, 'How was that last bit for you?' He will usually say, 'The meal was good, but that last mouthful was some-what bitter tasting.' This, of course, will lead to the request for dessert, or for the only vice the man seems to have – chocolate!![82]

Since his eyesight was impaired he no longer drives; but those who were driven by him often found it a knuckle-whitening experience. Those who chauffered him (assuming he was not asleep) would find him anxious not to waste time by dawdling. For one who expounded the Christian's duty to the State, and who knew the apostle Peter's call to 'obey every man-made authority for the Lord's sake',[83] he was skilled at convincing himself that speed limits applied only to other people, or different circumstances, or perhaps were only suggestions or approximations. After a lecture at a summer school in Vancouver he was once having his usual free-for-all of questions from the floor:

> I vividly remember one young man stepping up to the microphone to ask, 'Is it ever permissible for Christians to exceed the speed limit?' John's reply had the audience in stitches. After offering the

usual thorough theological grounding and hedging, he came to the point: at night, if streets are clear and there is no danger to anyone, he thought it might be permissible for Christians 'to exceed the speed limit just slightly ...'[84]

Though born and bred a Londoner, and thoroughly at home in cities, John Stott has from early childhood always been more than urban man. Even before the days of Robbie Bickersteth he was a student of the natural world, with a love of wild places. Regarded primarily as a thinker, he was always happy to be a man of action. In a BBC programme, while he was still Rector, he described a particular incident:

> I was driving home to the West End one night from Hampstead. It must have been about 11 o'clock. I wasn't thinking about anything in particular, when suddenly my attention was arrested by a gang of youths who were obviously warming up for a fight. It looked a rather ugly situation. So I slowed down to see what was happening. At that moment, I saw a hulking young man knock a smaller fellow over onto the pavement and proceed to kick him viciously in the side. He then started man-handling a girl.

John Stott stopped the car and went over and remonstrated, to find himself attacked instead; a call for the police, and a few people at a bus stop watching, were enough for the gang to move away. 'My friends tell me I was a silly ass even to attempt to intervene,' John Stott added; 'the bully might have had a knife' – and he went on to make the point that 'Christianity is all about getting involved'.[85]

At The Hookses, in his late seventies, he was still never happier than with some labour-intensive, and preferably messy, job on his small estate. 'It is just glorious at Hookses this week,' Frances Whitehead wrote in 1999. 'We have had almost unbroken sunshine: we are revelling in the beauty and the peace. In the afternoons John has been humping damp pond weed from there, up the steps and round to the compost heap – he counted twelve loads one day and thirteen the next! I don't know how his back survives!'[86] Often study assistants, perhaps fifty years his junior, would find it hard to keep pace. New arrivals would come, having heard they were likely to be introduced to serious birdwatching, but with little idea of what that might mean: 'from dawn to dusk, we tramped miles of tundra and bush in relative silence'. Indeed, birds and the pursuit of birds have featured everywhere in his life. Even in London, on the steps of All Souls, he and his churchwarden would find their attention straying:

> People were streaming out after Morning Service, with John at his

usual place on the right and myself opposite him – where I could keep an eye on things and tactfully detach the occasional visitor who tried to monopolise him. Suddenly, above the human chatter and the noise of traffic, a kestrel's call rang out loud and clear, giving me a rare chance of pointing out a bird call that he did not know.[87]

He could be distracted by them at a prayer meeting in a Chilean prison as easily as in a classroom at Rugby or on a golf course in America with Billy Graham. What Margaret Clarkson called 'the fraternity of the field-glass'[88] put him in touch with fellow-ornithologists wherever his travels took him. 'I am not ashamed to recommend birdwatching to you', he told a group of Latin American student leaders,[89] just as, twenty years before, he had declared unhesitatingly that 'every Christian should take an interest in natural history'.[90] But where others find they cannot share his enthusiasm, this is taken in good part. Lorne Sanny of the Navigators once received a book from him inscribed to a 'dear friend and failed bird watcher'.[91]

'His secret agenda is always birds,' reflected a study assistant after a visit to an East African game park: 'Our poor driver has probably never had a passenger so enamoured with the bird life. Several times we have stopped to watch a bird for some time, only to look behind us and see a line of vans trying to discover what animal we have spotted! ... there are often times when we go an hour or two without seeing any game, but we always see birds.'[92] Over the years he has made himself a skilled bird-photographer; something which began with his father's present of a modest camera when he was still at prep school, then fell into abeyance during the war, since film was unobtainable, and was resumed when he set himself up with 35mm equipment in the 1950s. Later, sometimes with the help of Richard Bewes, he prepared a series of tape and slide presentations on his travels, with a strong ornithological emphasis.

The overseas diaries are always strong on bird life. Quotations in earlier chapters represent only a fraction of such entries. Here is a final glimpse of John Stott the bird-lover, at the University of Manitoba's field station at Delta Marsh:

I've been lent one of the bicycles belonging to the university, and each morning I've sallied forth along one of the gravel roads which intersect the marsh. It is unbelievably peaceful and beautiful. With no pressures, and no timetable to keep except lunch and dinner, I have been able to watch and photograph birds to my heart's content. One morning, wearing waist-high waterproof boots, I plunged into the marsh up to my middle, invading a colony of Yellowheaded Blackbirds, which gradually got used to my intrusion and posed nicely before my camera. Words cannot adequately describe the beauty of Bobolinks, Wilson's Phalaropes, Redwinged Blackbirds and other species ...[93]

5

'I owe my very soul to the Scripture Union,' John Stott has said on occasion, remembering that Bash was a staff-worker for them.[94] In the early days his Bible reading was guided by SU daily notes, but in *I Believe in Preaching*, published in 1982, he described what had by then long become his own practice:

> I am personally grateful to Dr Martyn Lloyd-Jones, formerly minister of Westminster Chapel, for introducing me perhaps twenty years ago to Robert Murray McCheyne's 'Bible Reading Calendar'. McCheyne produced it in 1842 for the members of St Peter's Church in Dundee, Scotland, which he was serving at that time. It enables one to read the whole Bible through every year, the Old Testament once and the New Testament twice ... McCheyne's lectionary sets four chapters to be read daily. His intention in those tranquil Victorian days was for two to be read in private devotions (morning and evening) and the other two in family prayers (also morning and evening) every day. My own practice has been rather to take three chapters each morning, if possible reading two and studying the third, and to keep the fourth chapter for the evening.[95]

Three chapters a morning indicates early rising. Interviewed at the Senior Evangelical Anglican Clergy Conference in 1990, John Stott was asked how he began the day:

> Well, you are taxing me! I listen to the World Service of the BBC from 5 to 5.30 every morning while I'm shaving and showering; it's a very good half-hour programme, 'News Desk' and '24 hours'; it's not only news but it's comment on the news ... and half an hour is exactly right for shaving and showering and dressing. I have a glass of orange juice and make myself a cup of coffee and then I have a quiet time, of I suppose about an hour, in Bible reading and prayer; then I move on to reading a book, another book, doing some more serious Bible study, sometimes dictating letters if I'm going out early to lecture and I need to dictate before I go.[96]

The very start of the day, even before the BBC World Service, will often include a threefold greeting to the Holy Trinity, followed by a sentence of worship and another of petition for the day ahead. Sometimes this will be followed by a recital of the Spirit's nine-fold fruit, a practice of long standing. As far back as 1975 he was writing:

> I think I may say with truthfulness that it has been my practice for many years to pray every day that God will fill me with his Spirit and cause more of the Spirit's fruit to appear in my life.[97]

Sometimes, too, in accordance with Paul's appeal in Romans 12 'to offer your bodies as living sacrifices', John Stott will take the apostle at his word and do exactly that:

> Almost the first thing I do when I awake in the morning, when my alarm clock goes off, is to swing my legs out of bed and sit on the side of my bed and present my body to God. And I sometimes go from limb to limb, the hand, the lips, the ears, the eyes, the feet, and present my body to God afresh for that day as spiritual worship.[98]

He has on occasion been cited as an example of 'evangelical spirituality',[99] but it is not a term which appeals to him.

> I've never liked very much the phrase *spiritual formation* [he told an American interviewer], any more than I like the word *spirituality*. They seem to me to perpetuate the disastrous division between spiritual and secular ... What we would want to infer is that there is nothing that is 'secular' or 'profane' and that there is no such thing as spirituality over against secular concerns or the secular world.
>
> The second reason I don't like it is because it's not really a biblical phrase. The biblical phrase for 'spirituality' and 'spiritual formation' is discipleship.[100]

But by whatever name, it is these early morning hours which sustain and nurture a walk with Christ marked by an inner spiritual – some would say mystical – quality of devotion.[101] They are also times of intercession, unhurried, aided by lists and prayer diaries, but never a mere string of names. Chua Wee Hian, when he was General Secretary of IFES (the International Fellowship of Evangelical Students), was talking with John Stott and noticed how he was 'mentioning various prayer requests which we had listed in the IFES "Praise and Prayer" bulletin. I discovered that he was using this regularly and that he was able to remember names of people who were being prayed for better than I did!'[102]

Prayer and worship, the reading and study of the Scriptures, all that the Anglican 'General Thanksgiving' speaks of as means of grace, served to focus and intensify a single aim. The story goes that early in the 1970s a 'hard-nosed TV interviewer' in Chicago asked a personal question which went something like this:

'Mr Stott, you've had a brilliant academic career; firsts at Cambridge, Rector at twenty-nine, Chaplain to the Queen; what is your ambition *now*?'

In a five-word reply, John Stott said it all: 'To be more like Jesus.'[103]

After that, what is there left to say?

6

To Archbishop Donald Coggan, the word that summed up John Stott was 'courtesy';[104] and perhaps that is simply one aspect of Christian humility. Such unfeigned humility is a quality John Stott covets for himself, for those he pastors, and for all who see themselves as evangelicals, gospel people.[105] It is of course a word beset by misunderstandings. John Baillie wrote once of how 'in an autobiographical work published in the year 1930 I read the words, "I have never lost the childlike humility which characterizes all truly great men"!'[106] To John Stott, certainly as far back as 1970, humility had come to mean 'nothing but the truth. Humility is a synonym for honesty, not hypocrisy.'[107] It implies, too, submission and dependence, beginning with submission to Scripture: 'an essential element in Christian humility is the willingness to hear and receive God's Word.'[108] It was a theme to which he often returned in his writing, as for example in the Coda to his *Evangelical Truth* on 'The pre-eminence of humility'; or, less accessibly (at least to non-American readers) but offering a fuller exposition, in his contribution to a *Festschrift* for James Houston on his seventieth birthday, 'Pride, Humility and God'.[109] Humility is not only honesty; but (by facing honestly our flawed humanity) is the antithesis of human vanity and egotism. 'Probably at no point does the Christian mind clash more violently with the secular mind than in its insistence on humility and its implacable hostility to pride.'[110]

It is with this background of understanding that so many who have worked with John Stott, or count themselves his friends, think of humility as one of his most striking and most endearing qualities. In the words quoted in the Foreword, 'he genuinely disengages from the high opinion others have of him'. Speaking to clergy and ministers at the Keswick Convention in 1975 he began by describing himself as 'always a sinner and often a failure',[111] and this is no perfunctory or formal self-depreciation. He says it because he believes it and knows it to be as true of himself as of others. Yet perhaps it is part of his personal humility that he can be too trusting of others, too confident that matters can safely be left in hands which (as subsequent history proves) are less sure and able than his own; too ready to believe that forms of words which convey to him a satisfactory resolution (as with the publication of *Gospel and Spirit*)[112] will put a difficult issue to rest. For himself, he is regretfully aware that, under pressure or out of sorts, harried by deadlines and unnecessary complications to his plans, he can be irritable or out of temper: the obverse of his care for detail and capacity for work. It is not that he is 'a man without faults', a younger colleague wrote of him, 'but even in his weaknesses, he makes no attempts to conceal or bury his blemishes. The few times he has hurt me he has been humble enough to ask for forgiveness.' But it remains a struggle, as it will do for all Christians until the end:

> Once, after returning to a particularly large stack of arrears following a long trip, John was unusually glum, in fact, even sour. Both Frances and I tried to steer clear of him that day. The next morning when I came to work I could see the cloud just beginning to lift and said apologetically, 'I am sorry that there is so much for you to do and that Frances and I couldn't have handled more of it for you.' John's immediate and insistent comeback was, 'No, no, I'm repenting of the sin of self-pity and I don't need you to get me back into it!' End of discussion.[113]

But it is significant that such days are rare enough to stick in the memory. Another study assistant wrote to him at the end of his period of service:

> People ask me, 'What is John Stott's secret?' This is an annoying question, to which there is no good answer. Instead of answering directly, I have taken to telling people that although you have no 'secret' there are several characteristics I have observed in you that I will seek to emulate for the rest of my life. The three things I always mention are rigorous self-discipline, absolute humility and a prayerful spirit. Perhaps the most important thing I have learned from you is that, by grace, faithfulness to God is a combination of these three qualities.

The ground of true humility is the Christian doctrine of grace, as shown in the first of the three texts that the seventh Earl of Shaftesbury chose for his simple monument at Wimborne St Giles: 'What hast thou that thou didst not receive?'[114] To be a debtor to grace is to be liberated from false ideas of self-worth.

Every afternoon at 4.30pm I bring Uncle John a cup of coffee [wrote one of his assistants]. As soon as I set the cup on his desk, he almost always says, somewhat playfully, 'I'm not worthy,' usually without moving his bowed head from his papers. One afternoon last week I felt that it was particularly silly for him to equate worthiness with a cup of coffee. When he said, 'I'm not worthy', I responded, 'Sure, you are.' After a few moments he said, 'You haven't got your theology of grace right.' I said back, 'It's only a cup of coffee, Uncle John.' As I went into his kitchen and began putting things away, I heard him mutter, still with his head bowed to his papers, 'It's just the thin end of the wedge.'

Brought up with servants from childhood – domestic servants in the family home, servants at school, college servants at Trinity – he is now uneasy being waited on and much prefers to do the serving himself. At The Hookses he regards the washing-up as his own prerogative:

He won't let the rest of us wash the breakfast or lunch dishes. He insists they be left for him until after dinner. He says it is his way of contributing to the meals, since he never cooks. This is true, but I think the other reason he insists on dish duty is because of the sheer joy he gets out of cleaning up the kitchen.[115]

A consequence of his own humility of mind is the respect and dignity which he naturally accords to those he meets, and which, sadly, can seem particularly striking in some parts of the world as coming from an Englishman. An IFES colleague from Latin America who worked with him in Cuba recalls how,

... after I finished five days of translating for him, he invited me to do some birdwatching with him but I fell very ill. What a privilege it was to be fed, cared for, prayed over, comforted and affectionately ministered to by him. I have the impression that the chambermaids in the hotel where we stayed thought that I must be an extremely important person because I was being taken care of by a distin-guished white, Anglo-Saxon gentleman – something they had never seen before.[116]

7

When Anthony Trollope came to the end of *Barchester Towers*, he concluded with a final word about the Reverend Mr Harding, Precentor of Barchester and pastor of the little church of St Cuthbert:

The Author now leaves him in the hands of his readers; not as a hero, not as a man to be admired and talked of, not as a man who should be toasted at public dinners and spoken of with conventional absurdity as a perfect divine, but as a good man without guile, believing humbly in the religion which he has striven to teach, and guided by the precepts which he has striven to learn.[117]

This is how Trollope, and indeed his readers ever since, are pleased to remember the gentle, saintly and very human Mr Harding. Who would not be content with such a farewell? But of John Stott, history will come to say more. For the later decades of the twentieth century he was a leader – in some senses *the* leader – of world evangelicalism at a time of growth in numbers, confidence and maturity unparalleled for generations. His influence will live on; and his book *Evangelical Truth* ('an attempt to summarize the essence of the evangelical faith') contains what he described as 'a kind of spiritual legacy ... how I would like to be remembered'.[118]

Meanwhile, as this book closes, he remains busy and active, very much alive. Overseas visits are planned; more books are contemplated; the scripts of his London Lectures for the millennial year are on his desk, the theme he has chosen a characteristic reflection of his lifetime's discipleship, *The Incomparable Christ*.[119]

That would be a fitting note on which to end; but many readers, surely, will want to identify themselves by way of postscript with a recent letter to John Stott from a former study assistant. After two or three pages of news from across the Atlantic about himself and his family, the letter ends, 'Thank you for your ministry to me ... I feel most blessed to be your friend. Please live for ever.'

Notes

The reference 'Taped interview', unless otherwise stated, is to a series of recorded conversations between John Stott and the author, mainly at The Hookses in the autumn of 1992, supplemented by later interviews. The numbers following (e.g. 8/18) indicate interview and page number of transcript; in this case, page 18 of the eighth interview.

Foreword

[1] Hooper (ed.) (1979), p. 494; letter dated 10 December 1942.

[2] For example, in a letter dated 2 November 1995, John Stott wrote, 'I myself seldom use the epithet "Christian", mainly because of the cultural baggage which the word carries in many parts of the world, and prefer to refer to the "disciples" or "followers of Jesus Christ".' He made the same point at the Washington National Prayer Breakfast, 1983.

[3] Boswell (1968), vol. 2, p. 173.

[4] Thurman (1982), p. 281. She had just had to admit defeat in the struggle to retain her African farm.

[5] The Cambridge mission of 1977, which features in chapter 5 of this book, marked fifty university missions completed in twenty-five years.

[6] For more information, up to the end of 1994, see Dudley-Smith (1995). Page numbers given in these endnotes always refer to the UK edition of a book cited unless otherwise stated. When books have appeared under more than one title, for example with US editions, only the UK title is used in the text, but the alternative is shown in the Bibliography (pp. 506ff.).

[7] Boswell (1968), vol. 1, p. 29.

[8] *The Times* diary, 23 September 1998.

[9] Quoted in Gere and Sparrow (eds.) (1981), p. 73.

[10] Letter dated 13 April 1866, quoted in Newsome (1993), p. 1.

[11] Dillistone (1980), p. 6. Canon Dillistone could write the more frankly since Max Warren had died three years before.

[12] Pollock (1962), p. 11.

[13] The leaves of the diary are written on both sides, but numbered only on the front. References to the verso of a page are therefore given by quoting the number from the front, but adding the letter 'a'. 'Page 12' therefore means the front of leaf no. 12; and 'page 12a' the back.

[14] Books on travel, and on the natural sciences of his day, feature in his journal. Perhaps

'Bishop Pontopidan's *Natural History of Norway*', which he looked into while at Canterbury (26 November 1761), contained descriptions of Scandinavian bird life as well as the 'craken and sea serpent'.
[15] Meyers (1996), p. 152.

Chapter 1. An Established Ministry: All Souls and Beyond

[1] See, for this epithet and for a useful summary, T. E. Yates (1994), pp. 163–164.
[2] Norman (1976), p. 416n., quoting Robinson (1970), p. 242.
[3] Stott (1982b), p. 55. There is also a summary in his 'Historical Introduction' to Stott (ed.) (1996), pp. xii–xiii.
[4] J. Wolfe, "Religion and 'Secularization'" in P. Johnson (ed.) (1994), p. 481.
[5] M. Howard and Louis (eds.) (1998), p. 169.
[6] Welsby (1984), p. 99. In America, 1965 was the year of publication of Harvey Cox's influential *The Secular City*.
[7] Marwick (1998), p. 802. The book is a major study by an academic historian of the cultural revolution during what he calls 'the long sixties', extending from about 1958 to 1974. References to the place of religion in this period are minimal in the extreme.
[8] Hastings (1991), p. 582.
[9] Mrs Caroline Bowerman. Taped interview, 18 May 1995.
[10] Memorandum to the author, September 1996.
[11] See also Thurman (1982).
[12] On her death, John Stott contributed an appreciation to *All Souls*, August 1974.
[13] Robbie Low, 'An Interview with Michael Harper', *New Directions*, October 1966.
[14] Michael C. Harper. Taped interview, 27 July 1994. On leaving All Souls Michael Harper became for ten years General Secretary and Director of Sharing of Ministries Abroad, teaching and promoting the charismatic experience. He became Canon of Chichester in 1984, and in the early 1990s was received into the Orthodox Church and became Dean of the new British Antiochian Orthodox Deanery.
[15] Robbie Low, 'An Interview with Michael Harper', *New Directions*, October 1966.
[16] John Stott. Taped interview, 9 September 1992. In a personal letter of 1994 John Stott referred to this incident and added: 'it has influenced my attitude to tongue-speaking ever since'. JRWS papers. Letter dated 24 October 1994.
[17] Luker (1979), p. 63.
[18] Michael Harper. Taped interview, 27 July 1994.
[19] Luker (1979), p. 18.
[20] *Ibid.*, pp. 23–24.
[21] G. A. R. Swannell. Letter to the author, 1993.
[22] Sir Norman Anderson. Taped interview, 17 January 1991. He added that John Stott continued for some years to write to him and Lady Anderson on the anniversary of Hugh's death. See also Anderson (1985), pp. 226–227.
[23] JRWS diary. 'A visit to African University Colleges, April–June 1962', p. 26.
[24] Robert Howarth. Memorandum to the author, 1996. He was ordained as curate to All Souls in 1972.
[25] John Stott. Letter to the author, 3 August 1998.
[26] John Wesley, *Journal*, 11 June 1739.
[27] Michael Wilcock. Taped interview, 10 June 1992.
[28] Memorandum to the author, 1996.
[29] Ted Schroder. Memorandum to the author, 2 August 1997.
[30] Stott (1992a), p. 103.
[31] Ted Schroder. Letter to the author, 13 August 1997. The letter goes on to point out that John Stott was not at all unaware of the importance of listening. His book *I Believe in Preaching* (1982b) makes this clear: 'We need, then, to ask people questions and get them talking … it is important for us to listen. Humble listening is indispensable to relevant preaching' (p. 192).

[32] John Stott. Memorandum to the author, September 1996.

[33] George H. Cassidy. Letter to the author, 22 March 1995. George and Jane Cassidy had been in Nairobi and returned so that he could train for ordination. Their temporary home was at 13 Bridford Mews, where John Stott later lived as Rector Emeritus, 'a very grotty run-down little mews flat above the Rectory garage'. After twelve years as Archdeacon of London, George Cassidy became Bishop of Southwell in 1999.

[34] For example, his book *The Contemporary Christian* (1992a) is sub-titled *An Urgent Plea for Double Listening.*

[35] Stott (1969); see pp. 82ff.

[36] *Ibid.*, p. 98.

[37] Luker (1979), p. 62.

[38] Letter to the author, 18 November 1996.

[39] George Skinner Ingram was a well-known figure in All Souls: 'After many years of service in India with the C.M.S. during which he was awarded the M.B.E. for his work among the "untouchables", George and his wife, May, returned to England in 1952.' Hocken (1986), p. 82.

[40] Taped interview, 18 February 1993.

[41] From an account of the interview entitled 'Serving Christ and his Church', *The Church of England Newspaper*, 16 May 1969.

[42] Letter to the author, 5 October 1995. Roger Simpson was ordained in 1979 as curate at All Souls and moved to a Canadian pastorate in 1995. He became Vicar of St Michael-le-Belfrey, York, in 1999.

[43] Michael Eric Marshall was consecrated Bishop of Woolwich in succession to David Sheppard in 1975; and in 1992 became Archbishops' Adviser for the 'Springboard' initiative of the Decade of Evangelism.

[44] Stott and Meeking (eds.) (1986).

[45] Bebbington (1989), p. 150. The chapter links Keswick holiness teaching with the faith-mission principle and premillennialism as an expression of the permeation of nineteenth-century evangelicalism by Romantic thought.

[46] McGrath (1997), p. 54. As an undergraduate Packer had been deeply troubled by Keswick teaching in his own search for spiritual maturity and power. See p. 23.

[47] J. I. Packer, *The Evangelical Quarterly*, July 1955, p. 153. See in full pp. 153–167. The book in question, Barabas (1952), had been reviewed in the same journal three years before by G. W. Bromiley, who found 'no basic discrepancy between the Reformed and evangelical doctrine and the message of Keswick'. *The Evangelical Quarterly*, October 1952, p. 231.

[48] J. I. Packer, *The Evangelical Quarterly*, July 1955, pp. 166–167.

[49] McGrath (1997), p. 77. See also pp. 22–23. Packer's own account puts it all a good deal more strongly ('hatred of the cruel and tormenting unrealities of overheated holiness teaching') while acknowledging Keswick's strengths and making it clear that he speaks of the past rather than the present. See his Preface to the centenary edition of J. C. Ryle's *Holiness* (1979), pp. vii–viii, reproduced at length in Packer (1984), pp. 148, 158.

[50] Elisabeth Earnshaw-Smith. Taped interview, 15 May 1995.

[51] Memorandum to the author, 2 February 1996. Note the final cautionary phrase.

[52] Taped interview, 8/18.

[53] Pollock (1964), p. 174.

[54] *Ibid.*, p. 175.

[55] E. R. Appleton. Conversation with the author, 15 September 1993.

[56] Charles and Shirley Horne. Letter to the author, 1995. For an account of these events see Horne (1973).

[57] The Very Revd Dr Peter C. Moore. Letter to the author, 28 March 1995. At earlier meetings of the Convention, both Graham Scroggie and Ernest Kevan had expounded these chapters.

[58] Balleine (1908), p. 198. Wilson's appointment in 1824 was much resented because he

was an evangelical with a vision for the whole community. At his first Confirmation he presented to the bishop 780 candidates!

[59] His address on 'The Church's Continuing Mission in the Parish' was published in the Report of the Conference, *The Church Extends her Frontiers* (1955).

[60] Editorial, *Crusade*, March 1964, p. 3.

[61] Editorial, *The Churchman*, September 1962, pp. 131–135. Alister McGrath adds that when this editorial was reprinted as a pamphlet it is estimated to have sold 39,000 copies. See McGrath (1997), p. 329, n. 20.

[62] According to Peter Hocken, George Ingram understood by the baptism of the Spirit an experience of entire sanctification, such as he had received as an undergraduate at Cambridge many years before. Hocken (1986), p. 84.

[63] *Ibid.*, p. 85.

[64] Letter to the author, 4 August 1995. The Revd Roopsingh Carr returned to India in 1971 after study at the London Bible College and St John's College, Nottingham; and in 1980 became Executive Director of the SALT (Scripture Applied Leadership Training) Institute, Madras.

[65] Hocken (1986), p. 88.

[66] Watson (1983), p. 58. See p. 57 for Lloyd-Jones's often-quoted 'Gentlemen, I believe that you have been baptized with the Holy Spirit'.

[67] Tidball (1994), p. 73.

[68] *Ibid.*, p. 112. Tidball adds that Michael Harper himself warned of this danger.

[69] JRWS papers. Letter in reply to Mr Edward Doring, dated 29 October 1995.

[70] J. Martin (1997), pp. 166–167.

[71] Stott (1964a), p. 5. Though the booklet, and the address on which it was based, were firmly directed to the mid-1960s, the main points on (for example) 'baptism of the Spirit' had been argued along identical lines twelve years before in his brief article 'The Spirit and the Church', *Inter-Varsity*, Autumn Term 1952.

[72] Stott (1964a), p. 6.

[73] *Ibid.*, p. 25.

[74] *Ibid.*, p. 35.

[75] 'Life in the Spirit of Truth': John Stott interviewed by Roy McCloughry, *Third Way*, October 1995. See also the joint statement *Gospel and Spirit* (1977).

[76] Stott (1975b), p. 9.

[77] Taped interview, 8/30.

[78] See, for example, 'Life in the Spirit of Truth': John Stott interviewed by Roy McCloughry, *Third Way*, October 1995.

[79] In R. P. P. Johnston (ed.) (1966), p. 12.

[80] *Ibid.*, p. 15.

[81] Palmer (1992), p. 271. See also Heath (1995), pp. 313–314, which attributes this summary to Sir John Hewitt, his Secretary for Appointments.

[82] In 1962 Mrs G. M. Blake, a lay member of the diocese, suggested his name for the See of Gloucester; in 1963 the Southwell Evangelical Clergy Union (invited to suggest names by the Prime Minister's Secretary for Appointments) put forward those of Canon T. F. C. Bewes, Vicar of Tonbridge; the Ven. Ivan D. Neill, Chaplain General to the Forces; and John Stott. In 1965 a lay member of Church Assembly, Kenneth P. Cutting, suggested John Stott's name for St Edmundsbury and Ipswich. Public Record Office, PREM 5/470, PREM 5/485, PREM 5/494.

[83] Public Record Office, PREM 5/485, 4 November 1963. Canon M. A. P. Wood became Bishop of Norwich in 1971, nearly eight years later.

[84] For example, C. W. J. Bowles, who accepted Derby at the end of the decade; Professor W. Owen Chadwick, who proved elusive; Canon Max Warren, who told Geoffrey Fisher in 1956 that 'quite a lot of the necessary work of a Bishop he would find not only uncongenial but frustrating, and he could not really put his heart into it …' Public Record Office, PREM 5/473; Archbishop Fisher to (Sir) David Stephens, 17 February 1956.

[85] E. Carpenter (1991), p. 227.
[86] Stockwood (1982), p. 97.
[87] Canon Michael Saward. Memorandum to the author, 31 October 1995.
[88] Chadwick (1990a), p. 104.
[89] Palmer (1992), p. 270.
[90] *Ibid.*, p. 272.
[91] Chadwick (1990b), p. 10.
[92] Chadwick (1990a), p. 142.
[93] H. Carpenter (1996), p. 341. It should be added that Bennett was a very troubled man at the time and that the Archbishop's comment was in a talk on the telephone. See the footnote on the same page quoting from Michael Baughen.
[94] Hastings (1991), p. 456.
[95] For example, in his personal diary during an American visit, he confessed that he had sometimes felt painfully 'in limbo', adding, 'Although it has been by quite deliberate decisions, I hope and believe in response to God's call, that I have turned away from a traditional career-climb in the ecclesiastical institution', yet his position, for all the love and recognition which were shown to him, was not without its pain and sense of rejection by the church of his baptism. JRWS diary. 'Bay Area, Vancouver and Alaska: 19 July to 31 August 1981', p. 43a. The comment is made that had he lived twenty or thirty years later it would have been a different story. (See for example Peter Forster, 'Evangelical Enigma', *Church Times*, 9 July 1999). Perhaps; but such speculations should not overlook the way in which his own ministry paved the way for the appointment of evangelical archdeacons and bishops in and beyond the 1970s. Not only had he played a decisive part in creating a new climate of opinion towards evangelical churchmanship, but in many instances he had contributed to the personal formation of individuals in a way which lent credibility to their nomination.
[96] Taped interview, 18/5.
[97] Taped interview, 19/48. See his address to the Islington Clerical Conference, 1964, cited above (n. 71).
[98] Terry Lovell, 'The Times and Travels of "an Ordinary Christian"', *The Christian Bookseller*, May–June 1993.
[99] Letter to the author, 3 August 1998. The author recalls John Stott describing this visit in a personal conversation during a walk through Knole Park, Sevenoaks, probably in the late 1960s. He repeated it in much the same words in response to a question from Paul Handley, editor of the *Church Times*, 26 March 1999.
[100] Memorandum to the author, 28 November 1999. Michael Baughen and Lord Runcie confirm this recollection. Letters dated 7 December 1999, 16 December 1999.
[101] Smyth (1940), p. 7, quoting from Sir G. O. Trevelyan, *Life and Letters of Lord Macaulay* (1908), p. 50n.

Chapter 2. Evangelical Leadership: Furthering the Gospel

[1] For example, Professor K. Walters FRS was present as a young lecturer at 'that exciting week in November … responding warmly to the quite outstanding presentations. I believe John Stott was at the height of his communicative powers … it was all so moving, so God-honouring, so effective.' Letter to the author, 30 July 1996.
[2] Geraint D. Fielder. Letter to the author, 30 July 1996.
[3] This was the mission in which the Oxford Humanist Society, which had no fewer than 1,000 members, put up posters and distributed leaflets across the university attacking the CU's mission with John Stott: "Join OICCU now. Membership fee: your intellectual integrity and your social conscience."' Lowman (1983), p. 96. The Humanist Society had chosen the wrong mission and the wrong missioner for such a slogan to be convincing. Lowman adds that 'it was the Humanist Society, rather than the CU, that was virtually defunct soon afterwards'.
[4] Alex Williams. Letter to the author, 6 January 1996.

[5] JRWS papers. Letter from (Sir) Brian Young, 12 March 1964. C. T. Studd was a celebrated missionary, an Etonian and one of the 'Cambridge Seven' who volunteered for overseas mission following the D. L. Moody mission in Cambridge, 1882.

[6] JRWS papers. Letter dated 19 March 1964.

[7] See T. Dudley-Smith and A. S. D. Pierssené, 'Boys' Club Leadership: A Neglected Christian Opportunity', *Inter-Varsity*, Summer Term, 1954, pp. 17–20; Venables (1958).

[8] Minutes of the first meeting, 18 June 1964. I owe this reference and much of this information to Michael Eastman, FYT Secretary and Development Officer, 1967–98.

[9] Michael Eastman. Letter to the author, 13 January 2000.

[10] Since 1999, FYT, long since firmly established, has resumed full independence and is no longer part of SU. The Cambridge University Mission was renamed in the 1990s as the Salmon Youth Centre.

[11] The story is told in some detail in McGrath (1997), pp. 101ff.

[12] *Ibid.*, p. 103. Besides J. I. Packer, Latimer House owed much to John W. Wenham, one of the seminal minds of evangelical Anglicanism in his day, who was among its founders and served as Warden 1970–73; and to Roger T. Beckwith (Librarian, 1963–73; Warden 1973–94), whose work there was recognized by a Lambeth DD, 1992.

[13] Wenham (1998), p. 172.

[14] In McGrath (1997), p. 115.

[15] For the early beginnings from 1958 onwards, see volume one, chapter 11.

[16] M. L. Loane was Bishop Coadjutor and later Archbishop of Sydney and Primate of Australia. A. J. Dain was consecrated Assistant Bishop of Sydney in 1965.

[17] *Church Times*, 20 October 1961, p. 1.

[18] John Stott, 'World-wide Evangelical Anglicanism', in King (ed.) (1973), p. 176.

[19] See Leighton (1995), pp. 3, 79. It is a story in which John Stott plays a minor but influential part.

[20] Taped interview, 8/5.

[21] John Stott, 'World-wide Evangelical Anglicanism', in King (ed.) (1973), p. 177.

[22] Brown (1988), p. 36.

[23] Taped interview, 8/9. Two or three titles, such as E. M. B. Green's *Called to Serve* (1964) and John Stott's *Confess Your Sins* (1964b) and *Our Guilty Silence* (1967b) were later reprinted independently of the series.

[24] Dudley-Smith, Packer and Stott (1967).

[25] Taped interview, 18/1.

[26] Letter to the author, 1 January 1996. W. M. D. Persson took over from R. C. Lucas as Secretary of the Church of England Evangelical Council in 1965. He was Bishop of Doncaster, 1982–92.

[27] JRWS papers. From notes of a talk on the EFAC bursary scheme given at the 100th bursar celebration, 14 October 1986.

[28] *Ibid.*

[29] These extracts appear by courtesy of Mrs Monica Matthews, A. T. Houghton's daughter. 'Church Society' means the offices of Church Society in Wine Office Court, off Fleet Street. 'Oliver B.' refers to Oliver Barclay of the IVF; 'Frank' is A. T. Houghton's brother, formerly Bishop of Eastern Szechwan, China, and later General Director of the China Inland Mission; 'Wilkie' is the Revd L. F. E. Wilkinson, Principal of Oak Hill Theological College; 'Stibbs' is the Revd Alan Stibbs, his Vice-Principal; 'Hewitt' is the Revd Thomas Hewitt, Secretary of Church Society; 'Mohan' is Canon T. G. Mohan, Secretary of the Church Pastoral-Aid Society.

[30] CEEC Minute Book. See volume one, chapter 11, for some account of how CEEC evolved from the earlier IVF 'Church of England Group'.

[31] A. T. Houghton. Diary, 27 January 1961.

[32] *Ibid.*, 12 October 1961. Bishop Taylor's presidency was cut short by his sudden death on 13 December, his seventy-eighth birthday. The Bishop of Tonbridge was R. B. White.

[33] Lambeth Palace Library, Ramsey vol. 30, ff. 230r–v.

[34] *Ibid.*, ff. 283–285.

[35] The other signatories were the Revd. R. P. P. Johnston as President of the Islington Clerical Conference, and Lord Brentford and Lt General Sir Arthur Smith as Presidents of Church Society and the Church Pastoral-Aid Society respectively.

[36] Lambeth Palace Library, Ramsey vol. 30, f. 236.

[37] *Ibid.*, f. 249.

[38] *Ibid.*, f. 242. Sir R. E. Manningham-Buller became Lord Chancellor as Viscount Dilhorne (1962–64) later the same month.

[39] John R. W. Stott, 'Prayer Book Revision', *Church Times*, 22 and 29 March, 1963; reprinted in Stott (1963). Draft Canon B15 sought to limit traditional hospitality offered to non-Anglican communicants.

[40] JRWS papers. 'Reservation: A Note for Discussion', circulated with the Agenda for the first meeting of the group.

[41] See especially Articles 25 and 28.

[42] JRWS papers. Memorandum dated 22 June 1966.

[43] *Ibid.*

[44] JRWS papers. Report dated 14 September 1966 over the signature of the Bishop of London.

[45] JRWS papers. Letter to the Revd R. T. Beckwith, 17 December 1970. Roger Beckwith at Latimer House had supplied memoranda to John Stott and the evangelical members of the group.

[46] The Church of South India was inaugurated in 1947 from a union of churches which included Anglicans. Non-episcopally ordained ministers would be full ministers of the uniting church without re-ordination, though all future ministers would be episcopally ordained. It was a path to unity strongly recommended by evangelical leaders, including John Stott, in the UK Anglican–Methodist discussions.

[47] Anglican–Methodist Unity Commission (1968), p. 182.

[48] Welsby (1984), p. 170, gives the figure as 'more than a third'. But Chadwick (1990a), p. 340, gives 68.5% as willing to take part in the service.

[49] See Welsby (1984), pp. 78–79 and 166–167.

[50] See Crowe (ed.) (1967). Keele described the proposed Service of Reconciliation as 'needless, misleading and a cause of offence' (p. 40). For an account of the Congress, see chapter 3 below.

[51] *All Souls*, September 1969.

[52] *Ibid.*

[53] See *Crockford's Clerical Directory, 1969–70*, p. viii. The Preface is dated 'Michaelmas 1970'. Chadwick (1990a), p. 339, fully acquits the evangelicals and Anglo-Catholics of 'horse-trading in ecclesiastical politics. Feelings deep inside the soul were engaged on both sides.'

[54] Hastings (1991), p. 536, citing Robinson (1963).

[55] See Clements (1988), pp. 143–144.

[56] See Norman (1976), p. 420. Norman is here quoting a hostile reviewer.

[57] *The Observer*, 24 March 1963. See Hooper (1996), p. 115.

[58] Chadwick (1990a), p. 371. The interview was conducted on 1 April 1963. See also the pamphlet published later that month, Ramsey (1963), and Norman (1976), pp. 419, for Ramsey's later assessment.

[59] He was also a member of a small group of evangelicals (probably deputed by CEEC) led by Professor J. N. D. Anderson, who met personally with Bishop John Robinson to discuss and debate the issues raised by the book.

[60] *All Souls*, August 1963.

[61] See, for example, Packer (ed.) (1965). James Packer was Warden of Latimer House and a number of the contributors were at some point members of CEEC.

[62] CEEC Minutes, 5 February 1970.

[63] King (1969), p. 124. John King was Editor of *The Church of England Newspaper*, 1960–68.

[64] Annex to the CEEC Minutes, March 1965.

[65] *Ibid.*

[66] Colin Craston, influential in the higher reaches of Synodical Government and the Anglican Communion, expressed his own disappointment with CEEC in a short paragraph in his autobiography. See Craston (1998), p. 73.

[67] Leith Samuel, a personal friend of Dr Martyn Lloyd-Jones and an 'elder statesman' of Independent evangelicalism. Letter to the author, 7 April 1995. See also his autobiography, L. Samuel (1993), pp. 173–174, and his contribution to '18th October 1966: I was there ...' in *Foundations*, Autumn 1996. This issue of *Foundations*, sub-titled *A Journal of Evangelical Theology Published by the British Evangelical Council*, is largely devoted to Dr Martyn Lloyd-Jones's address at the Second National Assembly of Evangelicals; and offers perhaps the most comprehensive account yet published from an Independent and Free Church perspective in sympathy with Dr Lloyd-Jones's appeal and regretful of John Stott's intervention as chairman.

[68] Contribution to '18th October 1966: I was there ...', *Foundations*, Autumn 1996.

[69] Murray (1990), p. 523. John Stott gave three Bible readings at this Congress. At the end of one of them, Dr Lloyd-Jones took him to one side and said that he would like him to be his successor at Westminster Chapel. Taken totally aback, John Stott could only stammer that, while greatly honoured, he had no sense of calling to leave All Souls, or indeed the Church of England. Martyn Lloyd-Jones never referred to the matter again. Memorandum from John Stott to the author, 7 September 1998.

[70] As reported in *The Christian and Christianity Today*, 21 October 1966, p. 9. The opening reference to John Stott's continuing membership of the Church of England is his own recollection in a memorandum to the author, September 1996.

[71] Basil Howlett, contribution to '18th October 1966: I was there ...', *Foundations*, Autumn 1966.

[72] *Ibid.*, and quoted also by Leslie A. Rawlinson, who was present at the time. Letter to the author, 18 August 1999.

[73] Murray (1990), p. 523. Murray's account, pp. 522–528, written after consultation with John Stott, is admirably objective; and includes a fairly comprehensive survey of the press reports. See also Murray (2000), pp. 44–45.

[74] Lloyd-Jones (1989), p. 246.

[75] From the opening sentence of the lead story, 21 October 1966, p. 1.

[76] Lloyd-Jones (1989), p. 256.

[77] Bebbington (1989), p. 267.

[78] Robert Horn, 'His Place in Evangelicalism', in C. Catherwood (ed.) (1986), p. 2.

[79] Memorandum to the author, September 1996.

[80] *The Christian and Christianity Today*, 21 October 1966. See also Hylson-Smith (1988), p. 345.

[81] James Packer, 'A Kind of Puritan', in C. Catherwood (ed.) (1986), p. 45.

[82] JRWS papers. Douglas Johnson sent him a copy of the memorandum with a friendly covering letter dated 31 October 1966.

[83] John Stott, 'An Appreciation', in C. Catherwood (ed.) (1986), p. 207. It is important to notice the nature of this apology ('not for what I had said'), which is not always made clear in later accounts of the incident. See, for example, L. Samuel (1993), pp. 173–174. This account, while rightly blaming contemporary press reports as inaccurate, wrongly cites David Winter as Editor of *The Christian*, whose account of the confrontation spoke of a call 'to form a united church'. David Winter was in fact Editor of *Crusade* and Editorial Secretary of the Evangelical Alliance (the sponsors of the Assembly) and contributed a two-page report to *The Life of Faith*. 'Feelings ran high in the audience on Tuesday night,' he wrote, 'and one trembled for open debate in the circumstances. In the event there was no need to worry ...' (27 October 1966).

[84] Letter to the author, 4 February 1992.

[85] *Ibid.* Morgan Derham believed that the account of the meeting in Iain Murray's second

volume of Lloyd-Jones's biography is at fault 'in that it asserts that MLJ kept to his brief, and omits to say that he went beyond it in making a direct and forceful appeal in the words of Revelation – "Come out from Babylon"'. There is in fact no such reference in the address as now printed: but it is still clearly a forceful appeal and exhortation to take action. See 'Evangelical Unity: An Appeal', in Lloyd-Jones (1989), pp. 250, 254, 256.

[86] McGrath (1977), p. 125.

[87] David Bebbington, 'Evangelicalism in its Settings: The British and American Movements since 1940', in Noll, Bebbington and Rawlyk (eds.) (1994), p. 370.

[88] *Ibid.*

[89] *Evangelicals Now*, January 1991, p. 11.

[90] J. Martin (1997), p. 75.

[91] James Packer, 'A Kind of Puritan', in C. Catherwood (ed.) (1986), p. 56.

[92] Memorandum to the author, September 1996. Morgan Derham was rightly critical of the brief account which appeared under the heading 'Breaking Point' in the EA brochure *Called to One Hope* (1996), celebrating their 150th anniversary. It reports that 'supporters of both Stott and Lloyd-Jones left the EA in droves', which suggests that at the time a good deal of responsibility for the incident was felt to lie with the organizers of the meeting.

[93] *Foundations*, Autumn 1996; see n. 67 above.

[94] See, for example, the summary of an address by Dr J. I. Packer to Reform in 1995, citing the two 'bad arguments' used by Dr Lloyd-Jones. Packer concludes: 'So when people used to ask me why are you in the Church of England when the Church of England is in such a mess today I used to reply, "I'm in the Church of England today for the sake of what under God it might be tomorrow".' See Steer (1998), pp. 287–288.

[95] Stott (1978a), p. 7.

[96] 'Subject for Sunday': Roy Trevivian talks to John Stott; BBC Radio 4, Sunday 11 May 1969, as reproduced in *The Church of England Newspaper*, 16 May 1969.

[97] Christopher Green, 'Preaching that Shapes a Ministry', in C. Green and Jackman (eds.) (1995), p. 18.

[98] Part of his resignation speech was reproduced in the Preface to the wartime *Supplement to Crockford's, 1941*, which had to serve in place of a 1942 edition. See *Crockford Prefaces* (1947), p. 27. The more personal account is in Lockhart (1949), p. 439.

[99] Blanch (1991), p. 15.

[100] Paul (1964).

[101] From the Head of the Statistical Unit of the Central Board of Finance. See Paul (1964), p. 288.

[102] Hastings (1991), p. 535. He offers some possible reasons for the decline.

[103] *Ibid.*

[104] A fuller account of the problems of the theological colleges will be found in McGrath (1997), pp. 141–142. There were at that time no women in training for ordination.

[105] This was the successor to the de Bunsen Commission. Robert Runcie was Bishop of St Albans; Kenneth Woollcombe, Principal of the Episcopal Theological College, Edinburgh; and Derek Wigram (an evangelical), Headmaster of Monkton Combe School and a former Chairman of the Headmasters' Conference.

[106] McGrath (1997), p. 133.

[107] JRWS papers. Letter dated 31 March 1969. John Stott had heard privately from his old friend Canon T. G. Mohan four days earlier, telling him to expect such an approach, and seeing it as the answer to many prayers.

[108] JRWS papers. Letter dated 3 April 1969.

[109] JRWS papers.

[110] JRWS papers. Letter dated 8 July 1969. On holiday, Stuart Blanch was a near neighbour of John Stott at The Hookses.

[111] McGrath (1997), p. 133.

[112] He was invited, for example, to accept the benefice of Islington when Maurice Wood

left to be Principal of Oak Hill Theological College in 1961. Six months later he was told unofficially that his name had been mentioned by members of the Chapter of Melbourne Cathedral as a possible Dean; and asked if he would agree to be nominated ('I should be very surprised if you were not elected'). Neither approach seemed right to him.

Chapter 3. Keele 1967: Pointing the Way Forward

[1] Social Surveys (Gallup Poll) Ltd (1964), pp. 47, 127.

[2] *Religion in Britain and Northern Ireland* (1970), pp. 26–27.

[3] Norman (1976), p. 417. Chapter 10, 'After 1960', includes detailed references to many contemporary sources.

[4] Welsby (1984), p. 104.

[5] Paul (1964), p. 17. The section contains a multiplicity of tabulated evidence. See also *Church and State* (1970), Appendix D.

[6] He spoke as chairman of the Organizing Committee: 'Statement to be Made at the 133rd Islington Clerical Conference', 10 January 1967. For this and other original minutes and documents in this section I am indebted to Canon Michael Saward, who was press officer for the Congress.

[7] Letter to the author, 7 October 1992.

[8] Raymond Turvey. Letter to the author, 22 November 1992.

[9] Taped interview, 11/2.

[10] CEEC Minutes, 13 March 1964. Much of what follows is from this source.

[11] CEEC Minutes, 21 May 1965.

[12] Letter to the author, 22 November 1992.

[13] Bishop Gavin Reid. Letter to the author, 24 September 1997.

[14] Letter to the author, 8 October 1997.

[15] Michael Botting. Letter to the author, 3 October 1997.

[16] *Ibid.*, quoting from a diary kept at the time.

[17] E. S. Shirras. Letter to the author, 20 September 1997.

[18] CEEC Minutes, 3 March 1996.

[19] McGrath (1997), p. 130.

[20] *Ibid.*

[21] Letter to the author, 22 November 1996. Michael Saward has published his own recollections, in Saward (1987), pp. 37–38, in his contribution 'Behind the Plenaries', to Yeats (ed.) (1995), pp. 18–19, and in his autobiography, Saward (1999), p. 250. He adds the names of Frank Entwistle, who was then Education Secretary of BCMS and later Chief Executive of IVP; together with Eddie Shirras, later Archdeacon of Northolt; and George Hoffman, later Director of TEAR Fund, who were both curates. Philip Crowe, later Principal of Salisbury and Wells Theological College, was then Tutor at Oak Hill Theological College; Michael Saward was Warden of Holy Trinity Inter-Church Centre, Liverpool; and Gavin Reid was Publications Secretary of CPAS.

[22] Letter to the author, 24 September 1997. To talk of the Organizing Committee, under John Stott's chairmanship, 'throwing in their hand' is wide of the mark (see Colin Buchanan, 'Anglican Evangelicalism: The State of the Party', *Anvil*, vol. 1, no. 1, 1984, p. 17, n. 13). They listened to, welcomed and acted on the suggestions made for a more participatory style. The major change was not in the chosen speakers but in the methodology.

[23] See his letter to speakers of 5 December 1966 quoted below. John Cockerton and George Marchant had criticized an early draft of the suggested programme as 'too textbook, lacking in a sense of the present need'. G. J. Marchant. Letter to the author, 16 August 1966.

[24] See John Stott, 'World-wide Evangelical Anglicanism', in King (ed.) (1973), p. 180.

[25] JRWS papers. Letter dated 10 May 1966. Douglas Webster was at that time Professor of Mission at the Selly Oak Colleges, and from 1969 to 1985 Canon of St Paul's Cathedral.

[26] JRWS papers. Letter dated 31 May 1966.

[27] Taped interview, 11/4.

[28] George Hoffman, 'The Story of the Congress', in Crowe (ed.) (1967), p. 7. See Packer (ed.) (1967).

[29] From a transcript attached to the Minutes of the NEAC Committee of 1 December 1966.

[30] For the Archbishop's address, and the closing service of Holy Communion, closed-circuit television was used.

[31] George Hoffman, 'The Story of the Congress', in Crowe (ed.) (1967), p. 9.

[32] The Rt Revd Colin O. Buchanan, later Principal of St John's College, Nottingham, 1979–85; Bishop of Aston, 1985–89; Area Bishop of Woolwich from 1996, Lambeth DD, 1993. Canon E. Michael B. Green, later Principal of St John's College, Nottingham, 1969–75, Archbishops' Adviser for the 'Springboard' initiative for the Decade of Evangelism, 1992–96, Toronto University DD, 1992, and Lambeth DD, 1996. The Rt Revd Gavin H. Reid, later Bishop of Maidstone, 1992–2000.

[33] *Church Times*, 31 March 1967.

[34] John Gladwin, Foreword, in Yeats (ed.) (1995), p. 3. The Rt Revd John W. Gladwin was Director of the Shaftesbury Project 1977–82; Secretary of the General Synod Board for Social Responsibility 1982–88; Bishop of Guildford from 1994.

[35] From the text of the address in the Lambeth Palace Library.

[36] *Ibid.* See MS, p. 11.

[37] Letter to the author, 3 October 1997.

[38] John Stott's recollection, though of the content rather than of the exact words of their conversation. Taped interview, 11/5.

[39] See Packer (ed.) (1967), pp. 41–66, for this and succeeding quotations.

[40] George Hoffman, 'The Story of the Congress', in Crowe (ed.) (1967), p. 12.

[41] Letter to the author, 6 October 1997.

[42] Letter to the author, 22 November 1992.

[43] John Gladwin, Foreword to Yeats (ed.) (1995), p. 3.

[44] In Crowe (ed.) (1967), p. 18.

[45] A phrase used to describe Anglican evangelicals by the Bishop of Manchester, W. D. L. Greer, in conversation with the author at about this time.

[46] In Crowe (ed.) (1967), p. 18.

[47] Hebert (1957), p. 27. He went on to offer a parallel and perhaps even more disturbing picture of SCM, 'bravely setting out to tackle the whole problem of Christian living, those of social life, and of Biblical criticism, and of the unity of all Christians, and all the rest; and these problems are so pressing and so complicated that, however much one tries to find the Christian way, one is in danger of becoming immersed in the discussion of problems and yet more problems, and losing sight of the one thing needful – the knowledge of God Himself.'

[48] *Church Times*, 31 March 1967.

[49] In Packer (ed.) (1967), pp. 213–214.

[50] Anderson (1985), p. 213.

[51] *Ibid.*, p. 214.

[52] *Ibid.*, p. 218.

[53] Anderson (1968). See p. 7 for 'the spark'. It should be noted, however, that (Sir) Fred Catherwood's *The Christian in Industrial Society* (1964) pre-dated Keele by three years.

[54] Roy McCloughry. Letter to the author, 24 November 1997. The first of John Stott's study assistants (see chapter 8 below), he trained and taught as an economist before becoming Director of the Shaftesbury Project on Christian Involvement in Society, 1982–88; and Director of the Kingdom Trust from 1988.

[55] Wright (ed.) (1978).

[56] *Ibid.*, p. 182.

[57] John Gladwin, Foreword to Yeats (ed.) (1995), p. 3.

[58] Letter to the author, 3 October 1997, quoting from his diary.

[59] Letter to the author, 6 October 1997.

[60] Letter to the author, 3 October 1997.

[61] Comments from observers appear on pp. 15–17 of the Statement.

[62] *Ibid.*

[63] John Stott, 'State of Play', *Idea* (the journal of the Evangelical Alliance), November–December, 1990, in an interview with Ian Coffey.

[64] John Stott, 'World-wide Evangelical Anglicanism', in King (ed.) (1973), p. 181. The same phrases are used in his contribution, 'Evangelicals in the Church of England', to Richter (ed.) (1972), p. 174.

[65] Hastings (1991), p. 554.

[66] 5 April 1967.

[67] Michael Richards, 'Evangelicals Observed', *The Tablet*, 22 April 1967. A few weeks later the *English Churchman*, the most Protestant of the weekly church press, reported that the Apostolic Delegate was 'bubbling over with enthusiasm' both for *Guidelines* and for the Congress Statement (9 June 1967).

[68] Trevor Beeson, 'Evangelical Marathon', *New Christian*, 20 April 1967.

[69] Bebbington (1989), p. 250.

[70] Editor's Introduction, in Yeats (ed.) (1995), p. 8. See also McGrath (1997), p. 131.

[71] David L. Edwards, 'Evangelicals All', a review of Manwaring (1985), in the *Church Times*, 29 November 1985.

[72] McGrath (1994), pp. 35–36.

[73] In Crowe (ed.) (1967), p. 15.

[74] Morgan Derham, 'Evangelical Fellowship Keele-Halled?', *The Church of England Newspaper*, 28 April 1967.

[75] See John Capon, 'People in Close-up: John Capon Talks to John Stott (2)', *Crusade*, June 1974.

[76] Taped interview, 11/8.

[77] John Capon, 'People in Close-up: John Capon Talks to John Stott (2)', *Crusade*, June 1974.

[78] *Evangelical Magazine of Wales*, August–September, 1975.

[79] King (1969), p. 120.

[80] Welsby (1984), p. 214.

[81] Manwaring (1985), pp. 188–189.

[82] Hylson-Smith (1988), p. 290. The footnote reference to p. 12 in King (1969) I take to be a misprint, since the passage appears to be from p. 120, as quoted above.

[83] David Wells, 'On Being Evangelical', in Noll, Bebbington and Rawlyk (eds.) (1994), p. 396. The reference cited is once again King (1969). David Wells makes the same point, plainly from the same source, in 'Guardian of God's Word', a seventy-fifth birthday tribute to John Stott, in the influential *Christianity Today*, 16 September 1996.

[84] In Reid (ed.) (1986), p. 17. The chapter was originally an address to the Guildford Diocesan Evangelical Fellowship in November 1984.

[85] Editor's Introduction, in Yeats (ed.) (1995), p. 14.

[86] 31 March, 7 and 14 April 1967. Though the paper had set its face against 'the Anglo-Catholic intransigence which had often disfigured the *Church Times* in the past' under Roger Roberts (Editor, 1960–68), it was a journal in which evangelicals at that time felt consistently under-represented. The coverage of Keele was therefore all the more welcome. See Palmer (1991), p. 276.

[87] Quoted in Dillistone (1975), p. 398, from an interview with Charles Ferris.

[88] McGrath (1997), p. 132.

[89] Hastings (1991), p. 554.

[90] Taped interview, 11/6.

[91] John Stott, 'Obeying Christ in a Changing World', in Stott (ed.) (1977), p. 22.

[92] David Edwards, reviewing King (1969) in the *Church Times*, 13 June 1969.

Chapter 4. Travels and Writing: God's Word for Today's World

[1] Marcus L. Loane. Memorandum to the author, 7 January 1991.

[2] *Ibid.* CEEC: the Church of England Evangelical Council. EFAC: the Evangelical Fellowship in the Anglican Communion.

[3] W. Martin (1991), p. 265.

[4] JRWS diary. 'Visit to the Holy Land, 1960', p. 39.

[5] JRWS diary. 'A Visit to African University Colleges, April–June 1962', p. 3.

[6] *Ibid.*, p. 7a.

[7] *Ibid.*, p. 13.

[8] David Gitari was from 1975 Bishop of Mount Kenya East and then Archbishop of Kenya and Bishop of Nairobi.

[9] JRWS papers. Letter from David Gitari to Christopher Catherwood, copied to John Stott, dated 13 May 1983.

[10] See volume one, chapter 14.

[11] JRWS diary. 'A Visit to African University Colleges, April–June 1962', p. 31.

[12] *Ibid.*, p. 36. Although there was no legal apartheid, John Stott had noticed hotels and restaurants – and even churches – for 'whites only'. In the University, designated as multiracial, there was little social integration, so that even at his meetings the hall tended to divide into racial groups. The diary records his pleasure at seeing three or four small African boys in the Cathedral choir.

[13] George K. Kinoti, Professor of Zoology, University of Nairobi. Contribution towards submission for the Templeton Prize, 1996.

[14] *All Souls*, August 1963.

[15] Chua Wee Hian, 'Reports on Stott's Mission', *The Way*, no. 4, 1963, reprinted from a supplement to *The Evangelical Student* of India, September–October 1963. The Revd Chua Wee Hian had been Associate Pastor of the Chinese Church in London in 1961, and at the age of twenty-four had just become the first staff worker of the Fellowship of Evangelical Students for Singapore and Malaya. He later became internationally known as the General Secretary of IFES in the 1970s and '80s.

[16] Postcard to John Lefroy, dated 28 August 1963.

[17] JRWS diary. 'Asian Student Mission, August–September 1963', p. 26a.

[18] *Ibid.*, p. 29.

[19] *Ibid.*, p. 36. A considerable exchange of letters several months earlier had resulted in John Stott, on reliable advice but with great reluctance, declining an invitation from IFES which he had originally provisionally accepted (JRWS papers, 20 November 1962 to 23 May 1963). On John Stott's second visit to Hong Kong the Bishop (a successor to Bishop Hall) agreed to be Patron of the mission. On his third visit he stayed at Bishop's House and at the Bishop's invitation addressed the clergy of the diocese.

[20] *Ibid.*, p. 37a.

[21] Stuart Barton Babbage, 'Evangelicals and the Church in Australia', *The Churchman*, June 1963, p. 118. Babbage was Master of New College in the University of New South Wales, 1973–82.

[22] *All Souls*, January 1965.

[23] Canon A. J. Dain had just been appointed Bishop Coadjutor in the diocese.

[24] JRWS diary. 'Visit to USA and Australia, December 1964 – January 1965', p. 17.

[25] *Ibid.*, p. 17a.

[26] *Ibid.*, p. 30a.

[27] *Ibid.*, p. 47a.

[28] Letter to the author, 26 May 1997.

[29] JRWS diary. 'A Visit to California, April 1961', p. 9a.

[30] *Ibid.*, p. 23.

[31] See Hunt and Hunt (1991), especially pp. 127–128, 236–237, 413. IVCF: InterVarsity Christian Fellowship, USA.

[32] 'Change, Witness, Triumph', *His* magazine, March 1965.

[33] *Ibid. His* magazine records that on the third day of the Convention the student told an IVCF staff member that he had decided to become a missionary.

[34] JRWS diary. 'Visit to USA and Australia, December 1964 – January 1965', pp. 5–5a.

[35] Hunt and Hunt (1991), p. 437, n. 2.

[36] JRWS diary. 'Visit to USA and Australia, December 1964 – January 1965', p. 7. John Stott had been asked to preside. 'I introduced them to a little liturgy.' Taped interview, 6/66.

[37] John W. Alexander. Letter to the author, 15 May 1998.

[38] See Stott (1973), an early volume in The Bible Speaks Today series.

[39] Letter to the author, 1 November 1995.

[40] Hastings (1991), p. 456.

[41] Pollock (1966), p. 280.

[42] JRWS. Memorandum to the author, 12 May 1997.

[43] *Ibid.*

[44] *All Souls*, October 1966. See also C. F. H. Henry (1967).

[45] C. F. H. Henry (1967), p. 2.

[46] JRWS. Memorandum to the author, 12 May 1997.

[47] John R. W. Stott, 'The Great Commission (John 20:19–23)', in C. F. H. Henry and Mooneyham (eds.) (1967), p. 40.

[48] *Ibid.*, p. 50.

[49] *Ibid.*, p. 51.

[50] *Ibid.*, p. 56.

[51] A. J. Dain. Taped interview, 8 March 1993.

[52] JRWS. Memorandum to the author, 12 May 1997.

[53] Chester (1993), p. 29.

[54] B. Graham (1997), pp. 566–567.

[55] T. E. Yates (1994), p. 194.

[56] JRWS. Memorandum to the author, 12 May 1997.

[57] C. F. H. Henry (1947).

[58] T. E. Yates (1994), p. 201.

[59] Stott (1982a), p. 5.

[60] *All Souls*, July 1968.

[61] John Stott, 'An Evangelical at Uppsala', *The Church of England Newspaper*, 16 August 1968. This article, the first of two, then moves on to some positive assessments.

[62] The 'Programme to Combat Racism', set up in 1969 as a result of the Uppsala Assembly, administered a controversial special fund, whose first beneficiaries included liberation movements engaged in armed struggle.

[63] *All Souls*, September 1968; *Church Herald* (USA), 6 September 1968.

[64] *Ibid.*

[65] John Stott, 'Does Section Two Provide Sufficient Emphasis on World Evangelism?', in McGavran (ed.) (1972), p. 266.

[66] John R. W. Stott, 'The Rise and Fall of Missionary Concern in the Evangelical Movement, 1910–1973', in Winterhager and Brown (eds.) (1974), p. 62.

[67] Published as Stott (1975c). See *ibid.*, p. 7.

[68] B. Graham (1997), p. 437.

[69] 'Learning to Fly Kites: *World Christian* Interviews John Stott', *World Christian*, October 1989.

[70] He was not of course by any means alone in this among evangelical leaders. The Evangelical Alliance Relief (TEAR) Fund was set up in 1968 to provide a vehicle for the expression of a great surge of Christian compassion and social concern among many who wished to see such concern firmly linked with a biblical gospel.

[71] Sir Timothy Hoare, Bt. Letter to the author, 11 April 1996. Montague Goodman and his elder brother George were veterans of the Children's Special Service Mission from the 1890s onward and well-known members of the Christian Brethren.

72 Stott (1964b), p. 82.

73 Stott (1967b), p. 14.

74 1 December 1967.

75 JRWS papers. Letter dated 4 December 1967. The Revd Roger Roberts had been Sixth Form Master at Rugby when John Stott was a pupil.

76 *Mobilizing the Church for Evangelism* (1961a); *Motives and Methods in Evangelism* (1962) – the substance of the Presidential Address at the IVF Conference, April 1962; *Personal Evangelism* (1964e); *The Meaning of Evangelism* (1964d) – revised and enlarged from an article in the *Christian Graduate*, June 1956; *Evangelism: Why and How* (1967a) – the US edition of *Motives and Methods in Evangelism*, above.

77 Stott (1961b).

78 William Barclay, 'Entre Nous', *The Expository Times*, February 1962.

79 Stott (1982b).

80 Letter to the author, 13 July 1995.

81 Stott (1966a). Canon Frank Colquhoun became known to a whole generation of clergy and parishes through his book of *Parish Prayers* (1967); perhaps the most widely used collection since Eric Milner-White and G. W. Briggs had published their *Daily Prayer* (1941), some twenty-five years before. John Stott contributed sixteen short prayers; and three more to later volumes in the series, Colquhoun (1975) and (1982), as well as four to Frank Colquhoun's new edition of the BBC collection for the broadcast daily service, Colquhoun (1976).

82 Stott (1988a).

83 *The Keswick Week 1962* on 1 Corinthians 1 – 6; *1965* on Romans 5 – 8; *1969* on 2 Timothy.

84 In Fromer and Welson (eds.) (1965); and *God's Men* (1968).

85 Stott (1964c). A revised edition, based on the New International Version text, was issued in 1988: Stott (1988b).

86 Leith Samuel, 'A Man Under the Word', in C. Catherwood (ed.) (1986), p. 195.

87 Barclay (1997), p. 72.

88 Later editions have changed the title to *Only One Way* (1973); to *The Message of Galatians: Only One Way* (1984); and to *Essential Freedom: The Message of Galatians* (1989).

89 Later *The Message of 2 Timothy: Guard the Gospel.*

90 Michael Wilcock. Taped interview, 10 June 1992.

91 Stott (1968), p. 7.

92 Stott (1964a).

93 *His*, December 1968 – March 1970.

94 See Dudley-Smith (1995), pp. 40–41.

95 Stott (1963a).

96 *All Souls*, April 1963.

97 Derek Brewer: 'The Tutor: A Portrait', in Como (ed.) (1980), p. 43.

98 Among the books listed in this chapter, the following translations were published or in preparation at the time this book was being written: *Baptism and Fullness*, twenty-four languages; *The Message of Galatians*, fourteen; *Men Made New*, eleven; *The Preacher's Portrait*, seven; *The Epistles of John*, six.

Chapter 5. New Departures: Changes at All Souls

1 Hastings (1991), p. 597. His book is the source of much of the information quoted in these paragraphs.

2 Longford (1972).

3 Hastings (1991), p. 602.

4 *Ibid.*, p. 599.

5 Cited by Chester (1993), p. 17.

6 David Bebbington, 'Evangelicalism in its Settings: The British and American Movements

since 1940', in Noll, Bebbington and Rawlyk (eds.) (1994), p. 377.

[7] Hastings (1991), p. 615.

[8] *All Souls*, January 1970.

[9] John R. W. Stott, 'Evangelicals in the Church of England: A Historical and Contemporary Survey', in Richter (ed.) (1972), p. 177.

[10] Ted Schroder. Memorandum to the author, 2 August 1977. The Pastoral Measure, approved by Church Assembly in 1968, provided for a Rector and Vicar (or Vicars) in the same benefice; but only in the case of a Team Ministry.

[11] JRWS papers. Memorandum, 'A proposed restructuring of the staff team', dated September 1969.

[12] Taped interview, 17/35–36.

[13] Baughen, Bewes and Wilson (eds.) (1969).

[14] Taped interview, 17/40.

[15] *All Souls*, June 1970.

[16] EFAC (Evangelical Fellowship in the Anglican Communion) archives. The Honorary General Secretary's letter to members of the Council, April 1971.

[17] Raymond Dawes. Taped interview, 9 August 1991. In the course of time other projects were subsumed under the charitable status of the Langham Trust, such as 'Prom Praise', 'Speed to Need', and the SALT Institute of India, while retaining their day-to-day autonomy of management.

[18] The Rt Revd Michael Nazir-Ali. Letter to the author, 19 June 1998. The early days of the Langham Trust are described in *All Souls*, December 1974.

[19] JRWS papers. Letter dated 30 April 1970.

[20] Inscribed as a gift from Bishop Marcus Loane. A full description of this print appears in Hopkins (1997), p. 55, including a reproduction on the back of the dust-jacket.

[21] Miss Elizabeth Evans. Taped interview, 19 May 1995.

[22] *All Souls*, September 1970, p. 9.

[23] Taped interview, 17/54.

[24] Memorandum to the author, 1996.

[25] David Trapnell, 'Meaning Building with God', *All Souls Broadsheet*, July–August 1982.

[26] Memorandum to the author, 2 August 1997.

[27] David Trapnell. Taped interview, 18 February 1993.

[28] Sir Norman Anderson. Taped interview, 17 January 1991, p. 31.

[29] David Trapnell. Taped interview, 18 February 1993.

[30] *Ibid.*

[31] For legal reasons, his licence was that of Public Preacher.

[32] Botting (ed.) (1996), p. 17.

[33] *The Daily Telegraph*, 4 February 1971.

[34] *Ibid.*, 5 February 1971.

[35] For a full account of the rebuilding, see Endersbee (1977). The summary of 'Which Way Forward?' appears on pp. 19–20. A twenty-four-page illustrated brochure was also published by the church, with photographs of every stage, and a detailed 'Project Diary '68–'76' describing the long process: Bidewell and Hunter (eds.) (1976).

[36] *All Souls*, January–February 1975, pp. 12–13.

[37] Letter dated 6 March 1972, given to the author (with correspondence quoted below) by Archbishop Loane, 16 February 1998.

[38] Letter dated Easter Day (April 2).

[39] JRWS papers. Statement dated 6 July 1975. On 15 December 1975 John Stott was licensed 'to perform the Office of Assistant Stipendiary Curate in the Parish Church of All Souls' with a yearly stipend of £5 to be paid quarterly.

[40] Michael Baughen's letter 'From No. 12', *All Souls*, September–October 1975.

[41] JRWS papers. Letter from 10 Downing Street, dated 22 September 1975.

[42] Luker (1979), p. 72.

[43] Writing his annual letter to the Friends of All Souls, Christmas 1970, John Stott

describes how Michael Baughen had preached on his first Sunday as Vicar from Joshua 1, 'where another change of leadership is described, although he was quick to add that in our case the former leader is not actually dead!'

[44] In April 1979, for example, the subject was 'What is "British" and what is "Christian" in our own discipleship?' with the note '(two or three Third World Christians to be invited to help us to answer this question)'. JRWS papers. Memo, 'Christian Concern, 1979', dated 21 December 1978.

[45] 'Relevant Biblical Preaching: The Art of Double Listening: An Interview with John R. W. Stott by Derek Morris', *Ministry* (USA), January 1997. See also the section 'Reading and Resource Groups' in Stott (1982b), pp. 194–195.

[46] David Turner. Letter to the author, 2 May 1999.

[47] As, for example, in the 'Open Letter' of June 1977 to the Archbishops and Bishops of the Anglican Communion, with John Stott among the signatories. See Beckwith, Duffield and Packer (1977).

[48] Michael Saward, 'Behind the Plenaries', in Yeats (ed.) (1995), p. 18. Such a claim was a considerable exaggeration, ignoring as it did a still active generation of senior leaders: the Bishops of Winchester and Norwich (J. V. Taylor and M. A. P. Wood) for example; or such evangelical archdeacons as H. W. Cragg, G. J. C. Marchant, F. G. Kerr-Dineen and R. G. Herniman; or leading members of Synod such as Canon R. C. Craston; or indeed the two evangelical Archbishops, Dr Coggan and Dr Blanch.

[49] John Stott, 'World-wide Evangelical Anglicanism', in King (ed.) (1973), p. 181.

[50] EFAC archives. Joint Honorary Secretary's letter to EFAC Council members, April 1976. The story of the founding of this seminary, Trinity Episcopal School for Ministry, is told in Leighton (1995). John Stott had supported the venture from the beginning and had suggested Bishop Stanway's name, and encouraged him to accept the position (p. 18). But even as late as 1995, in spite of accreditation, more than half the dioceses of the American Episcopal Church would not allow their ministerial students to train at Trinity (p. 85).

[51] Barclay (1997), p. 85. The Revd A. M. Stibbs, after seven years with the China Inland Mission, was Vice-Principal of Oak Hill Theological College, 1938–65 (then Senior New Testament Lecturer), and a noted biblical teacher and scholar, one of the original editors of the *New Bible Commentary* (1953).

[52] Canon Philip D. King. Letter to the author, 11 May 2000. He became General Secretary of the South American Missionary Society in the mid-'70s, and of the General Synod Board for Mission from 1989. He felt that John Stott's use of the phrase 'evangelicals and charismatics' seemed to imply that the two categories were necessarily totally distinct.

[53] Hick (ed.) (1977).

[54] *Tools for Evangelism* (1973), pp. 2–9.

[55] Bishop D. S. (later Lord) Sheppard. Letter to the author, 26 February 1997.

[56] See McGrath (1997), pp. 245–246.

[57] See General Synod (1981), p. 10.

[58] John Stott, 'The Maturity of Love', *The Church of England Newspaper*, 13 December 1974; a published version of part of John Stott's address at SEAC.

[59] *Gospel and Spirit* (1977), p. 2.

[60] Michael Harper. Taped interview, 27 July 1994.

[61] Interview with John Stott: 'A Call to Balanced Biblical Christianity', *Impact* (Singapore), August–September, 1987.

[62] *Ibid.*

[63] Dr J. D. C. Anderson. Letter to the author, 24 January 1996.

[64] Hylson-Smith (1988), p. 307.

[65] Clements (1988), p. 22.

[66] Harper (1997), p. 31.

[67] John Stott, 'Is the Incarnation a Myth?', *All Souls*, October–November 1977. In

accordance with his practice at this time, the same material appeared in *Christianity Today*, 4 November 1977.

[68] See the trenchant and entertaining account in Hastings (1991), pp. 650–651.

[69] See McGrath (1997), p. 212. The symposium was E. M. B. Green (ed.) (1977). It was Stephen Neill who estimated that 'about equal numbers' of the two books were sold: see Neill (1991), p. 323.

[70] Donald English, 'Profile: John Stott – Christian Communicator Extraordinary', *The Epworth Review*, May 1993, p. 31.

[71] JRWS papers. Letter dated 27 November 1978.

[72] CEEC Minutes, 5 April 1979. There had been another meeting some months earlier between seven contributors to *The Myth of God Incarnate* and seven of their critics. John Stott refers to this 'seven-a-side rugby match' in 'The Mythmaker's Myth', *Christianity Today*, 7 December 1979.

[73] John Stott, 'Is the Incarnation a Myth?', *All Souls*, October–November 1977.

[74] Issued by the Church of England Evangelical Council (1978). No author is given, but the booklet was drafted by John Stott and approved by CEEC. Substantial extracts appeared as an article under his name using the same title in *Christianity Today*, 10 March 1978. A copy of the booklet was sent by CEEC to every bishop attending the 1978 Lambeth Conference.

[75] *Ibid.*, p. 13.

[76] Colin Craston gives a personal account in his autobiography, Craston (1998), pp. 71–72.

[77] Vol. 1, Stott (ed.) (1977); vol. 2, Cundy (ed.) (1977); vol. 3, Kaye (ed.) (1977). In all, over 40,000 copies were sold.

[78] CEEC Minutes, 3 March 1977.

[79] JRWS papers. Letter to Sir Marcus Loane, Archbishop of Sydney, 5 August 1977.

[80] *Church Times*, 15 April 1977.

[81] *The Guardian*, 16 April 1977.

[82] *The Nottingham Statement* (1977).

[83] Clifford Longley, 'Evangelical movement takes a critical look at itself', *The Times*, 2 May 1977.

[84] *Ibid.*

[85] Watson (1983), p. 102.

[86] *Ibid.*

[87] Saunders and Sansom (1992), p. 186. John Stott was not one of 'the lions'. In his presidential address to the Evangelical Alliance later in the year he went out of his way to explain and defend what David Watson sought to say at NEAC '77: 'The 16th century Reformers were very reluctant schismatics. They dreamed of a biblical reformed Catholicism. This is what David Watson meant at Nottingham when he referred to the Reformation as a "tragedy". Although he was much misunderstood he was quite right! Of course the Reformation was a wonderful recovery of long-lost biblical truth (that was the glory of it), but it was *at the expense of schism* (that is where the tragedy lay). The Reformers could not help it. The major fault was not theirs. But it was tragic nevertheless …' See Stott (1978b), p. 15.

[88] See, for example, Bebbington (1989), p. 268. It is perhaps significant, also, that the word 'Protestant', in Resolution K7 on 'Establishment' in the Nottingham Statement, met with opposition from a number of delegates.

[89] Stott (1977b), pp. 3–5.

[90] *Ibid.*

[91] *The Church of England Year Book, 1978*, p. xxvi.

[92] Dr John Rodgers, 'An American Observation on Nottingham '77', *EFAC Bulletin*, July 1977. John Rodgers became Dean of TESM in the following year.

[93] Barclay (1997), p. 101. See also Murray (2000), especially pp. 10–11 on church and baptism. The reference to p. 19 of the Nottingham Statement (para. E3) must be read in

context. See, for example, para. G2, where baptism is described as an expression of faith.
[94] McGrath (1997), pp. 213–217.
[95] *Ibid.*, pp. 215–216.
[96] Barclay (1997), p. 103.
[97] JRWS papers. Letter dated 12 July 1977.
[98] A few years later 'a member of the staff' of St John's College, Nottingham, described their experiences. See General Synod (1981), p. 21: 'There were some odd or worrying goings on. One or two of the charismatic students were inclined to find demons under every bed, and indulged in exorcistic activity in the neighbourhood. We gave lecture space to an itinerant healer who some students felt was manipulating students into an experience of being "slain in the Spirit" (literally manipulating – he pushed them over!).'
[99] JRWS papers. Letter to Archbishop Sir Marcus Loane, 5 August 1977. Archbishop Loane had been gazetted KBE the previous year.
[100] See Capon (1972), p. 15. For a striking description of the purpose and origin of the Festival of Light, including the launching rally attended by 4,000 people (to which Archbishop Michael Ramsey declined to send a message of blessing), see Chadwick (1990a), pp. 162–163. Ramsey did send a prayer for the following Trafalgar Square rally of some 30,000 supporters. Lance Bidewell, as Editor of *All Souls* (April 1973, p. 15), was critical of the Festival as 'fairly disastrous in terms of its public image'.
[101] In 1971–72, when it was still IVF, and in 1977–78 when the name had been changed to UCCF. He had earlier been President in 1961–62.
[102] John Wesson, 'Students – The Great New Factor of Our Time', *All Souls*, September 1973.
[103] See D. Johnson (1979), p. 13, and chapters 5–7. Douglas Johnson recalled how as a London undergraduate at just this time, he asked at the start of his second term for the use of a room in the university where six evangelical students might meet for Bible study. The Secretary and the Provost of King's College, 'both ex-SCM men', refused. 'DJ' then invited Bishop J. Taylor Smith, a household name as Chaplain-General throughout the First World War, to come and speak. The university authorities, faced with his acceptance, quickly made a room available, and by the end of the meeting some forty members of the college signed up to express further interest. See S. Bruce (1980), p. 239.
[104] S. Bruce (1980), Appendix II. This and the other quotations above are used by permission.
[105] John R. W. Stott, Foreword to Hunt (1991), pp. 9–10.
[106] The Revd John Samuel. Letter to the author, 15 June 1998. John Samuel was the undergraduate President of the CICCU that year.
[107] Letter to John Samuel, 18 March 1977.
[108] Canon A. W. A. Knowles. Letter to the author, 12 June 1998. Andy Knowles was then curate of Holy Trinity, Cambridge.
[109] John Stott, 'Cambridge Mission', *All Souls*, April–May, 1977.
[110] This was C. Mark Jones, later ordained. See Elworthy (1980), p. 15.
[111] John Stott, 'Cambridge Mission', *All Souls*, April–May, 1977.
[112] JRWS papers. Letter dated 14 March 1977. Professor Steve Bruce makes the point, with reference to the strength of evangelical youth work, that 'the key to evangelical success does not lie in the extension of the boundaries of christendom, in the conversion of the heathen, so much as in the preservation of the next generation within the paths of righteousness'. Even for work among children and adolescents, this is not a universal truth; and John Stott's university missions over these twenty-five years clearly show 'the conversion of the heathen' from backgrounds containing no Christian, let alone evangelical, influence. See S. Bruce (1980), p. 382.
[113] JRWS diary. 'Visit to USA, September–December 1972', p. 32.
[114] *All Souls*, December 1973.
[115] JRWS. Personal newsletter, August 1975.
[116] See John Stott's tribute to Myra Chave-Jones on her retirement: 'Versatile pioneer we

shall deeply miss', *The Church of England Newspaper*, 30 September 1983.
[117] Published as Stott (1961b).
[118] Taped interview, 10/22.
[119] *All Souls*, May 1974.
[120] *Ibid.*
[121] Letter from Mrs Avril Smith, *The Church of England Newspaper*, 3 December 1976.
Patrick Dearnley's response, 10 December 1976.
[122] JRWS. Memorandum to the author, 28 April 1999. One of Malcolm Muggeridge's
biographers places his 'moment of illumination' – his conversion – in the Church of the
Nativity in Bethlehem while filming in 1967, though he himself speaks of 'more a series of
happenings than one dramatic one'. As an adolescent he had read the Bible in secret; and
had lived for a time in Cambridge at the Oratory of the Good Shepherd, sometimes acting
as server when Wilfred Knox was the celebrant at the daily service of Holy Communion.
He was finally received into the Roman Catholic Church in November 1982. See Muggeridge (1988), p. 14, and Wolfe (1995).
[123] Wolfe (1995), p. 387.
[124] *Ibid.*
[125] JRWS papers. Letter dated 17 November 1976.
[126] JRWS papers. Letter dated 17 November 1976.
[127] Muggeridge (1977), pp. 121–122.
[128] JRWS papers. Summary by Tom Cooper, October 1979.
[129] Christopher Idle. Letter to the author, 29 February 1996. See his description of the
ASB as 'the thirteen-hundred page slab of staleness' in *Churchman* 107 (1993), p. 279,
quoted by D. A. Carson, 'Observations of a Friend', in Tinker (ed.) (1995), p. 216.
[130] Christopher Idle. Letter to the author, 29 February 1996.
[131] Preface, *The Church of England Year Book, 1979*, p. xxvi.
[132] See *Lambeth Conference, 1978* (1978), pp. 33–52, 92–94.
[133] Memorandum to the author, 7 September 1978.
[134] Archbishop Sir Marcus Loane, 'Reflections on the Lambeth Conference, 1978', *EFAC
Bulletin*, November 1978.
[135] JRWS papers. Memorandum written at the time. See also Murray (1990), p. 768.
[136] Stott (1979c). For Lloyd-Jones's *Ephesian Studies* see Murray (1990), p. 801.
[137] JRWS papers. Memorandum written at the time.
[138] John Stott, 'An Appreciation', in C. Catherwood (ed.) (1986), pp. 206–207.

Chapter 6. Australia to the Arctic: A Worldwide Parish
[1] *All Souls*, April 1970, p. 9.
[2] Published in Stott and others (1972).
[3] JRWS diary. 'Visit to USA, Australia and Asia, 26 December 1970 – 26 February 1971',
pp. 2, 4a.
[4] *Ibid.*, p. 7a.
[5] Bishop A. J. Dain. Taped interview, 8 March 1993.
[6] JRWS diary. 'Visit to USA, Australia and Asia, 26 December 1970 – 26 February 1971,
p. 10a.
[7] *Ibid.*, p. 14.
[8] This conviction found expression twenty years later, in his exposition of Acts 2 as
demonstrating the formal and the informal, joy and reverence, in the worship of the infant
church. See Stott (1990), pp. 85–86.
[9] JRWS diary. 'Visit to USA, Australia and Asia, 26 December 1970 – 26 February 1971',
p. 17.
[10] The public lecture in Singapore a few days later was published under this title (Stott
1971).
[11] JRWS diary. 'Visit to USA, Australia and Asia, 26 December 1970 – 26 February 1971',
p. 26.

[12] The Revd R. K. Hyatt. Letter to the author, 2 September 1998.

[13] JRWS diary. 'Visit to USA, Australia and Asia, 26 December 1970 – 26 February 1971', p. 30.

[14] *Ibid.*, p. 41a.

[15] *Ibid.*, p. 47a.

[16] In contrast to Paul's description of Tarsus in his day as 'no ordinary city' (Acts 21:39).

[17] JRWS diary. 7 April 1978.

[18] JRWS. Memorandum to the author, 14 April 1999.

[19] JRWS diary. 'Bermuda and USA, January 1978', p. 34a.

[20] Professor David Wells. Letter to the author, 30 July 1998.

[21] 'The State of the Union', *Time*, 9 October 1972.

[22] Thomas H. Englund, President of the Consortium. Letter to the author, 31 August 1998.

[23] JRWS diary. 'Visit to USA, September to December 1972', p. 9.

[24] *Ibid.*, p. 25.

[25] David F. Wells. Letter to the author, 30 July 1998.

[26] JRWS diary. 'Visit to USA, September to December 1972', p. 34a.

[27] 'I never knew a professor to be so honoured by the students!' David Wells. Letter to the author, 30 July 1998.

[28] Between 1964 and 1989 he gave fifteen of these TV addresses: see Dudley-Smith (1995), p. 40.

[29] Stott (1972c).

[30] *Ibid.*, p. 11.

[31] JRWS personal newsletter, September 1972.

[32] JRWS diary. 'Visit to USA, September to December 1972', p. 37.

[33] Letter to the author, 13 August 1998.

[34] JRWS personal newsletter, January 1973. The cost of the Arctic visit was defrayed by generous friends in Canada.

[35] JRWS diary. 'Toronto, 17–21 June 1973', p. 48a.

[36] For a striking view of Bathurst Inlet Lodge taken from the air, see Stott (1999a), pp. 92–93.

[37] JRWS diary. 'Bathurst Inlet, 28 June – 5 July 1973', p. 56a.

[38] *Ibid.*, p. 64. See also John Stott's 'Cornerstone' article, 'Freeing a stalwart people from fatalism', *Christianity Today*, 5 October 1979.

[39] See Scott (1951). The purpose of his expedition was to learn more about Ross's Geese, at that time a threatened species. Peter Scott and his companions stayed at Bathurst Inlet Lodge when it was still the Hudson Bay Post (pp. 7, 21).

[40] JRWS diary. 'Bathurst Inlet, 28 June – 5 July 1973', p. 68.

[41] *Ibid.*, p. 70. John Ryder was Professor at Lakehead University, Thunder Bay, on Lake Superior, Canada's southern border. In a letter to Sir Peter Scott of 31 July 1973 John Stott transcribed the message they had found in the cairn: 'July 9, 1965. We, Gordon K Hornby, pilot PWA Yellowknife NWT, and John P Ryder, Canadian Wildlife Service, Edmonton, found what is probably the largest known nesting colony of Ross's Geese. In view of this, we hereby name this lake after the Eskimo name for Ross's Goose, *Karak* Lake.' For an account, and photograph, of Ross's Goose at Lake Karak, see Stott (1999a), p. 70.

[42] JRWS diary. 'Bathurst Inlet, 13–20 June 1974', p. 50.

[43] *Ibid.*, p. 52a.

[44] JRWS diary. 'Canada and USA, June–July 1976', pp. 40–40a, from which this and the following extracts are taken.

[45] JRWS diary. 'Canada, July 1979', p. 15.

[46] *Ibid.*, p. 21.

[47] See John Stott, 'In North and South America', *All Souls*, March 1974.

[48] See John Stott, 'Jesus Christ and the Authority of the Word of God', D. M. Howard

(ed.) (1974). The address was also published separately as a booklet (Stott 1974).
[49] JRWS diary. 'Visit to North and South America, 27 December 1973 – February 1974', p. 11a.
[50] *Ibid.*, p. 28.
[51] *Ibid.*, p. 29a.
[52] *Ibid.*, p. 41a.
[53] John Stott, 'In Latin America', *All Souls*, September 1977.
[54] JRWS diary. 'A Visit to the Americas, June and July 1977', p. 25a.
[55] The diary says that *Cristo Rey*, 'Christ the King', was a phrase with strong Fascist associations in General Franco's Spain!
[56] JRWS diary. 'A visit to the Americas, June and July 1977', p. 31.
[57] See Darwin (1928), p. 379.
[58] John Stott, 'In Latin America', *All Souls*, September 1977.
[59] John Stott, 'A Visit to Latin America', *Christianity Today*, 9 September 1977.
[60] John Stott, 'Unhooked Christians', *Christianity Today*, 7 October 1977.
[61] JRWS diary. 'A Visit to North and South America, 27 December 1973 – February 1974', p. 45a.

Chapter 7. World Evangelization: The Lausanne Vision

[1] John Stott, 'Personal Impressions of the Nairobi Assembly', *All Souls*, January–February 1976.
[2] *Ibid.*
[3] JRWS diary. 'WCC Fifth Assembly, November 1975', p. 3a.
[4] *Ibid.*, p. 4a.
[5] *Ibid.* See also John Stott, 'Antwort auf die Ansprache von Bischof Mortimer Arias', in Kruger (ed.) (1976), p. 153. For Bishop Arias's paper, and responses (in English) from Rahantavololon Andriamanjato of Madagascar and John Stott, see *The International Review of Mission*, January 1976. The official Report, published by the WCC, gives John Stott's five points in slightly more detail; see *Breaking Barriers* (1975), pp. 18–19.
[6] For ten years he had been Secretary of the Missionary and Ecumenical Council of the Church Assembly.
[7] Taped interview, 13/1.
[8] Memorandum to the author, May 1999.
[9] John Stott, 'PACLA', *All Souls*, January–February 1977.
[10] Published in *Facing the New Challenges* (1978).
[11] John Stott, 'Global Vision', *All Souls*, April 1974.
[12] See Dudley-Smith (1995), p. 136, for six publications containing one or more of these addresses.
[13] John Stott, 'PACLA', *All Souls*, January–February 1977.
[14] *Ibid.*
[15] John Stott, 'Theological Tension Points in Ecumenical – Evangelical Relationships', *Facing the New Challenges* (1978), p. 251.
[16] See John Stott, 'World Evangelisation: Signs of Convergence and Divergence in Christian Understanding', *Third Way*, December 1977.
[17] John Stott, 'Evangelicals and Roman Catholics', *Christianity Today*, 12 August 1977.
[18] *Ibid.*
[19] A full list of participants is appended to the final Report, Stott and Meeking (eds.) (1986). The Report was also published in full in *The International Bulletin of Missionary Research*, January 1986.
[20] Stott and Meeking (eds.) (1986), p. 10.
[21] *ARCIC: The Final Report* (1982), p. 1. Julian Charley, one of John Stott's early curates (1957–64), was a member of ARCIC from 1970 to 1982 and so a signatory to this Report. In his own commentary he wrote: 'Being the only evangelical appointed, I was all the more conscious of the weight of responsibility laid upon me.' Charley (1983), p. 3. John

Stott respected and valued Julian Charley's work on the Commission, while remaining critical of the theological inadequacies of successive Reports.

[22] John R. W. Stott, 'Anglican – Roman Catholic Agreement?', *All Souls*, March 1972.

[23] Taped interview, 12/37. The 'Chalcedonian Definition', from the Council of Chalcedon, AD 451, is a major foundation of orthodox classical Christology in defining the person of Christ as human and divine.

[24] Taped interview, 12/38.

[25] Jack Dain made it clear that this was more than another conference on evangelism. 'This is not a congress on evangelism: it is a congress on *evangelization*, and there is a difference.' See Pollock (1979), p. 191. The book includes a stimulating account of Lausanne, its origins and follow-up.

[26] 5 August 1974. Quoted in Stott (ed.) (1996), p. xi.

[27] See B. Graham (1997), pp. 568ff., from which much of this description is taken.

[28] Edwards (1969), pp. 39–40.

[29] By 1977, firmly associated with Billy Graham's worldwide crusade ministry.

[30] John Capon, 'Lausanne '74', *Crusade*, September 1974. This eleven-page feature by the Editor gives a vivid account from an experienced observer, not unsympathetic but not uncritical, through each of the ten days of the Congress.

[31] John Stott, 'The Whole Christian', in Ng (ed.) (1980), p. 7. He added: 'I say without fear of contradiction that it's totally unbiblical ... you have got to declare what you are singing it about, then you can sing Hallelujah.'

[32] See Chester (1993), p. 71.

[33] B. Graham (1977), p. 571.

[34] See John R. W. Stott, 'The Biblical Basis of Evangelism', in Douglas (ed.) (1975), p. 65. A much expanded study formed his Chavasse Lectures in World Mission (Stott 1975c).

[35] John R. W. Stott, 'The Biblical Basis of Evangelism', in Douglas (ed.) (1975), p. 65.

[36] John Capon, 'Lausanne '74', *Crusade*, September 1974.

[37] *Ibid.*

[38] John Stott, 'The Lausanne Congress', *All Souls*, September 1974. For a summary of the background to this statement, see Padilla and Sugden (eds.) (1985).

[39] Taped interview, 10/41.

[40] Taped interview, 10/41.

[41] Interview with Fergus Macdonald, 'Only the Holy Spirit could have brought it about', *World Evangelization*, September–October, 1994.

[42] Preface to Stott (1975d), p. 1. The figure of 3,000 replies is taken from Pollock (1979), p. 208. Key documents from the Lausanne movement, including the Covenant with exposition and commentary, have been collected in Stott (ed.) (1996).

[43] Iremonger (1948), p. 416. Iremonger tells of the response of one American delegate to William Temple's 'parlour trick' in action: 'Archbishop, you tickle me pink!' See also Stephen Neill's autobiography for a reference to his own 'fatal flair for drafting', and a perceptive reflection on how 'there is much to be said for committing the whole work of drafting to a single individual, who, by divine inspiration, may catch the mind and mood of an assembly and translate it into intelligible form'. Neill (1991), pp. 134, 212.

[44] Letter to the author, 12 March 1993.

[45] W. Martin (1991), p. 448.

[46] *Ibid.*

[47] *Ibid.*

[48] Reproduced in the official Report, Douglas (ed.) (1975), p. 1294.

[49] John Capon, 'Lausanne '74', *Crusade*, September 1974.

[50] Pollock (1979), p. 210.

[51] Taped interview, 7 June 1993. Tom Houston had returned from Africa in 1971 to be Communications Director (and later Executive Director) of the Bible Society. In 1984 he became President of World Vision International and in 1989, following the Manila Congress, International Director of the Lausanne movement.

[52] P. Sathkeerthi Rao. Letter to the author, 20 February 1996.

[53] John Stott, 'The Lausanne Congress', *All Souls*, September 1974.

[54] Stott (ed.) (1996), p. xviii. On p. 37 of the same book John Stott explores the meaning of the phrase 'simple lifestyle' (as against, for example, 'simpler lifestyle', which was one of the alternative proposals). Accepting that concepts such as 'poverty', 'simplicity' and 'generosity' are all relative, and that Scripture lays down no absolute standards, he firmly defends the wording of the Covenant. The passage (pp. 37–38) repays study; while pp. 139ff. contain a report of the Consultation 'An Evangelical Commitment to Simple Lifestyle' of March 1980.

[55] W. Martin (1991), p. 449. John Stott rejected the suggestion of 'simpler' as offering no solution. It simply prompted the question 'Simpler than what?'

[56] John Stott, 'Introduction to the Covenant', in Douglas (ed.) (1975), p. 2.

[57] *All Souls*, September 1974.

[58] Taped interview, 10/42.

[59] T. E. Yates (1994), p. 200.

[60] 'A Challenge from Evangelicals', *Time*, 5 August 1974.

[61] John R. W. Stott, 'Ten Years Later: The Lausanne Covenant', in Dayton and Wilson (eds.) (1984), p. 66.

[62] C. F. H. Henry (1947), p. 84. Quoted in T. E. Yates (1994), p. 201.

[63] The four metaphors are listed, with their proponents, in Chester (1993), p. 76.

[64] Paul Henry, *Christianity Today*, vol. 14, no. 7, January 1970, p. 28. See also P. Henry (1974). Quoted in Chester (1993), p. 47.

[65] W. Martin (1991), p. 453. A number of printed sources are cited. See also the autobiography by F. Graham (1995), pp. 118–119.

[66] Hastings (1991), p. 616. The Covenant expressly and comprehensively affirms the 'divine inspiration, truthfulness and authority' of the Old and New Testaments. For John Stott's commentary, see Stott (ed.) (1996), pp. 13–14.

[67] Memorandum to the author, 7 September 1998, quoting his own letter of 9 September 1971.

[68] *Ibid.* By 1998 FEET had over 500 members.

[69] 72%. See Stott (ed.) (1996), p. xvi.

[70] JRWS diary. 'India, Nepal, Mexico and USA, 26 December 1974 – 3 February 1975', p. 22. WEF: World Evangelical Fellowship.

[71] *Ibid.*, p. 23.

[72] JRWS. Memorandum to the author, 28 April 1999.

[73] JRWS diary. 'India, Nepal, Mexico and USA, 26 December 1974 – 3 February 1975', p. 23.

[74] *Ibid.*, pp. 27–27a.

[75] *Ibid.*, p. 28.

[76] *Ibid.*, p. 29a. Jack Dain, disturbed lest his support of John Stott on this personal issue might have been taken amiss, wrote anxiously to assure Billy Graham of the warmth of his loyalty and friendship. Dr Graham replied, 'Nothing could ever come between us. I hope we can be next-door neighbours in heaven!' See Pollock (1979), p. 251.

[77] JRWS diary. 'India, Nepal, Mexico and USA, 26 December 1974 – 3 February 1975', p. 30a.

[78] A detailed account of the nature and purposes of these can be found in Stott (ed.) (1996). For an overview, see the Historical Introduction, pp. xvii–xx.

[79] Including, for example, *How Churches Grow* (1959) which speaks in terms of 'whole people' churches versus conglomerate churches (p. 54); and *Understanding Church Growth* (1980), which speaks of the 'homogeneous unit' (p. 225).

[80] JRWS diary. 'A Visit to the Americas: June and July 1977', p. 3.

[81] John Stott (ed.) (1996), p. 66. The first publication of the Report appears to have been in the journal *Missiology*, October 1977. John Stott wrote later: 'The essential point in the HUP debate was, I think, that *in evangelism* it is legitimate to recognize homogeneous

units, but *in the church* it is important not to acquiesce in them, but to work conscientiously towards homogeneity.' Memorandum to the author, 23 February 2001.

[82] JRWS diary. 'Bermuda and USA, January 1978', p. 3a.

[83] *Ibid.*, p. 4.

[84] From *The Willowbank Report*. See Stott (ed.) (1996), p. 78. The seventeen preliminary papers are published in Stott and Coote (eds.) (1980).

[85] Stott (1979).

[86] See chapter 10 below.

[87] Pollock (1979), p. 253. The same chapter illustrates some of the worldwide initiatives which sprang from Lausanne.

[88] Reginald Heber, Bishop of Calcutta 1823–26, in his famous missionary hymn 'From Greenland's icy mountains', written in 1819 for the Society for the Propagation of the Gospel. In the first draft Heber wrote 'the savage' but changed it to 'the heathen'. It was still being included in some post-1970 hymnals.

[89] Interview with John R. W. Stott, *His* magazine, October 1975.

[90] July 1975.

[91] Paragraph 6 of the Lausanne Covenant.

[92] John R. W. Stott, 'Ten Years Later: The Lausanne Covenant', in Dayton and Wilson (eds.) (1984), p. 70.

[93] JRWS papers. From the script of an address, 'Twenty years after Lausanne: some personal reflections', given at the Overseas Ministries Study Center, New Haven, Connecticut, on 1 February 1995, later published in their journal.

[94] David F. Wells, 'Guardian of God's Word', *Christianity Today*, 16 September 1996.

[95] The sub-title he chose for his book *The Contemporary Christian* (1992a).

[96] Douglas (ed.) (1975), p. 1294.

[97] Taped interview, 7 June 1993.

Chapter 8. Christ and the Scriptures: Letting the Bible Speak

[1] Broadcast 29 January 1978. Published as Stott (1978c), p. 4. *Cf.* Stott (1986a), p. 335.

[2] 'John Stott Speaks Out': interview with Michael G. Maudlin, *Christianity Today*, February 1993.

[3] Ridley (1895), p. 25, quoting John Foxe. Ridley also offered money to those who would learn chapters by heart, just as he himself as an undergraduate in Cambridge had learned by heart much of the New Testament, walking in the gardens of 'Pembroke Hall'.

[4] See Packer (1991), p. 400; Drummond (1992), pp. 435–437. I owe these instances to John Stott, who discovered them only long after ELT was founded.

[5] The original Deed of Settlement is dated 30 April 1971, between John Stott, Oliver Barclay, Timothy Dudley-Smith and John Laird, who had retired as General Secretary of Scripture Union three years before.

[6] See Stott (1982b), p. 115.

[7] JRWS. Memorandum to the author, 12 May 1997.

[8] *Ibid.*

[9] Roy McCloughry. Memorandum to the author, 8 September 1994.

[10] *Ibid.* The tradition also owed something to the custom John Stott had found in parts of Africa and Asia during his visits in the 1960s, whereby an adult friend or visitor is addressed as 'uncle'. See Stott (1996), p. 125, which offers a biblical warrant for recognizing the generation gap in some such way.

[11] Todd Shy seems to have been the first to be so described. See JRWS newsletter, May 1989.

[12] Roy McCloughry. Memorandum to the author, 8 September 1994.

[13] Hick (ed.) (1977).

[14] Roy McCloughry. Memorandum to the author, 8 September 1994.

[15] For the Reading Group, see Stott (1982b), p. 196. The account gives a number of examples of books and films studied by the group, mostly contemporary, but including the Qur'an.

[16] Roy McCloughry. Memorandum to the author, 8 September 1994. Following the study group, John Stott wrote to John Fowles, taking up from the book, and from the teaching of Jesus, the meaning of true freedom. JRWS papers. Letter dated 19 November 1979.

[17] Roy McCloughry. Memorandum to the author, September 1994. Toby Howarth was asked on his first morning as study assistant whether he possessed binoculars, a wristwatch and a Filofax (he felt the order of the list to be significant). Having only the first, he was sent out to buy himself the others. Letter to the author, 24 September 1998.

[18] Letter dated 16 September 1979.

[19] Jude 3, New English Bible.

[20] See *e.g.* Philippians 1:27.

[21] Taped interview, 8/21.

[22] Stott (1970).

[23] *Church Times*, 24 April 1970.

[24] *British Weekly*, 2 April 1970. A month later Erik Routley took up office as President of the Congregational Church in England and Wales.

[25] JRWS papers. Letters dated 17 April and 20 April 1970. For Erik Routley, see the Memorial Tribute: Leaver, Litton and Young (eds.) (1985).

[26] *Church Times*, 24 April 1970.

[27] 'Friends of All Souls' newsletter, February 1970.

[28] Stott (1972b). The complicated publishing history is set out in Dudley-Smith (1995), pp. 12–13.

[29] Stott (1979a).

[30] *Ibid.*, pp. 15–16.

[31] The lecture was given in Trinity College, 7 January 1944, when John Stott was away at camp, and published as Atkinson (n.d. [1944]).

[32] David Edwards, 'Seeking a Living Lord', *Church Times*, 27 April 1979.

[33] Stott (1991b).

[34] JRWS papers. Letter dated 12 July 1986 from the Revd Christopher Green.

[35] Christopher Green. Letter to the author, 31 October 1998. He was appointed Vice-Principal of Oak Hill Theological College in 2000.

[36] Stott (1975b). Fuller references to both editions appear in chapters 1 and 4 above.

[37] Stott (ed.) (1977).

[38] Stott (1975c), pp. 7–8. A US edition was published the same year with the sub-title *What the Church Should be Doing Now*.

[39] *Ibid.*, p. 11. It was the Lausanne Planning Committee who specifically asked that the opening address should provide a biblical definition of these five words.

[40] *Ibid.*, p. 12.

[41] *Ibid.*, p. 23. For such a review, see that by Robert T. Coote, Associate Editor of *Eternity*, September 1976.

[42] Stott (1984) and (1992a). Both books are considered more fully in subsequent chapters.

[43] See the section 'The Great Reversal' in Stott (1999), pp. 8–9.

[44] Taped interview, 20/6.

[45] JRWS newsletter, January 1973. The completion of the New Testament series was celebrated at a Service of Thanksgiving at St Peter's, Vere Street, on 27 October 2000.

[46] Later editions have changed the title to *Only One Way*; to *The Message of Galatians: Only One Way*; and to *Essential Freedom: The Message of Galatians*.

[47] Stott (1973).

[48] JRWS papers. 'The Bible Speaks Today (memorandum to contributors)', August 1972. The quotation comes in Moule (1892), p. 97.

[49] JRWS papers. 'The Bible Speaks Today (memorandum to contributors)', August 1972.

[50] J. A. Motyer (1974), Kidner (1976), Goldingay (1978), Wallace (1979).

[51] Letter to the author, 4 November 1998.

[52] Stott (1978a).

[53] James F. Nyquist, Letter to the author, 7 January 1998.

[54] *Church Times*, 23 March 1978. The Most Revd Richard F. Holloway, from 1992 Primus of the Episcopal Church in Scotland, was then Rector of Edinburgh Old St Paul. His later views appeared to embrace extremes of radicalism and theological liberalism.

[55] JRWS papers. Letter from the Revd Derick Bingham, 21 April 1983.

[56] JRWS papers. Letter dated 22 May 1987.

[57] Stott (1979c).

[58] *Ibid.*, p. 10.

[59] JRWS papers. Letter from John Thorpe, 4 September 1995.

[60] Stott (1972c). The US edition (1973) made a small book rather than a booklet.

[61] Stott (1982b), p. 55.

[62] Barclay (1997), pp. 48, 87–88.

[63] Chester (1993), p. 90. Blamires (1963).

[64] See chapter 6 above.

[65] Stott (1992a), p. 118.

[66] Stott (1975a).

[67] Stott (1978b). This exposition of John 17 was considerably elaborated under the title 'Dimensions of Church Renewal' in Stott (1992a), pp. 257–258.

[68] Stott (1975e), produced in association with TEAR Fund to accompany a soundstrip.

[69] Stott (1975d). This, together with other Lausanne papers, can be found collected in Stott (ed.) (1996).

[70] 'Evangelicals and Roman Catholics', *Christianity Today*, 12 August 1977.

[71] '"Unhooked" Christians', *Christianity Today*, 7 October 1977.

[72] 'Following Paul in Turkey', *Christianity Today*, 21 July 1978.

[73] For dates and titles of both series see Dudley-Smith (1995), pp. 72–75.

[74] Stott (1984), p. xi.

[75] Newbigin (1969), p. 8.

[76] Donovan (1978), p. 51. The word 'orporor' describes a restricted age-group brotherhood within a Masai clan line.

[77] McGrath (1997), p. 279. The final phrase is Dr Packer's own, as is another, 'the pain of brainwork', which he traces to Ecclesiastes.

[78] From his address at 'An International Tea in honour of John Stott' at the Christian Booksellers Association Convention, Dallas, Texas, 28 June 1992.

[79] See chapter 2 above.

[80] JRWS personal newsletter, October 1979.

[81] The Revd Geoffrey N. Shaw had been seven years as Tutor and Vice-Principal at Oak Hill Theological College before moving to Oxford. He was succeeded there as Principal by Canon R. T. France in 1989 and by Professor Alister E. McGrath in 1995.

[82] JRWS papers. Letter of invitation from Hudson T. Armerding, 5 October 1979. John Stott's reply, 12 October 1979.

[83] Lady Hilton, Joy's elder sister. Letter to the author, 1 June 1999.

[84] *Ibid.*

[85] JRWS. Memorandum to the author, 2 February 1996.

[86] JRWS papers. Letter dated 11 July 1979.

[87] JRWS papers. Letter to John Stott from the Revd Geoffrey Griffith, 21 February 1979.

[88] JRWS personal newsletter, October 1979.

Chapter 9. Thinking Christianly: The London Institute

[1] Addressing the UN General Assembly, 7 December 1988. See Campling (1990), p. 55, for this and much other information quoted.

[2] Bible Society (1980), p. 29.

[3] Saward (1987), p. 34, suggests 51% in the mid-1980s. He cites figures suggesting that in the 1980s almost 30% of the 'working clergy' (as opposed to the retired) identified themselves with Anglican evangelicalism (p. 35). But this is bound to be a very broad-brush assessment.

[4] See Williams (1984), p. 8.

[5] Wenham (1998), p. 218.

[6] S. Bruce (1996), p. 129.

[7] *Ibid.*, p. 163.

[8] By his encyclical *Apostolicae Curae* of 1896 Pope Leo XIII condemned Anglican Orders as invalid, and this remains the official position of the Church of Rome.

[9] See the Preface, *The Church of England Year Book, 1988*, p. xxv.

[10] *Faith in the City* (1985).

[11] *The Times*, 3 December 1985.

[12] Stott (1984), p. 2.

[13] See volume one, chapter 14: 'The Hookses: A Writer's Retreat'.

[14] JRWS personal newsletter, 1 May 1986, gives this pattern of what he there calls 're-firement'.

[15] JRWS papers. Letter dated 10 November 1980.

[16] 27 April 1981. 'Devaluation Day' is a reference to his reading that day in Leviticus 27.

[17] JRWS personal newsletter, October 1981.

[18] JRWS papers. Letter dated 10 March 1981.

[19] JRWS papers. Letter dated 23 March 1981.

[20] The Revd Paul D. A. Weston. Letter to the author, 10 April 1999. The Revd A. C. J. Cornes was then Senior Curate and Director of Training. The new Rector, the Revd R. T. Bewes, thirteen years younger than John Stott, had long been a close friend and shared a background which included camp, Cambridge, Ridley Hall and the Eclectic Society. The son of well-known missionary parents, he had spent his early years in Kenya; John Stott described him as 'a gifted communicator by both tongue and pen ... he retains a love for Africa and for the whole Third World'. JRWS personal newsletter, November 1982.

[21] JRWS personal newsletter, November 1982.

[22] JRWS diary. 'Sandringham, 8–10 January 1983'.

[23] Letter to the author, 24 September 1998.

[24] JRWS papers. Letter dated 21 February 1983. R. J. Palmer, Lambeth Librarian and Archivist, letter to the author 26 January 1996. John Stott found it ironic that because Archbishop Runcie was a graduate of Oxford the academic dress of his new doctorate should be that of an Oxford DD.

[25] JRWS papers. Letter dated 3 March 1983.

[26] An example would be Gordon College, Massachusetts, which offered him such a degree in 1993. He did, however, accept an Honorary DD that year from Wycliffe College, Toronto (Canada being a different country); and in 1997 from Brunel University (at the request of the London Bible College).

[27] Wendy Nelles, 'What's a Nice Theologian Like You Doing in a Place Like This?', *Christianity Today*, 21 October 1983.

[28] Letter dated 2 September 1983.

[29] 28 June 1984.

[30] His address was published by the Committee under the title *What is Man?* and reproduced as 'The Glory and the Shame' in *Third Way*, December 1990 – January 1991. Michael Alison MP and his wife Sylvia Mary had attended National Prayer Breakfasts in Washington DC, and had helped to introduce the idea to British public life. See Alison (1984), pp. 24–25. John Stott had attended more than one of these US National Prayer Breakfasts ('Can you imagine sitting down to breakfast in the Washington Hilton with 3,000 people?'), and in 1983 addressed a seminar of some 1,000 of them over lunch ('though with a decent interval in between'). See JRWS personal newsletter, May 1983, and his published address, Stott (1983a). On reflection he was somewhat disenchanted by the experience ('mingling with the mighty, etc.') and the uncritical adulation given to political figures. Memorandum to the author, 28 April 1999.

[31] Letter to the author, 28 April 1999. In a letter from 10 Downing Street to thank Richard Bewes, Mrs Thatcher wrote of how it was 'an inspiration to hear the words of

testimony and hope in Jesus Christ'. All Souls archives, 16 February 1988.

[32] Timothy Dudley-Smith, 'John Stott Reaches 65: An Appreciation', *The Church of England Newspaper*, 25 April 1986.

[33] JRWS papers. Card dated 7 May 1986. The Secretariat referred to is the Vatican Secretariat for Promoting Christian Unity, which nominated the Roman Catholic participants in ERCDOM. Basil Meeking was joint editor with John Stott of the final Report (1986).

[34] Dr A. M. McCutcheon. Taped interview, 24 May 1993.

[35] Letter dated 10 July 1987, convening a first meeting. It was AGE, at one of their earlier meetings, who decided to sponsor an 'authorized biography' of John Stott and to look for someone to write it.

[36] Ten years later John Wyatt gave the London Lectures in Contemporary Christianity for 1997, published as Wyatt (1998).

[37] Letter to the author, 2 May 1999.

[38] JRWS personal newsletter, 1 November 1984.

[39] JRWS personal newsletter, May 1983.

[40] 1978–83. 'Nationwide' replaced the word 'National' in the original title to indicate that its main concern was with local initiatives. See Hylson-Smith (1988), p. 315.

[41] See Clark (1994), p. 28. John Stott served also as a member of the preliminary 'Lambeth Group' (1976/7) and of the NIE Council of Reference (1978–81).

[42] John Stott, 'Reviving Evangelism in Britain', *Christianity Today*, 12 December 1980. For the text of the joint Statement 'The Gospel we Affirm Together', see Whitehead and Sneddon (1990), pp. 117–118.

[43] *Crockford's Clerical Directory, 1977–79*, p. x.

[44] Welsby (1984), p. 263. Dr Runcie declined to follow Archbishop Donald Coggan as Chairman of NIE, but agreed to speak at the Nottingham Assembly. 'As Michael Barling led the worship and during the singing of the chorus "Let there be love shared among us", Pastor Jack Glass of Glasgow and several followers advanced on the platform with placards reading "Runcie is a Romanizer" ...' See Whitehead and Sneddon (1990), p. 37. Dr Runcie said afterwards that for an awful moment he had read the final word as beginning not with R but with W!

[45] Welsby (1984), p. 263.

[46] John Stott, 'The Crucial Decision' (an extract from one of his conference addresses), *IFES Overview, 1988/89*.

[47] John Stott, 'Our Challenge for Today', *World Evangelization*, November–December 1988.

[48] Crowe (ed.) (1967), p. 37.

[49] *The Nottingham Statement* (1977), p. 40.

[50] *Ibid.*, pp. 44–45.

[51] John Stott, 'Evangelicals and Roman Catholics', *Christianity Today*, 12 August 1977.

[52] JRWS personal newsletter, Easter Day 1982.

[53] Stott and Meeking (eds.) (1988). The significance of their work can be judged from the fact that almost half *The International Bulletin of Missionary Research* for January 1986 was given to printing the Report in full. Spanish and French translations have since been published.

[54] JRWS personal newsletter, May 1984.

[55] Bishop Basil Meeking to Dr A. M. McCutcheon, 8 August 1996, as part of the submission for the Templeton Prize for Progress in Religion.

[56] CEEC Minutes, 7 June 1979.

[57] JRWS personal newsletter, Easter Day 1982.

[58] Church of England Evangelical Council (1982).

[59] *Ibid.*, pp. 4, 6, 7, 10, 11.

[60] John Stott, 'After the papal euphoria, let's look at the small print', *The Times*, 4 June 1982. (The choice of headline seems likely to have been a sub-editor's.) See also letters in reply: *The Times*, 10 June 1982, from Bishop B. C. Butler, a Roman Catholic member of ARCIC (appreciative and friendly in tone), and J. R. M. Moorman, Bishop of Ripon

1959–75 (distinctly less so). John Stott's reply to Bishop Butler, pleading for mutual and penitent submission to Scripture, exists in photocopy among his own papers but was not published, even if submitted.
[61] Stott and others (1988), addressed to all the Archbishops and Diocesan Bishops of the Anglican Communion, Easter 1988.
[62] *Ibid.*, pp. 14, 4.
[63] *The Times*, 30 April 1988. Amid a certain amount of ecclesiastical euphoria over the work of ARCIC, the Bishop of Birmingham showed that it was not only evangelicals who had misgivings, or wished attention to be paid not just to 'Agreed Statements' but also to what he called 'the different stances, attitudes and dogma of the two Communions in certain matters of faith and morals'. Montefiore (1986), p. 130.
[64] Malcolm Watts, 'The Crumbling of Evangelicalism', *Sword and Trowel*, the quarterly journal of the Metropolitan Tabernacle (unofficially known as 'Spurgeon's Tabernacle') London, September 1986, pp. 24–25.
[65] Russell (1915), p. 124.
[66] See Harper (1997), pp. 28–29; and Kemp, Harper and Stott (eds.) (1988).
[67] Baxter (ed.), Stott and Greenacre (consultant eds.) (1987).
[68] *Ibid.*, p. 178; John Stott's hand is evident in much of the drafting. See also *Lambeth Conference, 1988* (1988), p. 231, for Lambeth Resolution no. 43, much of the support for which came from Third World delegates: 'This Conference, recognising that evangelism is the primary task given to the Church, asks each Province and diocese of the Anglican Communion, in co-operation with other Christians, to make the closing years of this millennium a "Decade of Evangelism" with a renewed and united emphasis on making Christ known to the people of his world.'
[69] Letter dated 5 December 1985.
[70] Wimber and Springer (1985), p. 117.
[71] Meeting between John Stott and John Wimber, 1 November 1988. John Wimber was the founder of the Vineyard Church in Southern California, which led to an international fellowship of such charismatic churches. He died in 1997. Account taken from John Stott's memorandum to the author, 7 September 1998. For the 'already' and the 'not yet', see Edwards and Stott (1988), p. 233. For a brief account of John Stott's views on miracles, contrasted with John Wimber's teaching, see Stott (1990b), pp. 101–102, and (1999c), p. 127. See also Phillip Jensen, 'John Wimber Changes his Mind', from the symposium Payne (ed.) (n.d. [1990]), p. 9, reprinted from *The Briefing*, April 1990.
[72] Edwards and Stott (1988). This is considered in more detail in chapter 11 below.
[73] Clements (1988), p. 231.
[74] For a brief account of the issues involved, see the pamphlet published at the time by the Warden of Tyndale House, Cambridge, M. J. Harris (1985).
[75] Michael Baughen, recently consecrated Bishop of Chester; Roger Beckwith, Warden of Latimer House, Oxford; R. T. France, Principal of Wycliffe Hall, Oxford. For a brief account of 'The Relevance of the Resurrection' in this context, see Stott (1992a), pp. 70–71.
[76] John Stott, 'Reflections on the Resurrection', *The Times*, 6 April 1985 (Easter Saturday).
[77] Stott (1985), p. 85. The second edition (1991) makes reference to more recent publications touching both the resurrection and the uniqueness of Christ.
[78] See his presidential address, Stott (1983), on the need to know the Trinitarian faith of the Scriptures and to believe, obey, adorn, defend and share it. He was President in 1961–62, 1971–72, 1977–78 and 1981–82.
[79] John Stott, Gilbert Kirby and Cliff Richard, on their new roles with TEAR Fund, *Tear Times*, Spring 1983. Gilbert Kirby was General Secretary of the Evangelical Alliance 1956–66 (President in 1979) and from 1966 to 1980 was Principal of the London Bible College. Sir Cliff Richard (knighted, 1995) was already deeply involved with field visits and gospel concerts in support of the Fund.
[80] John Stott, 'Mission', in Prior (ed.) (1978). The chapter was abridged from Stott (1975c), chapter 1.

[81] Stott (1975e).
[82] Stephen Rand, Prayer and Campaigns Director, TEAR Fund. Letter to the author, 21 May 1998.
[83] *Ibid.*
[84] See Manwaring (1985), p. 208, and J. Martin (1977), pp. 84, 207. Steer (1998), p. 291, seems to generalize altogether too sweepingly, across a period of twenty years, based on John Martin's assessment above.
[85] Bebbington (1989), p. 270.
[86] *Anglican Evangelicals and their New Assembly* (1983), p. 1.
[87] *The Times*, 7 January 1983.
[88] Sceats (ed.) (1985), p. 55. Gordon Kuhrt suggested that CEEC needed a Chairman who was a member of General Synod: 'I agreed with him, and that was the major reason for my decision to retire from the chair.' Memorandum from John Stott to the author, 31 May 2000.
[89] Canon Colin Day, then Executive Officer of AEA/CEEC, carried the main day-to-day burden of preparation and execution, 1986–88.
[90] Report of General Planning Committee, 14 October 1986.
[91] Bishop G. H. Reid. Letter to the author, 28 April 1999.
[92] Minutes of Executive Committee, 9 December 1986.
[93] Memorandum to the author, 28 April 1999.
[94] JRWS personal newsletter, October 1981.
[95] Memorandum to the author, 28 April 1999.
[96] Toby Howarth. Memorandum to the author, 29 April 1999.
[97] Stott (1988c).
[98] John Yates III, study assistant to John Stott. Memorandum to the author, 21 April 1999.
[99] JRWS papers. 'Listening' report sent in by Michael Green during NEAC '88.
[100] Derek Pattinson, Preface, *The Church of England Year Book, 1988*, p. xxix.
[101] Derek Pattinson, Preface, *The Church of England Year Book, 1989*, p. xxix.
[102] *Church Times*, 6 May 1988.
[103] *The Times*, 'Runcie warning over doctrine', 30 April 1988.
[104] Melvin Tinker, Chaplain of Keele University, 'NEAC 3: A Conference Too Far?', *Churchman*, vol. 102, no. 4, 1988.
[105] Peter Williams, Vice-Principal of Trinity College, Bristol, 'NEAC 3: Retrospect and Prospect', *Anvil*, vol. 5, no. 1, 1988 (original footnotes here omitted). Dr Williams' contribution on John Stott to Elwell (ed.) (1993) remains the best short study of his life and thought.
[106] The description given by the chairman of the Executive Team, David D. Sceats, in his Preface to Stott (1988c).
[107] Memorandum to the author, 28 April 1999.
[108] Letter to the author, 20 July 1992.
[109] *Ibid.*
[110] John Stott stayed with Tom Cooper and his wife Karen a year after their return to the US; and met their firstborn, 'embarrassingly named Jonathan Thomas Stott Cooper'. JRWS diary. 'Bay Area, Vancouver and Alaska, 19 July to 31 August 1981', p. 1a.
[111] Steve Andrews. Taped interview, 10 June 1993.
[112] Mark Labberton. Memorandum to the author, 12 November 1994.
[113] *Ibid.*
[114] Paul Weston. Letter to the author, 10 April 1999.
[115] Memorandum to the author, 29 April 1999.
[116] Todd Shy. Taped interview, 10 September 1985.
[117] Memorandum to the author, 29 April 1999.
[118] Mark Labberton. Memorandum to the author, 12 November 1994.
[119] *Ibid.*
[120] Toby Howarth. Memorandum to the author, 29 April 1999.

[121] *Ibid.*

[122] For the story of A Rocha see P. Harris (1993).

[123] Steve Andrews. Taped interview, 10 June 1993.

[124] Toby Howarth. Memorandum to the author, 29 April 1999.

[125] Steve Andrews. Taped interview, 10 June 1993.

[126] Toby Howarth. Memorandum to the author, 29 April 1999.

[127] Letter dated 15 May 1986.

[128] Memorandum to the author, 29 April 1999.

[129] Press release, 11 January 1982.

[130] 'People in Close-up: John Capon Talks to John Stott, 1', *Crusade*, May 1974.

[131] J. R. W. Stott, 'God's Gospel in a Time of Crisis', *The Keswick Week, 1969*, p. 138.

[132] The Revd John Andrew Kirk had ministered in Argentina since 1966, after ordination and a curacy in England. He was Professor at the Facultad Evangélica de Teología, Buenos Aires; but by the time the Institute opened he was working in London for the Church Missionary Society as Theologian Missioner, and was named as Associate Director of the London Institute.

[133] Andrew Kirk. Letter to the author, 26 July 1999.

[134] After this meeting he circulated a 'rough sketch' of a possible way forward under the title 'Community of Concern', 30 March 1977.

[135] Andrew Kirk. Letter to John Stott, 23 November 1977.

[136] Os Guinness, Senior Fellow at the Trinity Forum, Burke, Virginia; writer and lecturer. Letter to the author, 12 July 1999.

[137] Confidential memorandum no. 4, circulated over the initials JRWS, 14 August 1980, to Oliver Barclay, Os Guinness, Andrew Kirk 'and possibly one or two others'.

[138] See McGrath (1997), p. 225. Chapter 10 gives an account of the origins of Regent College, with detailed references to source documents.

[139] *Ibid.*, p. 227.

[140] See Arthur Dicken Thomas Jr, 'James M. Houston, Pioneering Spiritual Director to Evangelicals', Part One, *Crux*, September 1993, p. 5.

[141] Letter to the author, 4 September 1999.

[142] McGrath (1997), pp. 222–232.

[143] Dr James Houston. Letter to the author, 24 August 1999. Dr Houston was Professor of Spiritual Theology and Spiritual Director at Regent College, Vancouver, from 1978. In 1993 a Chair was endowed in his name to perpetuate his work.

[144] JRWS papers. Letter from Dr James Houston, 24 January 1980.

[145] Stott (1968).

[146] JRWS. Memorandum to the author, 28 April 1999.

[147] Stott (1982b). See chapter 11 below.

[148] JRWS. Memorandum to the author, 28 April 1999.

[149] JRWS personal newsletter, October 1981.

[150] *Ibid.*

[151] 'Struggling with Contemporary Issues'; an interview with Alex Mitchell, *Third Way*, February 1982.

[152] JRWS personal newsletter, Easter Day 1982.

[153] JRWS personal newsletter, November 1982.

[154] Dr A. M. McCutcheon. Taped interview, 24 May 1993. He was Bursar from 1984 to 1989.

[155] The Revd James B. Notkin. Letter to the author, 19 June 1999.

[156] Lancelot (1929), p. 110.

[157] JRWS papers. Letter from James B. Notkin, Princeton Theological Seminary; dated (received) 2 April 1986.

[158] G. H. Cassidy, later Archdeacon of London, 1987–99, and Bishop of Southwell from 1999.

[159] Taped interview, 18/34.

[160] As always, there had been setbacks along the way. Writing to his US supporters of the Langham Foundation, John Stott described how the need to strengthen the galleries with steel girders (to bear the weight of the library), together with additional fire precautions required by the local authority, added £200,000 to the costs. Letter from John Stott to supporters, 1 June 1983.

[161] Taped interview, 18/36.

[162] JRWS papers. Notes of a conversation with Prof. John Wyatt.

[163] Memorandum to the author, 8 July 1999.

[164] JRWS papers. From a conversation with Saúl and Pilar Cruz.

[165] JRWS personal newsletter, November 1985.

[166] JRWS personal newsletter, October 1986. The promised 'day off' did not long live up to these good intentions.

[167] St Peter's, Vere Street, the home of the London Institute, continued to use the title Institute for Contemporary Christianity; and perhaps partly for this reason the name Christian Impact never really took hold. The Nottingham office (the base of the former Shaftesbury Project) was closed following financial difficulties in the early 1990s, and the name Christian Impact was discontinued in 1997.

[168] Griffiths (1982).

[169] O'Donovan (1984).

[170] Letter to Dr A. M. McCutcheon (for the Templeton Prize submission, 1995) from Andrew Kirk; at that time Dean and Head of the School of Mission and World Christianity, Selly Oak Colleges, Birmingham.

Chapter 10. A Global Ministry: Travels in Six Continents

[1] Stott (1958).

[2] Stott (1991a), p. 127.

[3] 'John Stott Speaks Out: An Interview with Michael G. Maudlin', *Christianity Today*, February 1993.

[4] JRWS papers. Letter from the Revd Dr Noel Jason, 22 May 1983; a Brahmin convert from Madras.

[5] From John Stott's endorsement of V. Samuel and C. Sugden (eds.) (1986). Chris Sugden. Letter to the author, 29 November 1999.

[6] EFAC files. Letter dated April 1981. Alan Neech was Chairman of the Keswick Council and had for five years served as Vice-Chairman of the Church of England's Board of Mission and Unity. BCMS: Bible Churchmen's Missionary Society, renamed Crosslinks in 1993.

[7] The Rt Revd David R. J. Evans, International Co-ordinator of EFAC. Letter to the author, 25 March 1993.

[8] John Stott, 'A New Beginning', *EFAC Bulletin*, Advent 1986. The title indicates a restructuring of Council and Secretariat to address anew the original vision. The EFAC bursary scheme, though still closely linked with EFAC, developed separately, and became the Studylink International Training Partnership. Both look to John Stott as their original founder. Letter from Bishop David Evans, 20 July 1999.

[9] 'Modernism Under a Scriptural Spotlight', *Church Times*, 23 July 1993.

[10] The papers of the Consultation, including a summary report of findings and five Bible expositions by John Stott (then recently retired as President of EFAC) are published as Stott and others (1996a). See p. 49 for the passage quoted.

[11] Ralph Waldo Emerson, 'Self-reliance', *Essays: First Series*, 1841.

[12] Stott (ed.) (1996), p. 143. See pp. 151–153 for a bibliography, and details of the papers and testimonies from the Consultation.

[13] Leighton Ford, Chairman, and Gottfried Osei-Mensah, Executive Secretary, of the ICWE in their joint introduction to the COWE Program issued to delegates.

[14] JRWS diary. 'COWE (Consultation on World Evangelization) at Pattaya, Thailand, June 16–26, 1980', pp. 3a–4. Pattaya is on the Gulf of Siam.

[15] This address was published in a condensed and adapted form in Winter and Hawthorn (eds.) (1981), and further abridged in *Decision*, April 1981.

[16] 'Consultation on World Evangelization: A Report by John Stott', *All Souls*, September–October 1980.

[17] *Ibid.*

[18] JRWS diary. 'COWE (Consultation on World Evangelization) at Pattaya, Thailand, June 16–26, 1980', p. 13.

[19] Letter to the author, 21 January 1998.

[20] See Stott (ed.) (1966), p. 155. The Statement is on p. 162.

[21] Martin Goldsmith, lecturer at All Nations Christian College, 1970–94: letter to the author, 20 March 1995.

[22] For a brief summary, see Stott (ed.) (1996), pp. xiv–xv.

[23] *Ibid.*, p. 170.

[24] JRWS diary. 'USA, June/July 1982', pp. 1a–2.

[25] A. P. Johnston (1978); *Christianity Today*, 5 January 1979. Dr Arthur Johnston was Chairman of the Division of World Mission and Evangelism and Director of the Paul Little Chair of Evangelism at Trinity Evangelical Divinity School, Deerfield.

[26] JRWS diary. 'USA, June/July 1982', p. 2.

[27] See Stott (ed.) (1996), pp. 225–249.

[28] JRWS papers. Summarized from John Stott's reply to Paul McKaughan, Associate Director and Congress Co-ordinator, LCWE, 13 March 1989.

[29] 'I felt confused and burdened but found relief in prayer, especially when I was brought by God's grace both to repent of my wounded pride and to surrender the document to God ... I no longer had a stake in it which I could not relinquish.' JRWS diary, pp. 6a–7.

[30] JRWS diary. 'Lausanne II in Manila, 11–21 July 1989', p. 9a.

[31] 'Learning to Fly Kites: *World Christian* Interviews John Stott', *World Christian*, October 1989.

[32] Letter to the Revd R. D. Wismer, 16 July 1989, from Manila.

[33] JRWS diary. 'Lausanne II in Manila; 11–21 July 1989', p. 10.

[34] *Ibid.*, p. 11a.

[35] For example, Roopsingh Carr, who for ten years was a member of All Souls. A presbyter of the Church of South India and founder of SALT (Scripture Applied Leadership Training), he persuaded John Stott to serve on his Council of Reference and to provide financial help for office equipment and the like. JRWS diary. 'A visit to India, Bangladesh and Egypt, January/February 1981', p. 5a.

[36] JRWS diary. 'A visit to India, Bangladesh and Egypt, January/February 1981', p. 34a.

[37] JRWS diary. 'Asia, 24 May – 22 June, 1987', p. 4.

[38] Published under the titles 'The Gospel', 'Evangelism and the Church', and 'Evangelism and Social Responsibility' in *Southern Cross*, the diocesan journal, May–October 1980.

[39] JRWS diary. 'Australia, May–June 1981', p. 3a.

[40] *Ibid.*, p. 5.

[41] *Ibid.*, p. 17.

[42] John Prince. Taped memorandum, 8 December 1994.

[43] Paterson (1901), p. 20.

[44] John Prince. Taped memorandum, 8 December 1994.

[45] JRWS diary. 'Visit to Kenya and Uganda, 30 August to 18 September, 1980', p. 20a.

[46] JRWS diary. 'A month in Africa, February/March, 1984', p. 19a. See also the brief account and dramatic pictures in Stott (1999a), pp. 84–85.

[47] JRWS diary. 'A month in Africa, February/March, 1984', p. 7.

[48] Dr Denis Osborne. Letter to the author, 2 August 1999. Dr Osborne was formerly Professor of Physics at the University of Dar es Salaam in Tanzania. He had become a Reader at All Souls in 1975; and from 1992 to 1999 chaired the Council of the London Institute for Contemporary Christianity.

[49] 'Michael Cassidy Interviews John Stott', *Africa Enterprise Update*, August 1988.

[50] JRWS diary. 'A visit to Kenya, Zimbabwe and South Africa, 11 June to 9 July 1988', p. 24. Seven years later South Africa returned to the Commonwealth with Nelson Mandela as its President. 'The whites had not been driven into the sea, nor had their homes been invaded. Black South Africa had proved to be remarkably forgiving.' Wm. Roger Louis, 'The Close of the Twentieth Century', in M. Howard and Louis (eds.) (1998), p. 326.

[51] James Allcock OBE. Letter to the author, 13 September 1996.

[52] John Stott added a comment in his diary that the name seemed to him misleading, and he hoped it might be changed: 'People naturally imagine that the Institute exists to study the works of C. S. Lewis, or at least to explore English Literature of which he had been Professor at both Oxford and Cambridge. But the C. S. Lewis Institute shares the same vision as the London Institute, and my own hope is that the two Institutes in the two capital cities will increasingly develop and work together. It is only because the C. S. Lewis Institute (like LICC) is a lay institute, and because C. S. Lewis was a lay theologian or Christian thinker, that his name was chosen ...' JRWS diary. 'USA, Canada, Philippines and Taiwan, May to June 1983', p. 2.

[53] For details of fifteen such broadcasts between 1964 and 1989 see Dudley-Smith (1995), p. 40.

[54] JRWS diary. 'Visit to USA, 20 January to 5 February, 1983', p. 1.

[55] JRWS diary. 'Bay Area, Vancouver and Alaska, 19 July to 31 August 1981', p. 6.

[56] *Ibid.*, p. 24.

[57] Gladys Hunt. Letter to the author, 12 August 1999.

[58] Letter to the author, 6 March 1997.

[59] JRWS diary. 'Visit to the USA, January to February 1984', p. 9a.

[60] Stott (1992a), p. 249. He adds, 'I realize that there may have been good reasons why the cathedral was closed. My concern is with the 'vibes' which were given off by that scene.'

[61] JRWS diary. 'Urbana '79, Chicago, Brazil and Patagonia, 27 December 1979 to 5 February 1980', p. 6. São Paulo had then a population of some six million. The provisional figure following the 1991 census just over ten years later was almost ten million.

[62] Letter to Frances Whitehead, dated 20 January 1980.

[63] JRWS diary. 'Urbana '79, Chicago, Brazil and Patagonia, 27 December 1979 to 5 February 1980', p. 18.

[64] JRWS diary. 'A Visit to Latin America and the Caribbean, January 1985', p. 3a.

[65] JRWS diary. 'Brazil, 25 August to 18 September 1989', p. 13a.

[66] *Ibid.*, p. 8.

[67] *Ibid.*, pp. 9–9a.

[68] John Prince. Taped memorandum, 8 December 1994.

[69] P. Harris (1993), p. 22. John Stott contributed a Foreword, and preached on 25 September 1993 at the tenth anniversary of the project. See John R. W. Stott, 'The Works of the Lord', in LeQuire (ed.) (1996), p. 78. Peter Harris accompanied John Stott on a birdwatching expedition to Gibraltar, Morocco and Portugal in April–May 1989.

[70] JRWS diary. 'Eastern Europe, May 1987', p. 12, gives an example of a Lutheran pastor who had attended All Souls when in London on a language course. John Stott invited him to his flat, and gave him a copy of *I Believe in Preaching*. Five years or so later he entertained John Stott in his home near Budapest, and showed him the completed manuscript of a Hungarian translation.

[71] JRWS diary. 'Eastern Europe, 9 April to 5 May 1980', p. 2a.

[72] See p. 48 above.

[73] Alex Williams. Memorandum to the author, 6 January 1996.

[74] Beeson (1974), pp. 212, 225. The Brethren Church was formed in 1918 by union between some Lutheran and Reformed Christians with former Roman Catholics. By 1970 it claimed some 270,000 members. It has no connection with the [Plymouth] Brethren assemblies of the UK.

[75] JRWS diary. 'Eastern Europe, 9 April to 5 May 1980', p. 19.

[76] *Ibid.*, p. 21.

[77] *Ibid.*, p. 24.

[78] *Ibid.*, p. 29.

[79] *Ibid.*, p. 32. Pavel Cerny later became President of the Brethren Church in the Czech Republic; but it was this visit, and Pastor Cerny's visit to England the same year, which ended what he called 'my isolation from the stream of worldwide Evangelical theology'. Letter to the author, 2 January 1998.

[80] An account in some detail of parts of this visit to Eastern Europe can be found in John R. W. Stott, 'Protestant Unity in Yugoslavia' and 'Poland's Power of the Proletariat', *Christianity Today*, 18 July and 10 October, 1980.

[81] Beeson (1974), p. 305.

[82] Alex Williams. Memorandum to the author, 6 January 1996.

[83] JRWS diary. 'Eastern Europe, May 1987', p. 12a. Four years later Canon Beeson was to write in his diary: 'It is not generally recognized, I think, just how repressively Ceausescu is ruling Romania. Attention is so much focussed on the Soviet Union that we tend to overlook the fact that the situation in Romania is every bit as bad. Church attendance there remains extraordinarily high, but the leadership of the Orthodox Church is very much in cahoots with the state, and dissident Baptists, in common with other dissidents, are severely treated. Ceausescu looks a nasty, ruthless piece of work ...' Beeson (1998), p. 70.

[84] JRWS diary. 'Eastern Europe, May 1987', p. 6.

[85] *Ibid.*, p. 13a.

[86] JRWS papers. Correspondence between July 1987 and September 1989.

[87] JRWS papers. Memorandum dated 30 May 1988.

[88] At SEAC, November 1978; from the Church Society recording C108, 'John Stott interviewed by Gavin Reid'.

[89] JRWS diary. 'Urbana '79, Chicago, Brazil and Patagonia, 27 December 1979 to 5 February 1980', p. 15.

[90] 'Rehabilitating Discipleship: An Interview with John Stott', *Prism* (the journal of Evangelicals for Social Action), July–August 1995.

[91] This is the word used to sum up a major aspect of John Stott's ministry on the ecumenical scene. See Mäkelä (1999), pp. 4, 261.

[92] John Stott (1999c), p. 115.

[93] JRWS papers. Letter dated 7 July 1987.

[94] JRWS papers. Letter dated 19 August 1987.

[95] JRWS papers. From his memoranda, 'A Visit to Africa' and 'A Visit to India', 7 September 1998.

[96] John Stott, 'The Christian and the Poor', a sermon preached on 16 February 1981. *All Souls Papers* (1981). See also Stott (1999d), p. 260.

[97] 'Learning to Fly Kites: *World Christian* Interviews John Stott', *World Christian*, October 1989.

[98] Memorandum to the author, 12 November 1994.

Chapter 11. Preacher and Writer: Publishing the Faith

[1] Quoted by Smyth (1940), p. 179, from Abner William Brown, *Recollections of the Conversation Parties of the Rev. Charles Simeon* (1863).

[2] Smyth (1940), p. 175. The Revd John Claude was 'a minister of the reformed religion' in France, whose 'essay' was originally translated into English in 1778 by Robert Robinson, a dissenting minister in Cambridge. Simeon published his own edition (omitting the translator's notes, which were 'four times as large as the original work') with one hundred of his own 'skeleton sermons' attached in 1796, and it was reissued (London: S. Cornish, 1837) a year after his death.

[3] Houston (ed.) (1986), p. xxvii.

[4] Jane Austen, *Mansfield Park* (1814; London: Folio, 1975), p. 273.

[5] Smyth (1959), p. 221.

[6] See volume one, p. 107.

[7] John R. W. Stott, 'The Ministry of the Word: Some Thoughts on Expository Preaching', *Christian Graduate*, September 1954, p. 106; reprinted in *Crusade*, January 1957.

[8] Stott (1961b), p. vii. A new edition appeared in 1995 in the Christian Classics series.

[9] Stott (1982b), p. 10. The Author's Introduction speaks of his having read 'nearly a hundred books on homiletics, communication and related themes'.

[10] Lloyd-Jones (1971).

[11] JRWS papers. Letter dated 12 May 1970.

[12] Stott (1982b), p. 178.

[13] *The Church of England Newspaper*, 12 February 1982. Dr Coggan, recently retired as Archbishop of Canterbury, had been influential in setting up the College of Preachers in 1960 and remained Chairman until 1980.

[14] JRWS papers. Letter from Hodder & Stoughton, 17 February 1982.

[15] Maurice A. P. Wood, Bishop of Norwich (personal knowledge).

[16] Extracts: 8 and 15 January. Review, 'The Power of the Pulpit', 5 February 1982.

[17] *Ibid.*

[18] Stott (1982b), p. 10.

[19] Prebendary R. C. Lucas, writing in the Proclamation Trust newsletter, September 1999. The Trust was the direct outcome of this first small conference. See the description of his remarkable work at St Helen's, Bishopsgate, in the opening chapter of the *Festschrift* written to mark Dick Lucas's seventieth birthday: C. Green and Jackman (eds.) (1995), pp. 11–23. He served as Rector of St Helen's, Bishopsgate, from 1961 to 1998. The Revd J. J. M. Fletcher was his curate from 1976 to 1981.

[20] Letter to the author, 1 September 1999.

[21] Editor's Note, *Christianity Today*, 12 June 1981.

[22] 'Rehabilitating Discipleship: An Interview with John Stott', *Prism*, July–August 1995.

[23] Canon Philip D. King. Letter to the author, 11 May 2000.

[24] Memorandum to the author, 14 April 1999.

[25] The Revd Dr M. A. Labberton, *John Stott – The Preacher* (unpublished; used by kind permission).

[26] Scots readers will be reminded of Mrs Macfadyen and the 'fower trumpets' which were her undoing. See 'The Collapse of Mrs Macfadyen' in Maclaren (1894).

[27] See Stott (1982b), p. 335, where this verse concludes the final chapter, for an account of how John Stott was introduced to it by the Revd Basil Gough.

[28] Perth, 18 April; Melbourne, 27 April; Canberra, 1 May; and published as Stott (1979b); republished in America two years later as *Culture and the Bible* (1981). From 1982 to 1986 John Stott was Vice-President for Europe of the United Bible Societies.

[29] Stott (1979b), p. 1.

[30] Stott (1982c).

[31] Stott (1989), the transcript of the address.

[32] Stott (1984).

[33] Crowe (ed.) (1967), p. 26.

[34] *Christianity Today*, July 1977 to June 1981.

[35] Taped interview, 8/38–39.

[36] Paul Weston. Manuscript, 'Reminiscences of the Hookses, 17–23 September 1983'. See Stott (1984), pp. 173–193; the reference to Solomon is on p. 174. Even Paul Weston's account does not fully convey the speed with which, once the research was done and the outline settled, John Stott would draft a book. He wrote to his study assistant, Bob Wismer, from The Hookses to report, '*Issues* is making good progress. I managed five chapters last week and one more yesterday …' (13 September 1983). See, however, p. xi of the Foreword to the first edition, where John Stott speaks of his difficulties in writing this book and how he was several times tempted to abandon it.

[37] *North–South: A Programme for Survival* (1980).

[38] Because of his family interest in medical matters, and the demands of a ministry to many doctors, nurses and paramedics, John Stott had written for *The Church of England*

Newspaper (29 October and 5 November 1971) on 'Reverence for Human Life', considering briefly both euthanasia and abortion.

[39] Autumn 1971; republished as Stott (1972a).

[40] *Marriage, Divorce and the Church* (1971).

[41] The most recent revision was in the 1999 revised edition of *Issues*, where the chapter was released in advance as Stott (1998).

[42] Stott (1999d), p. 312.

[43] See chapter 13 below.

[44] Taped interview 8/42. The revised US second edition appeared under the title *Decisive Issues Facing Christians Today* (1990).

[45] *The Church of England Newspaper*, 24 May 1985.

[46] At this time Hon. Curate of Clifton-on-Teme as well as Publisher at the Oxford University Press and Senior Deputy Secretary to the Delegates.

[47] *Church Times*, 25 January 1985.

[48] Lewis and Calabria (1989), p. 83. Letter dated 10 August 1953.

[49] Stott (1982b), p. 166.

[50] Taped interview, 8/48.

[51] Gordon (1991), p. 301.

[52] Stott (1986a), pp. 11–12.

[53] Stott (1958a), pp. 98–99.

[54] In spite of this unpopularity in academic circles, it is recognized as the teaching of the Church of England. The Doctrine Commission in their most recent Report make this clear: 'The view of the atonement reflected in the Thirty-Nine Articles is *substitutionary* in that Christ acts in our place and stead.' *The Mystery of Salvation* (1995), p. 212.

[55] Stott (1986a), p. 10, quoting especially from Taylor (1940).

[56] Stott (1986a), p. 168.

[57] Michael Green, 'The Centrality of the Cross', *Church Times*, 28 November 1986.

[58] *Christianity Today*, 4 September 1987.

[59] Edwards and Stott (1988), pp. 107–168.

[60] Translations were authorized in a dozen languages from Chinese to Urdu.

[61] JRWS papers. Letter dated 27 April 1987.

[62] Canon R. W. Hanlon to George and Maureen Swannell, 25 March 1991.

[63] JRWS papers. Letter from Ajith Fernando, 30 April 1987.

[64] JRWS papers. Letter from Dr D. A. McHardy, 21 February 1995.

[65] JRWS papers, 26 November 1987. The Very Revd James Stuart Stewart was then Professor Emeritus of New Testament Language, Literature and Theology, University of Edinburgh. He was a Chaplain to the Queen in Scotland (1951–66) as John Stott was in England.

[66] Stott (1999b) from the Preface to the Combined Edition, p. 4.

[67] Stott (1985).

[68] John R. W. Stott, 'I Believe in the Church of England', in Reid (ed.) (1986).

[69] *Ibid.*, p. 17.

[70] *Ibid.*, p. 21. The chapter was adapted from an address originally given to the Guildford Diocesan Evangelical Fellowship in November 1984.

[71] *Ibid.*, pp. 31–32.

[72] The Very Revd David L. Edwards was then Provost of Southwark, a prolific writer and editor. He had earlier been Editor to the SCM Press and SCM General Secretary, Canon of Westminster and Dean of Norwich.

[73] Edwards and Stott (1988), p. ix.

[74] JRWS papers. Original letter from David Edwards, dated Epiphany 1987.

[75] Letter to the Revd R. D. Wismer, 26 August 1987. Those named were Bishop of Thetford, Vice-Principal of the London Bible College, and Warden of Latimer House, Oxford.

[76] Taped interview with the Very Revd Dr S. G. W. Andrews, 10 June 1993.

[77] From the tape-recording of the conference at the London Institute.

[78] See volume one, p. 357, for a fuller quotation of this passage, from Edwards and Stott (1988), p. 104.

[79] Edwards and Stott (1988), p. 104.

[80] From the tape-recording of the press conference.

[81] Vol. 91, July 1988.

[82] *Church Times*, 6 May 1988.

[83] *Themelios* (an international journal for theological students, edited by David Wenham and co-published by UCCF and IFES), vol. 14, no. 1, 1988.

[84] O. R. Barclay, *Faith and Thought Bulletin*, vol. 14, no. 2, 1988; reprinted in the *Evangelical Review of Theology*, July 1989.

[85] 8 September 1989.

[86] Edwards and Stott (1988), p. 327.

[87] C. S. Lewis, who would have liked to follow his 'teacher', George MacDonald, along the road of universalism, found himself unable to do so for the same reason: 'a higher authority – the Dominical utterances themselves – seemed to me irreconcilable with universalism'. Personal letter, Lewis to the Revd Alan Fairhurst, then Tutor of St John's College, Durham, 6 September 1959; first quoted by Kendall Harmon, 'Nothingness and Human Destiny: Hell in the Thought of C. S. Lewis', in Mills (ed.) (1998), p. 253.

[88] Edwards and Stott (1988), pp. 314–315; the four arguments may be pursued on *ibid.*, pp. 315–320.

[89] *Ibid.*, p. 320.

[90] Gerstner (1990), p. 57.

[91] See Packer (n.d.), p. 12. The disagreement was particularly painful to both men in the light of longstanding personal friendship, and many battles fought side by side. It did not prevent each continuing to commend the other's writings with enthusiasm, nor did it lead to any lasting break of fellowship. 'In this', John Stott wrote to James Packer, 'you have been a model which I gratefully acknowledge and applaud.' JRWS papers. Letter dated 11 August 1997. For the text of Dr Packer's Chicago address, see Packer (1998), pp. 179–198.

[92] See 'What does it mean to be an Evangelical?', *Christianity Today*, 16 June 1989. The vote could well have gone the other way had not a representative of the Advent Christian General Conference pleaded that they would be excluded by such a resolution.

[93] For some of the history, see Robert A. Peterson, 'Basil Atkinson: A Key Figure for Twentieth Century Evangelical Annihilationism', *Churchman*, vol. 111, no. 3, 1997. John Stott writes: 'If my own memory is correct, I never read Basil's book, or heard him speak on this subject, although of course I knew something of his views.' Letter to the author, 17 November 1977.

[94] C. S. Lewis's second letter to Alan Fairhurst, 9 September 1959, quoted by kind permission. Lewis added a PS: 'To picture the foolish virgins in perpetual torment is perhaps just as blunderingly prosaic as to picture its wise ones as perpetually at supper! Both are prosaic, therefore false, extensions of the real poetic image which simply seizes the moment of "Come inside" or "Go away" …'

[95] *The Mystery of Salvation* (1995), pp. 198–199. This reference too I owe to Canon Alan Fairhurst. The Commission included evangelical scholars within its membership and was at pains to show that the Report was unanimous (p. x). See also the report of the Evangelical Alliance Commission on Unity and Truth among Evangelicals (2000) especially no. 19 of the 'Conclusions and Recommendations', p. 134.

[96] 'Many people went into print without even having bothered to read what I had written.' John Stott in an interview with Roy McCloughry, 'Life in the Spirit of Truth', *Third Way*, October 1995.

[97] JRWS papers. 'A Statement about Eternal Punishment', for private circulation, April 1993. An early summary of his thoughts towards annihilationism was published in the terminal letter of the Theological Students' Fellowship, Autumn 1958, and some notes on an address, 'The Last Judgment', given at the TSF Conference 1957–58.

[98] Professor of Biblical History and Literature, Sheffield, 1955–59; Rylands Professor of

Biblical Criticism and Exegesis, 1959–78. Looking back on his life he wrote, 'I should not find the career of a Bible teacher so satisfying as I do if I were not persuaded that the Bible is God's Word written.' F. F. Bruce (1980), p. 311.

[99] Foreword to Fudge (1982), pp. vii–viii.

[100] JRWS papers. Letter dated 26 October 1989.

[101] S. Bruce (1995), p. 104. By no means all these books were Christian. 'Occult' titles, New Age and the like represented nearly a fifth of all 'religious' books.

[102] Stott (1988a), originally Stott (1966a).

[103] Hopkins (1977), p. 60.

[104] See Hooper (1996), p. 747. The reference there given is to Owen Barfield's thinly disguised account of C. S. Lewis's difficulties with the Inland Revenue in the early days of such charitable gifts. See Tennyson (ed.) (1989), pp. 153–154.

[105] See Phillips (1984), pp. 171, 194.

[106] W. Martin (1991), p. 565.

[107] Personal knowledge.

[108] Taped interview, 19/22.

[109] Taped interview, 19/24.

Chapter 12. Seventy Plus: Pressing On

[1] *The Times*, 21 January 1936.

[2] Wm. Roger Louis, 'The Close of the Twentieth Century', in M. Howard and Louis (eds.) (1998), p. 332.

[3] Brierley (ed.) (1999). The population of China alone, or of India alone, is now equal to the entire population of the world two centuries ago. *The Times* reported in 1999 that according to UN demographers, 'the population of India will officially top one billion by this weekend' (issue of 13 August 1999).

[4] David B. Barrett and Todd M. Johnson, 'Annual Statistical Table on Global Mission: 1999', *The International Bulletin of Missionary Research*, January 1999.

[5] Ralph Dahrendorf, 'Towards the Twenty-First Century', in M. Howard and Louis (eds.) (1998), p. 334.

[6] John Stott believed that 'the 20th century may well go down in history as having been characterized by violence and brutality'. Personal newsletter, New Year 2000.

[7] Fox (ed.) (1999), pp. 17–18.

[8] S. Bruce (1995), pp. 37, 71.

[9] *The Independent*, 25 February 2000, quoting a survey commissioned by Voluntary Service Overseas. I owe the reference to Mrs Christina Rees, who cited it on BBC Radio 4's 'Thought for the Day' the following morning.

[10] *Church Times*, 31 March 2000, quoting a MORI Poll commissioned by Nestlé.

[11] George Turnbull, 'If They Never Go, They'll Never Know', *Business Matters*, Spring 1994, a journal of the Associated Examining Board. The information is taken from *Children 1990*, published by the Children's Defence Fund (USA), 1990. I owe the quotation to Alasdair Barron, 'The Personal Money Management Crisis', in Vale (ed.) (1998), pp. 118–119.

[12] David Bebbington, 'Evangelicalism in its Settings: The British and the American Movements Since 1940', in Noll, Bebbington and Rawlyk (eds.) (1994), p. 378.

[13] Chris Sugden, 'Where is the next John Stott?', *The Church of England Newspaper*, 21 September 1990.

[14] Eden and Wells (eds.) (1991); V. Samuel and Sugden (eds.) (1991).

[15] JRWS personal newsletter, May 1991.

[16] V. Samuel and Sugden (eds.) (1991), p. vii. Dr Graham also sent to All Souls Church a cable of warm admiration affirming John Stott's gifts and achievements, beginning, 'I never dreamed that my long time and beloved friend and colleague John Stott has already reached 70. He still looks like the young colleague I remember from when we held a mission at Cambridge University together in 1955 ...' British Telecom Telemessage, 15 April 1991.

[17] V. Samuel and Sugden (eds) (1991), pp. vii–viii.

[18] Colin Craston in the Preface to *The Church of England Year Book, 1992*, p. xxv.

[19] Pratt (ed.) (1865). The Society itself dated back to 1783.

[20] *Ibid.* See for example pp. 211, 404, 496.

[21] In common with most of Her Majesty's Chaplains, John Stott's personal contacts with the Royal Family were very limited. He used his position, however, 'as having been a Chaplain to the Queen for thirty-five years', to write personally to both the Prince and Princess of Wales, following her BBC *Panorama* interview of 1995, urging 'a new possibility – not for divorce but for reconciliation. For reconciliation is at the heart of the gospel of Christ.' JRWS papers, 21 and 28 November 1995.

[22] JRWS papers. Letter from the President Elect, 11 March 1994.

[23] 2 March 1994, 'A Biblical Vision for the Church', Acts 2:42–47. Canon C. M. Ruston had been succeeded in 1987 by the Revd M. H. Ashton.

[24] Letter from David B. Jones to the author, 8 January 1999.

[25] The original Deed of Settlement was signed by John Stott, Oliver Barclay, Timothy Dudley-Smith and John Laird, 30 April 1971.

[26] Nigel Sylvester was a former International Secretary of Scripture Union. David Cansdale (son of George Cansdale, Churchwarden of All Souls in the 1940s and '50s – see volume one, pp. 243–244) had retired two years before as Assistant Chief Constable in Hertfordshire.

[27] JRWS personal newsletter, March 1993.

[28] 'An Address by John Stott' at an International Tea in his honour hosted by InterVarsity Press, Dallas, 28 June 1992.

[29] St Peter's, Vere Street, as the home of the educational work of Christian Impact, retained its name as the London Institute for Contemporary Christianity.

[30] Taped interview, B16/4.

[31] 'Christian Impact – Response Forms', dated 21 October 1991. The report noted the need to encourage action: 'Some scepticism is expressed as to whether in fact we make or stimulate any "Christian Impact".' The name was dropped in 1997. EA: Evangelical Alliance. CARE: Christian Action, Research and Education. UCCF: Universities and Colleges Christian Fellowship.

[32] From the Application Form for the 1998 CMW course.

[33] John Stott. 'A letter from the President to supporters of LICC', February 1999.

[34] Lesslie Newbigin, 'Mission to Six Continents', in Fey (ed.) (1970), p. 185.

[35] *Ibid.*, p. 192. This was to provide 'an ecumenical agency dealing with Christian literature from a world base'.

[36] Memorandum to the author, 7 September 1998.

[37] W. Ward Gasque, 'Stott on Theological Education', *Christian Week* (Canada), 18 March 1997. The writer of the article, himself Dean of Ontario Theological Seminary, went on to describe how 'During the past quarter century, some of the leading seminaries around the world have been reclaimed for the evangelical cause ... Meanwhile, God has raised up new theological educational institutions that are equipping a new generation of church leaders to serve the world faithfully and to blaze new paths in mission.'

[38] 'An Admonition from John Stott', *Fellowship of Langham Scholars Newsletter*, March 1996.

[39] David B. Jones. Letter to the author, 8 January 1999.

[40] *Ibid.* David Jones recalls how, walking together into a church or hall for such an event, John Stott would turn to him and say, 'Here we are again, lurching unsteadily from one crisis to the next!'

[41] *Ibid.* David Spence had by this date succeeded Dr David Wells as chairman.

[42] Letter dated 8 October 1996.

[43] Sara 'Dee Dee' MacLean (founder member of the Board). Letter to the author, 5 February 2000.

[44] David B. Jones. Letter to the author, 8 January 1999, quoting the object of John Stott

Ministries. The words 'sincerely believe' are a slightly later addition, made at John Stott's request.

[45] JRWS diary. 'A visit to China, October 1996', p. 1.

[46] JRWS diary. 'Austria, June 1990', p. 6.

[47] JRWS diary. 'Cuba, 4–16 March 1996', p. 15.

[48] JRWS diary. 'India to Australia, February 1990', p. 11a.

[49] JRWS diary. 'Egypt, 10–26 November 1996', p. 2.

[50] John Stott, 'Christ and Culture', *LICC Annual Review*, 1966.

[51] JRWS diary. 'Kenya, 23 January – 20 February 1998', p. 17.

[52] JRWS diary. 'India, Singapore, Sabah, Malaysia, May 1994', p. 16.

[53] JRWS diary. 'Seattle, Vancouver and Korea, 4–31 July 1993', p. 14a.

[54] JRWS diary. 'Kenya, 23 January – 20 February 1998', p. 5a.

[55] JRWS diary. 'Canada and USA, June–July 1991', p. 11. By the time he wrote *The Birds our Teachers* (1999a) he was less enthusiastic: 'But still no Snowy Owls; only a brief glimpse of a single bird in flight perhaps half a mile away' (p. 31).

[56] JRWS diary. 'USA and Canada, June–July 1996', p. 5a.

[57] *Ibid.*, p. 7. Some of these photographs are reproduced in Stott (1999a), pp. 26–27.

[58] Stott (1999a), p. 32.

[59] JRWS diary. 'USA and Canada, June–July 1996', pp. 28–29. For the substance of the two addresses, see Stott (1999a), chapter 2.

[60] 'People in Close-up: John Capon Talks to John Stott (2)', *Crusade*, June 1974.

[61] JRWS diary. 'The Falkland Islands, the Antarctic, Chile and the U.S., December 1990 – February 1991', p. 3a.

[62] *Ibid.*, p. 26.

[63] JRWS personal newsletter, May 1991.

[64] David B. Jones. Letter to the author, 8 January 1999. He added that this 'Southern boy' was in professional life one of the world's foremost hand surgeons.

[65] JRWS. Letter as Chairman Emeritus to 'Friends of ELT' in the *Evangelical Literature Trust Report, 1996*.

[66] Jonathan Spence, 'China', in M. Howard and Louis (eds.) (1998), p. 226.

[67] See B. Graham (1997), pp. 595–596.

[68] JRWS diary. 'A Visit to China, October 1996', p. 6. Much of this section is drawn directly from information in this fifty-eight-page diary.

[69] JRWS. Memorandum to the author, 16 September 1998.

[70] JRWS diary. 'A Visit to China, October 1996', pp. 17–17a. Bibles could still not be sold generally in bookshops, but were distributed through forty-five Christian Centres across China.

[71] 'Basic Stott', issue of 8 January 1996; adapted from *Third Way*, October 1995.

[72] JRWS diary. 'A Visit to China, October 1996', p. 28.

[73] In the Taipei Fortuna Hotel a large sign in the lobby welcomed 'Dr John Stott' as a guest. His study assistant, John Yates, was amused to see John Stott, while waiting to meet someone in the lobby, sidle over to the sign and surreptitiously turn it to face the wall. John Stott in his turn was amused to find the Chinese comparing John Yates to Leonardo DiCaprio!

[74] John Yates III. Memorandum to the author, 1999.

[75] JRWS diary. 'Mexico, Jamaica, Trinidad and the US, January–February 1992', p. 1a.

[76] *Ibid.*, p. 4.

[77] A moving account of Armonía, including the story of Saúl and Pilar's call to work there, appears in Rand (1998), pp. 186–193. The LICC tape library stocks two cassette recordings of Saúl and Pilar Cruz talking on 'Urban Regeneration: A Mexican Story' and answering questions (28 September 1999).

[78] JRWS diary. 'Mexico, Jamaica, Trinidad and the US, January–February 1992', p. 6.

[79] JRWS. Memorandum to the author, 28 April 1999; based on an interview in Mexico, 5 March 1999.

[80] *Ibid.*

[81] JRWS personal newsletter, July 1992.

[82] JRWS diary. 'The Baltics, Kiev, Moscow and Novosibirsk, 9–30 June 1997', p. 1.

[83] *Ibid.*, p. 1a.

[84] JRWS diary. 'East and Central Europe, 27 October – 11 November 1997', p. 8. His four addresses were published under the title 'Church with a Mission' in Gaborné (ed.) (1999).

[85] JRWS diary. 'Seattle, Vancouver and Korea, 4–31 July 1993', p. 22.

[86] *Ibid.*, p. 19.

[87] *Ibid.*, p. 25a.

[88] Volume one of this biography, Dudley-Smith (1999), had been translated into Korean and published in paperback, all in a matter of weeks, to be available at the World Assembly.

[89] JRWS diary. 'Korea, 10–25 July 1999', p. 16.

Chapter 13. Still in Print: Serving the Contemporary Christian

[1] JRWS manuscript, 15 October 1995.

[2] Stott (ed.) (1996).

[3] Todd Shy. Taped interview, 22 April 1992, p. 13. John Stott refers in Stott (1991c) to his 'characteristically painstaking work' (p. 10).

[4] See Stott (1999d), pp. xii, xv, xvii.

[5] John Stott, *Your Confirmation* (1958c; revised 1991); and *Christian Basics* (1991a). *Your Confirmation* in the 1991 revision was also reissued as a small paperback in a third edition, 1995.

[6] JRWS personal newsletter, November 1990.

[7] Stott (1999e).

[8] Stott (1982c).

[9] Dr Dowley wrote to introduce himself, and to propose such a book, on 23 September 1986, explaining that the design and editorial partnership Three's Company specialized in creating full-colour books for Christian publishers.

[10] Stott (1990c), reissued from the same title (1958).

[11] Stott (1991b), reissued from Stott (1979a), described in chapter 8 above.

[12] Stott, revised S. Motyer (1994), p. 9. The original edition (1954) used the same title.

[13] Examples would be Stott (1986b) in Korean; Stott (1992b); or (in Romanian, with John Stott on 'The Paradox of our Humanness' as one of four contributors) Stott and others (1996b).

[14] Stott (1990a), appendix 1, p. 5.

[15] Dudley-Smith (ed.) (1995). A full bibliography was published at the same time, but as a separate volume: Dudley-Smith (1995).

[16] For *The Cross of Christ* (1986a) see chapter 11 above. For *The Contemporary Christian* (1992a) see section 2 of this chapter.

[17] Dorsett (ed.) (1988).

[18] JRWS personal newsletter, May 1990.

[19] Stott (1999d).

[20] Luke Bretherton, 'Good News?', *Third Way*, May 1999. Luke Bretherton, International Secretary of CARE, 1992–97, was lecturing in Christian Ethics at King's College, London.

[21] Stott (1984), p. 312.

[22] Stott (1984), 1990 edition, p. 353.

[23] JRWS diary. 'Seattle, Vancouver and Korea, 4–31 July 1993', p. 2a.

[24] Spong (2000), p. 103.

[25] Rick Hiebert, 'A typically old-fashioned Saviour? A liberal and a conservative debate the Bible's views on homosexuality', *British Columbia Report* news magazine, 2 August 1993.

[26] Spong (1991), p. 14.

[27] *Ibid.*, pp. 21–22, 117.

[28] Spong (1988), pp. 131, 154.

[29] *Topic*, the journal of the Diocese of New Westminster, September 1993.

[30] Dr Spong's highly subjective report of the evening in his autobiography cites the Dean as 'the moderator for this event'; but in fact the Dean was simply the host. The account, as might be expected, is pityingly critical of the 'dreadful performance' of his fellow-debater: 'John became more and more uncomfortable and his answers more and more bizarre.' See Spong (2000), pp. 396–398.

[31] This and other quotations from the dialogue are taken from the published transcript, *Crux*, September 1993, pp. 18–19.

[32] 'Religious dishonesty, religious hostility', *The Voice*, March 1994. See also Spong (2000), p. 398: 'They justified this subterfuge with the incredible claim that I had violated the rules of the debate by introducing new ideas in my concluding remarks to which John Stott did not have an opportunity to respond. They were, therefore, in the name of fairness giving their champion an opportunity to address this imbalance. I was amazed yet again to discover the basic lack of integrity and honesty in conservative evangelicals.' Further references to this, and to John Stott personally, appeared in Bishop Spong's article 'Farewell, John Stott!' posted on the Internet on 25 September 2000: www.beliefnet.com/author/author_44.html.

[33] JRWS papers. Letter dated 2 November 1995.

[34] Stott (1994), p. 88.

[35] JRWS papers. Letter from the Revd Dr H. S. D. Robinson, Rector of St John's, Shaughnessy, Vancouver, 1978–92, 30 July 1993.

[36] Michael Ingham, 'Two Views of the Bible', *Crosstalk*, August 1993.

[37] JRWS papers. Letter dated 13 October 1993.

[38] Maxine Hancock, 'Some Reflections on the Use of Language in the Stott–Spong Dialogue', *Crux*, December 1993.

[39] Stott (1999d), p. 383.

[40] Vasey (1995).

[41] Stott (1998). The Archbishop commended the book as a 'masterly study of homosexuality in the light of Scripture'. Bishop Spong suggested, in the days leading up to the Lambeth Conference, that the Archbishop's 'weak and ineffective leadership' on the homosexual issue 'reflected his own rampant homophobia'. Spong (2000), p. 425.

[42] Timothy Bradshaw, 'The Illiberal Reaction to Lambeth '98', *EFAC Bulletin*, January 1999. Dr Bradshaw was then Dean of Regent's Park College, Oxford. Lambeth Resolutions 1.10(d) and (e) rejected homosexual practice as 'incompatible with Scripture' and advised against legitimizing same-sex unions or ordaining those involved in them. See *Lambeth Conference, 1998* (1999), p. 381.

[43] Mervyn Stockwood, the likeable but maverick Bishop of Southwark, conducted as bishop a ceremony of blessing on a homosexual partnership, according to one biographer: see De-la-Noy (1996), p. 183.

[44] Glyn Paflin, 'Spong blames leadership for gay "hysteria"', *Church Times*, 5 February 1999.

[45] Stott (1992a).

[46] 1984 edition, p. 234; 1990 edition, p. 254.

[47] See, for example, John Stott, 'Secular Challenges to the Contemporary Church', *Crux*, September 1991; 'Evangelism through the Local Church', in C. Wright and Sugden (eds.), (1990); 'The Biblical Basis for Declaring God's Glory', in D. M. Howard (ed.) (1977).

[48] James I. Packer, 'Stott's Return to the Basics', *Christianity Today*, 7 February 1994.

[49] Issue of 30 October 1992. Peter Forster, formerly a tutor at St John's College, Durham, became Bishop of Chester in 1996.

[50] Letter from the Revd John Burrows, 21 January 1998.

[51] Based on a letter to a BST author, 1998.

[52] The Revd Simon Manchester, then curate to R. C. Lucas, who was at The Hookses with them. Letter to the author, 29 August 1997.

[53] JRWS personal newsletter, May 1990.

[54] *The Evangelical Times*. Review by Stephen V. Rees, February 1991; letter from K. Kaye, March 1991.

[55] Stott (1991c), p. 9.

[56] *Ibid.*, p. 10.

[57] Letter to the author, 10 September 1995.

[58] *Dictionary of National Biography*, 1897, vol. XLIX, p. 21, cites this as part of his 'alleged address' to the departing pilgrims.

[59] Stott (1994). Even without the Study Guide, it is one page longer than *The Message of Acts* (Stott 1990b).

[60] Stott (1994), Author's Preface, p. 10. For the Keswick Bible readings, see Stott (1966b).

[61] Stott (1966b), p. 41.

[62] *Ibid.*, p. 43. For the full argument and exegesis, see Stott (1966b), pp. 40–52; or Stott (1994) (which here echoes the earlier book), pp. 168–179.

[63] Stott (1966b), p. 76.

[64] Stott (1994), p. 205.

[65] The phrase is used in his memorandum to the author, 28 April 1999. For the full argument and exegesis, see Stott (1994), pp. 189–190.

[66] Stott (1994), p. 210.

[67] Letter to the Revd R. D. Wismer, 6 December 1992.

[68] JRWS personal newsletter, March 1994.

[69] Letter to the Revd Denis Shepheard, 29 March 1992.

[70] Stott (1999c), p. 10.

[71] Stott (1977), p. 14, the booklet based on his closing address to the National Evangelical Anglican Congress 1977 at the University of Nottingham.

[72] Stott (1999c), pp. 17ff. 'Originally "fundamentalist" was an acceptable synonym for "evangelical",' he writes (p. 20); before suggesting ten points of current divergence, decisively repudiating what the term has come to mean.

[73] *Ibid.*, pp. 54, 55, 67.

[74] The sub-title of the US edition is *A Personal Plea for Unity, Integrity and Faithfulness*, which the author hoped might also be used on any UK second edition.

[75] Stott (1964a) and (1975b).

[76] Stott (1999c), p. 104.

[77] JRWS papers, 29 December 1995.

[78] JRWS papers. Letters dated 8 August 1995 and 8 April 1995. See also 'Life in the Spirit of Truth: Roy McCloughry talks to the Rev. Dr John Stott', *Third Way*, October 1995.

[79] JRWS papers. Letter dated 1 July 1993.

[80] Zahl (1998), p. 54.

[81] 'Leave it to Jeeves', *My Man Jeeves* (London: Newnes, 1919), The book was ghost-written for Muriel: 'It was certainly some book. It had a red cover with a fowl of some species on it, and underneath the girl's name in gold letters.'

[82] Stott (1999a).

[83] *Ibid.*, p. 25.

[84] The Christian Booksellers Convention voted it their 'book of the year' for 1999, as they had done with *The Contemporary Christian* in 1992.

[85] JRWS personal newsletter, February 1999.

[86] The sermon, delivered 25 September 1993, is reproduced in LeQuire (ed.) (1996), pp. 78–83.

[87] John Stott, Foreword to P. Harris (1993), p. x.

[88] Stott (ed.) (1996).

[89] Letter to the author, 29 April 1996.

[90] *Ibid.* René Descartes coined the epigram *Cogito, ergo sum* ('I think, therefore I am') three centuries before. John Stott's borrowed version, substituting the name of a major supermarket company, and particularly appropriate for today's consumer society, might be

rendered, 'I shop, therefore I am.'

[91] JRWS papers. Letter dated 20 March 1995.

[92] JRWS papers. Fax to Dr John Akers, 16 September 1999. In the event John Stott acceded to a personal invitation from Billy Graham himself, and gave the plenary address on the first morning, 'The evangelist's message is Bible-based'.

[93] 'Theologian says Western church has "lost the fizz"', *The Grand Rapids Press*, 28 January 1995.

[94] See volume one, p. 239. John Stott had been awarded a Lambeth DD (which is not an honorary degree, but a degree dispensing the recipient from the normal university requirements of residence and examination) in 1983.

[95] 'A Tribute to John Stott', 14 October 1997.

[96] Press release, International Bible Society, 17 July 1997.

[97] *Third Way*, November 1991.

[98] David F. Wells, 'Guardian of God's Word', *Christianity Today*, 16 September 1996.

[99] Professor of Genetics, University of London, since 1974. Member of the General Synod, 1970–90.

[100] Dr A. M. McCutcheon. Letter to the author, 26 September 1996.

[101] Taped interview, 18/48.

[102] JRWS diaries. 'The Falkland Islands, the Antarctic, Chile and the US, December 1990 to February 1991', p. 64.

[103] Letter to the author, 1 June 1998.

[104] JRWS papers. 'Guidelines and Medical Report', September–October 1998.

[105] JRWS diaries. 'East Asia, January to February 1999'. He felt 'rotten and short of energy for my last address at Nanjing and on the flight home. But a visit to the doctor, antibiotics, an inhaler, plus a day in bed have put me on the road to recovery!'

[106] JRWS personal newsletter, New Year 2000.

[107] *Ibid.*

[108] JRWS papers. 'John Stott Ministries (USA) and the Langham Trust (UK). An Easter 1999 memorandum from JRWS about the future: Five Third World Ministries'.

[109] Corey Widmer. Memorandum to the author, 24 November 1999.

[110] The Steering Committee appointed at the Horsleys Green consultation consisted of David Spence and (as Convenor) David Jones (JSM); Bishop Michael Baughen and John Stott (LT UK); Nigel Sylvester (ELT), and two IFES advisers, with power to co-opt. Early in the new millennium they were able to report the formation of the Langham Partnership International, bringing together the Langham ministries in Canada, the US, the UK and Australia, together with the Evangelical Literature Trust; and the appointment of Dr Chris Wright as its first International Ministry Director.

[111] Pratt (ed.) (1865), p. 97.

Chapter 14. Leader, Pastor, Friend, Disciple: Life in Christ

[1] Lyall (1954), p. ix.

[2] *Ibid.*, p. x. See Torrey (1923); John Stott cites it as a booklet valued by Bash, in Eddison (ed.) (1983), p. 65.

[3] Stott (1952).

[4] Kidner (1979), p. 62.

[5] Stott (1988b), p. 12. The comparison is borrowed from the Foreword of Dudley-Smith (ed.) (1995), p. 9.

[6] Stott (1996), p. 9.

[7] Taped interview, 17/2.

[8] Originally from *Hymns and Sacred Poems, 1749*, in twenty-two stanzas, under the title 'After preaching (in a church)', and beginning 'Jesu, accept the grateful song'. John Wesley published it as 'Jesus, the name high over all' (stanza 9) as a hymn of seven verses, much as it is sung today, in his famous *A Collection of Hymns for the Use of the People called Methodists* (1779).

[9] Stott (1975e), p. 3.

[10] Stott (1990b), p. 233.

[11] Stott (1992a), p. 213.

[12] Quoted in Stott (1982b), p. 34.

[13] Letter to Dr Andrew Forbat, 19 August 1993.

[14] Houston (ed.) (1986).

[15] *Ibid.*, p. xxxix, quoting Carus (ed.) (1848), pp. 651–652.

[16] See, for example, Loane (1988), p. 14.

[17] Letter to the author, 29 May 1999.

[18] *Insight*, a journal of Wycliffe College, June 1993.

[19] See especially Stott (1992a), Part II, 'The Disciple', pp. 99–157.

[20] Gardner (1996), pp. 8–9. It was the Revd Tom Houston who drew my attention to this book as relevant to my subject. The quotations that follow are from pp. 32, 285–290.

[21] V. Samuel and Sugden (eds.) (1991), p. viii.

[22] The Revd Dr Vinay Samuel to LICC, 19 July 1996. Dr Samuel was at that time Executive Secretary of Partnership in Mission, Bangalore.

[23] Stott (1984).

[24] Letter to the author, 31 March 2000.

[25] Whistler (1993), p. 6.

[26] 'Face to Face with John Stott'; recorded interview, Senior Evangelical Anglican Clergy Conference, 1990.

[27] 'John Stott speaks out', *Christianity Today*, February 1993. For Bishop Spong's view of John Stott, see his article 'Farewell, John Stott!' posted on the Internet on 25 September 2000: 'So John Stott has decided to retire. What he needs to recognize is that all of his major ideas have also retired long before him ...' www.beliefnet.com/author/author_44.html.

[28] Conversation with the author, 15 April 2000.

[29] For example, René Padilla: 'I was wakened by a strange sound – John was cleaning my muddy shoes with a brush. "What are you doing, John?" I said. "My dear brother," said John, "there is no need for me to wash your feet, but let me at least brush your shoes".' Letter to the author, 6 September 1995. John Stott liked to use the image of shoe-cleaning as an example of cultural transposition. See Stott (1979b), p. 28.

[30] For example, when interviewed by Gavin Reid at SEAC, 1978. Church Society tape C108.

[31] Interview with Roy McCloughry, 8 June 1995. The edited version was published in *Third Way*, October 1995. Quotations from the interview are generally taken from the transcript of the recording rather than from the shorter, published version.

[32] 'An Address by John Stott' at the International Tea in his honour, Dallas, Texas, 28 June 1992, during the Christian Booksellers Association Convention.

[33] From Dessain (1961–84), quoted in Newsome (1993), p. 102.

[34] JRWS papers. Letter from Pastor Emiola Nihinlola, Nigeria, 18 September 1990.

[35] Walter Hooper (ed.), Preface to Lewis (1975).

[36] Peter Williams, 'John R. W. Stott', in Elwell (ed.) (1993), p. 343.

[37] 'People in Close-up: John Capon Talks to John Stott (2)', *Crusade*, June 1974.

[38] 'Struggling with Contemporary Issues', an interview with Alex Mitchell, *Third Way*, February 1982.

[39] 'John Stott speaks out', *Christianity Today*, February 1993.

[40] Interview with Roy McCloughry, 8 June 1995.

[41] Corey Widmer, journal of visit to East Africa, 31 January – 21 February 2000.

[42] *Ibid.*, Nairobi, 3 February 2000.

[43] H. Carpenter (1996), p. 183.

[44] Interview with Roy McCloughry, 8 June 1995.

[45] Toby Howarth. Letter to the author, 13 June 2000.

[46] Chua (1992), p. 147. Chua Wee Hian was recalling missions in Singapore and Malaysia in 1963, when he served as assistant missioner.

[47] The Revd Roger Simpson. Letter to the author, 12 September 1995.

[48] Stott (1999c), p. 107.

[49] Memorandum to the author, 28 April 1999, quoting Lewis (1955), p. 215.

[50] Ursula Parry. Letter to the author, 22 February 1996.

[51] The Revd Jonathan J. M. Fletcher. Letter to the author, 13 March 2000.

[52] Peter Chappell. Letter to the author, 4 June 1999.

[53] Colossians 1:28, New English Bible.

[54] Letter to the author, 14 February 1996.

[55] JRWS papers. Letter from the Revd Dale Van Deusen, 21 February 1991.

[56] JRWS papers. Letter to Mr Cook Kimball of New York, 3 January 1996.

[57] JRWS papers. Letter to the Revd J. A. K. Millar, 8 July 1997.

[58] Stott (1975a), p. 21.

[59] Letter to the Revd R. D. Wismer, 1 September 1989.

[60] Canon John Wheatley Price. Letter to the author, 11 July 1999.

[61] Keith and Gladys Hunt. Letter to the author, 6 March 1997.

[62] Stott (1984), 1990 edition, p. 273. The second sentence does not appear in the original 1984 edition.

[63] Corey Widmer, journal of visit to East Africa, 31 January – 21 February 2000.

[64] JRWS papers. Susan Larson, on behalf of Melissa Larson. Letter dated 15 June 1983.

[65] Taped interview with Rosemary Bird, 26 February 1996.

[66] The Revd Roopsingh Carr. Letter to the author, 4 August 1995.

[67] At question-time following an interview by Gavin Reid at SEAC 1978. Church Society tape C108. Canon K. A. A. Weston was then Rector of St Ebbe's, Oxford.

[68] C. S. Lewis, 'The Novels of Charles Williams', in Lewis (1982), p. 51. Lewis (1985), p. 64.

[69] Stott (1988b), p. 5.

[70] Os Guinness. Letter to the author, 12 July 1999.

[71] Toby Howarth. Memorandum to the author, 29 April 1999.

[72] Letter to the author, 30 September 1999. This gift for answering a variety of questions off the cuff stood him in good stead with journalists. In an interview in Canada in 1976 he replied in turn to questions on, among other things, fundamentalism, racial division, political leadership, Jimmy Carter, Donald Coggan, Malcolm Muggeridge, Christian feminism, women's ordination, church buildings, neo-Pentecostalism, the modern State of Israel and capital punishment! *Province*, a Vancouver BC daily newspaper, 17 July 1976.

[73] Roger Simpson. Letter to the author, 12 October 1995.

[74] C. René Padilla. Letter to the author, 6 September 1995.

[75] Letter to the author, 30 September 1999.

[76] E. M. B. Green, reviewing *The Message of Galatians* (Stott [1968]) in *The Christian*, 23 August 1968. A more recent example might be John Stott's Foreword to Berry (ed.) (2000), pp. 7–8. In just two pages complementary expressions are multiplied with a facility approaching legerdemain: Psalm 24 with Psalm 115, deification/exploitation/ co-operation, creation/delegation, respect/reverence, creation/destruction/dominion, culture/ nature, creation/Creator. Were it not for other factors in the writing, such a passion for order might become restrictive, even artificial.

[77] The Revd E. S. Shirras. Letter to the author, 20 September 1997.

[78] Stott (1999c).

[79] David Turner. Letter to the author, 2 May 1999.

[80] Taped interview, 20/45–46.

[81] For his comments on discrimination in choice of plays and films, see Stott (1982b), p. 193.

[82] David B. Jones. Letter to the author, 8 January 1999.

[83] 1 Peter 2:13, J. B. Phillips.

[84] Dr Markus Bockmuehl. Letter to the author, 24 April 1995.

[85] JRWS papers. Draft script, 'Getting involved with People', marked 'BBC, October 1970'.

[86] Letter to the author, 24 June 1999.

[87] George Cansdale. Letter to the author, 19 June 1989.

[88] See John Stott's Foreword to Clarkson (1975), p. 7.

[89] See John Stott, 'Maintaining Spiritual Freshness', *InterVarsity's Student Leadership*, Winter 1992.

[90] In his Foreword to Cansdale (1970), p. 9.

[91] Lorne Sanny. Letter to the author, 15 November 1995.

[92] Corey Widmer, journal of visit to East Africa, 31 January – 21 February 2000.

[93] JRWS diary. 'Canada and the USA, May–July 1986', pp. 33a–34.

[94] Tony McCutcheon. Taped interview, 24 May 1993.

[95] Stott (1982b), p. 183.

[96] Taped interview. 'Face to face with John Stott', SEAC 1990.

[97] Stott (1975b), p. 118.

[98] John R. W. Stott, 'An Appeal which Cannot be Ignored', Chicago Sunday Evening Club TV transcript, 13 February 1983.

[99] For example, Gordon (1991).

[100] 'Rehabilitating Discipleship: An Interview with John Stott', *Prism*, July–August, 1995.

[101] The Revd Tom Houston. Taped interview, 7 June 1993.

[102] Chua (1992), p. 149.

[103] Dr D. H. Trapnell. Taped interview, 18 February 1993.

[104] Personal conversation, 21 November 1997.

[105] See Stott (1999c), p. 147: 'Already I think I can see the wry smile on my readers' faces. For we have to confess that our reputation is very different. Evangelical people are often regarded as proud, vain, arrogant, and cocksure.'

[106] Baillie (1960), p. 70.

[107] Stott (1970), p. 125.

[108] Stott (1992), p. 184.

[109] Stott (1999c). Packer and Wilkinson (eds.) (1992).

[110] Stott (1984), p. 37. The words appear unchanged in the revised editions of 1990 and 1999.

[111] From a transcript of the recording, sent to me by David Cranston. The address does not appear in *The Keswick Week* for 1975.

[112] The statement on the charismatic movement published jointly by the Fountain Trust and the Church of England Evangelical Council, April 1977. See chapter 5 above.

[113] The Revd Dr Mark Labberton. Letter to the author, 12 November 1994.

[114] 1 Corinthians 4:7, Authorized Version. The others are 1 Corinthians 10:12 and Revelation 22:20.

[115] John Yates III, in Yates Gaskins and S. A. Yates (1998), p. 130.

[116] Jorge Atiencia. Letter to the author, 14 April 1966.

[117] Trollope (1995), p. 476. We meet Septimus Harding again in later chapters of the Barsetshire Chronicles.

[118] JRWS personal newsletter, New Year 2000.

[119] Published as Stott (2001).

Bibliography

The books listed are usually those referred to in the text or notes.

Alison, Sylvia Mary (1984), *God is Building a House*, Basingstoke: Marshalls.

All Souls Papers (1981), London: All Souls Church.

Anderson, J. N. D. (1968), *Into the World: The Need and Limits of Christian Involvement*, London: Falcon.

—— (1985), *An Adopted Son: The Story of My Life*, Leicester: IVP.

Anglican–Methodist Unity Commission (1968), *Anglican–Methodist Unity, 2: The Scheme*, London: SPCK and Epworth.

ARCIC: The Final Report (1982), London: Catholic Truth Society and SPCK.

Atkinson, Basil (n.d. [1944]), *A Theology of Prepositions*, London: Tyndale.

Baillie, John (1960), *Invitation to Pilgrimage*, Harmondsworth: Pelican. First published 1941.

Balleine, G. R. (1908), *A History of the Evangelical Party in the Church of England*, London: Longmans Green.

Barabas, Steven (1952), *So Great Salvation: The History and Message of the Keswick Convention*, London: Marshall, Morgan & Scott.

Barclay, Oliver (1997), *Evangelicalism in Britain 1935–1995: A Personal Sketch*, Leicester: IVP.

Baughen, Michael, Bewes, Richard, and Wilson, David (eds.) (1969), *Youth Praise 2*, London: CPAS.

Baxter, Christina (ed.), Stott, John, and Greenacre, Roger (consultant eds.) (1987), *Stepping Stones: Joint Essays on Anglican Catholic and Evangelical Unity*, London: Hodder & Stoughton.

Bebbington, D. W. (1989), *Evangelicalism in Modern Britain: A History from the 1730s to the 1980s*, London: Unwin Hyman.

Beckwith, R. T., Duffield, G. E., and Packer, J. I. (1977), *Across the Divide: An Exposition of the Open Letter on Relations between Evangelical Churchmen and Roman Catholics, Orthodox and Old Catholics*, Basingstoke: Lyttleton.

Beeson, Trevor (1974), *Discretion and Valour*, London: Fontana.

—— (1998), *Window on Westminster*, London: SCM.

Berry, R. J. (ed.) (2000), *The Care of Creation*, Leicester: IVP.

Bible Society (1980), *Prospects for the Eighties: From a Census of Churches in 1979,*

London: Bible Society.

Bidewell, Lance, and Hunter, Elrose (eds.) (1976), *Inside Story*, London: All Souls Church.

Blamires, Harry (1963), *The Christian Mind*, London: SPCK.

Blanch, Stuart (1991), *Future Patterns of Episcopacy*, Oxford: Latimer House.

Boswell, James (1968), *The Life of Samuel Johnson*, London: Folio edition. First published 1791.

Botting, Michael (ed.) (1996), *Bishop Michael and Myrtle: From Chester with Love*, Bramcote: Grove, for Chester Diocesan Board of Finance.

Breaking Barriers, Nairobi 1875: The Official Report of the Fifth Assembly of the World Council of Churches (1975), London: SPCK; Grand Rapids, MI: Eerdmans, in collaboration with WCC.

Brierley, Peter (ed.) (1999), *UK Christian Handbook: Religious Trends 2000/2001, No. 2*, London: Christian Research and HarperCollins.

Brown, Roger L. (1988), *The Evangelical Fellowship in the Church in Wales: The First 21 Years*, Cardiff: EFCW.

Bruce, F. F. (1980), *In Retrospect*, London: Pickering & Inglis.

Bruce, Steve (1980), *The Student Christian Movement and the Inter-Varsity Fellowship: A Sociological Study of the Two Movements*, unpublished PhD thesis, Department of Sociology, University of Stirling.

———— (1995), *Religion in Modern Britain*, Oxford: Oxford University Press.

———— (1996) *Religion in the Modern World*, Oxford: Oxford University Press.

Campling, Elizabeth (1990), *Portrait of a Decade: The 1980s*, London: Batsford.

Cansdale, G. S. (1970), *Animals of Bible Lands*, Exeter: Paternoster.

Capon, John (1972), *And There Was Light: The Story of the Nationwide Festival of Light*, London: Lutterworth.

Carpenter, Edward (1991), *Archbishop Fisher: His Life and Times*, Norwich: Canterbury Press.

Carpenter, Humphrey (1996), *Robert Runcie: The Reluctant Archbishop*, London: Hodder & Stoughton.

Carus, William (ed.) (1848), *Memoirs of the Life of the Revd Charles Simeon*, London: Hatchard.

Catherwood, Christopher (ed.) (1986), *Martyn Lloyd-Jones: Chosen by God*, Crowborough: Highland.

Catherwood, H. F. R. (1964), *The Christian in Industrial Society*, London: IVP.

Chadwick, Owen (1990a), *Michael Ramsey: A Life*, Oxford: Clarendon.

———— (1990b), *The Spirit of the Oxford Movement*, Cambridge: Cambridge University Press.

Charley, Julian (1983), *Rome, Canterbury, and the Future*, Bramcote: Grove.

Chester, Timothy (1993), *Awakening to a World of Need: The Recovery of Evangelical Social Concern*, Leicester: IVP.

Chua Wee Hian (1992), *Getting through Customs: The Global Jottings of Chua Wee Hian*, Leicester: IVP.

Church and State: Report of the Archbishops' Commission (1970), London: CIO.

Church Extends her Frontiers, The (1995), the Report of the 121st Islington Clerical Conference, London: Marshall, Morgan & Scott.

Church of England Evangelical Council (1978), *Truth, Error and Discipline in the Church*, London: Vine Books (an imprint of Church Society).

———— (1982), *Evangelical Anglicans and the ARCIC Final Report: An Assessment and Critique*, drafted by John Stott, Bramcote: Grove.

Church of England Evangelical Council and Anglican Evangelical Assembly (1983), *Anglican Evangelicals and their New Assembly*, London: CEEC and AEA.

Church of England Year Book, The (1978, 1979), CIO; (1988, 1989, 1992), Church House Publishing.

Clark, Geoffrey L. (1994), *An Examination of the Work and Writings of John Stott and an Assessment of his Influence on Evangelical Spirituality in English Church Life from 1967 to 1989*, unpublished MTh thesis, University of Oxford.

Clarkson, Margaret (1975), *Conversations with a Barred Owl*, Grand Rapids, MI: Zondervan.

Clements, Keith W. (1988), *Lovers of Discord: Twentieth Century Theological Controversies in England*, London: SPCK.

Colquhoun, Frank (1967), *Parish Prayers*, London: Hodder & Stoughton.

———— (1975), *Contemporary Parish Prayers*, London: Hodder & Stoughton.

———— (1976), *New Every Morning*, London: BBC.

———— (1982), *New Parish Prayers*, London: Hodder & Stoughton.

Como, James T. (ed.) (1980), *C. S. Lewis at the Breakfast Table*, London: Collins.

Craston, Colin (1998), *Debtor to Grace*, London: Silver Fish Publishing.

Crockford Prefaces (1947), London: Oxford University Press/Church House Publishing.

Crockford's Clerical Directory, 1969–70 (1971), *1977–79* (1980), London: Oxford University Press.

Crowe, Philip (ed.) (1967), *Keele '67: The National Evangelical Anglican Statement*, London: Falcon.

Cundy, Ian (ed.) (1977), *Obeying Christ in a Changing World*, vol. 2: *The People of God*, London: Collins. General editor John Stott.

Darwin, Charles (1928), *The Origin of Species by Means of Natural Selection*, Everyman edition, London: Dent. First published 1859.

Dayton, Edward R., and Wilson, Samuel (eds.) (1984), *The Future of World Evangelization*, Monrovia, CA: Marc.

De-la-Noy, Michael (1996), *A Lonely Life*, London: Mowbray.

Dessain, C. S. (ed.) (1961–84), *The Letters and Diaries of John Henry Newman*, Oxford: Clarendon.

Dillistone, F. W. (1975), *Charles Raven*, London: Hodder & Stoughton.

———— (1980), *Into All the World: A Biography of Max Warren*, London: Hodder & Stoughton.

Donovan, Vincent J. (1978), *Christianity Rediscovered: An Epistle from the Masai*, London: SCM.

Dorsett, Lyle (ed.) (1988), *The Essential C. S. Lewis*, London: Macmillan.

Douglas, J. D. (ed.) (1975), *Let the Earth Hear his Voice: Papers and Responses of the Lausanne International Congress on World Evangelization, 1974*, Minneapolis, MN: World Wide Publications.

Drummond, Lewis (1992), *Spurgeon, Prince of Preachers*, Grand Rapids, MI: Kregel.

Dudley-Smith, Timothy (1995), *John Stott: A Comprehensive Bibliography*, Leicester: IVP.

———— (1999), *John Stott: The Making of a Leader*, Leicester: IVP. Volume 1 of the present biography.

Dudley-Smith, Timothy (ed.) (1995), *Authentic Christianity: From the Writings of John Stott*, Leicester: IVP.

Dudley-Smith, Timothy, Packer, James I., and Stott, John R. W. (1967), *Evening Prayer: A Conservative Translation into Modern English*, London: Falcon.

Eddison, John (ed.) (1983), *'Bash': A Study in Spiritual Power*, Basingstoke: Marshalls.

Eden, Martyn, and Wells, David F. (eds.) (1991), *The Gospel in the Modern World: A Tribute to John Stott*, Leicester: IVP.

Edwards, David L. (1969), *Religion and Change*, London: Hodder & Stoughton.

Edwards, David L., with a response from John Stott, (1988), *Essentials: A Liberal–Evangelical Dialogue*, London: Hodder & Stoughton. US title *Evangelical Essentials*, 1989.

Elwell, Walter A. (ed.) (1993), *A Handbook of Evangelical Theologians*, Grand Rapids, MI: Baker.

Elworthy, John (1980), *Billy Graham in Oxford and Cambridge*, London: Regal.

Endersbee, Mary (1977), *Hidden Miracles at All Souls*, London: Lakeland.

Evangelical Alliance Commission on Unity and Truth among Evangelicals (2000), *The Nature of Hell*, London: Acute.

Facing the New Challenges: The Message of PACLA (1978), Kisumu, Kenya: Evangel.

Faith in the City (1985), London: Church House Publishing.

Fey, Harold E. (ed.) (1970), *The Ecumenical Advance: A History of the Ecumenical Movement*, vol. 2: *1948–1968*, London: SPCK, on behalf of the Committee on Ecumenical History of the WCC.

Fox, Shirley (ed.) (1999), *Families and the Labour Market: Trends, Policies and Pressures*, London: Family Policy Studies Centre, Joseph Rowntree Foundation.

Fromer, Paul, and Weldon, Ellen (1965), *Change, Witness, Triumph*, Downers Grove, IL: IVP.

Fudge, E. W. (1982), *The Fire that Consumes*, Houston, TX: Providential.

Gáborné, Naszádi (ed.) (1999), *Tanítványság és Szolgálat*, Budapest: Harmat.

Gardner, Howard (1996), *Leading Minds: An Anatomy of Leadership*, London: Harper-Collins.

General Synod (1981), *The Charismatic Movement in the Church of England*, London: CIO.

Gere, J. A., and Sparrow, John (eds.) (1981), *Geoffrey Madan's Notebooks: A Selection*, Oxford: Oxford University Press.

Gerstner, John H. (1990), *Repent or Perish (With a Special Reference to the Conservative Attack on Hell)*, Ligonier, PA: Soli Deo Gloria.

God's Men: From All Nations to All Nations (1968), Downers Grove, IL: IVP.

Goldingay, John (1978), *Songs from a Strange Land: Psalms 42 – 51*, Leicester: IVP.

Gordon, James M. (1991), *Evangelical Spirituality: From the Wesleys to John Stott*, London: SPCK.

Gospel and Spirit: A Joint Statement (1977), Esher and London: Fountain Trust and the Church of England Evangelical Council.

Graham, Billy (1997), *Just As I Am*, London: HarperCollins.

Graham, Franklin (1995), *Rebel with a Cause*, Nashville, TN: Nelson.

Green, Christopher, and Jackman, David (eds.) (1995), *When God's Voice is Heard: Essays on Preaching Presented to Dick Lucas*, Leicester: IVP.

Green, E. M. B (1964), *Called to Serve: Ministry and Ministers in the Church*, London: Hodder & Stoughton.

———— (2000), *The Message of Matthew: The Kingdom of Heaven*, Leicester: IVP. A revision of *Matthew for Today*, London: Hodder & Stoughton, 1988.

Green, E. M. B. (ed.) (1977), *The Truth of God Incarnate*, London: Hodder & Stoughton.

Griffiths, Brian (1982), *Morality and the Market Place: Christian Alternatives to Capitalism and Socialism*, London: Hodder & Stoughton.

Harper, Michael (1997), *The True Light: An Evangelical's Journey to Orthodoxy*, London: Hodder & Stoughton.

Harris, Murray J. (1985), *Easter in Durham: Bishop Jenkins and the Resurrection of Jesus*, Exeter: Paternoster.

Harris, Peter (1993), *Under the Bright Wings*, London: Hodder & Stoughton.

Hastings, Adrian (1991), *A History of English Christianity 1920–1990*, London: SCM.

Heath, Edward (1995), *The Course of My Life*, London: Hodder & Stoughton.

Hebert, Gabriel (1957), *Fundamentalism and the Church of God*, London: SCM.

Henry, Carl F. H. (1947), *The Uneasy Conscience of Modern Fundamentalism*, Grand Rapids, MI: Eerdmans.

———— (1967), *Evangelicals on the Brink of Crisis: The Significance of the World Congress on Evangelism*, Waco, TX: Word.

Henry, Carl F. H., and Mooneyham, W. Stanley (eds.) (1967), *One Race, One Gospel, One Task: The World Congress on Evangelism, Berlin, 1966*, vol. 1, Minneapolis, MN: World Wide Publications.

Henry, Paul (1974), *Politics for Evangelicals*, Valley Forge, PA: Judson.

Hick, J. (ed.), (1977), *The Myth of God Incarnate*, London: SCM.

Hocken, Peter (1986), *Stream of Renewal*, Exeter: Paternoster.

Hooper, Walter (1996), *C. S. Lewis: A Companion and Guide*, London: HarperCollins.

Hooper, Walter (ed.) (1979), *They Stand Together: The Letters of C. S. Lewis to Arthur Greeves*, London: Collins.

Hopkins, Hugh Evan (1977), *Charles Simeon of Cambridge*, London: Hodder & Stoughton.

Horne, Shirley (1973), *An Hour to the Stone Age*, Chicago, IL: Moody.

Houston, James M. (ed.) (1986), *Evangelical Preaching: An Anthology of Sermons by Charles Simeon*, Portland, OR: Multnomah.

Howard, David M. (ed.) (1974), *Jesus Christ: Lord of the Universe, Hope of the World*, Downers Grove, IL: IVP.

————— (ed.) (1977), *Declare His Glory Among the Nations*, Downers Grove, IL: IVP.

Howard, Michael, and Louis, Wm. Roger (eds.) (1998), *The Oxford History of the Twentieth Century*, Oxford: Oxford University Press.

Hunt, Keith, and Hunt, Gladys (1991), *For Christ and the University*, Downers Grove, IL: IVP.

Hylson-Smith, Kenneth (1988), *Evangelicals in the Church of England 1734–1984*, Edinburgh: T. & T. Clark.

Iremonger, F. A. (1948), *William Temple, Archbishop of Canterbury: His Life and Letters*, London: Oxford University Press.

Issues in Human Sexuality (1991), London: Church House Publishing.

Johnson, Douglas (1979), *Contending for the Faith*, Leicester: IVP.

Johnson, Paul (ed.) (1994), *20th Century Britain*, London: Longmans.

Johnston, Arthur P. (1978), *The Battle for World Evangelism*, Wheaton, IL: Tyndale House.

Johnston, R. P. P. (ed.) (1966), *Bishops in the Church: Addresses at the 132nd Islington Conference*, London: Church Book Room Press.

Kaye, Bruce (ed.) (1977), *Obeying Christ in a Changing World*, vol. 3: *The Changing World*, London: Collins. General editor John Stott.

Kemp, Eric, Harper, Michael, and Stott, John (eds.) (1988), *Towards a Renewed Church: A Joint Statement by Catholic, Charismatic and Evangelical Anglicans*, Bramcote: Grove.

Keswick Week, The, 1962, 1965, 1969, 1975, London: Marshall, Morgan & Scott.

Kidner, Derek (1976), *A Time to Mourn, and a Time to Dance: Ecclesiastes and the Way of the World*, Leicester: IVP. Later *The Message of Ecclesiastes: A Time to Mourn and a Time to Dance*.

————— (1979), *Ezra and Nehemiah: An Introduction and Commentary*, Tyndale Old Testament Commentaries, Leicester: IVP.

King, John C. (1969), *The Evangelicals*, London: Hodder & Stoughton.

King, John C. (ed.), (1973), *Evangelicals Today*, Guildford and London: Lutterworth.

Kruger, Hanfried (ed.) (1976), *Jesus Christus Befreit und Eint: Fünfte Vollversammlung des Ökumenischen Rates der Kirchen in Nairobi*, Frankfurt: Lembeck Verlag.

Labberton, Mark A., *John Stott – The Preacher*, unpublished.

Lambeth Conference, The Report of, 1978 (1978), London: CIO.

Lambeth Conference, The Report of, 1988 (1988), London: Church House Publishing.

Lambeth Conference, The Report of, 1998 (1999), Harrisburg, PA: Morehouse.

Lancelot, J. B. (1929), *Francis James Chavasse*, Oxford: Blackwell.

Leaver, Robin A., Litton, James H., and Young, Carlton R. (eds.) (1985), *Duty and Delight: Routley Remembered*, Norwich: Canterbury Press.

Leighton, Janet (1995), *Lift High the Cross: A History of Trinity Episcopal School for Ministry*, Wheaton, IL: Harold Shaw.

LeQuire, Stan L. (ed.) (1996), *The Best Preaching on Earth: Sermons on Caring for Creation*, Valley Forge, PA: Judson.

Lewis, C. S. (1955), *Surprised by Joy*, London: Bles.

———— (1975), *Fern-Seed and Elephants*, London: Fontana.

———— (1982), *Of This and Other Worlds*, London: Collins.

———— (1985), *Letters to Children*, London: Collins.

Lewis, C. S., and Calabria, Don Giovanni (1989), *Letters: A Study in Friendship*, trans. Martyn Moyniham, London: Collins.

Lloyd-Jones, D. Martyn (1971), *Preaching and Preachers*, London: Hodder & Stoughton.

———— (1989), *Knowing the Times: Addresses Delivered on Various Occasions 1942–1977*, Edinburgh: Banner of Truth.

Loane, M. L. (1988), *These Happy Warriors*, Blackwood, South Australia: New Creation Publications.

Lockhart, J. G. (1949), *Cosmo Gordon Lang*, London: Hodder & Stoughton.

Longford, Lord (1972), *Pornography: The Longford Report*, London: Coronet.

Lowman, Pete (1983), *The Day of His Power: A History of the International Fellowship of Evangelical Students*, Leicester: IVP.

Luker, Raymond (1979), *All Souls: A History*, London: All Souls Church.

Lyall, Leslie T. (1954), *John Sung*, London: China Inland Mission.

McGavran, Donald (1959), *How Churches Grow*, London: World Dominion Press.

———— (1980), *Understanding Church Growth*, revised edition, Grand Rapids, MI: Eerdmans.

McGavran, Donald (ed.) (1972), *The Eye of the Storm: The Great Debate in Mission*, Chicago, IL: World Books.

McGrath, Alister (1994), *Evangelicalism and the Future of Christianity*, London: Hodder & Stoughton.

———— (1997), *To Know and Serve God: A Biography of James I. Packer*, London: Hodder & Stoughton.

Maclaren, Ian (1894), *Beside the Bonnie Brier Bush*, London: Hodder & Stoughton.

Mäkelä, Matti (1999), *Mission According to John R. W. Stott: A Study with Special Reference to the Ecumenicals and the Evangelicals*, Abo, Finland: Abo Akademi University Press.

Manwaring, Randle (1985), *From Controversy to Co-existence: Evangelicals in the Church of England 1914–1980*, Cambridge: Cambridge University Press.

Marriage, Divorce and the Church (1971), the Report of the Archbishops' Commission, London: SPCK.

Martin, John (1997), *Gospel People? Evangelicals and the Future of Anglicanism*, London: SPCK.

Martin, William (1991), *The Billy Graham Story: A Prophet with Honour*, London: Hutchinson.

Marwick, Arthur (1998), *The Sixties*, Oxford: Oxford University Press.

Meyers, Jeffrey (1996), *Robert Frost: A Biography*, London: Constable.

Mills, David (ed.) (1998), *The Pilgrim's Guide*, Cambridge: Eerdmans.

Milner-White, Eric, and Briggs, G. W. (1941), *Daily Prayer*, Oxford: Oxford University Press.

Montefiore, Hugh (1986), *So Near and Yet So Far*, London: SCM.

Motyer, J. A. (1974), *The Day of the Lion: The Message of Amos*, London: IVP. Later *The Message of Amos: The Day of the Lion*.

Motyer, Stephen: see Stott, revised by Stephen Motyer (1994).

Moule, H. C. G. (1892), *Charles Simeon*, London: Methuen.

Muggeridge, Malcolm (1977), *Christ and the Media*, London: Hodder & Stoughton.

———— (1988), *Conversion: A Spiritual Journey*, London: Collins.

Murray, Iain (1990), *David Martyn Lloyd-Jones*, vol. 2: *The Fight of Faith 1939–1981*, Edinburgh: Banner of Truth.

———— (2000), *Evangelicals Divided*, Edinburgh: Banner of Truth.

Mystery of Salvation, The (1995), Report of the Doctrine Commission, London: Church House Publishing.

Neill, Stephen (1991), *God's Apprentice: The Autobiography of Stephen Neill*, ed. E. M. Jackson, London: Hodder & Stoughton.

Newbigin, Lesslie (1969), *The Finality of Christ*, London: SCM.

Newsome, David (1993), *The Convert Cardinals*, London: Murray.

Ng, L. M. (ed.) (1980), *Proceedings of the International Conference of Christian Medical Students, 1980*, London: ICCMS and Christian Medical Fellowship.

Noll, Mark A., Bebbington, David W., & Rawlyk, George A. (eds.) (1994), *Evangelicalism: Comparative Studies of Popular Protestantism in North America, the British Isles, and Beyond, 1700–1990*, New York: Oxford University Press.

Norman, E. R. (1976), *Church and Society in England 1770–1970*, Oxford: Clarendon.

North–South: A Programme for Survival (1980), the Report of the independent Commission on International Development Issues under the chairmanship of Willy Brandt, London: Pan.

Nottingham Statement, The (1977), London: Falcon.

O'Donovan, Oliver (1984), *Begotten or Made?*, Oxford: Clarendon.

Packer, J. I. (1984), *Keep in Step with the Spirit*, Leicester: IVP.

—— (1991), *Among God's Giants*, Eastbourne: Kingsway.

—— (1998), *Celebrating the Saving Work of God: Collected Shorter Writings of J. I. Packer*, vol. 1, Carlisle: Paternoster.

—— (n.d.), *The Problem of Eternal Punishment*, Disley, Cheshire: Fellowship of Word and Spirit. The Leon Morris Lecture for the Evangelical Alliance (Victoria), delivered 31 August 1990.

Packer, J. I. (ed.) (1965), *All in Each Place: Towards Reunion in England*, Abingdon: Marcham Manor.

—— (ed.) (1967), *Guidelines: Anglican Evangelicals Face the Future*, London: Falcon.

Packer, J. I., and Wilkinson, Loren (eds.) (1992), *Alive to God: Studies in Spirituality*, Downers Grove, IL: IVP.

Padilla, René, and Sugden, Chris (eds.) (1985), *How Evangelicals Endorsed Social Responsibility*, Bramcote: Grove.

Palmer, Bernard (1991), *Gadfly for God: A History of the Church Times*, London: Hodder & Stoughton.

—— (1992), *High and Mitred: Prime Ministers as Bishop-Makers, 1837–1977*, London: SPCK.

Paterson, A. B. (1901), *The Man from Snowy River and Other Verses*, Sydney: Angus & Robertson.

Paul, Leslie (1964), *The Deployment and Payment of the Clergy*, London: CIO.

Payne, Tony (ed.) (n.d. [1990]), *John Wimber: Friend or Foe?*, London: St Matthias Press.

Phillips, J. B. (1984), *The Price of Success*, London: Hodder & Stoughton.

Pollock, J. C. (1962), *Hudson Taylor and Maria*, London: Hodder & Stoughton.

—— (1964), *The Keswick Story*, London: Hodder & Stoughton.

—— (1966), *Billy Graham: The Authorized Biography*, London: Hodder & Stoughton.

—— (1979), *Billy Graham: Evangelist to the World*, San Francisco, CA: Harper and Row.

Pratt, John H. (ed.) (1865), *Eclectic Notes: Or Notes of Discussions on Religious Topics at the Meetings of the Eclectic Society, London, 1798–1814*, London: James Nisbet. First edition 1856.

Prior, Ian (ed.) (1978), *The Christian at Work Overseas*, London: TEAR Fund.

Ramsey, Michael (1963), *Image Old and New*, London: SPCK.

Rand, Stephen (1998), *Guinea Pig for Lunch*, London: Hodder & Stoughton.

Reid, Gavin (ed.) (1986), *Hope for the Church of England?*, Eastbourne: Kingsway.

Religion in Britain and Northern Ireland: A Survey of Popular Attitudes (1970), London: ITA.

Richter, H. (ed.) (1972), *Die Kommende Ökumene: Theologische Untersuchungen*, Wuppertal: Rolf Brockhaus.

Ridley, Nicholas (1895), *A Brief Declaration of the Lord's Supper*, ed. H. C. G. Moule, London: Seeley.

Robinson, John A. T. (1963), *Honest to God*, London: SCM.

—— (1970), *Christian Freedom in a Permissive Society*, London: SCM.

Russell, G. W. E. (1915), *A Short History of the Evangelical Movement*, London: Mowbray.

Ryle, J. C. (1979), *Holiness*, centenary edition, Welwyn: Evangelical Press. First published 1890.

Samuel, Leith (1993), *A Man under Authority*, Fearn, Ross-shire: Christian Focus.

Samuel, Vinay, and Sugden, Chris (eds.) (1986), *Sharing Jesus in the Two Thirds World*, Grand Rapids, MI: Eerdmans.

—— (eds.) (1991), *AD 2000 and Beyond: A Mission Agenda*, Oxford: Regnum.

Saunders, Teddy, and Sansom, Hugh (1992), *David Watson: A Biography*, London: Hodder & Stoughton.

Saward, Michael (1987), *Evangelicals on the Move*, Oxford: Mowbray.

—— (1999), *A Faint Streak of Humility*, Carlisle: Paternoster.

Sceats, David D. (ed.) (1985), *Proceedings of the Anglican Evangelical Assembly 1985*, London: CEEC.

Scott, Peter (1951), *Wild Geese and Eskimos*, London: Country Life.

Smyth, Charles (1940), *The Art of Preaching*, London: SPCK.

—— (1940), *Simeon and Church Order*, Cambridge: Cambridge University Press.

—— (1959), *Cyril Forster Garbett*, London: Hodder & Stoughton.

Social Surveys (Gallup Poll) Ltd, on behalf of ABC Television (1964), *Television and Religion*, London: University of London Press

Spong, John Shelby (1988), *Living in Sin?*, San Francisco, CA: Harper and Row.

—— (1991), *Rescuing the Bible from Fundamentalism: A Bishop Rethinks the Meaning of Scripture*, New York: HarperSanFrancisco.

—— (2000), *Here I Stand*, New York: HarperSanFrancisco.

Steer, Roger (1998), *Church on Fire: The Story of Anglican Evangelicals*, London: Hodder & Stoughton.

Stibbs, A. M., et al. (eds.) (1953), *New Bible Commentary*, London: IVF.

Stockwood, Mervyn (1982), *Chanctonbury Ring*, London: Hodder & Stoughton.

Stott, John (1952), *Ezra the Scribe*, London: Berean Band.

—— (1954), *Men with a Message: An Introduction to the New Testament and its Writers*, London: Longmans. See Stott, revised by Stephen Motyer (1994).

—— (1958a), *Basic Christianity*, London: IVF. Revised 1971.

—— (1958b), *What Christ Thinks of the Church: Expository Addresses on the First Three Chapters of the Book of Revelation*, London: Lutterworth. See Stott (1990c).

—— (1958c), *Your Confirmation*, London: Hodder & Stoughton. Revised 1971. See Stott (1991a).

—— (1961a), *Mobilizing the Church for Evangelism*, London: All Souls Church.

—— (1961b), *The Preacher's Portrait: Some New Testament Word Studies*, London: Tyndale. Reissued Leicester: IVP, 1995.

—— (1962), *Motives and Methods in Evangelism*, London: IVF. See Stott (1967a).

—— (1963a), *Beginning a New Life with Christ*, London: Falcon. Revised 1974.

—— (1963b), *Intercommunion and Prayer Book Revision*, London: Falcon.

—— (1964a), *The Baptism and Fullness of the Holy Spirit*, London: IVF. See Stott (1975b).

—— (1964b), *Confess Your Sins: The Way of Reconciliation*, London: Hodder & Stoughton.

—— (1964c), *The Epistles of John: An Introduction and Commentary*, Tyndale New Testament Commentaries, London: Tyndale. See Stott (1988b).

—— (1964d), *The Meaning of Evangelism*, London: Falcon. Revised 1973.

—— (1964e), *Personal Evangelism*, Downers Grove, IL: IVP. Originally London: IVF, 1949.

—— (1966a), *The Canticles and Selected Psalms*, London: Hodder & Stoughton. See Stott (1988a).

—— (1966b), *Men Made New: An Exposition of Romans 5 – 8*, London: IVF.

—— (1967a), *Evangelism: Why and How*, Downers Grove, IL: IVP. US edition of Stott (1962).

—— (1967b), *Our Guilty Silence: The Church, the Gospel and the World*, London: Hodder & Stoughton.

—— (1968), *The Message of Galatians*, London: IVP. Later *The Message of Galatians: Only One Way*.

—— (1969), *One People: Clergy and Laity in God's Church*, London: Falcon. Revised (US) 1982.

—— (1970), *Christ the Controversialist: A Study in Some Essentials of Evangelical Religion*, London: Tyndale. Reissued Leicester: IVP, 1991.

—— (1971), *Following Christ in the Seventies*, Singapore: James Wong. New edition, Sydney: Anzea, 1972.

—— (1972a), *Divorce: The Biblical Teaching*, London: Falcon.

—— (1972b), *Understanding the Bible*, London: Scripture Union. Revised 1976 and 1984. Revised (US) 1999.

—— (1972c), *Your Mind Matters: The Place of the Mind in the Christian Life*, London: IVP.

—— (1973), *Guard the Gospel: The Message of 2 Timothy*, London IVP. Later *The Message of 2 Timothy: Guard the Gospel*.

—— (1974), *The Authority of the Bible*, Downers Grove, IL: IVP. Extracted from D. M. Howard (ed.) (1974).

—— (1975a), *Balanced Christianity: A Call to Avoid Unnecessary Polarisation*, London: Hodder & Stoughton.

—— (1975b), *Baptism and Fullness: The Work of the Holy Spirit Today*, London: IVP. Revised and enlarged edition of Stott (1964a).

—— (1975c), *Christian Mission in the Modern World*, London: Falcon. Reissued Eastbourne: Kingsway, 1986.

—— (1975d), *Explaining the Lausanne Covenant*, London: Scripture Union. US title *The Lausanne Covenant: An Exposition and Commentary*.

—— (1975e), *Walk in His Shoes: The Compassion of Jesus*, Leicester: IVP. US title *Who Is My Neighbor?*, 1976.

—— (1977), *What is an Evangelical?*, London: Falcon.

—— (1978a), *Christian Counter-Culture: The Message of the Sermon on the Mount*, Leicester: IVP. Later *The Message of the Sermon on the Mount: Christian Counter-Culture*.

—— (1978b), *Essentials for Tomorrow's Christians*, London: Scripture Union

—— (1978c), *The Uniqueness of Jesus Christ*, Chicago, IL: Chicago Sunday Evening TV Club.

—— (1979a), *Focus on Christ: An Enquiry into the Theology of Prepositions*, London: Collins. US title *Understanding Christ*, 1981. See Stott (1991b)

—— (1979b), *The Authority and Relevance of the Bible in the Modern World*, Canberra: The Bible Society in Australia. US title *Culture and the Bible*, 1981.

—— (1979c), *God's New Society: The Message of Ephesians*, Leicester: IVP. Later *The Message of Ephesians: God's New Society*.

—— (1982a), *Evangelism and Social Responsibility: An Evangelical Commitment*, Exeter: Paternoster, on behalf of LCWE and WEF.

—— (1982b), *I Believe in Preaching*, London: Hodder & Stoughton. US title *Between Two Worlds*.

—— (1982c), *The Bible: Book for Today*, Leicester: IVP. US titles *God's Book for God's People*, 1983; *You Can Trust the Bible: Our Firm Foundation for Belief and Experience*, 1991.

—— (1983a), *In Christ: The Meaning and Implications of the Gospel of Jesus Christ*, Washington: National Prayer Breakfast Committee.

—— (1983b), *Make the Truth Known*, Leicester: UCCF.

—— (1984), *Issues Facing Christians Today*, Basingstoke: Marshalls. US title *Involvement*, 2 vols., 1985. Revised and enlarged edition, London: Marshall Pickering, 1990. US title *Decisive Issues Facing Christians Today*. For third edition see Stott (1999d).

—— (1985), *The Authentic Jesus: A Response to Current Scepticism in the Church*, Basingstoke: Marshalls.

—— (1986a), *The Cross of Christ*, Leicester: IVP.

—— (1986b), *The Whole Christian* (in Korean), Seoul: IVP Korea.

—— (1988a), *Favourite Psalms*, Milton Keynes: Word. Revised and illustrated edition of Stott (1966a).

—— (1988b), *The Letters of John: An Introduction and Commentary*. Tyndale New Testament Commentaries, Leicester: IVP. Revised edition of Stott (1964c).

—— (1988c), 'What is the Spirit Saying …?', Chippenham: CEEC.

—— (1989), *God's Word for our Time*, London: Hodder & Stoughton.

—— (1990a), *The Lordship of Christ in South Africa: A Challenge to Christians to Think and Act Biblically*, Pietermaritzburg: Africa Enterprise.

—— (1990b), *The Message of Acts: To the Ends of the Earth*, Leicester: IVP. US title *The Spirit, the Church and the World*.

—— (1990c), *What Christ Thinks of the Church*, Milton Keynes: Word. Revised and illustrated edition of Stott (1958b).

—— (1991a), *Christian Basics: A Handbook of Christian Faith*, London: Hodder & Stoughton. Revised edition of Stott (1958c). Also adapted for the US with the sub-title *A Handbook of Beginnings, Belief and Behaviour*, 1991.

—— (1991b), *Life in Christ*, Eastbourne: Kingsway. Revised and illustrated edition of Stott (1979a).

—— (1991c), *The Message of Thessalonians: Preparing for the Coming King*, Leicester: IVP. US title *The Gospel and the End of Time*.

—— (1992a), *The Contemporary Christian: An Urgent Plea for Double Listening*, Leicester: IVP.

—— (1992b), *Los Problemas del Liderazgo Cristiano*, Buenos Aires: Ediciones Certeza.

—— (1994), *The Message of Romans: God's Good News for the World*, Leicester: IVP. US title *Romans: God's News for the World*.

—— (1996), *The Message of 1 Timothy and Titus: The Life of the Local Church*, Leicester: IVP.

—— (1998), *Same Sex Partnerships? A Christian Contribution to Contemporary Debate*, London: Marshall Pickering. A chapter from Stott (1999d).

—— (1999a), *The Birds our Teachers*, London: Candle.

—— (1999b), *The Essential John Stott*, comprising *The Cross of Christ* (1986a) and *The Contemporary Christian* (1992a), Leicester: IVP.

—— (1999c), *Evangelical Truth: A Personal Plea for Unity*, Leicester: IVP.

—— (1999d), *New Issues Facing Christians Today*, London: Marshall Pickering. Third edition of Stott (1984). Published in the US in two volumes: vol. 1: *Human Rights and Human Wrongs: Major Issues for a New Century*; vol. 2: *Our Social and Sexual Revolution: Major Issues for a New Century*.

—— (1999e), *Understanding the Bible*, Grand Rapids, MI: Zondervan. Second revision. First published 1972.

—— (2001), *The Incomparable Christ*, Leicester: IVP.

Stott, John, revised by Stephen Motyer (1994), *Men with a Message: An Introduction to the New Testament and its Writers*, Grand Rapids, MI: Eerdmans. See Stott (1954).

Stott, John, and others (1972), *Christ the Liberator*, London: Hodder & Stoughton.

—— and others (1988), *ARCIC: An Open Letter to the Anglican Episcopate*, Bramcote:

Grove.
———— and others (1996a), *The Anglican Communion and Scripture*, Oxford and Carlisle: Regnum and EFAC in association with Paternoster.
———— and others (1996b), *Logos and Heresy: Romanian–British Contribution to a Theology of Postmodernity* (in Romanian), Bucharest: Editura Anastasia.
Stott, John (ed.) (1977), *Obeying Christ in a Changing World*, vol. 1: *The Lord Christ*, London: Collins. General editor John Stott.
———— (ed.) (1996), *Making Christ Known: Historic Mission Documents from the Lausanne Movement 1974–1989*, Carlisle: Paternoster.
Stott, John, and Coote, Robert (eds.) (1981), *Down to Earth: Studies in Christianity and Culture*, London: Hodder & Stoughton.
Stott, John, and Meeking, Basil (eds.) (1986), *The Evangelical–Roman Catholic Dialogue on Mission: A Report*, Exeter: Paternoster.
Taylor, Vincent (1940), *The Atonement in New Testament Teaching*, London: Epworth.
Tennyson, G. B. (ed.) (1989), *Owen Barfield on C. S. Lewis*, Middletown, CT: Wesleyan University Press.
Thurman, Judith (1982), *Isak Dinesen: The Life of Karen Blixen*, London: Weidenfeld & Nicholson.
Tidball, Derek J. (1994), *Who are the Evangelicals?*, London: Marshall Pickering.
Tinker, Melvin (ed.) (1995), *The Anglican Evangelical Crisis*, Fearn, Ross-shire: Christian Focus.
Tools for Evangelism (1973), from the National Study Week on Strategy for Evangelism at Morecambe, London: Church Book Room Press.
Torrey, R. A. (1923), *Why God Used D. L. Moody*, Chicago, IL: Moody.
Trollope, Anthony (1995), *Barchester Towers*, Folio edition. First published 1857.
Vale, Allister (ed.) (1998), *Our National Life*, London: The National Club with Monarch.
Vasey, Michael (1995), *Strangers and Friends*, London: Hodder & Stoughton.
Venables, G. J. (1958), *Christian Service in Youth Clubs*, London: Crusade.
Wallace, Ronald S. (1979), *The Lord is King: The Message of Daniel*, Leicester: IVP. Later *The Message of Daniel: The Lord is King*.
Watson, David (1983), *You Are My God*, London: Hodder & Stoughton.
Welsby, Paul A. (1984), *A History of the Church of England, 1945–1980*, Oxford: Oxford University Press.
Wenham, John (1998), *Facing Hell: An Autobiography 1913–1996*, Carlisle: Paternoster.
Whistler, Theresa (1993), *Imagination of the Heart*, London: Duckworth.
Whitehead, Roger, and Sneddon, Amy (1990), *An Unwanted Child: The Story of NIE*, London: BCC/CCBI.
Williams, Derek (1984), *Billy Graham in England, 1984*, Northwood: Creative Publishing.
Wimber, John, and Springer, Kevin (1985), *Power Evangelism*, London: Hodder & Stoughton.
Winter, Ralph D., and Hawthorn, Steven C. (eds.) (1981), *Perspectives on the World Christian Movement: A Reader*, Pasadena, CA: William Carey Library.
Winterhager, J. W., and Brown, Arnold (eds.) (1974), *Vocation and Victory: An International Symposium Presented in Honour of Erik Wickberg, General of the Salvation Army*, Basle: Brunnen.
Wolfe, Gregory (1995), *Malcolm Muggeridge – A Biography*, London: Hodder & Stoughton.
Wright, Christopher, and Sugden, Christopher (eds.) (1990), *One Gospel – Many Clothes*, Oxford: EFAC and Regnum.
Wright, David F. (ed.) (1978), *Essays in Evangelical Social Ethics*, Exeter: Paternoster.
Wyatt, John (1998), *Matters of Life and Death: Today's Healthcare Dilemmas in the Light of Christian Faith*, Leicester and London: IVP and CMF.
Yates Gaskins, Allison, and Yates, Susan Alexander (1998), *Thanks Dad, for Everything*, Ann Arbor, MI: Servant.

Yates, Timothy E. (1994), *Christian Mission in the Twentieth Century*, Cambridge: Cambridge University Press.

Yeats, Charles (ed.) (1995), *Has Keele Failed?*, London: Hodder & Stoughton.

Zahl, Paul F. M. (1998), *The Protestant Face of Anglicanism*, Cambridge: Eerdmans.

Index

Numbers in italics refer to photographs in the illustrations sections.

Authentic Christianity

From the writings of John Stott

Compiled and introduced by
Timothy Dudley-Smith

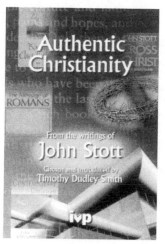

'*Nothing sets the heart ablaze like fresh vistas of truth,*' observes John Stott in one of his many books.

This personal selection by Timothy Dudley-Smith captures the many vistas of truth that John Stott has explored in fifty years of writing.

His arrangement of nearly a thousand extracts covers topics ranging from the cross of Jesus to marriage and divorce. It captures the passion and clarity of John Stott, an author who never fails to illuminate the central concerns of authentic Christianity.

Here is biblical, evangelical thought in its full spiritual and intellectual vitality.

0–85111–155–6
432 pages
Large paperback

Inter-Varsity Press

Praise for volume one

JOHN STOTT

THE MAKING OF A LEADER

Timothy Dudley-Smith

Winner of the John Pollock Prize for Biography, 2001

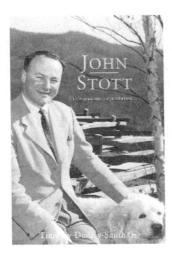

Here, happily, is the biography for which I personally have been eagerly waiting. The telling of the story by Timothy Dudley-Smith, with all its fascinating detail, is, in my view, a masterly achievement. For one thing, it was John Stott who, from the early fifties, first modelled for his ministerial contemporaries the power and primacy of expository preaching. Worldwide, our debt to this glorious and good man is immeasurable.

DICK LUCAS

For a generation, John Stott has been a source of inspiration, insight and information for literally millions of Christians around the world. It is hard to overestimate the breadth, depth and value of his influence. But, most importantly, he is an extraordinary example of a person absolutely dedicated to Christ and serving the church. I commend this compelling account of the real man, his life and influences, to you. It makes fascinating reading.

STEVE CHALKE

Four things stand out ... First, John's confidence in the gospel, his commitment to preaching it and to bringing people to Christ. Secondly, his commitment to the Bible and his desire to use all his gifts to study and teach it. Thirdly, his social conscience which is evident both in his pacifism and in his heart for the homeless. And, fourthly, here is a man who has sought to exploit every gift of intellect, communication and time he possesses for the glory of God.

DEREK TIDBALL

Not many books are written by bishops about people who are not bishops. If such a genre exists, this may be the best yet. But it is an outstanding biography in any class, and while not the final word ... it will remain a standard reference-point, as well as a delightful read, for many years to come ... To read this book is to be challenged more than once about our own commitment, our understanding of the Bible, and our desire, or lack of it, to share the faith which others have shared with us.

CHRISTOPHER IDLE

The author writes superb English and the book is most readable, not least because he laces the story with thumbnail sketches of the state of the world in which Stott grew up, and of the church and its theological drift within which Stott ministered and to which he, more than anyone, brought new confidence in the Word of God and in the gospel. This book will delight, inform and challenge.

KEITH WESTON

John Stott would have made his mark in many fields ... Yet the chief impression one is left with is of a humble Christian, with an immense passion for Christ and the gospel. I found this a rich and rewarding read ... Timothy Dudley-Smith, a long-time friend and intimate, has done a superb job in showing not merely the facts, but revealing the man.

CHRISTIAN LITERATURE CRUSADE REVIEW

0–85110–757–0 512 pages Hardback

Inter-Varsity Press

John Stott:
A Comprehensive Bibliography

Compiled by
Timothy Dudley-Smith

This bibliography is the first
attempt to compile a complete
account of John Stott's writings,
including books he has written or
edited or to which he has
contributed, his booklets and pamphlets, his contributions to
periodicals, and his prayers, verses and hymns.

For those who have followed and appreciated the work and
ministry of John Stott, this bibliography will be a treasured
map of his active life as a leader.

0–85111–156–4
156 pages
Large paperback

Inter-Varsity Press

The Cross of Christ

John Stott

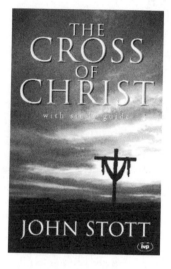

The universal symbol of the Christian faith is not a crib or a manger but a gruesome cross. Yet many people are unclear about its meaning, and cannot understand why Christ had to die. In this magisterial book John Stott explains the significance of Christ's cross and answers the objections commonly brought against biblical teaching on the atonement.

First, Dr Stott shows from the four Gospels how Jesus himself understood the cross. Next he argues that 'Christ in our place' is the heart of its meaning. Then he demonstrates what the cross achieved, and finally he explores what it means to live under the cross.

Whether as superb biblical exposition, or as a characteristically thoughtful study of Christian belief, or as a searching call to the church to live under the cross, John's Stott's modern classic continues to have a wide appeal.

With study guide

0–85110–674–9   416 pages   Large paperback

Inter-Varsity Press

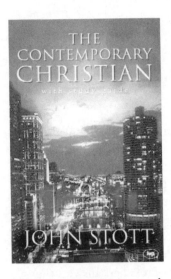

The Contemporary Christian

An urgent plea for double listening

John Stott

The Contemporary Christian is John Stott's definitive and passionate plea to the church. Before we attempt to teach or evangelize, he urges, we must listen to God's Word and God's world. Only then shall we be able to communicate the authentic gospel effectively. John Stott himself models this 'double listening' as he tackles five key questions:

- Amid scepticism inside the church as well as outside, what is the authentic gospel?

- In a world torn by pain and need, what characterizes the obedient disciple?

- Now that the Bible is often set aside as culturally irrelevant, how can we relate it with integrity to contemporary society?

- Given the church's general lack of credibility, what is her calling and how can she fulfil it?

- In a pluralistic society and a hungry world, what is the church's mission?

With study guide

0–85110–973–X
432 pages
Large paperback

Inter-Varsity Press